W9-BQX-990

OLD ENGLISH LITERATURE AND THE OLD TESTAMENT

Old English Literature and the Old Testament

Edited by Michael Fox
and Manish Sharma

UNIVERSITY OF TORONTO PRESS
Toronto Buffalo London

ISBN 978-0-8020-9854-2

Printed on acid-free, 100% post-consumer recycled paper with vegetable-based inks.

Library and Archives Canada Cataloguing in Publication

Old English literature and the Old Testament / edited by Michael Fox and
Manish Sharma.

(Toronto Anglo-Saxon series)
Includes bibliographical references and index.
ISBN 978-0-8020-9854-2

1. English literature – Old English, ca. 450–1100 – History and criticism.
2. Christian literature, English (Old) – History and criticism.   3. Bible – In
literature.   4. Christianity and literature – England – History – To 1500.   I. Fox,
Michael, 1967–   II. Sharma, Manish, 1973–   III. Series: Toronto Anglo-Saxon series

PR173.O54 2011   829.09'38221   C2011-902772-0

University of Toronto Press gratefully acknowledges the financial assistance of the
Centre for Medieval Studies, University of Toronto, in the publication of this book.

This book has been published with the help of a grant from the Canadian
Federation for the Humanities and Social Sciences, through the Aid to Scholarly
Publications Program, using funds provided by the Social Sciences and Humanities
Research Council of Canada.

University of Toronto Press acknowledges the financial assistance to its publishing program of the Canada Council for the Arts and the Ontario Arts Council.

Canada Council   Conseil des Arts
for the Arts   du Canada

ONTARIO ARTS COUNCIL
CONSEIL DES ARTS DE L'ONTARIO

University of Toronto Press acknowledges the financial support of the Government
of Canada through the Canada Book Fund for its publishing activities.

Contents

Abbreviations

ASE	*Anglo-Saxon England*
ASPR	G.P. Krapp and E.V.K. Dobbie, eds., *The Anglo-Saxon Poetic Records*, 6 vols. (New York: Columbia University Press, 1931–42)
BT	Joseph Bosworth and T. Northcote Toller, *An Anglo-Saxon Dictionary* (Oxford: Oxford University Press, 1898)
BTS	T. Northcote Toller, *An Anglo-Saxon Dictionary: Supplement* (Oxford: Oxford University Press, 1921)
CCCC	Cambridge, Corpus Christi College
CCCM	Corpus Christianorum, Continuatio Mediaevalis
CCSL	Corpus Christianorum, Series Latina
CH	*Ælfric's Catholic Homilies*, ed. Peter Clemoes and Malcolm Godden, 3 vols., EETS s.s. 17–18 (Oxford: Oxford University Press, 1979–2000). Vol. 1: *The First Series*. Text. ed. Clemoes, 1997. Vol. 2: *The Second Series*. Text. ed. Godden, 1979. Vol. 3: *Introduction, Commentary, and Glossary*, ed. Godden, 2000.
CSASE	Cambridge Studies in Anglo-Saxon England
CSEL	Corpus Scriptorum Ecclesiasticorum Latinorum
DOE	*Dictionary of Old English: A to G* online, ed. Angus Cameron, Ashley Crandell Amos, Antonette diPaolo Healey et al. (Toronto: Dictionary of Old English Project, 2007)
EEMF	Early English Manuscripts in Facsimile
EETS	Early English Text Society
o.s.	old series
s.s.	supplementary series
ELN	*English Language Notes*

ES	*English Studies*
JEGP	(formerly) *Journal of English and Germanic Philology*
JMLat	*Journal of Medieval Latin*
LS	*Ælfric's Lives of Saints*, ed. W.W. Skeat, EETS o.s. 76, 82, 94, and 114, 2 vols. (Oxford: Oxford University Press, 1881–1900; repr. 1966)
MGH	Monumenta Germaniae Historica
MLN	*Modern Language Notes*
NM	*Neuphilologische Mitteilungen*
PL	*Patrologia Latina*, ed., J.P. Migne, 221 vols. (Paris, 1844–64)
PMLA	*Publications of the Modern Language Association*
PQ	*Philological Quarterly*
RES	*Review of English Studies*
SP	*Studies in Philology*

OLD ENGLISH LITERATURE AND THE OLD TESTAMENT

Introduction

MICHAEL FOX AND MANISH SHARMA

It would be difficult to overestimate the importance of the Bible to the medieval world view. Augustine, the undisputed 'father' of the Western medieval understanding of the Bible, felt that the it was the expression of God's will; all that could profitably be known was contained within its verses. Specifically, through literal and figurative expression, the Bible contained eternal truths, history, prophecy, and commands or warnings about what we were to do. At the same time, however, all of scripture could be distilled into the simple commandment to love God with all our heart, and our neighbours just as ourselves.[1] In the late eighth century, the transplanted Anglo-Saxon Alcuin put the connection between the Word and God in different terms, but just as strongly: 'Ignorantia scripturarum ignorantia Dei est' (Ignorance of scripture is ignorance of God).[2]

After the pioneering work in the 1950s and 1960s of scholars such as D.W. Robertson and Bernard F. Huppé in which the influence of the Bible and the Augustinian interpretation of it were found to be behind most medieval works from Old English poetry to Chaucer, there was a strong reaction against such methods of interpretation. Although primary texts continued to be edited and studied (including, most significantly, biblical commentaries), proclamation of the Bible's primary influence on other, more 'literary' texts went out of fashion. Recently, however, scholarship

---

1 See *De Genesi ad litteram* I.i.1; *De Genesi contra Manicheos* II.ii.3; and *Confessiones* XII.xxv.35.
2 Ernst Dümmler, ed., *Alcuini epistolae*, MGH, *Epistolarum Tomus* IV, *Epistolae Karolini aeui* II (Berlin: Weidmann, 1895), Epistle 129 (Alcuin to Archbishop Æthelhard at Canterbury, 797).

has become receptive once more to the rich possibilities offered by such an approach, and the focus is often on the less explicable manifestations of biblical learning. Thus, in an assessment of Middle English biblical literature, James Morey comments that, although lay knowledge of the Bible before Wycliff has been assumed to be minimal, 'biblical allusions and models and large-scale appropriations of biblical narratives pervade nearly every medieval genre, intended for both learned and lay audiences.'[3]

It has long been recognized that, as Thomas Hall puts it, biblical study was 'the starting point for [Anglo-Saxon] literary endeavours of virtually any kind.'[4] That the Old Testament had a deep and productive influence upon surviving Old English literature is also well known. Malcolm Godden, in an excellent overview, summarizes the situation as follows: 'In terms of quantity, at least, the Old Testament was the major influence on Old English literature: it was a source for about a third of the extant poetry and for a large part of the prose, as well as influencing other writings.'[5] Over the course of the last forty years, approaches to understanding that influence have changed dramatically. The major change has been the gradual merging of what had been seen as two distinct literary traditions: Anglo-Latin and Old English. Largely as a result of this broader view of Anglo-Saxon literary culture (and the concomitant understanding that any writer of Old English must have had a thorough grounding in Latin scriptures and certain common school texts), the range of literature that might be considered to have been influenced in some way by biblical texts and traditions includes almost everything written in Old English. As Godden also observes, this influence even extends to the way in which literature might be read: 'Old Testament reading invited an imaginative and individual response to literature.'[6]

This volume provides a collection of essays by scholars engaged in the investigation of Old Testament influence upon Old English literature from different perspectives. Although contributions generally focus on individual works, authors, or trends, each finally speaks to the vernacular corpus as a whole, suggesting approaches and methodologies for further study. The essays address Old English writings in three categories: the Old Testament and Old English prose; the Old Testament and the poems of the

---

3 James Morey, *Book and Verse*, 1.
4 Thomas N. Hall, 'Biblical and Patristic Learning,' 327.
5 Malcolm Godden, 'Biblical Literature,' 206.
6 Ibid., 207.

Junius manuscript; and the Old Testament and other poems.[7] Latin orthography has been regularized throughout.

The remainder of the introduction will seek first to contextualize and then to summarize the essays in this collection.

The Old Testament and Old English Prose

Alfred

The Alfredian literature that formed the core of the cultural renascence orchestrated by Alfred in the ninth century includes a paraphrase in Old English prose of the first fifty psalms.[8] Along with the linguistic and stylistic evidence that indicates Alfred's authorship,[9] William of Malmesbury, writing in the twelfth century, mentions that Alfred was working on a translation of the psalms at the time of his death.[10] The first fifty psalms certainly are appropriate to the besieged king as they contain David's lamentations over the threat posed by foreign enemies and a cry for faith and learning.

Alfred's translations are found in the unique Paris Psalter (Paris, Bibliothèque nationale, MS Fonds Latin 8824), the most extensive extant collection of Old English translations of the psalms.[11] Each page of the manuscript contains double columns: on the left side of the page is the Latin text of the psalm, and on the right, the translation. While Psalms 1–50 have been translated into prose, Psalms 51–150 have been translated into verse. The translations, however, do not derive from the accompanying Latin, and the three parts of the manuscript seem to have discrete origins.[12] According to Robert D. Fulk and Christopher M. Cain, Alfred's

---

7 This introduction and the collection itself could be much expanded. Godden, for example, remarks that 'in many ways the most imaginative response to the Old Testament is to be seen in *Beowulf*, which draws on biblical stories ... to form part of its mythic structure' ('Biblical Literature,' 207). For a further sense of the situation with regard especially to the Old English poetry not treated here, see Godden.

8 Patrick P. O'Neill, ed., *King Alfred's Old English Prose Translation*.

9 Janet Bately, 'Lexical Evidence for the Authorship of the Prose Psalms,' 69–95; P. Pulsiano, 'Psalters,' 77–9.

10 Roger A.B. Mynors, Rodney M. Thomson, and Michael Winterbottom, eds., *William of Malmesbury*, vol. 1, book 2, cap. 123.2.

11 Bertram Colgrave, ed., *The Paris Psalter*.

12 See B.J. Douglas, 'The Anglo-Saxon Version of the Book of Psalms,' 43–164; Patricia Bethel, 'Regnal and Divine Epithets,' 1–41.

translations are given priority, and the verse translations 'seem to have been added to the prose translation to fill out the collection.'[13] Only one hand appears, and the manuscript is dated on the basis of palaeographical evidence to the second quarter of the eleventh century.[14] Both poetic and prose translations seem intended for lay consumption, and the manuscript thus supplies an important witness to lay piety.[15]

In the course of his translation, Alfred used an Old Latin version of the Roman Psalter that likely was brought to England by Augustine in the late sixth century; there is evidence that he also consulted glosses of the Gallican Psalter. He is sometimes literal and sometimes expansive, incorporating patristic exegesis in his paraphrase in order to clarify the spiritual significance of the text. Each psalm (except Psalm 1) is introduced by an Old English passage that includes the psalm's historical context and provides a three- or four-fold interpretation.[16] These introductions are modelled adroitly on a rather rigid structure used by Irish psalmic commentators.[17]

An important component of the Alfredian cultural resurgence was Alfred's law code.[18] While Alfred does not substantially revise existing statutes, his code is remarkable for its preface.[19] The typical opening to legal codes before and after Alfred's reign was concise: prefaces identified the ruler authorizing the code, noted that its issuance followed deliberation, and sometimes explained the conditions surrounding its issuance. The preface to Alfred's law code, by contrast, begins with an expansive Old English translation of Exodus, chapters 20–3, which contains the Ten Commandments followed by other moral and civil decrees. The translations of the New Testament that come after indicate the fulfilment of the old dispensation by the new (that is, Matthew 5:17 and Acts 15). The organization of the preface makes explicit Alfred's nuanced understanding

---

13 Robert D. Fulk and Christopher M. Cain, *A History of Old English Literature*, 61.

14 See Krapp, *The Paris Psalter*, ASPR V, xi.

15 See Gatch, *Preaching and Theology*, 48–9; Fulk and Cain, *A History of Old English Literature*, 121.

16 See O'Neill, ed., *King Alfred's Old English Prose Translation*, 31–4 and 34–40.

17 See Patrick P. O'Neill, 'The Old English Introductions to the Prose Psalms,' 20–38.

18 Felix Liebermann, ed., *Die Gesetze der Angelsachsen*. See further Patrick Wormald, *The Making of English Law* and '*Lex Scripta* and *Verbum Regis*,' 105–38.

19 See M. Treschow, 'The Prologue to Alfred's Law Code,' 79–110; Simon Keynes and Michael Lapidge, trans., *Alfred the Great*, 303–5; Felix Liebermann, 'King Alfred and the Mosaic Law,' 21–31.

of the law as an instrument of justice tempered by mercy: 'The principle of mercy, which had been proclaimed in the Christian era as the essence of Christian law, in that if it was fully possessed no other law would be needed, is not allowed to dominate but is circumscribed by a concern to maintain the discipline of justice.'[20]

Ælfric

Ælfric, monk of Cerne and Abbot of Eynsham, was a product of the Benedictine reform of the late tenth century and the greatest vernacular homilist of the Anglo-Saxon period. His immense prose output, mainly homilies and saints' lives, includes many translations of Old Testament passages.[21] Better known is his participation in a joint translation of most of the first six books of the Old Testament. Ælfric translates up to Genesis chapter 24, Numbers chapters 13–36, and the book of Joshua.[22] Mostly fragmented versions of this collaborative project, the Old English Hexateuch, survive in seven manuscripts.[23] The identity of the other participants in this endeavour is uncertain. Peter Clemoes suggests that Byrhtferth of Ramsey was Ælfric's co-translator, but Richard Marsden argues that at least three translators were responsible for the non-Ælfrician sections.[24]

In his vernacular preface to the Hexateuch, Ælfric reluctantly submits to the behest of his patron, Æthelweard, that he translate Genesis up to the sacrifice of Isaac, observing that someone else has translated the rest of the book. His reluctance is generated by the possibility that unlearned readers will submit to the law of the old dispensation and ignore the doctrine of

---

20 Treschow, 'The Prologue,' 89.
21 See James Hurt, *Ælfric*, 93–100.
22 Ælfric, in his *Libellus de ueteri testamento et nouo*, states that he has translated the first seven books of the Old Testament, Maccabees, and parts of Kings, Daniel, Job, Esther, and Judith. For precise details on what Ælfric translates, see Richard Marsden, *The Text of the Old Testament in Anglo-Saxon England*, 404.
23 Samuel J. Crawford, ed., *The Old English Version of the Heptateuch, Ælfric's Treatise on the Old and New Testament and his Preface to Genesis*. Crawford generates a 'Heptateuch' by including Ælfric's homily on Judges (Oxford, Bodleian Library, Laud Misc. 509).
24 Peter Clemoes, 'The Composition of the Old English Text,' 42–53; Richard Marsden, 'Translation by Committee?' 41–89. On Alcuinian and Old Latin influence on the Hexateuch, see Marsden, 'Old Latin Intervention in the Old English *Hexateuch*,' 229–64; and *The Text of the Old Testament*, 413–36.

the new.[25] Indeed, Clemoes notes that for Ælfric, as for all Christians, 'the primary importance of the Old Testament was its preparation for the New.'[26] Much of his preface, therefore, is devoted to educating readers about appropriate Christian reading practices – the manner with which the spiritual meaning of the Old Testament should be uncovered in its literal narrative. Ælfric's caution also manifests itself in leaving untranslated or glossing over parts of Genesis deemed too scandalous for a lay audience (for example, the sin of the Sodomites).[27] As Thomas N. Hall observes, despite Ælfric's concern in his preface to produce a faithful translation that adds nothing new to the original, his biblical translations 'are at times free enough to qualify as paraphrases, and it is not unusual for him to abridge or expand the Latin to clarify obscure passages, encourage certain interpretations, or bring the text into conformity with the prosodic and alliterative requirements of his own rhythmical prose.'[28]

The Old Testament and the Poems of the Junius Manuscript

As has often been observed, the body of scriptural verse attributed by Bede in his *Historia ecclesiastica* to the unlettered and divinely inspired cowherd Cædmon resembles the early-eleventh-century collection of poetry found in Oxford, Bodleian Library, MS Junius 11. These poems are known to modern readers as *Genesis A, Genesis B, Exodus, Daniel*, and *Christ and Satan*. The Dutch scholar Franciscus Junius, who published the manuscript in 1655, first attributed the Old Testament verse to Cædmon. Cædmon's authorship of any of these poems now seems highly unlikely, but *Genesis A, Genesis B, Exodus*, and *Daniel* all speak to the suitability of Old Testament narratives for Germanic-heroic treatment and to the capacity of poets composing in the vernacular to put a native and secular tradition to work for religious purposes.[29] Indeed, though the event is in fact extra-scriptural, the creation and fall of the angels is an example of an episode that particularly appealed to the Anglo-Saxon

---

25 Ælfric overcomes these reservations regarding biblical translation by the time of his *Letter to Sigeweard*, which exhibits no anxiety over the propriety of his efforts.
26 Peter Clemoes, 'The Chronology of Ælfric's Works,' in *Old English Prose: Basic Readings*, ed. Paul E. Szarmach, 29–72, at 53.
27 On the strategic alterations to the text, see Rebecca Barnhouse, 'Shaping the Hexateuch Text for an Anglo-Saxon Audience,' 91–108.
28 Hall, 'Biblical and Patristic Learning,' 330. See also Richard Marsden, 'Ælfric as Translator,' 319–58.
29 See Jeff Opland, *Anglo-Saxon Oral Poetry*, 120.

imagination as it receives treatment three times in the Junius manuscript (*Genesis A*, *Genesis B*, and *Christ and Satan*) and is often alluded to elsewhere, most significantly in the poetic *Solomon and Saturn*.[30]

The Old Testament narrative poetry is copied by a single hand using a single set of fitt numbers, which suggests that the copyist viewed all the poems as part of one composition. Linguistic and metrical evidence, however, indicates separate authorship for each poem (for *Genesis B*, a special case, see below), while palaeographical evidence indicates that the copyist was working with a single exemplar. *Christ and Satan* is the odd one out in this collection: two or three new hands intervene in its transcription, and studies of the codex have demonstrated that most of the gathering within which it is contained differs from the rest of the manuscript.[31] *Christ and Satan* also departs from the other poems in the manuscript in terms of theme and structure. Instead of being based (however loosely) on an Old Testament narrative, the last poem in the collection deals lyrically and dramatically with a number of well-known New Testament and extra-biblical Christian themes: the lament of the fallen angels, the Harrowing of Hell, the Resurrection, the Ascension, and Judgment Day. Nevertheless, the manuscript as a whole has been thought to possess a 'theological unity,' having been compiled in order to fashion from discrete compositions an 'epic of redemption.'[32] The manuscript is richly illuminated and in forty-eight drawings represents episodes in the book of Genesis from Creation to Abraham and Sarah's approach to Egypt.[33]

Even though *Christ and Satan* can be distinguished readily from the Old Testament–based poems in Junius 11, the question of the sources of the biblical poems is still a pressing one because of the heterogeneity of scriptural texts that circulated in early medieval England. In an important study that establishes the groundwork for future scholarship, Paul Remley surveys the various routes of scriptural transmission and reception in Anglo-Saxon England. He contends that once the heterogeneous milieu of

---

30 Robert J. Menner, ed., *The Poetical Dialogues of Solomon and Saturn*, lines 434–66. See also Michael Fox, 'Ælfric on the Creation and Fall of the Angels,' 175–200.

31 See Barbara C. Raw, 'The Construction of Oxford, Bodleian Library, Junius 11,' 187–207.

32 J.R. Hall, 'The Old English Epic of Redemption: The Theological Unity of MS Junius 11,' 185–208; reprinted in *The Poems of MS Junius 11*, ed. Roy M. Liuzza, 20–52. See also, in the same volume, Hall, 'The Old English Epic of Redemption: Twenty-Five-Year Retrospective,' 53–69.

33 For a detailed study of the illuminations in Junius 11 and their relationship to the poetry, see Catherine Karkov, *Text and Picture in Anglo-Saxon England*.

scriptural circulation has been acknowledged, 'nearly all of the verse of Junius 11, including many passages that have so far resisted convenient explanation ... may be seen to reflect an intelligible and not infrequently intelligent set of responses to problems engendered by the words of the Bible themselves.'[34]

Genesis A

The first poem in Junius 11 generally is thought to be an early (that is, eighth century) composition; *Genesis A* resembles in style, metre, and vocabulary other compositions that are considered early (*Exodus*, *Daniel*, and, perhaps, *Beowulf*) and differs markedly from Old English poetry that is known to have been written later in the Anglo-Saxon period. The poem follows in a linear fashion a mixed Old Latin-Vulgate version of the book of Genesis[35] from Creation to the sacrifice of Isaac (22:13), although there are numerous omissions and additions and, according to Fulk and Cain, 'scripture is by no means given a slavish translation.'[36] Lines 235–851, now called *Genesis B*, constitute a distinct, interpolated composition based on an Old Saxon source and deal mainly with the temptation and fall of Adam and Eve.

Until the intervention of Huppé's *Doctrine and Poetry*,[37] scholarship on the relationship of *Genesis A* to the Old Testament tended to debate the extent to which the poet transformed the biblical narrative into traditional Germanic and heroic verse.[38] According to Alger N. Doane, the poem's most recent editor, Huppé's contribution placed *Genesis A* 'in an appropriate intellectual setting' by contending that the text 'is steeped in the exegetical techniques and presuppositions of allegorical biblical commentary in the "Augustinian" tradition.'[39] In this way, the composition of *Genesis A*, and indeed of all Old English Old Testament poetry, is seen to be informed by patristic reading practices that conjoin literal text and spiritual signification in a highly traditional and systematic manner. *Genesis A*, for Doane and Huppé, is the product of a writer trained to read

---

34 Paul G. Remley, *Old English Biblical Verse*, 93.
35 See ibid., 148–9.
36 Fulk and Cain, *A History of Old English Literature*, 113.
37 Bernard F. Huppé, *Doctrine and Poetry*.
38 See, for instance, Henry Bradley, 'The "Cædmonian" Genesis,' 7–29; Arthur S. Skemp, 'The Transformation of Scriptural Story,' 423–70.
39 Alger N. Doane, ed., *Genesis A*, 42.

the words of the Old Testament *in Christo* and able to give fluid expression to extra-literal meaning and typological significance in the course of a predominantly literal paraphrase. However, while Doane approves of Huppé's contextualization, he criticizes the 'flat assumption of ideational unity' in Huppé's insistence that Augustine's doctrine of the two cities is the governing theme of the poem. Doane instead advocates an approach to *Genesis A* that acknowledges the patristic backdrop but is at the same time sensitive to the text's traditional Germanic elements and its varied, rather than univocal, exegetical response to features and episodes of the Old Testament.[40] Doane's assessment notwithstanding, scholars are far from unanimous in their estimation of the poet's debt to biblical commentary or how attentive a putative audience would have been to its figural dimensions (see Charles D. Wright's essay in this collection, pp. 121–71). Nevertheless, in a reading that follows Doane's methodological prescriptions, Andy Orchard finds in the traditionally heroic depiction of Abraham in *Genesis A* considerable evidence both for the poet's familiarity with patristic texts and for his reliance on Latin biblical narrative poets; authors such as Juvencus, Cyprianus Gallus, Caelius Sedulius, Arator, and Prudentius, Orchard argues, could have supplied to the *Genesis A* poet further models for allegorical interpretation of Genesis.[41]

Genesis B

Eduard Sievers discovered the interpolation of *Genesis B* within *Genesis A* in 1875 and theorized that the former was a West Saxon transcription of an Old Saxon exemplar, on the basis of comparison with the *Heliand*.[42] His hypothesis was confirmed dramatically in 1894 by Karl Zangemeister, professor of classics at Heidelberg, who found several Old Saxon fragments in a ninth-century Vatican manuscript (Vatican, Biblioteca Apostolica, MS Palatinus Latinus 1447), including twenty-six lines that overlap with *Genesis B*.[43] At some point in the copying of *Genesis A*, *Exodus*, and *Daniel*, perhaps into a manuscript predating Junius 11 by three-quarters of a century or so, a scribe interpolated episodes from a complete Saxon Genesis to make up for lacunae in *Genesis A*; namely, the fall of Satan, the

---

40 Ibid., 43.
41 Andy Orchard, 'Conspicuous Heroism,' 119–36.
42 Eduard Sievers, *Der Heliand und die angelsächsische Genesis*.
43 See Karl F. Zangemeister and Wilhelm Braune, 'Bruchstücke der altsächsischen Bibeldichtung aus der Bibliotheca Palatina,' 205–94.

Prohibition, and the fall of Adam and Eve.[44] Unlike *Genesis A*, however, *Genesis B* is not a continuous doubling of a scriptural source. Although it follows the plot provided by Genesis, chapter 3, the poem may more properly be described as a creative conglomeration and 'explanatory re-narrativization' of biblical and extra-biblical material.[45] While the influence of Augustine's interpretation of the third chapter of Genesis seems likely, the extra-biblical material has been difficult to source, suggesting the originality of the Saxon poet.[46] Nevertheless, scholars have proposed that this material bears some relationship to exotic apocryphal and exegetical works on the fall, perhaps associated with a continental centre that was a destination for Anglo-Saxon and Irish missionary activity.[47]

Exodus

The most immediate source for the Old English *Exodus*, an account of the departure of the Israelites from captivity in Egypt and the crossing of the Red Sea, at the level of narrative, is the book of Exodus 13:20–14:31. Linear narration, it must be said, is not a main concern, and *Exodus* is foremost a striking display of stylistic and imagistic variation by a poet exploring the limits of his literary register. The poem's most recent editor, Peter J. Lucas, summarizes the debt of the poet to the Old Testament beyond Exodus 13:20–14:31, while acknowledging that the poet possesses 'a close knowledge of the Bible as a whole':[48]

> [T]he poem draws on the rest of Exodus as appropriate, notably Exodus XV.1–21, the Song of Moses, and the later chapters which describe the Tabernacle of the Tent of the Presence of the Lord (*feldhusa mæst* 85). The stories of Noah (362–79), Abraham and Isaac (380–446), and Joseph (140–1

---

44 See Barbara Raw, 'The Probable Derivation of Most of the Illustrations in Junius 11,' 187–207; Alger N. Doane, ed., *The Saxon Genesis*, 38–42.
45 Doane, *The Saxon Genesis*, 93. On Vulgate and Old Latin echoes, see Remley, *Old English Biblical Verse*, 157–65.
46 On the influence of traditional Genesis commentary on *Genesis B*, see John Vickrey, '*Selfsceaft* in *Genesis B*,' 154–71; Rosemary Woolf, 'The Fall of Man in *Genesis B*,' 187–99; Thomas D. Hill, 'The Fall of the Angels and Man,' 279–90; Glenn M. Davis, 'Changing Senses in *Genesis B*,' 113–31.
47 See Brian Murdoch, 'An Early Irish Adam and Eve,' 146–77; Kathleen E. Dubs, '*Genesis B*,' 47–64; Doane, *The Saxon Genesis*, 98–107; Remley, *Old English Biblical Verse*, 165–7.
48 Peter J. Lucas, ed., *Exodus*, 55.

and lacuna, 142–7, 588) are based on the relevant parts of Genesis, and the allusion to the building of the Temple at Jerusalem (389–96) implies familiarity with the relevant parts of Kings and Chronicles.[49]

The abruptness with which the so-called patriarchal digression breaks into the narrative at lines 362–446 (dealing with Noah and the flood and the sacrifice of Isaac) has generated considerable critical debate, especially over the poem's relationship to the baptismal liturgy. James W. Bright was the first scholar to propose that *Exodus* was 'based on Scripture selected to be read on Holy Saturday' on account of the presence and placing of Genesis material.[50] His hypothesis did not meet with much approval until it was revived with some reservations by Lucas, who asserts that 'although Bright probably overstated his case (as, for example, when he claimed *Exodus* to be a *carmen paschale*), there can be little doubt that the poem reflects a knowledge of the liturgy.'[51]

Remley develops Bright's argument and suggests ways in which Old Latin lections of early medieval Holy Saturday services could provide clues to the rationale behind the composition of the main narrative and to the source and position of the patriarchal digression.[52] However, Daniel Anlezark has pointed out recently that the pairing of the flood and the sacrifice of Isaac in the patriarchal narrative 'is not unique to the Easter liturgy, ... and the association of Noah and Abraham has Biblical precedents in the books of Wisdom and Sirach (Ecclesiasticus) and in the epistle to the Hebrews, where the authors present synopses of earlier scriptural history.'[53] The Easter lectionary, therefore, may not be the poet's only source for the juxtaposition of Noah, Abraham, and Moses. Anlezark also proposes that the *Exodus* poet's use of the phrase *niwe flodas* (new waters [line 362]) to describe the flood may indicate the influence of Aldhelm's Riddle LXIII, *Corbus* (Raven), but does not cite Remley's provocative hypothesis that Aldhelm may have been the author of *Exodus*.[54]

Scholarship has also given rise to contention over the extent of *Exodus*'s reliance on patristic commentary on the Old Testament; the matter is

---

49 Ibid., 52.
50 James W. Bright, 'The Relation of the Cædmonian *Exodus* to the Liturgy,' 97–8. The readings for Holy Saturday have also been connected to *Beowulf*, via *Exodus*, by Allen Cabaniss, '*Beowulf* and the Liturgy,' 195–201.
51 Lucas, *Exodus*, 59–60.
52 Remley, *Old English Biblical Verse*, 227–30.
53 Daniel Anlezark, 'Connecting the Patriarchs,' 172.
54 Paul G. Remley, 'Aldhelm as Old English Poet,' 90–108.

complicated somewhat by the fact that the poet explicitly calls for a spiritual interpretation of his text at lines 523–6 within a homiletic digression. As with *Genesis A*, one side privileges the literal or historical dimensions of the text while the other argues for the priority of the figural and allegorical.[55] The question of priority aside, it is difficult to argue that the immense typological significance of the exodus for the church fathers and later commentators had but a small impact on the *Exodus* poet.[56] Phyllis Portnoy recently has demonstrated how 'the learned reader will find typology confirmed at every point in *Exodus*' and how the unlearned reader is educated in typological understanding by the connections implicitly engendered by the poem's chiastic symmetry (that is, ring composition) – thus establishing a compelling link between vernacular modes of poetic composition and Christian hermeneutics.[57] Portnoy's argument also persuasively answers questions regarding the poem's structural integrity that are engendered by the seemingly intrusive place of the patriarchal digression and the homiletic digression (lines 516–48), thought by some scholars to be interpolations.[58]

Daniel

Robert T. Farrell, the last editor of *Daniel*, concludes that '[t]he *Daniel*-poet is not a translator of the biblical text, and his accomplishment goes far beyond mere paraphrase; he has written a poem which is carefully constructed and which presents a very distinctive reworking of the first five chapters of the book of Daniel.'[59] Both Farrell and Remley discuss the possibility of the poet's reliance on an Old Latin version of Daniel, a biblical book that has its own complex textual history;[60] following Bright and J.R. Hall, Portnoy argues that, like the other Old Testament poems in

---

55 For an account of the history of the exegetical approach to *Exodus*, see John P. Hermann, *Allegories of War*, 57–89. Resistance to the allegorical approach has come most powerfully from Edward B. Irving, ed., *The Old English Exodus*, 28–35; Thomas A. Shippey, *Old English Verse*, 134–54; Nicholas Howe, *Migration and Mythmaking*, 72–107; Judith N. Garde, *Old English Poetry in Medieval Christian Perspective*, 25–56.

56 For a summary of patristic exegesis on the exodus, see Lucas, *Exodus*, 55–9.

57 Phyllis Portnoy, 'Ring Composition and the Digressions of *Exodus*,' 307.

58 See Lucas, *Exodus*, 30–3; Remley, *Old English Biblical Verse*, 170.

59 Robert T. Farrell, ed., *Daniel and Azarias*, 36.

60 See ibid., 22–9; Remley, *Old English Biblical Verse*, 328–33.

Junius 11, *Daniel* corresponds to sections of the Easter lectionary.[61] Whatever the poet's scriptural source, he departs from the Old Testament by considerably elevating Nabuchodonosor's importance. The action of the narrative and the thematic concerns of the Old English poem revolve around the recalcitrant Chaldean king rather than the eponymous protagonist.[62] Even though the influential commentary of Jerome on the book of Daniel resulted in the prominence of the prophetic material in the Middle Ages, the poet is intent on illustrating the pride and eventual humbling of Nabuchodonosor.

This idiosyncratic approach to the source material could be accounted for by the poem's somewhat abrupt conclusion. Although Farrell rejects this view, scholars have argued that the poem ends imperfectly and in its original state continued past Daniel's grim warning at Belshazzar's feast (lines 741–64).[63] The internal structural integrity of *Daniel* and its reliance on a unified biblical exemplar have also been challenged. The poem provides two separate accounts of an angel rescuing the three youths from Nabuchodonosor's fiery furnace (at lines 271–7 and 335–56), and Azarias's prayer for deliverance (lines 279–332) occurs after the first description of rescue (lines 271–8). These inconsistencies have suggested to critics, before and after Farrell's defence of integrity,[64] that parts of the poem were interpolated after the time of its first composition.[65] Remley argues for single authorship but provides much evidence for the poet's reliance on several liturgical exemplars, along with a more or less continuous text of the first five chapters of Daniel.[66]

---

61 Phyllis Portnoy, '"Remnant" and "Ritual,"' 408–21. See further John Bugge, 'Virginity and Prophecy,' 127–47, who 'adds to Bright's original contention that *Daniel* is a *carmen paschale* by showing it to be a baptismal poem as well' (143).

62 On the centrality of Nabuchodonosor in the poem, see Graham Caie, 'The Old English *Daniel*,' 1–9; Gillian R. Overing, 'Nabuchodonosor's Conversion,' 3–14; Manish Sharma, 'Nabuchodonosor and the Defiance of Measure,' 103–26.

63 See Farrell, *Daniel and Azarias*, 5–6 and 32–4; Raw, 'The Construction,' 187–207; Peter J. Lucas, 'On the Incomplete Ending of *Daniel*,' 46–59 and 'A Daniel Come to Judgement?' 71–91.

64 Farrell, *Daniel and Azarias*, 22–32. See also Robert E. Bjork, 'Oppressed Hebrews and the Song of Azarias,' 213–26.

65 See Stanley B. Greenfield and Daniel G. Calder, *A New Critical History of Old English Literature*, 217.

66 Remley, *Old English Biblical Verse*, 334–434.

The Old Testament and Other Old English Poems

The Canticles of the Three Youths

A poem of 191 lines in the Exeter Book (Exeter, Cathedral Chapter Library, MS 3501) between *Guthlac B* and *The Phoenix*, *The Canticles of the Three Youths* (earlier known as *Azarias*) paraphrases the Songs of Azarias and the Three Children from the book of Daniel, the narrative material introducing and connecting them, and concludes with Nabuchodonosor's request that they emerge from the furnace (Daniel 3:24–90).[67] The poem clearly has some relationship to the Old English *Daniel* as lines 1–72 of *The Canticles of the Three Youths* closely resemble *Daniel* lines 278–361 in their wording. The precise nature of this relationship is controversial, but, according to Farrell, 'it is reasonable to suppose that they are influenced by a common tradition in English,' although *Daniel* appears to be more faithful to scripture and thus is likely earlier.[68] In a meticulous study of the texts' interrelationship, with wide-ranging implications for the dating and scribal milieu of Junius 11 and the Exeter Book, Remley's tentative conclusion is that he is 'inclined to regard the common antecedent text of *Daniel* and *The Three Youths*, a text already standing at some distance from a hypothetical archetype of Daniel, as a production emerging before the period of vigorous Benedictine reform marked by (say) Æthelwold's consecration as bishop of Winchester in 963. The transmitted text of *The Three Youths*, by contrast, is most easily viewed as a product of the reform years.'[69]

Judith

The Old English *Judith*, a fragment of 349 lines, is the only other verse text in the *Beowulf* manuscript (London, British Library, MS Cotton Vitellius A.xv) and is copied by the second scribe of *Beowulf* (Scribe B). *Judith* occupies the final folios of the manuscript and accompanies three prose

---

67 On the basis that the poem includes two separate hymns, one by Azarias and one by the Three Youths, the poem's most recent editor supplies this alternative title, *The Canticles of the Three Youths*: see Bernard J. Muir, ed., *The Exeter Anthology of Old English Poetry*, vol. 2, 461. See also Paul Remley, '*Daniel*, the *Three Youths* Fragment,' 82, who argues that the poem should be called *The Three Youths*.

68 Farrell, *Daniel and Azarias*, 41.

69 Remley, '*Daniel*, the *Three Youths* Fragment,' 160.

pieces:[70] *The Life of St. Christopher*, *The Wonders of the East*, and *Alexander's Letter to Aristotle*.[71] Mark Griffith, the text's most recent editor, tentatively dates the poem on linguistic grounds to the late ninth or tenth century.[72] The primary source of *Judith* is a version of the deuterocanonical book of Judith 12:10–16:1 that 'undoubtedly resembled the Vulgate.'[73] Since the poem is missing its beginning and employs less than a third of its biblical source, some scholars have conjectured that almost a thousand lines of the original have been lost. The modern consensus is far more conservative, based primarily on the fact that *Judith* throughout is a selective retelling of its scriptural antecedent.[74] The principle informing the poet's selectivity is clear: he ignores the details (for example, only Holofernes and Judith are named) and the characterization (for example, Judith's flirtatiousness is suppressed) of the original and avoids engaging its figural potential in order to focus on the climactic beheading of Holofernes and the heroic triumph of God's representative over heathen evil.[75]

Metrical Psalms of the Paris Psalter, and Psalm 50

As noted above, accompanying Alfred's translation of the first fifty psalms in the Paris Psalter are verse translations of Psalms, chapters 51–150. Occasional verse translations from the Psalms in an eleventh-century Benedictine monastic work found in Oxford, Bodleian Library, MS Junius 121, are almost certainly transcribed from the Paris Psalter. Dating the vernacular verse of the psalter has proven challenging on account of its idiosyncratic metre, although a relatively late date of composition (that is, late ninth to early tenth century) generally is accepted.[76] In the course of

---

70 There is some question as to the original position of *Judith* in the manuscript; see Peter J. Lucas, 'The Place of *Judith* in the *Beowulf*-Manuscript,' 463–78, which argues that *Judith* originally came before *Christopher* – a juxtaposition that would suggest that Judith be read as a saint *ante Christo*.

71 For a detailed overview of scholarship on the *Beowulf* manuscript and *Judith*'s place within it, see Andy Orchard, *A Critical Companion to Beowulf*, 12–56.

72 Mark Griffith, ed., *Judith*, 44–7.

73 Ibid., 48. On the canonicity of the book of Judith for the Anglo-Saxons, see Eric G. Stanley, 'Ælfric on the Canonicity of the Book of Judith,' 439.

74 See Martina Häcker, 'The Original Length of the OE *Judith*,' 1–18.

75 Ælfric, by contrast, associates Judith allegorically with the Church Militant and tropologically with chastity. See Mary Clayton, 'Ælfric's Judith,' 215–27; Hugh Magennis, 'Contrasting Narrative Emphases in the Old English Poem *Judith*,' 61–6.

76 See Robert D. Fulk, *A History of Old English Meter*, 410–14.

his composition, the poet seems to have relied on interlinear glosses of the psalms.[77] Scholarly estimation of the quality of the verse is quite low,[78] particularly when compared to the *Kentish Psalm 50*, found in British Library, MS Cotton Vespasian D.vi.[79] *Psalm 50* is a 157-line poetic paraphrase of the Vulgate Psalm 50 and likely a product of the tenth-century Benedictine reform.[80] Unlike the metrical psalms of the Paris Psalter, *Psalm 50* evinces the skill of a poet who has absorbed and put to good use vernacular compositional practices. The poem begins by recounting traditional exegetical interpretation of the psalms as an act of repentance by David for his adulterous relationship with Bathsheba. An expansive paraphrase of the psalm follows, and the poem concludes with a prayer to God, asking that he forgive the poet and others just as he forgave David.

Contributions

The first section, considering Old English prose, begins with Michael Fox's observation that Ælfric's translation of Alcuin's *Quaestiones in Genesim* is in fact the first vernacular translation of a biblical commentary into any language. Although the *Interrogationes Sigewulfi* has not received a great deal of critical attention, it does seem – with five surviving manuscripts – to have been relatively popular. Fox thus addresses many aspects of Ælfric's translation, beginning with the unusual decision to translate this sort of text at all. As it cannot be coincidence that Ælfric ends his commentary with the abrupt observation that he has now written about 'the most necessary questions,' his evocation of King Alfred's version of *Regula pastoralis* by Gregory suggests that he felt there was some affinity, at least, between his overall purpose and Alfred's. Also, Ælfric's translation is hardly mechanical: where Alcuin wrote 281 questions from Genesis 1:1 to the blessings of the patriarchs, Ælfric includes only 69 questions from Genesis 1:1 to the temptation of Abraham, in Genesis chapter 22. Even in the 69 questions that Ælfric does translate, the material is significantly reorganized and rewritten, although the words of Augustine can sometimes be traced intact as they are quoted by Bede, then passed to Alcuin, and translated by Ælfric.

---

77 See M.J. Toswell, 'The Relationship of the Metrical Psalter,' 297–315.
78 On the substandard versification of the Paris Psalter, see Greenfield and Calder, *A New Critical History*, 231–2; M.S. Griffith, 'Poetic Language and the Paris Psalter,' 167–86.
79 Dobbie, ed., *The Anglo-Saxon Minor Poems*, 88–94.
80 Greenfield and Calder, *A New Critical History*, 232.

In the next chapter, Paul Szarmach suggests that Ælfric's paraphrase of the book of Judith fashions something that is neither a homily nor a saint's life but incorporates compositional features of his earlier writing experience. The influence of virgin martyr stories is part of this retelling, most notably in the treatment of Judith's beauty, and certainly the hitherto unexamined alliterative prose is an important Ælfrician element, but Szarmach also examines the function of the story as an exemplum. The Old Testament narrative is the point of comparison, but the poetic *Judith* offers another literary context: the two *Judiths* form an *opus geminatum*. Szarmach thus poses the question, did Ælfric know the poetic version? Via a recursive analysis of the intertextual relationship between the two versions, Szarmach seeks to illuminate both texts and heighten appreciation of the less-studied prose account.

Samantha Zacher considers how the Anglo-Saxons might have understood the Jewish practices and rituals of the Old Testament, particularly circumcision, which were rejected or reformulated by the Christian church. Beginning with the Old Testament references to the rite of circumcision and Paul's rejection of it in Galatians, Zacher proceeds to show that even the vocabulary involved in enumerating the details of the ritual is problematic. The surviving Old English evidence (for example in the translation of the Heptateuch) demonstrates (largely by selective omissions from the translation, in Genesis chapter 34 and Exodus chapter 4, for example) that the subject matter was difficult or uncomfortable. However, Ælfric in fact tackles circumcision on quite a few occasions, in his portion of the Heptateuch translation and, most significantly and probably originally, in his homily *Octabas et circumcisio Domini* (The Octaves and Circumcision of the Lord; *CH* I.6). While Ælfric clearly has the most to say about circumcision, Zacher also considers evidence from anonymous homilies and the poetry of the Junius manuscript. Reactions to the ritual are remarkably varied, but 'the rite of circumcision continued to signify and stress precisely those values of membership, community, and identity that were so prized in Anglo-Saxon literature.'

As we have seen, criticism of *Genesis A*, since the appearance of B.F. Huppé's *Doctrine and Poetry*, has been divided between interpretations *in Christo* (allegorical or typological readings) and *ad litteram* (literal or historical readings). However, Charles Wright, opening the section on the Old Testament and the poems of the Junius manuscript, argues that the allegorical or typological model advanced by Huppé does not provide a satisfactory context for the poem. His essay examines the question of the poet's approach to his biblical source, and the relative merits of Huppé's method and other attempts to discover a principle of composition for *Genesis A*; he finally suggests an alternative model that may have informed the Anglo-Saxon poet's conception of scriptural paraphrase: the genre of the world chronicle or universal history.

Manish Sharma acknowledges the debt of *Exodus* scholarship to typological and allegorical readings but suggests that a fuller understanding of the relationship between the poem's patriarchal and homiletic digressions can come from placing the poem within a philosophical context. Observing that Augustine's allegorical reading paradigm was founded on his linguistic epistemology, Sharma aims to outline the epistemological concerns of the *Exodus* poet in terms of the arguably Augustinian contrast that he establishes between human and divine language. Noting that the distinction between human and divine word is regulated by a heroic gift economy, Sharma seeks to demonstrate at the same time the poet's remarkable deployment of the heroic register in order to mediate reception of the Anglo-Saxon intellectual inheritance.

Like Wright and Sharma, Phyllis Portnoy offers new ways to understand the problematic dislocations, digressions, and incongruous details attending the reworking of scriptural narrative, this time in *Daniel*, the final Old Testament poem in Junius 11. Beginning with the question, why Daniel? Portnoy goes further to consider the manuscript context of the poem. She demonstrates that through ring composition the poet reorganizes the rather intractable scriptural and apocryphal materials and centralizes the episode of the three Hebrew youths in the fiery furnace, a subject which she argues is the key to the Junius 11 program. The episode incorporates phraseology from Deuteronomy that Portnoy suggests may derive in part from the poet's exposure to liturgy and art. Accordingly, Portnoy reconstructs a process of composition whereby the *Daniel* poet infuses his version of the furnace miracle with imagery recollected from both recitation and pictorial representation of the biblical canticles from both Deuteronomy and Daniel.

To begin the section on the Old Testament and other Old English poems, Damian Fleming explores the use of the so-called superlative genitive in Old English literature, concentrating on its incorporation into vernacular poetry. This construction, so easily recognizable (for example, 'King of kings,' 'Lord of lords,' 'Song of songs'), has been little studied in the fields of literature or grammar. Although it appears in a number of ancient languages, its great influence on the Latin world, and thence upon the English world, is directly tied to the frequency of its use within the Hebrew Bible. After briefly surveying the primarily negative evidence of the study of this construction in early medieval grammatical texts, Fleming examines how different Old English poets use this construction and suggests that certain poets must have been aware of its biblical origin. In particular, the poet Cynewulf seems to exploit the Hebraic nature of the construction and to use it in his poem *Elene* to distinguish the 'language' of Jewish men from that of Christian men.

Robin Waugh then argues that the miraculous behaviour of the cities in *Andreas* is due at least in part to their existence as texts that convey civic and scriptural authority. He employs O'Brien O'Keeffe's arguments concerning body and law in Anglo-Saxon England, in order to consider the role of public space as a participant in the oft-noted tendency for a body to be marked by law (such as the Old Testament laws) and made into a text. In *Andreas* this bodily text has a relationship with the cities that Andrew reads, transforms, writes over, and forces to speak.

Russell Poole proposes that the early-eleventh-century poet Sigvatr Þórðarson, an Icelander in the immediate entourage of Óláfr Haraldsson, the second great missionary king of Norway, probably benefited from specifically English modes of preaching and teaching. In his polemics against Óláfr's opponents Sigvatr deploys themes from the Old Testament story of the rebellion of the angels. Poole further argues that Anglo-Saxon recourse to the Old Testament to find models of militant secular leadership in pursuance of a just war, Judith prominent among them, would have helped Sigvatr to formulate his advocacy for Óláfr's forcible evangelization and unification of Norway. The poet combines these materials with New Testament themes such as the Entry to Jerusalem and the betrayal of Christ by Judas Iscariot.

Noting that the psalms are the songs of the elect to the Lord and, as such, stand as stylistic and generic paradigms for any song directly or obliquely invoking the Christian god, Stephen Harris observes that stylistic features such as refrains, formulae, stock images, parallelism, and apposition are shared between the psalms and Old English poetry; some lexical and phrasal echoes can be found through the rich glossed psalter tradition. However, there is also the matter of the psalms in which toil and rest, suffering and exaltation, are understood according to the promises of deliverance, judgment, and salvation. Psalm 43, for example, reminds war-ravaged readers that 'they got not the land in possession by their own sword' but by holding fast to the Lord's promise of deliverance to the righteous. Harris investigates, therefore, pertinent battle images in the psalms – their lexica and their thematic contexts. With these, he suggests a possible reception for *The Battle of Maldon*, arguing that it is written in the tradition of Psalm 43 to remind readers both of their suffering and that steadfastness in faith, not the sword, will ultimately deliver a people from its enemy.

In the concluding contribution, Jane Toswell explores the nexus between song and religion as it plays out in one Anglo-Saxon psalm translation, the so-called *Kentish Psalm*, a translation of Psalm 50. She observes that the translator seems to be aware of the patterns of repetition and balance in the Latin psalter, based on similar binary structures in the Hebrew and Assyriac originals, and suggests that he tries to replicate those in his Old English interpretation. Unlike the Paris Psalter poet, however, the Kentish translator wants to interpret and explicate every word and phrase of the text, a desire that affects the attempt to translate the register as well as the content of the source text. Via an innovative deployment of Itamar Even-Zohar's theory of the polysystemic nature of textual interrelation, Toswell argues that the *Kentish Psalm* translator, by adopting a more leisurely, almost prose-like approach, weakens the poetic import of the text while improving its homiletic efficacy as psalm explication rather than psalm.

Certain contemporary trends in scholarly emphasis are apparent in this volume; for instance, the verse *Judith* is featured in three of the essays summarized above. More important, perhaps, the great range of approaches evident in this collection reflects the lack of any sort of methodological hegemony in the field. It is difficult to deny that this eclecticism is a strength of Anglo-Saxon studies. The comparative, intertextual, historical, source-critical, and oral-formulaic studies that the reader will encounter here indicate the responsiveness of Anglo-Saxonists to the local challenges of particular texts and corpora and their unwillingness to subscribe to a single way of reading and understanding Old English literary culture.

The Old Testament and Old English Prose

Ælfric's *Interrogationes Sigewulfi*

MICHAEL FOX

The first book of the Old Testament has been the subject of frequent and diverse exegesis. If Augustine of Hippo may accurately be called the major figure in the Western understanding of Genesis, then this is due at least in part to the fact that he himself returned to the book again and again, making it a significant concern in five of his works, from *De Genesi contra Manichaeos* (388 or 389) to *De ciuitate Dei* (books XI–XIV, written between 417 and 420), and including his *Confessiones* (written between 397 and 401) and his master work on Genesis chapters 1–3, *De Genesi ad litteram* (401 to 414).[1] Augustine's various commentaries, supplemented often by Jerome's *Hebraicae quaestiones in Genesim* (389–92) and less frequently by Ambrose's various works pertaining to Genesis, provided the foundation for most subsequent treatments of the early medieval period. Bede, for example, relied heavily on Augustine in his *In Genesim* (composed in stages, probably between 703 and 731)[2] and was, in fact, one of the last authors to demonstrate direct knowledge of *De Genesi ad litteram*

---

1 R.J. Teske, trans., *Saint Augustine on Genesis*, offers a similar summary of Augustine's work on Genesis (3). The fifth work is his *De Genesi ad litteram imperfectus liber*, which ceases at Gen. 1:26. In addition to the works mentioned here, the interpretation of Genesis also features prominently in Augustine's *Quaestiones in Heptateuchum* and *Locutiones in Heptateuchum*. The former, in the section on Genesis, contains 173 questions on Gen. 4–50. The latter contains 213 *locutiones* on Gen. 1–50 (most of which discuss scriptural variants).

2 See C.W. Jones, ed., *Bedae uenerabilis opera, pars II, opera exegetica: Libri quatuor in principium Genesis*, vi–x.

before the twelfth century.³ Alcuin's *Quaestiones in Genesim* (ca 796) was at the forefront of a Carolingian explosion in biblical commentary, and Genesis, being the subject of commentaries also by Wigbod, Claudius of Turin, Hrabanus Maurus, Angelomus of Luxeuil, Haimo of Auxerre, and Remigius of Auxerre, certainly received its share of treatment. After the Carolingian period, however, the only named author who can be said to demonstrate a sustained interest in Genesis before 1100 is in fact the Anglo-Saxon monk Ælfric,⁴ who not only translated the opening chapters but also returned repeatedly to the book (and especially to Genesis chapters 1–3) in works such as *De initio creaturae* (*CH* I.1), the *Exameron*, the *Letter to Sigeweard*, the *Letter to Wulfgeat*, *De creatore et creatura*, and *De temporibus anni*.⁵ Ælfric also had the distinction of being, so far as I am aware, the first author to translate a work of Latin exegesis into any vernacular language, for Ælfric selectively translated and adapted Alcuin's *Quaestiones in Genesim* into Old English in his *Interrogationes Sigewulfi*.⁶

The *Interrogationes Sigewulfi* has not been the subject of much study. First edited by Karl Bouterwek in 1858,⁷ and in fact edited four times in the latter half of the nineteenth century, the standard edition of the

---

3 When *De Genesi ad litteram* was cited, it often was known only through intermediate sources (such as Bede, as we shall see) or via florilegia and epitomes. On the latter, see Michael Gorman, 'An Unedited Fragment of an Irish Epitome,' 76–85, and his remarks in 'The Encyclopedic Commentary on Genesis,' 178–9.

4 Genesis, however, was also an productive text for Old English poetry. A work such as *Beowulf*, for example, may contain reference in its opening lines to Gen. 11:1–9 (the tower of Babel), Gen. 1 (Creation), Gen. 4:1–16 (Cain's killing of Abel), Gen. 6:1–7 (the giants who struggle against God), and Gen. 7 (the flood). See also the introduction herein.

5 Katherine O'Brien O'Keeffe makes a similar point with a slightly different set of works but suggests that the group 'attest[s] to Ælfric's lifelong interest in the exegesis of Genesis' ('Three English Writers on Genesis,' 70–1). O'Keeffe subsequently posits what the relationship and different audiences of these texts might be (71–8).

6 Historically there has been some confusion in the titles of Ælfric's work and its source, Alcuin's question-and-answer commentary on Genesis. However, Alcuin's title is certainly *Quaestiones in Genesim* (not the invented *Interrogationes et responsiones in Genesim* of the *PL* edition), which therefore means that the rubric *Interrogationes Sigewulfi* may be used for Ælfric's translation without risk of confusion.

7 Bouterwek imagines Alcuin's *Quaestiones in Genesim* to have only 278 questions, which must indicate that he was working from a sixteenth-century edition of Alcuin's works edited by Marguerin de la Bigne (in *Sacra bibliotheca sanctorum patrum*, 2nd ed. [Paris, 1589], vol. 3, cols. 1065–1102), which was the first to include numbers for Alcuin's questions and the only one to tally 278.

commentary remains George MacLean's 1883–4 edition. However, the commentary, along with *De creatore et creatura* and *De sex aetatibus huius saeculi*, was best edited and discussed in a dissertation by William P. Stoneman, which, though unpublished, ought to be the edition of choice for those interested in the work.[8] Other critical study of the commentary is limited to comments in passing in general treatments of Ælfric and his writings, most significantly by Peter Clemoes, and to an insightful article by Katherine O'Brien O'Keeffe that assesses Ælfric's 'theological legacy' as the third prominent Anglo-Saxon to write on Genesis.[9]

Although modern interest has perhaps been lacking, the manuscript evidence suggests that the *Interrogationes Sigewulfi* was not an unpopular text; it survives complete in five different manuscripts.[10] Bouterwek's first edition was printed from the best-known manuscript of the group, and one of the two earliest, British Library, Cotton Julius E.vii, the principal manuscript for Ælfric's *Lives of Saints*. From the table of contents it is clear that three works were appended to the end of the *Lives of Saints*, the *Interrogationes*, *De falsis diis* (Pope XXI), and *De duodecim abusiuis*,[11] though only the *Interrogationes* and lines 1–140 and 150–91 of *De falsis diis* remain in the manuscript.[12] Clemoes terms these three texts an appendix to the *Lives of Saints* and suggests that 'Ælfric himself must have issued

---

8 See K. Bouterwek, *Screadunga*; George MacLean, 'Ælfric's Version of *Alcuini interrogationes Sigeuulfi in Genesin*'; F.H. Mitchell, *Älfrics Sigewulfi Interrogationes in Genesin*; A. Tessman, *Aelfrics altenglische Bearbeitung*; and W.P. Stoneman, 'A Critical Edition of Ælfric's Translation of Alcuin's *Interrogationes Sigwulfi presbiteri*.' All citations are from Stoneman; where I give citations by line number rather than question number, I will also provide line numbers from MacLean. For the relationship between Bouterwek, MacLean, Mitchell, and Tessman, see L.M. Reinsma, *Ælfric*, 100 and 237–8. With the exception of Bouterwek's edition, all of these were PhD dissertations.

9 See Peter Clemoes, 'The Chronology of Ælfric's Works,' in *The Anglo-Saxon*, 212–47; reprinted in Paul E. Szarmach, ed., *Old English Prose*, 29–72. See also O'Keeffe, 'Three English Writers.'

10 For more detailed information, see Appendix C to this chapter.

11 This work has been edited twice, but CCCC 303, Hatton 115, and Hatton 116 have not been collated in either edition. See R. Morris, ed., *Old English Homilies and Homiletic Treatises*, 107–19 and 299–304; and R.D.-N. Warner, ed., *Early English Homilies from the Twelfth Century MS Vespasian D.xiv*, 11–16. For an overview of the work and its relationship to *De octo uitiis*, see A. Kleist, 'Ælfric's Corpus,' 124–5.

12 The table of contents lists these three works as items XXXVII, XXXVIII, and XXXVIIII, respectively.

the set in this form.'[13] The other early manuscript is Cambridge, Corpus Christi College, MS 162, though the *Interrogationes Sigewulfi* here was in fact removed from Cambridge, Corpus Christi College, MS 178 by Matthew Parker.[14] CCCC MS 178, then, is slightly later than Cotton Julius E.vii and places the *Interrogationes* in completely different company; the manuscript opens with Ælfric's *De initio creaturae* (*CH* I.1), the *Hexameron*, and the *Interrogationes*. Taken together, these three works provide an excellent starting point for the interpretation of Genesis, and this must have been the compiler's aim. CCCC MS 178 also contains *De falsis diis* (though preserving a version different from Cotton Julius E.vii) and *De duodecim abusiuis* (with the addition of a discourse on the eight vices), but they are not consecutive or even proximate. The other three manuscripts are difficult to classify in terms of their contents. Oxford, Bodleian Library, MS Hatton 115, from the second half or third quarter of the eleventh century, is largely a collection of homilies, mainly from Ælfric, and has a great deal of overlap with CCCC MS 178 and with Oxford, Bodleian Library, MS Hatton 116, the first of two early twelfth-century manuscripts of the *Interrogationes*. The final manuscript, CCCC MS 303, is another collection of homilies, but it also contains five items from Ælfric's *Lives of Saints* and concludes with an incomplete version of his homily on Judith.

Overall, it is worth noting that we find *De duodecim abusiuis* and *De auguriis* (*Lives of Saints* XVII) in all five manuscripts, *De falsis diis* in four of the five, and the *Exameron* preceding the *Interrogationes* in two manuscripts.[15] Further, there is evidence that at least one person read the commentary closely, as CCCC MS 178, Hatton MS 115, and Hatton MS 116 were glossed by the 'tremulous hand,' who, in CCCC MS 178, also added a mark in the margin to indicate the beginning of each new question.[16] CCCC MS 178 also preserves an intriguing marginal

---

13 Clemoes also suggests that the order of the texts may reflect their order of composition. Although he notes that the 'same mixture occurs, though not as an organized set,' in Cambridge, University Library, MS Ii.1.33, that manuscript contains only one item of the 'appendix' of Cotton Julius E.vii, *De falsis diis* on fols. 175v–84v, with its ending imperfect ('The Chronology of Ælfric's Works,' 220 and 224n1).

14 See R.I. Page, 'Anglo-Saxon Texts in Early Modern Transcripts,' 79–82.

15 There are also two excerpts, as well as an early collation of Hatton MS 115 with Hatton MS 116 made by Franciscus Junius.

16 On the tremulous hand, see C. Franzen, *The Tremulous Hand of Worcester*. On these later manuscripts generally, see M. Swan and E. Treharne, eds, *Rewriting Old English in the Twelfth Century*, especially the contributions by E. Treharne ('The Production and

note signed 'Coleman' that supplements Ælfric's translation of Alcuin's *Interrogationes* 15. (*ÆInt.* 12).[17]

Although the central text of the *Interrogationes* is remarkably stable in the five manuscripts, there is one substantial and unresolved issue. CCCC MS 178 and Hatton MS 116 add a conclusion in rhythmical prose, the so-called doxology on the Trinity (lines 550–88; MacLean, lines 511–45), which is not present in Julius E.vii, Hatton MS 115, or CCCC MS 303. The passage is, however, integral to *De sancta Trinitate et de festis diebus per annum* (Pope XIa),[18] which Pope describes as follows: 'Whoever compiled this homily has joined together, at some points interwoven, three passages that can be found separately in Ælfric's extant writings and three shorter passages (probably segments of a single passage) that appear nowhere else but are equally characteristic of Ælfric ... I think Ælfric did not put it together.'[19] Since Clemoes feels the selection of texts in Julius E.vii to have been an authorial appendix, and because a line near the end ('Þæs we him þanciað on urum þeowdome' [line 585; MacLean, lines 541–2]) seems to refer to the incarnation and man's redemption, Clemoes argues that the passage makes sense in Pope XIa but not in the *Interrogationes*: 'It seems to me clear that the passage in question was written for *De sancta Trinitate* and transferred from there (not necessarily by Ælfric ...) to the version of *Interrogationes* represented by CCCC 178 and Hatton 116.'[20] Pope, however, having published *De sancta Trinitate* subsequent to Clemoes's remarks, argues that the passage was definitely intended for the *Interrogationes*. Pope reasons that the ending is overly abrupt without the passage (following MacLean), that the rhythmic conclusion balances the rhythmic introduction, that the emphasis on the Trinity makes sense as a supplement to an account of Genesis naturally emphasizing God only, and that the author of the colophon in CCCC MS 178, who admits to additions to *De auguriis* and *De octo uitiis*, says nothing about the *Interrogationes*.[21] Pope's arguments are persuasive in themselves, but one

---

Script of Manuscripts Containing English Religious Texts in the First Half of the Twelfth Century,' 11–40) and S. Irvine ('The Compilation and Use of Manuscripts Containing Old English in the Twelfth Century,' 41–61).

17 See W.P. Stoneman, 'Another Old English Note Signed "Coleman,"' 78–82.
18 The homily survives uniquely in London, British Library, Cotton Vitellius C.v, fols. 1r and 4r–5v.
19 J.C. Pope, ed., *Homilies of Ælfric*, vol. 1, 453.
20 Clemoes, 'The Chronology of Ælfric's Works,' 230n3.
21 Pope, ed., *Homilies of Ælfric*, vol. 1, 457–8. On the issue of these additions, see also M. Clayton, 'Ælfric's *De auguriis*,' II. 376–94.

might add that an account such as *De initio creaturae* (*CH* I.1) also begins with an introduction to God and the Trinity before treating the broad sweep of Christian history, primarily emphasizing God, and then Christ as redeemer, in words that are in fact adapted for inclusion in the *Interrogationes*.[22] It seems to me safe to conclude that the original form of the *Interrogationes* is the longer version found in CCCC MS 178 and Hatton MS 116.

If this is the case, then Ælfric clearly does intend to bracket his translation of Alcuin with two passages in his so-called rhythmical prose.[23] The first, which introduces the commentary, is in fact a combination of Ælfric's original introduction to the author of the Latin commentary and some comments culled from the prefatory letter of Alcuin to Sigewulf. Where Ælfric might have seen this letter, however, is unclear. Curiously, only one surviving manuscript of the *Quaestiones in Genesim* was definitely in England before 1100, and that is Oxford, Bodleian Library, MS Barlow 35, a composite manuscript of the tenth and eleventh centuries.[24] While MS B of the group, which includes Alcuin's *Quaestiones*, is from the tenth century and could theoretically have been Ælfric's source, this seems unlikely. Barlow 35, first of all, was written on the continent and may not even have been in England in the tenth century. Further, the prefatory letter to Sigewulf is not preserved in the manuscript, which demonstrates without doubt that Ælfric at least saw another manuscript of the commentary and paraphrased Alcuin's letter from memory; however, it more likely suggests that he had a different exemplar altogether. Barlow 35 contains an

---

22 See especially P. Clemoes, ed., *Ælfric's Catholic Homilies, The First Series(CH)* I.1.16–21, and compare *CH* I.1.241–4 with *Interrogationes*, 580–2 (MacLean, 'Ælfric's Version,' 537–40). Tellingly, in Cotton Vitellius C.v, Pope XIa opens the collection and is followed by *CH* I.1. Also similar to the conclusion of the *Interrogationes* is *CH* I.15.183–94.

23 The issue of what to call Ælfric's particular prose style – and how to present it in print – remains in contention. The major discussions are as follows: A. McIntosh, 'Wulfstan's Prose,' 109–42; P. Clemoes, 'Ælfric,' 202–6; J.C. Pope, ed., *The Homilies of Ælfric*, vol. 1, 105–36; S.M. Kuhn, 'Was Ælfric a Poet?' 643–62 (reprinted in his *Studies in the Language*, ed. R.E. Lewis, 186–205); T. Cable, *The English Alliterative Tradition*, 42–52; S. Brehe, 'Rhythmical Alliteration,' 65–87; P.E. Szarmach, 'Abbot Ælfric's Rhythmical Prose and the Computer Age,' 95–108; T.A. Bredehoft, 'Ælfric and Late Old English Verse,' 77–107, and also his *Early English Metre*, 81–90, which provides the most recent comment on the matter: 'The conclusion that Ælfric's rhythmical compositions are, indeed, late Old English verse seems impossible to avoid' (90).

24 See F. Madan, H.H.E. Craster, and N. Denholm-Young, *A Summary Catalogue of Western Manuscripts*; H. Gneuss, *Handlist of Anglo-Saxon Manuscripts: A List of Manuscripts*, item 541.

incomplete and disordered version of the *Quaestiones*, as it omits *Interrogationes* 93–4 and ends at *Int.* 262 (containing, in order, *Ints.* 1–92, 95–242, 265–80, 254, 257, and 261–2); the manuscript does, therefore, omit one question that Ælfric translates (*Int.* 94). Barlow 35 belongs to the β family[25] of Alcuin manuscripts, but unfortunately Ælfric does not translate those questions that are the best indicators of manuscript families, and thus it is also difficult to determine with certainty what version of the commentary Ælfric saw. However, given that it could not have been only Barlow 35, and given that Ælfric does paraphrase Alcuin's letter to Sigewulf, which seems only to have circulated with the α family, it is highly probable that the version Ælfric saw was in a now-lost manuscript of the α family.

Ælfric's rhythmical prose introduction begins with a brief, but artful, description of Alcuin:

> Sum geþungen lareow wæs on Engla lande
> Albinus gehaten and hæfde micele geþincða.
> Se lærde manega þæs Engliscan mennisces
> on boclicum cræfte, swa swa he wel cuþe,
> and ferde siþþan ofer sæ to þam snoteran kyninge,
> Karolus gehaten, se hæfde micelne cræft
> for Gode and for worulde, and he wislice leofode.
> To þam com Albinus, se æðela lareow,
> and on his anwealde ælþeodig wunode
> on Sancte Martines mynstre, and þær manega gelærde
> mid þam heofonlican wisdome þe him se hælend forgeaf. (lines 1–11)

[A certain distinguished teacher in the land of the English was called Albinus, and he had great merit. He instructed many of the English folk in book knowledge, such as he well understood, and then travelled over the sea to that wise king, called Karolus, who had great skill both for the things of God and of the world and lived wisely. Albinus, the noble teacher, came to him and lived as a foreigner in his kingdom, in the minster of St Martin, and taught many there with the heavenly wisdom which the Lord himself had granted him.]

---

25 On the manuscripts of Alcuin's commentary, see M. Fox, 'Alcuin the Exegete,' 39–60

Ælfric seems to organize his opening passage around the chiastic repetition of *lærde manega* and *manega gelærde* but also repeats *hæfde micele
gepincða* and *hæfde micelne cræft* in a way that emphasizes the comple-
mentary talents of Alcuin and Charlemagne. Alcuin's primary role as
lareow is twice stated, once with the adjective *gepungen*, and once with
æðela. Ælfric's choice of emphasis here may have been suggested to him
by his exemplar and other manuscripts of Alcuin's work that he had seen,
for those manuscripts of Alcuin's works that contain attributions almost
always introduce him as 'Albinus magister' or 'Alcuinus magister.' One
might nevertheless wonder precisely what semantic range Ælfric intends
in his use of *lareow*. This is perhaps clarified first by *on boclicum cræfte*;
in his *Grammar*, Ælfric observes that *grammatica* (*stæfcræft*) is *ealra
boclicra cræfta ordfruma and grundweall* (the starting point and foundation of all book knowledge).[26] Second, the phrase *se æðela lareow*, as Ælfric
must surely have been aware, refers often in the Old English corpus, especially in Alfredian prose, to the apostle Paul;[27] Ælfric himself uses the
phrase to describe Augustine![28] Finally, the somewhat unusual description
of Alcuin as *ælpeodig* may also include a hint of approbation, for this word
glosses *peregrinus* in Ælfric's *Glossary*.[29]

The remaining eight lines of the introduction are a rough paraphrase of the
salient points of Alcuin's prefatory letter to Sigewulf, in which Alcuin explains that he has gathered together the questions Sigewulf has asked him
over a period of time, so that Sigewulf might have a portable collection of
'precious pearls of wisdom' to carry with him. Significant also is Alcuin's
understanding of the nature of the questions that he has answered, for he
clarifies to Sigewulf that he has avoided the 'many most difficult questions'

26 'GRAMMA on grecisc is LITTERA on leden and on englisc stæf, and GRAMMATICA
    is stæfcræft. Se cræft geopenað and gehylt ledenspræce, and nan man næfð ledenboca
    andgit befullon, buton he þone cræft cunne. Se cræft is ealra boclicra cræfta ordfruma and
    grundweall' (Julius Zupitza, ed., *Ælfrics Grammatik und Glossar*, 289).
27 For example, *se æðela lareow Sanctus Paulus* appears in Vercelli VIII, and Paul is *se æpela
    lareow* repeatedly in Blickling IV (eight times), Blicking V (twice), and also in the
    Old English version of Gregory's *Cura pastoralis*. See Donald Scragg, ed., *The Vercelli
    Homilies*, VIII.14; Richard Morris, ed., *The Blickling Homilies of the Tenth Century*;
    Henry Sweet, ed., *King Alfred's West-Saxon Version of Gregory's Pastoral Care*, chapters
    30 (205.5–6), 33 (222.7), 35 (237.18), 47 (361.25), 51 (401.18–19; here Paul is *se æðela ðioda
    lareow* [the noble teacher of nations]), and 62 (457.30).
28 *Natiuitas sanctae Mariae uirginis* (Assmann 3), 510. See Bruno Assmann, ed., *Angel-
    sächsische Homilien und Heiligenleben*, repr., 24–48.
29 Zupitza, *Ælfrics Grammatik*, 303.

of Genesis and concentrated on those which are 'mainly historical' and require only 'a simple response.'[30] Ælfric reports only that Alcuin has collected these *cnottan* (literally, knots) and gathered both *axunga* (questions) and *swutelunga* (explanations) into one text. As we shall see, though, Ælfric in fact renders a text that Alcuin already considered mainly 'historical' (or literal) and 'simple' into a much more basic exegetical primer.

First of all, there is the question of scope: Alcuin wrote 281 questions and answers treating material from Genesis 1:1 through to the blessings of the patriarchs in Genesis 49. *Interrogatio* 281, however, though I think clearly assembled by Alcuin, has often been considered a separate treatise and indeed is sometimes so rubricated in the manuscripts as *De benedictionibus patriarcharum*. Oddly, though the models from which Alcuin was working in his final question were complete, the commentary ends in all extant versions at the same place – at Dan – omitting commentary on Gad, Aser, Nephthalim, Joseph, and Benjamin. In other words, Alcuin's *Quaestiones* did not come to Ælfric with a perfectly logical structure, if a selective set of questions and answers possibly could have a structure satisfying to all readers, and it might therefore be less surprising that Ælfric ceases to translate Alcuin long before the conclusion of the commentary; Ælfric's last question is *Int.* 201, on the contradiction between Genesis 22:1 and James 1:13. Genesis 22:1, of course, would have seemed to Ælfric a natural place to conclude because the model of Bede's *In Genesim* before him, his own translation of Genesis, and even the poetic *Genesis A* all conclude at roughly the same point in the narrative. As Peter Clemoes has suggested, the primary motivation for Ælfric's commentary may have been to redress the troubling *nacedan gerecednisse* that resulted from his translation of Genesis.[31] In addition, there remains the fact that Alcuin's *Quaestiones* changes considerably in flavour and, I suspect, in interest after *Int.* 201, becoming little more than a pastiche of quotations from Augustine's *Quaestiones in Heptateuchum* and Jerome's *Hebraicae quaestiones in Genesim*. Indeed, one can perhaps detect Ælfric's

---

30 'Sunt in eodem libro difficillimae quaestiones plurimae, quas ad presens tangere non libuit uel etiam non licuit, uel quia me de illis non interrogasti. Hae etiam maxime historicae sunt et simplici responsione contentae, illae uero maioris inquisitionis et longiorem habere indigent tractatum' (Epistle 80, ed. E. Dümmler, *Epistolae* IV, *Epistolae karolini aeui* II, 122–3).

31 Clemoes, 'The Chronology of Ælfric's Works,' 225. This point is still valid, I believe, despite the fact that Richard Marsden has since shown that Ælfric translated as far as Gen. 24, and perhaps to Gen. 25:18, further than had previously been believed. See Marsden, 'Ælfric as Translator,' 328n34.

impatience in his translations, which are fairly faithful to Alcuin in the earliest questions but become more and more his own in the last part of the *Interrogationes*.[32] In the end, Ælfric translates 69 of Alcuin's 281 questions and breaks off his efforts suddenly and with a flourish: 'Nelle we na swiðor embe þis spræcan, forþan þe we habbað þa nydbehefestan axunga nu awritene' (We do not wish to speak about this any further, for we have now written the most necessary questions). His choice of words is surprising in this context, for Ælfric again must have known that he was echoing the preface of King Alfred's version of Gregory's *Cura pastoralis*, in which Alfred mentions his efforts to see translated *suma bec, ða þe nidbeðyrfesta sien eallum mannum to witanne* (some books, those which might be most necessary for all men to be knowing).[33]

Although, perhaps somewhat surprisingly, a detailed analysis of every question in Ælfric's translation[34] yields constant and often remarkable results, such an analysis is clearly not possible here. Since I have discussed elsewhere in some detail how Ælfric deals with the issue of the angelic creation and fall,[35] I will confine my current remarks to other attributes and features of the commentary, mainly as they relate to the creation and fall in Genesis, chapters 1–3, which was clearly central to Ælfric's concerns, because almost two-thirds of his translation is either introductory or related to hexameral issues.[36]

---

32 See Appendix B to this chapter.

33 Sweet, *King Alfred's West-Saxon Version*, preface (6.6–7 and 7.6–7). So far as I can tell, these are the only two such superlative uses of *nydbehefestan/nidbeðyrfesta* in the surviving corpus of Old English.

34 While I will consider what Ælfric translates rather than how, his approach to translation has been the subject of much comment, especially with regard to his *Preface to Genesis*, which has been related to Jerome's statement on translation – 'non uerbum e uerbo, sed sensum exprimere de sensu.' See the comments by Marsden, 'Ælfric as Translator,' 322–8; Jonathan Wilcox, ed., *Ælfric's Prefaces*, 63–5; H. Minkoff, 'Some Stylistic Consequences of Ælfric's Theory of Translation,' 29–41, and 'An Example of Lating [*sic*] Influence on Ælfric's Translation Style,' 127–42; Mark Griffith, 'Ælfric's Preface to Genesis,' 215–34; the detailed treatment in Robert Stanton, *The Culture of Translation*, 144–71, though Stanton does not at all mention Ælfric's translation of Alcuin; and Tristan Major, 'Rebuilding the Tower of Babel,' 47–60.

35 M. Fox, 'Ælfric and the Creation and Fall of the Angels,' 175–200.

36 Alcuin's *Int.* 1–25 are 'introductory,' and the commentary proper begins with Gen. 1.1 at *Int.* 26; the last hexameral question is *Int.* 82 on Gen. 3:24. *Int.* 93–4, which address the first evil will in the angels and the nature of evil, might also be included here, though it is significant that Alcuin places these questions in the context of Cain's killing of Abel instead of in a discussion of the rebel angels or the transgression in Eden.

The Creation of Man and His Placement in Paradise

The questions in Ælfric's *Interrogationes* that pertain to Creation *in principio* do not explicitly mention the creation of man; however, the moment of creation of heaven and earth in Genesis 1:1 refers, among other things, to the creation of unformed matter (*ungehiwod antimber* or, simply, *antimber*). Ælfric's theory of the timing of man's creation relies exclusively on one question:[37]

> *ÆInt.* 16: On hu manegum wisum is Godes weorc?
> On feower wisum. Ærest on Godes wordes gefadunge on þam ecan geþeahte. Eft on þam ungehiwodum antimbre þe he þa gesceafta of gesceop, swa swa hit [a]writen is: 'Qui uiuit in aeternum creauit omnia simul'; 'Se þe leofað on ecnysse gesccop ealle þincg togædere.' Þæt ðridde wæs þa þa God todælde mislice gesceafta on þære syx daga gesceapennysse. Þæt feorðe is þæt God gescypð symle edniwan of þam ærran þæt hi ne ateorian.

> [In how many ways is God's work? In four ways. First, in the disposition of God's word in that eternal counsel. Second, in that unformed matter from which he shaped creation, as it is written: 'Qui uiuit in aeternum creauit omnia simul' (He who lives in eternity created all things at once) (Sirach 18:1). The third was when God distinguished various creations in the creation of the six days. The fourth is that God creates anew continually from earlier things, that they not perish.]

> *Int.* 19: Quot modis est operatio diuina?
> Quatuor. Primo, quod in uerbi [Dei] dispensatione omnia aeterna sunt. Secundo, quod in materia informi '*qui uiuit in aeternum, creauit omnia simul.*' Tertio, quod per opera dierum sex uarias distinxit creaturas. Quarto, quod ex primordialibus seminibus non incognitae oriuntur naturae, sed notae saepius, ne pereant, reformantur.

In other words, the creation of man, as one of God's works, is an eternal fact in the disposition of the word of God. *In principio*, in Genesis 1:1, the unformed matter that will eventually become man's body is made. Then,

---

37 To distinguish between the two commentaries, I will use *ÆInt.* for questions from Ælfric, and *Int.* for those from Alcuin. I will cite Ælfric, then Alcuin (if necessary), and give a translation only of the Old English.

on the sixth day, the body of man is created from earth, and his soul is created from nothing.[38]

One can see that while Ælfric is translating Alcuin fairly closely, there are some significant changes to the passage. The first is his perceived need to introduce the quotation from Sirach 18:1 with a tag that will explain the inclusion of the Latin (*swa swa hit [a]writen is*), probably because this is the first biblical quotation for which Ælfric has included the Latin. Further, the concept of *primordialia semina* (which I believe comes ultimately from Augustine's theory of causal reasons in *De Genesi ad litteram* [*DGnL*]) is clearly one Ælfric feels he ought to avoid.[39] Indeed, the difficulty of the dual account of man's creation that occasions Augustine's theory of 'causal reasons' is completely ignored: Ælfric omits Alcuin's explanation that the account of Genesis 2:7 is a recapitulation with added detail of the account in Genesis 1:26 (*Int.* 49). The final alteration of note is the clarification that Ælfric adds (*þe he þa gesceafta of gesceop*), most likely taken from Alcuin's main source, Bede's *De natura rerum (DNR)* I.7.[40]

Following Alcuin, Ælfric focuses most of his attention on the account of Creation in Genesis 1:26.[41] Where Alcuin devotes six questions to man's creation (*Int.* 36–41), Ælfric translates five and incorporates material from the sixth question (*ÆInt.* 25–9). Although the majority is translated faithfully, Ælfric makes some interesting additions. For example, Ælfric follows Alcuin's assertion that God's words at the creation of man (*faciamus* rather than *dixit Deus*) indicate man's innate nobility and his creation according to the plan (*consilium* or *geþeaht*) of God. However, Ælfric classifies God's creation of other creatures, specifically on account of the repetition of *fiat* and *dixit*, as creation *þurh hæse* and concludes therefore that the active participation evinced by the phrase *faciamus hominem* means that God creates man *þurh his agene handa*,[42] an innovation not seen in Alcuin, or in Augustine or Bede.

---

38 Ælfric chooses to dismiss the question of the material from which the body of man was created. Owing to the interchangeability of the terms *unformed matter* and *earth* in Gen. 1:1, it is not clear which is the primary ingredient of the body of man in Gen. 2:7.

39 See, for example, *DGnL* VI.i.1–vi.1 and *DGnL* VII.xxviii.42 (Joseph Zycha, ed., *De Genesi ad litteram*, 1–456).

40 'Secundo, quod in materia informi pariter elementa mundi facta sint "ubi qui uiuit in aeternum creauit omnia simul"' (*DNR* I.7; Charles W. Jones, ed., *Bedae opera didascalica*, vol. 1, 174–234.

41 Ælfric omits Alcuin's two main questions on Gen. 2:7, *Int.* 8 and *Int.* 50.

42 *ÆInt.* 25: 'Hwi is gecweden on þæs mannes gesceapennysse "Uton wyrcan mannan," and be þam oðrum gesceaftum is awriten þæt God gecwæð and hi wurdon þurh his

Ælfric combines Alcuin's *Int.* 37 and *Int.* 40 on the Trinity and the unity of the Trinity, which is signified by the use of the plural (*faciamus*) and the singular image (*ad imaginem nostram*).[43] Creation according to both the image (*anlicnyss*) and the likeness (*gelicnyss*) of God is again evidence of eternity (in image) and custom (in likeness), but Ælfric again adds a detail that is unique in this context:

ÆInt. 27. On hwam is se man his scyppendes anlicnys?
On þam inran men, þæt is on þære sawle; seo hæfð on hyre þreo þing on annysse æfre wyrcende, þæt is gemynd and andgit and wylla.[44]

[In what (way) is the man the image of his creator?
In the inner man, that is in the soul; it has in it three things that work always as one, that is, memory, understanding, and will.]

Int. 38: In quo est homo conditoris sui imago? In interiori homine.

The notion of the tripartite soul does not, of course, originate with Ælfric and is commonplace in discussions of the Trinity. For example, both Augustine and Isidore discuss the component parts of the soul – *memoria, intellegentia* (or *intellectus*), and *uoluntas* – with reference to the Trinity.[45]

---

hæse gesceapene? Witodlice forþan þe þæs mannes wurðscipe and æþelborennys is toforan þam oðrum gesceaftum, and forþi wolde mid geþeahte and þurh his agene handa hine gescyppan.' *Int.* 36: 'Quare de solo homine dictum est: "Faciamus hominem"; de aliis autem creaturis legitur: "Dixit Deus?" Vt uidelicet, quae [*Ms.*, quia] rationabilis creatura condebatur, cum consilio facta uideretur, et ut eius nobilitas ostenderetur.'

43 See *ÆInt.* 26. Ælfric makes virtually the same comment in *Preface to Genesis* 64–9 and *Exameron* 329–40.

44 Stoneman notes that the manuscript has been glossed with *memoria, intellectus,* and *uoluntas.* See also *CH* I.20, 192–200; *Lives of Saints* I.112–14; King Alfred's *Boethius* XIV.ii; and Byrhtferth's *Enchiridion* IV.i.381–3, a passage which Baker and Lapidge note is taken from Haimo's *Homilia de tempore* XXVIII. I owe the latter two references to Stoneman, 'A Critical Edition,' 258.

45 See Augustine, *DGnL* VII.viii.11; *De Trinitate* X.xi.18, XV.vii.11–12, and XV.xx.39; Isidore, *Etymologiae* VII.iv.1. The comment in Isidore's *Etymologiae* is especially interesting because Ælfric's concluding passage on the Trinity is closest in substance (though direct borrowing is difficult to discern) to the same section of Isidore (*Etymologiae* VII.iv.1–8). On Augustine's influence upon Ælfric's conception of the Trinity, see B. Raw, *Trinity and Incarnation in Anglo-Saxon Art and Thought,* 35–9.

Ælfric omits both Alcuin's quotation of Jerome on the creation of para-dise *in principio* and Alcuin's explanation of man's function in paradise (*ut operaretur et custodiret illum*).[46] In terms of Augustinian influence, the omission of the latter is most significant. Alcuin's response, a quotation from Bede's *In Genesim*, appears to be one of the few in which Alcuin is careful to preserve the precise language of two of the more important and recognizable concepts that originate with Augustine's *De Genesi ad litteram*.[47]

The condition of Adam and Eve in paradise, however, is treated with almost the same thoroughness as it is in Alcuin. Both Alcuin's and Ælfric's primary line of enquiry concerns the tree of knowledge and God's injunc-tion not to eat of it. Alcuin considers this issue in three questions that form part of the introduction to the *Quaestiones* (*Int.* 5–7), and Ælfric con-denses them into two:

ÆInt. 5. Hwi wæs se man betæht to his agenum cyre?
To þan þæt he wære hi[m] sylfum ealdor swa to life, swa to deaðe, forþan gif he wære neadunga Gode underþeod, þonne næfde he nan wuldor for godum weorcum, ne nan wite for yfelum, ac wære þonne swilce an nyten.

[Why was man given into his own care?
In order that he might be lord unto himself, either to life or to death. Because if he were necessarily a servant of God, then he might have no glory for good works, nor any punishment for evil, but would then be like a beast.]

Int. 5. Cur homo suae potestatis auctor est creatus? Vt sibi ipse auctor esset [siue] ad uitam, siue ad mortem. Si uero necessitate [*Ms.*, necessitati] esset subiectus, tunc nec boni operis haberet gloriam, nec mali poenam, sed esset quasi unus [*Al.*, unum] ex pecoribus.

ÆInt. 6. Hwi wæs Adame an treow forboden þa þa he wæs ealles oþres hlaford?
To þan þæt he hine ne onhofe on swa micclum hlafordscipe, ac wære on ge-healdsumnysse þæs bebodes his scyppende underþeod, and þurh þæt wiste þæt he him hyran sceolde.[48]

---

46 See *Int.* 27 and *Int.* 51, respectively.
47 That is, that man did not suffer the affliction of labour in paradise but rather felt an exhilaration of the will, and that man should guard paradise lest he admit anything by which he might merit expulsion. See *Int.* 51.
48 See also *CH* I.1, 74–83 and *ÆInt.* 37, below.

[Why was one tree forbidden to Adam when he was lord of all else?
In order that he might not exalt himself in such great lordship, but might be
a servant to his creator in obedience of the command and, through that, might
know that he should obey him.]

Int. 7: Quare Adam mundi dominus legem accepit? Vt non tanto extolleretur
dominio, sed in obseruatione mandati sciret se subiectum creatori [*Ms.*, con-
ditori] suo.

ÆInt. 5 is an almost verbatim translation of Alcuin's *Int*. 5; only the
specific words that Ælfric chooses require comment. Where Alcuin asks
why man was created *suae potestatis auctor*, Ælfric substitutes *to his
agenum cyre*, which is precisely the phrase that appears in Ælfric's account
of the angelic fall, and which is also substituted for *liberum arbitrium* in
ÆInt. 37. In Alcuin's response, which suggests that man is *auctor* of his
own life or death, Ælfric translates *him sylfum ealdor*, suggesting that
Ælfric deliberately alters the form of the question to accord with his other
writings and, specifically, his idea of free will.

Alcuin's *Int*. 6 concerns the creation of the two trees and their respective functions *quasi medicina* and *ut ueneno*, functions that are meant
to echo man's choice of life or death in the preceding question. Ælfric,
no doubt perplexed by Alcuin's language (as all subsequent readers of
Alcuin seem to have been), which might suggest some form of evil to
inhere in the tree of knowledge, omits the question. However, in *ÆInt*.
6, Ælfric substitutes Alcuin's reference to the injunction (*lex* – an unusual term for the commandment) for a more straightforward question,
and one that supplies the referent from the omitted *Int*. 6. Ælfric also
tacks on a somewhat redundant phrase emphasizing man's role as an
underþeod.

In a related question, which appears much later in both commentaries
(within the context of the temptation), Ælfric again addresses man's choice:

ÆInt. 37. Hwi wolde se æþela scyppend æfre þone mannan to his agenum
cyre lætan?
Forþan þe se scippend nolde þæt se man þeow wære, se þe to his anlicnysse
gesceapen wæs, ac wære þurh godne willan herigendlic oððe of yflum willan
nyðergendlic.[49]

---

49 Compare Alcuin's *Int*. 64: 'Cur homo factus est in liberum arbitrium? Quia noluit
    creator hominem cuiuslibet seruum creare, quem ad imaginem suam fecit, quatenus
    ex uoluntario bono, laudabilis appareret, uel appetitu malo damnabilis.' On human and

[Why would the noble creator ever leave man to his own care?
For the reason that the creator did not wish man, he who was created to his likeness, to be a servant, but (that) he might be praiseworthy on account of a good will, or damnable on account of an evil will.]

The distinction between this comment and the earlier questions is important: although man should recognize himself to be subject to God (*underþeod*), he is not compelled to be a servant of God (*þeow*). In my opinion, Ælfric's version of the question, which changes the subject from man to God, better suits the tone of the response. And, because Ælfric includes a comment on the component parts of the soul in an earlier question (*ÆInt.* 27, quoted above), the juxtaposition of *anlicnyss* and *willa* places man's choice in a wider context.[50]

There are two further questions that pertain to man's original condition in paradise, and Ælfric makes only minor changes to each. Having avoided Alcuin's unusual description of the two trees, Ælfric closely translates the orthodox description of the tree of knowledge, preserving both the Latin and the English terms for the tree and stressing the Augustinian binary of the good of obedience and the evil of disobedience.[51] Finally, God's threat is explained as the death of the soul and the death of the body, a twofold death that is destroyed by the single death of Christ.[52]

---

angelic free will, see also *CH* I.7, 137–61. For a detailed treatment of free will in Ælfric's works and Anglo-Saxon England, see Aaron Kleist, *Striving with Grace*, esp. 166–212.

50 Ælfric omits Alcuin's companion question which explains that freedom from sin is to be considered the greatest liberty (*Int.* 64).

51 *ÆInt.* 30: 'Hwi wæs þæt treow, þe Adam on agylte, gehaten "lignum scientiae boni et mali," þæt is on Englisc, "treow ingehydes yfeles and godes?" Næs þæt treow on his gecynde gesceadwis, ne hit næfde ingehyd godes oððe yfeles, ac þæt se man mihte on þam treowe, þe him forboden wæs, tocnawan hu mycel god is on gehyrsumnysse and hu micel yfel on ungehyrsumnysse.' See Appendix A, item 1.

52 *ÆInt.* 31: 'Hwæt is getacnod on þam worde þe God cwæð to Adame ær þan þe he agylte: "Þu scealt deaðe sweltan gif þu of þam treowe geetst?" Se twifealde deað wæs mid þam getacnod, þære sawle and þæs lichaman. Þære sawle deað is þonne hi God forlæt for sumere synne, and heo siððan sceandlic wunað. Þæs lichaman deað is þonne [seo] sawl him of gewit, and þisne twyfealdan deað towearp Crist mid his anfealdan deaðe, se þe wæs soþlice dead on lichaman and næfre on þære sawle, forþan þe he næfre ne syngode.' The only substantial addition that Ælfric makes to Alcuin's text is 'and heo [the soul] siððan sceandlic wunað,' which perhaps anticipates the soul's immortality.

The Mechanics of the Human Fall

The fall of man is passed over briefly in Alcuin's *Quaestiones* but receives even less treatment in Ælfric. Where Alcuin devotes seven questions to the fall sequence, Ælfric translates only two, thereby omitting the principal Augustinian elements in the exegesis of the fall. As Ælfric pays little more attention to the fall sequence in his other works on Genesis, it would seem that he felt that the scriptural account, with a few supplementary details, provided sufficient explanation for the temptation and man's consent. The devil's enmity towards man (an issue that falls outside Alcuin's series of seven questions) is explained by his feelings towards God, man, and himself: 'Hwi is se deofol swa onwerd þam men? For þære hatunge þe he hæfð to his scyppende, and for þam andan þe he hæfð to þam men, and orwennysse his agenre hæle.'[53] The specific terms that Ælfric is uses in this question – *inuidia* becomes *anda(n)*, and *desperatio* becomes *orwennyss* – recur frequently in Ælfric's other works. Alcuin's *Int.* 13 appears to have had a lasting influence upon Ælfric's treatments of Genesis.[54]

In the *Quaestiones*, the seven questions that pertain to the mechanics of original sin address, in order, the wisdom of the serpent, God's motivation for allowing the temptation, the serpent's comprehension of the words spoken through it, Eve's repetition of the injunction, Eve's ability to believe the serpent's words, Eve's look at the tree of knowledge, and Adam's consent to eat. Of these seven questions Ælfric chooses to translate only the second and third, explaining the serpent's ability to understand its

---

53 *ÆInt.* 10: 'Why is the devil so opposed to men? On account of the hatred that he has towards his creator, and on account of the envy that he has towards men, and despair for his own health'; *Int.* 13: 'Cur diabolus tam infestus est hominum saluti? Propter odium in creatorem et inuidiam in hominem, et desperationem suae salutis.'

54 The description in *De initio creaturae* is perhaps most complete: 'Þa ongeat se deofol þæt Adam and Eua wæron to ðy gesceapene þæt hi sceoldon mid eadmodnysse and mid gehyrsumnysse geearnian ða wununge on heofenan rice ðe he of afeoll for his upahefednysse, þa nam he micelne graman and andan to þam mannum, and smeade hu he hi fordon mihte' (*CH* I.1, 125–9). See also *Exameron* 449 (*De creatore et creatura* 215) – the devil was *waa on his awyrgedum mode*, and the speech of St Vincent, where the devil is said to act *mid niðfullum andan* (*Lives of Saints* XXXVII.82). The description in one of Ælfric's homilies is of particular interest because it is an adaptation of a Latin excerpt found in Boulogne-sur-Mer, Bibliothèque municipale 63, and includes Wisdom 2:24, the scriptural source for the devil's 'envy' towards man: '"Inuidia autem diaboli mors intrauit in orbem terrarum"; Ac ðurh þæs deofles andan se deað com on ðas woruld' (Pope XI.109–10).

speech and the reason God allows the temptation:

ÆInt. 35. Hweþer seo næddre þurh hire agen andgit to Euan spræce?
Nis hit na geleaflic þæt se wurm þurh his agen andgit Euan bepæhte, [ac] se
deofol spræc þurh þa næddran, swa swa he deð þurh wodne man, and heo ne
undergeat þa word þe ma þe se woda deð.[55]

[Did the serpent speak to Eve through its own intellect?
It is not believable that the worm deceived Eve through its own intellect,
(but) the devil spoke through the serpent, just as he does through one possessed, and it (the serpent) did not understand those words any more than a
possessed man does.]

ÆInt. 36. Hwi geþafode God þæt se man afandod wære, þa þa he wiste þæt
se man wolde abugan?
Forþan þe se man nære herigendlic gif he forþi ne syngode þe he ne mihte, ac
he wære herigendlic gif he nolde syngian þa þa he mihte. Git dæghwamlice
drecð deofol mancyn mid mislicum costnungum þ[æt] þa beon herigendlice
and halige, þe him wiðstandað, and þa beo[n] genyþerode, þe nellað him
wiðstandan.[56]

[Why did God permit the man to be tested when he knew that the man would
fail?
Because the man would not be praiseworthy if he did not sin for the reason
that he could not, but he would be praiseworthy if he did not wish to sin even
though he could. Even today the devil torments mankind with various temptations in order that he who withstands them might be praiseworthy and
holy, and he who does not wish to withstand them might be brought low.]

In the *Interrogationes*, the order of these two questions is reversed.
When Ælfric omits Alcuin's question on Genesis 3:1 – how the serpent

---

55 *Int.* 62: 'Si serpens sonum uerborum eius qui per eum loquebatur intelligere potuit?
    Non est credibile eum intelligere potuisse quae per eum diabolus agebat; sed sicut
    daemoniacus et mente captus loquitur quae nescit, ita serpens uerba edebat quae non
    intelligebat.'
56 *Int.* 61: 'Cur tentari Deus hominem permisit, quem consentire praesciebat? Quia magnae
    laudi [*Ms.,* laudis] non esset, si ideo homo non peccasset, quia malefacere non potuisset.
    Nam et hodie sine intermissione [per uniuersum] genus humanum ex insidiis diaboli
    [homines] tentantur [*Edit.,* tentatur], ut ex eo uirtus tentati probetur, et palma non
    consentientis gloriosior appareat.'

might be most wise among the beasts – his commentary makes the abrupt leap from Eve's creation to God's decision to allow the temptation. In order to provide at least some transitional material and to introduce the agent of the temptation, Ælfric must invert Alcuin's *Int.* 61 and *Int.* 62, despite the fact that doing so defies the chronology of the scriptural narrative.[57] In addition, Ælfric slightly alters the first clause of Alcuin's answer in order to explain, as Alcuin does in the omitted *Int.* 60, that the serpent is not acting of its own volition.

ÆInt. 36, except for two additions, is a close translation and thus represents one of the few passages that can be traced back to *De Genesi ad litteram*.[58] Ælfric's changes (he twice adds contrasting clauses) have a twofold purpose. First of all, I would suggest that the addition of *ac he wære herigendlic gif he nolde syngian þa þa he mihte* is intended to emphasize the possibilities of creation, *non posse peccare* and *posse non peccare*.[59] The second addition (*and þa beo[n] genyþerode, þe nellað him wiðstandan*) functions in a similar manner. Where Alcuin offers only one of the two possibilities for man, Ælfric balances Alcuin's answer by offering the second. In a work intended for *rudes lectores*, Ælfric may have felt this clarification necessary.

Ælfric's interest in the concept of the temptation and the praise that comes to those who resist the devil's advances is further illustrated by his decision to include (and end with) Alcuin's *Int.* 201. Where Bede ends his *In Genesim* in Genesis 21:9–10 (just after the birth of Isaac), Ælfric includes the testing of Abraham in Genesis 22:1. In fact, Ælfric completely rewrites Alcuin's explanation to highlight Abraham's obedience in his 'testing' and to show that the devil is the one who 'tempts.' Where the Latin verb in both verses is *temptare*, Ælfric appears to distinguish between testing and temptation by using the verbs *afandian* and *costnian*.[60]

---

57 That is, God must have permitted the temptation before the devil could speak through the serpent.

58 See Appendix A, item 2.

59 See also *Exameron* 413–17.

60 *ÆInt.* 69 (from *Int.* 201): 'Hit is awriten on Genesis þæt God afandode Abrahames, and se apostol Iacob awrat on his pistole þæt God ne costnað nænne man. Hu mæg beon ægþer soð? God afandað þæs mannes, na swilce he nyte ælces mannes heortan ær he his fandige, ac he wile þæt se man geþeo on þære fandunge and his ingehyd beo geopenod. God afandode Abrahames swa þæt he het hine niman his leofan sunu Isaac, and geoffrian Gode to lace, and siððan ofslean on þa ealdan wisan. Þa wæs Abraham Gode gehyrsum, and wæs him leofre þæt he Godes hæse gefylde þonne he his leofan bearne gearode, and

The Aftermath of the Fall

Of the fourteen questions (*Int.* 69–82) that Alcuin devotes to Genesis 3:7–24, Ælfric translates six (*ÆInt.* 38–43). Having omitted Alcuin's observation that Adam and Eve were not ashamed of their original nudity, because they had not yet experienced any law in their members as being at war with the law of their minds (*Int.* 59), Ælfric also omits the companion questions explaining that the eyes of Adam and Eve are opened to 'reciprocal concupiscence' (*Int.* 69) and that the donning of fig leaves signifies the loss of simple chastity and the onset of the double itch of lust (*Int.* 70).

Ælfric's first two questions concern Adam and Eve's attempt, upon hearing the voice of God, to hide themselves from him. Both questions follow Alcuin closely and are remarkable for the preservation of Augustine's words in *De Genesi ad litteram*.[61] In *ÆInt.* 38, Ælfric explains that God enquires about the whereabouts of Adam as a reproof, not as one who is ignorant, in order to make him understand where he then stands and from what state he has fallen; *ÆInt.* 39 explains that Adam's attempt to hide himself is the result of the foolishness (*stuntnys*) brought on by sin.[62]

After excluding Alcuin's question on the transfer of blame from Adam to Eve and from Eve to the serpent (Genesis 3:11–13), Ælfric translates two of Alcuin's five questions concerning God's curse.[63] The first considers the serpent's role in the human fall:

---

he wæs þa afandod and gerihtwisod and gewuldorbeagod, swa þæt God him cwæð to: "On þinum ofspringce beoð ealle eorðlice mægða gebletsode." Þus afandað God his gecorenan, na swilce he nyte heora ingehyd, ac he wile þæt hi beon þe geþungenran on þære fandunge. Oþer is seo fandung, þe Iacob se apostol embe spræc; þæt is seo costnung, þe gewemð þone man to syngigenne, ac God ne costnað nænne man, forþan þe he nele nænne to synnum gebigan, ac þeos costnung is of þam niðfullan deofle and of yfelum lustum, and se lust acenð þa synne, and seo syn, þonne heo bið geendod, acenð þone ecan dead.'

61 That is, *ÆInt.* 38–9 contain quotations from *DGnL* that have passed from Bede to Alcuin to Ælfric. See Appendix A, items 3–4.

62 *ÆInt.* 38 (*Int.* 72): 'Hwi axode God Adam æfter his gylte hwær he wære, swilce he nyste? Þæt he dyde for þreaginga, na swilce he nyste, and þæt Adam understode hwær he þa wæs and hwanon he afeolle'; *ÆInt.* 39 (*Int.* 73): 'Humeta wende Adam þæt he mihte hine behydan fram Godes gesihðe? Seo stuntnys him gelamp of his synne wite þæt he wolde hine bediglian þam þe nan þincg nis digle.'

63 I exclude *ÆInt.* 8 (*Int.* 10), which explains, with reference to our future baptism, why the earth, instead of the water, is cursed as a result of Adam's sin.

ÆInt. 40. Hwi [ne] axode God þa næddran hwi heo þa men forlærde, swa swa he axode Euan hwi heo Adame þone æppel sealde?

Forðan þe seo næddre be agenum willan þæt ne dyde, ac se deofol þurh hi, and forþi cwæð God hire to: 'Þu bist awyrged, and þu scealt gan on þinum breoste, and þu ytst þa eorþan eallum dagum þines lifes.' Se deofol, þe spræc þurh ða nædran, wæs on þære næddran awyrged; he gæð on his breoste, þæt is þæt he færð on modignysse, and mid þære men beswicð, and he yt þa eorðan, forþan þe þa belimpað to þam deofle þa þe þa eorðlican grædignysse and gælsan ungefohlice gefremmað.

[Why did God not ask the serpent why it led men astray, just as he asked Eve why she gave the apple to Adam?

Because the serpent did not act by its own will, but the devil (acted) through it, and for that reason God said to it: 'You are cursed and you shall go on your breast, and you will eat the earth for all the days of your life.' The devil, who spoke through the serpent, was cursed in the serpent; he goes on his breast, that is that he fares in pride and deceives men with it; and he eats the earth, because those who exist excessively in earthly greed and luxury belong to the devil.]

Int. 75. Quare non est interrogatus serpens cur hoc fecerit?

Quia forte id non sua natura uel uoluntate fecerat, sed diabolus de illo et per illum fuerat operatus. Ideo dicitur ei: '*Super pectus tuum gradieris et terram comedes*,' siquidem in pectore calliditas nequitiarum eius indicatur; qui et terram deuorat, dum luxuria et libidine peccantium pascitur et delectatur [*Al*., dilatatur]. Nam [et] sicut diabolus per serpentem loquebatur, ita et in serpente maledicitur.

Ælfric makes several changes to Alcuin's text, but the sense of the explanation remains the same.[64] In order to introduce properly the topic of the question, Ælfric supplies the parallel between the interrogation of Eve (the topic of the omitted *Int*. 74) and the interrogation of the serpent. The answer is rearranged slightly: Ælfric, by inverting the order of Alcuin's final two sentences, chooses to follow the order of Alcuin's source, Bede's *In Genesim*, rather than Alcuin.[65] Only in the explanation of the serpent's

---

64 The first part of the question comes from *DGnL*. See Appendix A, item 5.

65 Alcuin's response comes from *In Genesim* I.2075–8, I.2083–7, I.2095–6, and I.2079–82 (Alcuin's final sentence is simply adapted from Bede rather than being a quotation). Bede's sources are Augustine's *DGnL* and Jerome's *Hebraicae quaestiones in Genesim* III.14 (though Jones failed to notice the latter).

curse does Ælfric make any significant changes: the fact that the serpent goes on his breast, instead of indicating the cleverness of his wicked ways, indicates that he fares in pride and deceives men by pride; the eating of earth signifies that those who exist excessively in earthly greed and luxury belong to the devil.

Ælfric's possible sources for these changes are potentially informative and certainly illustrative of problems in their study and identification. That the chest signifies pride is not found in either Alcuin or Bede. M.B. Bedingfield has suggested that the idea may come from Isidore's *Quaestiones in Vetus Testamentum* (*QVT*), but it seems equally possible in this instance that the source is Augustine's *De Genesi contra Manichaeos* (*DGcM*) because Augustine was also Isidore's source for the passage.[66] Bedingfield identifies at least two other instances in which Ælfric may have been borrowing from Isidore's *QVT* to supplement Alcuin, *ÆInt.* 43 (discussed below) and *ÆInt.* 68. In the first of these, Isidore is again borrowing from *DGcM*. In the second, Isidore is not borrowing from *DGcM* but rather from Augustine's *Contra Faustum* (*CF*).[67] While that would seem to suggest that Isidore is the more likely source for all three, one possible use of Isidore that Bedingfield does not mention is in *ÆInt.* 22, where Isidore's source is again *DGcM*. To complicate matters, this use hints that it is at least possible that Ælfric is using *DGcM* rather than *QVT*[68] and thus also that there is a chance that Ælfric knew and used both *DGcM* and *CF* as he translated Alcuin; I have detected no independent

---

66 'Nomine pectoris significatur superbia mentis, nomine autem uentris significantur desideria carnis; his enim duabus rebus serpit diabolus aduersus eos quos uult decipere, id est, aut terrena cupiditate, et luxuria aut superbiae insana ruina' (Isidore, *QVT* V.4; *PL* 83.220D–221A). Compare *DGcM* II.xvii.26. A detailed treatment of Ælfric's sources and of parallels between the *Interrogationes* and his other works can be found in the database of *Fontes Anglo-Saxonici* (contributed by M.B. Bedingfield; http://fontes .english.ox.ac.uk/).

67 Compare *DGcM* II.xxiii.35 and *QVT* V.13–14, and *CF* XLI and *QVT* XV.5–6.

68 The issue is certainly open to debate. Ælfric adds 'swa [swa] he sylf cwæð on his god-spelle to þam Iudeiscum, þa þa hi axodon hwæt he wære. He cwæð: "Ic eom angin þe to eow sprece"' to his answer. Bede has 'interrogantibus se Iudeis quid eum credere deberent, respondit, "Principium,"' et cetera. (*In Genesim* I.26–7). Isidore has 'sicut ipse in euangelio Iudaeis interrogantibus respondit: "Ego principium,"' et cetera (*QVT* I.2), and Augustine has 'cum eum Iudaei quis esset interrogassent, respondit: "Principium,"' et cetera (*DGcM* I.ii.3). Isidore's *in euangelio* and *ego* are in Ælfric, but only Augustine has *quis esset*, though of course Ælfric could get *quis es* from John 8:25, and all of these differences are not such that a source need be assumed.

evidence that he used *QVT*. The weight of the evidence overall, however, most likely points to Isidore's *QVT*.[69]

Ælfric's second and final question on the curses pronounced by God considers the enmity between the wife's heel and the serpent's head and contains one of the two lengthy additions to the commentary.[70] In this case, I cite Alcuin first:

Int. 77. Caput serpentis est illicitae suggestionis cogitatio, quod nos omni intentione conterere atque allidere dcbemus ad petram, qui est Christus. Calcaneum mulieris est extremum uitae nostrae tempus, quo diabolus nos acrius impugnare satagit, cui si uiriliter resistimus, uictoriam perseuerantiae cum salute nostra accipiemus.

[The head of the serpent is the idea of forbidden suggestion, which we, with all effort, ought to crush and dash upon the rock, which is Christ (I Cor. 10:4). The heel of the woman is the last period of our lives, in which the devil most keenly attempts to ensnare us. If we resist him strongly, we shall receive the victory of perseverance with our salvation.]

ÆInt. 41. Ðære næddran heafod getacnað þæs deofles tihtinge, þa we sceolan mid ealre geornfulnysse sona tobryton, forþam gif heo þæt heafod innan þone man bestingð, þonne slingð heo mid ealle inn. Swaþeah ne bescyt se deofol næfre swa yfel geþoht into þam men þæt hit him to forwyrde becume, gif hit him ne licað, and gif he winð mid gebedum ongean. He sæwð foroft manfullice geþohtas into þæs mannes heortan þæt he hine on orwennysse

---

69 See the analysis of *ÆInt.* 43, below. There is scant other evidence that Ælfric knew of either *DGcM* or *CF* or that they were at all known in late Anglo-Saxon England. For example, Godden's summary list of sources for the *Catholic Homilies* lists neither work, and Gneuss's *Handlist of Anglo-Saxon Manuscripts* contains only one (very) late manuscript of each. While Isidore's *QVT* and *Etymologiae* (the latter certainly seems to be the source of Ælfric's conclusion on the Trinity here and perhaps in *ÆInt.* 27 as well) are not well represented either, Godden at least finds some evidence that Ælfric may have known them. See M. Godden, ed., *Ælfric's Catholic Homilies: Introduction, Commentary and Glossary*, xlvi–lxii, and H. Gneuss, *Handlist of Anglo-Saxon Manuscripts*, items 550 and 271.

70 The other is a long passage from Bede's *De natura rerum* on the seven wandering stars, which supplements *ÆInt.* 21. It is worth noting that in *ÆInt.* 21 Ælfric indicates clearly that he is interrupting Alcuin's commentary to make good a lacuna from his prior work, *De temporibus anni*.

gebringe, ac hit ne bið þam men derigendlic gif he to his drihtne clypað. Swa
se man swiþor bið afandod, swa he selra bið. Þæs wifes ho getacnode þæt se
deofol wile on fyrste, gif he æt fruman ne mæg, þone man beswican, and
swa near his lifes geendunge, swa bið þam deofle leofre þæt he þone man
forpære, ac us is to hopigenne [on] þæs hælendes gescyldnysse, [se] þe us
tihte þus: 'Confidite ego uici mundum.' Truwiað and beoð gebylde ic ofer-
swiðde þisne middaneard. Eft he cwæð: 'Þyses middaneard[es] ealdor com
to me, and he on me naht his ne funde.' Se deofol is þæra manna ealdor, þe
þisne middaneard ungemetlice lufiað, and he com to Criste cunnode hwæðer
he ænig þing his on him gecneowe; þa ne funde he on him nane synne, ac
unscæððignysse, þæt þæt we ne magon þurh us þæt we magon þurh Crist,
se þe cwæð: 'Omnia possibilia credenti.' Ealle þing synd þam geleaffullum
acumendlice. We sceolon winnan wið þone deofol mid fæstum geleafan, gif
we willað beon gehealdene, and se þe him onbihð bið soðlice beswicen.

[The head of the serpent signifies the suggestion of the devil, which we
should with all diligence immediately crush, because if the serpent pushes
that head into a man, then it worms all the way in. However, the devil never
implants evil thought into men such that it brings them to destruction, not
if it does not please the man and if he struggles against it with prayer. The
devil often sows sinful thoughts in the heart of a man such that he might
bring him to despair, but it will not be harmful to the man if he calls to his
Lord. As the man is tempted more, so will he be better. The wife's heel signifies that the devil desires to deceive the man eventually, if he might not at
first; the nearer the end of his life, the keener the devil will be that he turn
the man, but we should be placing our faith in the protection of the Saviour,
he who urged us thus: 'Confidite ego uici mundum.' 'Trust and be encouraged, I have conquered this earth' (John 16:33). Again he said: 'The lord of
this earth came to me, and he found nothing of his in me' (John 14:30). The
devil is the lord of those men who improperly love this earth, and he came
to Christ seeking to know whether he might recognize anything of his in
him; then he found no sin in him, but purity, that which we may not attain
by ourselves but may through Christ, he who said: 'Omnia possibilia credenti.' 'All things are possible to the faithful' (Mark 9:22). We shall struggle
against the devil with firm belief if we wish to be preserved, and he who
serves the devil will be truly overcome.]

The sources of Alcuin's response are difficult to identify. There are general
similiarities to Bede (*In Genesim* I.2129–34) and a slightly stronger resemblance to the beginning of a comment in Paterius's *Expositio ueteris et*

nouis testamenti (I.25),[71] but the comment is largely his own.[72] The moment seems perfect for original composition, for Ælfric interweaves a lengthy explanation into his translation, an addition for which I have been unable to locate any probable source. M.B. Bedingfield suggests that perhaps Gregory's *Moralia in Iob* lies behind part of the passage, but the parallel is not convincing, and the Gregory does not contain the verses from John or Mark. Curiously, though, Mark 9:22 does appear at the end of Alcuin's prefatory letter to Sigewulf, where he advises his dear brother to be content with what he has done.[73] Stoneman, for his part, observes simply, 'The elaboration is uniquely Ælfrician.'[74] Indeed, the passage, which is unlike any other explanation that I have seen, seems more homiletic than exegetical, bringing the conflict between Eve and the serpent into the New Testament struggle between Christ and the devil.

The final two questions in Ælfric that pertain to events immediately after the eating of the fruit concern Genesis 3:21 and 3:24. Although Ælfric augments Alcuin's terse remarks on the fashioning of skins for Adam and Eve in Genesis 3:21, his answer is the same: the dead skins signify their new mortality.[75] The placing of the cherubim and the fiery sword at the

---

71 Paterius would suggest Gregory's *Moralia in Iob* as a possibility, but the version in Paterius is much closer to Alcuin than that in Gregory (compare *PL* 79.694B and *Moralia in Iob* I.xxxvi.54). One might also compare Isidore, *QVT* V.5–7.

72 The phrase *conterere atque allidere debemus ad petram, qui est Christus* is oddly rare in this context, appearing otherwise, so far as I can tell, only in the pseudo-Bede *De psalmorum libro* (*PL* 93.736A). Opinions of this work seem to be mixed, with some suggesting it is a twelfth-century composition and others suggesting the work has been around since the ninth century. See Marcia Colish, '*Psalterium Scholasticorum*,' 533 ('internal references to contemporary events such as the investiture controversy place its date at the turn of the twelfth century'), and Michael Gorman, 'The Canon of Bede's Works,' 438–9 ('The commentaries on the Psalms ... were culled from two extant manuscripts, Munich Clm 14387, fol. 20–94, written at St Amand or Salzburg in the first decade of the ninth century ... and Stuttgart Theol. phil. fol. 206, written about the year 1100 in Zweifalten').

73 'His tantum, dilectissime frater, esto contentus, et si quid in eis perperam dixerim, tu fraterno stilo corrigere studeas; si quid uero bene, non mihi, sed largitori gratias age, qui et te proficere, et me tibi sufficere ex donis suis faciat; sine quo nihil possumus; in quo "omnia possibilia sunt credenti"; qui creditam suae nobis pecuniae largitionem in laudem nos et gloriam sui nominis multiplicare faciat' (Ep. 80, ed. Dümmler, *Ep.* IV, *Epistolae karolini aeui* II, 122–3).

74 Stoneman, 'A Critical Edition,' 266.

75 *ÆInt.* 42 (from *Int.* 80): 'Hwi worhte God pylcan Adame and Euan æfter þam gylte? Þæt he geswutelode mid þam deadum fellum þæt hi wæron þa deadlice for þære forgægednysse.'

gate of paradise is again treated as in Alcuin, but Ælfric supplements his answer with further figurative significations from Augustine's *DGcM* or Isidore's *QVT* and Bede's *In Genesim*:

> *ÆInt*. 43. Hwæt is þæt God gelogode cherubin and fyran swurd and awendendlic to gehealdene þone wæg þe lið to lifes treowe?
> Þæt is þæt neorxnewonges get is gehealden þurh engla þenunge and fyrena hyrdrædene, and þæt is anwendendlic forþan þe hit bið aweg gedon, and se weg bið us gerymed. Cherubin is gereht gefyllednyss ingehydes, þæt is seo soðe lufu, and þæt fyrene swurd getacnode þa hwilwendlican earfoðnyssa, þe we her on life forberað, and we sceolon þurh þa soðan lufe Godes and manna and þurh earfoðnysse to þæs lifes treowe eft becuman. Þæt lifes treow is se leofa hælend Crist, se þe is soð lif on hine lifigendum.[76]

[Why is it that God placed the cherubim and the fiery and turning sword to hold the way that lies to the tree of life?
That is that the gate of paradise is kept through the ministry of angels and a fiery guard, and it is turning because it will be taken away, and the way will be opened to us. Cherubim is interpreted as fullness of mind, that is, the true love, and that fiery sword signifies transitory difficulties that we endure in this life, and we shall through the true love of God and of men and through difficulty come again to the tree of life. That tree of life is the dear Lord Christ, he who is true life, living in him.]

Conclusions

Of Alcuin's first twenty-five questions in *Quaestiones* (those that precede the ordering of the commentary according to the scriptural narrative) Ælfric translates twenty-one. Ælfric's omissions, in each case, can be readily explained: he omits Alcuin's unusual (and widely avoided!) remark on the tree of knowledge, a repetitive question on the effect of God's curse on earthly and aquatic creatures, and two fairly insubstantial questions on the creation of man's soul and the perfection of a creation in seven days. The changes that Ælfric does make, with the exception of the lengthy addition

---

76 See *Int*. 82, which supplies the first sentence of Ælfric's answer, Augustine's *DGcM* II.xxiii.35–6 and Isidore's *QVT* V.14 (the latter's *per charitatem Dei et proximi* much abbreviates Augustine and is a more likely source), and Bede's *In Genesim* I.2298–310 (which seems certainly to provide the *lignum uitae* as Christ).

from Bede's *De natura rerum* (*ÆInt.* 21), are relatively minor and tend to be limited to restructuring syntax or adding clarifying phrases or clauses.

After *Int.* 26, however, Ælfric becomes much more selective, and his choices reveal his agenda. For example, Alcuin's ten questions on the original creation of the world (Genesis 1:1–5) become three, but Ælfric then translates every one of Alcuin's remarks concerning the creation of man and the evidence for the participation of the Trinity in his creation, even adding some comments of his own. Ælfric omits all ten questions on Genesis 2:1–8 – verses that include man's placement in paradise and occasion substantial comment from Augustine, Bede, and Alcuin – but then translates five of six questions on diverse topics, from the trees in paradise to God's warning and the creation of Eve.

In the most crucial part of the commentary, in the series of questions related to Genesis 3:1–24, Ælfric translates only nine of the twenty-three questions, and for the most part I am unable to discern any abiding principle of selection behind his omissions.[77] It is interesting, however, that many of the questions Ælfric excises are those that I would term explicitly Augustinian. If one considers only those questions in which Alcuin quotes Augustine (either directly or, in most cases, through Bede), Ælfric translates only five of eighteen possible questions, a percentage that is significantly lower than Ælfric's rate of translation overall.[78]

In my view, Alcuin's *Quaestiones in Genesim* preserves nine important Augustinian hexameral concepts in Augustine's words. Ælfric chooses to translate only two of these: one on the good of obedience versus the evil of disobedience (*ÆInt.* 30), and the other on God's decision to permit the temptation (*ÆInt.* 36). It does seem possible, when such significant concepts as reciprocal concupiscence, Eve's 'inexcusabilis praeuaricatio,' and pride and love of self as prerequisites for sin are omitted, that the omission of material is not coincidental. Although Ælfric may well have intended his *Interrogationes* to clothe the 'nacedan gerecednisse' of his vernacular Genesis, he perhaps did not consider suitable for his audience Augustine's

---

77 However, O'Keeffe states: 'Ælfric ignores questions which seem to be simple exposition and concentrates instead on the "cnottum." He generally omits questions on minuter points in Genesis in favour of questions on the three major events in the book: the fall, the flood and the covenant' ('Three Old English Writers,' 72).

78 Of eighty-four questions (*Int.* 1–82 and 93–4) Ælfric translates forty-four (*ÆInt.* 1–43 and 47), or somewhere just over 50 per cent, as opposed to 28 per cent of the Augustinian questions. I include the five passages that have been transmitted from Augustine to Ælfric in Appendix A.

somewhat sophisticated exegesis – which, as we have seen, had already been much abridged and simplified by the time Alcuin finished his commentary.[79] Of course, the principles of selection in all early medieval exegetical works might be said to be arbitrary and inexplicable to varying degrees (Alcuin's *Quaestiones in Genesim* is an excellent example), and it may be that no clear motivation for Ælfric's choices existed.[80]

In any case, even if some of the more complicated Augustinian concepts are omitted, I do not mean to suggest that Ælfric's *Interrogationes Sigewulfi* is a simple work. Ælfric clearly recognized its place within the body of his writing because he uses the *Interrogationes* as an opportunity to reverse a decision not to discuss the planets in *De temporibus anni*. He introduces and concludes the commentary with original passages in his rhythmical prose and manages to put his own stamp on the work as he makes those choices. Where Alcuin had not had much to say about the Trinity in his commentary, for example, Ælfric supplements one of Alcuin's questions and adds a lengthy 'doxology' at the end instead to highlight the significance of the Trinity. Where Alcuin discusses the punishment by water and fire (the flood and the Sodomites) in their scriptural sequence, Ælfric combines and supplements the two responses in a highly original and contrastive way.[81] Further, as I hope this analysis has shown, both the sensitivities of his translation choices and the complexity of his possible sources demonstrate that Ælfric was a master at his craft by the time he translated Alcuin. I think the argument could be made that this is a later work than Clemoes supposed. In any case, the commentary is the first translation into the vernacular of any Latin work of exegesis, an achievement that is noteworthy in itself and which suggests also that Ælfric was very much aware of the tradition of Anglo-Saxon exegesis and his place in it.

---

79 An illustrative change might be seen in *ÆInt.* 51. When Alcuin discusses Gen. 8:3 and the coming and going of the waters, he explicitly mentions interpretation according to the literal sense; Ælfric translates Alcuin's *Videtur iuxta litteram* as *Wen is þæt*.

80 I would like to thank the first anonymous reader of my manuscript for these cautionary remarks. The reader added that Ælfric's homilies do preserve complex Augustinian ideas on occasion, and it is certainly not clear that we are looking at different audiences for the *Interrogationes* and the homilies.

81 See *ÆInt.* 67, from *Int.* 187 and 97 and with substantial original material.

APPENDIX A
The transmission of Augustine's *De Genesi ad litteram* from Bede to Ælfric

1. On the reason for God's injunction against the tree of knowledge

Augustine, *De Genesi ad litteram* VIII.vi.12	... disceret quid interesset inter oboedientiae bonum et inoboedientiae malum.
Bede, *In Genesim* I.1494–6	... disceret quid interesset inter oboedientiae bonum et inoboedientiae malum.
Alcuin, *Interrogatio* 52	... experiri et scire potuit quid esset inter obedientiae bonum et inobedientiae malum.
Ælfric, *ÆInterrogatio* 30	... to cnawan hu mycel god is on gehyrsumnysse and hu micel yfel in ungehyrsumnysse.

2. On God's decision to allow the temptation

Augustine, *De Genesi ad litteram* XI.iv.6	Si ergo quaeritur, cur Deus temtari permiserit hominem quem temtatori consensurum esse praesciebat ... non mihi uidetur magnae laudis futurum fuisse hominem, si propterea posset bene uiuere, quia nemo male uiuere suaderet.
Bede, *In Genesim* I.1886–90	Si ergo quaeritur, cur Deus temptari permiserit hominem quem temptatori consensurum esse praesciebat, occurrit ratio uera: non magnae laudis futurum fuisse hominem, si propterea posset bene uiuere, quia nemo male uiuere suaderet.
Alcuin, *Interrogatio* 61	Cur tentari Deus permisit, quem consentire praesciebat? Quia magnae laudi non esset, si ideo homo non peccasset, quia malefacere non potuisset ...

| Ælfric, *ÆInterrogatio* 36 | Hwi geþafode God þæt se man afandod wære, þa þa he wiste þæt se man wolde abugan? Forþan þe se man nære herigendlic gif he forþi ne syngode þe he ne mihte, ac he wære herigendlic gif he nolde syngian þa þa he mihte. |

3. On the voice of God asking Adam where he might be

Augustine, *De Genesi ad litteram* XI.xxxiv.45	Increpantis uox est, non ignorantis.
Bede, *In Genesim* I.2023–4	Non utique ignorando quaesiuit, sed increpando admonuit ut adtenderet ubi esset in quo Deus non esset.
Alcuin, *Interrogatio* 72	Non utique ignorando quaesiuit, sed increpando admonuit ut attenderet ubi esset et unde cecidisset.
Ælfric, *ÆInterrogatio* 38	Þæt he dyde for þreaginga, na swilce he nyste, and þæt Adam understode hwær he þa wæs and hwanon he afeolle.

4. On Adam's attempt to hide himself from God

Augustine, *De Genesi ad litteram* XI.xxxiv.46	Et talis adfectio de peccati poena erat eum latere uelle, quem latere nihil potest …
Bede, *In Genesim* I.2041–3	Et talis adfectio de peccati poena erat eum latere uelle, quem latere nihil potest …
Alcuin, *Interrogatio* 73	Haec ei insipientia de peccati poena accidit, ut eum hoc latere putet, quem latere nihil potest.
Ælfric, *ÆInterrogatio* 39	Seo stuntnys him gelamp of his synne wite þæt he wolde hine bediglian þam þe nan þincg nis digle.

5. On God's failure to interrogate the serpent

Augustine, *De Genesi ad litteram* XI.xxxvi.49	Proinde quod serpens, cur hoc fecerit, non est interrogatus, potest uideri, quod non ipse utique id in sua natura et uoluntate fecerat, sed diabolus de illo et per illum et in illo fuerat operatus.
Bede, *In Genesim* I.2075–7	Quia serpens cur hoc fecerit non est interrogatus, potest uideri quod non ipse utique id sua natura et uoluntate fecerat, sed diabolus de illo et per illum fuerat operatus.
Alcuin, *Interrogatio* 75	Quare non est interrogatus serpens cur hoc fecerit? Quia forte id non sua natura uel uoluntate fecerat, sed diabolus de illo et per illum fuerat operatus.
Ælfric, *ÆInterrogatio* 40	Hwi [ne] axode God þa næddran hwi heo þa men forlærde, swa swa he axode Euan hwi heo Adame þone æppel sealde? Forþon þe seo næddre be agenum wille þæt ne dyde, ac se deofol þurh hi.

APPENDIX B
Ælfric's translations from Alcuin's *Quaestiones in Genesim*

Items in normal font have been translated without significant change, items in italics with minor changes, and items in bold with major changes; items with an asterisk contain substantial or noteworthy original material.[82]

Alcuin *Quaestiones in Genesim*	Ælfric *Interrogationes Sigewulfi*
Int. 1	**ÆInt. 1**
Int. 2	*ÆInt. 2*
Int. 3	*ÆInt. 3*
Int. 4	*ÆInt. 4*
Int. 5	ÆInt. 5
Int. 6	omitted
Int. 7	*ÆInt. 6*
Int. 8	omitted
Int. 9	ÆInt. 7
Int. 10	ÆInt. 8
Int. 11	omitted
Int. 12	ÆInt. 9
Int. 13	ÆInt. 10
Int. 14	*ÆInt. 11*
Int. 15	*ÆInt. 12*
Int. 16	*ÆInt. 13*
Int. 17	ÆInt. 14
Int. 18	***ÆInt. 15**
Int. 19	*ÆInt. 16*
Int. 20	ÆInt. 17
Int. 21	ÆInt. 18
Int. 22	ÆInt. 19
Int. 23	ÆInt. 20
Int. 24	***ÆInt. 21**
Int. 25	omitted

---

82 In total, there are 21 questions translated without significant change, 27 with minor changes, and 26 with major changes (the numbers do not add up to the 69 questions of Ælfric's *Interrogationes Sigewulfi* because some of Alcuin's questions are combined in Ælfric's answers). Ten further questions contain significant original material.

Int. 26	**ÆInt. 22**
Int. 27–8	omitted
Int. 29	*ÆInt. 23*
Int. 30–2	omitted
Int. 33	*ÆInt. 24*
Int. 34–5	omitted
Int. 36	*ÆInt. 25*
Int. 37	ÆInt. 26
Int. 38	****ÆInt. 27***
Int. 39	*ÆInt. 28*
Int. 40	ÆInt. 26
Int. 41	ÆInt. 29
Int. 42–51	omitted
Int. 52	*ÆInt. 30*
Int. 53	*ÆInt. 31*
Int. 54	omitted
Int. 55	ÆInt. 32
Int. 56	ÆInt. 33
Int. 57	*ÆInt. 34*
Int. 58–60	omitted
Int. 61	**ÆInt. 36**
Int. 62	*ÆInt. 35*
Int. 63	omitted
Int. 64	*ÆInt. 37*
Int. 65–71	omitted
Int. 72	ÆInt. 38
Int. 73	ÆInt. 39
Int. 74	omitted
Int. 75	***ÆInt. 40**
Int. 76	omitted
Int. 77	***ÆInt. 41**
Int. 78–9	omitted
Int. 80	*ÆInt. 42*
Int. 81	omitted
Int. 82	***ÆInt. 43**
Int. 83–6	omitted
Int. 87	***ÆInt. 44**
Int. 88	ÆInt. 45
Int. 89	**ÆInt. 46**
Int. 90–3	omitted

Int. 94	**ÆInt. 47**
Int. 95–6	omitted
Int. 97	*ÆInt. 67*
Int. 98	omitted
Int. 99	ÆInt. 48
Int. 100–4	omitted
Int. 105	**ÆInt. 49**
Int. 106	**ÆInt. 49**
Int. 107–22	omitted
Int. 123	ÆInt. 50
Int. 124–5	omitted
Int. 126	*ÆInt. 51*
Int. 127–31	omitted
Int. 132	**ÆInt. 52**
Int. 133	*ÆInt. 53*
Int. 134	ÆInt. 54
Int. 135	*ÆInt. 55*
Int. 136–40	omitted
Int. 141	*ÆInt. 56*
Int. 142	*ÆInt. 56*
Int. 143–7	omitted
Int. 148	***ÆInt. 57**
Int. 149	omitted
Int. 150	**ÆInt. 58**
Int. 151–3	omitted
Int. 154	*ÆInt. 59*
Int. 155	**ÆInt. 60**
Int. 156	omitted
Int. 157	**ÆInt. 61**
Int. 158–63	omitted
Int. 164	**ÆInt. 62**
Int. 165	*ÆInt. 63*
Int. 166–8	omitted
Int. 169	**ÆInt. 64**
Int. 170	omitted
Int. 171	*ÆInt. 65*
Int. 172–8	omitted
Int. 179	**ÆInt. 66**
Int. 180–6	omitted
Int. 187	***ÆInt. 67**

Int. 188	*ÆInt. 68
Int. 189–200	omitted
Int. 201	ÆInt. 69
Int. 202–81	omitted

APPENDIX C
Manuscripts of Ælfric's *Interrogationes Sigewulfi**

Cambridge, Corpus Christi College, 162, pp. 139–60, saec. x ex. or xi in., SE England (Ker 38; Gneuss 50 [pp. 1–138] and 54 [pp. 139–60])
The *Interrogationes Sigewulfi* in this manuscript was removed from CCCC 178 by Matthew Parker. Parker wrote in the Latin letter of Alcuin to Sigewulf, then pasted in the commentary, beginning on the second half of page 139.

Cambridge, Corpus Christi College, 178, pp. 1–270, saec. xi¹, prov. Worcester (Ker 41; Gneuss 54 [pp. 1–270] and 55 [pp. 287–457])
A manuscript in two parts, both of which have been glossed by the 'tremulous' hand and may have already been together in the thirteenth century. Part A contains two sets of homilies (general occasions, pp. 1–163; festivals, pp. 164–270);[83] Part B contains the Rule of St Benedict in Latin and Old English.

Major Contents (pp. 1–163)
1. *CH* I.1 (*De initio creaturae*), pp. 1–15
2. *Hexameron*, pp. 15–30 (+ CCCC 162, p. 139)
3. *Interrogationes Sigewulfi* (including rhythmic passage on the Trinity; now in CCCC 162)
4. *CH* I.24, pp. 33–43 (+ CCCC 162, p. 160)
5. *CH* I.19, pp. 43–54
6. Pope XI, pp. 54–73

---

* In the compilation of this material, I have used N.R. Ker, *Catalogue of Manuscripts*, and Stoneman, 'A Critical Edition,' 3–41. For a much more detailed description of these manuscripts, the latter should be consulted.

---

83 'This manuscript comprises, in essence, twenty-four homilies by Ælfric arranged in two groups, the first consisting of twelve items for any occasion, and the second of twelve homilies for specific occasions in the church year' (Jonathan Wilcox, 'Transmission of Literature and Learning,' 64–5).

7. *De octo uitiis et de duodecim abusiuis* (basically *De duodecim abusiuis* with *Lives of Saints* XVI.267–381; Morris, *Old English Homilies*, 299–304),[84] pp. 73–88

8. *Lives of Saints* XVII.1–267 (*De auguriis*) with an addition on Macarius and the Magicians and on Saul and the Witch of Endor (Pope XXIX), pp. 88–101[85]

9. Pope XVIII (*Sermo de die iudicii*), pp. 101–14

10. Pope XXI.1–313, 318–676 (*De falsis diis*), pp. 142–63

Cambridge, Corpus Christi College, 303, pp. 317–27, saec. xii[1], Rochester (Ker 57)

Largely a collection of homilies, most from the two series of *Catholic Homilies*. Includes five pieces from *Lives of Saints* and ends with an interrupted version of Ælfric's homily on Judith.

Major Contents

1. *CH* I.33, pp. 279–83
2. *CH* I.35, pp. 283–90
3. *Lives of Saints* XVI, pp. 290–6
4. *De duodecim abusiuis* (Morris, *Old English Homilies*, 299–304), pp. 296–301
5. Pope XIX (*De doctrina apostolica*), pp. 301–6
6. Pope XXI.1–140, 150–296, 299–301, 304–514, 565–676 (*De falsis diis*), pp. 306–17
7. *Interrogationes Sigewulfi*, pp. 317–27
8. *Lives of Saints* XII, pp. 327–33
9. *Lives of Saints* XIII, pp. 333–8
10. Assmann IX.1–393 (Ælfric's homily on Judith), pp. 356–62

London, British Library, Cotton Julius E.vii, fols. 230–8, saec. xi in., S England, prov. Bury St Edmunds (Ker 162; Gneuss 339)

This is the principle manuscript of Ælfric's *Lives of Saints* (*LS*). Appended at the end of *LS* were three items: *Interrogationes Sigewulfi*, *De falsis diis*, and *De duodecim abusiuis*, but only *Interrogationes Sigewulfi* (fols. 230–8) and a portion of *De falsis diis* remain (Pope XXI.1–140, 150–91, fols. 238r–240v).

---

84 Richard Morris, ed., *Old English Homilies and Homiletic Treatises*.
85 On *De duodecim abusiuis* and *De augurus* and the composition of CCCC 178 as a whole, see Clayton, 'Ælfric's *De auguriis*,' II.376–94.

Oxford, Bodleian Library, Hatton 115, fols. 121r–131v, saec. xi¾ or xi² and xii med., prov. Worcester (Ker 332; Gneuss 639 [fols. 1–147]) + Lawrence, University of Kansas, Kenneth Spencer Research Library, Pryce C2: 2

Another collection largely of homilies, most from Ælfric's two series of *Catholic Homilies* and many of which (as Ker observes) are also in CCCC 178 and Hatton 116. Glossed by the 'tremulous' hand.

Major Contents

1. *Hexameron*, fols. 1–10
2. *CH* I.19, fols. 10–16
3. *CH* I.20, fols. 16–23
4. Pope XVIII (*Sermo de die iudicii*), fols. 23r–30v
5. Pope XIX (*De doctrina apostolica*), fols. 35v–40v
6. *Sermo ad populum* (Ælfric's *Letter to Wulfgeat* [Assmann I] adapted to form a homily), fols. 95r–99v
7. *De duodecim abusiuis* (Morris, *Old English Homilies*, 299–304), fols. 116–21
8. *Interrogationes Sigewulfi*, fols. 121r–131v
9. *Lives of Saints* XVIII (*Sermo excerptus de libro Regum*), fols. 131v–139v

Oxford, Bodleian Library, Hatton 116, pp. 300–29, saec. xii¹, W England, prov. Worcester (Ker 333)

Another collection largely of homilies, most from Ælfric's two series of *Catholic Homilies* and many of which (as Ker observes) are also in CCCC 178 and Hatton 115. Glossed by the 'tremulous' hand.

Major Contents

1. *CH* I.38, pp. 239–52, 279–90
2. Homily for the Common of a Confessor (Assmann IV), pp. 290–4, 253–61
3. *Hexameron*, pp. 261–78, 295–300
4. *Interrogationes Sigewulfi* (including rhythmic passage on the Trinity), pp. 300–29
5. *De octo uitiis et de duodecim abusiuis* (basically *De duodecim abusiuis* with *Lives of Saints* XVI.267–381; Morris, *Old English Homilies*, 296–304), pp. 329–47
6. *Lives of Saints* XVII.1–267 (*De auguriis*, with an addition on Macarius and the Magicians, and on Saul and the Witch of Endor [Pope XXIX]), pp. 347–65

7. Pope XXI.1–150, 645–76 (*De falsis diis*; 'almost certainly a lost quire' [Ker]), pp. 365–73

Excerpts and Transcriptions

London, British Library, Harley 3271, fols. 90r–90v, saec. xi[1] (Ker 239.7; Gneuss 435)
Contains an extract of twenty lines on Noah's ark and where the flood waters went as they receded (*ÆInt.* 49 and 51)

Oxford, Bodleian Library, Hatton 114, fol. 19, saec. xi¼ (Ker 331.38; Gneuss 638)
Contains four lines on free will (from *ÆInt.* 5), copied on the bottom margin

Oxford, Bodleian Library, Junius 104
Contains a collation by Junius of Hatton 115 with Hatton 116

Ælfric's *Judith*

PAUL E. SZARMACH

Now that Bruce Mitchell and Fred Robinson have included the anonymous poem *Judith* in the sixth and seventh editions of their standard reader-grammar, and Peter Baker and Richard Marsden have done the same in their respective new textbooks, it cannot be too long before Ælfric's prose treatment of Judith will likely and eventually take its rightful place in the grand discussion, gathering momentum as well from recent scholarly work.[1] Extant in only two manuscripts, one seriously burned, and absent from the great homiletic cycles associated with the monk of Eynsham (and, until recently, with resultant editorial disregard), the retelling of this Old Testament narrative can illuminate Ælfric's narrative style in, it would seem, his late career, as he fashions something that is neither a homily nor a saint's life but incorporates compositional features of his earlier writing experience. The hint – or the tease – of virgin martyr stories is part of this retelling, most notably in the treatment of Judith's pulchritude, and

---

1 Bruce Mitchell and Fred C. Robinson, eds, *A Guide to Old English*, 313–25; Peter S. Baker, *Introduction to Old English*, 251–62 (selection 18); Richard Marsden, *The Cambridge Old English Reade*, 147–63 (selection III.19); and, of course, there is the venerable *Sweet's Anglo-Saxon Reader*, rev. Dorothy Whitelock, 136–48 (selection xxiii). One must note with appreciation Ian Pringle, '"Judith,"' 8–97, for his early discussion of many relevant themes with particular reference to Viking issues, where Judith is an example of resistance to the invaders. Mary Clayton, 'Ælfric's *Judith*,' 215–27, finds a disjunction between Ælfric's *Judith* and its possible meanings. Stacy S. Klein, 'Ælfric's Sources and His Gendered Audiences,' 111–19, sees Ælfric as revealing his 'deep-seated desires about male heterosexual desire and female sexuality' (117); also online at www.luc.edu/publications/medieval/vol13/13ch10.html. And now Margaret Hostetler offers new directions in her '*Nimað eow bysne be þyssere Iudith*,' 152–64, with her consideration of the problematical ending.

certainly the hitherto unexamined alliterative prose confers an indelible Ælfrician stamp to the account; not to be lightly dismissed is the necessary point of comparison, of course, but the poetic *Judith* offers another literary context. Metaphorically, at least, the two Old English *'Judiths'* form an *opus geminatum*, and the speculative and unanswerable question can be, did Ælfric know the poetic version? Practically, the two versions can create an intertextual or a comparative relationship, yielding a recursive analysis that will illuminate both texts and lead perhaps to a heightened understanding and appreciation of the less studied prose version, which is the intention here. Any discussion must necessarily begin with an introduction to the manuscript witnesses.

The two manuscript witnesses are:[2]

Cambridge, Corpus Christi College 303 [Ker 58 art. 73], pp. 356–62, entitled *Incipit de iudith quomodo interfecit olofernem*, from Rochester, xii[1]; hereafter cited as C.

London, British Library, Cotton Otho B.x [Ker 178 art.1; Gneuss 356], fols. 29, 30 [formerly fols. 143–151 (or 151v)], from Worcester, xi[med]; hereafter cited as O.

Bruno Assmann and Stuart Lee use C as the manuscript base in their respective editions.[3] Neither manuscript gives what would ostensibly be the complete text. Cambridge ends imperfectly at *7 god þe gestrangode for þære clænnesse*, which is line 393 in Assmann's edition. Ker notes that 'leaves are missing at the end,' while Clemoes is more specific, indicating that the current text ends at a quire break.[4] Assuming that another quire of eight would (typically) follow, one might be able to speculate that the

---

2 Ker, *Catalogue of Manuscripts*; Gneuss, *Handlist of Anglo-Saxon Manuscripts*. John Collins Pope offers useful comments on the scribes of C in *The Homilies of Ælfric*, vol. 1, 18–20. He observes that the scribe operating in the relevant section Corpus 303 is inconsistently archaic, sometimes producing 'sheer chaos.' Pope believes that the '*Judith* homily' belongs to the years when Ælfric worked on the *Lives of Saints*.

3 Assmann, ed., *Angelsächsische Homilien und Heiligenleben*, proceeding from Assmann's 'Abt Ælfric's angelsächsische Homilie über das Buch Judith,' 76–104; the reprint has an important supplementary introduction by Peter Clemoes, xi–xxxv. Stuart Lee, ed., *Ælfric's Homilies on Judith, Esther, and the Maccabees*. For purposes of convenience, I cite Assmann's lines in parentheses, and I provide translations for Assmann. See below on the issue of lineation of Ælfric's rhythmical prose.

4 Ker, *Catalogue of Manuscripts*, no. 57, p. 105; Clemoes, introduction to repr. of *Angelsächsische Homilien und Heiligenleben*, ed. Assmann, xxvii.

ending of art. 73 could be farther away from where Assmann had to leave C. To compensate for the loss of an ending in their base text, Assmann and Lee individually incorporate what they can from London, which is one of the manuscripts to survive in fragments from the oft-lamented Cotton Library fire of October 1731. With help from Humfrey Wanley's catalogue (W),[5] which provides text for the incipit and explicit of the London version, Assmann and Lee can work towards the ending of the piece. Ker notes further complications, however. The two leaves now surviving and considered part of O may in fact come from another manuscript altogether, for these leaves contain glosses written in the 'tremulous hand,' who was active in Worcester.[6] These interventions would seem to point to an independent manuscript, which joined the Cottonian detritus of Otho B.x.[7] In short, the ending of Ælfric's *Judith* offers a measure of indeterminacy. Given that Ælfric often reused his own materials and reshaped them – not to mention the scribes who took their own independent way with his works despite Ælfric's explicit wishes – we can only observe with absolute certainty that the edited text as we have it, and as we are accustomed to treat it, is an editorial composite. It may very well be the case that the coda as we know it, with its direct address to *min swustor*, its particular emphasis on Judith as a *bysen* (model), and its citation of Malchus, may reflect varying possibilities to conclude the core account.[8]

A set of further misdirections lies in any characterization of Ælfric's *Judith* as a homily. Clemoes observes that Ælfric does not use *cwyde*, which is his usual word for 'homily,' to describe the piece, but rather uses the phrase *on þisum gewritum*.[9] Ælfric also uses *racu* (424) and *spel* (404). The direct address *Leofan men*, which opens O and W, but not C, is not an Ælfrician form of direct address, never apparently occurring in his corpus,

5 Humfrey Wanley, *Librorum Veterum Septentrionalium Catologus*, vol. 2, 192, col. 1.
6 Christine Franzen, *The Tremulous Hand*, esp. 53–4.
7 See Lee, ed. *Ælfric's Homilies*, 2.
8 Hugh Magennis, 'Contrasting Narrative Emphases in the Old English Poem *Judith*,' 61–5, esp. 64–5, is likewise struck by the 'detachable nature [of the ending] and by its narrowness of interpretation.' Mary Clayton sees the explanations at the end of the text as 'appendages' ('Ælfric's *Judith*,' 219). See Hostetler, '*Nimað eow bysne be þyssere Iudith*,' for a discussion of how this coda reflects audience issues.
9 Clemoes, introduction to repr. of *Angelsächsische Homilien und Heiligenleben*, ed. Assmann, xxviii.

except here, according to the *Dictionary of Old English Corpus*.[10] If Worcester is a likely place of origin of O, it is probable that a scribe added the 'house' opening phrase, no doubt under the influence of that most illustrious member of the house, Wulfstan, whose *Leofan men* is his signature opening.[11] Now Ælfric offers many examples of the 'running-gloss' homily, where after a presentation of the biblical passage for the day he takes the passage apart more or less verse by verse, often ending with a moral exhortation. Along the way there are various possible amplifications of an idea or a point deriving from the text at hand, or even omissions of possible ideas or verses embedded in the passage. Ælfric's retelling of *Judith* shows no influence of the running-gloss paradigm, flexible as it can be. Rather, Milton McC. Gatch's suggestion has thus far proven to be the most fruitful for an understanding of the genre and context of the piece when he suggests that 'Ælfric's Old Testament translations and paraphrases ... are intimately connected with the monastic calendar's cycle of Old Testament readings ... [e.g.,] Judith and Esther in September.'[12] Subsequently amplifying his suggestion, Gatch sees Ælfric's Old Testament writings as 'an adaptation of materials from the monastic devotional life to the devotional life of laymen and non-monastic clergy.'[13] Ælfric's overt description of the liturgical need in the *Letter to the Monks of Eynsham* confirms at least in a general sense the function of *Judith* and explains in part the narrative flexibility that is inherent, as will be apparent, in the piece.

Yet another set of problematic issues surround the primary source, the Old Testament Judith. Richard Marsden has found no firm evidence for

---

10   The *Dictionary of Old English Corpus*, s.v. Cameron number B1.4.28, found within the Ælfric canon and cited by the *Dictionary of Old English (DOE)*, is nevertheless of doubtful attribution according to Pope, *The Homilies of Ælfric*, vol. 2, 772.

11   *Dictionary of Old English Corpus*, s.v. 'Leofan men.'

12   Milton M. Gatch, *Preaching and Theology in Anglo-Saxon England*, 203n53. C.A. Jones provides updated support to Gatch's suggestion in his edition of *Ælfric's Letter to the Monks of Eynsham* where para. 74 (in the run of paras. 70–80, which treat readings and responsories for the Night Office) names Judith, Esther, and Esdras as assigned to the fourth week from the Kalends of September. See C.A. Jones, ed., *Ælfric's Letter to the Monks of Eynsham*, 146 (English trans. *en face*) and 223n351. The Latin is, 'In quarta septimania ponimus Iudith, Hester et Esdras, et canimus "Tribulationes" et cetera'; the Jones's translation is, 'To the fourth week we assign Judith, Esther and Esdras and sing "[We have heard] the tribulations" and the rest.' It must be noted, however, that Ælfric does not explicitly explain *why* one observes the fourth week in the way one must.

13   Milton M. Gatch, 'The Office in Late Anglo-Saxon Monasticism,' 362.

'specific Vulgate textual traditions' for the poem *Judith*.[14] He does not consider Ælfric's *Judith* in his extensive discussion, and while it is hazardous to make the easy assumption that the same lack of specific connection could be said of the prose, it is certainly beyond the scope of this essay to track down any possibilities among the early medieval witnesses to the text. Edwin Edgar Voigt gives an indication of the difficulties, in his discussion of the relations of the Vulgate, Old Latin, Greek, and Chaldaic (Aramaic) versions, while dismissing the existence of the book of Judith in the Hebrew Apocrypha.[15] Pro tempore, the analysis here will assume a Latin Vulgate version in the main textual stream. Such a Latin version nevertheless would extend the problematic nature of source relations. Simply put, the original Vulgate source has many deficiencies in the text. Jerome says, 'huic [i.e., the book of Judith] unam lucubratiunculam dedi, magis sensum e sensu quam ex uerbo uerbum' (I put a little night work into this book, translating more sense for sense than word for word), and '[m]ultorum codicum uarietatem uitiossimam amputaui' (I lopped off the defective variety of the many manuscripts).[16] Anglo-Saxonists may warm to the translation formula also cited in Alfred's *Preface to the Pastoral Care* and Ælfric's *Latin Preface to the Catholic Homilies I*,[17] but the piety is misplaced, for Jerome is describing something like an abbreviated patristic 'all-nighter.' Carey A. Moore describes the procedure as 'simultaneous translation': 'As the Aramaic text was being translated aloud into Hebrew by a Jewish scholar, Jerome was dictating to his secretary a Latin translation of it.'[18] Jerome evidently used the same procedure in his translation of Tobit, only there it took him a day.[19] One might observe that divine inspiration has a tough row to hoe when human agency is so lax and

---

14   Richard Marsden, *The Text of the Old Testament in Anglo-Saxon England*, 442.
15   Edward Edgar Voigt, *The Latin Versions of Judith*. See especially 46–54 for observations on the Vulgate.
16   *Praefatio Hieronymi Liber Iudith*, PL 29.39–40.
17   Alfred's preface to the *Pastoral Care* is available in many an introductory reader, as well as in the still serviceable Henry Sweet, ed., *King Alfred's West-Saxon Version of Gregory's Pastoral Care*, part I, 6 (Cotton version) or 7 (Hatton version). Ælfric invokes the formula for the Latin prefaces to the *Catholic Homilies* and for the *Lives of Saints*, which are available respectively in Peter Clemoes, ed., *Ælfric's Catholic Homilies*, 173, and W.W. Skeat, ed., *Ælfric's Lives of Saints*, vol. 1, 6–7 (Latin and English *en face*). See also Jonathan Wilcox, ed., *Ælfric's Prefaces*, for the Latin preface to *Catholic Homilies I* (107) and for the Latin preface to the *Lives of Saints* (120).
18   Carey A. Moore, *Judith*, 95. The translations of the book of Judith are mine.
19   Ibid.

sloppy. Here, the ultimate source offers its own kind of indeterminacy to the would-be vernacular translator, which one might call error. Whether all problems should be attributed to Jerome or not, Voigt makes this observation about the tradition: 'Of the 340 verses in the Greek text the Vulgate omits 42 entirely and large parts of 45 more.'[20] If there are basic difficulties in the divine text, then what is a vernacular translator to do and how is he to do it? Is a leap over the gap possible with an appeal to sense for sense (as long as one predetermines the necessary sense)?

Before entertaining these questions, it is necessary to point out in an aside that Aldhelm's works on virginity offer something of an authoritative basis for the story of Judith in Anglo-Saxon England. Aldhelm's *Carmen de uirginitate* and *Prosa de uirginitate* form an *opus geminatum*, though there are noticeable differences between them generally and specifically in the treatment of Judith. Aldhelm gives a precis of Judith's life in *Prosa*, chapter 57 (in some manuscripts, chapter 56) and a more concise version in the eight-capital-sins portion of *Carmen*.[21] Ehwald consults some twenty-one manuscripts of *Prosa* and some twenty manuscripts of *Carmen* in his edition, not taking particular notice in his apparatus of the Old English glosses.[22] The two Aldhelmian passages give witness to the general knowledge of Judith, but they are insufficient to serve as sources for Old English poetry or prose.

These questions naturally suggest that the first step in analysis rightly must be a discussion of Ælfric's *Judith* relative to the original source. Whatever practical, temporal limits there may have been to the presentation of his *Judith*, Ælfric begins in direct, flat-footed explanatory mode by saying that the first thing to do is to distinguish between the two Nabuchodonosors: the Nabuchodonosor of the Babylonian Captivity and the second Nabuchodonosor, aka. 'Cambises,' King of the Assyrians, who is the potentate in question in *Judith*. This initial move presents the sort of factual or historical information that, as Thomas D. Hill reminds

---

20 Voigt, *The Latin Versions*, 46. For an appreciation of the book of Judith, see Toni Craven, *Artistry and Faith in the Book of Judith*.

21 Rudolph Ehwald, ed., *Prosa*, in *Aldhelmi Opera*, 316–17; *Carmen*, in *Aldhelmi Opera*, 457. For translations, consult Michael Lapidge and Michael Herren, *Aldhelm*, 126–7; Michael Lapidge and James L. Rosier, trans., *Aldhelm*, 159.

22 Ehwald, *Prosa*, 225; *Carmen*, 349. For glosses, see now Scott Gwara, ed., *Aldhelmi Malmesbiriensis prosa de uirginitate*; and Gwara's 'Glosses to Aldhelm's *Prosa de uirginitate*,' 561–645.

us, is part of exegesis.[23] Unfortunately, Ælfric is historically incorrect in his distinction of the two Nabuchodonosors: there is only one in reality, and that is the Nabuchodonosor of the Babylonian Captivity.[24] The 'first' Nabuchodonosor mentioned in *Judith* has no role in *Judith*, but the audience learns much about him in the twenty-one opening lines. This pre-history suggests some later themes in the narration, for example, the relation between the Israelites and the one True God, and divine punishment administered through political foes, exile, and servitude. The biblical action begins with the account of Nabuchodonosor, King of the Assyrians, and his partial success as a warlord. The success is partial because Nabuchodonosor's military victories do not automatically lead to the submission of other nations, and so he orders Holofernes to subjugate them with all deliberate ferocity. Nabuchodonosor (Judith 3:13) wishes all gods destroyed so that he may be *ipse solus Deus*. Holofernes meets success, but he comes to the Israelites who have prepared a defence, including some guerilla tactics in the mountains. Infuriated, Holofernes wants to know more about his enemy, and Achior, *dux omnium filiorum Ammon* (the leader of all the sons of Ammon), responds with a sympathetic and broad account of Israel from its beginnings to its recent successes. Achior even gives Holofernes the key to undermining the Israelites, which is the discovery of *aliqua iniquitas* in the sight of their Lord. Holofernes, ever the mad tyrant, seems not to hear what Achior says and banishes him to Bethulia, to die with the Israelites when Holofernes will destroy them. The ensuing siege of Bethulia creates deep hardship for its inhabitants, who wish to be delivered of their predicament by a merciful God but yet complain to Ozias *princeps* for his refusal to seek peace with the Assyrians. Ozias asks his countrymen to wait five days for God's mercy before capitulating. All these events take up chapters 1–7 in the Vulgate, nearly half of the whole. Ælfric follows these highpoints of the plot line until about halfway through the C version (22–191). Without getting bogged down in the details of military campaigns or siege warfare or in static moments in plot movement (for example, how Achior was greeted in Bethulia), Ælfric

---

23 Thomas D. Hill, 'Literary History and Old English Poetry,' 7–8: 'a great deal of this [biblical] exegesis is purely factual and philological.'

24 See Moore, *Judith*, 123–4, for a discussion of errors in this passage, and 129: 'the historical Nabuchadnezzar [alternate form of the name] was king of the Babylonians, not the Assyrians; he never ruled from Ninevah.' Enid M. Raynes, 'MS. Boulogne-sur-Mer 63 and Ælfric,' 69–71, discusses the two Nabuchodonosors as found in the Boulogne manuscript, which shows Ælfrician connections.

offers a trim narrative line that keeps the story moving. One may note here that the poetic *Judith* has not yet begun.

Much of the rest of the Old Testament book puts the narrative focus on Judith. The opening of Judith chapter 8 gives a static set-piece portrait of Judith in eight verses, stressing her begats, qualities, virtues, and attributes. Judith engages Ozias and the elders on their decision to give God a five-day deadline on granting mercy, with the fine theological point: 'Et qui estis vos, qui tentatis Dominum?' (Judith 8:11) [And who are you to tempt the Lord?]. She continues to scold them about their reactions to the situation and promises a plan, undetailed, which the elders endorse. Judith prays to God for the success of her plan (in the whole of Judith chapter 9) and then goes into action. Judith dresses up in a most stunning fashion, *non ex libidine, sed ex uirtute* (Judith 10:4), leaves Bethulia, accompanied by her maid, and enters Holofernes' camp, announcing that she has come to tell Holofernes how to overcome the Israelites. In the first encounter Judith explains that God is angry with the Israelites, and gives information on the situation within the Israelite camp. Holofernes and his men are taken by Judith's looks, beauty, and wise words (Judith 13:19). Judith and her maid get free passage to go in and out of the Assyrian camp for three days, ostensibly to pray. On the fourth day Holofernes invites Judith to attend a banquet. Drink gets the best of his desire, and in his chamber Judith takes Holofernes' sword and dispatches him with two strokes on the neck. She takes the head, orders her maid to place the head in the food bag they had been carrying, and the two return to Bethulia in triumph. When Vagao, Holofernes' eunuch, discovers the headless corpse, panic spreads through the Assyrians, who flee, pursued by the Israelites. The Israelites rejoice, and Judith sings a canticle to the Lord (Judith 16:1–21). The final verses describe the continuing peace for Israel, the death of Judith (and the liberation of her maid), and the continuing memorial celebration of the victory. If the title in C, 'How Judith killed Holofernes,' has meaning, then this second half of *Judith* has more significance. Clearly, Ælfric here too has much to abbreviate. The prayer to God for courage in chapter 9 surprisingly disappears, while chapter 16, which Ælfric tells his audience contained a song of praise for the heavenly God, does not offer the canticle beyond the mere mention.[25] There are other adjustments or omissions, as

---

25　For canticles and the breviary in Anglo-Saxon England, see Alicia Corrêa, 'Daily Office Books,' in *The Liturgical Books of Anglo-Saxon England*, esp. 52–60; in the same volume see also Philip Pulsiano, 'Psalters,' with the connections to canticles, 80–84. For a brief overview see the entry 'Canticles, Biblical,' in the *New Catholic Encyclopedia*, vol. 3 (New York: McGraw Hill, 1967), 69–70. Canticles are known in the West as early as

discussed below. When the Old English equivalent to the book of Judith appears to come to an end at 403, Ælfric continues on with a kind of envelope, much as he began, outside of the text at hand, only here considering biblical canonicity and possible moral applications.

The foregoing discussion comparing the mainline narratives in Ælfric's *Judith* and the Old Testament book underlines the major structural difference between the pair and the poetic *Judith*. As Mark Griffith demonstrates in his excellent discussion of source relations, the poetic *Judith*, as we have it, is in parallel to Judith 12:10–16:1.[26] True enough, the beginning of the poetic *Judith* has been lost, which is something of a counterpoint to Ælfric's *Judith* without its ending. How long the lost opening may have been is open to speculation; the opening as we have it occurs in section IX, but the section numbering scheme may have referred to the manuscript, not to the work.[27] Griffith's best guess is that the poem, now 349 lines, may have been some 450 lines and 'presumably dealt with Holofernes' assault on the Hebrews, the siege of Bethulia, Judith's journey to the Assyrian Camp, and her first three days' in the camp.[28] Such an opening, summarizing nearly three-quarters of the Old Testament book, which would imitate Ælfric's narrative strategy, would seem somewhat inconsistent with the poet's otherwise brilliant response to the source, for, as Griffith puts it, 'the poet concentrates on the key dramatic event and makes consistent changes to the source which show that he has his own coherent interpretation of it.'[29] The poetic *Judith* essentially depicts the *agon* between Holofernes and Judith, the kind of conflict between two opposing characters around whom all narrative features, motifs, themes, et cetera organize themselves. Without overarguing the point, this structure is oral at its root, such as when Beowulf and Unferth exchange pleasantries or when Beowulf takes on Grendel. Through the welter of narrative detail in the Old Testament, the *Judith* poet perceives an essential story. Strictly speaking, he has created an *imitation*, not a translation or a paraphrase.

---

the fourth century, and Judith 16:15–21 is a canticle in the Roman breviary for *feria quarta ad Laudes I*.

26 Mark Griffith, ed., *Judith*, 47–61. Griffith's edition replaces B.J. Timmer, ed., *Judith*, and all subsequent references to the poem are to Griffith. *Beowulf and Judith* is edited by E.V.K. Dobbie for the benchmark series Anglo-Saxon Poetic Records, vol. 4 (New York: Columbia University Press, 1953).

27 Griffith, *Judith*, 3–4.

28 Ibid., 4.

29 Ibid., 51.

Biblical source study *in magno* characterizes the major difference between Ælfric's *Judith* and the poetic *Judith*. The former work seeks to follow the main narrative line of the Old Testament in some form of concision, while the latter reshapes it in some form of poetic interpretation. To round out the description of Ælfric's *Judith* and to establish its further distinguishing characteristics, it is useful, if not necessary, to consider several points and issues in a reading of Ælfric's *Judith* that are necessarily selective in their respective emphases. Perhaps the central problem for all who have ever read the book of Judith is Judith's sexuality.[30] Without doubt, the Old Testament is unsubtle about Judith's plan to free the Israelites from Holofernes and his army. The set-piece description of Judith (8:1–8) describes her as a widow recluse, living shut away with servants, who fears the Lord *ualde*. The two identifying details of this description are that Judith's husband, Manasses, left her a widow when he died of heatstroke while supervising a harvest, and that she was rich with *eleganti aspectu*. The first detail, however gratuitous it appears, nevertheless particularizes Judith, while the second, seemingly only a part of a list of attributes, awaits its fulfilment of meaning in the seduction of Holofernes. In her prayer to God for courage, Judith suggests the ultimate result when she petitions that Holofernes' pride be cut off by *gladio proprio*, and 'capiatur laqueo oculorum suorum in me, et percuties eum ex labiis charitatis meae' (Judith 9:13). [Let him be caught by the snare of his eyes on me, and strike him through by the lips of my love.] Judith prepares for her plan by a total 'makeover' from her widow's weeds, which has more than divine sanction: 'Cui etiam Dominus contulit splendorem: quoniam omnis ista compositio non ex libidine, sed ex virtute pendebat' (Judith 10:4). [The Lord furthermore conferred bright beauty because all this planning came not from *libido* but from virtue.][31] Judith and God cooperate in the preparation and plans. Indeed, the next stages in the narrative stress Judith's beauty when Ozias and the elders see her (10:6), when Holofernes' guards see her and hear her words (11:18–19), and implicitly when Holofernes desired her (cf. 12:16). After the beheading of Holofernes, Judith's beauty receives further praise in the canticle when, in partial recapitulation of the narrative, she sings that Holofernes was not brought down by young men, sons of

---

30 For the sexuality of saints, see now Virginia Burrus, *The Sex Lives of Saints*, and Alexander Kazhdan, 'Byzantine Hagiography and Sex in the Fifth to the Twelfth Centuries,' 131–43.

31 I hesitated to translate *compositio* as 'make-up,' choosing a more general sense.

Titans, or giants, but 'Iudith filia Merari in specie faciei suae dissolvit eum' (16:8). [Judith, daughter of Merari, destroyed him by the beauty of her face.]

In the face of all this overt planning for seduction and the successful execution of Holofernes, Ælfric certainly came up against a compositional problem. After all, by the time of his *Judith*, Ælfric had likely written on the lives of women saints whose glory was chastity and the avoidance of sexual relations of any sort, even when they were confronted with torture. Ælfric retains the set-piece description of Judith found in the Old Testament, including the particularizing detail of Manasses' death, her living situation, her widowed chastity, and her beauty:

> Heo wæs swiðe wlitig   and wenlices hiwes ... (line 205)

> [She was very beautiful with a good figure ...]

having introduced the 'Judith' half of his narration with

> Ða wæs on þære byrig   on þam ylcan timan
> an ænlic wimman   on wudewanhade. (lines 191–2)

> [At that same time there was an elegant woman living as a widow in the city.]

Ælfric, often cited for his tendency to abbreviate sources, exercises this stylistic option in rendering Judith's personal preparations to visit Holofernes. The Old English audience learns only that

> heo awearp hire hæran   and hire wudewan reaf
> and hi sylfe geglængede   mid golde and mid purpuran
> and mid ænlicum gyrlum.   And eode hire syððan
> mid anre þinene. (lines 228–31)

> [She threw down her hairshirt and her widow's weeds and adorned herself
> with gold and purple and with splendid clothing. And she went with a maid.]

There is a certain speed and vigour in the description of Judith's transformation, as opposed to the more detailed Old Testament presentation, underlined by the simple verbs and mid-phrases. In indirect speech, Judith's voice calls her coming visit to Holofernes a *fær* (233), which Bosworth and Toller (*Supplement*) glosses in sense 4 as 'expedition' or 'enterprise,' citing this passage as the example. Klaeber gives 'sudden attack' as the first meaning (as in *Beowulf* 1068, the song about Finn and Hengest, and in *Beowulf* 2230, the rifling of the dragon's treasure) and associates *fær* compounds with 'sudden attack' or sudden actions.[32] Ælfric gives Judith's makeover a heroic cast rather than a sartorial one. In fact, *fær* most aptly describes a Viking attack, which in another sense is inappropriate because there is all too much planning for this *fær*! What Ælfric leaves out in this form of heroic misdirection is the Lord's cooperation in giving Judith more beauty (as above, Judith 10:4). The difficult moral or theological point of the Lord's participation in the seduction simply disappears.

The narrative motif of Judith's beauty continues, for when she leaves Bethulia, the elders,

> hi ealle wundrodon   hire wlites swiðe (line 235)

> [they all marvelled much over her good looks]

as do Holofernes' guards:

> Hi ða wundrodon   hire wlites swiðe
> and hire wislicra worda. (lines 242–3)

> [They all marvelled much at her good looks and her wise words.]

The virtually total repetition of the same line within so short a space has a telling effect, and it furthermore links both sides of the masculine world in their common reaction to what is established as a fact of the text, viz. Judith's beauty. The guards join beauty and wisdom together in their reaction to her 'wise words.' Holofernes fulfils Judith's prayer (Judith chapter 9) – which Ælfric does not give his audience:

> Sona swa he beseah   on hire scinendan nebbwlite,
> swa wearð he gegripen   mid ðære galnysse
> his unstæððigan heortan. (lines 245–7)

> [As soon as he looked on her radiant face, he was caught in the grip of fornication in his fickle heart.]

---

32 Friedrich Klaeber, ed., *Beowulf*, glossary s.v. 'fær.' *The Dictionary of Old English, A–F*, noting twenty-four occurrences (frequently in poetry), gives for sense 1 'sudden or unexpected danger; peril, calamity,' and sense 1a 'specifically: sudden attack of disease.'

Like his guards, Holofernes receives Judith's words approvingly because, when she apparently betrays her people, he believes her words (line 262). Holofernes' thegns, presumably not the same group who are the guards, add their approval to what they have seen and heard, saying:

> swylc wimman nære
> on ealre eorðan   swa fægeres wlites
> and swa wis on spræce. (lines 263–5)

[There are not such women in the whole wide world so fair in looks and so wise in speech.]

Judith's presentation is so winning that she gets free passage to come and go as she pleases in and out of the Assyrian camps, which includes permission for her maid servant to come and go with the food bag that will eventually prove so serviceable. This freedom unfolds as a stratagem, never perceived by the Assyrians and eventually revealed to the audience, to allow Judith and her maid to escape on the last day with Holofernes' head as if, in the eyes of any Assyrians observing the standard procedure, they were going to prayer.

The last scene to mention Judith's beauty is the banquet beheading. Holofernes orders his chamberlain (*burðegn*) to bring Judith to him:

> Heo com þa geglenged   for nanre galnysse
> and stod him ætforan   swiðe fægres hiwes,
> and his mod sona   swiðe wearð ontend
> on hire wilnunge   to his galnysse ...
> and het his beon bliðe   on his gebeorscipe,
> and heo him behet   þæt heo swa wolde. (lines 287–93)

[She came then dressed up for no fornication and stood before him with her very fair figure, and his mind was greatly inflamed and in desire for her because of his fornication, and he ordered her to be merry at his drinking party, and she promised him that she would.]

These six lines encapsulate the related issues in the depiction of Judith's sexuality: Judith comes for no lustful purpose, but yet she promises to join Holofernes in his feasting; she comes in beauty, while Holofernes burns in lust. What you see is not what you get. Judith's purpose is to kill Holofernes; it is not to lust physically in any number of *senses*, with no little irony. I take line 290a to be Holofernes' misprision that Judith has physical lust for him, reciprocating his lust for her. The word *bliðe* is freighted with concupiscence, and Judith would appear to acquiesce. Ælfric must have been aware of these problems in a moral reading, for he does not fail to render Judith's speech upon her return to Bethulia, which is her recapitulation of what occurred in the Assyrian camp. Judith attributes her continuing purity to the angel of God and to God himself (lines 326 and 328; Judith 13:30), both of whom are otherwise not evident in the actual telling of the events. Cecelia, after all, had her guardian angel to protect her from her husband.[33] Like Beowulf's account of his Danish expedition, this speech is an amplification of narrative events, providing new information. God and his angel were simply not at the banquet in the first telling. Commenting on the book of Judith, Moore observes: '[Judith] was also – for the sake of her God and her people – a shameless flatterer (11:7–8), a bold-faced liar (11:12–14, 18–19), and a ruthless assassin (13:7–8), with no respect for the dead (13:9–10, 15).' A moral explanation of all these things is necessary in the Old English too, thus the presence of God and his angel.

The beheading of Holofernes and its immediate aftermath in the Assyrian camp combine to provide the climactic scene in the book of Judith. The Old Testament relates the beheading in thirteen verses, which are paratactic in nature, beginning with *et* or the particle *–que*, and sometimes including coordinating elements in verses with multiple independent clauses. The narrative movement can be swift: Vagao the eunuch shuts the door; they are all drunk; Judith is alone; Holofernes is dead drunk; Judith orders her maid to stand outside. This quick camerawork, so to speak, takes but five verses.[34] The cinematography slows as Judith stands before the bed in tearful prayer, praying God to give her strength to fulfil her plan as she had thought she could *per te* (Judith 13:7). Judith loosens Holofernes' sword from the pillar, pulls his head up by the hair, and, uttering *Confirma me Domine* a second time, goes to work:

> Et percussit bis in ceruicem eius, et abscidit caput eius, et abstulit conopeum eius a columnis, et euoluit corpus eius truncum. (Judith 13:10)

---

33 Skeat, *Ælfric's Lives of Saints*, vol. 2, 356–77, esp. 358, lines 32–4, where Cecilia speaks to her bridegroom:

> Ic hæbbe godes encgel þe hylt me on [lufe]
> and gif þu wylt me gewemman . he went sona to ðe,
> and mid gramum þe slihð þæt þu sona ne leofast..
> [I have God's angel who holdeth me in love,
> and if thou pollute me he will quickly turn to thee,
> and will slay thee in anger, that thou silt cease to love.
>   trans. Skeat, *en face* (line 359)]

34 See Alain Renoir, '*Judith* and the Limits of Poetry,' 145–55.

[And she struck at his neck twice, and cut off his head, and took off the net from the pillars, and rolled his maimed body.]

Ordering her maid to put Holofernes' head in their customary food bag, Judith and her maid go as if to prayer (thus making their way through the guards), but arrive instead at the gates of Bethulia to announce their triumph. Even in the moments of prayer, the Old Testament verses emphasize vigorous action and, within the context, the stasis of prayer, making both action and reflection mutually emphatic. Ælfric by contrast focuses on action exclusively in the more or less equivalent passage (lines 298–310). While in either account there are details of time and place that are left unexplained or unaccounted for, Ælfric has Holofernes brought to Judith by his thegns, whereas the Old Testament describes them as together in his chamber where Holofernes overdrinks. Ælfric gives an apparently unnecessary observation that Holofernes' thegns *na swiðe ne gymdon syððan heora hlafordes* (line 300) [they did not pay much attention to their lord thereafter], which implicitly seems to criticize the thegns as deficient (if not inebriated) bodyguards. The presence of this contribution to the narrative goes to a form of narrative probability. Ælfric's Judith does not stop to pray at length or in brief but moves quickly *to ræde* (line 302). Once again, Ælfric abbreviates the narrative by excising a prayer. Judith kills the sleeping Holofernes with *his agen swurd* and in two swings. The biblical detail that Judith had lifted Holofernes' head, which has its practical advantages in this sort of assault, is absent. Ælfric forgoes the iconic moment.[35]

When he relates the beheading, the *Judith* poet is not at all bound to the paratactic style of the Old Testament or otherwise to the action-driven narrative of Ælfric. At this level of text, the *Judith* poet amplifies what he has at hand in the best tradition of Anglo-Saxon biblical poets. Klaeber complained that *Beowulf* lacked a steady advance, and he might say the same of *Judith*, but he could not say the same of Ælfric.[36] The *Judith* poet uses the resources of Old English poetry and his own imagination to create an *imitation* of the biblical text, producing a world full of more

---

35 See the cover to Griffith's edition, which reproduces the beheading of Holofernes by Judith from the Winchester Bible. Margarita Stocker, ed., *Judith, Sexual Warrior*, surveys the subject. See Nathaniel Harris, *The Life and Works of Gustav Klimmt*, page 33, for Klimmt's *Judith and Holofernes* (1901) and page 61 for his *Judith* II (1909). Ann W. Astell discusses Holofernes' head in 'Holofernes' Head,' 117–33, and 'rhetorical strategies appropriate to a militaristic tropology' (118).

36 Klaeber, *Beowulf*, lvii.

objects, scenes, and mental states, and a world that he reflects upon. The narrative line is there, but it runs underground, having already been abstracted from the Old Testament, as suggested above. The drinking that sets up the beheading scene is perhaps the first example of the differing compositional approach. It is another project altogether to prove that the drinking scene is a 'displaced banquet scene,' that is, a type scene as in *Beowulf*, and that the *Judith* poet shows his art to turn a banquet with excessive drinking to an Old Testament design and a Christian purpose. The book of Judith and Ælfric's *Judith* say little more than that the Assyrians drank a great deal. The Old Testament does say that Holofernes drank more than he had ever had in his life (Judith 12:20), and Ælfric observed that the wine was strong (line 295), but neither goes much farther than these details in their general description of heavy drinking. In the poetic *Judith*, the passage 15b–34a, on the other hand, describes a remarkable drinking scene including this description of Holofernes:

> Ða wearð Holofernus,
> goldwine gumena,   on gytesalum:
> hloh ond hlydde   hlynede ond dynede,
> þæt mihten fira bearn   feorran gehyran
> hu se stiðmoda   styrmde ond gylede
> modig ond medugal,   manode geneahhe
> bencsittende   þæt hi gebærdon wel. (lines 21–7)

[Then Holofernes, gold-friend of men, became joyful at drink: he laughed and shouted, made noise and roared, such that children of men might hear from far away how the stern-minded one stormed and yelled, proud and drunk with mead; he frequently exhorted the bench-sitters that they might conduct themselves well.]

Line 23, with its alliteration (the consonant cluster *hl-* might very well have been as striking and as difficult then as now) and rhyme, goes far in depicting Holofernes as a drunken fool. Holofernes is *stiðmod* under the influence, but in line 30 he is the echoic *swiðmod*. Presumably, a lord urges bench-sitters to be brave at the appropriate time, but here Holofernes is urging the men to do or be what exactly? The ironic foreshadowing in the description of the *duguð* as overdrunk *swylce hie wæron deaðe geslegene* (line 31) is almost too obvious. Whatever the final moral point of drunken soldiers might be, the *Judith* poet would seem to enjoy describing the traffic in *bunan and orcas* (line 18).

The precise moment of the beheading demonstrates again the *Judith* poet's inclination to amplify and elaborate. Judith first thinks before she acts:

> þearle gemyndig
> hu heo þone atolan   eaðost mihte
> ealdre benæman (lines 74–6)

[(She) was exceedingly thoughtful about how she might most easily deprive that terrible man of life.]

The implication here is that the 'plan' (Ælfric's *ræd*) is not quite fully thought through, and, like Beowulf contending with Grendel's mother, Judith seizes a most opportune sword. As in the Old Testament, but not in Ælfric, Judith prays to God with some tearful emotion, but the *Judith* poet gives more insight into her mind. She prays:

> 'Þearle ys me nu ða
> heorte onhæted   ond hige geomor
> swyðe mid sorgum gedrefed.' (lines 86–8)

['My heart is now exceedingly troubled, and my spirit sad, very much beset by sorrows.']

She says that she has never had need of more *miltse* from God than now, and the *Judith* poet says that God inspired her *mid elne* (line 95) so that she might accomplish the deed. The return of moral themes to the beheading scene sharply differentiates it from Ælfric's account, but one ought not to assume that an amplifying piety is at work. Just as the *Judith* poet shows vigour in his description of the banquet scene, he invests the beheading proper with a certain enthusiasm in describing Judith's two strokes. Lines 103b and 108b join to offer a parallel passage for each of the two strokes: '*Sloh ða wundenlocc ... Sloh ða eornoste.*' The parallelism recalls the coming of Grendel and its similar repetition of *com*.[37] The *Judith* poet explains, somewhat ingenuously, that the second stroke was necessary because the first did not accomplish the task: the neck was only half cut after all; the second killed the *heathen hound* (line 110), and his head rolled on the floor. God and piety return to the beheading scene along with the details of slaughter, all of which contrast with Ælfric's bald, almost factual account.

---

37 Ibid., lines 702, 710, 720.

The discovery of Holofernes' body may provide the last selective point of comparison. In the Old Testament the narrative is a tour de force of timing and a grim comedy much in the spirit of Hitchcock, perhaps. The audience knows why Holofernes cannot get up, and so there is an absurd joke on the retainers when they try to wake up a dead man. When the guards see the Israelites on the attack, they rush to Holofernes' tent to tell him. They do not call out his name (presumably to do so would be a sign of disrespect), but they make a noise instead. When the senior officers come, they order the chamberlains to go into his chamber. The eunuch Vagao goes into the chamber and with great tact claps his hands. When there is no movement, Vagao lifts the curtain and sees the headless Holofernes, much to his horror. And he quickly finds out also that Judith is not in her chamber.

The *Judith* poet takes the discovery scene in his own direction. The first battle or skirmish between the Assyrians and the Israelites takes on a life of its own in the poetic *Judith*. The poet elaborates the fighting so that the incident becomes a very pressing military reason to wake up the Assyrian leader. The warriors gather around Holofernes' tent, but none dare to wake him,

> oððe gecunnian   hu ðone cumbolwigan
> wið ða halgan mægð   hæfde geworden. (lines 259–60)

[or to discover how it had turned out for that warrior against the holy maiden.]

The poet changes the focus to the coming of the Israelites to increase the pressure on the Assyrians. The warriors, now *sweorcenferhðe*,

> Hi ða somod ealle
> ongunnon cohhetan,   cirman hlude
> ond gristbitian—   gode orfeorme—
> mid toðon, torn þoligende.   Þa wæs hyra tires æt ende,
> eades ond ellendæda. (lines 269b–73a)

[Then, together, they all began to cough and cry out loudly and gnash their teeth, lacking good things, and suffering grief. Then it was the end of their glory, happiness and brave deeds.]

This passage is the poet's contribution to the absurd scene with his emphasis on coughing and gnashing of teeth, a register of reactions from the most courteous (or so it would seem) to the most despairing. The *Judith* poet seizes a great opportunity for his amplifying aesthetic. He loses sight of Judith in his version, but his emphasis is on the Assyrians and their remarkable situation. Ælfric, avoiding complications, gives but the bare narrative facts in his treatment. He says that the Assyrians wished to wake their lord, found the doors locked, made noise unsuccessfully, and ordered a chamberlain to be sent in. The chamberlain finds Holofernes but not Judith. Here Ælfric gives just enough unelaborated narrative information to keep his story going.

If Ælfric's compositional moves do not suggest an awareness of the problematics of the book of Judith, then his overt statements do. With some apparent defensiveness, he begins the closure of his *racu*:

Nis þis nan leas spel: hit stent on leden.
[þus] on þære bibliothecan.   Þæt witon boceras,
þe þæt leden cunnon,   þæt we na leogað. (lines 404–6)

[This is no lying story: it stands in the Latin, and thus in the Bible. Learned men who know Latin know that we are not lying at all.]

Here I accept E.G. Stanley's emendation of Assmann's *his* to *þus*.[38] Bosworth and Toller (BT) and BT *Supplement* (BTS) give two meanings for *bibliothecan*, namely 'library' and 'Bible.' Stanley suggests 'Bible,' as does Gatch.[39] *The Dictionary of Old English, A–F*, gives further information in sense 2: 'in MSS of s.x. and later: the Bible; in Ælfric, specifically: the Scriptures in Jerome's canon.' It notes some twenty-three occurrences 'mainly in Ælfric.' Ælfric is clearly seeking to validate the story and to establish his own authority to tell it.

The canonicity of the book of Judith was an issue in the patristic period. Not in the Hebrew canon, the book of Judith received a 'mixed reception'

---

38 E.G. Stanley, 'Ælfric on the Canonicity of the Book of Judith,' 439. Stanley used ultraviolet light to achieve the reading *þus* on a difficult and dark passage in Cotton Otho B.x. Assmann saw *nis*, which may be an instance of his mind seeing what his eyes did not because he was predisposed to regarding the book of Judith as non-canonical. In other words, Assmann was expecting Ælfric to doubt canonicity because Assmann himself personally did. This observation of a psycho-visual reading is, of course, a guess. Assmann's reading makes no sense.

39 Stanley, ibid.; Gatch, 'The Office in Late Anglo-Saxon Monasticism,' 355n48, noting that the word is used to signify the entire canon in Ælfric's *Letter to Sigeweard on the Old and New Testament*, in *The Old English Version of the Heptateuch*, ed. S.J. Crawford (1922; repr. 1969), line 724 (46), and also line 835 (51).

among the Fathers, where in general the West (Hilary of Poitiers and Augustine of Hippo, for example) accepted the book, and the East (Origen, Cyril of Jerusalem, for example) rejected it.[40] There is an appeal to Latinity in lines 2, 22, 396, and 440. The first two instances concern the problem of the two Nabuchodonosors; in sorting them out, Ælfric tried to show how he knows his Latin and his Bible (if errant on the particular point of the two Nabuchodonosors). The second two instances are forms of citation. In line 396 Ælfric merely cites the canticle of Judith in its context, while in line 440 he cites Paul's teaching about fornicators and adulterers, producing the only Latin in the text, 'Fornicatores et adulteros iudicabit Deus' (Hebrews 13:4). One can also reasonably infer that Ælfric's audience may not have had much Latin and, reciprocally, would have accepted the authority of Latinity.

In the rendering of the book of Judith, Ælfric, as the above discussion describes, creates a denotative narrative that is by and large plain story or, as he himself puts it in the preface to Genesis, *þa nacedan gerecednisse* (the bare story).[41] Ælfric removes high points such as prayers, compresses incidents, and keeps to the surface of events. He does not rely on figurative language particularly, and similes are rare. When Achior describes the Crossing of the Red Sea (Judith 5:12), he says that the God of heaven parted the waters so that they stood *quasi murus*, which Ælfric dutifully renders as *swylce stanweallas* (line 104). When Judith describes the hapless state of the Israelites as akin to sheep who have no shepherd (11:15), Ælfric gives the Old English equivalent, *swa swa hyrdeleas sceap* (line 260). For his part, Ælfric invests the language with no particular colouring. A word such as *ænlic* and its forms, which occur five times (lines 19, 44, 192, 230, and 378), has the status of a motif word that gives texture and resonance. Ælfric applies the word four times in relatively positive contexts: to the Temple (line 19), to Judith herself (line 192), to Judith's clothes (line 230), and to the victory of the Israelites (line 378). These occurrences carry the overlapping meanings of 'singular,' 'incomparable,' and 'beautiful' (so BT, BTS); *The Dictionary of Old English, A-F*, gives sense 3 'unique, peerless, incomparable,' and specifically 3c 'of humans or angels and their physical appearance: peerless, beautiful,' but does not cite Assmann 9 as an example.[42] Ælfric also uses

---

40 Moore, *Judith*, 86–91, surveys the canonicity. The phrase is Moore's.

41 Wilcox, *Ælfric's Prefaces*, 117.

42 See Paul Beekman Taylor, 'The Old English Poetic Vocabulary of Beauty,' 211–21. Taylor places *ænlic* in the second of his four categories where the words listed suggest 'Beauty in an Appealing Physical Form' (218).

the word to describe the reaction of Nabuchodonosor's 'yes-men' to his speech in which he proposes to take over the world: *he ænlice spræce* (line 44). Of course, Nabuchodonosor's speech is anything but beautiful, but it is singular in its moral stupidity. There is then an ironic touch to this use that is a counterpoint to the eventual Israelite victory, which is truly *ænlice*.

In line with the straightforward denotative narrative, Ælfric offers a straightforward, if multiple, moral conclusion. Assmann signals his apparent discomfort with the ending by leaving several blank lines between line 403, which clearly ends the story of Judith, and line 404, which continues with concluding remarks; as well there is a horizontal line as if to offer an exclamation point on its side in order to emphasize further the discontinuity (cf. the comments above on the textual state of the ending). The first meaning that Ælfric sees in the book of Judith is the fulfilment of Matthew 23:12, 'Qui autem se exaltaverit, humiliabitur: et qui se humiliaverit, exaltabitur' (Whoever shall exalt himself shall be humbled: and he that shall humble himself shall be exalted), which is the equivalent of lines 408–9. As a pithy moral summary of the entire book of Judith, the New Testament verse seems more than adequate. Ælfric links Judith's humility to her purity (line 410a), which becomes the logical connection to Ælfric's first allegorical reading. In her victory over Holofernes, Judith betokens the believing church, which is Christ's bride, who with *cenum geleafan* (line 415) decapitates the old devil, ever serving Christ in purity. These allegorical equivalences, where Judith is the church (the bride of Christ), and Holofernes the devil, are traditional.[43] Ælfric continues with a problematical explanation of Judith's promise to Holofernes to bring him to her people: 'Ac hit næs na ealles leas' (line 420). It would appear that Ælfric means that Judith's promise is not a lie, because the issue is really about how God helped her, not about how she did not keep a promise to Holofernes. It is no doubt appropriate to address one of those glaring moral difficulties in the account. Another reading of Ælfric's words, whose grim and sardonic humor pushes the limit of interpretation, suggests that when Judith brought Holofernes' head into Bethulia, she did, so to speak, keep her promise to bring him to her people! Such a reading seems too clever by half. At

---

43 Hrabanus Maurus was the first to offer a full commentary on the book of Judith, *PL* 109.539–92, *Expositio in Librum Judith*. See Griffith's general discussion of the Christian tradition (*Judith*, lines 70–82), and especially his valuable notes (lines 240, 245, and 247).

this point Ælfric exclaims praise to God and utters, 'Amen' (line 423).
After these total interpretations of the book of Judith, Ælfric takes a
narrower focus to explain one point in the text and its meaning. The
Bethulians gave Judith *Holofernes þing* (line 382b; Judith 15:14), and the
Old Testament lists what those things are: gold, silver, clothing, gems,
and household goods. When Judith makes an offering in Judith 16:23,
she gives up the *uniuersa uasa bellica* and the canopy. Ælfric refers only
to the garments, saying that she would not have them and would not
wear them:

nolde þurh his hæþenscype   habban ænige synne. (line 428)

[She would not through his heathenism have any sin.]

Ælfric makes Judith's actions to be gestures of a personal choice, whereas
in the Old Testament her actions are part of the offerings of thanks given
by the community, not a repudiation of heathendom. Ælfric gives a compressed account of the Bethulian celebrations (when he gives it) in proper
narrative order, and effectively he resumes that account in the coda with
his specific interpretation. Since what Judith is wearing at a given time is
a recurrent motif (widow's weeds, seductive clothing), her rejection of
Holofernes' clothing and its connection with sin is an appropriate closure
to this motif. Narration and interpretation, in the main separated in
Ælfric's *Judith*, come together here.

There is an apparent logical or compositional gap between the discussion of Judith's rejection of Holofernes' tainted clothes and what follows
in line 429 when Ælfric begins a discussion of nuns, their moral behaviour, and Judith as a *bysen* who lived chastely before the birth of Christ.
The direct injunction *[n]imað eow bysne*, as well as the direct address *ge*,
and *min swustor*, come close to suggesting a particular occasion for the
presentation of the story of Judith.[44] The link between the story and the
interpretation or moral application of it is less in the text than in the audience. Clothing, the taint of sin, and particular nuns' behaviour form a set
of associative themes perhaps best understood as a reflex of a specific time
and place.

---

44 See note 8 to this essay. Mary Clayton discusses the addressee of Ælfric's *Judith*, concluding that 'the woman to whom the epilogue is addressed must, therefore, have been
   a dedicated virgin living among a community of *nunnan*' ('Ælfric's *Judith*,' 225–7).

This essay means to serve as a literary introduction to Ælfric's *Judith* with special emphasis on the work as a narration. Although there are problematical features of Ælfric's *Judith*, particularly as a physical text in the ending, the main body of the work is a 'plain vanilla' story in so far as a rendering of a biblical text can finally be for a teacher such as Ælfric. With the poem *Judith* as a point of comparison, Ælfric's intention is manifest: 'þa nacedan gerecednisse.' Poetic amplification, elaboration, or improvisation on a theme yields to prose abbreviation, concision, and even elimination. In the long history of biblical study, where faithfulness to the words of Holy Writ has proved to have fatal repercussions for some, Ælfric is freewheeling indeed, suggesting in this context that for him less is indeed more. Whether Ælfric is in deep imitation of the Bible, where, as Auerbach has taught us, there is meaning in what is not said as well as in what is said, may still remain to be proven.[45] No doubt Ælfric is fretful over ignorant clergy who cannot distinguish between the Old Law and the New Law, thus his remarks in the preface to the translation of Genesis.[46] Ælfric may be seeking to compensate for unexplained narration by offering moral points after he finishes his narration. Be that as it may, Ælfric has nevertheless produced an example of narration that is plain on the surface, such as haunted C.E. Wright in his search for *The Cultivation of Saga in Anglo-Saxon England*.[47]

Yet there is clearly more to say about Ælfric's *Judith* than this description of narrative. When the elder Ioachim praises Judith for acting *uiriliter* (Judith 15:11), then there is biblical warrant indeed for the obvious feature of Judith's heroic work and almost any of the varieties of gender criticism.[48] At least one potential area for study is the idea of the male gaze, which is a theme linking both the Assyrians and the Israelites: is it blasphemy to suggest that God *himself* participates in that gaze when he gives Judith more 'bright beauty'? Although there would seem to be enough discussion of Judith as a symbol of resistance to the Vikings and/or as *Ecclesia*, the avoidance of allegory in Ælfric's *Judith* seems to invite more

---

45 Erich Auerbach, *Mimesis*, 3–23, in the chapter entitled 'Odysseus' Scar,' wherein Auerbach contrasts Homeric and biblical styles.
46 Wilcox, *Ælfric's Prefaces*, 116–19.
47 C.E. Wright, *The Cultivation of Saga in Anglo-Saxon England*.
48 See Klein, 'Ælfric's Sources and His Gendered Audiences,' for more on the problematic ending, and Mary Dockray-Miller, 'Female Community in the Old English *Judith*,' 165–72, with emphasis on Judith and her maid.

commentary. Ælfric can be an easy allegorist as, for example, in his Purification Homily, *CH* I.9 (based on Bede), but his avoidance of allegorizing Achior or Judith's maid is worthy of note. Achior as a symbol of a pagan (read, Viking) who converts, or the maid as the soul of obedience, invites Alexandrian options. In what sense can Judith be seen as an Old Testament saint? Rosemary Woolf has suggested that the poetic *Judith* 'shows unmistakably the influence of the life of the virgin martyr,' and Marie Nelson subtitles her *Judith, Juliana, and Elene* as *Three Fighting Saints.*[49] Is there a theological basis for the consideration of Judith as a saint, perhaps within the theories of the three dispensations, before the Law, the Old Law, and the New Law? In his retelling of 2 Maccabees chapter 7 and the killing of the seven brethren and their mother at the hands of Antiochus, Ælfric observes:

Manega halgan wæron under moyses æ
ac we nabbað heora remynd mid nanum mæssedæge
Buton þyssera gebroðra þe swa bealdlice ðrowodon.

[Many saints were (there) under Moses' law,
but we hold not their commemoration on any massday,
except of these brethren, that so boldly suffered.][50]

How far ahead of the theological curve is Ælfric here?[51] How does the prose *Judith* function within the context of Ælfric's other Old Testament narratives? Does Ælfric adopt a different narrational stance when he relates stories from under the Old Law? And finally, one can bring up the vexed matter of Ælfric's rhythmical prose. Lee is uncomfortable in presenting the text in verse lines, whereas Assmann has no apparent

---

49 Rosemary Woolf, 'Saints' Lives,' 37–66, esp. 64; Marie Nelson, *Judith, Juliana, and Elene*. See also Nelson's note in 'Judith: A Story of a Secular Saint,' 12–13. The connection between the poetic *Judith* and saints' lives receives influential endorsement from Stanley B. Greenfield and Daniel G. Calder, *A New Critical History of Old English Literature*, 219.

50 Skeat, *Ælfric's Lives of Saints*, vol. 2, 80, with Skeat's translation *en face* at 81.

51 At the 6 July 2006 session of 'Holy Men and Holy Women,' a National Endowment for the Humanities summer seminar held at the Department of Anglo-Saxon, Norse, and Celtic, Teresa Webber observed that the standard category for Old Testament figures is 'prophets and patriarchs.'

discomfort.[52] However, the struggle to set up the lines, especially after a closer look at manuscript punctuation, may assist the understanding of Ælfric's stylistic development.[53] All in all, there are many ways to go forward in furthering the understanding of an important and significant prose incorporation of the Old Testament into vernacular literature.

---

52 Lee, *Ælfric's Homilies*, 1: 'when attempting to shoe-horn Ælfric's prose into a series of verse lines, each containing balanced half-lines, one comes across some troublesome decisions as an editor.'

53 See my 'Abbot Ælfric and His Rhythmical Prose in the Computer Age,' 95–108.

Circumscribing the Text: Views on Circumcision in Old English Literature

SAMANTHA ZACHER

Anglo-Saxons seem to have seen few Jews; the solitary allusion to the presence of a single Jew at the court of King Athelstan only underlines their exotic and unfamiliar nature.[1] Unlike many patristic authors, who could claim direct knowledge of Jews or Jewish practice, including the Hebrew language, those living in Anglo-Saxon England could for the most part only recapture a sense of what it was to be a Jew through reading and imagination, and largely through the distorting lens of an inherited Christian perspective. Yet, considerable interest in the subject of Jewish nationhood, religion, rituals, and language seemed to permeate the literature of Anglo-Saxon England. Several recent studies have focused on the stereotypes (both negative and positive) that surround the depiction of the Jew in Anglo-Saxon texts, thereby exposing the dissonance between what we might suppose are real attitudes towards Jews as unknown 'others' and what can be seen as merely (or perhaps especially) a series of rhetorical stances inherited from patristic contexts.[2]

---

1 See David J. Wasserstein, 'The First Jew in England,' 283–8. Wasserstein argues the presence of a Jew at the court of King Athelstan on the basis of a questionable reference to an 'Israel' (also identified as a *Iudeus Romanus*, or a Roman Jew) in a text known as the *Alea euangelii* (Gospel Dice) preserved in the twelfth-century manuscript in Oxford, Corpus Christi College 122. This interpretation, however, is summarily dismissed by Lapidge, 'Israel the Grammarian in Anglo-Saxon England' (99), who argues that the Israel in question reflects a botched reference to the famed Breton scholar, Israel the Grammarian.

2 Comprehensive overviews are offered by Andrew P. Scheil in 'Anti-Judaism in Ælfric's *Lives of Saints*,' 65–86, and *The Footsteps of Israel*. See too Nicholas Howe, *Migration and Mythmaking in Anglo-Saxon England*; Heide Estes, 'Lives in Translation,' as well as her 'Feasting with Holofernes,' 325–50. There has likewise been a recent resurgence of

By contrast, I focus here on a relatively neglected area with respect to Anglo-Saxon writings on Jews, namely those highly conflicted commentaries on individual Jewish practices and rituals. Perhaps not surprisingly, these texts tend to single out precisely those rituals commanded in the Old Testament (such as the observance of the Sabbath, circumcision, the sacrifice of the paschal lamb, special dietary laws, and treatment of the temple as the dwelling place of God),[3] which were either prohibited by the Christian church or comprehensively reinterpreted in what were held to be new Christian spiritual contexts. These rituals, even to Anglo-Saxons remote from the original identity-building ethos of the apostolic period, continued to symbolize highly effectual marks of both behavioural and cultural difference first between Jews and Gentiles and later between Jews and Christians. Of the various responses by sundry Anglo-Saxon authors to these Jewish rituals, surely the most interesting are those on the subject of bodily circumcision, which must have seemed the most foreign and outlandish of these rites.[4] For some of them, discussion of this practice fuelled the impression that the Jew represented both the spiritual and the physical other. Moreover, such impressions may have been deepened by the repeated biblical emphasis upon the rite as a sign of difference: in the

---

scholarly appreciation of the extent to which the Hebrew language was prized in Anglo-Saxon England. On the influence of the Hebrew Psalter on Anglo-Saxon versions, see Sarah Laratt Keefer, 'Hebrew and the *Hebraicum* in Late Anglo-Saxon England,' 67–80. For the use of Hebrew in onomastic and paronomastic puns, see Roberta Frank, 'Some Uses of Paronomasia in Old English Scriptural Verse,' 207–26. Also see the three articles by Fred C. Robinson, 'The Significance of Names in Old English Literature,' 'Anglo-Saxon Onomastics in the Old English *Andreas*,' and 'Some Uses of Name-Meanings in Old English Poetry,' repr. in his *Tomb of Beowulf and Other Essays on Old English*, 185–218, 224–7, and 228–35. For studies on the use of Hebrew in diverse commentaries on biblical and homiletic materials, see David Howlett, '*Tres linguae sacrae* and Threefold Play in Insular Latin,' 94–115. For the use and influence of Hebrew grammar and alphabets in Old English texts, see Damian Fleming. '"The Most Exalted Language,"' as well as his essay in this volume, '*Rex regum et cyninga cyning.*'

3 A glossed Old English version of a portion of Isidore's *De fide catholica contra Iudaeos* in *Old English Glosses*, ed. A.S. Napier, no. 40, Anecdota Oxoniensia, Mediaeval and Modern Series 11 (Oxford, 1900; repr. Hildesheim, 1969), lines 205.1–207.11, contains just such a list of Jewish rituals. The inclusion in this list of an entry for animal sacrifice (a ritual outlawed in a Jewish context after the destruction of the second Jewish Temple in 70 AD) suggests that these lists were more interested in stressing cultural difference than in historical accuracy.

4 The topic of circumcision in Old English literature has been treated briefly by Rebecca Barnhouse, 'Shaping the Hexateuch Text for an Anglo-Saxon Audience,' 103–5, and by Susan Kim, 'Bloody Signs,' 285–307.

Old Testament, circumcision was celebrated as a means of separating the elect and the faithful from the unclean, and in the New Testament it came to be viewed critically as an exclusionary measure that hindered Gentile conversion.

Although, as we shall see, Anglo-Saxons inherited a copious body of Latin (and Greek) patristic writings on the subject (with many of these writings having been filtered through the prolific meditations on the subject by such Anglo-Latin writers as Bede and Alcuin), there is an intriguing dearth of material in Old English texts on the subject. Indeed, aside from a few scattered references to circumcision in glosses and glossed texts, there are only a handful of references to the rite of circumcision in biblical and homiletic works, mostly associated with Ælfric. This shortage of materials would not in and of itself be so remarkable if not for the fact that inherited liturgical practice included a feast day on 1 January for the Circumcision of Christ; one would imagine that even rudimentary explication of the ritual would be necessary for educating Anglo-Saxon lay audiences.[5] In the following, I wish to explore the double dynamic of representation and censorship for an audience that was undoubtedly cut off (as it were) from both the sight and practice of this Jewish rite. I shall focus in turn on a series of representations, misunderstandings, and especially omissions on the subject of circumcision in a range of writings in Old English, including glosses, homilies, and poems, in an attempt to offer an overview of the changing range of Anglo-Saxon attitudes to the topic throughout the period. I have chosen deliberately to concentrate on vernacular texts and renderings because these offer a better index of more commonly held attitudes than do their more rarefied and learned Anglo-Latin counterparts. Although it has elsewhere been shown that Anglo-Saxon writers could sometimes be gratuitously vocal about their thoughts on Jews, it seems to be the peculiar nature of this touchy subject that their silences and omissions speak more loudly than words.

Circumcision in the Old Testament momentously marks the first covenant between God and Abraham, as revealed in Genesis 17:9–14. The terms of this rite are such that every male, in every generation (including slaves), is to be circumcised at the age of eight days. This rhetoric of initiation

---

5 The feast of the circumcision is discussed in Ælfric's homily *Kalendas ianuarii octabas et circumcisio Domini* in his *Catholic Homilies* I.6 (Peter Clemoes, ed., *Ælfric's Catholic Homilies*, 224–31), hereafter *CH* I.6, and alluded to in the Latin antiphon designated for this feast day in the Exeter Book poem *Christ I*, lines 417–38 (lyric XII), in *The Anglo-Saxon Poetic Records*, ed. George Philip Krapp and Elliott Van Kirk Dobbie, vol. 3.

serves to establish circumcision as a visible sign of nationhood, since, as verse 13 states, it is 'to be marked in the flesh as an everlasting pact.' Likewise, Genesis 17:14 (and later Leviticus 12:3) makes it clear that any failure to keep the rite will result in a veritable excision from the tribe, since the soul (Hebrew *nephesh*) of the apostate is literally to be 'cut off' from the nation. This theme is rehearsed elsewhere in Exodus 12:48, where it is further stated that circumcision was necessary for all non-Israelites who wished to take part in the feast of Passover, and again in Genesis 34:14–16, which stipulates the same for those who wish to marry a Jew.

Although references to the rite in the Old Testament tend to stress the importance of the physical sign, in certain contexts circumcision is importantly imbued with spiritual significance. In Deuteronomy 10:16, the Lord reminds the Israelites of their covenant, stating that they must 'circumcise the foreskin of [their] hearts.' By the same token, the Hebrew term *arel*, meaning 'uncircumcised,' is used not only to signify those nations and individuals who fall outside of the terms of the covenant but also to signify spiritual 'uncleanliness.' So, for example, Jeremiah 9:26 warns that 'for all these nations are uncircumcised [*arelim*], but all the house of Israel are uncircumcised of heart [*arlei- lev*].'[6] This same spiritual interpretation of circumcision is adapted to new ends in the New Testament, where it is used to undercut the need for physical circumcision, and to give credence to the idea of a purely asomatic celebration of the ritual.[7] Officially, the Christian church rejected the physical rite of circumcision at the Council of Jerusalem, as recorded in Acts, chapter 15. However, the rhetoric of displacement – shifting the issue from the body to the soul – is pervasive throughout the New Testament epistles. Of paramount importance to this topic are Paul's letters to the Romans and Galatians, in which he most assertively addresses the question as to whether Gentiles must

---

6   The biblical quotation is from the *JPS Hebrew-English Tanakh* (Philadelphia: Jewish Publication Society, 1999). For a list of the Old Testament references to circumcision from Genesis through Judges, see my table below. Also see further the Vulgate books of prophets in 1 Sam. 14:6, 17:26, 17:36, 31:4; 2 Sam. 1:20; Isa. 52:1; Jer. 4:4, 6:10, 9:25–6; Ezek. 28:10, 31:18, 32:19, 32:21, 32:24–32, 44:7–9; and also 1 Chron. 10:4; as well as the apocryphal Jth. 14:6; 1 Macc. 1:51, 1:63–4, 2:46, 2 Macc. 6:10.

7   The topic of circumcision in the New Testament has been amply treated by, for example, J.N.B. Carleton Paget, 'Barnabas 9:4,' 242–54; R. Jewitt, 'The Agitators and the Galatian Congregation,' 198–212; Judith M. Lieu, 'Circumcision, Women and Salvation,' 358–70; John M.G. Barclay, 'Paul and Philo on Circumcision,' 536–56. For a treatment of the rite through the lens of (especially) Lacanian and Foucaultian theories, see Kathleen Biddick, *The Typological Imaginary*.

become Jews before they become Christians.[8] Although speaking as a Jew himself, Paul does not negate the historical significance of circumcision as a sign of the original covenant, he does refute its continued significance as a prerequisite for salvation by Christ. Typical of his view is his statement in Romans 2:26–9 that spiritual circumcision is far more potent than the physical rite:

> If, then, the uncircumcised keep the justices of the law, shall not this un-circumcision be counted for circumcision? And shall not that which by na-ture is uncircumcision, if it fulfill the law, judge thee, who by the letter and circumcision art a transgressor of the law? For it is not he is a Jew, who is so outwardly; nor is that circumcision which is outwardly in the flesh: But he is a Jew, that is one inwardly; and the circumcision is that of the heart, in the spirit, not in the letter; whose praise is not of men, but of God.[9]

Paul argues that faith in Christ has the effect of superseding the Law of the Jews who shared in the original covenant with God, since under the New Law all who place their faith in Christ are to be included among the elect. In his letter to the Galatians, Paul takes a more exclusionary stance than in Romans, when he outlines the negative consequences for new con-verts seeking to undertake the physical rite of circumcision. Paul's more aggressive rhetoric reflects his desire to correct the Judaizing tendencies of teachers in the churches of Galatia and Asia Minor (unaffiliated with the Pauline mission), who insisted that faith in Christ must include adherence to Mosaic Law.[10] Thus, in Galatians 5:1–6, Paul states that circumcision is 'a yoke of slavery' from which Christ is the sole redeemer:

---

8 New Testament references to circumcision include Luke 1:59 and 2:21; John 7:22–3; Acts 7:8, 10:45, 11:2, 15:1, 15:5, 16:3, 21:21; Rom. 2:25–9, 3:1, 3:30, 4:9, 4:10–12, 15:8; 1 Cor. 7:18–19; Gal. 2:3, 2:7–9; 2:12, 5:2–3, 5:6, 5:11, 6:12–15; Eph. 2:11; Phil. 3:2–5; Col. 2:11, 3:11, 4:11; and Titus 1:10.

9 'Si igitur praeputium iustitias legis custodiat nonne praeputium illius in circumcisionem reputabitur; et iudicabit quod ex natura est praeputium legem consummans te qui per litteram et circumcisionem praeuaricator legis es; non enim qui in manifesto Iudaeus est neque quae in manifesto in carne circumcisio sed qui in abscondito Iudaeus et circumci-sio cordis in spiritu non littera cuius laus non ex hominibus sed ex Deo est.' All Vulgate references are cited from *Biblia sacra iuxta uulgatam uersionem*, ed. R. Weber et al., 4th ed. Unless otherwise indicated, all Vulgate translations are from the Douay-Rheims edition of the Old and New Testament (New York: P.J. Kennedy, 1950).

10 Bruce Metzger and Roland E. Murphy, eds., *New Oxford Annotated Bible with the Apocryphal/Deuterocanonical Books: New Revised Standard Version* (New York: Oxford University Press, 1991 [repr. from 1973]), 263.

Stand fast, and be not held again under the yoke of bondage. Behold, I Paul tell you, that if you be circumcised, Christ shall profit you nothing. And I testify again to every man circumcising himself, that he is a debtor to the whole law. You are made void of Christ, you who are justified in the law: you are fallen from grace. For we in spirit, by faith, wait for the hope of justice. For in Christ Jesus neither circumcision availeth any thing, nor uncircumcision: but faith that worketh by charity.[11]

In this passage, Paul inverts the Old Testament view of circumcision as a visible sign of inclusion among God's elect (extending back to Genesis 17:14 and Leviticus 12:3), by stating that under the New Law the act of circumcision serves literally to excise one (*excidere*) from Christ.[12]

While the early church recommended a stringent break from the Old Law on the topic of physical circumcision (as a means of cutting themselves off, the more clearly to claim a new faction), this view is mitigated in the writings of some of the later church fathers who assert that in place of the physical ritual, baptism can serve as the new *sphragis*, or the seal of the covenant.[13] Jean Daniélou has written extensively on the symbolism of this typology and cites the words of Cyril of Jerusalem (in his *Mystagogic Catechesis*) as being representative of these writings: 'after faith, we like Abraham, receive the spiritual *sphragis*, being circumcised in baptism by

---

11 'State et nolite iterum iugo seruitutis contineri; ecce ego Paulus dico uobis quoniam si circumcidamini Christus uobis nihil proderit testificor autem rursum omni homini circumcidenti se quoniam debitor est uniuersae legis faciendae; euacuati estis a Christo qui in lege iustificamini a gratia excidistis; nos enim spiritu ex fide spem iustitiae expectamus; nam in Christo Iesu neque circumcisio aliquid ualet neque praeputium sed fides quae per caritatem operator.'

12 Paul's understanding of circumcision as forming a debt to the law likewise finds vivid and intensified expression in the later writings of patristic writers such as Ambrose of Milan, who in his Letter to Constantius (*PL* 16.1246A) maintains that the salvific exchange of Christ's blood shed at the circumcision compensates for that of all Christians: 'Sed quia pretium pro omnibus solutum est, posteaquam passus est Christus Dominus, iam non opus est, ut uiritim sanguis singulorum circumcisione fundatur' (Since the price has been paid for all after Christ the Lord suffered, there is no longer need for the blood of each individual to be shed by circumcision). According to Ambrose's typological formulation, Christ's spilling of his blood through his own circumcision effectively serves as the first of his wounds to be incurred as a symbolic precursor to his crucifixion. In setting up this typological reading of the circumcision as a precursor for the passion of Christ, it becomes possible to implicate the Jew in both bloodlettings. For this argument, see further Ruth Mellinkoff, *Outcasts*, 43 and 106–7.

13 See further Thomas D. Hill, 'The *Sphragis* as Apotropaic Sign,' 147–51, who discusses the role of the *sphragis* as the symbol of the cross in Old English literature.

the Holy Spirit.'[14] By establishing baptism as a second *sphragis*, the church (however much individual writers continued to invoke a rhetoric of displacement) sought to imbue the ritual with the properties of cleansing from lust and sin.

As we shall see, discussions of circumcision in Old English texts tend to absorb both strains of this rhetoric: on the one hand, Anglo-Saxons continued to highlight a perceived lack of spirituality for those Jews who could not assimilate the spiritual significance of God's command, and, on the other, they seemed eager to cling to the idea that circumcision still served as a powerful assurance of the covenant with God for all generations. However, before examining in detail some of these passages on circumcision, it is prudent to examine the lexical tools available to Anglo-Saxons writing on the subject in Old English; such a survey presents an illuminating index for evaluating how the Anglo-Saxons both understood and found the means to explain the rite.

The most accurate descriptions of the ritual itself can be found in two verbal calques for the Latin *circumcido* (whence *circumcisio*), in the terms *ymbceorfan* (meaning 'cut' or 'carve around') and *ymbsniðan* (snip around).[15] By contrast, we find a good deal of confusion surrounding Old English terms for 'foreskin,' in that they rarely describe anatomical reality with any precision. Consider the evidence from the glossed texts: for example, in the *Cleopatra* glosses we find a translation of the Latin *praeputium* (foreskin) as *scama, þa wæpenlican limo*.[16] The term *scam[u]* (which elsewhere more generally means 'shame,' 'disgrace,' and 'shameful circumstance,' but here

---

14 For an edition of the fourth-century Greek text, see PG 33.513A, translated by Jean Daniélou, *The Bible and the Liturgy*, 63–9.

15 For the citations given I am indebted to the invaluable online *Dictionary of Old English* (http://www.doe.utoronto.ca/, last accessed July 2009); I borrow their abbreviations here. Works containing the Old English gloss *ymbceorfan* (in all of its variant spellings) include *The Lindisfarne Gospels* for Luke (LkGl [Li] C8.1.3) 1:59 and 2:21, John (JnGl [Li] C8.1.4) 7:22–3, and also the *Lindisfarne* commentaries containing the 'Argument to Matthew' (MtArgGl [Li] C8.1.5) line 1, the 'Headings to Readings in Matthew' (MtHeadGl [Li] C21.3) line 40, and the 'Headings to Readings in Luke' (LkHeadGl [Li] C21.8) line 7; *The Rushworth Gospels* for Luke (LkGl [Ru] C8.2.3) 1:59 and 2:21 and also John (JnGl [Ru] C8.2.4) 7:22–3. Texts containing the Old English gloss *ymbsniðan* (in all of its variant spellings) include Isidore, *De miraculis Christi* (IsGl C19) at 205.7 and 206.6. The term *ymbsniðan* likewise glosses other Latin words, such as *ancisus* in Abbo's, *Bella Parisiacae urbis* (Abbo C1) line 109.3, and in the *Antwerp Glossary* (AntGl 1 [Kindschi] D1.1) entry 3, where *ancisus* and *circumcisus* are juxtaposed as synonyms.

16 *Cleopatra Glossary* (ClGl1 [Stryker] D8.1), lines 4887 and 4918.

'private part') does not so much describe the foreskin itself but rather stands metonymically for the entire 'locus of "shame,"' while the appositive term *wæpenlican limo* apparently refers generally to the 'male member.'[17] The *Corpus Glossary* similarly interprets the Latin *praeputii* with the misfit gloss *testi* (the latter presumably a form of *testis* or 'testicle'), thereby comparing terms for 'foreskin' and 'testicle.'[18] A similar indeterminacy can be detected in the *Collected Glossaries*, where *praeputium* is glossed simply as *felcyrf* (cut-skin);[19] it seems impossible on the basis of this term alone to determine which bit of skin is implied.

Ælfric apparently developed or adopted a fuller phallic vocabulary. He seemed particularly fond of the term *fylmen* to represent the foreskin, since all four attested examples of this usage can be found in his *Homily on the Circumcision* and in his Old English translation of the *Heptateuch*.[20] Elsewhere, the ongoing *Dictionary of Old English* records the use of this word for any membrane, including that of the body, the stomach, parchment, or fruit. Ælfric may have adapted this highly specialized use of the term from a reference in Leviticus 19:23, which forbids the consumption (and holy use) of fruit taken from newly planted trees for at least three years; in the Vulgate, the forbidden fruits of these trees are termed *praeputia* or 'uncircumcized,' roughly translating the Hebrew (*peroth ... arelim*; 'fruit uncircumcised').[21] But even here we note that the precise nature of this fruity skin is far from clear.

17   For a refreshing discussion of several words describing the genitalia, as well as a treatment of circumlocution and euphemism in modern-day translations, see further Roberta Frank, 'Sex in the *Dictionary of Old English*,' 302–12.

18   *Corpus Glossary* (CorpGl 2 [Hessels] D4.2), line 14.695. The entry is problematic since the cases do not seem to match.

19   *Collected Glossaries* (CollGl 11 [Voss] D11), line 39. Indeed, Ælfric improves upon the latter term in his *Homily on the Circumcision* (*CH* I.6), 225.52, in which he uses *fell-* and *forcyrf-* separately to achieve greater precision.

20   Typical is the following statement from his *CH* I.6, 226.64: 'Swa hwilc hysecild swa ne bið ymbsniden on þam fylmene his flæsces, his sawul losað: for þan ðe he aydlode min wed' (Whatsoever male child is not circumcised in the foreskin of his flesh, he will lose his soul, because he has disregarded my covenant). The other three references include his *CH* I.6, 226.82, and his *Heptateuch* Gen. 17:11, 17:14.

21   The full reference from Lev. 19:23 is as follows: 'Quando ingressi fueritis terram et plantaueritis in ea ligna pomifera auferetis praeputia eorum poma quae germinant inmunda erunt uobis nec edetis ex eis' (When you shall be come into the land, and shall have planted in it fruit trees, you shall take away the first fruits of them. The fruit that comes forth shall be unclean to you: neither shall you eat of them [trans. Douay-Rheims]). An explanatory note for this passage in the Douay-Rheims Version states that

Elsewhere, Ælfric combines phrases to help pinpoint the location of the foreskin. In his *Homily on the Circumcision* he explains the injunction in Genesis that one must *forcurfe sumne dæl þæs felles ætforeweardan his gesceape* (cut off a certain portion of the fore-skin of his genitals). While the term *felles ætforeweardan* presents a good calque for the Latin *praeputium*, the word *gesceap* is more elusive; the *Dictionary of Old English* records several meanings for this word, including 'shape,' 'created being,' 'creature,' 'condition,' 'sex,' and 'genitalia.' Despite the clumsiness of Ælfric's phrasing, it is clear that he understood what he was describing: in his homily *De doctrina apostolica*, Ælfric uses the truncated phrase *gesceapu forceorfan* to refer instead to castration.[22]

The problems exhibited above with regard to lexical representation seem congruent with other difficulties surrounding the representation of the ritual. Perhaps the single greatest resource on the subject of circumcision in Old English is the Heptateuch, which presents translations of all five canonical books of the Bible, together with Joshua and Judges, made by Ælfric and an anonymous translator.[23] In a recent study Rebecca Barnhouse argues that both 'Ælfric and the anonymous translator delete many examples of circumcision' since passages 'would need too much explication in order to be understood figuratively.'[24] Barnhouse shows that although excerpts have been retained from Genesis chapters 17 and 21 and Joshua chapter 5, all of which describe the terms of the rite, many others have been omitted on account of their general difficulty. The excised passages include the problematic Exodus 4:24–6, which describes Sephora's circumcision of her son as a means of saving her husband, Moses, and also Genesis 34:14, which narrates the rape of Dinah by the prince of Sichem, an event that resulted in the circumcision of his men.[25] Even where the

---

the term *proeputia*, translated as 'firstfruits,' literally means 'foreskins,' since 'it alludes to circumcision, and signifies that for the first three years the trees were to be as uncircumcised, and their fruit unclean: till in the fourth year their increase was sanctified and given to the Lord, that is, to the priests.' The King James Version presents a more literal translation of the phrase *praeputia eorum poma*; it states that 'And when ye shall come into the land, and shall have planted all manner of trees for food, then ye shall count the fruit thereof as uncircumcised: three years shall it be as uncircumcised unto you: it shall not be eaten of.'

22 John C. Pope, ed., *The Homilies of Ælfric*, 625 (line 61).

23 S.J. Crawford, ed., *The Old English Version of the Heptateuch, Ælfric's Treatise on the Old and New Testament.*

24 Barnhouse, 'Shaping the Hexateuch Text,' 103.

25 Ibid.

descriptions of the rite seem particularly full, one can detect occasional hesitancy in handling the topic. Ælfric thus uncharacteristically interpolates into his otherwise close translation of Genesis chapter 17 the anachronistic comment *nu secge we betwux þisum þæt nan Cristen man ne mot nu swa don* (now we say about this matter [circumcision] that no Christian man may do so now).

While Barnhouse is certainly correct in pointing out the suppression or disappearance of many of the biblical descriptions of circumcision, her assessment that these passages are uniformly omitted because they are too difficult requires much more careful and detailed analysis, since the reactions of the Heptateuch authors are far more varied than her account suggests. Table I contains all references to circumcision in the Old Testament books from Genesis to Judges. Items in bold represent citations included from the Vulgate in the Old English Heptateuch. Citations that are underlined represent passages attributed to Ælfric according to the most recent estimation by Richard Marsden.[26]

Table I. References to Circumcision in the Vulgate and the Old English Heptateuch

Genesis	**17:10, 11, 12, 13, 14,** 23, **24, 25, 26, 27**
	21:4
	34:14, 15, 17, 22, 24
Exodus	4:26
	[6:12, 30 (referring to lips)]
	12:44, 48
Leviticus	12:3
	[26:41 (referring to hearts)]
Deuteronomy	10:16
	[21:12 (referring to nails)]
	30:6
Joshua	**5:2, 3, 4, 5, 6, 7, 8**
Judges	**14:3**
	15:18

It is surely striking that the Heptateuch contains only two clusters of references to circumcision and that both have been attributed to Ælfric. While the anonymous author(s) of the Heptateuch regularly jettisoned references to circumcision, Ælfric discerningly chose the passages he

---

26   Richard Marsden, 'Translation by Committee?' 41–90.

wished to translate. Ælfric's first grouping in Genesis chapters 17 and 21 reports the establishment of the covenant between God and Abraham, while his second in Joshua 5:2–4 narrates the 'second circumcision' (as it is called in Joshua 5:3), an event that marked the mass circumcision of Israelites after their passage over the Red Sea, as a renewal of the original covenant and ritual that had lapsed while the Hebrews wandered in the desert. The thematic link between these passages may suggest their perceived importance to Ælfric as an attestation of covenant and renewal, topics that (as we shall see) were central both to patristic and Anglo-Saxon interpretations and depictions of the rite. Ælfric's precision on the matter is likewise demonstrated by his inclusion of an esoteric Hebrew etymology from Joshua 5:3, which explicates the location of the 'second circumcision': the Hebrew *Gibeath Haaralot* (literally 'the hill of foreskins') is rendered in the Vulgate as *colle praeputiorum*, and in Ælfric's Heptateuch simply as *Preputiorum*. This Latin term for 'foreskin' occurs nowhere else in the corpus of Old English outside of glossaries. Ælfric once again shows surprising accuracy in rendering the terms of the rite.[27]

It may also be possible to suggest a rationale for Ælfric's omission of certain passages in his portion of the Heptateuch: for example, the excision of the tale-end passages from Joshua 5:5–8 seems merely indicative of Ælfric's practice of condensing long narratives. Moreover, while Ælfric omits both references to circumcision in Judges 14:3 and 15:18, these verses refer to the condition of being *uncircumcised*, a term that would been difficult or awkward to render in Old English, given the aforementioned lexical difficulties in rendering the practice. Perhaps too, the persistent association in the Old Testament of those who are uncircumcised (in Hebrew *arel*) with uncleanness may have appeared unnecessarily offensive to his (uncircumcised) contemporary Anglo-Saxon audience.[28]

Beyond his biblical translations, Ælfric displays similar selectivity in his homiletic treatments of the rite of circumcision. For example, he leaves out all references to circumcision from his two homilies on the apocryphal

---

27 Ælfric also keeps the reference to the place name Gilgal (meaning 'circle') in Josh. 5:9, though he probably would not have realized the putative etymological connection to circumcision.

28 For the use of the term *uncircumcised* as a phrase of censure in the Vulgate Old Testament, see further 1 Rg. 14:6, 17:36, 31:4; 2 Rg. 1:20; Isa. 52:1; Ezek. 28:10, 31:18, 32:19, 32:21, 32:24–32, 44:7, 44:9.

Maccabees and Judith.[29] In Judith, the omission occurs at the end of the narrative after Achior, having witnessed the decapitation of his lord Holofernes, converts to Judaism through circumcision.[30] Ælfric gets around the problem of having to explain the rite by merely stating that Achior began to believe in the Law of Moses: 'Ac he blissode sona and bletsode Iudith and gelyfde siððan on þone lyfigendan god æfter Moyses æ' (But he rejoiced immediately, and blessed Judith, and he believed afterwards in the living God, according to Moses's Law). The omissions in Maccabees are of a generally similar nature, in that Ælfric avoids discussing the topic by lumping circumcision under the host of Jewish rituals that were outlawed by Antiochus. It is also worth noting that some of the citations to the rite in Maccabees are especially technical and difficult to render, as can be seen from a passage in 1 Maccabees 1:16, which includes a discussion of epispasm, a procedure entailing the restoration of the foreskin by stretching out the residual skin, a technique practised by Jews who wished to be accepted by Gentile society.[31] This practice, so far from the world of Ælfric, was apparently common among Jewish Hellenists attempting to pass themselves off as Greeks.

However, if Ælfric in his previous homilies shies away from some of the more difficult and nuanced discussions of circumcision, he is forced to encounter the topic head-on in his *Catholic Homilies*, in I.6, 'The Octaves and Circumcision of our Lord.' As the title suggests, the majority of the homily is devoted to the explication of Christ's circumcision on the eighth day after his nativity, as narrated uniquely in Luke 2:21. Since the feast day falls on 1 January, the homily also treats themes relating to the discussion of the church's departure from pagan rituals for New Year's Day, and the

29   For a discussion of Ælfric's various omissions and changes to the apocryphal material in Maccabees, see Jonathan Wilcox, 'A Reluctant Translator,' 1–18.

30   See the passage in the Vulgate, Jud. 14:6: 'Tunc Achior uidens uirtutem quam fecit Deus Israhel relicto gentilitatis ritu credidit Deo et circumcidit carnem praeputii sui et adpositus est ad populum Israhel et omnis successio generis eius usque in hodiernum diem' (Then Achior seeing the power that the God of Israel had wrought, leaving the religion of the Gentiles, he believed God, and circumcised the flesh of his foreskin, and was joined to the people of Israel, with all the succession of his kindred until this present day).

31   See further the Vulgate, 1 Macc. 1:16: 'Et fecerunt sibi praeputia et recesserunt a testamento sancto et iuncti sunt nationibus et uenundati sunt ut facerent malum' (And they made themselves prepuces, and departed from the holy covenant, and joined themselves to the heathens, and were sold to do evil [trans. Douay-Rheims]). For discussions of this procedure, see for example, Leonard B. Glick, *Marked in Your Flesh*, 31–2, and Shaye J.D. Cohen, *The Beginnings of Jewishness*, 39–46.

fittingness of the calendrical celebration of New Year's Day. Malcolm Godden's notes on the homily succinctly outline the major sources for the piece, showing its main source to be Bede's homily 1.11, though the homily also draws on such other texts as Haymo of Auxerre's *Homiliae de tempore* 14, and Martin of Braga's *De correctione rusticorum*.[32] While Godden summarizes Ælfric's major omissions, additions, and changes to the homily, there is still more to gain by looking at some of Ælfric's discussions of circumcision through the lens of the previously surveyed texts on the subject.

An analysis of Ælfric's various departures from his sources reveals tensions unique to Ælfric's version; these betray Ælfric's anxieties both about having to explain to his lay audience the rite of circumcision and about its reception of the topic. In several places Ælfric calls attention to the potential ignorance of his audience on this subject. He writes (in lines 79–86):

Nis nu alyfed cristenum mannum þæt hi ðas ymbsnidenysse lichamlice healdon: ac þeah hwæðere nan mann ne bið. soðlice cristen buton he þa ymbsnidenysse on gastlicum þeawum gehealde; Hwæt getacnað þæs felmenes ofcyrf on þam gesceape: buton galnysse wanunge; Eaðe mihte ðæs cwede beon læwedum mannum bediglod: nære seo gastlice getacnung; Hit þincð ungelæredum mannum dyslic to gehyrenne: ac gif hit him dyslic þince þonne cide he wið god þe hit gesette: na wið us þe hit secgað.

[It is not allowed now that Christian men might observe this bodily circumcision: nevertheless no man is a true Christian unless he observes circumcision in a spiritual manner; what betokens the cutting of the foreskin on the penis except the waning of lust? Easily might this discussion be hidden from laymen if not for the spiritual meaning. It seems to laymen foolish to hear; but if it seems foolish, he should chide God who established it, not us who say it.]

While elsewhere Ælfric's homilies display anxiety about the possibility of *gedwyld* (heresy) and the *dysigness* (stupidity) of opinion, particularly

---

32 For editions of the listed sources, see Malcolm Godden, ed. *Ælfric's Catholic Homilies: Introduction, Commentary, and Glossary*, 47. According to Godden, Ælfric's major sources include Bede's Homily 1.11, *Bedae homiliae euangelii*, ed. D. Hurst, 73–9; Haymo of Auxerre's *Homiliae de tempore* 14 (*PL* 118.90–107); and Martin of Braga's *De correctione rusticorum*, in *Martini episcopi Bracarensis opera omnia*, ed. C.W. Barlow (New Haven, CT: Yale University Press, 1950), 183–203.

among the unlearned, his apprehension here about the reception of a legitimate biblical practice by a lay audience seems excessive, even for Ælfric.[33] To help solve the problem of introducing this subject to his uninformed audience, Ælfric inserts large portions of explanatory material (in lines 14–32), drawn primarily from Genesis chapter 17, in order to explain the scriptural history and workings of the procedure. As Godden has shown, Ælfric later recycles his translation of this scriptural material nearly verbatim in his Heptateuch Genesis.

One could, however, perhaps make too much of Ælfric's protestations and warnings. As we shall see, Ælfric does not simply dumb down his homily; ever the clever exegete, Ælfric uses his imported scriptural material from Genesis to flesh out a carefully schemed discussion of the typology associated with circumcision in the Old Testament. It is noteworthy that Ælfric situates his commentary on the circumcision in the context of two interpolated references to other landmark covenants from Genesis in Noah's flood (lines 13–14) and the near sacrifice of Isaac (lines 27–8), since all three biblical episodes are joined by the same divine promise of the continuation and multiplication of the line of Israel through the repetition of the words of the original covenant. The insertion of these bracketing allusions perhaps indicates a special trend among Anglo-Saxon writers because (as we shall see) the linking of these three episodes also serves as an important framing device in the Old English biblical poetry. For the moment, Ælfric seems here to be building, through his rearrangement of this biblical material, a link that serves to establish very clearly the Christian

---

33 In his *Catholic Homilies* II.36 for the sixteenth Sunday after Pentecost, for example, Ælfric worries about whether a gospel passage on the transience of earthly goods will seem extraordinary to foolish men (in Malcolm Godden, ed., *Ælfric's Catholic Homilies: The Second Series*, 304–9): 'Þis godspel ðincð dysegum mannum sellic. ac we hit secgað swa ðeah. weald ðeah hit sumum men licige' (this gospel will seem marvellous to foolish men, but nevertheless we say it, since it may please some men). By contrast, in another passage from Ælfric's homily on the dedication of a church, Ælfric recognizes that the belief in Christ as God may seem foolish to Jews and heathens (in R. Brotanek, ed., *Texte und Untersuchungen zur altenglischen Literatur und Kirchengeschichte*, 93): 'He cwæþ, we bodiaþ Crist þe wæs on rode ahaggen, Nu þincþ hit iudeiscum mannum tallic, & hæþenum hit þincþ dyslic, ac þa þe synd geleaffulle on gode, of iudeiscre þeode & of hæþenum leodum, þam þincð þæt crist is godes miht & godes wisdom' (He said, we pray to Christ, who was hanged on the cross; now it will seem stupid to Jewish men, and foolish to heathen men, but those who are believing in God of the Jewish people and of the heathen people, to them it will seem that Christ is God's Might and God's Wisdom).

inheritance of the terms of the covenant as promised first to Abraham in the Old Testament.

Ælfric continues to develop this emphasis upon Christian inheritance achieved through spiritual circumcision by linking the various namings and name changes mentioned in the Old and New Testament in conjunction with the fulfilment of circumcision as the sign of the covenant. Both Ælfric and Bede begin their homilies by explaining the significance of Christ's given name, Jesus (interpreted here as *hælend*, 'saviour,' echoing the standard etymology of the name from the Hebrew *Yehoshua*, meaning 'the lord will rescue or deliver'), in conjunction with his circumcision on the eighth day. As we have seen already, redemption into the membership of the Lord is a topic associated with the covenant. From this point Bede goes on to discuss the nativity of Jesus and his baptism, while Ælfric strategically turns immediately to the Bedan passage (lines 33–42) explaining the biblical name change from Abram (meaning *healic fæde*, 'high father') to Abraham (*manegra ðeoda fæder*, 'father of many nations'), and Sarai (*min ealdor*, 'my chief') to Sarra (*ealdor*, 'chief'). Both these name changes importantly signify through their Hebrew etymology the selfsame inheritance of a nation. Ælfric's concentration on the changing of names anticipates the climax of the piece. Both authors use this pattern of name changing to demonstrate that the good Christian who practises spiritual circumcision can also merit a name change. Ælfric's commentary is as follows (lines 106–16):

Gif we swa fram leahtrum ymbsnidene beoð þonne bið us geset niwe nama. swa swa se witega isaias cwæð; God gecigð his þeowan oþrum naman; Eft se ylca witega cwæð; ðu bist geciged niwum naman. þone ðe godes muð genemnode; Se niwa nama is cristianus. þæt is cristen; Ealle we sind of criste cristene gehatene: ac we sceolon þone arwurðfullan naman mid æðelum þeawum geglengan. þæt we ne beon lease cristene; Gif we þas gastlican ymbsnidenysse on urum þeawum healdað þonne sind we abrahames cynnes æfter soþum geleafan. swa swa se ðeoda lareow paulus cwæð. to geleaffullum; Gif ge sind cristes þonne sind ge abrahames sæd: and æfter behate yrfenuman.

[If we are thus circumcised from sins, then a new name will be established for us, just as the prophet Isaiah said, 'God will call his servants by other names.' Again, the same prophet said, 'You will be called by a new name, which God's mouth has named.' That new name is 'Christianus,' that is, Christian. We are all called Christians from Christ, but we should embellish that honourable name with noble customs, so that we are not false Christians. If we observe this spiritual circumcision in our customs, then we are of Abraham's kin, according to the true faith; just as Paul, the apostle of the gentiles, said to the faithful, 'If you are Christ's, then you are of Abraham's seed, and heirs according to the promise.']³⁴

Ælfric (like Bede) uses the words of Isaiah to recast the part of those Christians who perform spiritual circumcision in the role of the newly chosen people. While traditionally Israel (as a nation) inherited the terms of the covenant through Jacob, whose name was momentously changed to Israel, just so under the new covenant the Christians stand to inherit the pact from Christ himself. In Ælfric's account (again following Bede) the words of Isaiah are supplemented by the words of Paul (from Galatians 3:29) in order to emphasize the Christian principle of universal inclusion, since as Paul states in the adjoining passage from Galatians 3:28, 'there is neither Jew nor Greek: there is neither bond nor free: there is neither male nor female. For you are all one in Christ Jesus.' In order to cement this rhetoric of displacement whereby the New Law is held to supersede the Old, one final step is required: both authors show that while circumcision was once able to offer remedy against the wound of original sin under the Old Law (never mind the Christological anachronism), baptism serves as the newly required salve for entry into the company of the saved. To explicate this change, both Bede and Ælfric cite the Harrowing of Hell, which demonstrates that Christ himself had to save those circumcised Jews who were locked out from salvation. This rather complicated symmetry makes room for the reinterpretation of the rite in favour of a more 'spiritual circumcision' (*gastlic ymbsnyd[enyss]*; line 113), which marks the practice of cutting off oneself spiritually from lust and sin, as an alternative to physical mutilation. In arguing for this semiotic exchange, both Ælfric and Bede (very much in the spirit of Paul's second letter to the Corinthians 3:6) invoke the familiar patristic paradigm that treats Jews as representing the letter of the law and Christians as representing the spirit of the law.

Much more could be said about the symbolism of this complex homily, and in particular the long second portion of the homily (lines 129–203) devoted to Ælfric's discussion of the pagan practices associated with New Year's Day. Of particular importance and relevance in this section is Ælfric's brief discussion of Christ's circumcision as a token of the final age of the world (lines 121–8). However, since Ælfric enlarges upon this same

---

34 The three biblical quotations are from Isa. 65:15 and 62:2, and Gal. 3:29, respectively.

theme in his *Catholic Homilies* II.4, for the second Sunday after Epiphany, an exploration of that text will suffice. Ælfric's *CH* II.4 takes its pericope from the parable of the marriage at Cana in John 2:1–11. The homily, which is derived principally (though not entirely) from Bede's homily 1.14, focuses on the symbolism of the six water vessels as tokens of the six ages of the world.[35] The discussion of circumcision can be found in the passage describing the sixth and final age of the world. This age is said to mark the nativity of Christ, as well as his circumcision on the eighth day. As Ælfric states (lines 281–9):

> Cristes ymsnydennys hæfð mænigfealde getacnunga and swa ðeah swiðost belimpð to ðam gemænelicum æriste on ðissere worulde geendunge, on ðære bið seo galnys forðwyrt, and on ðære ablind ælc hæmed. and bið ure deadlica lichama awend to undeaðlicnysse. and we beoð æfter ðam gemænelicum dome geferode to gesihðe þæs godcundlican mægenðrymmes mid urum lacum. þæt is mid godum weorcum. and we symle syððan on ðam heofonlicum temple þurhwuniað.

[The circumcision of Christ has multiple significations and yet most greatly concerns the common resurrection at the end of this world, in which lust will be eradicated and in which all fornication will end; and our mortal body will be turned to immortality; and we shall after the common judgment be lifted to the sight of the divine glory with our gifts, that is, with good works; and we shall always after continue to reside in the heavenly temple.]

As circumcision is able to cleanse from lust and sin, Ælfric shows that this sixth age points ahead to the time of the Last Judgment and Resurrection, where those who are purified are able to enjoy their eternal rewards in heaven.[36] Bede, in his homily, however, makes much more of the symbolism

---

35 For an edition of Bede's homily 1.14, see *Bedae Homiliae euangelii*, ed. D. Hurst, 95–104. For a discussion of the relationship between Ælfric's *CH* II.4 and its sources in Augustine, Smaragdus, Haymo, and Bede, see Godden, *Introduction, Commentary, and Glossary*, 370–80; as well as C.L. Smetana, 'Ælfric and the Early Medieval Homiliary,' 34, and his 'Ælfric and the Homiliary of Haymo of Halberstadt,' 463–4; and Joyce Hill, 'Ælfric and Smaragdus,' 203–37.

36 Cf. Ælfric's *CH* I.6, which aligns the circumcision instead with the eighth age of the world, undoubtedly to create a more clear parallelism with the eighth day on which the circumcision takes place. In conflating the event of the circumcision with the eighth age, Ælfric departs somewhat from his source in Bede's homily 1.11, where Bede links the seventh age with the *aetas quiescentium* (age of rest) while he describes the eighth age as

of circumcision. In the Latin text the circumcision of Christ serves as an important turning point between the Old and New Law. As Bede states:

> Verum si in octaui diei circumcisione baptisma quod in mysterium dominicae resurrectionis a peccatorum nos morte redemit intellegis in inductione in templum et oblatione hostiae purificantis figuratum cognoscis fideles quosque de baptisterio ad altare sanctum ingredi ac dominici corporis et sanguinis uictima singulari debere consecrari, uino quidem de aqua facto et quidem meracissimo donatus es.

> [But in the circumcision of the eighth day you may understand baptism, which has redeemed us from the death of our sins into the mystery of the Lord's resurrection. In (Jesus's) being led into the temple and the offering of the sacrificial victims of purification, you may recognize a prefiguration of any of the faithful entering from the baptistery to the holy altar and needing to be consecrated by an exceptional sacrificial victim, the Lord's body and blood. (If you have this understanding of the story,) you have been granted wine made from the water, and it is a most undiluted wine.][37]

Bede's more detailed explanation makes better sense in the overall scheme of the parable. He links this baptismal imagery with that of the water vessels themselves, since their stated purpose within the parable is to cleanse and purify 'secundum purificationem Judaeorum' (according to the Jews' [rites of] purification). At the same time, Bede interprets the water vessels anagogically, so that they come to represent the saving waters

---

follows: 'Octaua autem aetas ipsa est dies resurrectionis sine ullo temporis fine beata quando uera omnimodae circumcisionis gloria coruscante non ultra corpus quod corrumpitur adgrauat animam non terrena inhabitatio deprimit sensum multa cogitantem sed corpus iam incorruptibile laetificat animam et subleuat caelestis inhabitatio totum hominem uisioni sui conditoris inhaerentem' (The eighth age is that blessed day of resurrection itself, without any temporal end, when, as the true glory of every sort of circumcision shines forth, *the body which is corrupted will no longer weigh down the soul, nor will the earthly habituation press down the mind which is thinking of many things* [Ws 9:15], but the then-incorruptible body will gladden the soul, and the heavenly habitation will raise up the whole human being, who is clinging to the vision of his Maker) [trans. Lawrence T. Martin and David Hurst, *Bede the Venerable: Homilies on the Gospels*, book I, 108–9; italics original]. Apparently, the Anglo-Saxons did not worry about the dilemma faced by the later church as to whether Christ's foreskin was resurrected together with his body.

37 Trans. Martin and Hurst, *Bede the Venerable*, 143.

of scripture.[38] Bede uses the event in the parable of Christ's turning the water into wine in order to mark a shift from the literal reading of the law by the Jews to its spiritual interpretation enabled through Christ, for as Bede states:

> Sed quantum inter aquam et uinum, tantum distare inter sensum illum quo Scripturae ante aduentum Saluatoris intelligebantur, et eum quem ueniens ipse reuelauit apostolis, eorumque discipulis perpetuo sequendum reliquit.

> [But as much as there is a difference between water and wine, by so much does the sense which the scriptures were understood before the Saviour's coming differ from that which he himself revealed to the apostles, and left to be perpetually followed by their disciples.][39]

Bede's complex symbolism shows a double teleological movement from circumcision to baptism and from the letter of the Law to its spiritual fulfilment. In doing so, Bede once again channels Paul's idea (as expressed in Galatians 3:24) of justification by faith as an alternative to the rigid adherence of the Law.

Although Ælfric writes more fully on the subject of circumcision than any other Old English author, a few additional examples can be found elsewhere in the corpus. For instance, there is a short treatment of circumcision found in the anonymous life of James the Greater (based upon the apocryphal Acts of James), which entwines narrative and doctrinal treatments of circumcision and baptism.[40] The narrative itself begins with an account of the imprisonment of James by the Jews for his preaching about

---

38 Cf. *CH* I.6, where Ælfric interprets the symbolism of the circumcision as follows: 'Ðæt stæncne sex. þe ðæt cild ymbsnað getacnode þone stan. þe se apostol cwæð; Se stan soðlice wæs crist; He cwæð wæs for þære getacnunge: na for edwiste; ðurh cristes geleafan. and hihte. and soðre lufe. beoð singallice estfulle heortan mid dæghwomlicere ymbsnidenysse afeormode fram leahtrum and þurh his gife onlihte.' (The stone knife, which circumcised the child, betokened the stone; concerning which the apostle said, 'The stone truly was Christ.' He said *was*, for its signification, not its substance; through the belief, hope, and true love of Christ, devout hearts are continually purified from their sins by daily circumcision and enlightened through his grace.)
39 Translation adapted from Marin and Hurst, *Bede the Venerable*, 139.
40 Rubie D.-N. Warner, ed., *Early English Homilies*. The Latin source for the text is the *Martyrdom of James the Great*, ed. Boninus Mombritius, *Sanctuarium seu Vitae Sanctorum*, 2nd ed., vol. 2, 37–40. For commentary on the apocryphal source and the Old English homily, see especially Frederick M. Biggs, *Sources of Anglo-Saxon Literary Culture: The Apocrypha*, 45–6. It is perhaps of interest that Ælfric uses the same apocryphal source as the basis for his *CH* II.27 on James the Greater, though he

Jesus and ends with the moments leading up to his beheading by Herod. The portion of the text that deals with circumcision occurs in James's defence of Christ as the true saviour and in his disparagement of the Jews who claim to be the rightful inheritors of Abraham's covenant with God. In making his case, James (in the Old English life) employs two prominent strands of Pauline rhetoric: on the one hand he champions justification by faith as opposed to works (as in Romans 4:1–12, Galatians 3:1–14 and 4:22–31), and on the other he cites Abraham as the paradigmatic Old Testament figure who privileges belief over deeds. James, following Paul (especially Romans chapter 4 and Galatians chapter 3), explains that if Abraham was accepted by God even before formal laws were in place, then faith alone must be sufficient to make one dear to God.

A less typical discussion can be found in the anonymous Napier homily 42, entitled *De temporibus antichristi* (On the Time of the Antichrist), which forges a damaging association between the ritual of circumcision and the evil and deceitful practices of the Antichrist.[41] The relevant passage in the homily is as follows:

> Ðonne færð he to Hierusalem þære burh mid miclum þrymme to ðan, þæt he wile eall cristen folc to him gebigan mid his lotwrencum and fram rihtum geleafan awendan, gif he mæg. And gif he þonne þæt ne mæg, þonne onginð he hy to pinianne on mistlicre wisan and eac fela ofslyhð haligra manna, forðam þe hi nellað gebugan fram þam soðan gode to him. he geedstaðelað niwe tempel, þær þær Salomon se mæra cyng hæfde ær arærd þæt mære tempel þam ælmihtigum gode to lofe; and þærinne he gesit and hine sylfne swa up ahefð, þæt he cwyð, þæt he sy þæs ælmihtigan godes sunu. And æfter Moyses lage he hine læt ymbsniðan mid scearpum flinte; and forþan he deð þæt, þæt he wile, þæt þa earman iudeiscan men scylan wenan, þæt he sy soð Crist, forðam he swa eadmodlice heora lage gefylð on ða wisan.

> [Then he will go to the city of Jerusalem with a great host, so that he will turn all Christian folk to him with his deceptions and turn them from right belief if he is able. And if he then might not, then will he begin to torment them in various ways, and he will also slay many holy men, because they will not wish to turn from the true God to him. He will erect a new temple, there

---

cuts precisely the portion of the text dealing with Jewish ritual and practice and chooses instead to concentrate on the legendary material.

41 Arthur S. Napier, ed., *Wulfstan*, 191–205.

where Solomon the famous king had before raised that famous temple to the almighty God as praise; and therein he will sit and he will raise himself up so much that he will say that he is the son of the almighty God. *And according to Moses's Law he will let himself be circumcised with a sharp flint, and therefore he does that, as he wishes, so that the wretched Jewish men must think that he is the true Christ, because he will so humbly fulfil their law in that manner* (emphasis mine).]

Here the homilist suggests that through circumcision, which is relegated to the Old Law, the Deceiver will be able to convince the Jews to place their belief in him as the true Messiah. This portion of the homily written on the topic of circumcision is drawn (as is much of the larger body of the homily) from the *Libellus de Antichristo* written by Adso of Montier-en-Der (ca 954).[42] Richard Emmerson, who has commented most fully on the relationship between the Latin and Old English texts, has shown that the Old English author significantly expands this passage on the circumcision in order to explain the ritual to his Anglo-Saxon audience.[43] Additions (like those in Ælfric's works) include the detail that the Antichrist self-circumcises *mid scearpum flinte* (with a sharp flint) and that this practice falls in line with Old Testament Law.[44] And yet, despite these localized embellishments, the Adso material is elsewhere more expansive on the subject of the circumcision of the Antichrist. In a second passage that has been omitted from the Old English translation, Adso has the Antichrist speak to the Jews in the persona of Christ himself, promising to gather them and join them in the

---

42 For an edition of Adso's commentary, see D. Verhelst, *Adso Dervensis, De ortu et tempore Antichristi*. Adso's commentary on the circumcision itself derives not from scriptural writings on the Antichrist but likely from patristic tradition. One of the earliest associations between the Antichrist and circumcision has been traced to a third-century commentary by Hippolytus of Rome, who also lists as its reason for the Antichrist's circumcision that it was performed in imitation of Christ. See Brother Linus Urban Lucken, *Antichrist and the Prophets of Antichrist in the Chester Cycle*, 15. Adso's *Libellus de Antichristo* was well known by the eleventh-century Anglo-Saxon homilist Wulfstan and his followers. In addition to the Napier homily 42 cited below, Dorothy Bethurum has shown that Wulfstan's homily 1a draws extensively from the *Libellus*, while Latin and Old English versions of the *Libellus* appear in no fewer than four manuscripts containing Wulfstan's 'Commonplace Book.' See Dorothy Bethurum, ed., *The Homilies of Wulfstan*, 282 (as cited by Richard Emmerson, 'From *Epistola* to *Sermo*,' 1.
43 Emmerson, 'From *Epistola* to *Sermo*,' 4–6. For more discussion of the relationship between Napier homily 42 and its source in Adso, see Jonathan Wilcox, 'Napier's "Wulfstan" Homilies XL and XLII' 1–19.
44 Emmerson, 'From *Epistola* to *Sermo*,' 5.

elect, so obviously parodying the biblical association between the ritual of circumcision and the principle of inclusion. Furthermore, according to Adso's text, the punishment to be received by those Jews who follow the leadership of the Antichrist is that they are to be branded on the forehead with a permanent mark of shame. This physical retribution externalizes the otherwise clothed sign of circumcision, serving to outcast further those 'wayward' Jews through the symbolic association between their punishment and the infamous mark of Cain.[45] In both the Latin and Old English texts, however, the Antichrist's self-circumcision (after Christ has already negated the historical and legal necessity for circumcision) surely serves to highlight the perversion of those Jews who continue to practise the rite.

A far more subtle, and certainly kinder, set of allusions to circumcision can be found in Old English biblical poetry. These references have for the most part escaped the attention of critics, precisely because they are so well disguised with euphemistic language that focuses generally on the covenant itself.[46] As can be seen from a passage in *Genesis A*, lines 2313–37 (which has been abbreviated from Genesis 17:1–15), these lines present a stunning exercise in circumlocution. In the following passage, God returns after thirteen years to speak with Abraham in order to urge him to maintain the terms of his covenant so that he may receive increased prosperity and divine protection:

> Sete sigores tacn   soð on gehwilcne
> wæpnedcynnes,   gif þu wille on me
> hlaford habban   oððe holdne freond   2315
> þinum fromcynne.   Ic þæs folces beo
> hyrde and healdend,   gif ge hyrað me
> breostgehygdum   and bebodu willað
> min fullian.   Sceal monna gehwilc
> þære cneorisse   cildisc wesan   2320
> wæpnedcynnes,   þæs þe on woruld cymð,
> ymb seofon niht   sigores tacne
> geagnod me,   oððe of eorðan
> þurh feondscipe   feor adæled,
> adrifen from duguðum.   Doð swa ic hate!   2325

---

45 For Latin commentaries conflating the mark of Cain with the circumcision, see Ruth Mellinkoff, *The Mark of Cain*, 92–8.

46 For an important exception, see A.N. Doane's edition in *Genesis A: A New Edition*, and especially his commentary on the passages that follow.

Ic eow treowige,   gif ge þæt tacen gegaþ
soðgeleafan.   þu scealt sunu agan,
bearn be bryde þinre,   þone sculon burhsittende
ealle Isaac hatan.   Ne þearf þe þæs eaforan sceomigan,
ac ic þam magorince   mine sylle   2330
godcunde gife   gastes mihtum,
freondsped fremum.   *He onfon sceal*
blisse minre   and bletsunge,
lufan and lisse.   Of þam leodfruman
brad folc cumað,   bregowearda fela   2335
rofe arisað,   rices hyrdas,
woruldcyningas   wide mære.

[*Set a true sign of victory on every male, if you wish to have in me a Lord or*
dear friend to your bold people. I will be shepherd and protector of this folk
if you will obey me in the thoughts, your heart, and desire to fulfill my laws.
Every man of that nation who is a male child, of those that come into the
world, shall be dedicated to me after seven nights with a sign of victory, or else
be cut off far from the world through hostility, and be driven from prosperity.
Do as I command: *I will be loyal to you if you carry out that sign of true faith.*
You shall have a son, a child by your wife, whom all city-dwellers will call
Isaac. There is no need for you to be ashamed of your son, for I will give that
youth my divine gift, by the power of my spirit, and for that good one a
wealth of friends. *He shall receive my favour and my blessing, my love, and*
grace. From that patriarch will come a mighty people, a multitude of rulers,
brave ones, shepherds of the kingdom, kings of the world, renowned afar[47]
(emphasis mine).]

The rite of circumcision is invoked in lines 2312–16, where it is cast as a
sigores tacn (a victory sign; lines 2313a and 2322b) that commemorates the
wær and *wed* (covenant and pledge) made between God and Abraham. As
A.N. Doane has rightly observed, the *Genesis* poet 'never translates *cir-*
cumcisio any more literally than this.'[48] Although it may be supposed from
the poet's opaque wording that he did not understand the terms of the rite,
the subsequent detail in lines 2320–5 that the *sigores tacn* is to be made

---

47 Translations of *Genesis A* and *Exodus* are adapted from Charles W. Kennedy, *The*
    Caedmon Poems.
48 Ibid., 306, lines 2312–14a.

ymb seofon niht (after seven nights),[49] demonstrates at least passing familiarity with the biblical laws regarding circumcision.[50] A similarly veiled passage appears in *Genesis A*, lines 2769a–70a, describing Abraham's circumcision of Isaac. Although the lines are adapted from Genesis 21:3–5, the sign of circumcision is once again described symbolically as a *beacen ... wuldortorht* (beacon ... wondrous bright). The poet for a second time thus deliberately suppressed the physical terms of the rite in order to emphasize its spiritual role as a *sphragis* or seal of the covenant. Moreover, in the first passage, the poet places recognizable emphasis upon redemption, inclusion, and the establishment of nobility. While fulfilment of the pact guarantees membership in fellowship with God, troth breakers are doomed to endure the familiar exile that sentences them (in words that recall the passage from Paul's address to the Galatians 5:1–6) 'to be cut off far from the world through enmity, and be exiled from prosperity.' This membership, we are told, is already secured for Isaac on account of his

---

49   The poet's awkward change from the biblical 'eighth day' was presumably designed to preserve the alliterative line, though the poet may have also had in mind other purification rituals that last for seven days (such as the period of separation commanded for menstruating women, as in Lev. 15:28). The poet's mention of the thirteen years that passed before God speaks to Abraham likewise highlights the precise year in which Ishmael received circumcision (Gen. 17:25–6).

50   Doane (*Genesis A*, 306, lines 2312–14a) shows that the poet's sign is to be understood 'in signum foederis.' He links the passage to Rom. 4:11 and perhaps also to Augustine's interpretation of the rite of circumcision as a sign of regeneration (as in the *De ciuitate Dei* XVI, 27 [CCSL 48, 532]). In fact, the poet's choice of the rare phrase *sigores tacn* (in lines 2313a and 2322b) may reveal an additional exegetical layer. The elements *sige-* and *tacn* are often associated with the Cross in Old English literature; however, the precise phrase *sigores tacn* is found in only one other Old English poem, in *Elene*, where it is used to describe each of the three crosses mentioned in the poem – namely, the cross that appears in the heavens to Constantine, the cross erected by Constantine in imitation of that vision, and the true cross itself (in lines 85a, 184b, and 1120b, respectively). In the case of the first cross, the *sigores tacn* is explained to be a token of God's 'wær' (covenant) with Constantine, promising him victory over his enemies. This pledge of protection and victory seems deliberately to recall the biblical pact that God makes with Abraham, especially since the cross here functions as a kind of *sphragis*, sealing Constantine's covenant with God. Although there does not appear to be a direct textual connection between the description of circumcision in *Genesis A* and the description of the crosses in *Elene*, it is just possible that when the *Genesis A* poet wrote about circumcision as a *sigores tacn*, he recalled a more familiar and celebrated victory emblem associated with baptism – the Cross. I thank an anonymous reviewer for suggesting this link.

circumcision, in terms drawn from Genesis 17:6, which show that he will inherit all the same provisions of the covenant.[51]

While the *Genesis* poet displays obvious skill at interweaving complex exegetical interpretations of the circumcision, he also deftly integrates these ideas within a much more widespread and readily available Anglo-Saxon Christian heroic ethos. The exile theme expressed in the above passage can also surely be read in the context of numerous Old English poems that discuss the harsh fate of exile from the community, as in *The Wanderer* (lines 20–1), *The Seafarer* (line 16), *Solomon and Saturn II* (line 381), *Exhortation to Christian Living* (line 27), *Christ III* (lines 1519–23), *Christ and Satan* (lines 625–6), and *Guthlac A* (lines 624–7).[52] In a similar vein, the reference above to the circumcision as a *beacen ... wuldortorht* (beacon ... wondrous bright; 2769a–70a) puts the Old Testament sign in direct comparison with other wondrous 'beacons' encountered elsewhere in Old English poetry (and some of these are likewise biblically derived); examples include the extraordinary fire in *Daniel* that does not burn the three youths (lines 487b), the speaking wall in *Andreas* (line 729b), and the talking cross in *The Dream of the Rood* (in lines 6b, 21b, 83a, and 118b). By couching his discussion of circumcision within more conventional poetic terms, the *Genesis A* poet highlights the strangeness of the Old Testament commandment, even as he renders the concept familiar within a wider Old English literary context.

A similarly allusive strategy can be found in the *Exodus* poem, in the portion of the text usually referred to as the so-called patriarchal digression, drawn primarily from Genesis 22:1–18. This interlude, which appears to interrupt the dramatic action of the poem, marking the account of the Israelites crossing the Red Sea, comprises two main narratives: the first describes the story of Noah and the flood, while the second narrates the would-be sacrifice of Isaac by Abraham. Part of the Abraham and Isaac interlude can be found in *Exodus*, lines 377–96:

---

51 Doane makes the excellent point that the *Genesis A* poet discriminates between the covenant of the body and that of the heart. As Doane demonstrates, the reference in *Genesis A*, lines 2367b–9a, to a 'haligu higetre[o]w' (holy covenant of the spirit) 'seems to distinguish Isaac as about to receive a new kind of covenant, one of the spirit, prophetical of the Christian promise and of Christ himself, for the previous covenants that Abraham and Noe received were old, according to the flesh,' 308.

52 See further the discussion of this exile topos in Samantha Zacher, 'Sin, Syntax, and Synonyms,' 53–76. All Old English poems are cited from *The Anglo-Saxon Poetic Records*, ed. George Philip Krapp and Elliott Van Kirk Dobbie.

Swa þæt wise men   wordum secgað
þæt from Noe   nigoða wære
fæder Abrahames   on folctale.
þæt is se Abraham   se him engla god   380
naman niwan asceop;   eac þon neah and feor
halige heapas   in gehyld bebead,
werþeoda geweald;   he on wræce lifde.
Siððan he gelædde   leofost feora
haliges hæsum;   heahlond stigon   385
sibgemagas,   on Seone beorh.
Wære hie þær fundon,   wuldor gesawon,
halige heahtreowe,   swa hæleð gefrunon.
þær eft se snottra   sunu Dauides,
wuldorfæst cyning,   witgan larum   390
getimbrede   tempel gode,
alh haligne,   eorðcyninga
se wisesta   on woruldrice,
heahst and haligost,   hæleðum gefrægost,
mæst and mærost,   þara þe manna bearn,   395
fira æfter foldan,   folmum geworhte.

[So wise men tell us in words that Abraham's father was ninth from Noah
according to genealogy. *That is the Abraham to whom the God of angels as-*
signed a new name; also he gave from near and far those holy tribes into his
keeping, and gave him dominion over nations. He lived in exile. Afterwards,
at the command of the Holy One, he led the most beloved of all beings; the
kinsmen scaled the highland, up to Mount Sion. *And there, as men have*
heard, they established a covenant and holy solemn pledge, and saw glory.
And there, in later years, the wise son of David, the glorious king, the wisest
of all earthly kings in the earthly kingdom, according to the teaching of the
prophets, built a temple to God, a holy sanctuary, the highest and holiest, the
most famous among men, and the greatest and most renowned of those
which the sons of men, humans upon the earth, ever built with their hands
(emphasis mine).]

As in Ælfric's short explication of the Old Testament circumcision in his
CH I.6, embedded within this section from *Exodus*, we can likewise detect
allusions to Genesis 17:5 and 17:6 outlining the terms of circumcision: in
line 382, the phrase *naman niwan* (new name) must refer to the name

change from Abram to Abraham after his circumcision, while lines 382–4 recall the language of the original covenant when God promises Abraham that he will be the father of many nations, here the *halige heapas* (holy tribes) and *werþeodas* (nations). By recalling the circumcision, the poet shows that that first spilling of Isaac's blood was not reduplicated in Isaac's physical sacrifice.

This seemingly misplaced discussion of circumcision in the context of the *Exodus* narrative perhaps becomes clearer when viewed (once again) through the lens of patristic interpretation. While it has previously been argued that baptismal imagery yokes together the two episodes of the patriarchal digression concerning Noah's flood and the crossing of the Red Sea, I would argue that the passages on the covenant present a strong third link supporting this rich symbolism.[53] That the poet thought of circumcision as a type of baptism seems to be supported by references elsewhere in the poem to the original Old Testament covenant of Genesis, chapter 17. For example, *Exodus*, lines 301b–305, reports that when the Israelites faced the wall of the water at the crossing of the Red Sea:

> Sæweall astah,
> uplang gestod   wið Israhelum
> andægne first,   yðholmes hleo.
> Wæs seo eorla gedriht   anes modes,
> fæstum fæðmum   *freoðowære* heold.   305

[The sea wall rose up, that protection of the billowing waves stood upright over against the Israelites for the space of one whole day. The company of the troop was of one mind, they held the *covenant* with a steadfast embrace (emphasis mine).]

---

53 The symbolism of the patriarchal digression has been abundantly mined by scholars. The first to link all three biblical figures to the baptismal liturgy for Easter was J.W. Bright in his 'Relation of the Cædmonian *Exodus* to the Liturgy,' 97–103. Paul G. Remley has revived this hypothesis in his *Old English Biblical Verse*, 78–87 and 168–230, where he has been able to trace the liturgical influence more specifically to the Roman series for these vigil lections. For further discussion of the patriarchal digression, see especially J.W. Earl, 'Christian Traditions in the Old English Exodus,' 541–70; Stanley R. Hauer, 'The Patriarchal Digression'; and, most recently, Daniel Anlezark, 'Connecting the Patriarchs,' 171–88.

The depiction of the Israelites holding the covenant *fæstum fæðmum* (with a steadfast embrace or perhaps even with a steadfast bosom) recalls the language of 2 Corinthians 3:3 that prescribes the inscription of the covenant in the heart,[54] while the detail of the crashing waves in the Red Sea reinforces the typological connection with baptism.[55] If we can accept this third layer of significance, then the poet in this digressionary sequence appears to be imposing the selfsame teleology that we find in patristic commentaries concerning the reinterpretation of circumcision as a spiritual rite. Although once again the poem contains no direct reference to circumcision, the subtext is arguably present and readable for those who know how, as close reading of patristic commentaries would have taught.

What we can perhaps learn from these various (mis)interpretations and circumlocutions on the subject of circumcision is that the rite continued to signify and stress precisely those values of membership and community that were so prized in Anglo-Saxon literature. While it is easy to imagine that Anglo-Saxon authors might have taken a thoroughly negative or disparaging view of so alien a practice, it is perhaps surprising to witness their remarkable variety of expression; as we have seen, the informed detachment brought to the topic in Bede's works is replaced by coy reticence and knowing allusion in the biblical poetry, and in Ælfric's works by a schoolmasterly precision with regard to a practice that Ælfric clearly deplored.

One can perhaps better gauge the specificity of Anglo-Saxon views on circumcision by contrasting the cited examples with the sometimes colourful and sensational narratives that developed in the later middle ages. If Anglo-Saxon authors occasionally recoiled from (or simply avoided) graphic description of the physical rite, writers and artists in the later

---

54 See, for example, 2 Cor. 3:3: 'Manifestati quoniam epistula estis Christi ministrata a nobis et scripta non atramento sed Spiritu Dei uiui non in tabulis lapideis sed in tabulis cordis carnalibus' (Being manifested, that you are the epistle of Christ, ministered by us, and written not with ink, but with the Spirit of the living God; not in tables of stone, but in the fleshly tables of the heart).

55 There may be one further reference to the covenant in the *Exodus* poem at line 487a, at the point in the poem where the walls of water crash over the Egyptians. The object of this crashing is usually taken to be *werge beornas* (accursed warriors); however, according to Peter J. Lucas, the manuscript reading is *wer beamas*. Lucas suggests an alternative reading in the genitive singular of *wærheam*, meaning 'covenant-pillar,' though he rejects the reading since 'even this explanation seems forced, and the sense and meter are incomplete' (*Exodus*, 136).

medieval period, by contrast, seemed to embrace the corporeal dimensions of the rite. Particularly expressive models can be found in the affective piety of the fourteenth-century female mystics writing on the Continent. Thus famously, Catherine of Sienna dubs herself a bride of Christ as she imagines herself converting Christ's foreskin into a wedding ring. Likewise Agnes Blannbekin records, on one aptly named feast of the circumcision, feeling the Lord's foreskin on her tongue, 'thin as the membrane of an egg,' and swallowing it 'about a hundred times' with great sweetness.[56] The high middle ages also saw the physical survival of Christ's foreskin on earth as an important sign of his humanation. Several important churches (for example) in Paris, Bologna, Bruges, and Antwerp laid competing claims to the ownership of this relic, thereby attesting to its increased iconic significance.[57]

Although clearly less spectacular than the accounts produced in the high middle ages, Old English treatments of the circumcision nevertheless reveal their own unique set of ideological interests and concerns that developed from the materials they inherited on the subject. Whether their discussions turned to the role of circumcision as a seal of the original covenant between God and Abraham, or to more eclectic and esoteric matters, such as the Antichrist's self-circumcision as a means of deceit, Anglo-Saxon authors continued to read circumcision as a spiritual marker of difference that could separate the clean from the unclean and exclude the latter. In contemplating their own collective and not-too-distant conversionary past, it seems that some Anglo-Saxon writers found in these biblical (and later patristic) accounts formulations of otherness that made them reflect upon their own conceptions of religious and ethnic difference.[58] And as the passages on circumcision in

---

56 A translation of Blannbekin's revelation concerning Christ's foreskin (chapter 37) can be found in Ulrike Wiethaus, *Agnes Blannbekin*, 35–6. For a more general discussion of these mystical treatments of the holy prepuce, see Felix Bryk, *Circumcision in Man and Woman*.

57 For a list of some of these claims by churches, see Marc Shell, 'The Holy Foreskin,' 356n18. A heated debate concerning the various representations of Christ's circumcision in medieval art has been waged between Leo Steinberg, *The Sexuality of Christ* in *Renaissance Art and in Modern Oblivion*, 52–64, and Caroline W. Bynum, 'The Body of Christ in the Later Middle Ages: A Reply to Leo Steinberg,' 79–119.

58 An earlier precedent for this type of identity politics could be found in the writings of the Venerable Bede, who in his *Ecclesiastical History* cited cultural and social differences to cast the *gens Anglorum* as the new chosen people and to mark off these conquering peoples from the native Britons. For treatments of this topos, see Patrick Wormald,

Genesis and *Exodus* would seem to indicate, Anglo-Saxon writers also sometimes productively invoked the Pauline model of spiritual explication as a means of fashioning their present-day Christian community as still newer inheritors of the covenant and as members in the community of Christ.

'The Venerable Bede and the "Church of the English,"' 13–32, and his 'Bede, the Bretwaldas and the Origins of the Gens Anglorum,' 99–129; Andrew P. Scheil, *The Footsteps of Israel*, 111–42; Stephen J. Harris, *Race and Ethnicity in Anglo-Saxon Literature*, 45–82 and 131–56; and Samantha Zacher, 'The Chosen Peoples.' I am grateful to Andy Orchard for his bright and helpful suggestions and comments on this essay. I also thank Peter Gilgen for providing valuable comments on the final draft.

The Old Testament and the Poems
of the Junius Manuscript

Genesis A ad litteram

CHARLES D. WRIGHT

Since the appearance of B.F. Huppé's *Doctrine and Poetry* in 1959,[1] criticism of *Genesis A* has been divided between interpretations *in Christo* and *ad litteram*. According to Huppé, the poem can be properly understood only in terms of the principles of allegorical exegesis codified by St Augustine. In Huppé's words, the poet 'intends to enlighten and enkindle the minds of his audience to perceive the traditional doctrinal meaning underlying Genesis,' and 'through figurative interpretation ... to set forth man's duty to praise God.'[2] The contrast between the city of God and the city of Man, according to Huppé, is the fundamental unifying theme of the poem, providing its principle of selection and emphasis and governing its elaboration of scriptural detail. Huppé's reading of the poem was endorsed by its most recent editor, A.N. Doane, in 1978.[3] Doane criticizes Huppé's a priori assumption of thematic unity and does not accept all of his allegorical or figural readings of individual passages, but asserts that his 'general approach [is] unqualifiedly right.'[4] Although Doane concedes that 'the specific approach of *Genesis A* is predominantly literal,' he argues that '[the poet's] task also included suggesting the

---

1 B.F. Huppé, *Doctrine and Poetry*. Chapter 5 (131–216) is devoted to *Genesis A*.
2 Ibid., 208, 135.
3 Alger N. Doane, ed., *Genesis A*.
4 Ibid., 42–3.

essential established non-literal significations of the literal meaning,'[5] and his commentary frequently proposes implicit spiritual meanings.[6]

In the past three decades various critics have defended or disputed Huppé's and Doane's spiritual interpretation of individual passages,[7] but there has been little sustained effort to articulate principles by which to test the validity of their approach to the poem or to identify possible generic and hermeneutic models alternative to the tradition of allegorical and figural biblical exegesis that, according to Huppé and Doane, must have informed the poet's conception of his task.[8] There has, of course, also been

---

5 Ibid., 53, 51. For similar statements, cf. 50–1 and 61n53. Doane's exegetical interpretation, like Huppé's, was in response to widespread neglect of Christian-Latin traditions in earlier criticism. Although I focus here on my disagreement with Doane, I wish to acknowledge the many virtues of his edition.

6 In the context of the four levels of exegesis (literal, allegorical, tropological, and anagogical) allegorical designates the level relating to the church in this world; in medieval usage, however, it can also refer to any trope in which one thing is said to signify another. The standard work on the four levels of exegesis is Henri de Lubac, *Exégèse médiévale: Les quatre sens de l'Écriture*, 2 vols. in 4 parts, Théologie 41, 42, 59 (Paris: Aubier, 1959–64); the first two volumes have been translated by Mark Sebanc and E.M. Macierowski as *Medieval Exegesis: The Four Senses of Scripture*. I will use the terms *extra-literal* and *spiritual* to refer generally to any of the higher levels of exegesis of Genesis, and distinguish broadly between allegorical and typological or figural interpretations rather than restricting the term *allegorical* to the second of the four levels. The term *typology* refers specifically to the foreshadowing of events of the New Testament in the Old. See especially Jean Daniélou, *From Shadows to Reality* and *Typology and English Medieval Literature*, ed. Hugh T. Keenan. Following Erich Auerbach's seminal essay 'Figura,' in *Scenes from the Drama of European Literature*, 11–76, the term *figural* has also been used to refer to the relation between historical type and antitype in interpretations of Old English Christian poetry. In 'Confronting *Germania Latina*,' 71–88, Joyce Hill distinguishes typological and allegorical interpretations in that the former are firmly rooted in (Old Testament) history; Hill finds typological readings of Old English biblical poems generally more admissible, not only because they do not diminish the significance of the particularized historical narrative but also because 'typological correspondences are relatively simple and were, moreover, more readily accessible to the potential audience for vernacular poems' (82).

7 The most vigorous opponents of this approach have been Bennett Brockman, '"Heroic" and "Christian" in *Genesis A*,' 115–28, and Nina Boyd, 'Doctrine and Criticism,' 230–8.

8 Some principles in relation to *Genesis A* have been briefly formulated by Brockman and Boyd, and by J.E. Cross in his review of Huppé's book, 'Doctrine and Poetry,' 561–4, and in his 'Old English Period,' 22. See also Judith Garde and Bernard J. Muir, 'Patrisitic Influence and the Poetic Intention in Old English Religious Verse,' 49–68, and Garde, *Old English Poetry in Medieval Christian Perspective*, 34–8. Although Garde and Muir reject allegorical and typological readings in favour of prophetic and catechetical ones, their approach is ultimately as reductive as Huppé's. Other general critiques of exegetical

valuable criticism of *Genesis A* that is not staked upon this long-standing debate; yet the stakes *are* high, with implications for how we define the poem's hermeneutic mode, its genre, and its implied audience. It is my belief that the poet's fundamentally historical approach to the biblical narrative rendered both allegory and typology peripheral to his concerns and that he does not, as a rule, prompt meditation on extra-literal meanings.[9] What does concern the poet are literal questions of credibility and morality that might trouble a less sophisticated audience, questions that he anticipates and resolves in a variety of resourceful ways. In what follows, I will attempt to vindicate a reading of the poem *ad litteram* in two ways: first, by critiquing the assumptions governing extra-literal interpretation of the poem as a whole and of allegorical or typological readings of specific passages in their immediate contexts; and second, by proposing a generic model for the kind of historical paraphrase of Genesis that the poet seems to have undertaken.

It is not my purpose to insist that in more than two thousand surviving lines the *Genesis A* poet never makes even a glancing allusion to a traditional extra-literal meaning of a biblical verse or passage or that readers intimately familiar with exegesis of Genesis could not have supplied such meanings, whether or not the poet encouraged them to do so. It is legitimate to speculate, if one wishes, as to how such readers might have responded to *Genesis A*. The poem's *readers* were all by definition literate, at least in the vernacular, but they would not necessarily have been literate in Latin, and even those capable of reading Latin would not necessarily have

---

interpretations include Philip B. Rollinson, 'The Influence of Christian Doctrine on Old English Poetry,' 271–84, and Wilhelm Busse, *Altenglische Literatur und ihre Geschichte*, 198–276. I am generally more in sympathy with critics who (like Cross in much of his work) have stressed the importance of the Christian-Latin (not only patristic) background of Old English religious poetry, but the approach has at times been misapplied, as Cross argued in the case of Huppé's reading of *Genesis A*. Unfortunately, Cross's brief but trenchant critiques of Huppé's book have often been overlooked. After the present essay was completed, I found that Katherine O'Brien O'Keeffe, in her unpublished dissertation 'The Book of Genesis in Anglo-Saxon England,' 172–205, makes a sustained case for a literal reading of *Genesis A*, focusing on three major episodes (the Fall of Adam and Eve, the Flood, and the story of Abraham). I have added references in the notes to specific arguments and evidence from her dissertation at points where they complement my own.

9 My discussion of specific passages will necessarily be selective, and I will avoid discussing passages whose literal significance has been defended by previous critics such as Brockman and Boyd, unless I have some additional contextual or comparative support to offer.

been intimately familiar with commentaries on Genesis. Rather than speculate about the responses of hypothetical readers of various capacities and backgrounds, therefore, I prefer to ask what kind of reader (or auditor) is implied by the poem itself.

It is also legitimate to focus on the reception and reading of the poem in the larger context of the Junius manuscript with its other biblical poems and program of illustrations and to bring to bear other literary and iconographic evidence dating from the second half of the tenth century.[10] There are, to be sure, inherent advantages in exploiting these codicological and historical contexts to interpret a poem that has not been securely dated or localized, and the results have often been illuminating.[11] One consequence of reading *Genesis A* through its manuscript context, however, has been a certain levelling of the poem's distinctiveness in favour of thematic or ideological links with the other poems in Junius 11, which were almost certainly composed at different times and places and in different social and institutional contexts. Yet *Genesis A* has relatively little in common with *Genesis B*, *Exodus*, *Daniel*, or *Christ and Satan* in terms of its approach to its biblical source or its narrative and stylistic resources – aside from the resources that almost all Old English poems share by virtue of being Old English poems. As synthesizing approaches tend to be reductive in direct proportion to their explanatory power, there are compensatory advantages to focusing on each poem in isolation, without privileging the manuscript context because it is the only immediately accessible one.

The implied audience of the surviving text of *Genesis A* may not be an infallible guide to the poet's intended or actual audience, but it is certainly a far better guide – whatever the poem's date or place of origin – than the other poems in the tenth-century compilation we know as Junius 11. To be sure, the process of transmission has altered the text of *Genesis A*.[12] In

---

10 Leslie Lockett, 'An Integrated Re-examination of the Dating of Oxford, Bodleian Library, Junius 11,' 141–73, has recently argued that the manuscript should be dated ca 960–ca 990. For a complete digital facsimile, see *MS. Junius 11*, ed. Bernard J. Muir.

11 The most sustained and sophisticated reading of the Junius 11 poems in relation to the drawings in the manuscript is Catherine E. Karkov, *Text and Picture in Anglo-Saxon England*. To the extent that Karkov proposes typological readings of episodes in *Genesis A*, they are usually grounded in the drawings and other external iconographic and literary traditions and presented as the likely responses of the artist or of a learned eleventh-century readership.

12 Paul Remley, *Old English Biblical Verse*, 27–8 and 29n47, argues that the sectional divisions and illustrations in Junius 11 imply at least four stages of transmission of the poems.

addition to various lacunae, one major and one minor interpolation (that is, of *Genesis B* and of the names of the wives of Noah and his sons in lines 1547–8) have been detected, and there are almost certainly other alterations that have not been detected and may be undetectable.[13] Even setting aside the known interpolations and lacunae, we cannot assume that the Junius 11 text of *Genesis A* is otherwise virtually identical to what the poet wrote – but neither can we assume that it is radically or even substantively different.[14] The close, often verse-by-verse rendering of the biblical Genesis in much of the poem militates against an assumption of extensive non-authorial revision on a structural level and, to a more limited extent, on the verbal level.[15] The uncertainty dictates that no single detail can bear the burden of establishing the poet's intention or the nature of his audience, but it does not obviate efforts to identify recurrent patterns of emphasis or to characterize in broad terms the poet's basic approach to the biblical narrative and the kind of audience presupposed by that approach. If the poem in its surviving form consistently refrains from invoking extraliteral levels of signification, this will almost certainly have been true as well for any earlier stage of its transmission, including the poem in its original form, however one defines *original*.

I will regard *Genesis A*, therefore, as a generally trustworthy though defective copy of a poem composed by a single author – an enabling assumption that is no less probable for being unprovable. The poem's general consistency of style and tone,[16] which has been acknowledged by

---

13 Remley, *Old English Biblical Verse*, 49n85, thinks that line 1601c may also be an embedded gloss. Remley lists (in 94n1) the certain and probable lacunae in *Genesis A* and *B*, with estimates of the numbers of lines lost.

14 One might argue that the known interpolations and lacunae already show that the poem is radically and substantively different from whatever the poet originally composed; I would argue that our knowledge of these interpolations and lacunae already shows that we can detect gross tampering and major losses or interpolations and that any losses and interpolations we cannot detect are likely to have been minor and would not, in any case, have obscured or fundamentally altered the poet's basic approach to the biblical narrative.

15 Doane (*Genesis A*, 61) concludes that 'the poet has systematically, virtually phrase by phrase, reproduced in traditional poetry the essential meaning of the Latin Genesis which he had before him as he worked,' that 'at almost every point the details of the Vulgate diction and syntax are influencing the style as well as the matter,' and that 'the poem appears to be remarkably free from corruption.'

16 As Doane (*Genesis A*, 35–6) points out, there are some linguistic differences between the section preceding *Genesis B* (part I, lines 1–234) and the section following it (part III, lines 852–9236), but he also states that '[part] I does not on grounds of style or

critics of various persuasions, is sufficient justification for interpreting it as a coherent response to the biblical text by a reader/author situated in a specific historical moment. Since the poem has not been precisely dated or localized, however, I will not assume that it is relatively early *or* late or that its surviving manuscript context necessarily tells us anything about the circumstances in which or the audiences for whom it was written. I will therefore privilege contexts deduced from evidence within the poem instead of contexts applied from evidence external to it.

The question of the poem's sources is a special case, for a poet's response to an established external source *is* a kind of internal evidence. It is evident, for example, that the poet was paraphrasing a Latin version of the book of Genesis, even if there is some doubt as to the exact nature of the version he consulted.[17] We can also be sure that he was familiar with non-biblical traditions because some of his elaborations on the Genesis narrative (such as the legend of the raven of the ark feeding on corpses) are widely paralleled.[18] What we cannot assume is that he derived such information from Latin biblical commentaries. Even if in some cases he did, we cannot assume that those commentaries interpreted such details figurally; and even if in some cases they did, we cannot assume that the poet wished to convey the figural interpretations along with those details. Early medieval biblical commentary was not as univalent and consistently figural as Huppé and Doane represent it, for there were alternative exegetical traditions (which

---

treatment of the source differ enough from III to justify a theory of diverse origin.' Doane would attribute the linguistic differences to an 'incomplete revision ... which brought the earlier poem into early West-Saxon forms.' On stylistic links between various passages spanning the greater part of the poem, see now Andy Orchard, 'Intoxication, Fornication, and Multiplication,' 333–54.

17 See especially Paul G. Remley, 'The Latin Textual Basis of *Genesis A*,' 163–89, and *Old English Biblical Verse*. Remley argues (*Old English Biblical Verse*, 114 and note 56), in my view rightly, that the poet's source must have been a Latin text of Genesis.

18 Compare the following comment by J.E. Cross: 'In medieval times, a body of material had accumulated in Hexameral writings, homilies, tracts, and verse-by-verse explanation of the text, which was really taken as the story of Scripture, and which was intimately associated with the Biblical text in the medieval mind. It was compounded of scientific lore, of history, of speculation about motive and reasons for the actions and thoughts, of information reaching back to Rabbinic stories, apocryphal legend and early history, and included, on occasions, spiritual interpretations as, for example, that the Ark typifies the Church of the faithful on the sea of the world. Our poet gives no clear hint of interest in spiritual interpretation but he often explains "literally" or "historically," in no way to modify the basic narrative but merely to make it more acceptable' ('The Old English Period,' 22).

I will describe briefly) that focused primarily on the literal level of Genesis. Biblical commentary does not, in any case, afford an appropriate generic model for the essentially narrative mode of *Genesis A*. A more suitable model, the catechetical *narratio*, has already been proposed by J.R. Hall and Virginia Day, and I will suggest another: the Universal History or World Chronicle, a medieval genre whose historical orientation towards the book of Genesis may also have informed the Anglo-Saxon poet's conception of scriptural paraphrase.

Exegesis or Eisegesis? Extra-literal Interpretation of *Genesis A*

Allegorical and figural readings of *Genesis A* depend heavily upon a priori assumptions that a Christian poet paraphrasing the Old Testament simply must have wanted to convey extra-literal Christian significations and that a learned audience would have been trained to supply them even without contextual prompting. If the presumed spiritual sense of a given passage is not clearly activated by the context, citation of patristic authorities is deemed sufficient to prove that it is inevitable or automatic. Thus Doane claims that an extra-literal dimension in *Genesis A* 'is simply a result of the poet's inevitable mental apparatus.' The poet's 'technique,' according to Doane, 'is not to impose a discursive spiritual interpretation ... but to allow for the fact that there inevitably is one in the mind of the reader or hearer; he leaves suggestive interstices of meaning, which may be filled with innumerable associations.' The poet, Doane concludes, 'handles all of his material in such a way as to suggest or allow the main outlines of extra-literal interpretations that were universally felt to be the soul of divine reading.'[19]

It is one thing to say that the poem allows for extra-literal interpretation by a reader so inclined, and quite another to say that the poet deliberately or consistently encourages it. The first assertion is beyond argument but has little value as criticism; the second carries the burden of proof. The poet would hardly have set out to *prevent* such interpretations, but that does not mean he wished to emphasize them. Whether the poem's interstices were suggestive or inert would depend on a given reader's (or listener's) predisposition and training, but the dual assumption of a covert allegorical aesthetic and a learned audience cannot be elevated to a self-confirming argument ex hypothesi (a tendency of Robertsonian criticism).

---

19 Doane, *Genesis A*, 50–4.

Yet the counterclaim that medieval authors who wished to convey extra-literal levels of meaning always made them explicit is equally self-confirming. There are no objective means for determining whether a medieval religious poem or biblical paraphrase that does not make extra-literal levels of meaning explicit nonetheless prompts them to be supplied by a knowledgeable reader. One has to rely on context – not simply the immediate context of a passage but also the larger context of the poem as a whole. A persuasive extra-literal reading will normally be supported by textual details that resist or are not adequately accounted for by a literal reading – that is, by something cryptic, incongruous, or supererogatory in the verbal or structural fabric of the text that is more satisfactorily captured by recourse to an extra-literal reading.[20] As Wilhelm Busse has noted, what constitutes (for example) an 'unrealistic collocation' is a subjective judgment; yet the critic is responsible for specifying its grounds, which are subject to evaluation, as are the consequent arguments for the collocation's fit with a given exegetical tradition.[21] An extra-literal reading supported by evidence that a specific image, word, or thing was traditionally interpreted in the way suggested will be more compelling than one that is unparalleled, but the mere existence of a commonplace spiritual interpretation of, say, Noah's ark does not establish that every reference to Noah's ark in a medieval text functions contextually as a figure of the church.

Allegorical or figural interpretation of Genesis was grounded upon verses in the New Testament that refer explicitly to Genesis or that were associated with verses in Genesis in Christian tradition. In his *Fontes Anglo-Saxonici* entry for *Genesis A*, however, Doane cites just one New

20 In his review of Huppé's book, Cross argues similarly that 'positive evidence' for extra-literal significations may include 'unusual structure, apparently incongruous or abrupt collocations of words or phrases' (*JEGP* 59 [1960]: 562). O'Brien O'Keeffe, 'The Book of Genesis,' 205, speaks more generally of 'verbal signals.' Cf. also Rollinson, 'The Influence of Christian Doctrine,' 383, who refers to 'a riddling inadequacy, inconsistency or impossibility in the literal text which impels the reader to seek a meaningful interpretation from traditional Christian symbolism.' Even an apparently incongruous collocation may, of course, have a literal foundation. For example, when the poet refers to the beasts subjected to Adam as *halig feoh* (201b, distinguished from *wilde deor*, 202a), he appears to have 'anticipated the distinction of clean and unclean animals from Genesis 7.2–3,' as Doane (*Genesis A*, 237–8) argues.

21 Busse, *Altenglische Literatur*, 218, citing J.E. Cross and Susie I. Tucker, 'Allegorical Tradition and the Old English *Exodus*,' 122–7, for the term *unrealistic collocations*. The term *unrealistic* was unfortunate, since *realistic* is not coterminous with *literal*.

Testament source, 2 Peter 2:7–8, which merely states that Lot was a right-
eous man who did not succumb to the sins of Sodom;[22] and though
Augustine did interpret Lot figurally, Doane points out in his edition that
'Bede literalizes this figure and reapplies it to the biblical situation, much
as the poet does.'[23] The *Genesis A* poet must also have been familiar with
the traditional correlation of Genesis 1:1 or 1:3 and John 1:1, which, as
Roberta Frank has shown, underlies the doctrine that Christ the Logos/
Verbum was the agent of Creation and informs the poet's assertion that
þeos woruldgesceaft/þurh word gewearð wuldorcyninges (lines 110b–
11).[24] Whether the interpretation of the words *in principio* as referring to
Christ was a mystical or historical interpretation of Genesis 1:1 was de-
bated by the major Western Fathers,[25] yet Christ, the Word and Wisdom
of God, was understood by all orthodox commentators to have been the
literal agent of Creation.

The only other convincing echo of a New Testament verse in this
lengthy poem, to my knowledge, is the statement that Adam and Eve
before the fall were *englum gelice* (like angels) [185]. As Frederick M.
Biggs has shown, this phrase derives from Luke 20:36, according to
which the just in heaven will not marry or die but will be *aequales enim
angelis*.[26] Since the poet emphasizes Adam and Eve's physical reproduction in lines 192–8a, the reference is clearly not to chastity; rather, as
Biggs argues, the poet must have been familiar with commentary that
linked the New Testament phrase to Genesis 1:27 (*et creauit Deus hominem ad imaginem suam*) as an index of man's rational nature, which he
shares with angels. These commentaries do not, however, interpret
Adam allegorically as Reason, and neither does the poet; the motif is not

---

22 'The Sources of *Genesis A* (Cameron A.1.1.1),' 1990, *Fontes Anglo-Saxonici: World
    Wide Web Register*, http://fontes.english.ox.ac.uk/, accessed September 2006 [Entry
    Reference C.A.1.1.1.077].
23 Doane, *Genesis A*, 293 (note to lines 1931b–44).
24 Roberta Frank, 'Some Uses of Paranomasia in Old English Scriptural Verse,' 207–26;
    repr. in *The Poems of MS Junius 11: Basic Readings*, 69–98, at 73.
25 See M.J. Clark, 'The Commentaries on Peter Comestor's *Historia scholastica* of Stephen
    Langton, Pseudo-Langton, and Hugh of St. Cher,' 346–58.
26 Frederick M. Biggs, '*Englum gelice*,' 447–52. As Biggs notes, the poet's use of the word
    gelice (rather than *swylce*) suggests that he is recalling the verse from Luke rather than
    the parallel verse in Matt. 22:30, whose wording is 'sicut angeli Dei in caelo.' My quota-
    tions from Genesis are generally from Doane's facing-page reconstruction of the poet's
    source; quotations from other biblical books are from *Biblia Sacra iuxta uulgatam uer-
    sionem*, 4th ed., ed. Robert Weber.

conducive to such an interpretation, for the simple fact that it applies equally to both Adam *and* Eve.[27]

Nor does Doane in his *Fontes Anglo-Saxonici* entry identify a single compelling patristic source that involves an extra-literal interpretation of a verse in Genesis. Many of the patristic texts he lists are cited only for the Old Latin biblical readings to which they attest, rather than for the associated commentary; most that do involve the commentary proper relate to literal expansions and explanations, and most are cited only as analogues or possible sources. A good case can be made for the poet's knowledge of Bede's commentary on Genesis, which does often the invoke spiritual sense, but everything that the poet may have drawn from Bede relates to the letter.[28]

More telling than the poet's failure to introduce extra-literal interpretation overtly, or to echo verbally the New Testament verses or the patristic

---

27 Compare the literal use of the motif in Pseudo-Augustine, *Sermo 49 ad fratres in eremo*, *PL* 40.1344 (God rebukes the body of a deceased sinner): 'paradiso uoluptatis te collocaui, uita angelica perfruebaris' (I put you in the paradise of pleasure. You enjoyed the life of the angels); trans. in Michael J.B. Allen and Daniel G. Calder, *Sources and Analogues of Old English Poetry*, 47.

28 Doane's suggestion (*Fontes Anglo-Saxonici*, entry reference C.A.1.1.1.102) that the word *fyrgebræc* (2562b) 'seems derived directly' from Bede's *fragorem flammarum* (*In principium Genesis* IV.xix.26, CCSL 118A, 227.1204) is convincing because the context is identical: in both works it describes what caused Lot's wife to look back and be turned into a pillar of salt. Yet the poet gives no hint whatsoever of Bede's figural equation of Lot's wife with those who turn back to the desires of the world after having embarked on the path of virtue, and Bede himself has just stated, 'Hoc uere iuxta litteram factum esse credendum est.' Instead, the poet blames Lot's wife for disobedience ('þæs heo wordum wuldres þegna / hyran ne wolde,' 2570b–1a). For an allusion to an extra-biblical but a literal tradition concerning Lot's wife, see note 45 below. Doane also cites Bede's commentary as a 'probable antecedent source' (SA2: see entry ref. C.A.1.1.1.077) for the poet's contrast between the fairness of the land of Sodom and the wickedness of its inhabitants, whose sins Lot refused to follow, fleeing their custom even while inhabiting their land (1933–43). This parallel is also close and compelling, but as previously noted, Doane himself concedes that Bede 'literalizes' the figure of Lot. I find completely unconvincing Doane's suggestion (source ref. C.A.1.1.1.085) that Bede's comment on the etymology of Isaac's name (*risus*, which Bede relates to the birth of Christ, since angels had told the shepherds not to fear, because they had come to announce great joy [Luke 2:10]) is a relevant analogue for *Genesis A*, lines 2196b–2200, in which God tells Abraham not to fear or be sad because a son will be born to him. The reference to Sara's laughter occurs nearly two hundred lines later (line 2382), and the immediate context is wholly adequate to explain God's words, for Abraham has just stated that he is oppressed by sorrow ('mec sorg dreceð,' line 2180b) that he will not have an heir.

sources upon which such interpretation was grounded, is his frequent emphasis on literal and ethical concerns that actually interfere with allegory and typology. In his account of Creation and the fall of the rebel angels, for example, the poet nowhere states or implies the Augustinian allegorical equation of the separation of the light from the darkness (Genesis 1:3–4) with good and evil angels. Doane's note to lines 34b–91 asserts the correspondence simply because the topic is 'traditional' and because the poet has described the good angels as bright (*fægre*, line 79a; *beorht*, line 89a) and the bad angels as dark (*swearte*, line 72a), enveloped in darkness (*þystrum beþeahte*, line 76a) and deprived of light (*leohte belorene*, line 86a).[29] What Doane must ignore is that the account of the fall of the rebel angels takes place *before* the creation of light and the separation of light and darkness (lines 121b–43a). Quite apart from the problem of narrative sequence, the poet's comment that, *after* their separation and naming, both day and night 'ever afterwards carried out and did the will of the Lord' (*siððan æfre / drugon and dydon drihtnes willan*, lines 140b–2), shows that he *could not have been* allegorically equating the darkness / night of Genesis 1:3–4 with the rebel angels. The exegetical topic that the poet introduces (overtly) here is not the allegorical equation of light and darkness with the good and bad angels but the hexaemeral theme of God's continuing governance of the natural world after he had ceased from the work of Creation,[30] which he attaches to Genesis 1:2–3 because light / day and darkness / night were the first things that God created. Characteristically, however, the poet expresses it in terms of their perpetual obedience to God's will.

In the poet's description of paradise there is no hint of the figural equation with the church. As Hugh Magennis has argued, '*Genesis A* shows no desire to pursue non-literal interpretations of paradise, but makes use of the traditional ideas current in the wider Christian tradition.'[31] The same is true of his (now unfortunately defective) paraphrase of the story of Adam and Eve. When, for example, the poet describes the creation of Eve from Adam's side, he emphasizes that the procedure was painless and bloodless:

---

29 For a refutation of Doane's allegorical reading of these images, see David N. Johnson, 'The Fall of Lucifer in *Genesis A* and Two Anglo-Latin Royal Charters,' 506 and note 23.

30 See Frank E. Robbins, *The Hexaemeral Literature*, 71. Compare the Leiden family glosses in *Glossae Biblicae*, ed. P. Vaciago, 1:297 (no. 16): 'cessauit a nouis faciendis creaturis non a gubernandis creatis'; the same gloss also occurs at 1:395 (no. 14). The allegorical equation is also found in some of these glosses (1:10 [no. 2]). On the Leiden family glosses, see note 45 below.

31 Hugh Magennis, *Images of Community in Old English Poetry*, 147–8.

he þæt andweorc   of adames
lice aleoðode   and him listum ateah
rib of sidan.   he wæs reste fæst
ond softe swæf,   sar ne wiste,
earfoða dæl   ne þær ænig com
blod of benne   ac him brego engla
of lice ateah   liodende ban
wer unwundod. (lines 176–83a)

[He removed material from Adam's body and skilfully drew a rib from his side. He was fast asleep and slept soundly, he did not perceive pain or a bit of hardship, nor did any blood flow from the wound, but the prince of angels drew the burgeoning bone from the unwounded man.]

What interests the poet is the miraculous nature of the operation through which Adam passed *unwundod*, not the conventional typological association between the creation of Eve from Adam's side and the establishment of the church in the water and blood that flowed from the pierced side of the 'sleeping' Christ.[32] The poet makes explicit the anaesthetic function of Adam's biblical *sopor* (Genesis 2:21), and his description of Adam as a *wer unwundod* who shed no blood, so far from suggesting or even allowing for typology, effectively obviates it. An explanation of this kind implies an audience that might wonder how Adam could have a rib removed from his side without suffering excruciating pain, loss of blood, and a potentially fatal wound – an audience, that is, more likely to wonder about the physical implications of the procedure than its figural potential. What the poet presumes is his audience's belief in the awesome power of God, as well as their interest in the marvellous, not their knowledge of typology.

Bennett Brockman has already discussed the predominantly literal and social implications of the Cain and Abel episode (lines 965–1054).[33] The poet's one major addition, a lurid image of 'branches' of sin sprouting from the blood of Abel (lines 982b–95a), might be regarded as a tropological

---

32 See Daniélou, *From Shadows to Reality*, 48–56; Hans-Martin von Erffa, *Ikonologie der Genesis*, vol. 1, 145–50. Nor is there any hint of the tradition of Adam's prophetic *exstasis* discussed by Daniélou and von Erffa; the poet simply ignores the crucial verse (Gen. 2:22; cf. Eph. 5:30) upon which the tradition was grounded. O'Brien O'Keeffe, 'The Book of Genesis,' 181–5, notes that the poet fails to translate certain words in the narrative of the Fall (such as *pelliceas*, Gen. 3:21, and *uersatilem*, Gen. 3:24) that were crucial for mystical exegesis by a commentator such as Bede.
33 Brockman, '"Heroic" and Christian.'"

expansion of the literal narrative. Yet there is a close parallel and possible source for the image in Aldhelm's *Carmen de uirginitate*, where Aldhelm represents Cain as the exemplar of all subsequent violence and social discord in human history – much as Augustine had identified the murder of Abel as the historical precedent or archetype of the murder of Romulus by Remus. As I have argued elsewhere, therefore, 'It is unnecessary ... to posit a separate tropological "level" in *Genesis A* in order to accommodate Cain's spiritual "descendants."'[34] The poet subsequently distinguishes the Cainite and Sethite genealogies, making it clear that *sethes cynn* (the line of Seth), the *bearn godes* (sons of God) remained blessed and dear to the Lord until they took wives from the kin of Cain (lines 1245–52). Yet the very fact that the poet identifies the *filii Dei* of Genesis 6:2 as *sethes bearn* (the sons of Seth) [line 1257b], and the *gigantes* of Genesis 6:4 as their hateful offspring, shows that his perspective is moral and historical rather than allegorical. Even Seth's progeny can fall away from God; his seed remains blessed, however, because Noah remains righteous (lines 1285–9a).[35]

In recounting the story of the flood (lines 1249–1554) the poet follows the biblical text fairly closely, occasionally elaborating on literal details or incorporating apocryphal expansions of the biblical narrative. When he describes the caulking of the ark, for example, he explains that the material (*eorðan lim*, 'bitumen') used was a special type that becomes harder the more severely the sea water beats upon it:

> þæt is syndrig cynn.
> Symle bið þy heardra   þe hit hreoh wæter,
> swearte sæstreamas,   swiðor beatað. (lines 1324b–6)

[That is an exceptional thing: the more the rough water and the dark seastreams pound upon it, ever the harder it is.]

---

34 Charles D. Wright, 'The Blood of Abel and the Branches of Sin,' 9. For Augustine's interpretation of Cain's fratricide as a historical archetype, see Marijane Osborn, 'The Great Feud,' 979.

35 Compare Magennis, *Images of Community*, 157–8. On the etymology of Seth's name ('seed') see 146 below. Karkov, *Text and Picture*, 87, suggests that the 'linking of Enoch's birth to his death [sic], or ascension,' associates him with Christ, but the poet's insistence that Enoch did *not* suffer death (lines 1205–6) instead dissociates him from Christ. Enoch and Elias are proverbially the ones who were born but did not die; cf. Martha Bayless and Michael Lapidge, ed. and trans., *Collectanea Pseudo-Bedae*, 122–3 (no. 5, with commentary at 202). I do not believe that the poetic paraphrasis for Enoch's birth (his mother 'brought him to men,' line 1213) is intended to suggest the birth of Christ, as Karkov further suggests.

Doane cites commentaries by Bede and Isidore to support his argument that 'the bitumen of the ark is *always* [emphasis mine] taken as one or more of the virtues, applying to Noe as the type of the Just Man and *figura Christi*,' and that by focusing on this particular detail the poet wished to suggest the ark's figurative significance. Nina Boyd contested this reading on the grounds that 'the poet's statement is merely a literal account of the properties of *eorðan lim*, the *bitumin* [sic] of Genesis 6.14,'[36] but Peter J. Lucas has reasserted that 'the juxtaposition of the emphasis on pitch and rough-sea weather would almost certainly be suggestive to an audience that knew its patristic exegesis.'[37] Since the function of pitch in caulking a wooden ship is, after all, to resist rough-sea weather, there is nothing cryptic, incongruous, or supererogatory in the juxtaposition sufficient to activate an extra-literal interpretation. The number of exegetes who interpreted bitumen as faith, or the sea beating on the ark as the temptations endured by the church in this world, matters only if something specific in the poet's description of the bitumen or its immediate context plausibly evokes that interpretation. A reader who was familiar with a comment such as Bede's might, of course, have brought it to mind, even without any prompt, and having done so might have interpreted Noah's obedience to God and the sinner's scornful rejection of Noah's warnings as exemplifying faith and disbelief respectively.[38] However, no reader lacking such specific biblical and exegetical knowledge could deduce from the poem itself that *eorðan lim* signified faith or any other virtue.

Similarly, when the poet alludes to the 'many years' (*wintra worn*, line 1320a) that elapsed before the ark was completed, the same learned reader might have thought of 1 Peter 3:20–1, which refers to the *increduli* who were counting on the patience of God in the days when Noah was building the ark, and which then compares the salvation of Noah and his family to the salvation of Christians through baptism.[39] The poet, however, associates the lapse of time not with the patience of God or the preaching of Noah but rather with the magnitude of the construction project: 'geseah

---

36 Doane, *Genesis A*, 263; Boyd, 'Doctrine and Criticism,' 234.

37 Peter J. Lucas, 'Loyalty and Obedience in the Old English *Genesis* and the Interpolation of *Genesis B* into *Genesis A*,' 134n9.

38 Boyd points out, however, that in lines 1285–91 the poet asserts that God tested Noah's *ellen* ('Doctrine and Criticism,' 234).

39 Geoffrey Shepherd, 'Scriptural Poetry,' 29, suggests that the naming of the wives of Noah and his sons invokes the 'sacred ogdoad'; these names are now generally thought to have been interpolated, and their closest analogues occur in literal glosses rather than allegorical expositions (see below, 167).

þa ymb wintra worn wærfæst metod / geofonhusa mæst gearo hlifigean' (lines 1320–1) [after many years the faithful Lord saw the greatest of ocean vessels towering, made ready]. He expects his audience to be aware that so gigantic a craft would take a very long time to build, so to validate the narrative's literal plausibility he is careful to specify that Noah and his sons had 'many years' to complete the job.[40] He cannot simply assert that it was a marvel of God, as in the case of the creation of Eve, because it was Noah who built the ark, albeit according to divine specifications.

Why, then, did the poet allude to the 'preaching of Noah,' if not to hint at the figural significance of bitumen? His purpose, I believe, was not only to justify God's *reðe wite* (harsh punishment, line 1319a) of unrepentant sinners but also to demonstrate Noah's concern for his kinsmen. Noah, he thereby assures his audience, was not insensitive to the fate of his kinsmen in his eagerness to save himself and his immediate family but tried his best to warn them; and God did not wreak his terrible vengeance without first giving sinners a chance to repent (and Noah time to finish the ark). The poet's treatment of the period preceding the flood, in other words, implies his awareness that the unadorned biblical narrative might run afoul of his audience's respect for kinship bonds and loyalties as well as their sense of justice, not to mention their common sense regarding shipbuilding.

Doane's justification for explaining the *eorðan lim* figuratively is that 'the expanded comment cannot be explained by reference to the literal level of the Vulgate,' but the detail *is* part of the literal level, as the material used to caulk the ark, and unfamiliar things mentioned in the Bible, often required literal explication.[41] The poet's reference to the material quality of bitumen is, in effect, a kind of scientific gloss – exegetical, to be sure, but not extra-literal – and one that can, *pace* Doane, be paralleled in biblical commentaries without reference to any figural associations. A series of glosses on the Pentateuch that 'bears an unmistakeably Anglo-Saxon character' and that Bernhard Bischoff and Michael Lapidge have shown to transmit the teachings of Theodore and Hadrian distinguishes between two types of bitumen, one of which is so hard that it can be dissolved only by menstrual blood:

De lignis leuigatis [IV.14]: .i. deuinctis tabulis bitumine inter iuncturas ubique extrinsecus ne aqua possit intrare. Bituminis autem sunt duo genera: alterum

---

40 The Carolingian chronicler Frechulf addressed the same concern by emphasizing that Noah had one hundred years to build the ark (see below, 164).

41 For similar comments see *Glossae Biblicae*, ed. Vaciago, 1:298 (no. 38); 1:396 (no. 38), and 2:386 (no. 25).

est naturale, quod in Mare Mortuo inuenitur et foris aqua iacitur in similitu-
dine bouis, quod non potest diuidi ullatenus nisi sanguine menstruali; alterum
est quod de lacu hauritur et in sole coquitur usque dum fuerit durum, bitu-
menque dicitur; ipsum potest dissolui facile et commiscere quolibet desideras.

[*Of timber planks* (IV.14): that is, with the planks fastened with pitch between the joints and all over the outside so that water cannot get in. Now
there are two sorts of pitch: one is natural, which is found in the Dead Sea and
is cast up by the water in the likeness of a cow, and it cannot be broken up at
all except with menstrual blood. The other kind is that which is dredged up
from the waters and is baked in the sun until it becomes hard: it is called bitumen. It can easily be dissolved and mixed with anything you wish.][42]

Such a gloss is hardly conducive to figural interpretation, and none is
given. It suffices to show that the *bitumen* of the ark and its waterproofing
function did not necessarily or automatically have a figural significance for
all Christian exegetes and that, notwithstanding Bede's comment, literal
explications of Genesis had some currency in early Anglo-Saxon England.
The person who compiled (apparently in Britain) the related 'Pent III'
glosses was certainly not thinking of bitumen as *fides* when he stated that
it was also used as mortar for the stones of Babylon![43] The Pent III glosses
do admit a few figural interpretations but are predominantly literal in
orientation, while the Canterbury glosses, as Lapidge points out,[44] are
manifestly within the Antiochene tradition of exegesis – a tradition that,
despite the authority and popularity of Alexandrian exegetes such as
Augustine, Isidore, and Bede, was perpetuated in early medieval biblical
glosses such as the Leiden glossary and its congeners.[45]

---

42 Bernhard Bischoff and Michael Lapidge, ed. and trans., *Biblical Commentaries from the
    Canterbury School of Theodore and Hadrian*, 316–17, with Lapidge's commentary on
    the passage at 450. O'Brien O'Keeffe, 'The Book of Genesis,' 187–8, cites passages from
    Isidore, Bede, and Alcuin as examples of literal glosses on the bitumen, but the first two
    of these are not apposite, because both do then supply extra-literal interpretations.
43 *Glossae Biblicae*, ed. Vaciago, 1:11 (no. 36); see also 1:514 (no. 28) for essentially the same
    comment in a later glossary. For the English origin of the Pent III series (Vaciago's Aᶜ),
    see Bischoff and Lapidge, *Biblical Commentaries*, 286.
44 Bischoff and Lapidge, *Biblical Commentaries*, 247.
45 The major Leiden family glossaries have now been published by Vaciago, *Glossae
    Biblicae*. They are predominantly literal but occasionally admit extra-literal
    interpretations. On these glossaries see Michael Lapidge, 'The School of Theodore and
    Hadrian,' 45–72; Bischoff and Lapidge, *Biblical Commentaries*, 173–5; and Remley, *Old
    English Biblical Verse*, 45–9. In a paper in preparation I argue that the *Genesis A* poet

It is likewise the literal information about pitch as a waterproofing sub-stance that fascinated the *Genesis A* poet. Speculating about how someone with Bede's knowledge might have read this passage makes for a diverting thought-experiment, but the poem affords little evidence that someone like Bede was its intended reader.[46] Its audience's familiarity with biblical exegesis would no doubt have varied from individual to individual, but any of them might have wondered how a wooden ship could withstand a flood of such magnitude and duration, and the poet evidently expected his audience to be impressed by the remarkable nature of the substance that Noah used to waterproof it.[47] The poet's focus on the caulking of the ark is motivated by the need to seal a potential crack in the surface logic of the narrative in order to preserve its historical plausibility. His insistence on the exceptional (*syndrig*) quality of the substance is, moreover, consistent with his interest in the marvellous nature of Adam's pain-free surgery.

The poet provides another literal gloss concerning the raven, which did not return to the ark because it had found a floating corpse to feed upon. Here again, he is responding to a straightforward problem raised by the biblical narrative: Why did the raven not return to the ark? Huppé inter-prets the raven as symbolic of 'those who dwell in Babylon, the enemies of God, and those who refuse the way of Redemption, which leads to Jerusalem.'[48] It is true that the poet does designate the raven as 'the enemy,' if we retain the manuscript reading *se feond* (line 1447a, emended by

---

was familiar – probably through a Canterbury School gloss preserved in several of the Leiden family manuscripts – with a tradition that the soul of Lot's wife remained in the pillar until the Day of Judgment (cf. *Genesis A* 2570b–4a with *Biblical Commentaries*, ed. and trans. Bischoff and Lapidge, 416–19).

46 Someone like Bede, for example, would surely have felt compelled to explain that an impassible God could not literally 'repent' of creating man, as Genesis 6:6 (*paenituit eum*) seems to suggest. The *Genesis A* poet, however, is content to translate the verb without reservation, even adding an intensifier (*hreaw hine swiðe*, line 1276b). Bede singled out this verse as a place where 'Scripture is suited to, and adapts itself to the lowly intelligence of duller persons, the multitude of whom is far greater' [*congruit tamen scriptura, et se coaptat humili intelligentiae tardiorum, quorum longe maior est multitudo*] (*In principium Genesis* II.vi.5–6, CCSL 118, 101.1017–19). See Calvin B. Kendall, 'The Responsibility of *Auctoritas*,' at 104 (translation Kendall's).

47 Here I agree with Boyd, 'Doctrine and Criticism,' 234: 'If the poet's audience are to accept the rather improbable claims made in the Bible for the enduring properties of the ark (an account of seafaring would undoubtedly engage their particular interest), such a piece of "scientific" knowledge lends credibility to the story.'

48 Huppé, *Doctrine and Poetry*, 175.

Krapp to *feonde*, 'rejoicing').[49] Yet, as Milton M. Gatch has pointed out, in early exegetical tradition the raven was normally associated with sinful Christians, for whom the term *feond* hardly seems appropriate.[50] Moreover, the contumelious and ill-omened raven has a venerable history quite apart from allegory, and the legend is found in other medieval vernacular contexts without spiritual explication.[51] The raven is a *feond* not only because of its proverbial ill nature but also because the description is focalized from the point of view of Noah, whom the raven failed to serve in the way it was intended (as emphasized by the formula *him seo wen geleah* and the echo *secan wolde ... secan nolde*):

> Noe tealde   þæt he on neod hine,
> gif he on þære lade   land ne funde,
> ofer sidwæter   secan wolde
> on wægþele.   eft him seo wen geleah
> ac se feond gespearn   fleotende hreaw.
> salwigfeðera   secan nolde. (lines 1442–8)

[Noah assumed that if it did not find land on the journey it would return to him over the broad water (back) on the deck of the ship. The expectation deceived him, for the enemy perched on a floating corpse; the dark-feathered one did not wish to return.]

---

49 *The Junius Manuscript*, ed. Krapp, ASPR 1.

50 Milton M. Gatch, 'Noah's Raven in *Genesis A* and the Illustrated Old English Hexateuch,' 3–15. Gatch implies that the raven was never interpreted as the devil, but there are examples; in a search of the electronic databases *Patrologia Latina* and *Library of Christian-Latin Texts*, I find four: Jerome, *Dialogus aduersus Luciferanos* 22 (*PL* 23.176); Eucherius, *Liber formularum spiritalis intelligentiae* (*PL* 50.749); Angelomus of Luxeuil (*PL* 115.161B); and Pseudo-Bede, *In Pentateuchum commentarii* (*PL* 91.226, already cited by Shepherd, 'Scriptural Poetry,' 29n1; Shepherd also refers to Sulpicius Severus's *Chronicle* and Rabanus Maurus's commentary on Genesis, but neither of these authors interprets the raven as the devil). Two examples from Greek Fathers are cited in a note at *PL* 99.253, and for another see Elias Steinmeyer and Eduard Sievers, *Die althochdeutschen Glossen*, vol. 5, 228.

51 See Anna Birgitta Rooth, *The Raven and the Carcass*, 112–45, who quotes many examples from medieval vernacular sources, including (199ff.) the Middle English *Cursor Mundi*, and the Middle Irish *Lebor Gabála Érenn* (on which see below), as well as *Genesis A*.

The poet's comment about the raven has more in common with Aldhelm's Riddle 63 ('Corbus') than with the allegorical commentaries cited by Doane. Aldhelm's raven describes itself as the one 'who first of all living things flouted the bonds of the law by refusing to bow my neck to the commandment of the patriarch.'[52] Instead of referring to an allegorical equation with the devil or sinners, Aldhelm invokes the aetiological legend that God punished the raven's disobedience by causing its feathers to turn black (the same legend is found in the Old English *Adrian and Ritheus* dialogue, likewise without any allegorical gloss).[53] In any case, the legend (first attested in Jewish sources) seems to have appealed to the *Genesis A* poet in the first place as a satisfying answer to a literal problem not resolved by the biblical narrative. Even Augustine, who allegorizes the raven elsewhere, refers to the legend in his *Quaestiones in Heptateuchum* strictly as a literal solution to the question of whether or not the raven had died (since the dove subsequently found no place to rest and had to return).[54] Moreover, the legend was conveniently homologous with the traditional Germanic 'Beasts of Battle' type scene, which the poet invokes in lines 1983b–5, mentioning, however, only the raven ('sang se wanna fugel ... hræs on wenan' [the dark bird sang ... in expectation of a corpse]) instead of the triad raven, eagle, and wolf.[55] In short, as Gatch concluded, 'there is no evidence that he wanted to do more than explain the raven's behavior, that he knew the typological or tropological applications of the explanation, or that the lines are a clue to some larger, allegorical reading of the verse-paraphrase of Genesis.'[56] By the same token, the poet explains why the dove did not return on the third occasion, simply by pointing out that, having found land and trees, it did not need to:

---

52 Rudolph Ewald, ed., *Aldhelmi Opera*, 126; trans. Michael Lapidge and James L. Rosier, *Aldhelm*, 83.

53 James E. Cross and Thomas D. Hill, eds., *The Old English Prose Solomon and Saturn and Adrian and Ritheus*, 37 (no. 21).

54 J. Fraipont and D. de Bruyne, eds., CCSL 33, 5; cited by Doane (271), who thinks that 'Augustine's comment, or some comment directly derived from it, was certainly known to the poet.' Augustine interprets the raven allegorically in his *Contra Faustum Manichaeum* (PL 42.264) and *Tractatus in euangelium Ioannis* (PL 35.1426).

55 Cf. Stanley B. Greenfield and Daniel G. Calder, *A New Critical History of Old English Literature*, 208. I cannot agree with Gatch's view ('Noah's Raven,' 6) that the exegetical cadaver theory rules out a relation to the motif of the Beasts of Battle.

56 Gatch, 'Noah's Raven,' 9.

> seo eft ne com
> to lide fleogan   ac heo land begeat,
> grene bearwas.   nolde gladu æfre
> under salwedbord   syððan ætywan
> on þellfæstenne   þa hire þearf ne wæs. (lines 1478b–82)

[It did not fly back to the ship, for it had caught sight of land, green forests. Gladdened, it wished never again to be in a planked hold under a deck blackened with pitch, since there was no need.]

I see no evidence from the context that the poet intended 'to emphasize the three stages or states of holiness which [the three flights of the dove] typify,' as Doane suggests.[57] The poet's explanation that it never again wanted to be in the hold of a ship is a natural one for a wild bird that has been thus confined for well over forty days and, when finally released, is *glæd* to have left. Augustine's comment that the third release of the dove 'figures the end of the world when the saints shall be in eternal safety with the Father'[58] does not explain anything that needs explaining in *Genesis A*, for the poet has explained the dove's behaviour naturally in a way that, while disarmingly simple, is also perfectly adequate.

There is no additional detail, as far as I can see, in the poet's account of the flood narrative that cannot be explained literally and adequately either by the biblical text and its legendary accretions or by simple extrapolation from the circumstances narrated.[59] The few distinctive non-biblical details serve straightforward narrative functions.[60] Since Augustine was mapping his spiritual explication on the same biblical narrative that the poet is (literally) paraphrasing, and since Augustine cannot propose a spiritual reading that contradicts any of the literal information in the Bible, some of what he says may be fortuitously congruous with what the poet says (or

---

57 Doane, *Genesis A*, 272.

58 As paraphrased by Doane, *Genesis A*, 272.

59 Compare Miranda Wilcox, 'Vernacular Biblical Epics and the Production of Anglo-Saxon Cultural Exegesis,' 195–6, who concludes that the poet dwells on themes that 'intersect to produce a vivid and multi-dimensional depiction of the ark, not as a type of the Church or prefiguring Christ's baptism, but as an actual crowded and chaotic space inhabited by a few heroic, seafaring people and their many animals.' I am grateful to Thomas N. Hall of Notre Dame University for drawing my attention to Wilcox's dissertation.

60 For example, there is the non-biblical detail that Noah first sent the dove out seven days after the raven, a detail paralleled in the Irish *Lebor Gabála Érenn*. In neither case is the number seven invested with any allegorical significance.

with what any translator of Genesis might say). Yet nothing in Augustine's spiritual explication necessarily or even advantageously applies to the specific details in the poet's paraphrase. If, on the first release of the dove, the bird could find no resting place on which to set its feet (lines 1456b–8a), this is because the Bible says 'non inuenisset ubi requiesceret pes eius' (Genesis 8:9, in a Vetus Latina reading), and it is the Augustinian interpretation (in Doane's words, 'the saints who are not promised rest in this world') that is supererogatory, not the literal detail.[61]

The typological values assigned by Augustine are similarly irrelevant in the embarrassing episode of Noah's drunkenness, which the poet characterizes as 'inappropriate' (*swa gerysne ne wæs*, line 1565). He does not shrink from criticism of the patriarch's lapse by taking refuge in a figurative allusion to the Passion of Christ but associates Noah's inability to cover himself with the Fall by alluding to the expulsion of Adam and Eve from paradise:

swiðe on slæpe   sefa nearwode
þæt he ne mihte,   on gemynd drepen,
hine handum self   mid hrægle wryon
and sceome þeccan   swa gesceapu wæron
werum and wifum   siððan wuldres þegn
ussum fæder and meder   fyrene sweorde
on laste beleac   lifes eðel.   (lines 1570–6)

[His spirit was so paralyzed that, dazed in mind, he was unable to cover himself with his garment and hide his shameful parts, as their natures were for men and women after the thane of glory shut the homeland of life against our father and mother with a fiery sword.]

This does not deny Noah's personal holiness (manifested by his obedience, not by his intemperance) but it effectively precludes typology.[62]

---

61 Paul Battles has cogently argued that the poet's treatment of the tower of Babel episode (lines 1649–1701) is not consistent 'with a programme of Augustinian exegesis' ('*Genesis A* and the Anglo-Saxon "Migration Myth,"' 47–51 and 65 [quotation at 51]).

62 On the poet's censure of Noah, see L.N. McKill, 'The Artistry of the Noah Episode in *Genesis A*,' 132–3, and Magennis, *Images of Community*, 91–2 and 153; Magennis (92n72) contrasts the poet's moral perspective with the typological tradition connecting the episode with the Passion of Christ. For the poet's emphasis on the obedience of Noah, see Lucas, 'Loyalty and Obedience,' 125–6. Compare Jonathan Wilcox's conclusion that the laughter of Sarah and mockery of Abraham, in reaction to God's message

The poet's selection of details to elaborate upon is driven by a fascination with the marvellous and with the need to explain literal problems raised by the biblical narrative: How could Adam have a rib removed without suffering and haemorrhaging? How could Noah and his sons have constructed so gigantic a craft? How could the ark withstand the punishing waves of a cataclysmic flood for more than forty days without breaking apart? Why did the raven not return to the ark if there was not yet any dry land for it to alight upon? Why did the dove fail to return on the third occasion, and why did Noah not curse it also? So far from insinuating figural significations, the poet is concerned to vindicate the internal consistency and historical veracity of the biblical narrative by anticipating questions such as these.

In addition to figural readings of major narrative episodes, critics of *Genesis A* have proposed allusions to patristic name etymologies and numerology. According to Huppé, in Melchisedech's blessing of Abraham the poet alludes to the allegorical significance of the number of warriors in Abraham's army (318, signifying Christ crucified, arrived at by converting the number to the Greek letters *TIH*):

> wæs ðu gewurðod   on wera rime
> for þæs eagum   þe ðe æsca tir
> æt guðe forgeaf.   þæt is god selfa ... (lines 2107–9a)

[Be honoured among the number of men in the eyes of the one who gave you the glory of spears in battle. That is God himself ...]

Huppé argues that the phrase *on wera rime* refers to the number of Abraham's small army; yet since the immediate sense of the phrase (as Huppé concedes) is that Abraham is to be 'blessed among men,' there is no contextual pressure to link it with the specific number of warriors in Abraham's army, especially considering that the alleged allegorical cue occurs more than seventy lines after the number being interpreted. Moreover, Huppé's translation of *wæs ðu gewurðod* as 'you have been honoured' is tendentious. Accepting the emendation of the manuscript reading *wærðu*, the word order indicates that *wæs* (or *wes*) is imperative, and unlike

---

that Sarah will bear a child in her old age (lines 2238–90a), is 'uncomplicatedly' derisive and that the poet 'shows no hint of the influence of Augustine and the Abraham apologists' ('The First Laugh,' 258–9). On this episode see also O'Brien O'Keeffe, 'The Book of Genesis,' 202–4.

Huppé's perfect tense, the poet's 'be honoured' does not refer to any specific event or circumstance in the past.[63]

As Huppé noted, the poet's praise of Abraham's victory against superior numbers does bear a striking resemblance to a comment in Bede's commentary on Genesis, in a passage occurring shortly before his exposition of the number 318 (which undoubtedly was a typological 'hot spot' for Christian exegetes):

> miraculum quidem est diuinae potentiae permaximum, quod cum cohorte tam modica tantam hostium stragem fecerit Abram.[64]

> [A very great miracle indeed of the divine power is that Abraham, with so small a band, caused the overthrow of so great an enemy.]

>   næfre mon ealra
> lifigendra her   lytle werede
> þon wurðlicor   wigsið ateah
> þara þe wið swa miclum   mægne geræsde. (lines 2092b–5)

> [Among all the living here who have attacked so great a force, never has a man achieved victory in battle more gloriously with a smaller troop.]

This is a close parallel indeed, if not so distinctive as to render borrowing beyond question. Yet even if we accept it as evidence of the poet's familiarity with Bede's commentary, the fact remains that the poet took from Bede only what was consonant with a literal and heroic understanding of Abraham as a military leader who had been victorious against overwhelming odds.[65]

---

63 Huppé, *Doctrine and Poetry*, 198. For other examples of Huppé's 'loose or inaccurate translation,' see Cross's review, 564. O'Brien O'Keeffe, 'The Book of Genesis,' 197–202, draws attention to different contextual reasons for scepticism of Huppé's allegorical readings of the episodes of Abraham, Lot, and Melchisedech, noting (202) for example that the poet does not render Melchisedech's offering of bread and wine directly but with the 'neutral' *lacum* (line 2103).

64 *In principium Genesis* III.xiv.14, CCSL 118A, 187.1585–7; trans. Huppé, *Doctrine and Poetry*, 196.

65 For a similar view, see Michael J. Swanton, *English Literature before Chaucer*, 90. As Malcolm Godden has pointed out, the passage is also reminiscent of the conclusion of *The Battle of Brunanburh*; see his 'Biblical Literature,' 210. On the historiographical background of these passages see Andrew P. Scheil, 'The Historiographic Dimensions of *Beowulf*.' Andy Orchard, in 'Conspicuous Heroism,' 45–58 (repr. in *The Poems of*

Doane passed over Huppé's suggestion in silence, but it has been revived recently by Andy Orchard.[66] Orchard does not address the grammatical or contextual difficulties involved in taking *wæs ðu gewurðod on wera rime* as a punning allusion to a long-distance number but supports Huppé's allegorical reading circumstantially by arguing that it is not wholly isolated as a figural element in the larger context of the poet's extended treatment of the War of the Kings. Doane had argued that allegorizations of the battle were 'sporadic and non-influential,'[67] but Orchard draws attention to Latin glosses in the Anglo-Saxon illustrated Prudentius in Cambridge, Corpus Christi College 23 (one of whose artists also worked on Junius 11) that interpret the four kings defeated by Abraham tropologically as the vices that the soul must conquer. The question, however, is not so much the availability of a figural reading of the biblical episode as it is its relevance within the local context of the passage in *Genesis A* and the larger generic context of the poem. Since the *Psychomachia* is the very definition of a tropological battle poem, it is not surprising that Prudentius's summary of the story of Abraham should attract tropological glosses. But does the *Genesis A* poet's treatment of the War of the Kings prompt a tropological reading?

The best evidence, perhaps, is the poet's assertion that the four kings are from the north, whereas Genesis seems to imply that they are from the east. Here, then, we have an apparently incongruous detail that might plausibly suggest an extra-literal signification. Doane, who stresses that 'the poet treats [the War of the Kings] in a secular spirit,' allows for both moral and literal dimensions of the poet's directional patterning, because the kings are 'men from a country on the left hand of Egypt, probably Babylon.'[68] I agree with Orchard that the traditional negative associations of the north are relevant. There is, however, a plausible Old Testament source for the idea in Jeremiah 25:9, which prophesies a battle between the Israelites and 'all the kindreds of the north' (*uniuersas cognationes*

MS Junius 11, ed. Liuzza, 119–36) – references are to the reprint, here 125–6 – cites a similar statement earlier in Bede's commentary, which explicitly links Abraham's victory against superior forces (*tantos reges cum paucis superauit*) with the power of faith (not with the number 318); however, this is not as close a parallel as Bede's later statement, and in any case the poet, unlike Bede, does not refer to faith in this context.

66 Orchard, 'Conspicuous Heroism,' 126ff.
67 Doane, *Genesis A*, 295.
68 Doane, *Genesis A*, 295–6.

aquilonis).[69] The enemies of the Israelites and of their progenitor Abraham are thus aligned symbolically, yet the symbolism is of the most basic and archetypal kind that can be appreciated without invoking a tropological level.[70] Abraham is a godly man and therefore can be associated with the south, but this need not mean he is a figure for the soul; the forces of the four kings are evil because they oppose the godly Abraham and therefore can be associated with Israel's prophesied northern enemies, and indeed with Satan, who wished to place his home and throne *on norðdæle* (line 32b, cf. Isa. 14:13), but this need not imply that they are allegorical ciphers of the Vices. The poet's emphasis in the episode as a whole is manifestly on the heroic and martial dimensions of the battle, and his symbolic way of stressing the duality of good and evil is also grounded in the literal level.

In *Genesis A* there is no hint of Prudentius's etymological play on Lot's name (*uinctus*, 'bound'), which is also alluded to in the second of the two Corpus 23 tropological glosses.[71] Orchard suggests, however, that the poet alludes generally to Jerome's association of the Elamites with 'the forces of worldliness,' and specifically to the etymology of Dan (*iudicium*), the place where the Elamites were defeated, in the phrase *dome bedrorene* (line 2082a).[72] The Elamites are undoubtedly worldly, yet the characterization is too broad to take as an etymological allusion without some supporting verbal cue, such as (for example) an alliterative collocation of *Elamitare* with *eorðe*. As for Dan equalling *iudicium* equalling *dom*, one immediate problem is that the context suggests that *dom* is to be taken in the sense of 'glory' ('judgment' is at best a sub-audition, but what would it mean to say the Elamites were 'bereft of judgment'?). Another difficulty is that the poet has chosen not to mention the name Dan, though he does

---

69 As Michael Lapidge has shown, Byrhtferth characterizes the English defeat at Maldon as a fulfilment of this very prophecy from Jeremiah ('Byrhtferth and Oswald,' 74). In this context the allusion functions as a kind of secular typology, but in the context of the biblical Genesis an allusion to another Old Testament tradition is symbolic but not typological. A note in *The Jerusalem Bible*, gen. ed. Alexander Jones, 1507 (note g), states that 'The north is the traditional invasion route' (citing Jer. 1:13–15 'etc.'; the verses in Micah 7:6 being commented upon are not, however, in the Vulgate). Doane (*Genesis A*, 296) cites other biblical verses and commentary that associate the gentiles with the north.

70 Compare with Magennis's remarks on the poet's imagery of the city and landscape as 'essentially symbolic in nature, but ... not guided by a predetermined allegorical or tropological approach' and lacking 'a developed concern with the subtleties of exegetical scholarship' (*Images of Community*, 159).

71 See Orchard, 'Conspicuous Heroism,' 129–30.

72 Ibid., 127.

refer to *domasco* (line 2082b), to which the Elamites were driven. One could argue, I suppose, that the etymology has been artfully substituted for the proper name, but an argument of this kind is inherently weaker than one based on positive evidence.

An inherently weak case such as Huppé's is not strengthened by debatable circumstantial evidence relating to other passages. With the exception of the specification of the northern origins of Abraham's enemies (which can be accounted for by another Old Testament passage), there are no cryptic, incongruous, or supererogatory details that resist or are not satisfactorily captured by a literal reading, and figural readings of unproblematic details are out of harmony with the poet's handling of the episode as a whole. A circumstantial case of this kind would be more compelling in *Exodus*, a poem studded with cryptic, incongruous, and supererogatory details that encourage extra-literal interpretation, and one whose author makes an explicit appeal to his audience to interpret with 'the keys of the spirit' (line 525).[73] The *Genesis A* poet's handling of the biblical narrative is strikingly different and is not conducive to extra-literal interpretation.

If there is insufficient contextual support for figural interpretations of numbers and names in the poet's rendering of the story of Abraham, the poet clearly does allude to the etymologies of at least two biblical names in other episodes. Fred C. Robinson has demonstrated that the poet's reference to the 'body of seedbearing Seth' (*sædberendes Sethes lice*, line 1145) reflects the etymology of *semen* (the poet apparently even substituted the Old English word for 'seed' for Seth's name in line 1133b: *sedes eafora*, 'seed's offspring').[74] Similarly, the etymology of Noah's name (*requies*, 'rest') is likely alluded to in God's instruction to Noah 'to clear a resting place' (*reste geryman*, line 1304a) for all creatures in the ark, and the description of the place in which the ark finds 'rest for the sea journey' (*lagosiða rest*, line 1486b).[75] Yet the poet seems to have restricted himself to etymologies suggested by the Bible itself and which are therefore part of

---

73 On this passage see James W. Earl, 'Christian Tradition in the Old English *Exodus*,' 541–70; repr. in *The Poems of MS Junius 11*, ed. Liuzza, 137–72, at 147; and Dorothy Haines, 'Unlocking *Exodus* ll. 516–32,' 481–98.

74 Robinson, 'The Significance of Names in Old English Literature,' *Anglia* 86 (1968): 14–58, at 29–30.

75 See Robinson, 'The Significance of Names,' 33, and Doane's notes on these lines. O'Brien O'Keeffe, 'The Book of Genesis,' 190–1, briefly discusses the play on Noah's name in the context of the poet's other references to the ark, or the second dove finding a 'resting place,' finding them too inconsistent to support 'hard and fast allegorization.'

the literal level.[76] As Robinson noted, in Genesis 4:25 Seth is termed 'another seed' to replace Abel, and in Genesis 5:29 Noah's name is said to signify the release from labour. The reference to the body of 'seed-bearing' Seth in the context of Seth's burial might arguably suggest the alternative etymology *resurrectio* and its figurative associations, but the poet alludes directly only to the biblically sanctioned etymology, *semen*. Etymologies of Hebrew names, moreover, were valued not just as allegorical ciphers but also as literal information concerning the three sacred languages of the Bible. Indeed, such etymologies often circulated separately in the form of lists without any spiritual explanations attached, and Jerome's *Liber interpretationis hebraicorum nominum*, the most fundamental of all such lists, does not supply extra-literal meanings.[77]

A different kind of onomastic punning on a divine name has been detected by Roberta Frank. While granting that 'the main concern of the *Genesis* poet was to narrate the historical truth of Old Testament events,' Frank argues that the poet 'highlighted potentially Christological episodes ... with multiple plays on "word" as if striving to make the Old English *word* more like the *Logos* in which all meanings were enclosed.'[78] As I have already noted, the doctrine of Christ as the Verbum/Logos is expounded in the beginning of the Gospel of John, verses closely associated by John himself with the opening verse of Genesis, and orthodox Christian interpretation of Genesis held that the Logos was the literal agent of Creation. As Eusebius emphasized in his *Ecclesiastical History*, however, the pre-incarnate Christ was also quite literally present in several of the theophanies related in the book of Genesis.[79] The Canterbury commentaries, for example, though consistently Antiochene in orientation,

---

76 Cf. Doane, *Genesis A*, 65. Huppé argues that the poet refers to the patristic interpretation of Cain as *possessio* (*Doctrine and Poetry*, 155), but as T.A. Shippey has pointed out in his review of Doane's edition (*Modern Language Review* 76.2 [1981]: 430–1, at 430), in the poem it is Abel who *æhte heold* (line 973b). Objecting to Huppé's claim for a similar play on the name of Sarah, J.E. Cross argued that it is 'irrelevant to a study of this poem that Sarah's name had a symbolic meaning to Biblical commentators, or even that the poet knew it, for if he did, he clearly rejected it for his purpose here because he gives no hint of the symbolic meaning' (review of Huppé, 562). It is worth noting that the poet actually suppresses the fact that Abraham's name was changed from Abram, passing up an excellent opportunity to exploit its figural significance.
77 P. de Lagarde, G. Morin, and M. Adriaen, eds., CCSL 72.
78 Frank, 'Some Uses of Paranomasia,' 76.
79 See the Latin translation by Rufinus, *Historia ecclesiastica*, ed. Theodor Mommsen, book 1.2.

identify the three angels who appeared to Abraham as 'the Son of God in the company of two angels.'[80] In a valuable but generally neglected essay on the Old English *Exodus*, Ruth M. Ames has shown how pervasive was the medieval assumption that the second Person of the Trinity was historically present (not simply prefigured) in Old Testament events.[81] Although I do not agree with the conclusions that Ames draws for interpreting *Exodus*, I find her approach to Anglo-Saxon representation of the Old Testament deity more convincing than that of Barbara Raw, who, despite noting several examples of Christ-type images of God in Anglo-Saxon illustrations of the Old Testament, argues on the basis of some rather ambiguous statements by Ælfric that 'it seems very unlikely that the Anglo-Saxons believed that the Old Testament appearances were of Christ rather than God the Father.'[82] Yet Anglo-Saxons who pondered this matter at all would hardly have regarded it as an either-or proposition. A striking and unambiguous example of the pre-incarnate Christ in Old English literature is afforded by Vercelli Homily XIX, which blandly states that 'Christ himself' warned Adam and Eve not to eat the forbidden fruit.[83] There can be no question of typology here (Christ cannot prefigure or covertly represent himself).[84] By the same token, when the *Genesis A* poet, expanding on Genesis 7:16, *inclusit eum Dominus deforis* (the Lord shut him in from outside), states that *nergend usser* (our Saviour) closed and blessed the door of Noah's ark, we can assume that he meant that the pre-incarnate Christ literally performed this action.[85] According to an Old English version

---

80 *Biblical Commentaries*, ed. and trans. Bischoff and Lapidge, 324–5 (Pent I, no. 106).

81 R.M. Ames, 'The Old Testament Christ and the Old English *Exodus*,' 33–50. Garde and Muir, 'Patristic Influence,' 55, without reference to Ames, argue similarly that in both *Genesis A* and *Exodus* 'Christ is perceived as already *historically* active ... in his Christological (Trinitarian) capacity as the Lord of Victories and Creator of Men' (emphasis in original). As Karkov notes (*Text and Picture*, 167–8), most of the drawings of God as Creator in Junius 11 have the cruciferous nimbus appropriate to Christ as the Logos.

82 Barbara C. Raw, *Trinity and Incarnation in Anglo-Saxon Art and Thought*, 104.

83 *The Vercelli Homilies and Related Texts*, ed. D.G. Scragg, 317, line 35.

84 Cf. R.A.S. Macalister, ed. and trans., *Lebor Gabála Érenn*, 1:190–1 [§45] (I have replaced Macalister's macrons with the fada): 'A doras assan sliss sóer, / amail ro ordaig Noé nóem; / dáig ro oslaiced a tóeb thair / ár Críst, ár Cenn, ár n-Athair' (Its door out of its free side, / as holy Noe ordained; / for he would open its side eastward, / our Christ, our Head, our Father).

85 Strictly speaking, in lines 1363–7b the door of the ark is closed by *heofonrices weard* / ... *sigora waldend* and blessed (*segnade*) by *nergend usser*. But here the three terms for the deity seem to be appositives, not an enumeration implicitly distinguishing the *nergend* from the other two persons of the Trinity.

of the Ordinals of Christ, Christ instituted the office of doorkeeper (*hostiarius*) when he closed and opened the door of the ark: 'Crist wæs hostiarius, þa he beclysde Noes arce wið þone geotendan flod and eft untynde' (Christ was a doorkeeper when he closed the ark against the surging flood and later opened it).[86] The connection with the ecclesiastical grades obviously associates the ark with the church, as a commentary on the Old English version makes explicit,[87] yet the form of the Ordinals presumes that Christ's action was historical, for the other sanctions all involve acts of the incarnate Christ from the Gospels. A Latin version of the Ordinals attributed to Theodore of Canterbury even introduces the list with a statement that Christ instituted these grades *in carne*, despite the fact that the first one mentioned is the *hostiarius*, which Christ instituted before his incarnation.[88] The *Genesis A* poet may well have been familiar with this sanction from the Ordinals, which unequivocally asserts Christ's literal presence in Old Testament history.

Extra-literal meanings might be conveyed not only by verbal hints but also by structural cues, that is, by conspicuous emphasis on or suggestive juxtaposition of biblical episodes of special typological significance in Christian tradition. Indeed, a distinctive selection or configuration of biblical episodes or verses can be compelling evidence of figural intent, especially when the same selection or configuration can be shown to have served traditionally as a dossier of scriptural proof texts for a specific typological correspondence, or as lections for a liturgical feast such as Easter. While the *Genesis A* poet sometimes adds or omits material, he generally adheres to the episodic and even verse sequence of the biblical narrative, especially in paraphrasing chapters 3 to 5 and 8 to 22, leading Paul Remley

---

86 Karl Jost, ed., *Die 'Institutes of Polity, Civil and Ecclesiastical,'* 225. On this ordinal see Roger E. Reynolds, *The Ordinals of Christ from Their Origins to the Twelfth Century*, 86. The same doorkeeper sanction also occurs in the several late Anglo-Saxon pontificals, including the Egbert Pontifical, ed. H.M.J. Banting, *Two Anglo-Saxon Pontificals*, 17: 'Ostiarius fuit quando conclusit et aperuit archam noe. et portas inferni aperuit. unde modo hostiarii qui dicuntur aecclesiae ostia et sacrarii et tangere signum ut occurrant omnes custodiri iubentur.' See Reynolds, *The Ordinals of Christ*, 84.

87 Reynolds, ed., *The Ordinals of Christ*, 87. The drawing of the ark on page 66 of the Junius manuscript includes features reminiscent of Anglo-Saxon church architecture (see Karkov, *Text and Picture*, 90–1), and the artist no doubt intended to invoke the typological association.

88 Jane Stevenson, ed., *The 'Laterculus Malalianus' and the School of Archbishop Theodore*, 146–8: 'Nam hostiarius fuit, quando ostium archae aperuit, et iterum clausit.' See Reynolds, *The Ordinals of Christ*, 44.

to conclude that his main source was 'almost certainly a continuous exemplar of Genesis I–XXII (or of III–V and VIII–XXII)' of a mixed Old Latin–Vulgate type.[89]

There is, however, considerable 'narrative dislocation' in the poet's narration of the Creation and of the flood, corresponding respectively to Genesis chapters 1 to 2 and 7 to 8.[90] The textual losses and possible dislocations in the second quire of the Junius manuscript make it very difficult to reconstruct the poem's original sequence for the Creation narrative, though Remley has proposed that the biblical order could largely be restored by moving lines 169–204 to follow lines 206–34.[91] Even without resorting to such a drastic editorial intervention, one can account for the poet's conflation of material in Genesis chapters 1 to 2 as an effort to harmonize the two 'Priestly' and 'Jahwist' accounts of Creation 'so as to produce a coherent synthesis of traditions on Creation.'[92] Unfortunately, most of the poet's account of the temptation and fall of Adam and Eve has been lost, but we can still draw an instructive contrast with *Genesis B*, which drastically reconfigures the biblical narrative so that the devil approaches Adam first, is rejected, and only then tempts Eve. The temptation is similarly modified in the Old French *Jeu d'Adam*, and it has been convincingly argued that in both cases the purpose was to suggest the allegorical equation of Adam with Reason, and Eve with the carnal appetite.[93] In *Genesis B*, this allegorical pattern is never overtly stated but (in Thomas D. Hill's words) is 'implicit in the relationship of the characters within the narrative;'[94] yet it is convincing precisely because the poet's radical revisions of the biblical narrative are consistent with it. By contrast, *Genesis A*, as we have seen, deploys the traditional exegetical motif that prior to the fall Adam and Eve were 'like angels' because they were both endowed with rational souls – a literal interpretation that in itself interferes with an allegorical reading of Adam alone as Reason.

As for the flood narrative, Remley argues that 'the biblical passages ... which are subject to the greatest amount of alteration in *Genesis A*

---

89 Remley, *Old English Biblical Verse*, 148.
90 Remley, *Old English Biblical Verse*, 120. Remley (105) defines 'narrative dislocation' as 'a shift in position of an Old English reflex of Genesis more than one verse forward or back, vis-à-vis the context of its biblical source.'
91 Ibid., 131–6.
92 Ibid., 128.
93 Rosemary Woolf, 'The Fall of Man in *Genesis B* and the *Mystère d'Adam*,' 191–3.
94 Thomas D. Hill, 'The Fall of Angels and Man in the Old English *Genesis B*,' 282.

correspond precisely to those encountered in drastically abridged forms among Latin lections that were commonly included among liturgical lections for the Easter Vigil.'[95] Some of the poet's omissions are paralleled in surviving flood lections, but his overall selection and arrangement of verses does not otherwise closely match any known series. Still, Remley's assumption that the poet was familiar with such abridged lections is entirely plausible – indeed, it would be remarkable if he were *not* familiar with the Easter liturgy – yet the poet's own abridgement appears to have been motivated by a concern for narrative coherence rather than liturgical resonance. In other words, his familiarity with abridged and harmonized flood lections may have inspired and facilitated his own effort to simplify 'the lengthy and somewhat intractable biblical account of the Flood.'[96] Remley concludes that the poet was not attempting either to translate a specific lectionary abridgement or 'to invoke the theology of the baptismal liturgy'; rather, his knowledge of Easter lections functioned 'at the level of style rather than meaning.'[97]

The poet's relatively few minor rearrangements of verses are likewise explicable as efforts to clarify the literal narrative. In lines 210–18, for example, the sequence Genesis 2:6, 2:5, 2:10 clarifies how the plants of paradise were watered before there had been any rain.[98] At lines 1635b–6, the poet inserts his rendering of Genesis 11:1 ('and there was yet a single language common to earthdwellers') between Genesis 10:10 and 10:20, which refer to Babylon as the beginning of Nemrod's kingdom and to the 'children of Cham.'[99] Michael J. Swanton argues that this rearrangement 'serves implicitly to identify Babel with Babylon and its ruler Nimrod, omitting any reference to him as a "mighty hunter before the Lord," so as to underline his role as the first tyrant and figuratively the devil.'[100] Yet, as Doane notes, although the Bible does not explicitly identify Nimrod as the tower's builder, 'a connection [is] taken for granted by all commentators.' 'By rearranging these verses,' Doane concludes, 'the poet is able to indicate Nimrod's literal role without interfering with the actual words of the

---

95 Remley, *Old English Biblical Verse*, 137–8.
96 Ibid., 142.
97 Ibid., 142–3.
98 See Doane's note on this passage.
99 Remley, *Old English Biblical Verse*, 113n53, characterizes this as the only 'narrative dislocation' in the entire paraphrase of Gen. 8–22.
100 Swanton, *English Literature before Chaucer*, 07.

text.'[101] Another such minor rearrangement occurs in the description of the blessing of Abraham in lines 1719–1810, where the poet has reversed the order of Genesis 12:2 and 12:3. His purpose, Doane suggests, was 'to stress Christian interpretation of the Blessing of Abraham, the second blessing being the greater.'[102] Doane is surely right that the blessing of Abraham's own progeny, the Israelites, would have been less relevant to an Anglo-Saxon audience than the promise that through Abraham all gentile nations would be blessed. To the extent that the historical destiny of those gentile nations, including the *gens Anglorum*, is understood to have been fulfilled through their conversion, the blessing is given a Christian interpretation; even so, it is neither a veiled allegory nor a shadowy figure, but a literal promise. (For the same reason that Christ cannot prefigure himself, an Old Testament 'type' cannot be the same as its New Testament anti-type.)[103] The poet's treatment of the blessing of Abraham, then, is not an exception to the rule formulated by Doane that the poet's 'rearrangements do not disturb the concept of a simple, linear narrative presentation: they are carried out with the simplest expository aims in view.'[104]

---

101 Doane, *Genesis A*, 281.
102 Doane, 'The Sources of *Genesis A*' [Source record C.A.1.1.1.074.01].
103 Garde, *Old English Poetry*, 37–8, emphasizes the historical nature of the promise to Abraham. The poet exalts both Abraham and Lot in two other passage that Doane sees as instances of 'mystical interpretation.' Doane (286) translates lines 1717b–18, 'forðon hie wide nu / dugeðum demað drihta bearnum,' as 'Therefore widely they now judge amidst (heavenly) hosts the sons of multitudes,' which he tentatively interprets as 'a comparison of the literal *past* (when Abraham and Loth shared the heritage of righteousness with their forebears in the time of the old covenant of the flesh) and the mystical *present* (when Abraham and Loth are among the blessed saints sharing the glories of God and judging the children of the new covenant).' Cf. also Karkov, *Text and Picture*, 97. I am aware of no precedent in Christian tradition for Lot and Abraham as heavenly judges, and it is hard to believe that the poet would allude to 'Abraham's bosom' in so imprecise a way. As Doane concedes, the line is 'obscure in context' (the genealogy of Thare), and I would suggest that *demað* is a scribal error for *temað* (induced by anticipation of double alliteration), yielding the sense 'Therefore they widely now have progeny among the hosts with sons of multitudes.' The statement would both anticipate the blessing of Abraham and also account for the biblical statement that Lot is the father 'usque hodie' of both the Moabites and Ammonites (Gen. 19:37–8). Subsequently, the poet says that the generations of men and the *fullwona bearn* (? sons of baptism) widely praise Abraham for his obedience (lines 1949b–51a), but even if we relate the obscure hapax legomenon *fullwona* to *fullwian* (baptize), the passage is an unremarkable, and hardly mystical, assertion that Abraham, the progenitor of the converted gentile nations, is still praised by them.
104 Doane, *Genesis A*, 62.

   The fact that *Genesis A* as it survives in the Junius manuscript ends with the sacrifice of Isaac – probably the single most Christologically resonant passage in Genesis for the Fathers – has often been regarded as a kind of implicitly typological structure, for even though the episode is narrated in biblical sequence, it is obviously marked by its climactic position. As Doane notes, Genesis chapter 22 is a 'natural stopping place' for Genesis transla-tions and commentaries[105] as well as for Genesis lections and pictorial cycles. This is, of course, due to the episode's Christological significance, and it would be perverse to deny that the poet was aware of this signifi-cance or that it would have been appreciated by most readers of *Genesis A*. It *may* be hinted at in the poet's rendering of Genesis 22:6, *imposuit* [name-ly, *ligna holocausti*] *super Isaac filium suum* (he lay the wood of the sacrifice upon his son), as *wudu bær sunu* (the son bore the wood, line 2887b). The double meaning proposed by Robert P. Creed ('the wood [Cross] bore the Son') is almost too good not to be true, and if there are any figural prompts in *Genesis A*, this is probably the most attractive one.[106] Even if the purpose of this syntactically reversible formulation was to suggest the Cross, how-ever, other verbal details seem at odds with it. As L.N. McKill notes, the description of Isaac as a *bearn unweaxen* who is *wintrum geong* (a un-grown child ... young in years, lines 2872a, 2889a) is more consonant with the human pathos of the scene than with an allusion to Christ crucified.[107]

   Stanley Greenfield and Daniel Calder have pointed out that the sacrifice of Isaac is also the climax of an ethical theme that the poet has developed very consistently and explicitly throughout the entire poem: the theme of obedience.[108] From the opening description of the fall of the wicked an-gels, the poet evaluates the central figures of biblical history according to their conformation to or rebellion against the will of God. Greenfield and Calder have illustrated this contrast in the first fit of the poem, which be-gins with a statement of man's obligation to praise God, and proceeds to describe the joy of the obedient angels and the misery of the rebellious. Even night and day after their creation are said 'to perform God's will ever afterward.' Peter J. Lucas has also traced the poet's elaboration of the theme of obedience to the covenant (*wær*) between God and the chosen

---

105 Doane, *Genesis A*, 324–5.
106 Robert P. Creed, 'The Art of the Singer,' 80.
107 L.N. McKill, 'The Offering of Isaac and the Artistry of Old English *Genesis A*,' 9n23. Cf. O'Brien O'Keeffe, 'The Book of Genesis,' 193–6.
108 Greenfield and Calder, *A New Critical History*, 209. See also McKill, 'The Offering of Isaac,' 8–9.

people.[109] The major episodes of the poem can be viewed in the same terms: the disobedience of Adam and Eve, and the contrast between Cain and Abel, between the genealogies of Seth and Cain, between Noah and the wicked whom God destroys in the flood, and even between the raven and the dove. In addition, as Greenfield and Calder point out, 'Abraham's willingness to sacrifice Isaac is literally consonant with Germanic notions of loyalty and obedience and provides a fitting conclusion.'[110] The poet understood that for Christians the sacrifice of Isaac was the climactic event of the book of Genesis, so he concluded his paraphrase with this episode; yet he chose to stress its exemplary value rather than its figural significance.

The biblical paraphrase of *Genesis A* may be termed Christological insofar as the poet assumed that all the acts of God in the Old Testament were the acts of a triune God and that the eternally begotten pre-incarnate Logos was present at Creation and throughout salvation history as it unfolded through the first five ages of the world. The *waldend* (ruler) is at the same time the *nergend* (saviour): He separated light from dark (lines 140b–1a), he shut the door of the ark (line 1367), and he tested the obedience of Abraham (2864b–5a).[111] For Swanton, the poet's use of the epithet *nergend* is 'quite illogical, in any narrative sense, prior to the Fall,' so it must be understood in relation to 'the figure of Christ.'[112] But the *nergend* of *Genesis A* is not a figure of Christ; he *is* Christ, the second person of the Trinity, in his preincarnate manifestation in human history.

If *Genesis A* is not figural, then neither is it secular.[113] The poet consistently emphasizes the duty of human beings to praise and obey God, and interprets human history as a series of decisive interventions by God – and by Christ – in human history. As Augustine explained, historical narratives describe human institutions, but history as a record of the order of time (*ordo temporum*) is not itself a human institution, because God is the founder and administrator of time.[114] Old Testament history is sacred because it recounts the deeds – the *gesta* – of both the righteous and the wicked in the first ages of the world, as well as the corresponding temporal

---

109 Lucas, 'Loyalty and Obedience,' 123–8.
110 Greenfield and Calder, *A New Critical History*, 209.
111 The poet uses the term *nergend* for the deity sixteen times (see Doane's glossary, s.v. *nergend*), often in conjunction with other epithets (such as *waldend, frea ælmihtig*) that by themselves often refer to God the Father.
112 Swanton, *English Literature before Chaucer*, 86.
113 I disagree with Boyd's claim ('Doctrine and Criticism,' 237) that the 'framework of moral values' is 'restricted to a purely secular concept of propriety and nobility.'
114 *De doctrina christiana* 2.28.44, ed. Joseph Martin, 63.

rewards and punishments that God meted out to each. From a Christian point of view, as already in the Pauline epistles, many of the events in the Old Testament are also types that have been fulfilled and supplanted in the New Testament. Yet a figural reading of an Old Testament event does not cancel its historical reality – on the contrary, a figural reading presupposes its historicity – and a Christian author may, for various reasons, concern himself with the historical level without invoking figural readings, neglecting them, that is, without negating them.

Augustine sought to do precisely this in his literal commentaries on Genesis. He first attempted to combat the Manichaean rejection of the Old Testament, in a commentary written in 388/389, by vindicating both the proper or historical sense of Genesis as well as its prophetic sense.[115] Augustine found it difficult to explicate the literal meaning consistently, however, especially in the Creation narrative, so a few years later (between 393 and 395) he tried to explicate the first three chapters historically in his *De Genesi ad litteram imperfectus liber*,[116] but abandoned the task because it was too daunting. Finally, in 401, he took up the task once more, this time completing it (through Genesis chapter 3) in fourteen years with his great commentary *De Genesi ad litteram libri duodecim*.[117] In his *Retractions* Augustine conceded that even this work raised more questions than it answered,[118] but he never wavered in his conviction that Genesis did have a proper historical sense and that it was important to recover it. Nor, of course, did he waver from his conviction that the figurative sense, where it was present, revealed a higher truth. However, in these two literal commentaries, when he does allude to a figural reading of a difficult verse in Genesis, he quickly recalls himself to his purpose: 'But this is an interpretation on the lines of prophetic allegory, which is not what we have

---

115 *De Genesi contra Manichaeos* (PL 34.173–220). All three of the Genesis commentaries discussed here are translated by Matthew O'Connell, *Saint Augustine: On Genesis*, ed. Edmund Hill.

116 J. Zycha, ed., *De Genesi ad litteram imperfectus liber*, 457–503.

117 Zycha, ed., *De Genesi ad litteram libri duodecim*, 1–435. See also the French translation with extensive commentary by P. Agaësee and A. Solignac, *La Genèse au sens littéral en douze livres*. In book 8.2.5 Augustine quotes his statement in the earlier commentary that he had resorted to figurative exegesis whenever he could not recover the literal sense but asserts that, after more careful consideration, he is now 'able to demonstrate how all these things were written straightforwardly in the proper, not the allegorical mode' (trans. E. Hill, *Saint Augustine*, 349).

118 Augustine, *Retractationes* 2.24.2, ed. A. Mutzenbecher, CCSL 57, 109; trans. Edmund Hill, *Saint Augustine*, 167.

undertaken in this work. We undertook, you see, to talk here about the scriptures according to their proper meaning of what actually happened, not according to their riddling, enigmatic reference to future events.'[119]

I invoke Augustine's *ad litteram* commentaries on Genesis not to suggest that they were sources or generic models for *Genesis A* but simply to demonstrate that even Augustine – whose approach to interpreting Genesis both Huppé and Doane elevate to virtually hegemonic status[120] – assumed that the immediate, proper sense of Genesis was the historical, and that Augustine could set aside the figurative sense for specific reasons or audiences, even within the generic context of the biblical commentary. In form, however, *Genesis A* is not a biblical commentary; it is a narrative, one whose generic models must therefore be sought in traditions of biblical paraphrase, to which I now turn.

Genesis as History: *Genesis A* and the Genre of the World Chronicle

The *Genesis A* poet's approach to biblical paraphrase may have been tailored to the needs, interests, and capacities of his intended audience, perhaps including a patron or patrons of higher social status but lower level of learning, but it probably also reflects the influence of generic models that allowed for narrative expansion and moralizing comment, yet constrained extra-literal interpretation. In speaking of generic models for biblical paraphrase, one thinks inevitably of the Late-Latin biblical poets who, according to Michael Lapidge, 'formed the core of the Anglo-Saxon school curriculum, at least down to the time of the Norman Conquest.'[121] The poetry of Juvencus, Arator, Sedulius, and Avitus 'defined the style of Anglo-Latin poetic diction,'[122] in Lapidge's words, and it is easy to assume that vernacular poets were indebted to the precedent they established for poetic expansion of biblical narratives. There is, however, surprisingly little concrete evidence for such influence (though Lapidge makes an appealing argument for reconsidering the case for the influence of Avitus on

---

119 Zycha, ed., *De Genesi ad litteram* I.xvii.34, CSEL 28.1, 25.3–6; trans. E. Hill, *Saint Augustine*, 183. Hill (159n20) gives a list of similar passages.

120 Doane goes so far as to suggest that only works in the 'Latin, Augustinian tradition' (which he defines as 'historical-allegorical') are useful for 'illustrating traditional content in *Genesis A*' (57).

121 Lapidge, 'Versifying the Bible in the Middle Ages,' 24; since Lapidge details editions of these poems and the major relevant scholarship, I forgo listing them here.

122 Ibid., 23.

the Old English *Exodus*). At any rate, while the study of these Latin poets, as Lapidge argues, would have made one 'deeply aware of the possibilities of figural interpretation of biblical and historical events … instinctively seeing Old Testament events as *figurae* of those in the New Testament,'[123] it would *not* have suggested an implicit or covert figural hermeneutic for Old Testament paraphrase, precisely because Arator, Sedulius, and Avitus are quite explicit about the figurative meanings that they all, to a greater or lesser extent, ascribe to Old Testament events (Juvencus's paraphrase of the gospels does not invoke Old Testament types). In narrating the creation of Eve, for example, Avitus elaborates on the depth of the sleep that God cast upon Adam, but then even more elaborately explicates its mystical significance as a figure of the death of Christ, from whose side flowed water and blood, signifying baptism and martyrdom.[124] Had the *Genesis A* poet's conception of biblical paraphrase been modelled on Avitus or the other major Christian-Latin poets, why should he, unlike them, avoid asserting in plain terms the figural significance of such Christological 'hot spots' in Genesis? As we have seen, however, the poet not only fails to express the typological equation in the way Avitus does, but also focuses on details that are incompatible with a figural interpretation. Doane himself cites the poem's faithfulness to the literal sense as evidence that the poet's 'method is entirely alien to' the tradition of Christian-Latin poetry.[125] Late-Latin biblical epics may have given the poet the idea for an extended poetic paraphrase, but they could not have inspired his historical and consistently non-figural approach to Genesis.[126]

If *Genesis A* does not adopt the figural mode characteristic of these Late-Latin biblical poems, were there any alternative well-established narrative approaches to the book of Genesis that corresponded more closely to the poet's literal and historical paraphrase? One attractive possibility is the catechetical *narratio*. As defined by St Augustine, the *narratio* was intended to provide a general survey of the cardinal moments of biblical history, beginning with the Creation.[127] According to Virginia Day, most

---

123 Ibid., 25.
124 Avitus, *Carmina de spiritalis historiae gestis* I.160–9, ed. R. Peiper, MGH Auctores antiquissimi 6.2, 207.
125 Doane, *Genesis A*, 58.
126 Wilcox, 'Vernacular Biblical Epics,' 187–94, suggests that the *Genesis A* poet might have encountered such details as the raven feasting on corpses and the waterproof nature of bitumen from these biblical epics, yet both details were widely available, as Wilcox concedes.
127 *De catechizandis rudibus* III.5–6, ed. J. Bauer, CCSL 46, 124–6.

early medieval examples of the genre deal with 'God and his creative powers, the creation, the fall of angels, and the creation and fall of man,'
together with other major events of biblical history culminating in the
Redemption.[128] Day sees the influence of the *narratio* primarily in the
opening section of the poem, while J.R. Hall has appealed to the same
tradition as an analogue for the contents of the Junius manuscript as a
whole.[129] Now Augustine stressed that the purpose of the *narratio* was to
provide the essential data of biblical history necessary for instruction that
focused on the Redemption, but its literary mode is narrative, and the emphasis is upon the literal history of Old Testament events and not upon
their potential extra-literal significance. Ælfric's sermon *De initio creaturae* is representative; though he alludes twice to the Redemption, Ælfric
avoids extra-literal exegesis of the Genesis narrative itself. In this respect,
the work differs markedly from his treatment of the biblical text in his
Preface to Genesis, which stresses the *gastlice andgit* (spiritual understanding) of the Old Testament.

Katherine O'Brien O'Keeffe has drawn attention to these differences as
a function of genre. In the *De initio creaturae*, Ælfric 'is careful to include
only those Old Testament events which require little exegesis to make a
simple point clear. The necessary typology of Abel, Abraham, and Isaac is
far too complex for the *populum*. For this reason, Ælfric restricts himself
to a simple exposition of how God has acted in history, explained at three
points in Genesis: the creation of man, the flood, and the Tower of Babel.
Each of these events, though open to higher exegesis, is also accessible at
the literal level of God's acting among men.'[130] O'Brien O'Keeffe's explanation of the discrepancy between these two works in terms of genre and
audience is convincing. I would disagree only with the premise that Abel,
Abraham, and Isaac had to be excluded because of their 'necessary typology'; the ark of Noah was as much a typological hot spot as the death of
Abel or the sacrifice of Isaac, yet Ælfric was able to summarize the story
of the flood without so much as an allusion to the church. Ælfric drew the

---

128 Virginia Day, 'The Influence of the Catechetical *narratio* on Old English, and Some
     Other Literature,' 51–61. Garde and Muir, 'Patristic Influence,' insist dogmatically
     that 'a *catechetical* perception of salvation history is common to the whole OE reli-
     gious collection, regardless of quality, genre or style' (63–4, original emphasis).
129 J.R. Hall, 'The Old English Epic of Redemption,' 185–208; repr. in *The Poems of MS
     Junius 11*, ed. Liuzza, 20–52, followed by J.R. Hall's 'Twenty-Five-Year Retro-
     spective,' 53–68.
130 O'Brien O'Keeffe, 'Three English Writers on Genesis,' 71.

figural equation explicitly elsewhere,[131] but the genre of *De initio crea-turae* and the social contexts of the *narratio* constrained exposition of extra-literal meanings.

Another tradition of biblical paraphrase that might have informed the poet's historical approach to Genesis is the World Chronicle or Universal History.[132] Early medieval histories and chronicles that survey biblical history often employ a literal, narrative mode instead of the exegetical mode of commentaries. The most influential such history for the early Middle Ages was the great *Chronicle* of Eusebius in the Latin version of Jerome,[133] which in the words of R. Howard Bloch 'stood as the dominant paradigm of world history for over a thousand years.'[134] The authentic Eusebius-Jerome *Chronicon* begins with Abraham and consists mainly of genealogical and regnal lists and timelines; Bede refers to it as a *descriptio temporum*.[135] At a very early date, however, a narrative summary of world history from Creation through Abraham was interpolated in some manuscripts.[136] This spurious *Exordium libri* treats the Old Testament as a record of the origins

---

131 *CH* I.35, in *Ælfric's Catholic Homilies: The First Series, Text*, ed. Peter Clemoes, 484; *CH* II.4, in *Ælfric's Catholic Homilies: The Second Series, Text*, ed. Malcolm Godden, 33.

132 See Karl Heinrich Krüger, *Die Universalchroniken*, with a Mise-à-jour (1985). For a list of early Latin chronicles, see E. Dekkers, *Clavis Patrum Latinorum*, 503–7. See also Michael I. Allen, 'Universal History, 300–1000,' 17–42; and Rosamond McKitterick, *Perceptions of the Past in the Early Middle Ages*, 7–33.

133 The standard critical edition of Jerome's version of the Eusebius *Chronicon* is R. Helm, *Eusebius Werke*, vol. 7, 3rd ed., Die griechischen christlichen Schriftsteller der ersten drei Jahrhunderte 47 (Berlin: Akademie-Verlag, 1984).

134 Bloch, *Etymologies and Genealogies*, 37.

135 *Epistola ad Plegwinum* 3, ed. Charles W. Jones, CCSL 123C (Turnhout, Belgium: Brepols, 1980), 618.

136 On the *Exordium libri*, reprinted in *PL* 27.61–76, see Alden A. Mosshammer, *The Chronicle of Eusebius and Greek Chronographic Tradition*, 41. I cite the text from *Eusebi chronicorum libri duo*, ed. Schoere, vol. 1, who lists manuscripts that contain the *Exordium* at XII–XIII. Arnaldus Pontacus, in his 1604 edition reprinted in *PL* 27.756, lists four manuscripts; *In Principio Incipit Index of Latin Texts* (Turnhout, Belgium: Brepols) lists four others (incipit: 'Incipiunt tempora totius saeculi'). According to Hermann J. Frede, *Kirchenschriftsteller: Verzeichnis und Sigel*, 514 (no. 3494: HI chr), the *Exordium* was written no later than the beginning of the sixth century. On the version of the Eusebius-Jerome *Chronicon* known to Bede, see John Morris, 'The Chronicle of Eusebius,' 80–93, who does not mention the *Exordium*; nor is it mentioned by McKitterick, who characterizes the Eusebius-Jerome *Chronicon* as the exception to the rule that medieval World Chronicles begin with Creation (*Perceptions of the Past*, 9).

and history of the human race and of God's interventions in human history, and so it adheres to the literal level, proceeding by way of narrative paraphrase, and often reverting to extensive direct quotation of the biblical text. Here is a part of the account of Noah and the flood:

> Cum foret autem Noe solus iustus, placens Deo in generationibus suis, decreuit Deus seruari de quancunque specie ad reparandum semen cuiuslibet animantium: caetera autem uniuersa per diluuium perdere ac ulcisci, ab homine usque ad pecus, tam uolatilium quam reptantium super terram. Instituit ergo Noe fabricari Arcam ex lignis elaboratis et leuigatis tabulamentis ... bitumine linitam intrinsecus et extrinsecus, diuisam in mansiunculas et tristega. In quam sic dispositam introiuit Noe cum filiis et uxoribus suis ... Septimo autem die ab ingressu Arcae, quae fuit XVII mensis secundi, excesserunt aquae terminos et confinia naturae, tantaque uis imbrium largissimorum est exorta, tam ingens aquarum abyssus inuasit continuo incremento per dies quadraginta, scissis cataractis coeli, donec nedum superficiem totius orbis, sed uniuersa montium cacumina sub undis inuoluerent cubitis XV altiores. (46–7)

> [And when Noah alone of his generation was just and pleasing to God, God ordered something from every species to be preserved to restore the seed of living things, but everything else to be punished and destroyed, both man and beast, those that fly as well as those that creep upon the earth. So Noah undertook to build an ark of timber planks, caulked with pitch inside and out, and divided into chambers and three-storeyed. After it was arranged in this way, Noah boarded it with his sons and their wives ... Seven days later, on the seventeeth day of the second month, the waters surpassed their bounds and the limits of nature, and with the cataracts of heaven opened such a huge and powerful torrent was unleashed, so vast a gulf of waters poured in, growing ever larger for forty days, until not merely the surface of the entire earth but all the mountain peaks were submerged fifteen cubits beneath the waves.]

Much of the remainder of the account consists of direct quotation from the Bible. It never alludes to the significance of the ark as the church, or to the flood as a figure of baptism.

Like the Eusebius-Jerome *Chronicon*, the brief world chronicles of Prosper of Aquitaine and Isidore of Seville focus on the succession of genealogies, kingdoms, and nations, but Prosper begins with Adam, and Isidore begins with Creation. Prosper's *Epitoma chronicorum* is barely more than a list of names, dates, and begettings, though Prosper does devote a few more developed sentences to events such as the flood, the tower of Babel, and the circumcision of Abraham.[137] He defines the circumcision as a corporeal sign of the promise that passed into (*transiuit*) the spiritual sacrament of the circumcision of the faithful heart after the birth of Christ, and he notes that Joseph on his death prophesied concerning Christ and the vocation of the gentiles; however, these are the only two such proleptic references in his survey of Old Testament history, and there is no allegorical interpretation.

Isidore's *Chronicon* takes the form of a narrative precis that highlights the main events in Old Testament history, ignoring their spiritual sense.[138] Isidore mentions that the etymology of Seth's name is *resurrectio* (I.4) but explains it in terms of the seed of the just sons of God after the death of Abel, not as a figure of the resurrection of Christ or of the resurrection of the dead at Judgment. Concerning Noah, Isidore says only that the flood occurred in his six-hundredth year, that his ark came to rest on an Armenian mountain range named Ararat, and that Noah had three sons from whom descended seventy-two nations (I.17–18). Isidore wrote a thorough-going allegorical commentary on Genesis, so the strikingly different treatment he accords the biblical narrative in his chronicle is plainly a function of genre.[139] One could argue that the brevity of Isidore's chronicle simply did not afford scope for exegesis; yet Isidore does find room to discuss the problem of Methuselah's whereabouts during the flood (since according to biblical chronology he survived the event, yet was not on the ark [I.10]), to relate the apocryphal legend (derived from Josephus) that antediluvian men inscribed their knowledge on columns of clay and stone so that one or the other would survive a catastrophic flood or conflagration (I.16), and to describe the marvellous dimensions of the tower of Babel (1.22).

The chronicle of Sulpicius Severus is considerably more expansive than Prosper's or Isidore's, offering a fully developed narrative summary

---

137 *Chronica minora, saec. iv, v, vi, vii*, ed. Theodor Mommsen, vol. 1, 385–485; *PL* 51.535–606.

138 José Carlos Martin, ed., *Isidori Hispalensis chronica*.

139 See Thomas O'Loughlin, 'Christ as the Focus of Genesis Exegesis in Isidore of Seville,' 156–7, who points out that Isidore reserved Christological interpretation for his commentaries, whereas his *Chronica maiora* and *De natura rerum* focus on world history and natural history, respectively. The minor chronicles edited by Mommsen, *Chronica minora*, and Karl Frick, *Chronica minora*, vol. 1, for the most part consist of little more than genealogies and lists of kings, tribes, and nations, though occasionally a major event in Genesis will generate a brief narrative summary – as a rule, unembellished with figural commentary.

of biblical history with occasional supplementary information on points of literal interest.[140] Some of Sulpicius's minor elaborations on Genesis are of the same nature as those found in *Genesis A*. He notes, for example, that the bitumen of the ark rendered it impenetrable by the waters of the flood, and he conjectures that the raven did not return to the ark, because it was occupied with the cadavers it found floating on the waters:

> Sed Noe, uirum iustum, uita innocens destinatae exemit sententiae. Idem admonitus a Deo diluuium terris imminere, arcam immensae magnitudinis ex lignis contexuit ac bitumine illitam impenetrabilem aquis reddidit; qua ille cum uxore ac filiis tribus et totidem nuribus est clausus. Volucrum etiam paria itidem diuersi generis bestiarum eodem claustro recepta. Reliqua omnia diluuio absumpta. Igitur Noe, cum iam imbrem uim destitisse et quieto in salo arcam circumferri intelligeret, ratus, id quod erat, aquas decedere, coruum primum explorandae rei gratia, eoque non reuertente – ut ego conicio, cadaueribus detentum – emisit columbam: quae cum consistendi locum non reperisset, reuersa est. Rursum remissa folium oliuae retulit, manifestum indicium nudari cacumina arborum. Tertio demum emissa non rediit: unde animaduersum aquas destitisse. Ita Noe arcam egressus est.[141]

> [But an innocent life saved Noah, a just man, from the sentence that had been decided. Warned by God that a flood was to threaten the earth, he constructed a wooden ark of immense size, waterproofed it with pitch, and shut himself inside along with his wife and his three sons and their wives. Pairs of birds and of a diverse stock of beasts were likewise sheltered in the same hold. Everything left outside was submerged by the flood. So when Noah realized that the torrential rain had ceased and that the ark was riding on calm seas, he surmised (as was the case) that the waters had subsided, so to test it he first sent out a raven. When it did not return (occupied, I presume, with the dead bodies) he sent out a dove, which came back when it could find no place to alight. Dispatched once more, it brought back an olive branch, clear evidence that the treetops were above water. The third time it did not return, from which Noah concluded that the waters had subsided. And so Noah left the ark.]

---

140 *Sulpice Sévère, Chroniques*, ed. Ghislaine de Senneville-Grave. The *Chronicon* survives in only a single eleventh-century manuscript, but a fragment from the second half of the ninth century has recently been published by Hartmut Hoffman, 'Der ältere Textzeuge der Chronik des Sulpicius Severus.' It was known to Frechulf, and Michael Gorman has recently shown that Adomnán copied a 'fairly long passage' verbatim ('Adomnán's *De locis sanctis*,' 34–5).

141 *Sulpice Sévère, Chroniques*, ed. De Senneville-Grave, II, 1–2 ; p. 94–6.

Sulpicius makes no reference to any spiritual significance for either motif or for the ark itself. In the entire paraphrase of the Old Testament (which runs to 192 pages in the critical edition) there are just three brief allusions to extra-literal meanings. To explain Deborah's unusual role as a female leader who ended the Israelites' twenty-year subjugation by the Canaanite king Jabin, Sulpicius notes that she is also a type of the church.[142] The other two are mere asides: Sulpicius mentions that *prudentes* interpret Lamech's slaying of an unnamed youth with reference to a 'future mystery' that he does not even bother to specify;[143] and he dismisses the change of Abraham's name with the remark that 'the mystery of the matter is not for the present work to expound.'[144] The *Genesis A* poet, we may recall, suppresses the change of names of Abraham and his wife, thereby simplifying the narrative and at the same time obviating any typological reading.

The genre of Universal History did not constrain figural interpretation for every early medieval chronicler or historian. Gregory of Tours, for example, periodically interrupts his narrative of biblical history in the *Historia Francorum* to point out figurative associations of selected events,[145] and Bede does so often in the chronicle inserted in his *De temporum ratione*.[146] Bede's work established an alternative model, yet to my knowledge only two early medieval chroniclers, the anonymous compiler of *The Chronicle of 741* and Ado of Vienne (d. 875), adopted Bede's approach.[147]

The persistence of the literal mode of Universal History after Bede is evident in the extensive *Historiae* of Frechulf of Lisieux, dating from 829/830.[148] Frechulf does not provide a continuous narrative summary of Genesis but focuses on selected episodes and verses. Although Frechulf (in a letter of ca 824) had asked Hrabanus Maurus to write a commentary on the Pentateuch dealing first with the literal sense and then with the

---

142 Ibid., I, 23.3; p. 148.
143 Ibid., I, 1; p. 92.
144 Ibid., V, 1; p. 100.
145 B. Krusch and W. Levison, eds., *Historia Francorum*, vol. 1, 1–9.
146 Charles W. Jones, ed., *De temporum ratione*, 463–544.
147 Unfortunately the Genesis section of *The Chronicle of 741* was omitted by Georg Waitz in his edition, *Chronicon universale 741*, MGH Scriptores 15 (Hanover: Hahn, 1881), but McKitterick, *Perceptions of the Past*, 23–8, indicates that it draws on Bede; her reproduction (fig. 4) of the beginning of the chronicle in Munich, BSB Clm 246, fol. 4v, shows that it includes a Christological interpretation of the etymology (*resurrectio*) of Seth's name. Ado's *Chronicon* is in *PL* 123.23–143.
148 Michael I. Allen, ed., *Frechulfi Lexoviensis episcopi opera omnia*.

spiritual, in his own work Frechulf set out to narrate only the *res gestae* of human history from Adam down to Pope Boniface's conversion of the Pantheon to a church dedicated to all martyrs. He adopts the Augustinian theme of the two cities as a broad framework for interpreting biblical history,[149] but his discussion of specific passages from the Old Testament, though often elaborate, rarely appeals to levels other than the literal. As he states in his preface, 'I have not neglected to elucidate difficult questions insofar as it pertains to the truth of history' (*quantum adtinet ad historiae ueritatem*).[150] On the few occasions when he does allude to a spiritual interpretation of Genesis, it is in the context of affirming the historicity of the literal narrative.[151] Throughout his account of Noah and the flood, Frechulf focuses on problems raised by the historical level, especially ones that have aroused scepticism as to its plausibility, such as how Noah would have had the ability or the time to build such a massive ship (Frechulf reminds doubters that Noah had a hundred years to complete the job and that men of the first age were very strong [I.1, 21]). At the end of book I and the beginning of book II, Frechulf restates his intention to recount the *historiae ueritas* from the beginning of the world to the birth of Abraham to the birth of Christ, with consideration of any difficult matter only 'insofar as it pertains to the narration of actual deeds and the reckoning of history' (*quantum adtinet ad rei gestae narrationem* [I.1, 57]; *quantum ad historiae rationem adtinet* [I.2, prol.]).[152]

My purpose in surveying these Latin chronicles and histories is not to suggest that the *Genesis A* poet was directly influenced by any one of

---

149 See Nikolaus Staubach, '*Christiana tempora*. Augustin und das Ende der alten Geschichte in der Weltchronik Frechulfs von Lisieux,' 167–206.

150 Allen, ed., *Frechulfi opera omnia*, 1:18.

151 Thus, although (*quamuis*) the Tree of Life, like the rock in the desert from which Moses struck water, mystically signifies Christ, it existed in paradise *corporaliter* (I.1, 4; ed. Allen, 1:30). Again, the sin of Lamech, which had been avenged to the seventy-seventh generation, is equated with the sin of the entire world, absolved by the shedding of Christ's blood, because the generations from Adam to Christ numbered seventy-seven 'according to the truth of history' (I.1, 17; ed. Allen, 1:44). And even if it mattered to 'the sacred mystery and the *figura* of the actual event' what precise numbers of such tiny creatures as flies and gnats were on board Noah's ark, that was God's concern, not Noah's! (I.1, 23; ed. Allen, 1:49).

152 Cf. I.7, 19: 'Hanc igitur annorum seriem, a protoplausto scilicet usque ad Domini aduentum, in singulis prout potuimus regnis ex celebrioribus factis enarrare curauimus.'

them[153] but rather to show that for many early medieval authors – even some who also wrote or commissioned allegorical commentaries on the Old Testament – the genre of Universal History dictated a literal approach to the biblical narrative. In the words of Henri de Lubac,

> Nor again will one forget, if one does not want to set up artificial oppositions everywhere, that there have always been certain writings that, owing to their very character or the particular end they have in view, contain exclusively or at least predominantly a literal exegesis ... It does not follow that the authors of such writings ought to be included among the 'literalists.' The same will be said for the redactors of chronicles: a certain Fréculphe of Lisieux in the ninth century announces his plan to restrict himself in his *Chronicle* to a short summary of the *historiae ueritas*; the same goes in the twelfth century for Godfrey of Viterbo in his *Pantheon*; in the chapters of his *Chronicon* where he summarizes the history of the Bible, Otto of Freising does not, at least not habitually, give himself over to allegory or morality; he informs the reader of the fact that his specialty is *historia*, not dogmatic or spiritual exposition.[154]

A similar approach to Old Testament paraphrase in the context of vernacular historiography is exemplified by the Middle Irish *Lebor Gabála Érenn* (Book of the Taking of Ireland), dating from about the middle of the eleventh century and surviving in three main recensions consisting of

---

153 There is, nonetheless, evidence for the circulation of some of these works in Anglo-Saxon England. Bede knew the chronicles of Eusebius-Jerome, Prosper, and Isidore; see Michael Lapidge, *The Anglo-Saxon Library*, 207, 212, 224. Isidore's chronicle was a source for annals in the Anglo-Saxon chronicle, according to Janet Bately, 'World History in the *Anglo-Saxon Chronicle*,' 188 (see also Susan Irvine's entry, 'The Sources of Anglo-Saxon Chronicle MS E,' 2002), and for passages in two Ælfrician homilies (ÆHomM11 [Assmann 4] and ÆHom 10 (ed. Pope); see Lapidge, *The Anglo-Saxon Library*, 261). Eusebius-Jerome and Prosper may have also been used in the Old English *Orosius* and by Ælfric, *Catholic Homilies* I.40 (see Lapidge, 257 and 263). Frechulf is listed as a possible source for the Orosius by the *Fontes Anglo-Saxonici*. There are, however, no surviving Anglo-Saxon manuscripts of any of these chronicles. The three manuscripts of part I of Frechulf listed by Helmut Gneuss, *Handlist of Anglo-Saxon Manuscripts: A List of Manuscripts and Manuscript Fragments Written or Owned in England up to 1100*, nos. 74, 724, 725, are all post-conquest. However, Lapidge (*The Anglo-Saxon Library*, 172) lists a ninth-century fragment of Frechulf's *Historia* that was in England (?Peterborough) before the conquest, and an entry, 'Fredulfus historiographus,' in a Peterborough booklist of s. xi/xii probably refers to this work (Lapidge, 144 and 146 [no. 25]).

154 Henri de Lubac, *Medieval Exegesis*, vol. 2, 214–15.

extended prose narrative that is supplemented by poems and glosses.[155] The *Lebor Gabála* is a synthetic history of Ireland whose closest models are the barbarian histories of the Germanic peoples, such as those by Cassiodorus, Isidore, and Fredegarius.[156] The *Lebor Gabála*, however, is also part Universal History, beginning with Creation and continuing through the Exodus. At several points it conflates biblical paraphrase with mythological narratives of the successive takings of Ireland and of the progenitors of the Irish people (such as Nél, who is said to have met Moses and married a daughter of Pharoah named Scota, from whom the *Scotti* derive their name). In the lengthy biblical narrative of *Lebor Gabála*, there is no question of extra-literal interpretation. One searches in vain the three major redactions with their prose paraphrase of Genesis, poems, and explanatory glosses for any kind of figural exegesis of the biblical narrative.[157]

Lebor Gabála, does, however, frequently expand the biblical narrative with pseudo-historical information drawn both from patristic and apocryphal sources. Like *Genesis A*, for example, *Lebor Gabála* inserts a description of the fall of Lucifer (17–19 and 26–7 [§3]). Some of the glosses, moreover, reflect practical concerns and interests similar to those of the *Genesis A* poet. A comment on the bitumen of the ark, for example, is material rather than spiritual:

> Is é imorro aigned fil isin bidamain, nach milleadh cruimi na gaetha na uisce na tes ngreine, na crand do curter inti. (108–9)

> [Now this is the nature that pitch possesses, that no worms, nor winds, nor water, nor sun-heat destroys the timbers that have been placed in it.]

What is remarkable about this comment is that it seems to have been borrowed from Bede but with Bede's spiritual interpretation removed,

---

155 *Lebor Gabála Érenn*, ed. and trans. R.A.S. Macalister. For a more recent translation of the first recension, see John Carey in *The Celtic Heroic Age*, ed. and trans. John Koch and John Carey, 226–71.

156 For a valuable recent study, see John Carey, *The Irish National-Origin Legend*.

157 Another medieval Irish universal history, *The Irish Sex Aetates Mundi*, ed. and trans. Dáibhí Ó Cróinín, composed ca 1090, is primarily literal but does include two prominent allegorical passages, one on the dimensions of Noah's ark (71/113 [§19]), omitted in the second and third recensions, and one on Babylon (93–5/129–30 [§§60–2]), which has been suspected as a late addition but is defended by Ó Cróinín (32–4).

suggesting that the glossator was only interested in the literal information.[158] Other glosses note that Noah sent out the dove seven days after the
raven (1:120–1 [§65.8] and 1:34–5 [§14]; cf. 243 note) and that he cursed
the raven for insubordination (not for being a demon in allegorical guise)
(1:121–3 [§65]); the dove's failure to return is rationalized in the same
straightforward terms as in *Genesis A* (1482): 'for there was no need' (*uair
na rangadar a les* [1:122–3 (§65)]). As in *Genesis A* we are told (in one of
the interpolated poems) that Christ opened the door of the ark (1:190–1
[poem V, stanza 45]); however, Christ is otherwise conspicuous by his
absence – except insofar as he co-dwells in every reference to the deity.

   Genesis A (1547–8) and *Lebor Gabála* (1:168–9 [poem I, stanza 2]; 186–7
[poem V, stanza 37]) both also supply, in closely similar form, apocryphal
names of the wives of Noah and his sons. Although Gollancz was probably right to regard this unmetrical list in *Genesis A* as an interpolation,[159]
it is telling that the one intrusive gloss that has been identified involves not
an allegorical or typological equation but a literal, pseudo-historical supplement. Aside from the compiler of the Junius 11 manuscript and the in-
terpolator of *Genesis B*, the Anglo-Saxon who added these names is the
only specific reader of *Genesis A* who has left us direct evidence of his response to the poem;[160] and to the extent we can extrapolate from this one

---

158 Compare Bede, *In principium Genesis* II.vi.14–15, CCSL 118A, 105–6, lines 1168–72:
     'Bitumen est feruentissimum et uiolentissimum gluten cuius haec uirtus est ut ligna
     quae ex eo fuerint oblita nec uermibus exedi, nec solis ardore, uel uentorum flatibus,
     uel aquarum possint inundatione dissolui. Vnde, quid aliud mystice in bitumine
     quam constantia fidei accipitur?' It is possible, of course, that Bede and the *Lebor
     Gabála* draw on a common source for the literal information and that Bede added
     the allegorical gloss.
159 Sir Israel Gollancz, *The Caedmon Manuscript of Anglo-Saxon Biblical Poetry, Junius XI
     in the Bodleian Library*, lxiii. Gollancz's suggestion is endorsed by Alfred Bammesberger,
     'Hidden Glosses in Manuscripts of Old English Poetry,' 44–5.
160 There is some other evidence within the poem for the responses of Anglo-Saxon read-
     ers prior to the compilation of Junius 11. Paul Remley has argued, for example, that
     the sectional divisions in *Genesis A* were added by a reviser familiar with sectional
     divisions similar to those surviving in early medieval copies of Genesis, including the
     Codex Amiatinus (*Old English Biblical Verse*, 119–20). This putative reviser's response
     to *Genesis A*, to the extent that we can reconstruct it, was therefore primarily at the
     level of narrative structure. Other readers have supplied some accent marks, but these
     afford little basis for reconstructing a notional response (beyond grammatical or met-
     rical parsing) of the poem; see Doane, *Genesis A*, 14–15, and Katherine O'Brien
     O'Keeffe, *Visible Song*, 182–3. Finally, we may be able to identify one other Anglo-
     Saxon reader of *Genesis A*, one whose own response to the Genesis narrative is at-
     tested independently: the *Beowulf* poet. Klaeber, a stern critic of the scholarly method

annotation, his response, though learned, involved a very different kind of learning from that postulated as normative by Huppé and Doane. Yet such non-biblical but not extra-literal information circulated widely in apocryphal narratives, in catechetical summaries, in question-and-answer dialogues, in concise notes that recur in Irish and Anglo-Saxon sources,[161] and in insular biblical paraphrases. The Middle Irish *Saltair na Rann*, a massive poetic survey of the Bible dating from the end of the tenth century, is as lavish with supplementary literal-historical data of this kind as it is sparing of figural interpretation.[162] The poet seems to regard such learning as the

---

of cataloguing *Parallelstellen*, was nonetheless convinced that the *Beowulf* poet was directly influenced by *Genesis A* ('Die *Ältere Genesis* und der *Beowulf*,' 321–38). Doane too has accepted that the 'extensive common vocabulary of the two poems places them together' and that the syntactic and contextual evidence adduced by Klaeber 'implies the priority of *Genesis A*' (37). As Theodore M. Andersson has suggested, 'If this dependence can be regarded as fairly established, the implications may not have been sufficiently appreciated. The connection suggests something about the *Beowulf* poet's literary culture and monastic models' ('Sources and Analogues,' 144). At the same time, the connection suggests something about the reception of *Genesis A* and potentially about the kind of audience for whom it was intended. The *Beowulf* poet's apparent borrowings from or echoes of *Genesis A* do not, of course, amount to a paraphrasable interpretation of that poem, but he seems to have shared with the *Genesis A* poet an interest in apocryphal narrative expansions of Genesis, and none of his allusions to Genesis involves an extra-literal signification.

161   Old English notes on biblical topics are conveniently indexed by N.R. Ker, *Catalogue of Manuscripts Containing Anglo-Saxon*, 520, s.v. 'Commonplaces.' The commentary in Cross and Hill, eds., *The Old English Prose Solomon and Saturn*, is particularly valuable for tracing such material in both Old English and Anglo-Latin. Remley, *Old English Biblical Verse*, 43–93, surveys various textual, liturgical, and pedagogical means by which biblical knowledge was transmitted in Anglo-Saxon England.

162   The only complete edition of the poem is not accompanied by a translation: *The Saltair na Rann*, ed. Whitley Stokes. Stokes's text is available online with corrections at CELT: The Corpus of Electronic Texts, http://www.ucc.ie/celt/published/G202001/index.html. The only published translation to date covers just the section on Adam and Eve: *The Irish Adam and Eve Story from Saltair na Rann*, ed. and trans. David Greene and Fergus Kelly, with commentary by Brian Murdoch. Murdoch has subsequently published a summary study of several following sections: 'From the Flood to the Tower of Babel,' 69–92. Through the generosity of Fergus Kelly, I have been able to consult unpublished draft translations of the sections narrating the stories of Creation, the Flood, the Tower of Babel, and the Exodus from Egypt (my citations are to Stokes's edition by line number; translations are by Greene and Kelly). In the stanzas devoted to paraphrasing the book of Genesis, totalling nearly three-thousand lines, the poet retails just one figural interpretation: the three days that Adam's body was without a soul are said to be a figure of Christ's resurrection (lines 1045–8; ed. and trans. Greene and Kelly, 24–5).

province of *senchaide*, the class of professional historians; he claims that in the time of Nimrod 'the historians [*senchaidi*] of the seed of Adam' related ancient 'stories' (*scela*), including the expulsion from paradise, the murder of Abel, and Noah's flood (2713–24), and he invokes 'reliable historians' (*senchad slán* [1059]) as sources for the statement that Eve was formed nine months after Adam's creation.

Saltair na Rann is not, of course, a history like *Lebor Gabála*, and neither is *Genesis A*. But the *Genesis A* poet's close adherence to the literal narrative can be understood as a consequence of an historiographical rather than an exegetical *modus tractandi*. The poet does incorporate details from biblical commentaries but chiefly to supplement the sometimes spare historical data of the Bible rather than to stimulate meditation on extra-literal levels of meaning. Other prominent features of the poem can be viewed in generic terms as well, notably the heavy emphasis on genealogies.[163] Although the poet condenses some genealogical matter from the Bible, most readers of *Genesis A* will be more impressed (if not depressed) by the amount of genealogical detail he does manage to versify and even elaborate upon. As Bloch has emphasized, 'the defining mode of universal history was that of genealogy ... [T]here is in the Eusebius-Jerome world-chronicle no way of separating the sequence of events from paternal succession ... Humanity evolves according to a process of accretion, beginning with a single set of parents.'[164] Genealogy was, of course, also a defining mode of secular history for the Anglo-Saxons, as is reflected in historical works such as Asser's *Life of Alfred*, which includes a genealogy reaching back to Adam,[165] and the Parker Chronicle for 855, which traces the lineage of Æthelwulf back to Adam through a special son of Noah, Hraþraing, who was born in the ark.[166] Again, battle narratives and migration scenes stimulate the author of *Genesis A* to poetic elaboration grounded in heroic rather than exegetical traditions. The manifest destiny of God's chosen people is proven by the martial valour of Abraham in the battle with the Five Kings and the rapid expansion of his progeny. The scattering of nations after the

---

163 On the relation between genealogy and history in the poems of the Junius manuscript, see Karkov, *Text and Picture*, 143–58, esp. 154. My suggestion was developed independently of Karkov, who also compares the genealogies in the Anglo-Saxon Chronicle.

164 Bloch, *Etymologies*, 37. Although the passage that Bloch quotes (38) to illustrate this is unfortunately from the spurious *Exordium libri*, his statement about the centrality of genealogy is valid for the authentic parts of the Eusebius-Jerome *Chronicon*.

165 *Asser's Life of King Alfred*, ed. W.H. Stevenson, 3–4.

166 Raymond W. Chambers, *Beowulf*, 202. See Thomas D. Hill, 'The Myth of the Ark-Born Son of Noe and the West-Saxon Royal Genealogical Tables,' 379–83.

Tower of Babel is recast in the form of a 'migration myth' that, in Paul Battles's words, 'places the biblical and Germanic migrations within a single historic continuum, situating the Anglo-Saxons' immediate, regional-tribal history within the larger framework of universal Christian history.'[167] The poet's moral perspective that calls attention to the exemplary rather than the typological value of the key figures of biblical history is likewise consonant with the medieval understanding of *historia* as a genre that attempts to inspire the reader 'to imitate the good' when it tells of 'good men and their good estate,' and 'to eschew what is harmful and perverse' when it tells of 'the evil ends of wicked men,' as Bede says in the preface to his *Historia ecclesiastica*.[168] So too, according to Bede, the poet Cædmon, who sang of creation and the origin of the human race and all the story or *history (tota historia)* of Genesis, intended 'to turn his hearers away from delight in sin and arouse in them the love and practice of good works.'[169]

There is also evidence that the poet was familiar with distinctive stylistic conventions of Anglo-Saxon historical writing. Thomas D. Hill has shown that the poet's elaborately varied circumlocutions for death that are applied to the good patriarchs have close parallels in Anglo-Latin historiography.[170] I believe that the poet also employs an historiographical formula in his rendering of the first verse of Genesis. In lines 112–13, after having described the fall of the rebel angels, the poet announces the beginning of world history with the words,

Her ærest gesceop   ece Drihten,
helm eallwihta,   heofon and eorðan.

[Here the eternal Lord, the protector of all things, first created heaven and earth.]

The poet's use of *her* with a preterite verb to record an event (the *primordial* event) is a striking anticipation, if not an appropriation, of the

---

167 Battles, '"Migration Myth,"' 65.
168 *Bede's Ecclesiastical History of the English Nation*, ed. and trans. Bertram Colgrave and R.A.B. Mynors, 2–3.
169 *Historia ecclesiastica* IV.24, ed. and trans. Colgrave and Mynors, 418–19. In Bede's summary of the content and purpose of Cædmon's poetic works there is no reference to higher exegesis.
170 Thomas D. Hill, 'The "Variegated Obit" as an Historiographic Motif in Old English Poetry and Anglo-Latin Historical Literature,' 102–24.

technical language of the *Anglo-Saxon Chronicle*, which introduces annal entries with the same formula.[171] The *her/hic* convention, which Peter Clemoes regarded as a technological innovation of the 890 chronicle,[172] can be traced back as far as the Franks Casket in a different application, as a formula for inscriptions or *tituli* accompanying an image (such *tituli* appear alongside several illustrations in the Junius manuscript).[173] However, the context of this passage in *Genesis A* suggests an historiographical formula, one whose placement at the very moment of Creation and the opening of Genesis signals the poet's conception of the biblical narrative, and of his own narrative, as history.

---

171 Remley, *Old English Biblical Verse*, 37 n. 62, notes that line 112 contains two apparent echoes of *Cædmon's Hymn* (l. 4a, *ece drihten*; l. 5a, *he ærest scop*). Assuming these are not fortuitous, the substitution of *her* for *he* could have been made by the poet himself, or by a later scribe or redactor familiar with the Chronicle convention.

172 Clemoes, 'Language in Context: *Her* in the 890 Anglo-Saxon Chronicle,' 27–36.

173 The *her* convention in the Chronicle is both temporal and spatial, referring not only to a given year but also to its physical entry on the manuscript page.

The Economy of the Word in the Old English *Exodus*

MANISH SHARMA

In recent years the focus of criticism on the Old English *Exodus* has undergone some contraction. Against the older tendency to outline in detail potential patristic and liturgical antecedents is a determined scholarly effort to rethink the text's relationship to its native milieu without reductive appeals to a prevailing Germanic-heroic ethos.[1] Thus, on the one hand, Paul Remley and Daniel Anlezark have investigated potential Anglo-Latin exemplars, especially from the Aldhelmian corpus.[2] On the other hand, Phyllis Portnoy has demonstrated how the poet's deployment of a native mode of poetic composition would have encouraged a typological reading of *Exodus* for an audience unversed in exegetics.[3] The present reading combines the older concern about patristics with the newer, nativist focus.

My first priority, however, is not to investigate how specific details of the text originate in biblical commentary but to argue that the poet's hermeneutic paradigm reveals a commitment to a linguistic epistemology similar to, and perhaps derived from, that of Augustine. I attempt initially, therefore, to place *Exodus* within a philosophical, rather than an

---

1 For an account of the history of the exegetical approach to *Exodus*, see John P. Hermann, *Allegories of War*, 57–89. Resistance to the allegorical approach has come most prominently from Edward B. Irving, ed., *The Old English Exodus*, 28–35; Thomas A. Shippey, *Old English Verse*, 134–54; Nicholas Howe, *Migration and Mythmaking*, 72–107; and Judith N. Garde, *Old English Poetry in Medieval Christian Perspective*, 25–56.

2 See Nancy J. Speirs, *Hermeneutic Sensibility and the Old English 'Exodus'*; Paul G. Remley, 'Aldhelm as Old English Poet: *Exodus*, Asser, and the *Dicta Ælfredi*,' 90–108; Daniel Anlezark, 'Connecting the Patriarchs,' 171–88. See further Michael Lapidge, 'Versifying the Bible in the Middle Ages,' 11–40, who reconsiders the case for the influence of the late antique poet, Avitus, on *Exodus*.

3 Phyllis Portnoy, 'Ring Composition and the Digressions of *Exodus*,' 289–307.

exegetical, context. Second, in the notorious patriarchal (lines 362–442) and homiletic (lines 516–48) digressions, I attempt to demonstrate that the *Exodus* poet expresses this linguistic epistemology through the idiom of an indigenous and 'heroic' economic register. Robert Bjork, relying on the anthropological work of Marcel Mauss, observes that due to 'the gift-based nature of Anglo-Saxon society' a 'gift economy resides in language,' involving the exchange of speeches in Old English narrative poems.[4] Language and words thus have a material status, akin to treasure, in the mechanisms of exchange, binding together Anglo-Saxon aristocratic culture. Bjork focuses on *Beowulf*, but exactly such a treatment of language is operative in the digressions of *Exodus*; the organization of this linguistic economy, I contend, reveals the epistemological underpinnings of the text – knowledge is a process of exchange. Portnoy has done much to establish how the digressions are structurally intrinsic through her detailed analysis of the chiastic symmetry of *Exodus*. My analysis also supports claims for the poem's structural integrity;[5] however, whereas Portnoy has argued that the poem's native compositional mode would have educated an unlearned audience to read allegorically, I argue that the poet's own understanding of scriptural allegory is founded on an epistemology discernible in the poem's native economic mode.

Linguistic Epistemology

Augustine's writings had a decisive impact on later investigations into the relationship between language and knowledge. Marcia Colish sums up the case: 'The thought of St. Augustine occupies a position of central importance in the development of linguistic epistemology in the medieval West.'[6] Eugene Vance points to the crucial and strategic place that language occupies in Augustinian thought: 'All of Augustine's endeavours in metaphysics, epistemology, and exegesis coincide with a relentless effort to

---

4 Robert E. Bjork, 'Speech as Gift in *Beowulf*,' 995. On the social phenomenon of gift giving, see further Marcel Mauss, *The Gift*; John M. Hill, *The Cultural World in Beowulf*, 85–107. For a review of scholarship on the function of the gift exchange in Old English poetry, see also John M. Hill, 'Social Milieu,' 255–70, esp. 258–60.
5 Portnoy, 'Ring Composition,' 289–90. On the debate over interpolation, see Peter J. Lucas, ed., *Exodus*, 30–3; Paul G. Remley, *Old English Biblical Verse*, 170. All citations from *Exodus* are from Lucas's edition.
6 Marcia Colish, *The Mirror of Language*, 8.

define the functions and limits of human language.'[7] The limits of human language will concern us here, and these become apparent in an early and seminal passage from Augustine's *De doctrina Christiana* (I.vi):[8]

> Et tamen deus, cum de illo nihil digne dici possit, admisit humanae uocis obsequium, et uerbis nostris in laude sua gaudere nos uoluit. Nam inde est et quod dicitur deus. Non enim reuera in strepitu istarum duarum syllabarum ipse cognoscitur, sed tamen omnes latinae linguae scios, cum aures eorum sonus iste tetigerit, movet ad cogitandam excellentissimam quamdam immortalemque naturam.

> [And yet God, although nothing worthy of His greatness can be said of Him, has condescended to accept the worship of men's mouths, and has desired us through the medium of our own words to rejoice in His praise. For on this principle it is that He is called *Deus* (God). For the sound of those two syllables in itself conveys no true knowledge of His nature; but yet all who know the Latin tongue are led, when that sound reaches their ears, to think of a nature supreme in excellence and eternal in existence.][9]

Although Augustine's *De doctrina Christiana* has long been held as a primary source for medieval literary theory, and possibly influenced Anglo-Saxon authors in this respect,[10] it is Augustine's epistemology that provides the foundation for his instruction on proper scriptural interpretation.[11] We will see that the same is the case for the *Exodus* poet. Augustine here identifies the limits of human language by elucidating its purely indicative function. Thus, the human sign does not have the power to encompass divine

---

7 Eugene Vance, 'Saint Augustine: Language as Temporality,' in his *Mervelous Signals: Poetics and Sign Theory in the Middle Ages*, 34.

8 CCSL 32.10.10–17. On the circulation of *De doctrina Christiana* in Anglo-Saxon England, see further J.D.A Ogilvy, *Books Known to the English, 597–1066*, 84. The *Fontes Anglo-Saxonici* database returns thirty-six records as of 5 June 2008. See also Michael Lapidge, *The Anglo-Saxon Library*, 285. Bernard F. Huppé, *Doctrine and Poetry*, argues throughout for the influence of *De doctrina Christiana* on Old English literature.

9 D.W. Robertson Jr, trans., *On Christian Doctrine*, 10–11.

10 See further Martin Irvine, 'Anglo-Saxon Literary Theory Exemplified in Old English Poems,' 157–81; reprinted in *Old English Shorter Poems*, ed. Katherine O'Brien O'Keeffe, 31–64; Malcolm B. Parkes, '*Rædan, areccan, smeagan*,' 1–22. For a recent assessment of Augustine's presence in Anglo-Saxon England, see Thomas N. Hall, 'Biblical and Patristic Learning,' 335–7.

11 See further Huppé, *Doctrine and Poetry*, 28–63.

nature, although it can direct the mind towards contemplation of that nature. Human language is alienated from the divine due to the necessarily arbitrary and mediated nature of signification; by contrast, divine 'language' exists in a relation of unmediated reflexive complementarity to its source.[12] For Augustine, human beings enjoyed an unmediated apprehension of God and things only before the Fall through a divine and incorporeal semiotics characterized by a transparent relationship between sign and referent. He tells us in *De Genesi contra Manicheos* (II.iv.5) that, in the Garden of Eden, God 'irrigabat eam fonte interiore loquens in intellectu eius, ut non extrinsecus uerba exciperet tamquam de supradictis nubibus pluuiam, sed fonte suo, hoc est de intimis suis manante ueritate satiaretur' [irrigated (the soul) with an interior spring, speaking in its intellect: not from outside did it receive words, as if rain from the above-mentioned clouds, but rather from its own spring, that is, by truth spreading from its own interior, it was satiated].[13]

In *De fide et symbolo*, Augustine makes more precise the distinction between limited, post-lapsarian human language and perfect divine signification. There exists a flawless and self-reflexive concord between the mind of God and his Word due to the fact that the Word partakes of his essence:[14] 'Deus uero cum uerbum genuit, id quod est ipse genuit; neque de nihilo, neque de aliqua iam facta conditaque materia; sed de seipso id quod est ipse' [When God begat the Word, he made that which is himself; he did not make the Word out of nothing nor out of any ready-made and found material; but he made from himself that which is himself]. However, for humans, 'inter animum autem nostrum et uerba nostra, quibus eumdem animum ostendere conamur, plurimum distat' [between our minds and our words, with which we try to show our minds, there is a great difference].[15] The material and formal properties of human language, in other words, interrupt cognitive self-reflexivity.

---

12 See Eric Jager, *The Tempter's Voice*, 51–98.

13 Dorothea Weber, ed., *Augustinus: De Genesi contra Manichaeos.*

14 CSEL 41.7.17–20. See also *De catechizandis rudibus* (II.iii): 'distet sonus oris nostri ab illo ictu intelligentiae, quando ne ipsi quidem impressioni memoriae similis est' (the sound of our speech is different from the impact of intellectual apprehension since it does not even resemble the memory impression [CCSL 46.123.32–4]).

15 On the circulation of *De fide et symbolo* in Anglo-Saxon England, see Ogilvy, *Books Known to the English*, 88; Lapidge, *The Anglo-Saxon Library*, 285. Augustine also juxtaposes finite human language and perfect divine language in *De doctrina Christiana* (I.xiii): 'Nec tamen in eundem sonum cogitatio nostra conuertitur, sed apud se manens integra, formam uocis qua se insinuet auribus, sine aliqua labe suae mutationis assumit.

The difference between the human mind and human language, however, is ultimately an effect of temporality. The reflexive relationship between God and his Word is absolutely punctual and timeless since God remains eternally present to himself as pure Being beyond the temporality he engenders. According to Vance, '[i]f divine knowledge of temporality occurs, unlike man's, without division or difference within the knowing mind, so too God's eternal Word, unlike human speech, produces itself without any succession of syllables unfolding in time.'[16] So Augustine writes in his *Confessiones* (XI.ix):[17]

> Vocas itaque nos ad intelligendum uerbum Deum apud te Deum, quod sempiterne dicitur, et eo sempiterne dicuntur omnia: neque enim finitur quod dicebatur, et dicitur aliud ut possint dici omnia; sed simul ac sempiterne omnia ... Non ergo quidquam uerbi tui cedit atque succedit quoniam vere immortale atque aeternum est.

> [So you call us to understand the Word, God, with you, O God, which is spoken eternally, and in which all things are spoken eternally. Nor is it the case that what was spoken is ended and that another thing is said, so that all things may at length be said: all things are spoken once and forever ... Therefore no part of your Word gives place to another or takes the place of another, since it is truly eternal and immortal.]

Books 11–13 of the *Confessiones* contain a meditation on the relationship between human time, creation, and eternity; that Bede cites repeatedly from this part of Augustine's work in his commentary on Genesis attests to knowledge of Augustine's speculations on temporality and language in early Anglo-Saxon England.[18]

Ita uerbum dei non commutatum, caro tamen factum est ut habitaret in nobis' (And yet our thought does not lose itself in the sound, but remains complete in itself, and takes the form of speech without being modified in its own nature by the change: so the Divine Word, though suffering no change of nature, yet became flesh, that He might dwell among us [CCSL 32.13.4–8]).

16 Vance, 'Language as Temporality,' 38.

17 CCSL 27.198.1–11. See further Ogilvy, *Books Known to the English*, 83; Lapidge, *The Anglo-Saxon Library*, 282. *Fontes Anglo-Saxonici* returns three records as of 5 June 2008. I use Vance's translation for this citation from the *Confessiones* and the following citation from *De Trinitate*.

18 See John F. Kelly, 'Augustine' in *Sources of Anglo-Saxon Literary Culture*, ed. Biggs, Hill, and Szarmach, 71.

The lack of succession in the divine Word must be kept in mind when Augustine points to the temporal predicament of created things and the consequence of temporality for language in his *De Trinitate* (IV.xxi):[19]

Sed plane fidenter dixerim, patrem et filium et spiritum sanctum unius eius-demque substantiae, deum creatorem, trinitatem omnipotentem insepar-abiliter operari: sed ita non posse per longe imparem maximeque corpoream creaturam inseparabiliter demonstrari; sicut per uoces nostras, quae utique corporaliter sonant, non possunt pater et filius et spiritus sanctus, nisi suis et propriis interuallis temporum certa separatione distinctis, quae suae cujusque uocabuli syllabae occupant, nominari.

[But I would like to affirm plainly that the Father and the Son and the Holy Spirit, being of one and the same substance – God the creator, the omnipotent Trinity – are inseparable in their works, but it is the creation, so greatly dis-similar and corporeal, which constrains them to become separate in their manifestation, just as, with our words, which are of course corporeal sonor-ities, the Father and the Son and the Holy Spirit cannot be named except by fractions of duration proper to each, and clearly separated and occupied by the syllables of each word.]

Human words cannot represent the timeless unity of the divine nature because 'corporeal sonorities' take time to utter. His recognition of the temporal predicament that prevents human language from naming the Trinity allows Augustine to identify precisely the distinction between human language and the divine Word in *De Trinitate* (XV.xv):[20]

Ac per hoc etiam si concedamus, ne de controuersia uocabuli laborare uidea-mur, iam uocandum esse uerbum quiddam illud mentis nostrae quod de nostra scientia formari potest, etiam priusquam formatum sit, quia iam, ut ita dicam, formabile est; quis non uideat, quanta hic sit dissimilitudo ab illo Dei uerbo, quod in forma Dei sic est, ut non antea fuerit formabile priusquam formatum, nec aliquando esse possit informe, sed sit forma simplex et simpliciter aequalis ei de quo est, et cui mirabiliter coaeterna est?

---

19 CCSL 50.202.7–15. See further Ogilvy, *Books Known to the English*, 94; Lapidge, *The Anglo-Saxon Library*, 287. *Fontes Anglo-Saxonici* returns six records as of 5 June 2008. On Alcuin's use of *De Trinitate*, see Whitney F. Bolton, *Alcuin and Beowulf*, 139–41, and Michael Fox, 'Alcuin's *Expositio in epistolam ad Hebraeos*.'

20 CCSL 50A.499.70–78. Translation taken from Stephen McKenna, *St Augustine: The Trinity*, 490.

[And, therefore, even if we should concede, in order that we may not appear to be engaged in a controversy about words, that something of our own mind is already to be called a word which can be formed from our knowledge even before it is formed, because it is, so to say, already formable, who does not see how great its unlikeness is here to that Word of God, who is so in the form of God that He was not previously formable before he was formed, nor can He ever be formless, but that he is a simple form, and simply equal to Him from whom He is, and to whom He is in a marvellous way co-eternal?]

The radical distinction between divine and human language is here elucidated by direct comparison. Once more, Augustine illustrates how for mortals the time of Creation precludes the possibility of linguistic self-reflexivity, the specular and timeless correspondence of being and language that, by contrast, constitutes the relationship between God and his Word. The language of God, then, perfectly manifests his will and his presence in the form of the Son.

Language and Economy

The crucial elements of the Augustinian distinction between human and divine signification are, therefore, as follows: (1) God and his Word are identical, and the former exists in a timeless and reflexive relationship to the latter; and (2) the representational capacity of human language, by contrast, is limited by temporality, and human words are shot through by division and difference. As Augustine says in *De doctrina Christiana*, human language, possessing only an indexical function, cannot provide any true knowledge of the divine nature and ultimate truth; in *De Trinitate*, this failure is linked intimately to time and the necessity of succession in creation. Divine language maintains its 'value' while human language always involves a *loss* of some kind because of the temporal mediation involved. The form of this Augustinian linguistic distinction may have influenced the *Exodus* poet's conception of language and its limits. This distinction is understood and expressed in the poem, I will argue, through a linguistic economy involving relative degrees of gain.

We should observe first how the narrative unfolds against the backdrop of a complex transactional matrix: Abraham's immolation of Isaac at lines 397–446 forms the basis of a positive economy whereby obedience is rewarded by God with property and treasure. The Christological dimension[21] of the

---

21 On the presence of Christ in the Old Testament, see Ruth M. Ames, 'The Old Testament Christ and the Old English *Exodus*,' 33–50, who argues also for a link

exchange underscores its structural authority in a text preoccupied by the struggle for salvation.²² The original transaction between Abraham and God secures the reward of both victory in battle and a homeland for his descendants; at line 19, accordingly, God is said to bestow the *handlean* (hand-reward) of victory on Moses and the Israelites by means of which they can dispossess their enemies of the Promised Land. The Egyptians, on the other hand, practise a false economy whereby they seek to repay (*gyldan* [line 150]) the Israelites for the services rendered on their behalf by Joseph (the *feorhlean* [line 150]) with treachery (*facne* [line 151]). For their disregard of an ordered principle of exchange, the Egyptians, in turn, receive from God a reward for actions (*dædlean* [line 263]) and a profound reward (*deop lean* [line 507]), the collection of which occurs, of course, under the Red Sea.²³ The poem closes with the Israelites' rejoicing amidst the spoils of war on the far side of the sea (lines 565–90), the proper distribution of wealth having been re-established as the drowned bodies of the Egyptians relinquish their treasures. God regulates the flow of wealth in the text's economy, occasionally diverting its course on behalf of his chosen people. John F. Vickrey's observations on the allegorical significance of the despoiling of the Egyptian host support this argument: the Israelites are the treasure of Pharoah, just as humankind belonged to the devil prior to the Redemption.²⁴ The movement of the *transitus* represents allegorically the impoverishment of Satan as he loses his 'riches' to Christ after the

---

between the *word* (word) imagery and the poet's subtle Trinitarianism. On the equation of *word* and Christ in Junius 11, see further Roberta Frank, 'Some Uses of Paronomasia in Old English Scriptural Verse,' 211–15.

22 See, for instance, *De Trinitate* (IV.xiii): 'Quam propterea dominus pro nobis indebitam reddidit ut nobis debita non noceret' (And, therefore, for our sake the Lord paid the tribute to death which was not due, in order that the death which was due might not injure us [CCSL 50.183.47–8]). The typological link between the sacrifice of Isaac and Christ is a patristic commonplace current in the Anglo-Saxon period; see Rabanus Maurus, *Commentariorum in Genesim*: 'Nam sicut Abraham unicum et dilectum filium Deo uictimam obtulit, ita Dominus unigenitum filium suum pro nobis omnibus tradidit' (For just as Abraham offered his only and beloved son to God, so God exchanged his only begotten son for us all [*PL* 107.568C]). On the theological 'economy' of the redemption, see further Stanislas Lyonnet and L. Sabourin, *Sin, Redemption, and Sacrifice*, 46–224.

23 The term *lean* occurs elsewhere in *Exodus*, at line 315, to describe the special 'reward' granted to the tribe of Judah.

24 See John F. Vickrey, '*Exodus* and the Treasure of Pharoah,' 159–65; '*Exodus* and the Robe of Joseph,' 1–17.

descensus.[25] The dynamic of transaction, profit, and loss, therefore, is a central structural principle in *Exodus*.

The focus of this essay is the participation of the *word* (word) in the poem, as a unit of exchange, within the poem's distributive scheme. The transfer of the *word* from God to Abraham fixes the covenant at line 428 in the patriarchal digression; the transfer of the *word* to the exegete at lines 523–6 in the homiletic digression conveys the profitable spiritual counsel without which, the poet tells us, we may not transcend this transitory and exilic existence. In both cases, words are described as material things, further attesting to the economic understanding of language that Bjork finds in Anglo-Saxon culture. However, as is not the case for the provision of land and treasure in the poem, the form of the exchange mutates, and the value of the *word* is susceptible to fluctuation. By tracing these fluctuations, we can perceive the manner with which the *Exodus* poet may have absorbed and transformed Augustine's epistemological distinction between human and divine signification.

In the opening passage of the poem, the famously ambiguous phrase *wræclico wordriht* at line 3 appears to denote, via syntactical parallelism with *Moyses domas*, the Mosaic 'word laws' of the Pentateuch that prefigure the new dispensation of Christ:[26]

Hwæt! We feor and neah   gefrigen habað
ofer middangeard   Moyses domas,
wræclico wordriht,   wera cneorissum,
in uprodor   eadigra gehwam
æfter bealusiðe   bote lifes,
lifigendra gehwam   langsumne ræd,
hæleðum secgan.   Gehyre se ðe wille. (lines 1–7)

[Lo! Far and near we have heard the laws of Moses, the wonderful word-laws, proclaim to the generations of men of the reward of life in heaven for each of the blessed after the perilous journey, of enduring counsel (or 'gain') for all living. Let him hear who will.]

---

25 It is striking that Augustine in *De doctrina Christiana* (II.xlii) argues that the wisdom of pagans should be appropriated for Christian use in the same way that the Israelites despoiled the Egyptians of their treasure by the command of God (CCSL 32.76.1–6).

26 On the syntactical arrangement of these lines, see Alfred Bammesberger, 'Die syntaktische Analyse von *Exodus* 1–7a,' 6–15.

Despite paralleling *Moyses domas*, it is impossible to read the term *wordriht* without acknowledging the series of – *riht* compounds in the text to which it belongs: *folcriht, landriht,* and *eðelriht*. The terms *eðelriht* at line 211 and *landriht* at line 354 both refer to the land promised to the Israelites to which they have a God-given 'right' on account of the obedience of Abraham. The *folcriht* at line 22 refers to the withdrawn 'folk right' or 'sovereignty' of the tribes that oppose the chosen people. Like the Promised Land, the *word* can be understood as that to which a proprietary right (*riht*) can attach; it is a unit of value that functions materially in the text's economy in a manner analogous to literal treasure.[27] The simplex *riht* appears with this sense also in *Exodus*: at line 338, the *frumbearnes riht* is the 'right of the first-born,' or patrimony, that Reuben forfeited on account of laying with Jacob's concubine (Genesis 49:3–4 and I Chronicles 5:1–2).[28] The sense of the compound, *wordriht*, is thus richer than has been recognized; their juridical significance aside, the *wordriht* have something in common with both property and patrimony.

The adjective *wræclic* that modifies *wordriht* intensifies the intratextual rapport of *wordriht* with the other –*riht* compounds; like Canaan, the rightful homeland from which the Israelites are alienated, the 'word rights' are both 'wondrous' and 'foreign.'[29] In this way, the *wordriht* are distanced; a hermeneutic, rather than spatial, estrangement is instituted, and only the *lifes wealhstod* (interpreter of life [line 523]), we are later told, can bridge it.[30] The value of the *word* derives from this initial inaccessibility, making it an object of desire (*Gehyre se ðe wille*) analogous to the Promised Land – the territory for which the Israelites are said at line 53 to endure 'a longstanding desire' (*langne lust*).

---

27 On the significance of the *landriht* and *eðelriht,* see L.L. Schücking, *Untersuchungen zur Bedeutungslehre der angelsächsischen Dichtersprache* 44: 'so ist *riht* nicht nur das Recht, sondern auch sein Gegenstand, neben Berechtigung auch Rechtsanteil, Besitz.'

28 The noun *riht* also appears at lines 186, 352, and 587; *riht* appears as an adjective ('straight') at line 126.

29 See Huppé, *Doctrine and Poetry*, 221, who translates *wræclico wordriht* as 'pilgrim law.' On the typological significance of *wordriht*, see Maxwell Luria, 'The Old English *Exodus* as a Christian Poem,' 600–6.

30 On the *lifes wealhstod* as Christ, see Dorothy Haines, 'Unlocking *Exodus* ll. 516–32,' 481–98, and Ames, 'The Old Testament Christ,' 33–50. As I have been arguing for the influence of Augustine's *De Trinitate* on *Exodus*, it is important to note that the phrase *mediator uitae* referring to Christ occurs eight times in book 4. The phrase occurs in only two other patristic works, both by authors referencing Augustine (Hincmar of Rheims and Eugippius of Africa).

To accept the *word* is to be granted access to a valuable benefit estimated in economic terms; only by means of the *word* may be attained the *bote lifes* (remedy / reward of life). Once the Israelites have crossed the Red Sea and symbolically attained their *landriht*, in the poet's compressed account of the exodus, they are said to have acquired a 'reward' or 'remedy' with the only other appearance of the term *bote* in the poem: *bliðe wæron   bote gesawon* (they were joyful, they perceived their reward/remedy [line 583]). In the latter context, moreover, the phrase *bote gesawon* stands in apposition to *heddon herereafes* (they took heed of the treasure [line 584]), both verses referring to the booty strewn over the far shore of the Red Sea. The phrase *bote lifes* at line 5 is syntactically paralleled by *langsumne ræd* at line 6, and this suggests that the poet is playing here on a secondary sense of *ræd*: not only 'counsel' or 'wisdom' but also 'profit' or 'gain.' Moses is said to provide *ece rædas* to the Israelites after the crossing of the Red Sea (line 516), and the poet seems to evoke both senses in this later passage also; the same phrase, for instance, appears at *Beowulf* line 1201 (*geceas ecne ræd*) and line 1760 (*þæt selre geceos, / ece rædas*) and both times means 'enduring gain(s).' Possession of the *word*, the poet plausibly is suggesting, brings with it profitable and enduring (*langsum*) returns. The opening seven lines of *Exodus*, therefore, orient desire towards the *wordriht* by comprehending their value in terms of treasure, land, and patrimony.

However, it is with the account of Abraham in the patriarchal digression that we first see the *word* operate as a unit of exchange:[31]

Ne sleh þu Abraham   þin agen bearn,
sunu mid sweorde.   Soð is gecyðed,
nu þin cunnode   cyning alwihta,
þæt þu wið waldend   wære heolde,
fæste treowe,   seo þe freode sceal
in lifdagum ' lengest weorðan
awa to aldre   unswiciendo.
Hu þearf mannes sunu   maran treowe?
Ne behwylfan mæg   heofon and eorðe
his wuldres word,   widdra and siddra

---

31 On the significance of the digression for the poet's larger thematic concerns, see Stanley
    R. Hauer, 'The Patriarchal Digression in the Old English *Exodus*, Lines 362–446,' 77–90.
    On the liturgical passages that may have inspired lines 427–31, see J.W. Bright, 'On the
    Anglo-Saxon Poem *Exodus*,' 17–18.

þonne befæðman   mæge foldan sceattas,
eorðan ymbhwyrft   ond uprodor,
garsecges gin   ond þeos geomre lyft. (lines 420–32)

[Do not slay, Abraham, your only child, your son with the sword. The truth
is revealed, now that the Almighty King has tried you, that you with the
Ruler held the covenant, the fast pledge; it shall turn into the most lasting
goodwill for you in the days of your life forever to eternity, unfailing. In what
way does the son of man need a greater pledge? Heaven and earth cannot
encompass his word of glory, which is more ample and spacious than the
earth's expanse, the circuit of the world and heaven above, the vastness of the
sea, and this sorrowful air can contain.]

In a manner reminiscent of that of the ideal Germanic retainer, Abraham's
compliance places lord over kin. The corresponding account of the angel's
speech in *Genesis A* stresses not only the value of this prioritization but
also the great profitability of the exchange:[32]

Mago Ebrea,   þu medum scealt
þurh þæs halgan hand   heofoncyninges,
soðum sigorleanum   selfa onfon,
ginfæstum gifum.   Þe wile gasta weard
lissum gyldan   þæt þe wæs leofre his
sibb and hyldo   þonne þin sylfes bearn. (lines 2917–22)

[Hebrew warrior, you yourself shall receive recompense through the blessed
hand of the king of heaven, true victory rewards and ample gifts. The guardian of spirits will repay you with favours because his love and protection was
more precious to you than your own son.]

The preoccupation of the *Genesis A* poet with the rich reward that accompanies the transaction is highlighted by comparison to the more laconic biblical account (Genesis 22:16–17): 'Per memetipsum iuraui, dicit
Dominus: quia fecisti hanc rem, et non pepercisti filio tuo unigenito propter me: benedicam tibi' (By my own self have I sworn, saith the Lord: because thou hast done this thing, and hast not spared thy only begotten son

---

32 Citation taken from Doane, ed., *Genesis A*.

for my sake: I will bless thee).[33] The *Exodus* poet, like the *Genesis A* poet, is also keen to demonstrate the great value of Abraham's sacrifice. Thus, Abraham receives from God 'the most lasting goodwill ... forever to eternity.' The *freod* of God is described in terms strongly reminiscent of the 'everlasting counsel' provided by the *wordriht* (line 6) or the 'enduring counsel' provided by Moses' words on the Red Sea shore at line 516. Nevertheless, the precise nature of this goodwill is not immediately apparent, on account of the elliptical syntax of the passage. It does seem to be the case that God is replacing the old pledge (*treow*) with Abraham regarding Isaac (line 424) for a new pledge (*treow*) regarding the Promised Land (line 427). Lines 428–32, arguably, expand upon this latter promise, of which the poet asks rhetorically, 'In what way does the son of man need a greater pledge?' The elements *treow* at line 427 and *word* at line 429, then, are syntactically apposed, and the poet goes on to describe the 'greatness' of the *word* in the following lines. If we accept this reading, we see the *Exodus* poet's originality in comparison to the laconic Vulgate account and the account in *Genesis A*. Instead of gaining God's blessing or great gifts, in *Exodus* the poet specifies that Abraham receives God's *word* for his sacrifice. And yet, as with the *Genesis A* account, Abraham's initial obedience returns an infinite profit, as God's word is said to be boundless, unable to be encompassed by heaven, earth, or sea. A 'greater pledge' (*maran treowe*) is impossible because God's *word* is infinite, requiring no supplement. Informed by the Anglo-Saxon conception of a linguistic gift economy, the word is described in material terms, and its great value is attested to by its infinite size.

The mastery of God over the boundaries of the universe is a motif anticipated by his exchange with Moses earlier in the poem (lines 22–9), an addition to the biblical narrative: addressing him for the first time 'with words' (*wordum*), God tells of the creation of the world, in particular the creation of the *eorðan ymbhwyrft ond uprodor* (line 26) – a verse that is repeated verbatim at line 430 in the passage cited above. The repetition appears strategic: both God and his word master and transcend earthly limits; both share the same nature. We saw above the correspondence between God and his word in Augustine's linguistic theory; this correspondence finds in *Exodus* a reflex in the shared infinitude of God and his word.

---

33 All citations from the Vulgate are taken from R. Weber, ed., *Biblia sacra*. All translations are taken from the Douay-Rheims Version (1582–1609).

Paul Remley recently has suggested, as a direct source for lines 427–31, three hexameters from Aldhelm's *Carmen de uirginitate*: 'Illum nec terrae nec possunt cingere caeli / Nec mare nauigerum spumoso gurgite uallat / Aut zonae mundi, quae stipant aethera celsa' (Neither the earth nor the sky can enclose him, nor can the navigable sea with its foaming flood surround him, nor the regions of the world, which press up against the lofty air).[34] If we accept Remley's proposal, and indeed the phrasing of the two passages is strikingly similar, the significance of the divergence between Aldhelm and *Exodus* is amplified. Aldhelm uses the boundaries of the world to describe the infinitude of God; the *Exodus* poet uses language almost identical to Aldhelm's but to describe the infinitude of God's *word*.

That lines 420–32 present God's word of glory in terms of quantitative measure underscores its material status; the *wuldres word* here is an immense treasure, the infinite size of which perfectly corresponds to the infinite tally of Abraham's descendants:

> He að swereð,   engla þeoden,
> wyrda waldend   and wereda god,
> soðfæst sigora,   þurh his sylfes lif,
> þæt þines cynnes   and cneowmaga,
> randwiggendra,   rim ne cunnon,
> yldo ofer eorðan,   ealle cræfte
> to gesecgenne   soðum wordum,
> nymðe hwylc þæs snottor   in sefan weorðe
> þæt he ana mæge   ealle geriman
> stanas on eorðan,   steorran on heofonum,
> sæbeorga sand,   sealte yða. (lines 432–42)

[He will swear an oath on his own life, the Prince of angels, the Ruler of the workings of Providence, the God of hosts, the Lord of victories fixed in truth, that of your tribe and kin, of your shield-warriors, men over the earth with all their skill will not be able to tell the number with true words, unless there should be someone so wise in his mind that he alone can number all the stones on the earth, the stars in the heavens, the sand of the sea cliffs, and the salty waves.]

---

34 Remley, 'Aldhelm as Old English Poet,' 92–3.

Where the previous passage stressed the boundless nature of the *wuldres word*, the poet here stresses the finitude of its human counterparts. We have seen that God's word is limitless; it exceeds the bounds of earth, heaven, and sea. God's infinite 'language,' we could say, partakes of his being. The words of men, however, are circumscribed by precisely the limits that the word of God transcends, being incapable of numbering the stones, the stars, and the waves. The corresponding Vulgate passage contains no such reference to inexpressibility (Genesis 22:17): 'et multiplicabo semen tuum sicut stellas cæli, et uelut arenam quæ est in littore maris: possidebit semen tuum portas inimicorum suorum' (and I will multiply thy seed as the stars of heaven, and as the sand that is by the seashore: thy seed shall possess the gates of their enemies). Genesis 13:16, however, also describes the Abrahamic covenant: 'faciamque semen tuum sicut puluerem terrae; si quis potest hominum numerare puluerem, semen quoque tuum numerare poterit' (And I will make your seed as the dust of the earth; if any man is able to count the dust of the earth, he will also be able to count your seed). While Genesis 13:16 provides a source for the reference to a man counting the uncountable, Daniel Anlezark has proposed the condensed version of the Abraham narrative in Hebrews 11:12 as a source for the Old English passage's reference to inexpressibility: 'tamquam sidera caeli in multitudinem, et sicut arena quae est ad oram maris innumerabilis' (as the stars of the heaven in multitude, and as innumerable as the sand which is by the shore of the sea).[35]

It is striking that Genesis and Hebrews account for everything in lines 432–42 of *Exodus* except for the poet's mention of 'true words' at line 438.[36] This addition, while subtle, is unlikely to be casual or accidental. Explicit reference to the failure of human language in this context suggests that the poet is intent on differentiating the illimitable word of God and limited human words, especially as the infinitude of God's word has been described only nine lines earlier and in terms that anticipate the finitude of human words (*heaven*, *earth*, and *sea* anticipate *stars*, *stones*, and *waves*). The close juxtaposition of linguistic infinitude and finitude argues against a formulaic deployment of the inexpressibility topos.

---

35 Anlezark, 'Connecting the Patriarchs,' 177. See also Remley, *Old English Biblical Verse*, 191, who suggests an Old Latin source for this passage. On the importance of counting and numbering to the *Exodus* poet, see further P.F. Ferguson, 'Noah, Abraham, and the Crossing of the Red Sea,' 282–7.

36 The phrase *soðum wordum* occurs elsewhere in *Exodus* at line 522, describing the Decalogue.

The infinitude of the word of God is conveyed by its physically massive stature (*widdra ond siddra*), which corresponds both to the infinite number of Abraham's descendants that it engenders and to God's own infinitude. The finitude of human words is conveyed in qualitative, rather than quantitative, terms by their inability to comprehend and represent reality. In this way, linguistic finitude is made a product of temporality by the poet: a state of affairs postulated via the absurdity that a mortal life could be sufficient to enumerate *in words* the particulate constituents of the universe. There is simply not enough time for such a linguistic feat to be accomplished. Paradoxically, we cannot understand Abraham's successful transaction with God, the exchange of Isaac for God's word of glory, without grasping the failure of words to account for it. The intrusion of time in this passage recalls Augustine's linguistic epistemology, where it is time that is the element that distinguishes human language from divine and reveals the epistemological limits on the former.[37] The phrase *soðum wordum* occurs once more in *Exodus* in a passage that again demonstrates the poet's concern to link language and time:

> Dægweorc ne mað
> swa gyt werðeode,   on gewritum findað
> doma gehwilcne,   þara ðe him drihten bebead
> on þam siðfate   soðum wordum. (lines 519b–22)

[The day's work was not concealed; accordingly the nations still find in scriptures each one of those laws which the Lord commended to them on that journey with true words.]

There is not enough time to number Abraham's descendants with true words, while the true words of God are untouched by time and can be found 'still' (*gyt*) in scripture. Temporality is once more the element that distinguishes human and divine language for the *Exodus* poet.

---

37 This enumerative (and representational) failure of the human word contrasts, perhaps ironically, with more modest success in this regard earlier in the patriarchal digression: 'Swa þæt wise men **wordum** secgað / þæt from Noe **nigoða** wære fæder / Abrahames on folctale' (Accordingly, wise men say with words that from Noah ninth in the line of descendants was Abraham's father [lines 377–9]). The poet refers to a similar intellectual limitation in the Noah digression where the different species aboard the ark are described as 'missenlicra þonne men cunnon' (more various than men know [line 373]).

Investment and Profit

The distinction made between the finitude and infinitude of the *word* in its manifestations in the patriarchal digression allows for a new perspective on the allusion to the Pauline trope of the Letter and the Spirit (II Corinthians 3:6) in a vexed passage from the homiletic digression:[38]

> Gif onlucan wile   lifes wealhstod,
> beorht in breostum,   banhuses weard,
> ginfæsten god   gastes cægon,
> run bið gerecenod,   ræd forð gæð;
> hafað wislicu   word on fæðme,
> wile meagollice   modum tæcan,
> þæt we gesne ne syn   Godes þeodscipes,
> Metodes miltsa.   He us ma onlyhð,
> nu us boceras   beteran secgað,
> lengran lyftwynna. (lines 523–32)

[If the interpreter of life, bright in the breast, the guardian of the bone-house, will unlock the good stronghold (or 'ample goods') with the keys of the spirit, the mystery will be explained, wisdom (or 'gain') shall advance; it (or 'he') has wise words in its (or 'his') grasp, it (or 'he') desires earnestly to teach our minds so that we shall not be lacking in God's fellowship (or 'doctrine'), the mercies of the Creator. He will grant us more; now, scholars tell us of better things, of the more lasting joys of heaven.]

This convoluted and ambiguous passage has long been understood as describing the process of Old Testament interpretation in general and the Pentateuch in particular.[39] The phrases *lifes wealhstod* (line 523) and

---

38 'Qui et idoneos nos fecit ministros noui testamenti; non littera, sed Spiritu: littera enim occidit, Spiritus autem uiuificat' (Who also has made us fit ministers of the new testament, not in the letter, but in the spirit. For the letter killeth, but the spirit quickeneth). See further J.R. Hall, 'Pauline Influence on *Exodus*, 523–48,' 84–8. On the influence of this fundamental trope on Anglo-Saxon thought, see further Huppé, *Doctrine and Poetry*, 3–64. On the metaphor of the keys of interpretation, see Burlin, *The Old English Advent*, 74–6; Haines, 'Unlocking *Exodus*,' 481–98.

39 Cf. *Andreas* lines 316 and 601, *Widsið* line 1, *Beowulf* line 259, and *The Meters of Boethius* VI.1. See also *Elene* lines 1249–50: 'bancofan onband, breostlocan onwand, / leoðucræft onleac' (he unbound the bone coffer, opened my breast-lock, unlocked the craft of poetry).

banhuses weard (line 524) usually have been accepted as referring to the human soul or intellect, which is then understood as the antecedent of *hafað* (line 527) and *tæcan* (line 528).[40] Pointing to the resultant 'awkward transition from a mind in general to a (learned?) mind which teaches other minds,' Dorothy Haines recently has attacked this long-standing interpretation, arguing that both *lifes wealhstod* and *banhuses weard* refer to Christ, who is, she suggests, the entity 'bright in our breasts.'[41] As Haines establishes from her survey of patristic and homiletic sources, Christ is identified consistently as the figure who unlocked the Old Testament so that the inner meaning of scripture can come forth. Haines's interpretation, while mostly convincing, cannot be called definitive as it does not directly confront the problem posed by the conditional, *gif*, at line 523. If Christ *already* has unlocked the Old Testament via his teaching, why does the passage in question present us with a hypothetical state of affairs? An attempt to solve all the difficulties that these lines have presented to scholars is beyond the scope of this essay. What remains here as a central concern, however, is the way that this passage communicates with lines 420–32, which, as we saw, describe God's giving of his word to Abraham in exchange for the sacrifice of Isaac.

One function of the conditional *if* at line 523 is that it generates a promise: if A is done, then B will follow. The poet is arranging a covenant of sorts, and as a result these lines echo the covenant formed between Abraham and God that is described at lines 420–32.[42] Just as Abraham was rewarded for his obedience to God, we will be rewarded for attentive reading of scripture. As suggested above, for his sacrifice Abraham receives God's *word* that his descendants will be uncountable. In the above passage it appears that *run*, *ræd*, and *word* are syntactically apposed: *if* the Old Testament is interpreted properly, the mystery will be revealed, wisdom shall go forth, and the 'wise words' (presently 'in its/his grasp') will be exchanged. In both the patriarchal digression and the homiletic digression, words are exchanged for deeds. Yet there is a revealing distinction between the two putative transactions. We saw that Abraham's gain was infinite; the poet told us that the word of God (*wuldres word*) that Abraham immediately received for his absolute obedience was greater than the world was able to contain (*befæðman* [line 429]). The contrast established by the above passage is precise: the *wislicu word* attained in

---

40 See Tolkien and Turville-Petre eds. and trans., *The Old English Exodus*, 75; Irving, ed., *The Old English Exodus*, 98; and Lucas, ed., *Exodus*, 142.

41 Haines, 'Unlocking *Exodus* ll. 516–32,' 498.

42 See further Zacharias P. Thundy, *Covenant in Anglo-Saxon Thought*.

exchange for correct interpretation is contained *on fæðme* at line 527.[43] The former, *wuldres word*, is uncontainable, the latter, *wislicu word*, is contained, although in both cases words are treated as material entities. Rather than being an infinite plenitude, the 'wise words' are circumscribed, and the value they bestow upon their possessor consequently is limited; ergo, *He us ma onlyhð*. The relatively limited benefit supplied in the present by the *wislicu word* must be supplemented in the future by God. The *boceras* can 'tell of better things, of the more lasting joys of heaven,' but the knowledge they provide awaits completion and fulfilment. We should observe in this regard another suggestive contrast with the patriarchal digression: speaking of God's word to Abraham, the angel at line 427 asks rhetorically, '*Hu þearf mannes sunu maran treowe?*' Unlike the 'wise words' received from scriptural interpretation, God's word requires no supplementation; it is complete in itself and awaits no addition.

The full return on the labour of exegesis, therefore, is indefinitely deferred, unlike the infinite and immediate gain received by Abraham, who is privileged to engage in a direct commerce with God. The poet seems to be alluding here to another famous Pauline passage, this time on the perfection of spiritual knowledge at the end of time (I Corinthians 13:12): 'uidemus nunc per speculum in enigmate tunc autem facie ad faciem nunc cognosco ex parte tunc autem cognoscam sicut et cognitus sum' (We see now through a glass in an obscure manner: but then face to face. Now I know in part: but then I will know even as I am known).[44] Both the *Exodus*

---

43 The noun *fæðm* occurs as a simplex or is compounded five times elsewhere in the narrative, each time indicating containment. At line 75, it is said that heaven is divided from the earth by the 'reaches' (*fæðmum*) of a cloud. At lines 293–4, Moses tells the Israelites that *Ofest is selost / þæt ge of feonda fæðme weorðen* (Haste is best, so that you escape from the grasp of enemies); likewise, the poet tells us that Pharoah *wolde heorufæðmum hilde gesceadan* (desired to decide the battle with hostile clutches [line 505]). The Israelites can resist Pharoah's clutches in part because they *fæstum fæðmum freoðowære heold* (held to the covenant with a fixed embrace [line 306]). Pharoah and his army, however, find it impossible to escape the *wælfæðmum* (deadly clutches [line 481]) of the Red Sea.

44 See also Augustine, *De Trinitate* (IV.xviii): 'Nunc ergo adhibemus fidem rebus temporaliter gestis propter nos et per ipsam mundamur et cum ad speciem uenerimus quemadmodum succedit fidei ueritas ita mortalitati succedat aeternitas. Quapropter quoniam fides noster fiet ueritas cum ad id quod nobis credentibus promittitur uenerimus, promittitur autem nobis uita aeterna' (Hence, we now practice faith in the things that were done in time for our sake, and by it we are cleansed, in order that when we have come to sight, as the truth follows the faith, so may eternity follow mortality. Wherefore, our faith will become truth when we shall arrive at that which is promised to us who believe, but what is promised to us is eternal life [CCSL 50.191.23–31]). Translation taken from McKenna, *The Trinity*, 160–1.

poet and Paul are describing the incompleteness of spiritual knowledge in the present. For Paul, this knowledge can only be completed after mortality has been left behind. The biblical intertext describes a flawless and immediate reflexivity ('but then face to face'); both Paul and the *Exodus* poet must look to the future for an immediate and timeless relationship between the self and truth. As Augustine observes, human understanding and human language are mediated and partial on account of their temporal situation; it is only God who sees himself face to face in his Word. The full significance of the compound *wordriht*, adumbrated in the first lines of the poem, is thus made clearer: just as the Israelites' attainment of the Promised Land looks forward allegorically to the final Christian reward (Christians are presently *eðellease* [line 534]), the correspondence noted above between the *eðelriht* and the *wordriht* anticipates the full attainment of a truth that can only be understood partially in the present.[45]

In this manner the poet generates two parallel economies: the unlimited economy of the Abrahamic covenant in the patriarchal digression and the limited economy of the 'hermeneutic covenant' in the homiletic digression. In *Exodus*, the operation of these two systems of profitable exchange is set against the institution of a debt that characterizes all human existence:

> Þis is læne dream,
> wommum awyrged,   wreccum alyfed,
> earmra anbid.   Eðellease
> þysne gystsele   gihðum healdað,
> murnað on mode,   manhus witon
> fæst under foldan,   þær bið fyr and wyrm,
> open ece scræf   yfela gehwylces,
> swa nu regnþeofas   rice dælað,
> yldo oððe ærdeað. (lines 532b–40)

[This is transitory (or 'borrowed') joy, cursed with sins, granted to exiles, a time of waiting for the wretched. Homeless we sorrowfully occupy the guest-house; we mourn in spirit; we are aware of the house of wickedness fixed under the earth where there is fire and the serpent, an eternally open pit of every sort of evil – just as now the arch-thieves share dominion, old age (or 'senility'), and premature death.]

---

45 Cf. Luria, 'Old English *Exodus*,' 600–1: '*The wordriht* which proclaims to men the reward of heavenly life is, surely, not really the Old Law of Moses, but the New Law of Christ, which is prefigured in that law just as Christ himself is prefigured in Moses.'

The motif of ephemeral happiness is so common in Old English poetry as barely to require comment; however, the economic logic perceived so far in the text demands that we attach a special significance to 'transitory' or 'borrowed joy.'[46] As we have seen, the labour required for spiritual understanding is rewarded ultimately with the 'more lasting joys of heaven' (*lengran lyftwynna*). The poet makes clear in the following half-line, however, that the joys of mortal existence participate in no such distributive system; they are not an everlasting reward for labour or obedience, but a 'loan.' The temporal structure of this loan deserves some comment. While exegetical labour is a long-term investment with full compensation occurring far in the future, the *læne dream* is granted to exiles (*wreccum alyfed*) in the present, during this 'time of waiting' (*anbid*). The form of the loan thus parallels the form of God's exchange with Abraham, also an exile (*He on wræce lifde* [line 383]), which returns immediate profits 'in the days of his life' (*in lifdagum* [line 424]). The *læne dream* is exactly the inverse of the *wuldres word*: both granted to exiles in the time of mortal existence, the former creates an unavoidable debt, and the latter provides gain without loss. God, moreover, is the source of Abraham's infinite profit, while the debt created by the *læne dream* ultimately must be settled with the 'arch-thieves' (*regnþeofas*), an epithet applied to the devil in its only other appearance in the extant Old English corpus (*Resignation*, line 15).

Opposed to the positive and profitable structures of exchange within which the *word* is inscribed is the absence of the very possibility of economy; in a world where it is thieves who 'share dominion' (*rice dælað*), after all, any ordered economy is threatened. Indeed, in their willingness to participate in a false economy with the Israelites, the Egyptians closely resemble the *regnþeofas*. The Egyptians robbed the Israelites of their reward for Joseph's services, and the *regnþeofas* rob human beings of life. The plight of the Israelites in captivity, therefore, anticipates the contemporary plight of Christians under the yoke of the arch-thieves.

Identifying the two arch-thieves, the collocation of senility and premature death (*yldo oððe ærdeað*) at line 540 in the homiletic excursus occurs nowhere else in the extant Old English corpus, though at first glance the doublet looks like a typical homiletic construction.[47] In *Exodus*,

---

46 The same formula appears in *Guthlac A*, lines 3 and 330; the collocation of *læn* or *læne* and *dream* occurs in *The Dream of the Rood*, lines 131–44; *Christ III*, lines 1585–6; and *The Seafarer*, lines 64–5.

47 Compare the homiletic sentiment in *The Seafarer*, lines 70–1, where old age is also personified: 'adl oððe yldo   oððe ecghete / fægum fromweardum   feorh oðþringeð' (disease or old age or violence / wrests away life from those fated to pass away).

however, this construction seems to bear a special function. Premature death (too little time) and old age/senility (too much time) together register the lack of perfect and timeless reflexivity that is, according to Augustine, a concomitant of the temporal predicament of human understanding and human language. As it is for Augustine, time is once more the crucial factor, and the poet ties in the intrusion of temporality with the motif of thievery – the antithesis of fair exchange. The assertion that these two arch-thieves share dominion sustains the text's reliance on an economic logic and points elegantly both to a theological state of affairs and an epistemological problem.

A linguistic and epistemological economy, therefore, informs the three temporal modalities of the poem: in the past we find the Abrahamic covenant of the *wuldres word*; in the present we find the hermeneutic covenant of the *wislicu word* and the reign of the *regnþeofas*; and the correspondence of *wordriht* and *eðelriht* points to the future and the perfection of spiritual knowledge. While direct commerce with God may not be possible, the *Exodus* poet is still committed to providing sound investment advice. Careful interpretation of the wise words of scripture will grant, in time, unlimited spiritual profit; in a market run by thieves, however, only a fool could expect lasting returns from borrowed joy.

Conclusion

It is too much to say that we find in *Exodus* a thorough and dogmatic expression of Augustinian linguistic epistemology. What is closer to the truth is that we find in this poem a culturally determined response to an available and influential linguistic model within a poem almost obsessively concerned with language and its limits. The *Exodus* poet thus demonstrates the remarkable capacity of the heroic register to mediate reception of the Anglo-Saxon intellectual inheritance, whether theological or philosophical. We saw how Augustine, particularly in *De Trinitate*, is keen to differentiate divine and human language. The same is the case for the *Exodus* poet, who describes both the infinitude of the divine word (lines 427–31) and the limits on human language (lines 432–42). For Augustine, moreover, the divine word partakes of the nature of its source, with which it is contemporaneous. For the *Exodus* poet, the divine word is infinite in size and, like God, transcends the boundaries of the world. Furthermore, if we accept Remley's proposal that Aldhelm's *Carmen de uirginitate* is the source for the description of God's word (lines 427–31), it is striking that Aldhelm's text describes the infinitude of God.

For Augustine, the finitude of human language is a product of temporal mediation. The same view seems to be the case for the *Exodus* poet; we are told at line 438, for instance, that the mortal lifespan is insufficient to number the descendants of Abraham 'with true words.' Likewise, in the homiletic digression at lines 523–32, the 'wise words' received from scriptural interpretation require supplementation in the future by God ('he will give us more [*ma*]' [line 530]). By contrast, the poet tells us that the infinite word of God requires no supplementation and is complete in itself ('In what way does the son of man need a greater [*maran*] pledge?' [line 427]). Throughout *Exodus*, this Augustinian distinction between human and divine signification relies for its expression on an indigenous gift economy, by means of which words are accorded materiality and value. The word of God is of infinite size and of infinite value, providing infinite gain when given to Abraham. In contrast, the poet indicates the finitude of the 'wise words' promised in exchange for scriptural interpretation and, thus, their finite value.

The intersection of a linguistic economy with the temporal mediation inherent in human language and understanding is set up early in the poem by the compound *wordriht* (line 3), strategically apposed to *Moyses domas* at line 2. The *wordriht*, like the *landriht* and *eðelriht* of the Israelites, have for the poet a material dimension, to which a proprietary right can attach. Thus, the Israelites' acquisition of the Promised Land (*eðelriht*) finds a parallel in the Israelites' acquisition of Moses' Laws (*wordriht*). The Promised Land, in turn, looks forward allegorically to final salvation, just as Moses' Laws look forward both to the new dispensation of Christ and the ultimate revelation only available in heaven. In this way, the *Exodus* poet's vivid depiction of the Israelites' struggle for salvation merges artfully with the struggle to attain a deeper knowledge of God and transcend, finally, the limits of human understanding.

Daniel and the Dew-Laden Wind:
Sources and Structures

PHYLLIS PORTNOY

Over the years the Old English *Daniel* has excited little admiration or even discussion. On its own it is considered 'unimaginative,' 'prosaic,' 'sluggish,' 'nebulous,' and 'diffuse.'[1] Viewed within Oxford, Bodleian Library, MS Junius 11, it suffers further in comparison with *Exodus*, its lively and difficult companion piece. The one passage in the poem considered worthy of remark is the rather beautiful simile of a summer wind laden with dew, but the passage is problematic, and at best it is seen as a poorly integrated lyric interruption of the poet's otherwise pedestrian efforts at biblical paraphrase.

The image of the dew in *Daniel* is in fact a central and well-integrated component of an elaborate ring structure that has yet to be noted in the poem. Ring composition is a classical structuring technique that gives balance, cohesion, and focus to narrative poetry by organizing long passages into symmetrical rhetorical 'rings.'[2] I suggest that an impressive use of this narrative device is one feature that *Daniel* has in common with *Exodus*. I hope to demonstrate that while *Daniel* may lack the drama and intensity of heroic epic, its skilfully executed ring structure goes some way towards challenging the prevailing criticism of the poem's organization and pace. It also helps explain the choice of the book of Daniel for the final Old Testament subject of Junius 11. I argue here that the *Daniel* poet uses ring

---

1 The comments are, respectively, T.W. Hunt, *Caedmon's Exodus and Daniel*, 13; F.A. Blackburn, ed., *Exodus and Daniel*, 33; H.J. Solo, 'The Twice-Told Tale,' 347; and Paul Remley, *Old English Biblical Verse*, 253 and 288.
2 For ring composition (cf. ring pattern, ring structure, envelope pattern) in classical and Old English poetry, see H. Ward Tonsfeldt, 'Ring Structure in *Beowulf*,' 143–52, and Phyllis Portnoy, 'Ring Composition and the Digressions of *Exodus*,' 289–307.

composition to refocus rather than paraphrase the book of Daniel, that the resulting emphasis on the episode of the Three Hebrew Youths in the Fiery Furnace is a key to the Junius 11 program, and that one source for both the episode and the program is the book of Deuteronomy, passages of which are linked with the books of Genesis, Exodus, and Daniel in early Christian liturgy and art.

The manuscript sequence Genesis-Exodus is a biblical given – but why Daniel? Scholars have cited the liturgical importance of the furnace miracle in early Christian religious practice, particularly in the observances for Easter.[3] The very frequent appearance of the miracle in both insular and continental art[4] is further evidence of the important role played by the story in the redemptive theology of the period.[5] While such rationales might account in part for the inclusion of so popular and familiar a subject for the Old Testament program of Junius 11, they do not explain the resulting collocation of *Exodus* and *Daniel*, an obviously non-biblical sequence that should strike a modern reader as very odd. Moreover, as Graham Caie has observed, the two poems appear to move very smoothly from one to the other[6] – indeed it has been suggested that the exordium of *Daniel* (lines 1–103) was composed (perhaps by the compiler or compilers) expressly to form a link with *Exodus*,[7] indicating that the juxtaposition of two biblical books so widely separated in scripture

---

3 See James Bright, 'The Relation of the Caedmonian *Exodus* to the Liturgy,' 97–103; Robert Farrell, 'The Unity of the Old English *Daniel*,' 131–4; Remley, *Old English Biblical Verse*, 79–87, 136–43, 216–30; Portnoy, '"Remnant" and "Ritual,"' 408–21, and *The Remnant*, 119–22, cf. reorientation in John Bugge, 'Virginity and Prophecy in the Old English *Daniel*,' 127–47.

4 For surveys of the theme in art, see Colum Hourihane, '*De Camino Ignis*,' 61–82; Ann Walton, 'The Three Hebrew Children in the Fiery Furnace,' 57–66. The familiarity and popularity of the story as an exemplum of faith is evident from Ælfric's introductory comments to his summary of the story in *De falsis diis: us is eac fulcuð* (it is also well known to us). See John C. Pope, ed., *Homilies of Ælfric*, EETS o.s. 260, 692. Ælfric treats the story at length in the second Christmas homily (II.19–22) and in the homily on the Nativity of St Clement (I.569–71). See Benjamin Thorpe, ed., *The Homilies of the Anglo-Saxon Church*, 2 vols.

5 See J.R. Hall, 'The Old English Epic of Redemption: The Theological Unity of MS Junius 11,' 185–208 and 'The Old English Epic of Redemption: Twenty-Five Year Retrospective,' 53–68; Catherine Karkov, *Text and Picture in Anglo-Saxon England*, 2; Manish Sharma, 'Nabuchodonosor and the Defiance of Measure in the Old English *Daniel*,' 124.

6 Graham Caie, 'The Old English *Daniel*,' 3.

7 See Remley, *Old English Biblical Verse*, 255–72, for discussion of the various arguments.

was perfectly acceptable to an Anglo-Saxon. This paper will explore the possibility that the link might in fact have been traditional.

Ring Composition

To begin, I take up the challenge presented by Paul Remley, who cautions that 'any argument asserting the unity of the central section of *Daniel* will be misdirected.'[8] I follow this path, however, secure in the knowledge that angels are treading it before me, for in fact one of the perceived problems in this part of the poem is the proliferation of angels. The first of these appears at line 236, when the three Hebrews, Annanias, Misael and Azarias, are thrown into the furnace by King Nabuchodonosor's servants. The angel saves the youths, the furnace is heated, the flames kill the servants, and the angel then saves the youths, transforming the blast of the furnace into a wind laden with dew. Azarias then sings a prayer for a deliverance that seems already to have occurred twice, the angel *then* enters the furnace, the servants are again incinerated, the angel saves the youths, transforming the heat of the furnace this time into a summer rain, and finally, the three sing a song of praise and the angel departs.

This section of the poem is an extended treatment of the furnace episode from the third chapter of the book of Daniel. The narrative seems to have unredeemable flaws: the angelic intercession occurs before it is requested, it recurs repeatedly, the furnace appears to require relighting, and the servants reburning. The redundancy of the angel is especially problematic, and several explanations have been advanced to account for it. Early editors considered the offending repetitions the result of the poet's inept interpolation of the Canticle (or Prayer) of Azarias into the court tale.[9] Others argue for the integrity of the poem's sequence, pointing out that the proleptic angelic rescue and the doublets of furnace and servants exist also in the biblical source. The biblical sequence is indeed very problematic: the furnace is heated at Daniel 3:19, then again at 3:46; the servants are killed at Daniel 3:22, then again at 3:48; the youths are walking about unharmed at Daniel 3:24 without the saving angel, singing their hymn of praise; at Daniel 3:50 the flames are rendered harmless by the angel, and the youths sing their hymn; Azariah's prayer for deliverance occurs after deliverance seems already to have taken place (at any rate, the fact that the

---

8 Ibid., 337.
9 Ibid., 338–41 and 349–56. Remley argues that the poem's redundancies are the result of the conflation of canonical and apocryphal details from liturgical exemplars.

three youths are alive and singing well before the petition for deliverance is voiced has occasioned biblical commentary and exegesis from earliest times); finally, the Canticle of the Three Hebrew Youths has no real connection with the furnace narrative.[10]

These inconsistencies, redundancies, and doublets in Daniel, chapter 3 resulted from the insertions of the Canticle of Azarias and the Canticle of the Three Hebrew Youths into the Greek versions of the Hebrew-Aramaic text of Daniel at verse 24, each with an introduction in prose (Daniel 3:24–5 and 3:46–50 of the deuterocanonical version). The additions (in italic below) appear also in the Vulgate, with a note from Jerome as to their apocryphal status.

Daniel 3:19 furnace heated
Daniel 3:22 death of servants
Daniel 3:23 youths fall bound into furnace
Daniel A3:24–5 prose introduction to canticle
Daniel A3:25–45 Canticle 1: Prayer of Azarias
Daniel A3:46–50 prose interlude: 3:46 furnace heated
3:48 death of servants
3:49–50 angel and dew-laden wind
Daniel A3:51–90 Canticle 2: Song of the Three Hebrew Youths
Daniel 3:24–5 King observes angel / Deliverance of youths

The resulting lack of coherence in this narrative notwithstanding, there is only one angel and one rescue; the biblical source therefore cannot absorb the blame for the *Daniel* poet's insistently reduplicated action of the angel.

Robert Farrell, the most recent editor of *Daniel*, has suggested that the poet developed a 'theme of the angel'[11] from the single mention of the angel in the Vulgate. Even so, the theme does not fit coherently into the narrative; indeed, as Remley notes, the second rescue narrates as if it were a

---

10 The one connection, in verse 88, is considered artificial by most scholars: 'he has rescued us from the midst of the burning fiery furnace; he has rescued us from the midst of the fire.' For the critical history of the additions, see J.J. Collins, *Daniel*, 180 and 198; R.H. Charles, ed., *The Apocrypha and Pseudepigrapha of the Old Testament in English*, vol. 1, 625–31.

11 Robert Farrell, 'The Unity of the Old English *Daniel*,' 129, and Farrell, ed., *Daniel and Azarias*, 29.

different miracle altogether.[12] Geoffrey Shepherd and Earl Anderson are closer to a vindication of the episode, I think, in their observation that the two well-noted accounts of the rescue (lines 255b–78 and 333–56) can be seen as framing devices deployed to set off the Canticle of Azarias (lines 283–332).[13] I suggest that the structural balancing goes beyond a single framing of the one canticle. Both the Canticle of Azarias and the Canticle of the Three Hebrew Youths (lines 362–408) appear, like the angel, to intrude upon and impede the narrative. Looking at the passages more closely and from a wider perspective, Remley observes that the passages that follow upon each angelic rescue (lines 279–82 and 356–61) in fact serve as integrated, balanced introductions to each of the two canticles. Remley's important point can be seen more clearly if we schematize the passage:

A Angelic rescue, lines 255b–78
   B Introduction to Canticle of Azarias, lines 279–82
      C Canticle, lines 283–332
A Angelic rescue, lines 333–56a
   B Introduction to Canticle of the Three Hebrew Youths, lines 356b–61
      C Canticle, lines 362–408

I shall have more to say about the symmetry of this repeated sequence, but first I would like to view the episode from a wider perspective yet, and also in more detail, to show that this patterned organization of the canticles is in fact only one part – the central part – of a complex ring pattern.

In classical ring composition, narrative elements are arranged symmetrically and chiastically, through verbal or 'idea echo,' into concentric 'envelopes' or 'rings' that frame a medial point, or 'kernel.' The balanced repetition and pairing establish relationships between ideas and events, and a crucial incident in this way becomes centralized in the foreground of the narrative as a static 'set piece.'[14] Thus the formal structure, in addition to being a convenient mnemonic device for an oral poet, can also serve as

---

12 Remley, *Old English Biblical Verse*, 335.
13 Geoffrey Shepherd, 'Scriptural Poetry,' 32; Earl Anderson, 'Style and Theme in the Old English *Daniel*,' 2–3. Farrell makes a similar observation about the weather similes in *Daniel and Azarias*, 28. See also Farrell, 'The Unity of the Old English *Daniel*,' 129; Remley, *Old English Biblical Verse*, 347 and 356.
14 For discussion of these various elements and effects of ring composition see note 2 above.

a subtle and indirect commentary or interpretive subtext. In one of the earliest studies of ring composition in Old English, H. Ward Tonsfelt notes, 'in the hands of a superior poet the enclosing circle of similarity ... becomes a means for subjecting the narrative materials to evaluation and comment.'[15]

While the original audience and readership of *Daniel* were perhaps not in the presence of such superior hands, they would very likely have been familiar with ring composition from *Beowulf* or *Exodus*, if not also from classical verse, and thus attuned to the suggestive effects of the structure. But to a modern reader unfamiliar with ring composition, the patterned placement of narrative components can appear to be merely senseless repetitions or circlings that disrupt, retard, and confuse the forward momentum of the narrative. Many of the apparent infelicities in the central section of *Daniel* can in fact be explained if we see the two essential components or dimensions of the narrative – spatial ordering and linear sequence – in the rhetorical context that the poet likely intended. Reading the furnace episode in schematized form, we can appreciate how the skilful manipulation of the two axes of composition into rhetorical rings works to shape and direct our understanding of the events.

The first detail to notice is that there are three, not two, instances of the saving action of the angel in the poem and that they are balanced in their presentation. The first and third instances correspond to the apocryphal addition at Daniel A3:49, where the angel is said to descend (*descendit*) into the furnace; the second instance corresponds to the resumption of the narrative proper at Daniel 3:25, where the angel is said to be walking about (*ambulantes*) with the three Hebrew youths. In the poet's corresponding passages the angel comes down from the high heavens (*of hean rodore ... becwom*; *of roderum ... cwom*)[16] and is 'walking about' (*hwurfon*) with the youths:

Angel 1 (lines 235–8) *of hean rodore ... becwom*   Daniel A3:49 *descendit*
Angel 2 (lines 270–3) *hwurfon*   Daniel 3:25 *ambulantes*
Angel 3 (lines 335–8) *of roderum ... cwom*   Daniel A3:49 *descendit*

15 Tonsfeldt, 'Ring Structure,' 446.
16 All citations to the poem are from Krapp, ed., *The Junius Manuscript*, ASPR 1. All translations are my own.

Thus, while the poet's manner of repeating the angel's actions may seem disruptive to the linear sequence of the narrative, from a spatial perspective it has a certain pleasing symmetry: the descent of the angel forms an envelope that frames the saving action.

This is true to a far greater extent for the poet's placement of the repetitions within the larger picture of the entire furnace episode (see schematization below). The poet's version of the episode contains all the problematic doublets and inconsistencies of the scriptural source, plus some of his own creation. Besides the repeated references to the angel, the poet adds repeated descriptions of the preservation of the youths by the angel, the miraculous weather in the furnace, the king's perception of the miracle, and the youths' protection by God. The repetitions are in fact key elements in a highly organized pattern of rhetorical rings that together give the episode more coherence – structurally at least – than it has in the biblical sequence where the events recur in tandem. In the process, the poet makes significant alterations to the scriptural order. For one thing, he moves the repeated detail of the servants' deaths to the beginning of the sequence, thereby avoiding the problem in the biblical account in which the same servants who are killed at verse 22 stoke the furnace at verse 48. Another major change is the placement of the two canticles symmetrically and prominently in the middle of the sequence. The balanced repetitions project the furnace miracle into the centre and foreground of the *Daniel* narrative, and the canticles into the centre and foreground of the miracle narrative.[17]

The repetitions also serve to set Nabuchodonosor's pagan spiritual blindness against the faith of the Hebrew youths. The king's involvement (at A) is the framing motif for each of the rings, each repetition serving both to end one ring and introduce the next. His perception of the miracle – a repetition that does not appear at all in scripture and which has not been noted before in the scholarship on the poem – frames the third to fifth rings. Within the frames the preservation of the youths by the angel alternates with preservation by God, another point repeated with insistence in the poem, but not in scripture.[18]

---

17 The furnace episode (lines 224–489) occurs almost exactly at the midpoint of the poem. Similarly, the middle 'ring' containing the two *Daniel* canticles (lines 268–418) occurs almost exactly at the midpoint of the furnace episode.

18 In fact, the poet omits the one reference to preservation by God in the apocryphal scriptural account, which occurs at the end of the Canticle of the Three Youths.

Ring 1

A Nabuchodonosor: command to heat furnace (line 224)
  B Youths unharmed (lines 232–4)
    C Angel's protection (lines 235–8)
  B Youths unharmed (lines 239–40)
A Nabuchodonosor: command to heat furnace (lines 241–7)

Ring 2

A Nabuchodonosor: command to heat furnace (lines 241–7)
  B Youths unharmed; heathen servants perish (lines 243–54)
    C God's protection (lines 260–1)
      D Furnace weather (line 263)
  B Youths unharmed; heathen servants perish (lines 266–7)
A Nabuchodonosor: perception of miracle (lines 268–70)

Ring 3

A Nabuchodonosor: perception of miracle (lines 268–70)
  B/C Angel's protection; youths unharmed (lines 272–3)
    D/C Simile; God's protection (lines 274–8)
      E Intro to canticle (lines 279–82)
        F Canticle (lines 283–332)

    C/B Angel's protection; youths unharmed (lines 335–42)
      D/C Simile; God's protection (lines 346–51)
        E Intro to canticle (lines 356–61)
          F Canticle (lines 362–408)
A Nabuchodonosor: perception of miracle (lines 409–26)

Ring 4

A Nabuchodonosor: perception of miracle (lines 409–26)
  B/C Youths unharmed; God's protection (lines 433–40a)
    *Angel returns to heaven (line 440b)
      *F Canticle (lines 444–6)
    *Youths returned to God (lines 452–5)
  C/B Youths unharmed; God's protection (lines 456–8)
A Nabuchodonosor: perception of miracle (line 459)

Ring 5

A Nabuchodonosor: perception of miracle (line 459)
    C God's protection (lines 465–6)
A Nabuchodonosor: perception of miracle (lines 473–85)
    C God's protection (lines 474, 480)
A Nabuchodonosor: perception of miracle (lines 487–8)

The repetition and pairing create a structural unity for the episode, isolating it as a static set piece and directing the focus to central ideas and images in the passages, often to ironic effect. In the first ring, for example, the angel's sheltering 'embrace' at C (*fæðmum* [line 238]) counters both the 'embrace' of the flames at B (*fæðm fyres lige* [line 233]) and Nabuchodonosor's commands to heat the furnace, which frame it at A. The envelope formed by the youths' unblemished condition at B also counters the envelope formed by the king's command. The structure becomes complexly and densely textured and more pointedly focused when details from one ring carry over into another. Thus in the second ring the poet shifts the focus to the youths by repeating the miracle of their preservation from the first ring, linking the angel's embrace of the youths with God's (*fæðm* [line 260]) through verbal echo, and contrasting their preservation with the deaths of the servants. He further demonstrates the powerlessness of the king's command from the first ring by balancing it with his stupefied amazement in the second ring, a detail that has been prepared at the end of the second ring (at A). Similarly, the 'unmarred beauty' (*wlite* [line 239]) of the youths in the first ring is a contrast to the 'reduced beauty' (*wlite* [line 267]) of the servants in the second ring.

The details of the angel's action from ring 1, along with the youths' unblemished state, the weather in the furnace, and God's protection from ring 2, reappear in ring 3 along with the canticle (E and F). The result is an almost exactly doubled parallel structure of Angel – Youths – Simile – God – Canticle. The 'shining beauty' of the angel in the second sequence (*wlitescyne* [line 337]) echoes and combines the details of shining and of beauty from the first sequence (*sunnan scineð* [line 275]; *wlitiga* [line 326]) and from rings 1 and 2 (*sunnan scima* [line 263]; *wlite* [lines 239 and 267]), and the summer wind and dew (lines 274–8) are balanced by the summer wind, rain, and showers (lines 346–9). Thus the poet actually 'improves' upon his source by transforming the problematic biblical redundancies into artful designs. The two details in the biblical sequence that are *not* repeated in scripture (the angel's descent and the moisture imagery) are given equal voice here with those that *are* (the heating of the furnace and the death of the servants), with the result that the canticles each acquire a very elaborate and symmetrical introduction. In this way, the narrative is retarded while our attention is directed to the canticles, the centrepiece of the design.

To be more precise, it is the king's attention that appears to be so directed, as a result of the rhetorical envelopes formed by his repeated gaze. The continued repetition in the final two rings of non-scriptural references to seeing, signs, and truth (*geseah, geseo to soðe, onget* [lines 411, 415, 459]; *gesawon* [line 473]; *beacen onget, swutol tacen godes* [lines 487–8]) creates a moment of possibility for the implacable Nabuchodonosor by linking his perception of truth to that celebrated by the youths in their canticles: *soðe* (lines 287, 401); *soðfæst* (lines 332, 383, 394). The king's perception of God's saving power forms two envelopes in ring 4 (at C) around two further striking and parallel additions to the biblical story: the return of the angel to heaven and the return of the 'remnant' to God. The angel's departure is not mentioned at all in scripture; in the poem it is imagined as an ascent to heaven:

þa gewat se engel up   secan him ece dreamas
on heanne hrof   heofon rices. (lines 440–1)

[Then the angel departed up to the high roof of the heavenly kingdom to seek eternal joys.]

The youths also return to God at this point in the poem, if only figuratively:

Agæf him þa his leoda lafe   þe þær gelædde wæron
on æht ealdfeondum   þæt hie are hæfdon. (lines 452–3)

[He gave to Him the remnant of his people who were led there into the possession of their old foes, that they should have favour.]

The doubled upward movement of these additions in ring 4 is accompanied by singing, as it frames what amounts to a reported reprise of the canticles (at F), another significant repetition that the poet has added to the biblical or apocryphal source:

Hyssas heredon drihten   for þam hæðenan folce,
septon hie soðcwidum   and him sædon fela
soðra tacna. (lines 444–6)

[The young men praised God before the heathen folk; they exhorted them with words of truth, and told them of many truthful signs.]

Ring 5 builds on the upward movement towards God, harmonizing Nabuchodonosor's recognition of *soðra tacna* with the *soðcwidum* and *soðra tacna* of the added canticle through pairing with the final, doubled repetition of the motif of God's protection, and the episode ends on a high and promising lyrical note. Indeed, the episode has taken on a hymnodic character partly from the hypotactic effect of ring structure, which has many of the same formal framing characteristics as musical structure, and partly from the poet's centralization of the two canticles, which quite naturally reflect the lyricism of their liturgical sources. The two canticle sequences (ring 3, B–F) form a second lyrical structure within the structure that adds to the quasi-liturgical choral quality of the episode. This paired parallel sequence of the two canticles mimics antiphonal singing, where one choral element of a set is chanted in response to the other, often in perfect metrical and harmonic balance.

Both the harmony and the upward movement of the episode are momentary, however; narrative hypotaxis has its limitations, and the poet immediately underlines the quick reversal of the moment with another non-biblical comment about the king: *no þy sel dyde / ac þam æðelinge oferhygd gesceod* (and yet he did no better; but pride ruled the prince [lines 488–9]). The king will ignore the example of the youths, the next generation will ignore the example of the (eventually converted) king, and the poem ends by coming full circle, comparing the impieties of Belshazzar, who began *deoflu drincan* (to drink to devils [line 749]), with those of the Israelites, whom *gylp beswac / windruncen gewit* (pride and drunken thoughts had seduced [lines 751–2]). This echo of the poem's beginning is well noted, as is the unconventionality of the *deofoldædum* and *druncne geðohtas* (devil deeds and drunken thoughts [line 18]) attributed to Israel in the poem's exordium. This same negative portrayal of Israel is the subject of the Canticle of Azarias, and connections between the canticle and the exordium are also well documented.[19] What has not been noticed is that along with other details also not associated with the biblical Daniel, the critique of Israel that is prominent in both of these sections of the poem has very close analogues in the book of Deuteronomy. Once we recognize the importance of Deuteronomy in *Daniel*, we will be able to appreciate why the poet has devoted so much of his poetic energies to the episode of the fiery furnace.

---

19 Remley, *Old English Biblical Verse*, 368–9.

Sources in Deuteronomy

Several sources have been proposed for the *Daniel* poet's negative portrayal of Israel,[20] but the correspondences are very general, and none account for the association of a fallen Israel with the book of Daniel, where the attitude to the captive Israelites is entirely positive and sympathetic. Deuteronomy compares very closely in several places with *Daniel*, however, in its imagery and phraseology as well as its attitude; moreover, the books of Deuteronomy and Daniel have a long history of close connection, as we shall see.

A cluster of motifs associated with divine favour – covenant obligation, the exodus from Egypt, prosperity, triumph over the enemy[21] – recurs repeatedly in Deuteronomy along with corresponding threats of exile, dispersal, and decimation as reprisals for apostasy. Similar ideas and images appear in the *Daniel* poet's version of the Canticle of Azarias as well as in the exordium of the poem. While the Old English of the canticle follows the Vulgate Latin in general, it departs significantly in several places, where it is much closer to the language of Deuteronomy. For example, the condition of the people as described in the poem's Canticle of Azarias – 'we are exiled throughout the wide earth,' 'scattered through many lands,' 'under many peoples' (*Daniel*, lines 300–5) – compares closely with the repeated statements in Deuteronomy that the people will be 'scattered among the nations' (Deuteronomy 4:27), 'taken away from their land, scattered through all nations, all peoples, to the ends of the earth' (Deuteronomy 28:63–4), 'cast out from their land' (Deuteronomy 29:28):

> Siendon we towrecene   geond widne grund,
> heapum tohworfene,   hyldelease;
> is user lif   geond landa fela
> fracoð and gefræge   folca manegum,
> þa usic bewræcon   to þæs wyrrestan
> eorðcyninga   æhta gewealde. (*Daniel*, lines 300–5)

[We are scattered over the wide earth, dispersed in bands without grace. Through many lands and peoples our life is infamous and vile; they have exiled us into bondage to the worst of earthly kings.]

---

20   Ibid., 256–69; D.A. Jost, 'Biblical Sources of Old English *Daniel* 1–78,' 257 61.
21   See Moshe Weinfield, *Deuteronomy and the Deuteronomic School*, 320–38 and 339–49.

atque disperget in omnes gentes et remanebitis pauci in nationibus. (Deuteronomy 4:27)

[And (the Lord) will scatter you among all peoples, and you shall be left few among the nations.]

remanebitis pauci numero ... auferamini de terra ... disperget te Dominus in omnes populos a summitate terrae usque ad terminos eius et servies ibi diis alienis. (Deuteronomy 28:62–4)

[You shall be left few in number ... you shall be carried from the land ... God will scatter you among all peoples from the farthest parts of the earth to the ends of it and there you will serve alien gods.]

et ejecit eos de terra sua ... projecitque in terram alienam. (Deuteronomy 29:28)

[And he has cast them out of their land ... and has thrown them into a strange land.]

The Old English renderings of these Deuteronomy passages in *The Old English Version of the Heptateuch*[22] are also close to the *Daniel* poet's in phrasing:

Ac Drihten eow todrifð geond ealle ðeoda, ðæt eower byð feawa on ðam lande to lafe & ge ðeowiað fremdum godum. (*Heptateuch*, Deuteuronomy 4:27–8)

[But God will drive you through all the peoples so that you will be few left in the land and you will serve foreign gods.]

... & forhwyrfð eow of ðam lande ðe ge inn farað to agenne. Drihten eow adrifð geond ealle ðeoda oð eorðan endas, & ge ðeowiað ðam godum ðe ge ne cunnon. (*Heptateuch*, Deuteuronomy 28:63–4)

---

22 Crawford, *The Old English Version of the Heptateuch*. Richard Marsden sees the *Heptateuch* as an editorial enterprise involving more than one anonymous translator and compiler; see 'Old Latin Intervention in the Old English *Heptateuch*,' 230–1, and 'Translation By Committee?' 41–90.

[And (God) will remove you from the land that you will go in to possess. God will drive you through all peoples to the ends of the earth, and you will serve gods that you do not know.]

Indeed the expressions of exile and diaspora in *Daniel* (*towrecene, tohwor-fene*, and *bewræcon*) are almost exact renderings of the Vulgate and Old English Deuteronomy passages (*disperget, auferamini, ejecit; forhwyrfð, todrifð, adrifð*), whereas the Latin Daniel canticle contains no mention at all of exile or scattering. The Latin canticle also contains no reference to foreign lands or peoples, as compared with *Daniel* (*geond widne grund* and *geond landa fela*), with the Vulgate Deuteronomy (*in omnes gentes, in omnes populos*, and *a summitate terrae usque ad terminos*), and with the *Heptateuch* Deuteronomy (*geond ealle ðeoda* and *geond ealle ðeoda oð eorðan endas*). Thus the poem's emphasis on dispersal seems to go beyond the conventional Old English theme of exile to embrace a central motif of the book of Deuteronomy: the scattering of the people.[23]

Other details in the Canticle of Azarias correspond far more closely with Deuteronomy than with the Latin Daniel canticle. One is the reference to the covenant given *to Abrahame and to Isaace and to Iacobe* (lines 313–14). This exactly parallels a formulaic repetition of the three patriarchs throughout Deuteronomy, whereas the Latin Daniel canticle refers to Abraham, Isaac, and *Israel* (Daniel A3:35, emphasis mine). The distinction between 'Jacob' and 'Israel' is an important one for the study of biblical narrative as it has served scholars in identifying various layers of biblical redaction;[24] here it is significant because it points to a biblical source for the poem other than the Latin Daniel canticle.

Another notable connection with Deuteronomy is the poem's focus on God's 'speech' and 'words.' In the closing verses of the canticle, where the Latin repeats the opening invocation of God's 'name,' *da gloriam nomini tuo Domine* (give glory to your name, O Lord [Daniel A3:43]), the poem has *Fyl nu frumspræce ... wlitiga þinne wordcwyde* (fulfil now your ancient word ... make beautiful your word-speech [lines 325–6]). The compounds *frumspræce* and *wordcwyde* are very suggestive of the compound invocation of the 'word' and the 'speech' of God in the opening lines of

23 See G. Widengren, 'Yahweh's Gathering of the Dispersed,' 227–45.
24 Other biblical passages that contain the variant *Israel* are considered late additions. See Martin Rist, 'The God of Abraham, Isaac and Jacob,' 289 ff.; Herbert Gordon May, 'The God of My Father,' 155.

the Canticle of Moses from Deuteronomy, a passage that also contains another and most striking congruence with *Daniel*:

> Audite caeli, quae loquor;
>   audiat terra uerba oris mei
> Concrescat in pluuia doctrina mea,
>   fluat ut ros eloquium meum
> quasi imber super herbam
>   et quasi stillae super gramina. (Deuteronomy 32:1–2)

[Hear, O heavens, what I speak; let the earth listen to the words of my mouth. Let my teachings gather as the rain, and my speech distil as the dew, like showers on the grass and like drops on the young plants.]

The water images in these lines are very similar to those of the paired weather similes that introduce the poem's two Daniel canticles:

Simile 1
                gelicost
efne þonne on sumera   sunne scineð
and deawdrias[25]   on dæge weorðeð
winde geondsawen. (*Daniel*, lines 274b–7a)

[most like when in summer the sun shines and dewfall comes during the day, spread out by the wind.]

Simile 2
                gelicost
þonne hit on sumeres tid   sended weorðeð
dropena drearung   on dæges hwile,
wearmlic wolcna scur. (*Daniel*, lines 346a–9a)

[most like the weather in the summer season when drops of rain are sent falling during the day, and warm showers from the heavens.]

---

25 *Deawdreas* is the reading given in Farrell's edition. See further below.

The images of dew and rain in the Deuteronomic Canticle of Moses are precisely those of the *Daniel* poet's doubled treatment of the single Vulgate *Daniel* passage, which states that the angel made the hot blast within the furnace as innocuous – indeed as beneficent – 'as though a dew-laden breeze were blowing through it' (*New American Bible*) or 'as a wind of dew blowing' (Vulgate: *quasi uentum roris flantem* [Daniel A3:50]). While the wind image must derive from the Latin canticle, the 'falling' conveyed in the compound *deawdrias* (dew fall [line 276]) is absent there, but present in the *stillae* (drops) of the Deuteronomic canticle. Deuteronomy's *stillae* and *imber* correspond even more closely to the 'drops' (*dropena*) of rain 'falling' (*drearung*) and the warm 'showers' (*scur*) from heaven that the *Daniel* poet adds to his second, entirely non-scriptural simile.

The relationship of the two similes both to each other and to the one biblical passage can perhaps shed some light on the controversial crux of the manuscript reading, *deawdrias*. As the second element of this *hapax legomenon* does not conform to any established Old English forms, editors have struggled to explain or harmonize it. Grein read *deaw-drias* as 'dew of the magician,' and Krapp emended *drias* to *dryge*, translating as 'when the dew becomes dry,' by reasoning that dew does not 'fall' during the day (*on dæge* [lines 276, 348]).[26] Given the poet's attention to structural symmetry, however, it is more likely that his images of dropping and falling in the second simile are purposeful, conceived with the intention of balancing a similar falling action in the first.

Moreover, the repetition and intensification of water imagery in the second simile suggest that the poet had in mind the traditional biblical association of rain fall and dew fall with the descent from heaven of divine blessing and grace – the notion behind the gentle dropping action of Shakespeare's 'quality of mercy,' and the doctrinal significance of the opening images of the Deuteronomic canticle, as well as the closing images of Moses' blessings: *Habitabit Israël confidenter ... cælique caligabunt rore* (Israel shall dwell in safety ... and the heavens shall be misty with dew [Deuteronomy 33:28]).[27] The theology of the dew image in fact requires

---

26 Krapp, *Junius Manuscript*, 225. For commentary see J.-A. George, '*Hwalas ðec herigað*,' 108–9. Peter Lucas emends to *deaw dryre*, a regular form of *dreosan*, with the same sense, 'dew fall' ('*Daniel* 276,' 390–1).

27 In scripture, dew is emblematic of God's miracles, for example, the dew falling on Gideon's fleece (Judg. 6:38). Dew represents God's grace (Hosea 14:5, Mic. 5:7, Zech. 8:12, Isa. 26:19; Sir. 18:16) and blessing (Gen. 27:28, Deut. 33:13, Isa. 18:4); its deprivation represents God's curse (I Kings17:1, Hag. 1:10). These attributes are treated

that the descent and spreading should occur not as in nature but mysteriously and miraculously at God's command, by which dew can materialize at any time of day. Krapp's notion of evaporation, with its attendant associations of dry as opposed to moist, and upward as opposed to downward movement, would destroy both the sense and the symmetry of the *Daniel* poet's passages. And perhaps Grein's summarily dismissed magical reading of the dew as 'the work of the fairies' has much to recommend it.[28]

The verb that the *Daniel* poet deploys for the rain fall and dew fall gives another indication that these passages are possibly inspired by the imagery of the Deuteronomic canticle. Where the Vulgate Daniel passage describes the miracle with the simple indicative statement *fecit medium fornacis quasi uentum roris flantem* ([the angel] made the interior of the furnace as a wind of dew blowing [Daniel A3:27]), the *Daniel* poet uses the subjunctive form of the verb *weorðan* (to come to be, to be made) in both weather similes. The action governing the dew fall and the drops of rain respectively, *deawdrias on dæge weorðeð* and *sended weorðeð/ dropena drearung*, literally translates as 'made to become,' giving a sense very close to that created by the Deuteronomy verb *concrescat*, which compares the bringing together of doctrine to the gathering of moisture into droplets before they are let to fall to the earth as raindrops. The poem's verb *sended* is similarly closer to the Latin *fluat*, which besides 'flow' indicates 'proceed,' 'issue.'[29]

In addition to the *Heptateuch* version of the Deuteronomic canticle, several other Old English versions, in the form of continuous glosses to the Latin psalter, provide support for these connections between the poem and the canticle in their similar usage of *scur* for *imber*, *dropan* for *stillae*, and

---

extensively in patristic commentary; see for example, Ambrose, *Enarrationes in Psalmos XII*, *Praefatio* 4, *PL* 14.923C; *in Psalmum XXXV* 55, col. 764; *in Psalmum XXXVI*, 26, col. 981A; Jerome, *Commentariorum in Isaiam prophetam*, *PL* 24.535D; and Rabanus Maurus, *Commentaria in Cantica*, *PL* 112.1133A–C, 1152A–C. Similar exegeses occur also in Latin psalter glosses; for example, the Eadwine Psalter gloss to Psalm 132:2 reads: *sicut ros Hermon, qui descendit in montem Sion: ros - caritas quae fluxit de spiritu sancto* (as the dew of Hermon which descends upon Mount Zion: dew – love which flows from the holy spirit). The Eadwine gloss is the standard commentary found in the *Glossa ordinaria*. See Margaret Gibson, T.A. Heslop, and Richard W. Pfaff, eds., *The Eadwine Psalter*, 108 and 119.

28 See the discussion in Jane Roberts, Christian Kay, and Lynne Grundy, eds., *A Thesaurus of Old English*, vol. 1, xxi.

29 According to BT, Old English *flowe* (*Heptateuch*, Deuteronomy 32:2) similarly conveys the notion of 'issuing forth.'

weax for *concrescat*.[30] Other details in the Deuteronomic canticle seem also to be reflected in the poem. In the verses introducing the canticle in Deuteronomy, Moses censures the people for their pride (Deuteronomy 31:27). The pride of Israel is also specified in the *Daniel* Canticle of Azarias (*oferhygdum* [line 297]) and in the exordium (*wlenco* [line 18]),[31] but not in the Latin Daniel canticle. Similarly, Moses states that the people will 'quickly' turn from God and provoke his anger (*declinabitis cito ... inritetis eum* [Deuteronomy 31:29]; *ad iracundiam concitauerunt* [Deuteronomy 32:16, 19]; cf. *in ira et in furore, et in indignatione maxima* [Deuteronomy 29:28]). These details are entirely absent from the Latin Daniel canticle but correspond very closely to the description in the exordium of *Daniel* of the Israelites' short-term belief (*gelyfdon / lytle hwile* [lines 28–9]) and God's consequent anger (*þa wearð reðemod* [line 33]). In both the Deuteronomic canticle and the poem, God's present anger is contrasted with his past favour towards his people, which in both are called 'beloved' (*dilectus* [Deuteronomy 32:15]; *dyrust* and *leofost* [lines 36–7]). Again in both, the overall sense of moral and spiritual failure is similar in expression: Israel is *gens absque consilio est et sine prudentia* (a nation without counsel and without wisdom [Deuteronomy 32:28]); it lacks *wisdom* (wisdom) and *ece rædes* (lasting counsel) [*Daniel*, lines 27–30].

---

30 The glossed psalters examined here are Vespasian (eighth century), Cambridge (early tenth century), Bosworth (late tenth century), Lambeth and Stowe (early eleventh century), Arundel and Vitellius (mid-eleventh century), Eadwine, or Canterbury (twelfth century). See Minnie Cate Morrell, *A Manual of Old English Biblical Materials*, and Phillip Pulsiano, 'Psalters,' 61–85, for categorization and descriptions of each psalter. The Vulgate/Gallican verb *concrescat* often appears in the earlier Old Latin/ Romanum texts as *expectetur* (be awaited, hoped for) and is glossed with forms of the Old English *abidan*. The psalters are quite varied in both the Latin and Old English for the opening images of Deuteronomy, chapter 32, with some elements closer than others to the poem. For example, the Romanum psalters (Vespasian, Cambridge, Bosworth, and Eadwine) have *nix* (snow) rather than *stillae* in the Latin, but have *imber*, glossed as *scur*. The Gallican Psalters (Stowe, Arundel, and Vitellius) have *stillae*, glossed as *dropan*, but they gloss *imber* as *hagol* (hail). *Daniel* compares exactly to the Lambeth Psalter, which has *imber*, glossed as *scur*, and *stillae*, glossed as *dropan*. The *Heptateuch* also translates *stillae* as *dropan*, but *imber* as *smylte ren* (gentle rain). The Lambeth Psalter, like the other psalters, might very well have belonged to a larger now lost sample of psalters with similar textual readings.

31 Indeed the pride of Israel is compared to the pride of Nabuchodonosor and Belshazzar: *wlenco* (line 678); *oferhygd* (lines 107, 489, 494, 614, 656). For a recent discussion of pride in the poem see Manish Sharma, 'Nabuchodonosor and the Defiance of Measure in the Old English *Daniel*,' 103–26.

Another feature that *Daniel* shares with the Canticle of Moses is that it includes heathen practices in its detailing of the apostasy of Israel. Moses states that the people *dereliquit Deum ... immolauerunt daemonibus* (they have forsaken God ... sacrificed to devils [Deuteronomy 32:15–18]). In *Daniel*, the people have *æcræftas forleton* (forsaken the laws) and turned to *deofoldædum* (devil deeds [lines 18–19]); *forleton drihtnes domas, curon deofles cræft* (they have forsaken God's laws, cultivated devil's craft (lines 31–2)].[32] In contrast, in the Latin Daniel canticle the sins of the people are not specified beyond the breaking of the commandments: *deliquimus in omnibus; et praecepta tua non audiuimus, nec obseruauimus* (we are delinquent in every way; and we have not paid attention to your commandments, nor have we performed them [Daniel A3:29–30]). Similarly, the poem is much closer to Deuteronomy than to the Latin Daniel canticle in its expression of God's retribution. In each case retribution takes the form of a decimation of the people, but again the phraseology of the Latin Daniel canticle, *imminuti sumus* (we have been diminished [Daniel A3:37]), is significantly different from that of the Latin and Old English Deuteronomy passages which read, respectively: *remanebitis pauci nationibus* (you will be left few among the nations [Vulgate Deuteronomy 4:27, 28:62]); *byð feawa on ðam lande to lafe* (you will be left few in the land [*Heptateuch* Deuteronomy 4:27, 28:62]). The Deuteronomy passages are both closer in diction to Azarias's statement in the poem that Israel has been reduced to only a 'few' (*heora fea* [line 325]).

This lowest point in the fortunes of Israel is the gist of the *Daniel* poet's treatment of Israel throughout the poem. As in the Old English versions of the Canticle of Moses from Deuteronomy (both the glossed psalters and the *Heptateuch* version), the poem describes the captive Israelites as *lafe* (remnants), and the condition in the poem of the 'wretched remnant' (*earme lafe* [lines 80 and 152]; cf. *wæpna lafe* [line 74) is very close to that described by Moses: *uidebit quod ... clausi quoque defecerunt residuique consumpti sunt* ([God] will see that ... the captured ones have also failed, and the remnant is consumed [Vulgate Deuteronomy 32:36]); *he gesyhð ... ða belocenan geteorodun &. ða lafa synd fornumene* ([God] will see ... that

---

32 The accusation of devil worship in the Canticle of Moses is possibly also behind the heathenism specified in the *Daniel* poet's Canticle of Azarias: *we nu hæðenra þeowned þoliað* (we now suffer in servitude to heathens [or in heathen lands], lines 306–7); this part of the poem might also reflect the many statements throughout Deuteronomy that the people will worship 'alien gods,' 'gods they did not know' (*diis alienis ... diis quos ignorabant* [Deuteronomy 32: 16–17 and passim]).

those who have been taken captive have failed in strength and the remnant is destroyed [*Heptateuch* Deuteronomy 32:36]). The reduction of an already decimated remnant is a popular expression in both the Pentateuch and Prophets for emphasizing the huge scale and the final ignominy of the destruction to be visited upon Israel: even the remnant of the people is reduced.[33] The *Daniel* poet would not have found the remnant motif anywhere in the court tales of the book of Daniel, and his many echoes of the Canticle of Moses suggest that the source for his very unconventional usage of this popular biblical motif might well have been Deuteronomy, the *locus classicus* in any case for the scattering and return of the remnant.[34] It is thus a significant signal of his interest in Deuteronomy that the poet chooses to end his version of the furnace miracle with the return of the 'remnant of the people' (*leoda lafe* [line 452]) to God;[35] these are the select 'people of inheritance,' according to Deuteronomy, whom God rescued from the iron furnace (*et eduxit de fornace ferrea Ægypti, ut haberet populum hæreditarium* [Deuteronomy 4:20]).

To sum up, then, when these correspondences between Deuteronomy and *Daniel* are tallied against the scriptural Daniel (see the table on pp. 216–17), they indicate that the prophecies and accusations of Deuteronomy, especially those concentrated in the Canticle of Moses, offer ample resource for the portrayal of a fallen Israel in *Daniel*, especially as recounted in the exordium and the Canticle of Azarias. Like the Canticle of Azarias, the exordium has also had a history of source-critical speculation, including arguments of interpolation. Both passages are distinguished from the rest

---

33 See Portnoy, *The Remnant*, chap. 3.

34 Ibid., 98–101. In the passages cited here from Deuteronomy, chapters 4 and 28, the Vulgate *remaneo* represents the Hebrew and Greek words for 'remnant.'

35 I argue elsewhere that the remnant in this passage represents only the three Hebrew youths, not the entire Israelite nation as assumed by Caie, 'The Old English *Daniel*,' 5–6, and R.E. Finnegan, 'The Old English *Daniel*,' 208. Both see a favourable reversal in the fortunes of the Israelites 'as a nation' in these lines, by assuming that Nabuchodonosor returns the same remnant that he took captive at the beginning of the poem. But in fact each recurrence of the remnant in the poem serves rather to distinguish Daniel and the three Hebrew youths from the original 'remnant of the weapons' (line 74): the youths are chosen from '*among* the wretched remnant of the Israelites' (line 80); Daniel is chosen leader '*of* the wretched remnant' (line 152). In progressively narrowing his focus, the poet has refined the remnant from the past sense of 'what the weapons left behind' of the Israelite people at the sack of Jerusalem to the more immediate sense of the 'wretched remnant' of that group in the narrative present at Babylon to the 'remnant' of that group selected by the king and centralized in the narrative of the furnace miracle. See Portnoy, *The Remnant*, 162–82.

of the poem by their complex structure, both contain many non-biblical details, and both are noted to be lyrical in character.[36] Remley suggests that for the exordium the poet combined encyclopedic knowledge and memory of the psalms and canticles of the daily Office, many of which advert to the fall of Israel, with an equally compendious knowledge and memory of the historical books of the Old Testament. With respect to the Canticle of Azarias, Remley argues that the infrequent liturgical use (and therefore the lesser degree of exact recollection) of this canticle likely accounts for the poet's significant deviation from the Latin. He concludes that the poet likely depended at least in part upon a text that differed considerably from any extant Latin texts of the canticle.[37]

Given the linguistic parallels detailed here, I suggest that this Latin text might have been the Canticle of Moses from Deuteronomy rather than, or in addition to, the Canticle of Azarias. It is not just that the Canticle of Moses is comparable to *Daniel* from its large concentration of parallel references to the fall of Israel, the rain and dew, and the remnant. The canticle has a history of textual and iconographic representation in liturgical manuscripts where it serves as a link between the miracles of the Red Sea and the fiery furnace. This link may have prompted the poem's introductory references to the exodus from Egypt (line 6), and it may also stand behind the sequence of Old Testament subjects in the program of Junius 11.

Exodus-Daniel in Liturgy and Art

Moses' song of apostasy and retribution resolves ultimately into praise and blessing in one very common manuscript 'program' of sorts: the series of canticles appended to the Latin psalter. Here the second Daniel canticle, the 'Song of the Three Hebrew Youths,' follows the Deuteronomic Canticle of Moses in a nearly standardized order of seven Old Testament canticles in which the canticles from Deuteronomy and Daniel are the sixth and seventh and the Canticle of Moses from Exodus, the fourth in the series. The seven canticles were chanted in the daily Office at lauds, one on each day of the week, and thus unlike the psalms they would have

---

36 Remley, *Old English Biblical Verse*, 255–78 and 369; Remley, '*Daniel*, the *Three Youths* Fragment, and the Transmission of Old English Verse,' 124.

37 Remley, *Old English Biblical Verse*, 271–2 and 359–63. Another impediment to recollection noted by Remley is that the Canticle of Azarias was subjected to an unusual degree of ad hoc centonization in the liturgy. See also Marsden, 'Old Latin Intervention,' 262.

Comparison of the Old English *Daniel* with Daniel 3 and Deuteronomy

Vulgate Deuteronomy	Heptateuch Deuteronomy	Old English Daniel	Vulgate Canticle of Azarias (Dan. A3:24–50)
4:27 disperget in omnes gentes et remanebitis pauci	**4:27** Drihten eow todrifð geond ealle ðeoda … byð feawa on ðam lande to lafe	**Lines 300–4** towrecene geond widne grund … heapum tohworfen … geond landa fela … bewræcon	
28:62–4 remanebitis pauci numero … auferamini de terra … disperget te Dominus in omnes populos a summitate terrae usque ad terminos eius	**28:62–4** forhwyrfð eow of ðam lande… Drihten eow adrifð geond ealle ðeoda oð eorðan endas		
29:28 et ejecit eos de terra sua … projecitque in terram alienam			
4:27; 28:62 pauci	**4:27; 28:62** feawa	**325** heora fea lifigen	imminuti sumus
Abraham, Isaac, et Iacob [passim]	Abrahame, Isaace and Iacobe	**313–14** Abrahame, Isaace and Iacobe	**3:35** Abraham … Isaac… et Israel
31:27 ceruicem durissimam	**31:27** geflit	**18** wlenco, **297** oferhygdum	
31:29 declinabitis cito	**31:29** sona forlæt	**28–9** Gelyfdon … lytle hwile	
32:1–4 uerba, loquor, doctrina, eloquium	**32:1–4** spece, word, lar, spæce	**325–6** frumspræce, wordcwyde	**3:43** nomini tuo
Concrescat in pluuia … fluat ut ros … quasi imber … quasi stillae	wax … swa ren; flowe … swa deaw & swa smylte ren & swa dropan	**276** deawdrias on dæge weorðeð; **346–9** weorðeð … dropena drearung … wearmlic wolcna scur	**3:50** quasi uentum roris flantem
32:15 dilectus		**36–7** dyrust, leofost	

Comparison of the Old English *Daniel* with Daniel 3 and Deuteronomy (*Continued*)

Vulgate Deuteronomy	*Heptateuch* Deuteronomy	Old English *Daniel*	Vulgate Canticle of Azarias (Dan. A3:24–50)
32:16, 19 ad iracundiam concitauerunt [cf. 31:29]	**32:16, 19** gremedon hine ... ða wearð he yrre	**33** þa wearð reðemod	
32:16–17 immolauerunt daemoniis	**32:16–17** offrodon deoflum	**18** deofoldædum; **32** deofles cræft; **749** deoflu drincan	
32:36 residuique consumpti sunt	**32:36** ða lafa synd fornumene	**80, 152** earme lafe	

acquired connections with each other from their contiguity both in the manuscripts and in liturgical recitation. Hundreds of Old English glossed psalters are thought to have been in circulation in Anglo-Saxon England, preserving a textual version of an oral-liturgical tradition that is thought to have been continuous from at least the eighth century.[38]

The *Daniel* poet might therefore have been very familiar with the two Canticles of Moses from either textual study or weekly recitation, or both – hence perhaps his references to Moses in his exordium and his substitution of ideas from the Deuteronomic canticle for the less familiar Canticle of Azarias. Moreover, the complex interrelationships among the Latin psalter texts and among the various Old English glosses suggest that the poem was likely part of a larger tradition in which liturgical influence altered biblical representation. Richard Marsden argues that the *Heptateuch* version of the Deuteronomic Canticle of Moses reflects readings from the Latin Roman Psalter in combination with Old English readings from the glossed psalters; in other words, the *Heptateuch* translator seems to have turned from a biblical exemplar to a liturgical exemplar for the canticle.[39] Sarah Larratt Keefer argues similarly that the Exodus Canticle of Moses in the *Heptateuch* also is based upon the psalter rather than on scripture. Keefer concludes that the glossed psalters had two functions similar to

38 Morrell, *A Manual*, 47–8; Pulsiano, 'Psalters,' 80–4.
39 Marsden, 'Old Latin Intervention,' 259–64; Marsden, *The Text of the Old Testament in Anglo Saxon England*, 435–8.

those of the *Heptateuch*, instruction and meditation.[40] Presumably a biblical poet would have benefited from such education; in any case, the poem's linguistic parallels with the *Heptateuch* and the glossed psalters described above, and the parallels between the *Heptateuch* and the glossed psalters, suggest very strongly that like the *Heptateuch* translator the *Daniel* poet likely used the psalter as his resource. Furthermore, if we consider the pervasive presence of Deuteronomy in *Daniel* as the intermediary link,[41] then the Junius 11 sequence, *Exodus–(Deuteronomy)–Daniel* is nearly identical to the psalter sequence of canticles from Exodus, Deuteronomy, and Daniel (numbers 4, 6, and 7).[42] This suggests that the Junius compiler or compilers, no less than the *Heptateuch* 'committee,'[43] might have been influenced by the psalter canticle tradition.

Nevertheless, must we assume that a poet had only words (written or oral, biblical or liturgical) in mind as he composed? In what remains of this essay I wish to explore another important element of the liturgical tradition as a possible resource for an Anglo-Saxon poet: psalter illumination. I am led to this line of enquiry from some notable pictorial analogues to *Daniel* and to Junius 11 presented by the illustrations of the Utrecht Psalter, an early ninth-century Gallican Psalter that was housed in Canterbury at the end of the tenth century, and of its twelfth-century copy, the Eadwine (Canterbury) Psalter. The Utrecht pictorial style is thought to have been based on a very early (fifth- or sixth-century) illuminated psalter or psalter tradition, making it a possible source or a record of a source or sources that could have served the *Daniel* poet, whatever the exact date of the poem.[44]

---

40 Sarah Larratt Keefer, 'Assessing the Liturgical Canticles from the Old English *Hexateuch*,' 109–43. See also Patrick P. O'Neill, 'Latin learning at Winchester in the Early Eleventh Century,' 162–4.

41 The influence of Deuteronomy has also been noted in the final lines of *Exodus*. See James Earl, 'Christian Traditions,' 559; Peter Lucas, ed. *Exodus*, 146; Fred C. Robinson, 'Notes on the Old English *Exodus*,' 378.

42 The intervening fifth canticle is the Canticle of Habakkuk.

43 Marsden, 'Translation by Committee?'

44 For reproduction and discussion of the Utrecht Psalter, see Ernest T. DeWald, *The Illustrations of the Utrecht Psalter*; F. Wormald, *English Drawings of the Tenth and Eleventh Centuries*, 20–1; E. Temple, *Anglo-Saxon Manuscripts 900–1066*, 81–3; Carol Gibson-Wood, 'The Utrecht Psalter and the Art of Memory,' 9–15; Van der Horst et al., *The Utrecht Psalter in Medieval Art*. For discussion of the insular-continental interconnection of artists and of biblical iconography, see the introductions by DeWald and Van der Horst; Veronica Ortenberg, *The English Church and the Continent in the Tenth and Eleventh Centuries*; Carol Neuman de Vegvar, *The Northumbrian Renaissance*.

The illustrations contain some striking pictorial parallels with verbal details in *Daniel*, and like the poem and like the Junius program, they make connections between the events of Exodus, Deuteronomy, and Daniel. The spectacular pen drawings bring the psalms and canticles to life in a manner that is startlingly literal and concrete and at the same time typological in effect. This is particularly well exemplified in the illustrations of the Canticles of Moses and of the Three Hebrew Youths, and it is not difficult to see how a poet viewing such lively pictorial representation of the canticles, or some like derivative or analogue, might have been inspired to unusual flights of fancy such as the *Daniel* poet's depictions of the dew and rain.

The dew and rain are both present in the depiction of the Canticle of the Three Hebrew Youths in the Utrecht tradition (fig. 1);[45] in fact they appear to be conflated – or perhaps interchangeable – pictorial motifs. The illustration seems to be depicting the rain and dew from the text of the canticle proper, *Benedicite, omnis imber et ros* (Every shower and dew, bless the Lord [Daniel A3:64]), but while the short vertical dashes may look more like rain, the presence in the drawing of the angel and the furnace requires the dashes to be read as the dew properly associated with the furnace miracle. The angel and the furnace derive from the apocryphal prose interlude that precedes the canticle and which is not present in the psalter text (and which contains no 'rain'). The conflation of the two passages in the illustration is a close pictorial analogue for *Daniel*, as the rain or dew pictorial image suggests visually the same sense of the paired water effects of dew and rain that the *Daniel* poet achieves by introducing the rain image into his centralized description of the furnace miracle.

The treatment of the angel in the Utrecht tradition presents another analogue to the poem. As in many insular and continental depictions of the furnace miracle,[46] the angel is placed centrally above the furnace, illustrating the scriptural statement that the angel 'descended' into the furnace (Daniel A3:49). Unlike the comparanda, however, the angel does not appear to be descending any further. Rather, he stands directly below Christ and gestures upwards towards Christ instead of downwards towards the youths. The inclusion of Christ produces a hierarchical configuration that

---

45 For the Utrecht Psalter image see fol. 87v of the DeWald online facsimile. Because the Utrecht images are very faint in print, I have used the illustrations from the Eadwine (Canterbury) Psalter here. The later psalms and canticles are not present in the Harley Psalter.

46 For examples, see above, note 4.

is unconventional and makes the role of the angel more of a mediating one, whereas in the absent prose interlude it is the angel alone that performs the crucial action: *et excussit flammam ignis de fornace et fecit medium fornacis quasi uentum roris flantem* (and he [the angel] drove the flames out of the furnace, and made the inside of the furnace as though a dew-laden breeze were blowing through it [Daniel A3:49–50]). In many depictions of the miracle the angel brings on the saving dew by touching the furnace with a cross-staff.[47] Here, however, the dew is falling directly from heaven; in other words, the saving action is not the angel's, but Christ's. The inclusion of Christ in the pictorial version of the furnace miracle is a parallel to the *Daniel* poet's inclusion of God in his version. There the repeated alternating motifs of God's protection and the angel's protection resolve in ring 5 with the final focus on God. And, granted that the depiction of dew carried by wind within a flaming furnace is no easy task, the final effect of the illustration is that the dew appears to fall, like raindrops, as it does in *Daniel*.

Another striking similarity to the poem is that the illustration of the Daniel canticle appears to quote (pictorially in this case) from the Canticle of Moses from Deuteronomy; the angel's intermediary position and supplicating stance are identical to those of Moses (fig. 2),[48] and the people of Israel are in the same lateral positions in both drawings. The Deuteronomy illustration also has the same symmetrical short vertical dashes on either side of the central figure, here depicting the dew or rain – or both, I would argue – of the canticle's opening verses.[49] Dew is configured similarly in the drawing for Psalm 132:2 (fig. 3), *sicut ros Hermon, qui descendit in montem Sion* (as the dew of Hermon which descends upon Mount Zion), but exactly the same image is used to depict rain in Psalm 146:8 (fig. 4), *et parat terrae pluuiam* (and who prepares rain for the earth).[50] The repeated use of the dash motif over the long period of the Utrecht copying thus indicates that rain and dew were conventionally paired and/or interchangeable

---

47 Ibid.
48 For the Utrecht Psalter image, see fol. 86r of the DeWald online facsimile.
49 DeWald, *The Illustrations of the Utrecht Psalter*, 69, reads the images as the fire of God's wrath from verse 22.
50 The same image appears in the illustration of Psalm 71:6, *Descendet sicut pluuia in uellus: et sicut stillicidia stillantia super terram* (He shall come down like rain upon the fleece: and as showers dropping upon the earth). For the Utrecht Psalter illustrations, see fols. 40v, 75v, and 81v in the DeWald online facsimile.

iconographically. Besides the similar collocations of the rain and dew, then, the parallel connections between the Deuteronomy and Daniel canticles – iconographically in the psalters and verbally in the Junius *Daniel* – suggest that the psalter illustrations, or some version of them, might have been known to the poet.

An Anglo-Saxon might also have made connections between these two canticles from their chanting one after the other, as already noted, in the Saturday-Sunday Office. A more concentrated and dramatic chanting would have occurred on Holy Saturday, when the two canticles formed the final two of the twelve Old Testament lections of the Easter vigil. In the liturgical ritual the focus of the audience advances from the mediating Moses to the mediating angel to direct contact with Christ as the readings progress from Deuteronomy to Daniel to the baptism (the ritual act of commitment to Christ). As these final two readings are liturgical canticles, as opposed to excerpted biblical passages, they were likely chanted rather than read, and thus they would have been heightened in dramatic effect and easily committed to memory.

The liturgical practice of antiphonal singing often took the form of physical as well as musical separation and balance, with parts of the choir stationed on opposite sides of the church (even as the Israelites are depicted in the Utrecht illustrations). The directions given in the *Regularis Concordia*, for example, indicate that the chanting of the canticles on Holy Saturday was to be divided between boy soloists and choir and sung from various parts of the darkened church.[51] One can imagine that the responsion would have been particularly impressive with the men taking the role of Moses and the boys, that of the three Hebrew youths. Familiarity from the daily Office would likely have further set these two readings apart in the liturgical experience and memory of any participant in the ritual and might therefore also have prompted the iconographical connections between the two made by the Utrecht artist, as well as the verbal connections made by the *Daniel* poet, and the programmatic connections made by the Junius compiler or compilers.

---

51 See Joyce Hill, 'Lexical Choices for Holy Week,' 122–3, and Lucia Kornexl, 'The *Regularis Concordia* and Its Old English Gloss,' 100–1.

Figure 1. Eadwine (Canterbury) Psalter, fol. 275b, Daniel Canticle. By permission of the Master and Fellows of Trinity College, Cambridge.

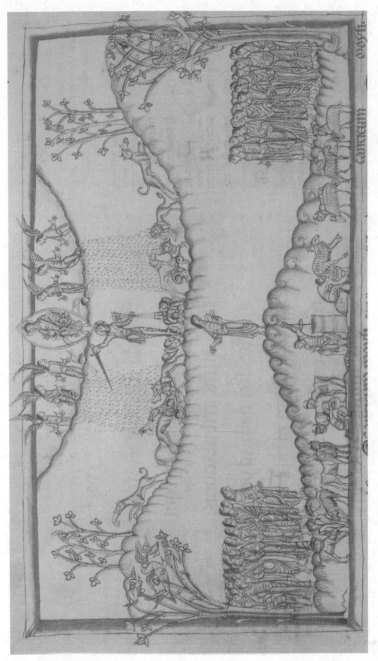

Figure 2. Eadwine (Canterbury) Psalter, fcl. 270b, Deuteronomy Canticle. By permission of the Master and Fellows of Trinity College, Cambridge.

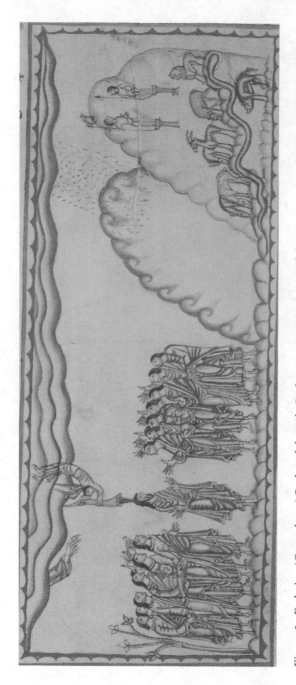

Figure 3. Eadwine (Canterbury) Psalter, fol. 238b, Psalm 132. By permission of the Master and Fellows of Trinity College, Cambridge.

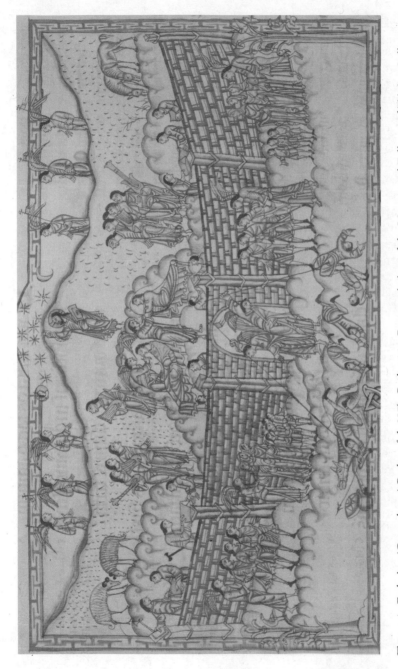

Figure 4. Eadwine (Canterbury) Psalter, fol. 257b, Psalm 146. By permission of the Master and Fellows of Trinity College, Cambridge.

Conclusion

If plotting a course through this labyrinth of verbal-iconographical links and parallels seems like an impossible task, it is also a measure of the amazing capacity of the Anglo-Saxon poet, because the complex pathways are most likely those of memory, or as Paul Remley has suggested, of *ruminatio*. In this process of recollection and contemplation, 'hearing certain words [of the Bible] ... sets up a chain reaction of associations ... and, in turn, a scriptural phrase will suggest quite naturally allusions elsewhere in the sacred books.'[52] Allowing that the mnemonic process might have been iconographic as well as verbal, we can reconstruct a process for the composition of *Daniel* in which the episode of the furnace miracle, chosen for structural elaboration from its importance in liturgy and art, recalls the familiar verbal and pictorial imagery from the Daniel canticle, which from collocation in the psalter, the Office, and the Easter vigil recalls the verbal and pictorial imagery of the Deuteronomic Canticle of Moses, which in turn recalls other passages of Deuteronomy.

Daniel Anlezark argues for such a method of composition underlying the vast and various mix of texts found to be reflected in *Exodus*. This eclecticism, he claims, suggests that Anglo-Saxon poets composed not by 'pulling books off the shelf in search of quotations, or "sources,"' but rather by 'ruminating on sacred history' and 'draw[ing] on vast memories, storing poems they had heard, texts they had studied in the classroom, or lections they had rehearsed annually in the liturgy.'[53] For *Daniel*, as for *Exodus*, one must follow the poet into each of these complexly interrelated areas and through his artful structures in order to appreciate how such a diffuse sense of 'source' might affect his re-creation. I regret to say that rather than simplifying the enterprise, I have added another layer to it: I suggest that the store of memory would very likely have included pictorial as well as textual and liturgical versions of Old Testament biblical narrative.

---

52 Remley, *Old English Biblical Verse*, 272–3.
53 Daniel Anlezark, 'Connecting the Patriarchs,' 188.

The Old Testament and Other
Old English Poems

Rex regum et cyninga cyning: 'Speaking Hebrew' in Cynewulf's *Elene*

DAMIAN FLEMING

The influence of the Bible, and in particular the Old Testament, on the surviving corpus of Old English poetry has long been acknowledged, as other articles in this volume amply demonstrate.[1] The *Genesis* poems, *Exodus, Daniel,* and the verse portions of the *Paris Psalter* alone constitute over nine thousand lines of Old English verse based directly on the Old Testament. This study examines the more subtle, linguistic influence that the Old Testament had on Old English poetry. Through the medium of Latin, a handful of Hebrew loanwords and loan translations entered Old English,[2] as did constructions based on Hebraic ways of expressing ideas.[3]

---

1 A version of this paper was read at 'A Symposium on the Study and Use of the Bible in the Middle Ages,' University of Western Ontario, 22–3 March 2002. I am thankful for the help of the following during the preparation of this article: Andy Orchard, Antonette diPaolo Healey, David Townsend, David McDougall, Ian McDougall, and Tess Owens Fleming.

2 See Helmut Gneuss, '*Anglicae linguae interpretatio*,' 109–48, esp. 123–5; Gneuss notes the Hebrew loanword (via Latin) *sabbat* and its parallel loan formation *ræstedæg*. Other Hebrew loanwords in Old English include *alleluia* and *fariseisc*; other loan formations on a Hebrew basis include *sundorhalga* for *Pharisaei* (= *divisi*), *rihtwisende* for *Sadducaei* (= *iusti*), and *hælend* for *Iesus* (= *salvator*); see Herbert Dean Meritt, *Fact and Lore about Old English Words*, 207–9.

3 See Richard Marsden, 'Cain's Face and Other Problems,' 2–51, esp. 38–43; for particular instances in the *Dictionary of Old English A–F on CD-ROM*, ed. Angus Cameron, Ashley C. Amos, and Antonette diP. Healey, see s.vv. *āfæstnian*, senses 2.d and 8; *andfangend; andfeng*, sense 2; *andfengnes*, sense 1.a; *āweorpan*, sense 1.a.iii.a.iii; *bearn*, senses I.C.1 and I.D.2; *belūcan*, sense 3.b.ii; *ēaland*, sense 3; *forweorpan*, sense 1.a.i; *fulnes*, sense 1; and *fyllednes*, sense 1. On Hebraisms in post-conquest English, see Marsden, '"In the Twinkling of an Eye,"' 145–72. On biblical Hebraisms in later English, see J. Isaacs, 'The Authorized Version and After,' 196–234, esp. 209–14.

The focus of this article is one specific type of Hebrew syntax adopted in Old English, the so-called augmentative or superlative genitive. In particular, I argue that Cynewulf seems to be aware of the biblical and Hebraic origin of this construction and uses it in his poem *Elene* to distinguish the diction of the Jewish characters from that of the Christian ones.

In the superlative genitive construction, a noun in any case is modified by the same noun in the genitive plural, raising the meaning of the first noun to the superlative; well-known examples include *king of kings*, *lord of lords*, and *Song of Songs*.[4] Although this construction is used as a means of 'superlation' in pre-Christian Latin,[5] its popularity and wide use in the Christian west is due to its use within the Hebrew Bible and the subsequent translation of the construction into Latin in the Vulgate.[6] The few modern grammars of medieval or ecclesiastical Latin that treat this construction generally attribute its origin to an imitation of the Hebrew.[7]

---

4 For an overview of this construction in ancient languages, see Gerd Schäfer, 'König der Könige' – 'Lied der Lieder'; see also Calvert Watkins, *How to Kill a Dragon*, 241–6. This syntactical construction is not explored in detail in Bruce Mitchell, *Old English Syntax*; discussion there is restricted to these remarks (§1296): 'Strictly speaking, the partitive genitive represents the whole from which a part is taken. Muxin … is right to point out the difference between what he calls the "partitive" genitive … from the "elective" – sometimes known as the "cognate" or "emphatic" genitive – e.g. CH I.2, 197.223 *ealra worulda woruld*, CH II.20, 191.35 *ealra goda God* (in which *one of a kind* is chosen). But we can reasonably use the term "partitive" for both' (Mitchell, vol. 1, 545). The only treatments of the subject in Old English that I have found are in Roberta Frank, 'Some Uses of Paronomasia in Old English Scriptural Verse,' 207–26, esp. 221–2, and Niilo Peltola, 'Observations on Intensification in Old English Poetry,' 649–90, esp. 686–90.
5 Jeffrey Wills, *Repetition in Latin Poetry*, 193, shows that the construction exists in classical Latin, citing uses in Plautus, Pliny, Seneca, Petronius, Martial, and Lucretius, which can be explained without reference to a foreign influence. Wills notes, however, that the use of the construction in classical Latin is marginal; see also J.B. Hofmann, *Lateinische Syntax und Stilistik*, §54, sec. γ.
6 On Jerome's translation techniques, see Benjamin Kedar-Kopfstein, 'The Vulgate as a Translation'; for this construction in particular see esp. 250, 'The noun in a construct state with its own plural is used to express a superlative degree. This was not unknown in L[atin]; V[ulgate] thus consistently follows Heb[rew]: Gn. 9:25; Dt. 10:17; 1 Rg. 6:16; Nm. 3:32; 1 Rg. 8:27.'
7 See Franz Kaulen, *Sprachliches Handbuch zur biblischen Vulgata*, 255, §138a, 'Durch Wiederholung des nämlichen Substantivs im Genitiv wird nach hebräischer Weise eine Steigerung des in demselben liegenden Begriffs hervorgebracht'; see also Albert Blaise, *Manuel du latin chrétien*, 83, §87, 'Génitif augmentatif; bien qu'il ne soit pas inconnu à la littérature profane … c'est avant tout un hébraïsme.' This is echoed by Alison Goddard Elliot, 'A Brief Introduction to Medieval Latin Grammar,' without reference to Hebrew, only that 'the construction becomes far more widespread in Christian Latin,' 18. John F.

Seow succinctly defines the Hebrew construction in reference to the opening of *Ecclesiastes* thus:

> The juxtaposition of the singular and the plural of the same noun is the standard way in Hebrew to express the superlative: e.g., 'king of kings' = 'supreme king' (Dan. 2:37; Ezra 7:12), 'servant of servants' = 'abject servant' (Gen. 9:25), and 'god of gods' = 'highest god' (Deut. 10:17). Thus, *hăbēl hăbālîm* refers to absolute or the ultimate *hebel*, a word that has been translated as 'vanity.'[8]

Presumably because of the rarity of the construction in pre-Christian Latin authors, it is not treated in the antique grammars, which primarily sought to explicate classical Latin usage. The majority of early medieval grammars are significantly dependent upon the pre-Christian grammars and thus also do not discuss the construction. As a result, it is not discussed in Priscian, Probus, or Donatus, or in the specifically Christian, insular grammars of Asporius, Tatwine, Boniface, the *Ars Bernensis*, Sedulius Scottus, Murethach, and the *Ars Laureshamensis*.[9] I have found this construction explained by only two early medieval grammarians; one of them is Virgilius Maro Grammaticus, an author who is known for his

---

Collins, *A Primer of Ecclesiastical Latin*, 307, states, 'In imitation of a Hebraic idiom, a noun in the genitive case may follow a different case of itself (e.g., *in saecula saeculōrum* "forever and ever").' W.E Plater and H.J. White, *A Grammar of the Vulgate*, 19–20, indicate that 'the genitive is also used to heighten the meaning of the first word and raise it to a superlative; so "cælum cæli, in saecula saeculorum," etc.' Regarding modern English, Isaacs notes, 'it is in the other phrases and categories of phrase that Hebrew idiom has left its mark; superlatives, such as "Holy of Holies," "Song of Songs," "King of Kings," and "Vanity of Vanities,"' ('The Authorized Version,' 210).

8 C.L. Seow, *Ecclesiastes*, 101; see also *Gesenius' Hebrew Grammar as Edited and Enlarged by the Late E. Krautzsch*, trans. A.E. Cowley, §133.i.; Ronald J. Williams, *Hebrew Syntax*, §47.

9 Priscian, *Institutiones grammaticae*, ed. H. Keil, in *Grammaticae Latini (GL)*, ed. II. Keil, 2:1–597, 3:1–377; Probus, *Instituta artium*, ed. H. Keil, in *GL*, 4:47–192; Donatus, *Ars Grammatica*, ed. H. Keil, in *GL*, 4:355–402; Asporius, *Ars*, ed. Hermann Hegan, in *GL*, 8.39–61; Tatwine, *Ars*, ed. M. DeMarco, 1–93; Boniface, *Ars grammatica*, ed. G.J. Gebauer and B. Löfstedt, 1–99; *Ars anonyma Bernensis*, ed. H. Hagen, in *GL*, 8:62–142; Sedulius Scottus, *Commentum Sedulii Scotti in maiorem Donatum grammaticum*, ed. Denis Brearley; Murethach, *In Donati artem maiorem*, ed. L. Holtz; *Ars Laureshamensis*, ed. B. Löfstedt. On these grammars and their use in Anglo-Saxon England, see Vivien Law, *Grammar and Grammarians in the Early Middle Ages* and *The Insular Latin Grammarians*. I am grateful to the late Dr Law for her invaluable advice via email at an early stage in the development of this article.

deviations from the norm.[10] He begins his section concerning the comparative and superlative degrees of nouns with a discussion of the formation and use of the superlative genitive construction:

> Nunc de conparatione pauca dicenda sunt. Possititiuus gradus cum genitiuo seruit – licet ex sollicismo –, tamen superlatiui facit opus, ut sapiens sapientum, quasi hoc diceret: sapientissimus sapientum.[11]

> [Now a few things have to be said about comparison. The positive degree works with the genitive, although this is a solecism, and does the job of the superlative, as 'wise man of wise men,' as if this should say: 'the wisest of wise men.'][12]

The Carolingian grammarian Smaragdus, writing in the ninth century, begins his discussion of the superlative in a similar fashion, and without the critical judgment of Virgilius's *licet ex sollicismo*; on the contrary, Smaragdus's presentation makes the construction seem like a natural part of the superlative degree:

> Superlatiuus gradus dicitur, eo quod positiuo et conparatiuo superferatur. Coniungitur namque genitiuo casui, suo semper generi et semper plurali, ut fortissimus rex regum et Dominus Dominorum.[13]

> [The superlative degree is named such because it surpasses the positive and comparative degrees. And it is joined to the genitive case, with its own gender and always plural, as the strongest 'king of kings and Lord of Lords.']

---

10   On Virgilius Maro Grammaticus, see Vivien Law, *Wisdom, Authority and Grammar in the Seventh Century*; on the influence and knowledge of his works in Anglo-Saxon England, see Law, *The Insular Latin Grammarians*, 49–52.

11   *Virgilius Maro Grammaticus: Opera omnia*, ed. B. Löfstedt, 143.

12   All translations are my own unless otherwise noted.

13   Smaragdus, *Liber in partibus Donati*, ed. B. Löfstedt, L. Holtz, and A. Kibre, 38–9. Joyce Hill has demonstrated the large influence that Smaragdus had on Ælfric in homiletic matters but does not discuss their grammars: Joyce Hill, 'Ælfric and Smaragdus,' 203–37. Vivien Law suggested to me that Smaragdus was widely used from the ninth through eleventh centuries in Anglo-Saxon England as well as on the continent (personal communication by email, 20 November 2001). However, Helmut Gneuss points out, as far as manuscripts are concerned, 'there is no evidence for the availability of the grammars of Alcuin, Hrabanus Maurus, and Smaragdus in pre-conquest England' ('The Study of Language in Anglo-Saxon England,' 12). On Smaragdus generally, and the possibility that he knew some Hebrew, see Fidel Rädle, *Studien zu Smaragd von Saint-Mihiel*, 51–60, esp. 60.

It is only after this explanation that Smaragdus explains the regular formation of superlative adjectives from the positive degree. Ælfric's vernacular grammar of the Latin language does not contain any occurrences or discussion of the superlative genitive construction.[14]

Although this construction is not discussed in most ancient and medieval Latin grammars, the early medieval reader would encounter it frequently and presumably be quite familiar with it; the Vulgate Bible has many examples that were as familiar to the Anglo-Saxons as they are to us: *seruus seruorum* (Genesis 9:25), *sancta sanctorum* (Exodus 26:34; 3 Regum 6:16), *princeps principum* (Numbers 3:32; 1 Paralipomenon 27:3), *Deus deorum et Dominus dominantium* (Deuteronomy 10:17), *caelum et caeli caelorum* (3 Regum 8:27), *uanitas uanitatum* (Ecclesiastes 1:2), *rex regum* (1 Ezra 7:12), *saeculum/-a saeculi/-orum* (Psalms, passim; Apocalypse, passim), and *rex regum et Dominus dominantium* (1 Timothy 6:15; Apocalypse 19:16). Not surprisingly, the use of this construction is more common and varied in the Old Testament books originally written in Hebrew than in the books of the New Testament, originally composed in Greek.[15] It is noteworthy that Smaragdus's claim that the second element in this construction is always plural (*semper plurali*) is not true; while singular + genitive plural is the most common form of the construction, the Old Testament's common *saeculum saeculi* shows that it is not absolute. It should also be noted that New Testament use of the construction does conform to Smaragdus's rule and is limited to positive terms, referring to God (*rex regum et Dominus dominantium*), eternity (*in saecula saeculorum*), or angels (*milia milium*).

This construction seems to have made a smooth transition from Latin into Old English. It is commonly used in Old English prose in imitation of its use in Latin. Thus, for example, the phrase *worulda woruld* is used over three hundred times in the psalter glosses to gloss *saeculum/-a saeculi/-orum*. The same phrase, again in imitation of the Latin, is commonly used in doxological contexts, especially as part of closing formulae to homilies.[16]

---

14 *Ælfrics Grammar und Glossar*, ed. Julius Zupitza.
15 In the Greek of the New Testament the use of this construction is also generally viewed as a Hebraism.
16 The ending of Ælfric's *CH* I.7 is typical: 'se þe leofað & rixað. mid fæder & halgum gaste. on ealra worulda woruld. AMEN.' Similar endings conclude his *CH* I.2, 7, 13, 17, 19, 24, 28, 30, 31, 35, 36, 40; II.6, 7, 13, 15, 28, 29, 30, 31, 32, 34, 36.1, 38, 40, 42, 44, 45; Ælfric's Lives of Saints Eugenia, Peter's Chair, Forty Soldiers, Book of Kings, Alban; Ælfric's homily 12, 31 (ed. Pope); Ælfric's homily 4, 12 (ed. Assmann). In total, Ælfric ends 37 of 151 homilies, or approximately one-quarter, with the phrase *on ealra*

Ælfric in particular uses superlative genitive names for God, often in doublets. Such formulations most likely originally stem from the New Testament's *rex regum et Dominus dominantium*; perhaps as a result, the doublets like this in Old English always include *cyninga cyning*. Ælfric uses the following titles for God:

> *ealra cyninga cyning & hlaforda hlaford* (*CH* I.1, 178.8–9)[17]
> *ealra biscopa biscop* and *ealra cyninga cyning* (*CH* II.1, 7.166–7)[18]
> *ealra cyninga cyning & ealra sacerda sacerd* (ÆIntSig 62.411).[19]

Similar doublets can also be found in anonymous texts, such as *ealra cyninga cyning & ealra wealdendra waldend*, in Vercelli homily 6.[20] Individually, the superlative genitive construction, by its repetitive nature, gives emphasis to any such title of God. In doublets, the emphasis is almost great enough to bring the homily to a stop; it is perhaps like a bit of song, a psalm, in the midst of prose.

The construction is not prevalent in the early Christian Latin poetry that would have been best known by the Anglo-Saxons, or in the Latin poetry composed by Anglo-Saxons themselves [see tables 1a and 1b].[21] Of course, a Latin poet would have to fit a phrase like *rex regum* into a strictly regulated quantitative line. This is not a problem for the Old English poet,

---

worulda woruld. Wulfstan and the anonymous homilists also frequently end their homilies *on (ealra) worulda woruld*.

17 *Ælfric's Catholic Homilies*, vol. 1, *The First Series: Text*, ed. Peter Clemoes, 178.

18 *Ælfric's Catholic Homilies*, vol. 2, *The Second Series: Text*, ed. Malcolm Godden, 7.

19 George Edwin MacLean, 'Ælfric's Version of *Alcuini interrogationes Sigeuulfi in Genesin*,' *Anglia* 7 (1884): 1–59 at 42–4.

20 *The Vercelli Homilies and Related Texts*, ed. D.G. Scragg, 128.

21 On the Anglo-Saxon curriculum texts, see Michael Lapidge, 'The Anglo-Latin Background,' 5–37, esp. 7. Editions consulted for tables 1a and 1b are Alcuin, *Carmina*, ed. E. Dümmler, 160–351; Aldhelm, *Opera*, ed. R. Ehwald; Arator, *De actibus apostolorum*, ed. A.P. McKinlay; Avitus, *Poematum libri VI*, ed. R. Peiper, 203–74; Æthelwulf, *De abbatibus*, ed. A. Campbell; Bede, *Bedas metrische Vita sancti Cuthberti*, ed. W. Jaager; Boethius, *Philosophiae consolatio*, ed. L. Bieler; Boniface, *Carmina*, ed. E. Dümmler, 3–19; Eusebius, *Aenigmata*, ed. Fr. Glorie, 211–71; Fridegod monachus, *Breuiloquium uitae beati Wilfredi*, ed. A. Campbell, 4–62; Juvencus, *Euangeliorum libri quattor*, ed. J. Huemer; K. Strecker, ed., *Miracula Nynie episcopi*, 943–61; Prosper of Aquitaine, *Epigrammata*, ed. J.-P. Migne, col. 498–532; Prudentius, *Psychomachia*, ed. M.P. Cunningham, CCSL 126, 149–81; Sedulius, *Opera omnia*, ed. J. Huemer, 14–146; Tatwine, *Aenigmata*, ed. Fr. Glorie, 167–208; Wulfstan Cantor [of Winchester], *Narratio metrica de sancto Swithuno*, ed. A. Campbell, 65–177.

Table 1a. Occurrences of the superlative genitive in Latin poetry read by Anglo-Saxons

Author, Work	Occurrences	Total Lines	Frequency
Sedulius, *Carmen paschale*	2	1753	1:876.5
Prudentius, *Psychomachia*	1	915	1:915
Avitus, *De spiritualis historiae gestis*	1	2552	1:2552
Juvencus, *Euangelia*	1	3134	1:3134
Boethius, *Philosophiae consolatio*	0	875	...
Arator, *De actis apostolorum*	0	2325	...
Prosper of Aquitane, *Epigrammata*	0	836	...

Table 1b. Occurrences of the superlative genitive in Anglo-Latin poetry

Author, Work	Occurrences	Total Lines	Frequency
Boniface, *Carmina*	1	521	1:521
Wulfstan of Winch., *Narratio de sancto Swithuno*	4	3382	1:845.5
Aldhelm, *Carmen de uirginitate*	1	2942	1:2942
Alcuin, *Carmina*	1	6583	1:6583
Aldhelm, other poetry	0	1813	...
Bede, *Vita S. Cuthberti*	0	979	...
Eusebius, *Enigmata*	0	282	...
Aethelwulf, *De abbatibus*	0	819	...
Miracula Nynie episcopi	0	504	...
Tatwine, *Enigmata*	0	213	...
Frithigod, *Breuiloquium Vitae beati Wilfredi*	0	1396	...

whose stress-based line would not hinder the use of such a phrase in the same way. Superlative genitive phrases are by their nature alliterative, a fact that makes their incorporation into Old English poetry easier. I have found that Old English poems of all sorts contain various forms of polyptoton and *figurae etymologiae*, just as Latin poems do, even though it means two of the main stresses of the line fall on a repetition of the same word or root.[22] In Old English poetry, superlative genitive phrases form a

---

22 On this subject in general, see Frank, 'Some Uses of Paronomasia.' All references to Old English poetry refer to *The Anglo-Saxon Poetic Records*, ed. Krapp and Dobbie. Following are examples of polyptoton in Old English verse: **bearn after bearne** (*Genesis A*, line1070a); **cynn æfter cynne** (*Exodus*, line 351a); **æðele be æðelum** (*Andreas*, line 360a); **stan fram stane** (*Andreas*, line 738a); *ne geald he yfel yfele* (*Elene*, line 493a); **halig is se halga** (*Elene*, line 750a); **weall wið wealle** (*Christ I*, line 11a); swa þæt leohte *leoht* (*Christ II*, line 592a); *frod wiþ frodne* (*Maxims I*, line 19a); *flod wið flode* (*The*

half-line per se, the *a* line in particular, with double alliteration, for example, *dryhtna dryhten* (*Andreas*, line 874a).[23] Owing to these factors the construction is not only possible but actually well suited to Old English verse. These considerations may also help to explain why it is much more prevalent in Old English verse than in Latin verse. The superlative genitive construction, however, is not indigenous to Old English, as far as the extant evidence suggests. Whereas one finds examples of repetition and polyptoton in various kinds of Old English poetry, the superlative genitive construction is exclusive to poems that are learned, Latinate (based on specific Latin sources), and wholly Christian; it does not occur in secular heroic poetry such as *Beowulf, Deor, Maldon, Widsith*, and *Brunanburh*.[24] Rather, the use of this construction in Old English verse seems to be an innovation of Christian Old English poets who borrow their syntax not from the Latin of Christian poetry but directly from the Latin of the Bible.

In the corpus of Old English poetry I count fifty-five occurrences of this construction in eighteen different poems (see table 2).[25] The most frequently occurring form is *worulda woruld*, a literal rendering of the Latin *saeculum/-a saeculi/-orum*, which constitutes twenty-two of fifty-five occurrences, appearing in seven different poems. The majority of these occurrences (fifteen) are found in the metrical psalms of the *Paris Psalter*.[26] *Worulda woruld* in the *Paris Psalter* renders the psalter text's frequently

---

Order of the World*, line 85a); *ecg wið ecge* (*Riddle 3*, line 42a); *feond his feonde* (*Riddle 50*, line 4a); *lað wið laþum* (*Beowulf*, line 440a); *wunder æfter wundre* (*Beowulf*, line 931a); *an æfter anum* (*Beowulf*, line 2461a); *be naman nemnan* (*Judith*, line 81a); *wese of dæge on dæg* (*The Paris Psalter*, line 67.19.2a); *of cynne on cynn* (*The Paris Psalter*, line 84.5.2a); *swelces and swelces* (*The Meters of Boethius*, line 28.50); *wigan wigheardne* (*Maldon*, line 75a); *wigan to wige* (*Maldon*, line 235a); *wigan on gewinne, wigend cruncon* (*Maldon*, line 302); *fyrd wið fyrde* (*Maxims II*, line 52a); *lað wið laþe* (*Maxims II*, line 53a); *wyrc þæt þu wyrce* (*An Exhortation*, line 16a).

23 See Andy Orchard, 'Artful Alliteration in Anglo-Saxon Song and Story,' 429–63.

24 One might therefore take issue with Seamus Heaney's translation of *Beowulf*, line 78, 'heal-ærna mæst; scop him Heort naman,' as '**the hall of halls**. Heorot was the name,' in *Beowulf: A New Verse Translation, Bilingual Edition*, 6–7.

25 See table 2 and the appendix to this essay; there are two occurrences in editions of *The Anglo-Saxon Poetic Records* that are not in the manuscripts and are thus not included in table 2 and the appendix: <*drihtna*> *drihten, dema mid unc twih* (*Genesis A*, line 2255a); and <*dryhtna*> *dryhten; and gedwolan fylgdon* (*Elene*, line 371a).

26 Occurrences of *worulda woruld* in the metrical *Paris Psalter* (psalm, verse, and line number) are 71.5.3a; 78.14.4a; 83.4.3a; 91.6.6a; 101.25.4a; 102.16.2a; 103.6.3a; 103.29.2a; 105.37.2a; 110.5.4a; 110.8.2a; 118.90.1a; 131.15.2a; 134.13.3a; 148.6.2a. Other superlative genitive phrases in the *Paris Psalter* (each of which renders a Latin superlative genitive title for God) are *ealra godena god* (135.2.2a, 135.28.1a), and *drihtna drihten* (135.3.2a).

Table 2. Old English Poems containing superlative genitive phrases, sorted by frequency

Poem	Occurrences	Total Lines	Frequency
A Prayer	3	79	1:26
A Summons to Prayer	1	31	1:31
The Kentish Hymn	1	43	1:43
The Gloria I	1	57	1:57
The Whale	1	88	1:88
The Judgment Day I	1	119	1:119
Christ II (Cynewulf)	3	427	1:142
Christ I	3	439	1:146
The Judgment Day II	2	306	1:153
Genesis B	1	617	1:167
The Phoenix	4	677	1:169
Christ and Satan	3	729	1:243
The Paris Psalter	19	5040	1:280
Elene (Cynewulf)	4	1321	1:330
Andreas	5	1722	1:344
Juliana (Cynewulf)	2	731	1:365
Guthlac B	1	561	1:561
Guthlac A	1	818	1:818

used *saecula saeculorum,* or a similar repetitive phrase in the psalms' Latin text, to express eternity. Most of the other occurrences of this construction in Old English verse can be grouped according to the narrative situation in which they occur. One such situation, probably derived from the construction's prevalence in the psalms, is the use of the construction in the context of prayers.[27] The clearest example of this is in the short poem simply known as *A Prayer,* where it is used three times within twenty-five lines. Another situation where the construction is commonly employed is in homiletic and especially doxological contexts within poems; such usage seems related to the use of the phrase in actual homilies, noted above.[28]

The most common usage of the construction in Old English poetry outside of the *Paris Psalter* is in descriptions of heaven and specifically in

---

27 Thus, *A Prayer,* lines 21a, 42a, 44a; *Andreas,* line 1151a; *Juliana,* line 594a; *A Kentish Hymn,* line 15a.

28 Thus, *Andreas,* line 1686a; *Christ and Satan,* lines 203b, 223a; *Christ II,* line 778a; *A Summons to Prayer,* line 19a; *Gloria I,* line 41a.

descriptions of the songs of angels.[29] Any Judeo-Christian description of a song of angels would likely be influenced by the vision of the throne of God as described by the prophet Isaiah, where the superlative genitive construction is not used, but *epizeuxis*,[30] the simple repetition of a word, is; this device shares the repetitious, religious, and ritualistic effect of superlative genitive constructions:

> Vidi Dominum sedentem super solium excelsum et eleuatum et ea quae sub eo erant implebant templum; seraphin stabant super illud ... et clamabant alter ad alterum et dicebat: '**Sanctus sanctus sanctus Dominus exercituum**, plena est omnis terra gloria eius.' (Isa. 6:1–3)[31]

> [I saw the Lord sitting upon a throne high and elevated: and his train filled the temple. Upon it stood the seraphim ... And they cried to one another, and said, **Holy, holy, holy, the Lord God of hosts**, all the earth is full of his glory.][32]

This particular song of angels is widely known as the *Sanctus* of the Mass, where it is also explicitly defined as a song of angels[33] and where the title of God is kept partly in Hebrew (*sabaoth* for the Vulgate's *exercituum*):

---

29 Thus, *Andreas*, lines 874a, 978a; *Christ and Satan*, line 313a; *Christ I*, lines 136a, 405a; *Christ II*, line 580a; *Guthlac A*, line 17a; *Guthlac B*, line 1103a; *The Phoenix*, lines 628a, 649a, 658a, 662a; *Judgment Day II*, lines 198a (describing hell), 248a.

30 See, for example, Bede, *De schematibus et tropis*, ed. C.B. Kendall, 147: '*Epizeuxis est eiusdem uerbi in eodem uersu sine aliqua dilatione geminatio*, ut: "Consolamini, consolamini, populus meus, dicit Dominus uester" [Is. 40:1]. Et iterum: "Eleuare, eleuare, consurge, Hierusalem" [Is. 51:17]. Et iterum: "Viuens, uiuens ipse confitebitur tibi" [Is. 38:19]. Et in psalmo: "Dies diei eructat uerbum" [Ps. 18:3]. Alibi repetitio eiusdem sermonis palilogiae optinet nomen.'

31 All quotations from the Bible are from *Biblia Sacra iuxta Vulgatam versionem*, ed. R. Weber, 4th ed. (Stuttgart: Deutsche Bibelgesellschaft, 1994).

32 All translations of the Vulgate are from *The Holy Bible: The Douay Rheims Version* (reprint, Rockford, IL: TAN Books, 1971).

33 The most common preface in the Roman Rite reads: 'Vere dignum et iustum est, aequum et salutare nos tibi semper et ubique gratias agere, domine sancte pater omnipotens, aeterne deus, per Christum dominum nostrum. Per quem maiestatem tuam laudant **angeli**, adorant **dominationes**, tremunt **potestates**, caeli caelorumque **uirtutes** ac beata **seraphin** socia exultatione concelebrant, cum quibus et nostras uoces ut admitti iubeas deprecamur supplici confessione dicentes,' Gregor Richter and Albert Schönfelder, eds., *Sacramentarium Fuldense saeculi X*, 1. The second most common preface reads: 'et ideo cum **angelis** et **archangelis**. Cum **thronis** et **dominationibus**. Cumque omni militia caelestis exercitus ymnum gloriae tuae canimus sine fine dicentes,' Nicholas Orchard, ed., *The Leofric Missal II: Text*, 106. On the preface, see *The Catholic Encyclopedia* (New York, 1912), s.v.

Sanctus sanctus sanctus dominus deus **sabaoth**. Pleni sunt caeli et terra gloria tua. Ossana in excelsis.[34]

[Holy, Holy, Holy, Lord God Sabaoth. The heavens and earth are full of your glory. Hosanna in the highest.]

The speech of angels and the superlative genitive construction are also directly linked in the Apocalypse of John:

Et uenit unus de septem angelis qui habebant septem fialas et locutus est mecum dicens ' ... hii cum agno pugnabant et agnus uincet illos quoniam **Dominus dominorum est et rex regum.**' (Apocalypse 17:1, 14)

[And there came one of the seven angels, who had the seven vials, and spoke with me, saying ' ... These shall fight with the Lamb, and the Lamb shall overcome them, because he is **Lord of lords** and **King of kings.**']

It is therefore not surprising that when Old English poets wish to express the language in songs of angels or to describe heaven, they employ the superlative genitive. The construction likely had, as it does for us, a feeling

---

. 34 The text is that of Richter and Schönfelder, eds., *Sacramentarium Fuldense*, 1; this text is cited because in the base manuscripts of the standard edition of the 'Hadrianic' Gregorian Sacramentary (Jean Dehusses, ed., *Le Sacramentaire grégorien*, vol. 1, *Le Sacramentaire*), as well as in the manuscripts (and thus the editions) of the earliest complete massbooks from Anglo-Saxon England (the Leofric Missal and the Winchcombe Sacramentary), the text of the *Sanctus* is abbreviated and never written out in full. On the ancient pedigree of the *Sanctus* in the Roman rite and its retention of the Hebrew *sabaoth*, see Joseph A. Jungmann, *The Mass of the Roman Rite*, 2:128–38; see also *Catholic Encyclopedia*, s.v. 'sanctus.' For a recent study of the history and development of the *Sanctus* in various liturgies, see Bryan D. Spinks, *The Sanctus in the Eucharistic Prayer*. On the liturgy and massbooks of Anglo-Saxon England, see Richard W. Pfaff, 'Liturgy,' and 'Liturgical Books,' in *The Blackwell Encyclopedia of Anglo-Saxon England*, ed. Michael Lapidge et al., as well as Pfaff's 'Massbooks: Sacramentaries and Missals,' in *The Liturgical Books of Anglo-Saxon England*, ed. Pfaff, 7–34. For the *Sanctus* in Old English contexts, see, for example, Ælfric's *Letter to Sigeweard*, 'We habbað nu gesæd be ðam circlican bocum on þære ealdan æ & eac on þare niwan: ða synd þa twa gecyðnyssa be Cristes menniscnysse & be þære halgan þrinnysse on soðre annysse, swa Isaias geseah on his gastlican gesihðe, hu God sylf gesæt & him sungon abutan duo seraphin, þæt sind twa engla werod: Sanctus, sanctus, sanctus, Dominus Deus **Sabaoth**, þæt ys on Englisc: Halig, halig, halig, Drihten weroda God,' S.J. Crawford, ed., *The Old English Version of the Heptateuch*, EETS 160 (1922; reprint with the text of two additional manuscripts transcribed by N.R. Ker, London: Oxford University Press, 1969), 68–9.

of things angelic, biblical, and possibly Hebraic. Thus in *Christ I*, the superlative genitive construction is added to an Old English poetic rendering of the *Sanctus*:

> Halig eart þu, halig,   heahengla brego,
> soð sigores frea,   simle þu bist halig,
> **dryhtna dryhten** ... Þu eart weoroda god. (lines 403–5a; 407b)

[Holy are you, holy, prince of high-angels, true lord of victory, ever are you holy, **lord of lords** ... You are the God of hosts.]

Another use of the construction in *Christ I* further suggests the connection between this type of diction and the speech of angels, the Old Testament, and specifically the Hebrew language. The Hebraic nature of the superlative genitive is highlighted in this case by its being bracketed by the Hebrew names *Emmanuel* and *Melchisedech* (lines 132a, 138b) in the context of an explicit reference to the Hebrew language (line 133a):

> Eala gæsta god,   hu þu gleawlice   130
> mid noman ryhte   nemned wære
> **Emmanuhel**,   swa hit engel gecwæð
> **ærest on Ebresc!** Þæt is eft gereht,
> rume bi gerynum: 'Nu is rodera weard,
> god sylfa mid us.'   Swa þæt gomele gefyrn   135
> **ealra cyninga cyning**   ond þone clænan eac
> sacerd soðlice   sægdon toweard,
> swa se mæra iu,   **Melchisedech**,
> gleaw in gæste   godþrym onwrah
> eces alwaldan. (lines 130–40a)   140

[O God of spirits, how wisely you were named with the right name, Emmanuel, as the angel said first in Hebrew. That is often interpreted broadly according to mysteries, 'Now is the guardian of the heavens, God himself with us.' Thus the old men of yore foretold the **king of all kings** and truly also the pure priest; so the great one of old, Melchisedech, wise in spirit, revealed the divine majesty of the eternal all-ruler.]

The distribution of the narrative use of these phrases suggests awareness among Old English poets of the biblical origin of the construction. Such awareness need not have been necessarily conscious; perhaps the superlative genitive construction had a certain biblical, archaic feel as I believe it does in modern English. A particularly striking use of the construction can be found in Cynewulf's *Elene,* where he seems to use it as a means of distinguishing the language of the Jewish, Hebrew-speaking characters from that of the Roman, Latin-speaking characters.

Elene tells the story of the discovery of the true cross in the holy land by Helena, mother of the Roman emperor Constantine. The substance of the poem is a poetic rendering of a Latin text known variously as the *Inventio Sanctae Crucis* or the *Acta Cyriaci.*[35] The narrative core of the poem (lines 276–801), and the part with which I am primarily concerned, tells of Elene's verbal battles with the Jews and in particular with their spokesman Judas in her attempts to discover the location of the cross. When Elene arrives in Jerusalem, she has the Jews gathered and rebukes them for their lack of belief in Jesus Christ in a rather insulting speech with quotations from three Old Testament prophets.[36]

---

35 On the source of *Elene,* see Susan Rosser, 'The Sources of Cynewulf's *Elene* (Cameron A.2.6),' and especially Gordon Whatley, 'The Figure of Constantine the Great in Cynewulf's *Elene,*' 161–202; Whatley notes, 'because Cynewulf treats the *Inventio* so freely, it will probably never be possible to determine on which manuscript of the legend he based his poem ... one can say with some confidence, however, that he was working from a text which could have differed only in minor ways from those surviving today,' 161. Texts of the *Inventio* can be found in a number of sources: Alfred Holder, ed., *Inventio sancta crucis*; B. Mombritius, ed., *Sanctuarium seu Vitae Sanctorum,* vol. 1, 376–9; Ángel Fábrega Grau, ed., *Passinario Hispánico,* vol. 2, 260–6; Stephan Borgehammar, *How the Holy Cross Was Found,* 201–302. My references are to Borgehammar's 'Inventio Crucis A' text; although he provides a composite text, his critical apparatus gives variants from up to twenty Latin manuscripts. Translations of the Latin *Inventio* are also now readily available: Borgehammar, *How the Holy Cross Was Found,* 154–61; E. Gordon Whatley, ed. and trans., 'Constantine the Great, the Empress Helena, and the Relics of the Holy Cross,' 77–95; Jan Willem Drijvers, *Helena Augusta,* 165–71; Michael J.B. Allen and Daniel G. Calder, trans., *Sources and Analogues of Old English Poetry,* 60–8.

36 Lines 332–95; within this speech, *The Anglo-Saxon Poetic Records* text contains a superlative genitive phrase, *dryhtna dryhten,* (line 371), where the manuscript simply has *dryhten,* leaving the line metrically deficient (see note 25 above); supplying *dryhtna* is a common and reasonable emendation, but this possible use of a superlative genitive phrase is not considered here because it lacks manuscript authority. Other emendations are obviously possible, which do not necessarily have to alliterate. F. Holthausen, *Cynewulfs Elene (Kreuzauffindung) mit Einleitung, Glossar, Anmerkungen und der lateinischen Quelle,* following Sievers, supplies *duguða*; the collocation *duguða dryhten* does occur, even within this same poem (see *Elene,* line 81a; *Andreas,* line 698a; *Christ II,* line 782a; and *Phoenix,* line 494a). Since the collocation occurs in a quotation attributed in the text to Moses, the reading *dryhtna dryhten* would not contradict my argument which follows.

After Elene's speech the Jews are sent into council to produce the information that Elene wants, namely the location of the cross. At this council Judas is first introduced. The Jews are depicted as genuinely confused, not knowing what Elene expects from them (lines 411–16). Judas explains to his countrymen that his grandfather and father have passed on to him the full record of the life, death, and identity of Jesus Christ. It is within this speech, which Cynewulf presents to us as direct speech within the direct speech of Judas, that Cynewulf first employs in the poem the superlative genitive construction.[37] Judas explains that his father had told him that when men who love Christ come looking for the cross, this will signal the beginning of the end for the Jewish people:

'Ne mæg æfre ofer þæt   Ebrea þeod
rædþeahtende   rice healdan,
duguðum wealdan,   ac þara dom leofað
ond hira dryhtscipe,
in woruld weorulda   willum gefylled,
ðe þone ahangnan cyning   heriaþ ond lofiað.' (lines 448–53)

['Beyond that point never will the Hebrew people, deliberating, control the kingdom, command hosts, but *their* fame shall be praised, and *their* mastery, into the **age of ages** *their* desires fulfilled, those who worship and praise the crucified king.'] (italics added)

This follows the Latin rather closely, although Cynewulf makes the subtle change of transferring the eternal reign (which in the Latin refers to Christ) to Christians generally:

Iam autem amplius Hebraeorum genus non regnabit, sed regnum eorum erit, qui crucifixum adorant. Ipse autem regnabit in saecula saeculorum.[38]

[Now the race of the Hebrews will reign no longer, but rule will be theirs, who love the crucified one. He himself will reign into the ages of ages.]

Judas's father then explains in greater detail who Jesus was and how the Jews had condemned him (and later his follower Stephen) to death. In this

---

37 Lines 419a–535, the longest speech in the poem; cf. his prayer at lines 725–801, the second longest speech in the poem, which also contains direct speech within direct speech.
38 Borgehammar, *How the Holy Cross Was Found*, 261.

section Cynewulf elaborates his source; his narrative details are from the Latin, but he chooses particular phrases that are additions to the Latin:

> Þa siððan wæs
> of rode ahæfen   rodera wealdend,
> **eallra þrymma þrym**,   þreo niht siððan
> in byrgenne   bidende wæs
> under þeosterlocan,   ond þa þy þriddan dæg
> **ealles leohtes leoht**   lifgende aras,
> ðeoden engla,   ond his þegnum hine,
> soð sigora frea,   seolfne geywde,
> beorht on blæde. (lines 481b–9a)

[Then afterward the ruler of the heavens, the **power of all powers**, was taken from the rood, and he waited for three nights in the dark enclosure, and on the third day the **light of every light** arose alive, the prince of angels, and he revealed himself to his servants, the true lord of victories, bright in his glory.]

The Latin is less detailed and contains no superlative genitive phrases:

> Ipse autem sepultus, post tertia die resurgens, manifestauit se suis discipulis.[39]

[He, however, having been buried, rising after three days, revealed himself to his disciples.]

It might also be noted that Cynewulf's *ealles leohtes leoht*, with its genitive element in the singular, is an example of the less common form of the construction, which is restricted within the Latin Bible to the Old Testament.

Immediately following this, Cynewulf continues to elaborate his source with biblical language in describing the martyrdom of Stephen. The Latin *Inventio* reads:

> Et tollentes eum multitudo lapidauerunt eum. Sed beatus ille, cum traderet animam, expandens manus ad caelum orabat dicens: 'Ne statuas illis ad peccatum, Domine.'[40]

---

39 Ibid., 262.
40 Ibid.

[And bearing him away, the crowd stoned him. But that blessed man, when he surrendered his soul, raising his hands toward heaven, prayed, saying: 'Oh Lord, set this not as a sin for them.']

Stephen's cry to heaven is a quotation from the story in Acts 7:59. Cynewulf here paraphrases Stephen's words, but before doing so, he includes a different biblical quotation, which is not found in the Latin:

> Þa for lufan dryhtnes
> Stephanus wæs   stanum worpod;
> **ne geald he yfel yfele,**   ac his ealdfeondum
> þingode þrohtherd,   bæd þrymcyning
> þæt he him þa weadæd   to wræce ne sette,
> þæt hie for æfstum   unscyldigne,
> synna leasne,   Sawles larum
> feore beræddon,   swa he þurh feondscipe
> to cwale monige   Cristes folces
> demde to deaþe. (lines 491b–500a)

[Then, for the love of the Lord, Stephen was pelted with stones; **he did not repay evil with evil**, but, enduring, interceded for his old enemies, asked the king of glory that he (God) not set vengeance on them for that woeful deed, that they, because of malice, deprived of life a man not guilty, free of sins, following Saul's teaching, just as he (Saul), by his enmity, condemned to slaughter and death many of Christ's people.]

Ne geald he yfel yfele renders Paul's epistle to the Romans 12:17, *nulli malum pro malo reddentes*, which is especially fitting here as Cynewulf, following his source, first introduces the character of Saul and then, elaborating on his source, describes the virtues of Paul after his conversion and name change (*Elene*, lines 500b–10). It is also noteworthy as an addition of polyptoton to his source, which would perhaps stand out aurally as a special type of discourse, in this case specifically biblical, following closely upon the three successive superlative genitive constructions.

It is important to keep in mind that this is a story told by a Hebrew to a group of Hebrew wise men about the wisdom of his father; the imagined language of discourse here must be Hebrew. The use of the superlative genitives is Cynewulf's way of showing this. Cynewulf, I believe, is doing what Fred Robinson has argued that the *Battle of Maldon* poet does with the speech of the Viking messenger, namely distinguishing it as different from that of the other characters by the use of special language and syntax.[41] Cynewulf is not simply amplifying the language of his source to make it fit into Old English verse; he is amplifying it in a specific and apt way, by putting language reminiscent of the Old Testament into the mouth of an ancient Hebrew. Such a reading is partly informed by the explicit interest that Cynewulf expresses in the language of the Jews, especially insofar as it is different. Hence, almost every time the noun *Ebreas* (the Hebrews) or the adjective *ebreisc* (Hebrew or Hebraic) is used within this poem, it is within the context of language or discourse, as the following examples illustrate:

> Ongan þa leoflic wif
> weras *Ebrea*   wordum negan ... (lines 286b–7)

> Hie þa anmode   ondsweredon:
> 'Hwæt, we *Ebreisce*   æ leornedon ...' (lines 396–7)

> Þa sio cwen ongan
> weras *Ebresce*   wordum negan,
> fricggan fyrhðwerige   ymb fyrngewritu ... (lines 558b–60)

> Word stunde ahof
> elnes oncyðig,   ond on *Ebrisc* spræc. (lines 723b–4)

[The dear woman began to address the Hebrew men with words ... They, all of one mind, answered, 'Lo, we Hebrews have learned the law' ... Then that queen began to address the Hebrew men with words, to ask those heart-weary ones about the old writings ... He forthwith took up words, not knowing of courage, and spoke in Hebrew.]

The only other occurrence of the root *ebrea-* in *Elene* is at line 448, cited above, in the first line of direct speech by Judas's father, immediately preceding the first use of a superlative genitive phrase in the poem. In that instance I would suggest there is an implied reference to speech; the father's language draws attention to itself through the superlative genitive phrase, as he draws attention to himself and his people as Hebrews. After Judas tells his countrymen the information he learned from his father, he

---

41 See Fred C. Robinson, 'Some Aspects of the *Maldon* Poet's Artistry,' 25–40, esp. 25–8.

becomes the spokesman of the Jews and refuses to reveal anything to Elene. He uses his skill with words (*wordes cræftig* [line 419]) to try to deceive her. Only after torture does he reveal his knowledge to her. He takes Elene to Calvary, but he does not know the exact location of the buried cross. He then begins a prayer, which comprises the second longest speech in the poem (lines 725–801).[42] This prayer is not the prayer of a converted man; it is the prayer of a man desperately searching for something specific. He is not yet a Christian, but he is still Jewish and doubtful; his prayer, though bold and eloquent, is a specific petition, and it is presented in a Hebrew mode. The speech is introduced by the final occurrence of the root *ebrea-* in the poem, as quoted above: 'Word stunde ahof / elnes oncyðig, ond **on Ebrisc** *spræc*' (lines 723b–4). Cynewulf here follows the Latin source in specifying that Judas prays in Hebrew ('leuauit uocem suam ad Dominum Hebraica lingua et dixit').[43] In fact, in many of the manuscripts of the Latin source, this sentence is followed by a string of 'pseudo-Hebrew' beginning '*Ai. acraac. rabri. milas. filo. nabonac.*'[44] Following this is a 'translation,' beginning 'Quod interpretatur: "Deus, Deus, qui fecisti caelum et terram,"' and ending 'in saecula saeculorum.' In *Elene*, the beginning of Judas's prayer closely follows the Latin source, which begins with praise of God as creator and moves to a description of the hosts of angels surrounding the throne of God, leading up to a conflation of the scene from Isaiah 6:1–3 cited above and the *Sanctus* of the Mass:

> Þara sint IIII   þe on flihte a
> þa þegnunge   þrymme beweotigaþ
> fore onsyne   eces deman,
> singallice   singaþ in wuldre
> hædrum stefnum   heofoncininges lof,
> woða wlitegaste,   ond þas word cweðaþ
> clænum stefnum,   (**þam is ceruphin nama**):
> 'Halig is se halga   heahengla god,
> weoroda wealdend!   Is ðæs wuldres ful
> heofun ond eorðe   ond eall heahmægen,

---

42 See note 37, above.

43 Borgehammar, *How the Holy Cross Was Found*, 265.

44 Borgehammar conveniently provides a synopsis of the variant versions of the Hebrew prayer (*How the Holy Cross Was Found*, 273–8); Whatley, 'Constantine the Great,' has noted that this prayer contains 'some phrases of recognizably Hebrew origin,' including, for example, *baruc. ata. adonai* and the Hebrew names *Israel*, *David*, and *Iesu*, 94.

tire getacnod.'   Syndon tu on þam,
sigorcynn on swegle,   **þe man seraphin**
be naman hateð. (lines 743–55a)

[There are four of them, who ever in flight perform their service in glory before the sight of the eternal judge; they sing praise of the king of heaven
continually in wonder with clear voices, the most beautiful of melodies, and
speak these words in pure voices (they have the name cherubim): 'Holy is the
holy God of high-angels, ruler of hosts! Heaven and earth are of full of his
glory and his high-might is revealed with glory.' There are two among them,
the victory-race in heaven, who are called seraphim by name.]

Although Cynewulf is following his source, the subtle changes he
makes are noteworthy.[45] Cynewulf carefully rearranges the Hebrew loanwords, the names of the orders of angels, to bracket the *Sanctus*. He also
expands the Latin's simple *sanctus, sanctus, sanctus* to a paraphrase of the
Sanctus, including *weoroda wealdend*, which renders *Dominus Deus exercituum* of Isaiah 6:3, or the macaronic *Dominus Deus* **Sabaoth** of the
Sanctus of the Mass. Cynewulf again expands the biblical and specifically
Hebraic feel of the language that he puts into the mouth of Judas.

In the Latin version Judas's prayer now refers to God's casting the rebellious angels into hell.[46] Cynewulf renders this passage[47] and then again
augments it with original details and specific language:

> He þinum wiðsoc
> aldordome.   Þæs he in ermðum sceal,
> **ealra fula ful,**   fah þrowian,

---

45 Cf. Latin: 'Et ipsa sunt uolatilia in aeriis cursibus, in lucem immensam, ubi humana
natura transpire non potest, quia tu es, qui fecisti ea ad ministerium tuum, sex animalia,
quae habent senas alas; quattor quidem ex ipsis quae uolant ministrantia et incessabili
uoce dicentia; "Sanctus, sanctus, sanctus," Cherubin uocantur; duo autem ex ipsis posu-
isti in Paradiso custodire lignum uitae, quae uocatur Seraphin' (Borgehammar, *How the
Holy Cross Was Found*, 265–6).

46 'Tu autem dominaris omnium, quia tua factura sumus, qui incredibiles angelos pro-
fundo tradidisti tartaro, et ipsi sunt sub fundo abyssi a draconum foetore cruciandi, et
tuo praecepto contradicere non possunt' (Borgehammar, *How the Holy Cross Was
Found*, 266).

47 'Þæs ðu, god dryhten, / wealdest widan fyrhð, ond þu womfulle / scyldwyrcende
sceaðan of radorum / awurpe wonhydige. Þa sio werge sceolu / under heolstorhofu
hreosan sceolde / in wita forwyrd, þær hie in wylme nu / dreogaþ deaðcwale in dracan
fæðme, / þeostrum forþylmed' (lines 759b–66a).

þeowned þolian.   Þær he þin ne mæg
word aweorpan,   is in witum fæst,
ealre synne fruma,   susle gebunden. (lines 766b–71)

[He rejected your authority. For this he, hostile, shall suffer in miseries, full of every foulness/**the foulness of every foulness**, endure bondage. There he cannot reject your words; he is fast in punishments, the source of all sins, bound in torment.]

Cynewulf calls Satan either 'full of every foulness' or the 'foulness of every foulness.'[48] Either way, Cynewulf creates a phrase that is aurally identical to a superlative genitive construction. Significantly, he uses this phrase to refer to Satan. Cynewulf here again follows the language of the Old Testament specifically as opposed to the general Judeo-Christian tradition that had taken up use of the superlative genitive.

In the Old Testament, superlative genitives are used to express both positive notions, such as God and eternity, and superlative negatives, such as *uanitas uanitatum* (Ecclesiastes 1:1) or *maledictus Chanaan, seruus seruorum erit fratribus suis* (Genesis 3:25). In the New Testament, however, the use of the superlative genitive is restricted to positives, in titles for God (*rex regum*) and the expression of eternity (*in saecula saeculorum*). On the whole, Old English usage of the construction seems generally influenced by the New Testament; thus, in extant Old English poetry, superlative genitive phrases are used only to refer to God, heaven, or eternity, apart from Cynewulf's use under consideration. In the extant corpus of all

---

48 The *Dictionary of Old English* prefers the former; see *Dictionary of Old English on CD-ROM, A–F*, s.v., fūl, *noun* sense 3; this is the reading preferred by a majority of editors and translators: thus Krapp and Dobbie, eds., *The Anglo-Saxon Poetic Records*, vol. 2, 144; R.V. Gordon, *Anglo-Saxon Poetry*, 249; Albert S. Cook, ed., *The Old English Elene, Phoenix, and Physiologus*, 93; Holthausen, *Cynewulfs Elene*, 29; S.A.J. Bradley, trans., *Old English Poetry*, 184. Three editors who support the reading 'foulness of every foulness' are Julius Zupitza, ed., *Cynewulfs Elene mit ein Glossar*, 28; Charles W. Kent, ed., *Elene*, 47; and P.O.E. Gradon, *Cynewulf's Elene*, who notes, 'ealra fula ful: an extension of such phrases as "eallra þrymma þrym." These are probably an imitation of the biblical use of an intensive genitive,' 55. A construction of the type 'full of every foulness,' with two words that are near homonyms used in a non-superlative genitive phrase, does occur elsewhere. There are a number of occurrences in the *Paris Psalter* of *goda god*, which must, for metre, mean 'good God,' although that does not keep a hearer or reader from thinking 'God of gods' (thus *Paris Psalter* 67.19.3a, 105.36.2a, 117.2.2a, 117.4.3a, 117.28.2a.); also cf. the metrical *Solomon and Saturn*, line 79a, *scyldigra scyld* (shield of sinners), referring to the Word of God.

Old English I have only discovered one negative use of the superlative genitive, and that is in Ælfric's rendering of Genesis 3:25 cited above as *awyrged is Channan, 7 he byð ðeowena ðeowa his gebroðrum*. Thus, I suggest that this is another instance of Cynewulf creating a specifically Old Testament, Hebraic voice for Judas, a Jewish, Hebrew-speaking character.

Cynewulf's source text itself invites such a reading. In both the speech concerning Judas's father and here, the narrative context is explicitly Hebraic. The first case was a speech within a speech told by a Jewish man about his Jewish father to a group of Jewish men. In this later instance, we are told explicitly, both in the Latin source and in the Old English, that Judas offers a prayer *in Hebrew*. Both his source and *Elene* contain Hebrew loanwords in this speech (*seraphim* and *cherubim*); after the passage quoted above, Cynewulf also includes his source's allusion to the rabbinic tradition of the story of Moses finding Joseph's bones by means of sweet-smelling smoke.[49] Judas's speech, in the source and in *Elene,* ends with a profession of his faith in Christ, but still in Jewish, Hebraic terms:

> 'Ic gelyfe þe sel
> ond þy fæstlicor   ferhð staðelige,
> hyht untweondne,   on þone ahangnan Crist,
> þæt he sie soðlice   sawla nergend,
> ece ælmihtig,   **Israhela cining,**
> walde widan ferhð   wuldres on heofenum,
> a butan ende   ecra gestealda.' (lines 795b–801)

['I shall believe the better, and the more firmly establish my heart, my undoubting hope, in the crucified Christ, that he truly is the saviour of souls, eternal almighty, king of Israel, who forever controls the eternal dwellings of glory on heaven without end.']

The narrative context of this scene is thoroughly Jewish. In addition, Cynewulf may have had a version of the *Inuentio* legend containing what alleged to be Hebrew writing. These factors suggest that we accept *ealra fula ful* as it sounds, that is, as a superlative genitive phrase, used by Cynewulf as one among other elements to create a speech that could sound Hebrew to a learned Old English audience.

---

49 See Whatley, 'Constantine the Great,' 32; Oliver Farrar Emerson, 'The Legend of Joseph's Bones in Old and Middle English,' 331–4.

Cynewulf, I would suggest, contrary to an anti-Jewish reading of this poem, evinces a keen interest in the Hebrew language, together with a certain amount of sympathy for the Jewish characters.[50] This interest in Hebrew, a language only minimally accessible to Anglo-Saxons, is not unique to Cynewulf. Ælfric, another author whose anti-Judaism has recently been examined, also demonstrates interest in knowing what little he could about the Hebrew language, and he transmits this information in his homilies.[51] Considerations of strains of anti-Judaism in Anglo-Saxon England need to be considered in the light of the fundamental importance of the Old Testament – the Hebrew scripture – in Anglo-Saxon England. From such a standpoint we can better understand Cynewulf's subtle use of the superlative genitive construction. While it had obviously become a fully integrated part of Latin Christian discourse, a careful reader and author like Cynewulf could see the construction's Old Testament origin and use it to enrich his already linguistically rich poetry, in particular giving a fitting voice to his Hebrew characters.[52]

---

50 Readings of this poem that construe it as quite anti-Jewish can be found in Andrew P. Scheil, *The Footsteps of Israel*, 219–28, and Heide Estes, 'Lives in Translation,' 33–45, 176–82; critics who find Cynewulf's treatment of the Jews far more sympathetic include John Gardner, 'Cynewulf's *Elene*,' 65–76, esp. 70; Catharine A. Regan, 'Evangelicism as the Informing Principle of Cynewulf's *Elene*,' 27–52, esp. 32–7; Gordon Whatley, 'Cynewulf and Troy,' 203–5, esp. 204; Thomas D. Hill, 'Bread and Stone, Again,' 252–7, esp. 257.

51 See Andrew P. Scheil, 'Anti-Judaism in Ælfric's *Lives of the Saints*,' 65–86. The present article is part of a larger project of mine concerning Anglo-Saxon attitudes towards and perceptions of the Hebrew language.

52 For an excellent review of Cynewulf's particular skill in executing *Elene,* see Samantha Zacher, 'Cynewulf at the Interface of Literacy and Orality,' 346–87.

APPENDIX
Occurrences of the Superlative Genitive Construction
in Old English Poetry

Genesis B	Line
drihtna drihten, *deaðbeames ofet*	638a
Christ and Satan	
ceosan us eard in wuldre *mid* **ealra cyninga cyninge,**	
se is Crist genemned	203b
geond **ealra worulda woruld** *mid wuldorcyninge*	223a
agan dreama dream *mid drihtne gode*	313a
Andreas	
dryhtna dryhten. *Dream wæs on hyhte*	874a
eallra cyninga cining, *þone clænan ham*	978a
dryhtan dryhtne, *þæs ðe he dom gifeð*	1151a
þær þe **cyninga cining** *clamme belegde*	1192a
in **woruld worulda** *wuldorgestealda*	1686a
Elene (Cynewulf)	
in **worulda weorulda** *willum gefylled*	452a
eallra þrymma þrym, *þreo niht siððan*	483a
eallra leohtes leoht *lifgende aras*	486a
ealra fula ful, *fah þrowian*	786a
Christ I	
ealra cyninga cyning *ond þone clænan eac*	136a
ealra cyninga cyning, *Crist ælmihtig*	215a
dryhtna dryhten. *A þin dom wuniað*	405a
Christ II (Cynewulf)	
in **dreama dream,** *ðe he on deoflum genom*	580a
ealra þrymma þrym. *Wæs se þridda hlyp*	726a
þurh woruld worulda, *wuldor on heofnum*	778a
Guthlac A	
ealra cyninga cyning *ceastrum wealdeð*	17a
Guthlac B	
ealra þrymma þrym, *ðraeta mæstne*	1103a
The Phoenix	
ealra þrymma þrym, *þines wuldres*	628a
in **lifes lif,** *leomum geþungan*	649a
in **dreama dream,** *þær hi dryhtne to giefe*	658a
þurh woruld worulda, *ond wuldres blæd*	662a

Juliana (Cynewulf)
ealra cyninga cyning   *to cwale syllan*   289a
dryhtna dryhtne.   *Þa se dema wearð*   594a
The Whale
dryhtna dryhtne,   *ond a deolflum wiðsace*   83a
The Judgment Day I
ealra cyninga cyning.   *Forþon cwicra gehwylc*   95a
The Judgment Day II
on **worulda woruld**   *wendað þær inne*   198a
and on **worulda woruld**   *wihta gesæligost*   248a
A Summons to Prayer
ealra cyninga cyningc,   *casta uiuendo*   19a
The Gloria I
et in secula seculorum
And on **worulda woruld**   *wunað and rixað*   41a
The Kentish Hymn
Ðu eart **cyninga cyningc**   *cwicera gehwilces*   15a
A Prayer
Æla, **leohtes leoht!**   *Æla, lyfes wynn!*   21a
ealra kyninga kyning,   *Crist lifende*   42a
ealra dugeða duguð,   *drihten hælend*   44a
The Paris Psalter
þurh **ealra worulda woruld**   *wunað him ece*   71.5.3a
and þe on **worulda woruld**   *wordum heriað*   78.14.4a
and þe on **worulda woruld,**   *wealdend, heriað*   83.4.3a
on **worulda woruld**   *and to widan feore*   91.6.6a
on **worulda woruld**   *well gerehtest*   101.25.4a
þurh **ealra worulda woruld**   *wislic standeð*   102.16.2a
on **worulda woruld**   *weorðeð ahlded*   103.6.3a
ond on **worulda woruld**   *wnie syððan*   103.29.2a
on **worulda woruld,**   *wealdend drihten*   105.37.2a
on **ealra weorulda weoruld**   *wurdan soðfæste*   110.5.4a
on **worulda woruld**   *wynnum standan*   110.8.2a
And on **worulda woruld**   *wunað ece forð*   118.90.1a
And þu þinra bearna   **bearn** *sceawige*   127.7.1
on **worulda woruld**   *wunian þence*   131.15.2a
on **ealra worulda woruld**   *wynnum standeð*   134.13.3a
ealra godena god,   *forðon ic hine godne wat*   135.2.2a
drihtna drihten   *dædum spedigast*   135.3.2a
And ge **ealra godena god**   *geara andettað*   135.28.1a
and on **worulda woruld**   *wolde healdan*   148.6.2a

The City as Speaker of the Old Testament in *Andreas*

ROBIN WAUGH

In a volume that depicts the books of the Old Testament in the Anglo-Saxon age as works subject to and deeply involved in radically transformative processes such as translating, glossing, versifying, and genre reclassifying, it should not be surprising to encounter an argument that deals with a particular Anglo-Saxon *representation* of part of the Old Testament – in this case, a city. In fact, one may readily interpret many of the cities described in Old English poetry as 'textual' cities. In *Elene*, for instance, Rome and Jerusalem do not work as typical settings; instead, they involve themselves intimately in the poem's process of establishing God's authority over speech, scriptures, laws, and judgments. No wonder, then, that researchers such as Andrew Scheil and Nicholas Howe have recently pursued projects that further detail the remarkably active roles of cities in Anglo-Saxon literature by examining the textual traditions of cities such as Babylon and Rome,[1] while the Old English *Andreas* would seem to provide particularly fruitful ground for this kind of examination. In this poem, cities participate in the action so much that one might even designate them as characters. For instance, a part of the ancient Jewish temple comes alive and speaks, upon God's command that it do so:

> ac of wealle ahleop,
> frod fyrngeweorc,   þæt he on foldan stod,

---

1 See Andrew Scheil, 'Babylon and Anglo-Saxon England,' 37–58, and Nicholas Howe, 'Rome: Capital of Anglo-Saxon England,' 147–72. For Old English poems other than *Andreas,* I use George Philip Krapp and Elliott Van Kirk Dobbie, eds., *The Anglo-Saxon Poetic Records.* This article is based in part on papers that I read at the 2002 MLA Annual Convention and the 2002 Conference of the Association of Canadian College and University Teachers of English.

stan fram stane.   Stefn æfter cwom
hlud þurh heardne,   hleoðor dynede,
wordum wemde (lines 736b–40a)

[but it leapt down from the wall, stone from stone, that wise, old creation, so that it stood on the ground. Then a loud voice emerged from that hard stone. The noise resounded, words were spoken.][2]

Later, the city of the Mermedonian cannibals, from which Andreas (Saint Andrew) eventually rescues Saint Matthew, actively contributes to the former's torture:

drogon deormode   æfter dunscræfum,
ymb stanhleoðo   stærcedferþþe,
efne swa wide   swa wegas tolagon,
enta ærgeweorc,   innan burgum,
stræte stanfage. (lines 1232–6a)

[They dragged the brave-spirited and determined (one) through mountain caves and upon stony slopes, even as far as the paths extended from inside the cities, those stone-paved roads, the ancient works of giants.]

Equally, the city then contributes to a miraculous triumph over his suffering: 'Stop on stræte   (stig wisode), / swa hine nænig gumena   ongitan ne mihte, / synfulra geseon' (lines 985–7a). [He walked on the street (the road guided his way), so that not any of the evil men could perceive or catch sight of him.][3] And the climax of the city's participation in the drama of this saint's life occurs when a flood blasts out of a column and submerges his tormenters:

---

2 I use the edition of Kenneth R. Brooks, *Andreas and the Fates of the Apostles*. Translations, unless otherwise credited, are my own. The poem is usually assigned a date in the ninth century. See Shannon N. Godlove, 'Bodies as Borders,' 139 and note 7. For relatively recent studies of *Andreas*, see Antonia Harbus, 'A Mind for Hagiography,' 127–40; Ivan Herbison, 'Generic Adaptation in *Andreas*,' 181–211; and Alison Powell, 'Verbal Parallels in *Andreas*.' Scott DeGregorio touches on some of my concerns in his '*Þegenlic* or *flæsclic*,' 449–64. The year 2009 saw the publication of two essays: Godlove, 'Bodies as Borders,' 137–60, and Alexandra Bolintineanu, 'The Land of Mermedonia in the Old English *Andreas*,' 149–64.

3 The passage describes Andreas's invisibility at this point in the narrative. The Old English poem is more obscure concerning Andreas's invisibility than the source is.

... se stan togan.   Stream ut aweoll,
fleow ofer foldan ....   duguð wearð afyrhted
þurh þæs flodes fær.   Fæge swulton (lines 1523–30)

[... the stone fractured. A flood blasted out and flowed over the earth ... the warriors were struck with fear because of the water's attack. Those who were fated to die perished.]

These miraculous events have often seemed bizarre to critics, who have frequently sought explanations for them in typology.[4] Lisa Kiser says that 'the special metaphorical weight which many of these images carry is central to an informed interpretation of *Andreas*.'[5] Penn Szittya asserts that the 'stone imagery' of the poem is meant specifically to recall Ephesians 2:20–2 and 1 Peter 2:4–8. In this critic's view, these images 'consistently' present, wherever they appear, 'the wall of the Temple of the Church, a structure built from living stones.' This kind of figural reading is certainly plausible in the light of well-known exegetical traditions that existed in Anglo-Saxon England. Bede, in his study of the Jewish Temple, *De templo Salomonis*, undertakes the exact kinds of figural connections between stories of buildings that Szittya proposes. Figures in stone, Szittya goes on to say, 'may be variously the prophets, the apostles, the priesthood, or simply members of the Church.'[6]

More recently, Christopher Fee has hinted that one might build on the discussion of typological connections in *Andreas* by linking the stone imagery to the body: 'The infliction of wounds upon [Andreas's] body ... parallels the inscription of his identity in the text. [This identity is as] a type of Christ, who is "the Word."'[7] These connections between word, body, and stone definitely contribute to one's understanding of the poem, but Fee's argument, which employs a number of Michel Foucault's ideas

---

4 See Penn Szittya, 'The Living Stone and the Patriarchs,' 167; John P. Hermann, *Allegories of War*, 119.
5 Lisa J. Kiser, '*Andreas* and the *Lifes Weg*,' 66.
6 Szittya, 'The Living Stone,' 169, 172. For other important typological studies of *Andreas*, see Frederick M. Biggs, 'The Passion of Andreas,' 413–27; James W. Earl, 'The Typological Structure of *Andreas*,' 66–89; Constance B. Hieatt, 'The Harrowing of Mermedonia,' 49–62; Thomas D. Hill, 'Figural Narrative in "Andreas,"' 261–73; Marie Walsh, 'The Baptismal Flood in the Old English "Andreas,"' 132–58; and Godlove, 'Bodies as Borders,' 137–60. For Mermedonia in particular as a figure of the soul's salvation, see Bolintineanu, 'The Land of Mermedonia,' 150, 153–6, 162–3.
7 Christopher Fee, 'Productive Destruction,' 55.

from *Discipline and Punish*,[8] only glances at the crucial role of the city in the saint's trials. I argue that the miraculous behaviour of the cities in *Andreas* is due at least in part to their existence as texts, and particularly texts that convey civic authority (a connection that Foucault notes generally but only touches upon in a rather enigmatic way).[9] For instance, when Andreas declares that the flood from the column represents a visitation of the law as one may read it in the Old Testament (lines 1498–1521), attitudes towards community, morality, and public execution of the law interact with the figure of his body, a martyr's body. The city is the essential context for this interaction. In fact, the city, as the *Andreas* poet depicts it, is as essential a 'document' to the career of Andreas as is his body. Although many connections between the saint's body and the urban landscape are possible, I shall limit this discussion by concentrating on the idea of the body's interior, after I provide the necessary legal background and briefly describe the larger analogies between city and body that the poem sets up.

   Daniel G. Calder and Anita R. Riedinger have already shown that the *Andreas* poet constructs the image of the city in the poem carefully, in both formulaic and thematic terms.[10] I here build on their ideas by using Katherine O'Brien O'Keeffe's arguments concerning body and law in Anglo-Saxon England, in order to consider the role of public space as a required participant in the oft-noted susceptibility for a body to be marked by the law. For instance, O'Brien O'Keeffe observes a tendency in the *Anglo-Saxon Chronicle* to ignore the body until, 'politically, the body makes its uncomfortable appearance in the record of years of turmoil caused by a challenge to the throne and then by the chaos resulting from an uncertain succession.'[11] She notes a change from the early codes, which

---

8 The most popular ideas from this extremely influential study seem to be that 'the body is … directly involved in a political field; power relations have an immediate hold upon it; they invest it, mark it, train it, torture it, force it to carry out tasks, to perform ceremonies, to emit signs. … [T]he mastery of its forces … might be called the political technology of the body.' Michel Foucault, *Discipline and Punish*, 25–6. See also Fee, 'Productive Destruction,' 55–9.

9 See Foucault, *Discipline and Punish*, 21.

10 Daniel G. Calder, 'Figurative Language and Its Contexts in *Andreas*,' 132, and Anita R. Riedinger, '*Andreas* and the Formula in Transition,' 184. After my article was written, Lori Ann Garner's 'The Old English *Andreas* and the Mermedonian Cityscape,' 53–63, and Bolintineanu, 'The Land of Mermedonia,' 156–60, appeared.

11 Her specific example occurs in the C manuscript of the *Anglo-Saxon Chronicle*. Under the entry for the year 1036, supporters of a rival candidate for the thronc of the Saxons blind Alfred æþeling. Katherine O'Brien O'Keeffe, 'Body and Law in Late Anglo-Saxon England,' 214.

largely concerned compensation for bodily injuries, to those laws that were influenced by later writers such as Wulfstan, where 'punishments ... take the form of mutilations.' According to O'Brien O'Keeffe, these mutilations 'enacted on the bodies of those convicted at once the penalty and ineradicable memorials of their crimes. Their mutilated bodies became texts of their behaviour and its lawful consequences.' She thus proposes that 'judicial mutilation' is a kind of informational drama. The spectacle of a mutilated body 'continually announces both crime and punishment.'[12] In her discussion of judicial bodies as 'spectacles,' however, O'Brien O'Keeffe (like Foucault) slights (though she does not completely omit or argue against) two crucial parts of the discussion, and both of these parts involve the consideration of early Anglo-Saxon society as being primarily oral.

My first addition to O'Brien O'Keeffe's ideas about law and the body is further acknowledgment of the audience that would be the necessary witnesses to legal spectacles. At this point, cities enter the discussion. Presumably, a spectacle of mutilation could take place anywhere, and political figures are typically surrounded by an entourage that could act as such an audience, but the logical and traditional locations for legal proceedings of any kind are assemblies. Since large groups of people are most easily found and assembled in cities, cities and towns would necessarily connect with legal characteristics and authority. Significantly, the poet strongly emphasizes the idea of a city in *Andreas* once the Mermedonians have been defeated and have decided to accept baptism.

Þa gesamnodon   secga þreate
weras geond þa winburg   wide ond side
...
Þa wæs mid þy folce   fulwiht hæfen,
æðele mid eorlum,   ond æ Godes
riht aræred,   ræd on lande
mid þam ceasterwarum. (1636–7; 1643–6a)

[Then the people joined together, from far and wide throughout the joyful town, in an assembly... Then for that people the true rite of baptism was enacted, and the sure counsel and law of God revered in that land by the city dwellers.]

---

12 O'Brien O'Keeffe, 'Body and Law,' 217 and 230.

City, law, and assembly are clearly connected. These connections receive further emphasis when the poet repeats the idea of the city throughout the passage (lines 1649–60). Indeed, the poem is almost obsessive about associating the Mermedonians with the city in which they live.[13] Words for city, taking only *burh* and *ceastre* as examples, appear forty times in this poem of 1722 lines, when there are only twenty instances of these same terms in a similar type of poem, *Elene*, of 1321 lines, which also involves a discussion of cities for thematic purposes. Accounting for the differences in the poems' lengths, one still comes up with a figure of about twenty-seven instances of the two city terms for *Elene* versus forty for *Andreas*.

My second addition to O'Brien O'Keeffe's ideas about the law and the body and to Fee's reading of *Andreas* as a moral drama that is inscribed upon the body of its hero is an adjustment of the focus of these two critics – who are concerned with the exterior of the body – to a focus upon the interior of the body. I believe that such an adjustment is necessary because Anglo-Saxon society was primarily oral. In such a society, a poet's 'word-hord,' as Old English texts call the poet's internal stock of stories, 'signifies not only the repertoire of language but the power of language symbolic of the speaker's power,' says Martin Irvine.[14] The people in such oral societies perceive the speech of others, with its signs and other sophisticated properties, as a physical and interior object that makes language.[15] Eric Jager helps to make my point when he proposes that Anglo-Saxon people tended to situate a person's speaking power, perhaps the soul itself, in the breast.[16] For this society the chest cavity was a physical, interior organ of speech. Certainly there is evidence in the literature of the Anglo-Saxons that they associated speaking power with a specific kind of physicality: the breath, body parts, and blood that move inside the chest cavity. Furthermore, in my view, this interior organ of speech functions as a kind of totem.[17]

If Anglo-Saxon society is primarily oral, then one is unlikely to encounter purely textual cities in Old England works. Instead, one would most likely encounter cities such as the Mermedonian one in *Andreas*: textual,

---

13 See Garner, 'The Old English *Andreas*,' 55–7, 60–1.
14 Martin Irvine, 'Medieval Textuality and the Archeology of Textual Culture,' 192. See also Garner, 'The Old English *Andreas*,' 55, and Godlove, 'Bodies as Borders,' 147.
15 Robin Waugh, 'Word, Breath, and Vomit,' 362.
16 Eric Jager, 'Speech and the Chest in Old English Poetry,' 850. See also Sarah Lynn Higley, 'The Mouthful of the Giants,' 284.
17 For example, Sigurðr kills Fáfnir, cuts out the dragon's heart, eats part of it, and so gains understanding of the language of nature, in *Volsunga saga*. See R.G. Finch, ed. and trans., *The Saga of the Volsungs*, 65–6.

oral, and anthropomorphized. It is textual because it is a marked body, like Andreas's. It is oral because it 'speaks' when it blasts out the flood. And, furthermore, the Old English poet has made changes to the sources so that the city in *Andreas* is recognizable as a kind of 'speaking body' well before the poem gets to the flood; this poet, as compared to the poem's sources, downplays the role of the city in Andreas's trials, *except* where the city seems to speak:

[T]res dies sunt hodie trahentes me, per omnes plateas et uicos huius ciuitatis, capilli mei deuellati sunt, per uicos aspersos, caro mea extirpata est, per plateas, sanguis meus aspersus.

[For three days they have dragged me through all this city's streets and squares. My hairs have been pulled out and scattered through the streets; my flesh has been stripped and my blood scattered through the squares.][18]

Sint me leoðu tolocen,   lic sare gebrocen,
banhus blodfag;   benne weallað,
seonodolg swatige. (lines 1404–6a)

[My limbs are dislocated; my body is terribly broken apart, a bone house painted with blood; wounds, deep, bloody wounds, pour out (blood).]

In the Old English version of this passage there is a complete lack of reference to the streets and squares of the Latin version, while the building imagery seems to be transferred into the body of the saint when it is called a *banhus* (bone house) in the Old English.

In order to spell out completely the analogy between a speaker's body and the Mermedonian city in *Andreas*: the interior of this city is the dungeon where both Andreas and Matthew are kept prisoner. Such a prison is analogous to the halls in Old English heroic literature that often resound with the noise of thanes. In *Beowulf*, for instance, the monster Grendel,

---

18 Franz Blatt, ed., *Die lateinischen Bearbeitungen der Acta Andreae et Matthiae apud anthropophagos*, 85. The translation of the Latin is from *Sources and Analogues of Old English Poetry*, ed. and trans. Michael J.B. Allen and Daniel G. Calder, 30. Biggs, 'The Passion of Andreas,' 418–19, drew my attention to this passage. For more on the poem's sources, see Garner, 'The Old English *Andreas*,' 54 and notes 5 and 6, and Bolintineanu, 'The Land of Mermedonia,' 150 and note 4. Bolintineanu notes that, in many spots elsewhere, the poet adds references to the city and its buildings to the accounts in the sources. See 'The Land of Mermedonia,' 155–6, 158.

maddened by the joyful sounds issuing from the Danish hall, violates the interior of this anthropomorphized space by entering Heorot through its 'mouth,' as if he were in search of the speaking totem inside the building. Thus, an early Germanic hall is (among other things) a kind of extension of both the heroic life and the heroic, speaking body.[19] Furthermore, the interior, speaking totem of the city or body in *Andreas* amounts to a kind of personified bible: the two apostles represent this text because they often quote from it and because their lives are not only re-enactments of it but also (in the end) parts of it; both of them appear in the gospels. The cannibalism of the Mermedonians is therefore even more ominous than it seems at first. They threaten not only to consume the bodies of God's messengers but also to eat that message itself; they threaten not only to destroy God's work and plans but also to eat words that represent God's breath and His gift of life when, like the *moððe* of 'Riddle 47' in *The Exeter Book*, they would 'ne wæs / wihte þy gleawra' (be not one bit the wiser [lines 5–6]) for their actions. It is thus entirely appropriate that the cannibals enact a kind of parody bible from a location next to the prison (they regulate their dietary practices and decide upon the death day of their victims, write it down, and, rather absurdly, stick to their established schedule so that the deaths of their victims amount to a kind of doomsday [lines 134–7]), and that the city ultimately 'speaks' scripture in the form of a flood. The poem explicitly describes this flood as a visitation of Old Testament justice (lines 1508b–21). More generally, the Mermedonian city can be anthropomorphized because the Bible anthropomorphizes the New Jerusalem that appears in the book of Revelation (chapter 21) as the bride of Christ.

Although the flood is the most obvious example of the participation of the city in speech, assembly, and law in *Andreas*, the poet foreshadows this event and hints at the idea of the city as a body, complete with an interior, earlier in the poem. Fit 10 begins as follows:

> Gewat him þa Andreas   inn on ceastre
> glædmod gangan,   to þæs þe he gramra gemot,
> fara folcmægen,   gefrægen hæfde,
> oððæt he gemette   be mearcpaðe,
> standan stræte neah,   stapul ærenne. (lines 1058–62)

---

19 See *Klaeber's Beowulf and the Fight at Finnsburg*, ed. R.D. Fulk, Robert E. Bjork, and John D. Niles, lines 88–9, 642–4, 724. The prison is called a *sele* (hall) at line 1311 of *Andreas*.

[Then Andrew walked joyfully into the city to where there was, he had learned, a meeting of those wicked folk, [he walked] until he got to a column of brass that was standing along the way, near to the path.]

The appearance of the column at this juncture seems puzzling. It does not seem to partake in the action, so its emphasis seems out of place, particularly when a more generalized description of the city has usually sufficed in *Andreas* so far. However, the scene provides crucial links between various events in the poem. Most obviously, the column prefigures the stone pillar that emits the flood, but the poet goes on to make further connections between the poem's various settings: 'þanon basnode under burhlocan / hwæt him guðweorca   gifeðe wurde' (from there [from the bliss of the angels] he [Andreas] expected any deeds of glory that he might be given, down in the prison [lines 1065–6]). At first glance, this passage would seem only to increase confusion. Readers might recall that *burhloca* is used to describe the dungeon from which Andrew rescues Matthew on two previous occasions (lines 940 and 1038), but the (re)appearance of this term for prison in the proceedings out by the monument is even more puzzling than the sudden appearance of the monument itself, even if one chooses to render *burhlocan* as something like 'the city walls,' as several translators do in order to make better sense out of the passage.[20] To my mind, the use of this compound at line 1065, when the compound in itself connects the two ideas of city and prison, must work as a verbal parallel with the word's other appearances. In fact, this term appears only in *Andreas* (three times) and one other poem (once). The related (generative?) term *ferðloca* (breast) also appears in *Andreas* three times (lines 58, 1570, and 1671). Hence, a connection in the reader's mind between the ideas of the interior of the body and of a prison is almost inevitable at this juncture of the poem. There is no other obvious reason to mention the prison here. Moreover, the passage also contains a reference (otherwise incongruous) to *engla blisse* (angels' bliss [line 1064b]), which might well recall the speaking statue that appears earlier in the poem as an *anlicnes engelcynna* (image of one of the angels [line 717])

Then the poem goes on to make many connections, as Fee has noticed, between body and voice during the trials of Andreas that follow the scene beside the brass monument. In order for the saint to achieve his new figural identity, his 'voice is silenced' during these tortures. Fee suggests that

---

20 See, for example, Brooks, ed., *Andreas*, 98. See Garner, 'The Old English *Andreas*,' 57–9 and note 23, for an extensive discussion of this issue.

this event is 'intimately related to the destruction' of the saint's body and voice; through this destruction the saint may become the blank page upon which God's word is eventually written, and he may speak in a new 'holy voice,' a *halgan stefne* (line 1399), once his old worldly voice has been removed.[21] In parallel fashion, once the city of the Mermedonians has taken part in Andreas's torture, it too has been written upon (with Andreas's blood) and thus can speak in a new, holy voice. The city's new voice duly appears when the flood blasts out of the pillar. Not only does such 'speech' fall into the pattern of the speaking stone image from earlier in the poem and into the tradition of 'the countless objects speaking in the Exeter Book riddles,' but such anthropomorphism also fits with the Greek analogue of the poem's story. In the Greek version, Andrew observes a statue on top of the pillar and prays that water will come out of its mouth.[22] However, this 'voice,' though new for the city, is actually old. It asserts and performs the Old Testament. Correspondingly, then, this voice goes out from *enta ærgeweorc* (the ancient work of giants [line 1235a]), a description of the city that conflates Old Testament history with the ancient history of the Anglo-Saxons.[23] The deluge is able then to work as the miraculous influence of both ancient biblical and Germanic heroic history, which the people of Mermedonia 'learn' and experience in an ironic fashion.

In the middle of this retribution, a phrase occurs that has caused difficulties in interpretation (at least, according to modern editions and translations), and these difficulties may be partially alleviated through a consideration of the various parallels that I have suggested so far. The manuscript reads (if one supplies the conventional line divisions, punctuation, and capitals) 'Fæge swulton, / geonge on geofene   guðræs fornam / þurh scealtes sweg' (lines 1530b–2a). The justifiable reaction of most readers to this passage is that, as George Phillip Krapp writes, 'The MS. *scealtes sweg* gives no meaning'; he therefore emends the last half-line of the passage to *þurh sealtne weg* (by the way of the salt) – a periphrastic phrase meaning 'the sea').[24] Kenneth R. Brooks, under the influence of

---

21 Fee, 'Productive Destruction,' 59.

22 Garner, 'The Old English *Andreas*,' 60. See note 28.

23 This description perhaps also associates the city with the body of a giant. See further Emily Thornbury, '*eald enta geweorc* and the Relics of Empire,' 82–92; Bolintineanu, 'The Land of Mermedonia,' 159–60; and Garner, 'The Old English *Andreas*,' 59. For the flood as both baptismal and Eucharistic (therefore, it is important that the Mermedonians ingest the water) see Godlove, 'Bodies as Borders,' 156–8.

24 Krapp, ed., *The Anglo-Saxon Poetic Records*, vol. 2, *The Vercelli Book*, 45, 121.

L. Ettmüller, emends the phrase to *þurh sealtnes swelg* (by the abyss of the salt).[25] Consequently, Krapp and Brooks attribute the battle deaths of the young warriors to the action of the water. However, another interpretation is equally possible, as S.A.J. Bradley indicates by translating the last phrase in the Old English sentence as 'because of the man's voice.'[26] Apparently, for Bradley, the phrase should read *scealces sweg*. This emendation was first suggested by Jakob Grimm in 1840, but it is not his preference. He originally goes for an emendation of the first term to *sealtes*, which has become the conventional emendation of the manuscript text at this juncture; after all, the scribe seems to mistake *scealte* for *sealte* earlier in the poem.[27] Yet *scealces* is an attractive emendation strategy. It allows sense to emerge with only one change to what the scribe wrote: a change from *t* to *c* in *scealtes*, making *scealces*. This change fits at least fairly well (semantically, but not as well metrically) with the following word in the manuscript, *sweg*. This same word is used to describe the sound of God's speech at line 93 of the poem, and elsewhere in Old English poetry it has connotations of emotional expression, often taking place in the hall.[28] Thus, by interpreting the phrase as *scealces sweg* at line 1530, one may interpret the flood not only as a kind of triumph of textual authority but also as an entirely appropriate speech act; the man's heroically described voice exactly parallels the 'voice' of the city. The voice of the saint is also an appropriate agent for the flood's action because of the remarkably succinct and violent conversion of the Mermedonians that follows:

> Þa þær ofostlice   upp astodon
> manige on meðle,   mine gefrege,
> eaforan unweaxne;   ðær wæs eall eador
> leoðolic and gastlic,   þeah hie lungre ær
> þurh flodes fær   feorh aleton.
> Onfengon fulwihte   ond freoðuwære,
> wuldres wedde   witum aspedde,
> mundbyrd meotudes. (lines 1625–32a)

---

25 Brooks, ed., *Andreas*, 49, 114.
26 S.A.J. Bradley, ed. and trans., *Anglo-Saxon Poetry*, 149.
27 See Krapp, ed., *The Vercelli Book*, 121, and Brooks, ed., *Andreas*, 70.
28 See Brooks, ed., *Andreas*, 114, and *Beowulf*, 129a, 642–4, 782b–3a, 1063, 1160b–1a, 1214.

[Then, right there in that group, those many young boys immediately stood up, as I have heard. Although, before this, they had lost their lives entirely because of the flood's tide, their ghostly and bodily portions were completely reunited. They received baptism, a covenant of peace, a promise of glory with release from pain, and God's protection.]

The textual city is spoken into action by God through his saint, and the Mermedonians' physical experience of this newly voiced Old Testament text kills them; Andreas's voice can now raise them from the dead because he is the succeeding conduit of God's word. Meanwhile, the power of that word as an oral entity is stressed through the parallels between the saint's speech and the flood, through the poet's references to *fyrhðlocan* (line 1570a) and *breost* (line 1574a) during the flood scene, and through the fact that the drowning Mermedonians would breathe in and ingest some of the flood water – that is, would bring it (and all that it represents) into their interiors. The scene as a whole would seem then to emphasize the idea that, in a society that values oral traditions, a text needs to be enacted with a voice in order to gain authority and force.

The flood is also significant more generally as a disruption of space. A kind of plan for space is systematically established by the Mermedonians, as actors within their city, through legalistic activities and quasi-legal language (lines 134–7). This civic space is systematically destroyed by a succession of divine and saintly figures in the course of the poem. Andreas's invisibility makes the point. Readers notice that the poet seems to bring up the fact of the saint's invisibility too late for ideal reader comprehension (line 986), but perhaps a disturbance of the reader's notions of space is exactly right for the poem's context; the poet may wish to put readers in the same place as the confused Mermedonians, who are forced to witness a voice that comes from, apparently, no space at all – a very disturbing situation (lines 1184–94). In fact, a voice from nowhere may well make an inhabitant wonder if parts of his or her city are actually talking, an illusion that becomes reality when the pillar starts blasting out water.

After the deluge, the speaking saint and the speaking city represent (among other things) a shift of oral language to a kind of 'pure' law, a kind of divine state. Critics have noticed this political evolution in which the cities themselves participate. By the end of the poem, Calder says, 'the poet sees Mermedonia in a triple image: it is the "winburg" ("wine-city" 1637a, 1672a), the "goldburg" ("gold-city" 1655), and the "wederburg" ("weather-city" 1697a, that is the city of fair weather) ... [T]he setting ... has undergone a complete metamorphosis from the place "morðre bewunden" [19b] to the island which combines attributes of a Christian civilization reflecting paradise.'[29] However, if one considers this city as not only a participant in the events in Andreas's life but also a speaker of them, one can take this symbolism further. In its changed form, that is, bathed in flood waters from within, the city in *Andreas* represents perfectly an ideal body that is in paradise because it is one with paradise; this city needs baptism just as its inhabitants do.

Thus, hagiographers are justified in their increasing analysis of the sections of saints' lives that one might call, after Foucault, 'spectacle[s] of the scaffold': torture as a kind of ritualistic, legal, and economic drama that needs an audience to fulfil its purpose and that is expressed through marks on the tortured one's body. Indeed, many critics have taken up Foucault's ideas in their readings of accounts of bodies from all periods of history. However, interpretations of the body of the early medieval age typically ignore the interior of that body (even in their long descriptions of tortures) and need to be rethought if they are to apply to this era. In addition, much work needs to be done concerning the descriptions of the interiors of bodies in medieval works, with particular attention to the associations between this bodily interior and speech.[30] *Andreas*, with its speaking city, suggests that saints' lives in general hold many possibilities for such research.

---

29 Calder, 'Figurative Language,' 132. See also Riedinger, '*Andreas* and the Formula,' 184.
30 See Foucault, *Discipline and Punish*, 3–69; cf. 12. For more on punishment and interiority, see Roberta Frank, 'The Blood-Eagle Again,' 287–9. For the reasons behind the relative lack of critical attention with regard to the body's interior, see Julia Kristeva, *Powers of Horror*, 17 and 52–5.

Cyningas sigefæste þurh God:
Contributions from Anglo-Saxon England
to Early Advocacy for Óláfr Haraldsson

RUSSELL POOLE

The cult of Óláfr Haraldsson (later styled Óláfr helgi) established itself with astounding speed in the early eleventh century. Already in his lifetime, the period on which I shall focus here, his court poet, Sigvatr Þórðarson (who was born and brought up in Iceland but spent his adult life in Norway in the service of Óláfr) freely associates him with Christ and evinces awareness of biblical 'examples' that relate to the evaluation of conduct on the part of both the king and his opponents. Such rhetoric cannot adequately be accounted for as a simple Christianization of traditional skaldic praises. Equally, the Norwegian church, still in its institutional infancy, could scarcely have developed its own distinctive mode of advocacy so early. In this essay I shall investigate to what extent Sigvatr could have learned the techniques and themes of advocacy using English vernacular sources.[1] This approach deals with only one part of a complex scene; Saxon contributions to the missionary effort in Norway, emanating from the archbishopric of Hamburg-Bremen, are in no way discounted,[2] and it is also acknowledged that many statements of Christian doctrine and exegesis take a fairly standard form right across Western Christendom. Nevertheless, certain aspects of the history and textuality suggest some

---

1 Cf. Lesley Abrams, 'The Anglo-Saxons and the Christianization of Scandinavia,' 213–50; Staffan Hellberg, 'Kring tillkomsten av Glælognskviða,' 18; Erich Hoffmann, *Die heilige Könige bei den Angelsachsen und den skandinavischen Völkern*, 79–80; Matthew Townend, 'Like Father, Like Son?' 476.

2 Cf. Abrams, 'Anglo-Saxons and Christianization,' 248; Halldór Halldórsson, 'Synd – An Old Saxon Loanword,' 60–4; Halldór Halldórsson, 'Some Old Saxon Loanwords in Old Icelandic Poetry,' 106–26; Halldór Halldórsson, 'Determining the Lending Language,' 365–78; Staffan Hellberg, 'Tysk eller Engelsk mission?' 42–9.

special closeness to English models on the part of Sigvatr, as also on the part of his royal patrons Óláfr Haraldsson of Norway and Knútr inn ríki of Denmark and England.

Records for the period indicate that the Norwegian missionary kings benefited very significantly and in a variety of ways from English support.[3] Óláfr Tryggvason was helped by Ethelred's payment of Danegeld and his sponsorship at confirmation, possibly also by provision of English clergy.[4] In the next phase, Óláfr Haraldsson, having assisted Ethelred's return to England from exile, himself returned to Norway accompanied by English missionary bishops, among them Grimkell[5] and Rodolf, who was later abbot at Abingdon.[6] Despite Óláfr's early successes in his native country, unrest developed against his rule, as we shall see, and eventually he was exiled to Sweden in 1028, being briefly supplanted by Hákon Eiríksson. In 1030, however, Grimkell supported Óláfr's return, an initiative that ended in the king's death at Stiklastaðir. Shortly afterwards, Grimkell certified Óláfr's sanctity. The skald Þórarinn loftunga, in his poem Glælognskviða, appears to be urging Sveinn, ruler of Norway after the king's death, to support the cult of Óláfr on the basis that 'the gift of Norway is within the power of Óláfr to grant to Sveinn.'[7] In the event, Óláfr's sanctity paved the way for his son Magnús to return to Norway and take up the kingship in 1034.

In England as well as in Norway, Óláfr began to be honoured as a saint almost immediately after the battle of Stiklastaðir.[8] All the versions of the Anglo-Saxon Chronicle that were being kept up in the early eleventh century record his death, while MS C adds an acknowledgment of his sanctity: 'Her wæs Olaf cing ofslagen on Norwegon of his agenum folce [ond] wæs syððan halig' (In this year King Óláfr was killed in Norway by his own people and was afterwards holy).[9] As Knútr inn ríki sought to consolidate his rule in England, he energetically patronized the cults of English saints, especially 'royal saints and/or those who had been martyred at the hands of Scandinavians,' such as Edmund of East Anglia and Ælfheah.[10]

---

3   Abrams, 'Anglo-Saxons and Christianization,' 221.
4   Theodore M. Andersson, 'The Viking Policy of Ethelred the Unready,' 284–95, at 1 and 4.
5   Abrams, 'Anglo-Saxons and Christianization,' 223.
6   Timothy Graham, 'A Runic Entry in an Anglo-Saxon Manuscript,' 16–24.
7   Townend, 'Like Father, Like Son?' 475.
8   Abrams, 'Anglo-Saxons and Christianization,' 245.
9   Katherine O'Brien O'Keeffe, ed., The Anglo-Saxon Chronicle, 105.
10   Townend, 'Like Father, Like Son?' 476; cf. M.K. Lawson, Cnut, 141–3.

Aside from Knútr and his entourage, at least some of the supporters of Ethelred would have had reason to cultivate Ólafr's memory, having benefited from his help in 1014.

Contemporary English preaching and teaching were notable for their inclusion of modes that would have been well suited to the needs of a poet working in newly Christianized Norway, since for some decades English preachers had been devoting considerable attention to educating the laity at all levels of society. Hagiography, revived by the Benedictine reformers, had become 'part of a remarkable movement to provide sermons for the common people,'[11] and if Ælfric's hagiographical writings represent 'a kind of managed popularization of the cult of saints,'[12] similar comments could be made about his exegesis of scripture and the liturgy. Old English homilies were remarkable for their 'mixed and all-encompassing audience' and 'democratic stamp.'[13] In these efforts of outreach, the vernacular enjoyed an accepted place, as witness the *West Saxon Gospels* and other early translations of scripture into English. Ælfric possessed an outstanding ability to use his native language in order to explain 'issues in ways which his audience will most readily understand.'[14] As observed by Michael Fox in this volume, Ælfric's partial translation of Alcuin's *Quaestiones in Genesim* in his *Interrogationes Sigewulfi* is the first vernacular translation of a biblical commentary into any language, insular or continental. It seems to have been relatively popular, as well as popularizing: Ælfric renders a text that Alcuin already considered mainly 'historical' (or 'literal') and 'simple' into a much more basic exegetical primer. The missionary corps in Norway, whether or not they themselves belonged to the Benedictine Reform faction, might have extended this policy by using the skills of Danish or Norse native speakers from England,[15] Grimkell, with his un-English name, possibly being an instance.[16] Such a practice would fit with attestations of Anglo-Saxonisms in contemporary skaldic poems, for example, *helvíti* (hell torment or, simply, hell).[17]

---

11 Geoffrey Shepherd, 'Scriptural Poetry,' 29; Hugh Magennis, 'Warrior Saints,' 49.
12 Magennis, 'Warrior Saints,' 50.
13 Jonathan Wilcox, ed., *Ælfric's Prefaces*, 21.
14 Wilcox, *Ælfric's Prefaces*, 20.
15 Abrams, 'Anglo-Saxons and Christianization,' 216.
16 Hellberg, '*Glælognskviða*,' 44; Abrams, 'Anglo-Saxons and Christianization,' 223.
17 Halldórsson, 'Determining the Lending Language'; see below for citation of this word in its verse context.

Some forms of the teaching pursued in England were specifically directed at the upper echelons of secular society. Leading churchmen, notably Wulfstan, incorporated homiletic material in their political and legislative statements, with evident effectiveness.[18] Ælfric, who likewise enjoyed 'strong connections to court through his primary patrons Æthelmær and Æthelweard,' placed 'increasing emphasis in his later works on using Biblical texts to provide political guidance for the king and his counselors.'[19] Given this access to not merely Anglo-Saxon but also Anglo-Danish aristocratic and royal circles, the teachings of Ælfric and Wulfstan could readily have percolated through to members of Óláfr's close entourage such as Sigvatr, who (like his father, Þórðr Sigvaldaskáld, before him) spent a significant amount of time in England, chiefly in association with Óláfr but also with the Norwegian king's great rival, Knútr.

Sigvatr's *Nesjavísur* (Verses [on the Battle] of the Headlands) expresses jubilation at Óláfr's victory at the Battle of Nesjar, which took place at a location in Oslofjorden on Palm Sunday 1016.[20] As the timing of the battle entails, references to the New Testament are plentiful; complementarily, as we shall see later in this essay, Sigvatr's advocacy for the king's just war depends on a line of interpretation of Old Testament militant secular leadership that was popularized by Anglo-Saxon poets and teachers.

Hirð Áleifs vann harða
hríð, en svá varðk bíða –
peitneskum feltk – páska –
palmsunnudag – hjalmi. (*Nesjavísur*, 14)[21]

[Óláfr's warband won a hard battle on Palm Sunday, and in this way I had to await Easter. I put on a Poitou-made helmet.]

18 M.K. Lawson, 'Archbishop Wulfstan,' 577; cf. Dorothy Whitelock, ed., *Sermo Lupi ad Anglos*, 16 and the references there given.
19 Stacy S. Klein, 'Beauty and the Banquet,' 79–80.
20 Bjarne Fidjestøl, *Det norrøne fyrstediktet*, 118–19, 227–8; Russell Poole, 'The *Nesjavísur* of Sigvatr Þórðarson,' 171–98.
21 Finnur Jónsson, ed., *Skjaldedigtning: Den norsk-islandske skjaldedigtning* A 1–2 (tekst efter håndskrifterne) and B 1–2 (rettet tekst) (Copenhagen: Gyldendal, 1912–15. Repr., Copenhagen: Rosenkilde og Bagger, 1967 [A], 1973 [B]), A1:232, B1:220. This edition will be henceforward abbreviated as *Skj*. Translations of Old Norse/Icelandic and Old English texts are my own unless otherwise indicated.

This is very far from the statements of victory found in older skaldic poetry. Sigvatr's stanza is a tissue of Christian references, not merely to Palm Sunday itself but probably also to the Easter vigil, a rite that would have been familiar to recently baptized Scandinavians, since baptism of converts and presentation of chrism clothing was frequently timed to coincide with this point in the church year.[22] Sigvatr plays on the timing of the battle by working into his poem a series of mentions of the sun (and, by way of wordplay, the moon), no doubt in the awareness that the sun symbolized Christ. Such a basic Christian trope could have been derived from a host of sources and figured dramatically in actual services throughout Christendom. Sigvatr might also have been aware that the palm traditionally symbolized victory, another fundamental trope with antecedents in antiquity. We note, however, that these points of doctrine figure prominently among those taken up by Ælfric in fully teacherly fashion in his instructions for Easter observance[23] and his homily on Palm Sunday (first series).[24]

A further Palm Sunday reference occurs in the following stanza from *Nesjavísur*:

Vasa sigmána Sveini
sverða gnýs at frýja,
gjóðs né góðrar hríðar
gunnreifum Áleifi,
þvít kvistingar kosta –
koma herr í stað verra –
áttu sín, þars sóttusk
seggir, hvárirtveggju. (*Nesjavísur*, 5)[25]

[There was no reason to reproach Sveinn for his fighting (din of swords) or battle-glad Óláfr for a good attack (storm of the falcon of the victory moon), since both parties had to commit themselves to a lopping of limbs, where men engaged; the force had not come into a worse place.]

22 See, for example, Janet L. Nelson, *The Frankish World*, 86; Simon Coupland, *Carolingian Coinage and the Vikings*, 110.

23 Christopher A. Jones, *Ælfric's Letter to the Monks of Eynsham*, 188.

24 Benjamin Thorpe, ed., *The Homilies of the Anglo-Saxon Church*, vol. 1, 218; Jones, *Ælfric's Letter*, 183.

25 Bjarni Aðalbjarnarson, ed., *Heimskringla*, vol. 27 (this edition henceforward abbreviated as ÍF 27): 61, v. 40; *Skj.* A1: 229, B1: 218.

The motif of a lopping of limbs is one that Sigvatr could arrive at by extending a standard kenning type where men are referred to figuratively as trees. The 'felling' of such man or warrior 'trees' in battle is a conventional extension of the metaphor. By contrast, the use of a word like *kvisting* (lopping of a branch or twig) is unique. When we look for possible inspirations for such a locution, it seems most likely to have been motivated by the Easter theme of the poem. In Matthew's account of Christ's entry into Jerusalem, some of the spectators *caedebant ramos de arboribus et sternebant in uia* (cut boughs from the trees and strewed them in the way [Matthew 21:8]). Ælfric mentions those who *ðæra treowa bogas heowon* (cut the branches of the trees) in his homily for Palm Sunday (first series).[26] Their actions could be envisaged vividly by anyone who had participated in the liturgy for Palm Sunday that was current in the Anglo-Saxon church. Ælfric explicitly enjoins that the congregation, both the learned and the laity, should carry palm twigs, emulating the palm- or branch-bearing Jerusalemites at the gates of the city.[27]

In another stanza by Sigvatr, Óláfr is depicted as the new ruler entering into his kingdom and able to lay down laws. The stanza is uniquely attested in *Heimskringla* and Snorri Sturluson's separate *Óláfs saga helga*[28] and is presented separately from *Nesjavísur* in *Edda Snorra Sturlusonar*, where it is placed among the poet's occasional verses,[29] and in *Skjaldedigtning*, where Finnur Jónsson refers it to a hypothetical *Óláfsdrápa*.[30] It may, however, be integral to *Nesjavísur* and form its climax.[31] The new ruler's entry to his kingdom is formulated in terms reminiscent of Christ's entry to Jerusalem on the original Palm Sunday.[32]

Loptbyggvir, mátt leggja
landsrétt, þanns skal standask,
unnar, allra manna,
eykja, liðs á miðli. (Sigvatr fragment 4)[33]

---

26 Thorpe, *The Homilies of the Anglo-Saxon Church*, vol. 1, 212–13.
27 Ibid., vol. 1, 218–19; Jones, *Ælfric's letter*, 124–5; M. Bradford Bedingfield, 'Reinventing the Gospel,' 24–5; M.R. Godden, ed., *Ælfric's Catholic Homilies: Introduction, Commentary and Glossary*, 118.
28 ÍF 27: 73, v. 52; *Óláfs saga Helga*, chap. 58.
29 Jón Sigurðsson et al., ed., *Edda Snorra Sturlusonar*, vol. 3, 346.
30 Finnur Jónsson, *Den oldnorske og oldislandske Literaturs Historie*, vol. 1, 587–8; Finnur Jónsson, ed., *Morkinskinna*, 205–6; cf. Fidjestøl, *Det norrøne fyrstediktet*, 122–3.
31 Poole, 'The *Nesjavísur* of Sigvatr Þórðarson.'
32 E.H. Kantorowicz, 'The King's Advent,' 206–31.
33 ÍF 27: 73, v. 52; *Skj.* A1: 240, B1: 226.

[Sea king (dweller of the stern of the draught animals of the wave, i.e., of the ships), you can lay down a law of the land that will stand between the contingent of all men.]

The stanza contains the explicit statement that Óláfr now possesses the power to 'lay down a law of the land that will stand between the contingent of all men.' It is not merely the newness of Óláfr's dispensation that parallels Christ's New Law but also the symmetry and universality of its application. John 13:34–5 states Christ's new commandment as follows: 'Mandatum nouum do uobis ut diligatis inuicem sicut dilexi uos ut et uos diligatis inuicem. In hoc cognoscent omnes quia mei discipuli estis si dilectionem habueritis ad inuicem' (A new commandment I give unto you: That you love one another, as I have loved you, that you also love one another. By this shall all men know that you are my disciples, if you have love one for another).[34] John clearly associates this commandment with Thursday of Easter week.[35] Sigvatr's knowledge of the commandment may have been mediated through the *West Saxon Gospels*: 'Ic eow sylle niwe bebod, þæt ge lufion eow betwynan swa ic eow lufode. Be þam oncnawað ealle menn þæt ge synt mine leornungcnihtas, gif ge habbað lufe eow betwynan' (I give you a new commandment, that you love between yourselves as I loved you. By that all men will know that you are my disciples, if you have love between you).[36] The Old Norse/Icelandic *milli* (between), which corresponds more closely to *betwynan* than to *inuicem*, may point to this mediation.

Also significant is the word *eykja*, genitive plural of *eykr* (draught animal), literally 'animal that bears the yoke,' here used to form part of a kenning for 'sea king,' viz., 'dweller of the stern of draught animals of the wave.' Insofar as Sigvatr is not elsewhere greatly given to kennings, this one is so extended that it draws attention to itself. The king is represented imagistically as one who rides on draught animals, as distinct from ordinary horses or steeds. This special formulation evokes Christ's entry into Jerusalem. As stated in Matthew 21:7, 'et adduxerunt asinam et pullum et inposuerunt super eis uestimenta sua et eum desuper sedere fecerunt' (and they brought the ass and the colt and laid their garments upon them and made him sit thereon). Compare Mark 11:7: 'Et duxerunt pullum ad Iesum et inponunt illi uestimenta sua et sedit super eo' (And they brought the

---

34 All translations are taken from the Douay-Rheims Version (1582–1609).
35 Hence the traditional English name of this day, Maundy Thursday, from *mandatum*.
36 R.M. Liuzza, ed., *The Old English Version of the Gospels*, vol. 1, 187–8.

colt to Jesus. And they lay their garments on him: and he sat upon him). Ælfric devotes considerable explication to these beasts in his homily for Palm Sunday (first series).[37]

It must have been difficult, all the same – and the stanza describing the lopping of limbs is a representative sample – for Sigvatr to depict Óláfr with any conviction as a Christ-like figure.[38] Óláfr's entry into Norway inevitably, in the eyes of many, put him in the role of aggressor.[39] Opposition from the magnates who had previously enjoyed power in their individual regions was acknowledged by Óláfr's staunchest advocates, and Sigvatr himself composed a poem lamenting the death of Erlingr Skjálgsson at Óláfr's hands.[40] Throughout *Nesjavísur* and other poems Sigvatr, like his fellow skalds, frankly describes Óláfr as a ruthless military leader, capable of instigating and performing homicide while in pursuit of victory. This was despite the fact that Christian teachings on homicide would have been readily accessible. Ælfric states in his homily on Palm Sunday (second series) that Christ 'forbead þæt gewinn mid wordum ðearle, þæt nan Godes þeow ne sceolde on him sylfum truwian, ne mid wæpnum winnan wið woruldlicum cempum, gif he Cristes fotswaðum filigan wile'[41] (strongly forbade the combat by his words, that no servant of God should trust to himself, nor with weapons strive against worldly soldiers, if he means to follow the footsteps of Christ).[42] This teaching would have been reinforced by the very popular story of St Martin, the noble soldier who abjured warfare, celebrated by Ælfric and other Anglo-Saxon writers.[43] Homicide always required justification and, in an extreme view, called for penitence no matter how just the cause, even for 'warriors who have fought "pro aecclesiastica justitia" or sought to repel pagan invaders.'[44]

It is true that Sigvatr evolves a rhetoric of at least partial justification for Óláfr's deeds of homicide. Some of it focuses on the alleged perjury or treachery of Óláfr's rivals, notably those based in Trondelag.

---

37 Thorpe, *The Homilies of the Anglo-Saxon Church*, vol. 1, 206–13.
38 Cf. Bjarne Fidjestøl, 'Kongetruskap og gullets makt,' 9.
39 Cf. Carla del Zotto, 'Vom rex iustus zum Märtyrer,' 123.
40 *Skj.* A1: 244–7, B1: 228–31; cf. ÍF 27: 314–19.
41 Thorpe, *The Homilies of the Anglo-Saxon Church*, vol. 2, 248–9.
42 Translation of Thorpe, modified.
43 Cf. Magennis, 'Warrior Saints,' 35–40.
44 J.E. Cross, 'The Ethic of War in Old English,' 280–1; cf. Fred C. Robinson, 'God, Death, and Loyalty in *The Battle of Maldon*,' 76–98, repr. in Fred C. Robinson, *The Tomb of Beowulf*, 112.

Né hœfilig, hreifa,
hykk dróttinsvik þóttu,
elds, þeims allvel heldu
orð sín, viðir, forðum. (*Nesjavísur* 13)[45]

[Men (trees of the fire of the hand), I think that betrayal of the lord did not seem becoming to those who had in the past kept their word very well.]

Also, Óláfr's partisans viewed him as the *þjóðkonungr* (nation king) (cf. *Nesjavísur*, verse 2, to be cited below), a term that must have carried the implication that he was rightful king of all Norway and therefore entitled to press his campaign. However, contemporary skaldic texts never hint at Óláfr's bridling of his battle anger, or his contrition at the killing of his enemies, or prayers to meet that contingency in advance, or the impropriety of fighting a battle upon so holy a day as Palm Sunday. Among contemporary leaders, an approximate counter-example is Henry II of Germany, who is said to have halted his Italian campaign in 1004 because he did not wish to shed Christian blood in Holy Week.[46] It is only in much later texts, such as the so-called *Legendary saga*, that considerations of that kind make themselves felt. The notion that a campaign against heathens constitutes a just war is also strangely muted. In the relatively extensive skaldic corpus dating from Óláfr's lifetime, it is remarkable that his Norwegian adversaries are never referred to as *heiðinn* (heathen) despite their often steadfast and determined defence of the ancestral religion. That distinction is reserved for the Swedes, notably in Sigvatr's *Austrfararvísur*. An obscure kenning in *Nesjavísur* may embody an allusion to sun worship on the part of Óláfr's opponents,[47] but predominantly attitudes of respect for Óláfr's opponents seem to have been maintained.

If the justness of the war is dubious, serious moral issues are also posed by the massive worldly riches that a leader like Óláfr evidently felt entitled to accumulate in order to cultivate personal prestige and build up a following. No doubt, however, advocacy for Óláfr could defend him as deploying 'just wealth' to pursue his 'just war,'[48] and in the following stanza Sigvatr states with evident approval that the king was capable of both angry intimidation and generous rewards.

---

45 Cf. *Skj.* A1: 232, B1: 220.
46 Lawson, 'Archbishop Wulfstan,' 566.
47 *samknúta sunnu* (one joined with the sun) in v. 11: see Russell Poole, 'Sigvatr, *Nesjavísur*.'
48 Cf. J.E. Cross, 'Oswald and Byrhtnoth,' 101.

Fekk meira lið miklu
mildr, en gløggr til hildar,
hirð þás hugði forðask
heið þjóðkonungs reiði,
en vinlausum vísa
varð, þeim es fé sparði –
háðisk víg fyr víðum
vangi – þunnt of stangir. (*Nesjavísur* 2)[49]

[The generous man (Óláfr) received a much larger force for the battle than the niggardly one (Sveinn) when the illustrious war band thought to escape the king of the nation's anger, whereas for the friendless leader, who stinted on payment, it became sparse around the standards. War was waged off the broad coastland.]

The terminology here has a distinctly English flavour. The stanza contains the earliest attestation of the word *hirð* (war band), which derives from Old English *hīred* (household, band of retainers). Óláfr most probably brought both the term and the institution it denotes to Norway at the end of his English campaigns.[50] Similar may be the case of *þjóðkonungs* (of the nation's king); although this word occurs in purportedly earlier skaldic poetry, associated in our sources with the era of Haraldr hárfagri, Sigvatr's use of it may have been reinforced by Old English *þēodcyning*.[51]

The source of Óláfr's copious wealth, like that of other Viking adventurers, was in itself morally dubious – being the ill-gotten gains of raiding and Danegeld.[52] He used it to win the personal loyalty of a large entourage, prominent among which were the skalds, with their skills in the creation of propaganda. Sigvatr speaks of himself (perhaps with an ironic side glance at St Martin) as donning a helmet from Poitou, a prestigious and valuable item. He alludes in *Nesjavísur,* verse 9, to the *auðván* (hope of riches) entertained by himself and other followers of Óláfr, and in verse 13 he uses a kenning for 'warriors,' *hreifa elds viðir* (trees of the fire of the hand; that is, trees of gold), that testifies to the wealth and munificence of their lord. The poet makes little apparent attempt to link these conspicuous treasures with

---

49 *Skj.* A1: 228, B1: 217.
50 Cf. Dietrich Hofmann, *Nordisch-englische Lehnbeziehungen der Wikingerzeit,* 83.
51 Ibid.
52 Bjarne Fidjøstøl, '"Har du høyrt eit dyrare kvæde?"' 61–73. Also in P. Foote trans., '"Have You Heard a Poem Worth More?"' 117–32, at 129.

Christian purposes. Such ingrained skaldic themes and ideologies were extremely resistant to modification, but then, as we shall see, some treatments of scripture embodied in the teachings of Ælfric and other English writers could have been construed as giving them continued legitimacy, even in the face of new orthodoxies.

As Óláfr's reign continued into the third decade of the century, wealth, if an effective and even justifiable weapon, would increasingly prove itself dubious for another reason. In a series of stanzas from his *Vestrfararvísur* Sigvatr speaks with surprising frankness about a golden offer that he himself received from Knútr, Óláfr's inveterate rival. The reference may not be simply personal but may be more broad, to Knútr's initiative in offering to chieftains and other influential Norwegians gold in return for their support against Óláfr.[53] Advocates for Óláfr could condemn Knútr's initiative as an assault by Mammon upon righteousness, represented by Óláfr,[54] but, given Knútr's early baptism[55] and energetic patronage of ecclesiastical institutions in England,[56] it would scarcely have been politically viable to anathematize him too strenuously.

> Knútr hefr okkr enn ítri
> alldáðgǫfugr báðum
> hendr, es hilmi fundum,
> Húnn, skrautliga búnar;
> þér gaf hann mǫrk eða meira
> margvitr ok hjǫr bitran
> golls (ræðr gǫrva ǫllu
> goð sjalfr), en mér halfa. (*Vestrfararvísur* 5)[57]

[The glorious Knútr, all prosperous in deeds, has adorned the arms of both of us finely, Bersi, when we met the king. Wise in many matters, he gave you a mark of gold or more and a sharp sword, and to me half (a mark): God himself entirely determines all things.]

---

53 Fidjestøl, 'Kongetruskap og gullets makt,' 4.
54 Ibid., 8–9.
55 Lawson, *Cnut*, 129; Michael Hare, 'Cnut and Lotharingia,' 268.
56 Lawson, *Cnut*, 129 and 135–6; Simon Keynes, introduction to *Encomium Emmae Reginae*, ed. Alistair Campbell, xxvi.
57 ÍF 27: 224, v. 86; *Skj.* A1: 242, B1: 227.

Knútr spurði mik, mætra
mildr, ef hánum vildak
hendilangr sem, hringa,
hugreifum Áleifi;
einn kvaðk senn, en sǫnnu
svara þóttumk ek, dróttin
(gǫr eru gumna hverjum
gnóg dœmi) mér sœma. (*Vestrfararvísur* 7)[58]

[Knútr, generous with fine rings, asked me if I would be serviceable to him as to the gracious Óláfr. I said one lord at a time was fitting for me, and I felt that I made a truthful answer. To each of men are there provided sufficient examples.]

The thinking here derives first and foremost from Matthew 6:24: 'Nemo potest duobus dominis seruire. Aut enim unum odio habebit et alterum diliget aut unum sustinebit et alterum contemnet. Non potestis Deo seruire et mamonae' (No man can serve two masters. For either he will hate the one and love the other, or he will sustain the one and despise the other. You cannot serve God and Mammon).[59] I shall return to the latter stanza presently.

Sigvatr obviously held considerable respect for Knútr, but elsewhere, in a series of occasional verses, he literally demonizes those who use their wealth in order to buy away and subvert support for Óláfr.[60] Correspondingly, we see a shift in Sigvatr's portrayal of Óláfr so that it now has more to do with the suffering Christ and less with the triumphant one seen in *Nesjavísur*.

Fjandr ganga þar þengils,
þjóð býðr opt, með sjóða,
hǫfgan malm fyr hilmis
haus ófalan, lausa;
sitt veit hverr, ef harra

---

58 ÍF 27: 293, v. 105; *Skj.* A1: 243, B1: 227.

59 *West Saxon Gospels*: 'Ne mæg nan man twam hlafordum þeowian oððe he soðlice ænne hatað and oðerne lufað; oððe he bið anum gehyrsum and oðrum ungehyrsum. Ne magon ge gode þeowian and woruldwelan' (Liuzza, ed., *The Old English Version of the Gospels*, vol. 1, 13).

60 Fidjestøl, 'Kongetruskap og gullets makt,' 6.

hollan selr við golli
(vert es slíks) í svǫrtu,
sinn, helvíti innan. (Sigvatr lausavísa 16)[61]

[The enemies of the king go there with loose purses; people often offer heavy metal for the head of the leader, which is not for sale; each knows his (reward) inside in black hell punishment if he sells his faithful lord in exchange for gold. It is deserving of such.]

Kaup varð daprt, þars djúpan,
dróttinrœkð, of sóttu
þeir es, heim, á himnum,
hás elds, svikum beldu. (Sigvatr lausavísa 17)[62]

[The reward in heaven was dismal, where they who ventured on betrayal of a lord with acts of treachery sought the deep home of high flame.]

Gerðisk hilmis Hǫrða
húskarlar þá jarli,
es við Áleifs fjǫrvi,
ofvægir, fé þægi;
hirð esa hans at verða
háligt fyr því máli;
dælla es oss, ef allir
erum vír of svik skírir. (Sigvatr lausavísa 18)[63]

[Then the house carles of the leader of the Hǫrðar would prove overbearing to the earl, when (= if) they accepted money in exchange for Óláfr's life. His court is not to be loudly accused in this way. It is better for us if all of us are clean from deceit.]

The compositional process in these three verses is in keeping with Anglo-Saxon style. It involves a conflation of biblical texts of the type practised by Ælfric, among other English preachers.[64] From the New

---

61 ÍF 27: 294–5, v. 106; *Skj.* A1: 270, B1: 250.
62 ÍF 27: 295, v. 107; *Skj.* A1: 270, B1: 250.
63 ÍF 27: 295 6, v. 108; *Skj.* A1: 270, B1: 250.
64 Bedingfield, 'Reinventing the Gospel,' 14–15 and 23–4; Paul G. Remley, *Old English Biblical Verse*, 33, 49–50, and 59–61.

Testament we have the allusion to Judas's betrayal of Christ for thirty silver pennies.[65] Ælfric comments on it thus in his homily for Palm Sunday (second series):[66] 'Forwel fela manna onscuniað Iudan belæwinge, and swa-ðeah nellað forwandian þæt hi ne syllon soðfæstnysse wið sceattum. Se Hælend sylf is eal soðfæstnys, and se ðe soðfæstnysse beceapað wið feo, he bið Iudan gefera on fyrenum witum, seðe Crist belæwde for lyðrum sceatte' (Very many men shun the treachery of Judas, and yet fear not to betray truth for money. Jesus himself is all truth, and he who sells truth for money will be the companion of Judas in fiery torments, who betrayed Christ for vile pelf).[67] The commercial terms *sellan* and *(be)ceapian* correspond exactly to Sigvatr's *kaup* and *selr*. Alongside this reference is one to Matthew 5:12: 'gaudete et exultate quoniam merces uestra copiosa est in caelis' (be glad and rejoice, for your reward is very great in heaven).[68] The corresponding verse in Luke (6:23) reads: 'gaudete in illa die et exultate ecce enim merces uestra multa in caelo' (be glad in that day and rejoice; for behold, your reward is great in heaven).[69] Sigvatr's adjective *daprt* (dismal) is evidently an irony taking its cue from *gaudete*, most probably mediated by the Old English translation *gefagniað*.[70] Complementarily, from the Old Testament and its apocrypha we have an allusion to the story of Lucifer's rebellion.[71]

In thematic as well as technical respects, these verses could have been composed in emulation of English sources. Loyalty had long been a topic of homilies and scriptural poems in Anglo-Saxon England. The rebellion of the angels, for instance, held an acknowledged place in the education and spiritual guidance of both clergy and laymen.[72] *Genesis* graphically depicts Satan's disloyalty to God and its repercussions in words that correspond quite closely to those used by Sigvatr: 'Forþon he sceolde grund gesecan / heardes hellewites, þæs þe he wann wið heofnes waldend.

---

65 Fidjestøl, 'Kongetruskap og gullets makt,' 9.
66 Thorpe, *The Homilies of the Anglo-Saxon Church*, vol. 2, 244–5; ÍF 27: 224, v. 86; *Skj.* A1: 242, B1: 227.
67 Thorpe's translation.
68 *West Saxon Gospels*: 'Geblissiað and gefægniað forþam þe eower med ys mycel on heofonum' (Liuzza, *The Old English Version of the Gospels*, vol. 1, 9).
69 *West Saxon Gospels*: 'Geblissiað and gefagniað on þam dagum, nu eower med is mycel on heofonum' (Liuzza, *The Old English Version of the Gospels*, vol. 1, 111).
70 Fidjestøl, 'Kongetruskap og gullets makt,' 7.
71 ÍF 27: 293, note to v. 105.
72 Michael Fox, 'Ælfric on the Creation and Fall of Angels,' 199; cf. Virginia Day, 'The Influence of the Catechetical *Narratio*,' 59.

/ Acwæð hine þa fram his hyldo and hine on helle wearp, / on þa deopan dala.'73 (Therefore he had to seek the bottom / of cruel hell torment, because he contended against the ruler of heaven. / He [God] rejected him from his favour then and cast him into hell, / into those deep valleys [lines 302–5].) Ælfric's sermon, *De initio creaturae*, describes Lucifer's descent into *helle wite* after he rebels against God's lordship; Ælfric goes on to complement it with a lengthy discussion of idolatry – as a betrayal of God – and a mention of the betrayal of Christ.74 Similarly, around the year 1000, Wulfstan added topicality to Ælfric's account of Old Testament history by commenting that the people had brought estrangement from God, the invasion of a heathen army, and ultimately the Babylonian captivity upon themselves through their sinfulness.75 Closest to Sigvatr's time, Wulfstan's *Sermo Lupi* (1014) deplores what he identifies as pervasive failures of loyalty.76 In the peroration his call for a purification of conscience and for truth and loyalty is immediately followed by an evocation of the Last Judgment, much as we see in Sigvatr's verses:

> ... utan word and weorc rihtlice fadian, and ure ingeþanc clænsian georne, ond að ond wed wærlice healdan, and sume getrywða habban us betweonan butan uncræftan; ond utan gelome understandan þone miclan dom þe we ealle to sculon, and beorgan us georne wið þone weallendan bryne helle wites.77

> [... and let us order our words and deeds rightfully, and cleanse our inward thoughts earnestly, and faithfully keep to oath and pledge, and have some loyalty between us without deceit; and let us constantly bear in mind the great judgment that we must all come before, and save ourselves earnestly from the surging fire of hell torment.]

Earlier in the homily, there is specific condemnation of *hlafordswice* (treachery/treason against one's lord),78 again in terms lexical and thematic, that Sigvatr could have picked up on.

---

73 This and further citations from Old English poetry are from *The Anglo-Saxon Poetic Records* edition.
74 Fox, 'Ælfric on the Creation and Fall of Angels,' 177.
75 Dorothy Bethurum, ed., *The Homilies of Wulfstan*, 149–50; M.R. Godden, 'Biblical Literature,' 218.
76 Whitelock, *Sermo Lupi*, 30, 31–2, and 42; cf. Robinson, 'God, Death, and Loyalty,' 119.
77 Whitelock, *Sermo Lupi*, 42.
78 Ibid., 31–2.

The nexus of ideas in *Vestrfararvísur*, verse 7 – namely, many good examples of people who faithfully follow one lord – could also derive from Anglo-Saxon teachings. Ælfric's general homily 'Memory of the Saints' (*Lives of the Saints*, homily XVI) explains the importance of saints' lives in precisely those terms: 'We magon niman gode bysne ærest be ðam halgum heahfæderum hu hi on heora life gode gecwemdon and eac æt þam halgum þe þam hælende folgodon.' (We may take good examples, first from the holy patriarchs, how they pleased God in their lives, and also from the saints who followed the Saviour.)[79] This provision of good examples is the controlling idea throughout Ælfric's collection,[80] and in his preface he likens God to a king of this world surrounded by his retainers and stewards, who serve him obediently. 'Hi synd ungeryme, swa swa hit gerisð Gode; ac we woldon gesettan be sumum þas boc, mannum to getrymminge and to munde us sylfum, þæt hi us þingion to þam Ælmihtigan Gode, swa swa we on worulde heora wundra cyðað.'[81] (They are countless, as befits God, but we intend to compile this book about some of them, as strengthening for men and for our own preservation, that they may intercede for us to Almighty God, as we in this world make their miracles known.)

What are the good examples that Sigvatr and others in Óláfr's circle could have regarded as setting an appropriate standard for their leader? The model for the later, eleventh-century Óláfr advocacy, following his death and martyrdom, was very clearly the saint and martyr Edmund of East Anglia. This highly productive prototype of a long series of lives of royal saints and martyrs enacts the new ideal of kingship in emulation of the suffering Christ.[82] That was an ideal, as we have seen, that could have been cogently applied to Óláfr in the latter years of his reign, when betrayal became an increasingly serious threat; however, earlier in his career, as a matter of pragmatic politics, a more militant model was called for. Ælfric appears to acknowledge similar pressures when, in his homily on the Maccabees, he 'clarifies the duty of Anglo-Saxon *bellatores* to defend their country against invaders, just as (he implies) the Maccabees were the *bellatores* of the hard-pressed Hebrews.'[83] In the same homily Ælfric defines *iustum bellum* (just war) as *rihtlic gefeoht wið ða reðan*

---

79 W.W. Skeat, ed., *Ælfric's Lives of Saints*, vol. 1, 336–7.
80 Wilcox, *Ælfric's Prefaces*, 46.
81 Ibid., 121.
82 Lawson, *Cnut*, 134.
83 Magennis, 'Warrior Saints,' 42.

flot-menn, oþþe wið oðre þeoda þe eard willað fordon (just war against the cruel seamen, or against other peoples who wish to destroy the land).[84] Ælfric evidently held respect for English leaders involved in active resistance, such as 'the nobleman Æthelweard, for whom he wrote *Lives of the Saints*,'[85] and at least in that context would not insist on the pacifism of Edmund as the only possible example for conduct.[86] Such teaching could also have commended Byrhtnoth, no matter what his personal faults, as an ealdorman galvanizing resistance to a heathen raiding party[87] (though, of course, scholarly opinion is very divided on all to do with Byrhtnoth)[88] and using 'just wealth' to obtain solidarity for the 'just war.'[89]

The Old Testament, which afforded the Anglo-Saxons 'a veiled way of talking about their own situation' and 'considering and articulating the ways in which kingship, politics and warfare related to the rule of God,'[90] was therefore the place to turn for numerous examples of militant secular leadership. The eligibility of Judith, the protagonist of the deutero-canonical book of that name,[91] as one such example is confirmed by Ælfric;[92] and Paul Szarmach, in his essay in this volume, examines the function of her story as an exemplum. In a treatise written sometime after 1005, Ælfric directs an Oxfordshire landowner and member of the laity called Sigeweard to consider her example, side by side with those of Esther and Judas Maccabæus, at a time of English indecisiveness in the resistance to the Danish heathens.[93]

> Iudith seo wuduwe, þe oferwann Holofernem þone Siriscan ealdormann, hæfð hire agene boc betwux þisum bocum be hire agenum sige; seo ys eac on

---

84 Skeat, *Ælfric's Lives*, vol. 2, 114; cf. Cross, 'Oswald and Byrhtnoth,' 93; James W. Earl, 'Violence and Non-violence in Anglo-Saxon England,' 134.

85 Magennis, 'Warrior Saints,' 42.

86 Cf. Earl, 'Violence and Non-violence,' 133 and 135.

87 Cf. Craig R. Davis, 'Cultural historicity in *The Battle of Maldon*,' 157.

88 Cf., to name only a very few studies, Donald Scragg, ed., *The Battle of Maldon*, 37–8; Fred C. Robinson, 'Lexicography and Literary Criticism,' 99–110, repr. in Robinson, *The Tomb of Beowulf*, 141; Robinson, 'God, Death, and Loyalty,' 111.

89 Rosemary Woolf, 'The Ideal of Men Dying with their Lord in the *Germania*,' 63–81; Joseph Harris, 'Love and Death in the Männerbund,' 99; Scragg, *The Battle of Maldon*, 22–3, and cf. 32 and 40; Robinson, 'God, Death, and Loyalty,' 115–19; Roberta Frank, 'The Ideal of Men Dying with their Lord in *The Battle of Maldon*,' 99 and 106.

90 Godden, 'Biblical Literature,' 225; cf. Klein, 'Beauty,' 78 and 81.

91 Mark S. Griffith, ed., *Judith*, 47.

92 Michael Swanton, 'Die altenglische Judith,' 291.

93 Wilcox, *Ælfric's Prefaces*, 40–1; Godden, 'Biblical Literature,' 218.

Englisc on ure wisan gesett eow mannum to bysne, þæt ge eowerne eard mid
wæmnum bewerian wið onwinnendne here.[94]

[The widow Judith, who overcame Holofernes, the Assyrian ealdorman, has
her own book among these books about her own victory; it is also set down
in English in our idiom, as an example to you people that you should defend
your land with weapons against the invading army.]

On the one hand, Judith is undeniably a servant of God in the sense used
by Ælfric in his *Lives of the Saints*, both as a true worshipper and as a symbol of the Church Militant.[95] On the other hand, where the issues of just war
and just wealth are concerned, she is emphatically not depicted as a saint and
martyr but as a pragmatic operator and, to that extent, a fit example for
Óláfr himself, not to mention Knútr. I shall consider in this light the two
extant Old English narratives of *Judith*, first the anonymous poetic version,
now generally agreed to be a composition of the mid- to late tenth century,[96]
and, second, Ælfric's prose homiletic version. While the latter would have
been more acceptable among the Anglo-Danish establishment and educated
elite, the former version has its own importance as indicating current senti-
ments at a more popular level. The church was not monolithic, and legendary tendencies that Ælfric would have been anxious to censor might have
been perfectly acceptable in other quarters;[97] in turn, they have influenced
advocacy such as Sigvatr's, with mediation through the clerics who provided
teaching and preaching to Óláfr's entourage and conceivably also to elite
members of the laity comparable with Ælfric's Sigeweard.

In the poetic version the heroine is the *nergendes þeowen* (the Saviour's
servant [lines 73b–4a]), in contrast to the licentious Holofernes, who
symmetrically is *nergende lað* (hateful to the Saviour [line 45b]).[98] It

---

94 S.J. Crawford, ed., 'Libellus de veteri testamento et novo,' in *The Old English Version
    of the Heptateuch*, 48–51.
95 Svanhildur Óskarsdóttir, 'The Book of Judith,' 82.
96 R.D. Fulk and Christopher M. Cain, *A History of Old English Literature*, 117;
    Swanton, 'Die altenglische Judith,' 289; Shepherd, 'Scriptural Poetry,' 12; David
    Chamberlain, '*Judith*,' 158.
97 Cf. Aidan Conti, 'An Anonymous Homily for Palm Sunday,' 377–80.
98 Cf. Andy Orchard, *Pride and Prodigies*, 8–9; Shepherd, 'Scriptural Poetry,' 44. Paul
    Szarmach comments in his essay in this volume that the poetic *Judith* essentially depicts
    the *agon* between Holofernes and Judith, the kind of conflict between two opposing
    characters around whom all narrative features, motifs, themes, et cetera organize
    themselves.

is significant then that Judith is shown as engaging in homicide of a cold-blooded, calculated type, and the act is fully, not to say gruesomely, described – if anything, with greater detail and graphic qualities than we find in Sigvatr's praises of Óláfr. Descriptions like this one would serve to signal the continuing acceptability of traditional skaldic emphases on warfare and slaughter.

>   Genam ða þone hæðenan mannan
> fæste be feaxe sinum,   teah hyne folmum wið hyre weard
> bysmerlice,   ond þone bealofullan
> listum alede,   laðne mannan,
> swa heo ðæs unlædan   eaðost mihte
> wel gewealdan.   Sloh ða wundenlocc
> þone feondsceaðan   fagum mece,
> heteþoncolne,   þæt heo healfne forcearf
> þone sweoran him,   þæt he on swiman læg,
> druncen ond dolhwund.   Næs ða dead þa gyt,
> ealles orsawle;   sloh ða eornoste
> ides ellenrof   oðre siðe
> þone hæðenan hund,   þæt him þæt heafod wand
> forð on ða flore. (lines 98–111)

[She seized the heathen man firmly by his hair, with her hands drew him to herself ignominiously, and craftily laid down the man full of evil, loathsome man, so that she might control the wretched being most readily. Then she of braided locks slew the hostile assailant, planner of enmity, with her shining sword, so that she cut halfway through his neck and he lay in a swoon, drunk and grievously wounded. He was not dead then as yet, totally lifeless; the lady strong in her courage struck the heathen dog then firmly a second time, so that his head rolled away on the floor.]

While the seductiveness and deceitfulness that the biblical Judith uses to achieve the killing of Holofernes are toned down by the poet,[99] the premeditation remains unmistakable. At the same time, though, other elements in the poem work to suggest that Judith is perpetrating a just homicide. Exerting leadership as a magnate rather than a queen,

---

99 Fulk and Cain, *A History of Old English Literature*, 117; Griffith, *Judith*, 57; Swanton, 'Die altenglische Judith,' 294, though contrast Karma Lochrie, 'Gender, Sexual Violence, and the Politics of War in the OE *Judith*,' 10–12.

somewhat analogously to the ealdormenn of tenth-century England, she reinforces militancy among her compatriots (*landbuend* and *eðelweardas* [lines 226a, 314a, and 320a]) in their defence of their native land (*eðle* [line 169a]). The words *hæþen* and *here* are repeatedly applied to the Assyrians in the poem, just as they are to the Danes in the *Anglo-Saxon Chronicle*.[100] The poet shows the defeated adversary on a direct course to hell and its torments, just as Sigvatr himself was to do:

> gæst ellor hwearf
> under neowelne næs   ond ðær genyðerad wæs,
> susle gesæled   syððan æfre,
> wyrmum bewunden,   witum gebunden,
> hearde gehæfted   in hellebryne
> æfter hinsiðe. (lines 112b–17a)

[The soul departed to a different place under the precipitous headland, and there it was abased, shackled in agony for ever afterwards, wound around by serpents, bound up with torments, cruelly confined in hell fire after his passing away.]

Victory is decidedly with Judith, as the poet expressly recognizes, even though hers can hardly be called a military victory in the ordinary sense:

> Hæfde ða gefohten   foremærne blæd
> Iudith æt guðe,   swa hyre god uðe,
> swegles ealdor,   þe hyre sigores onleah. (lines 122–4)

[Judith had then won pre-eminent fame in battle, as God granted her, king of heaven, who bestowed victory upon her.]

The victory motif is redoubled later in the poem when, engaged in full-scale combat against heathen opponents,[101] Judith and her people achieve a signal victory: *on ðam sigewonge* (on the victory field [line 294]); *sigore geweorðod* (honoured with victory [line 298]); *sigorlean in swegles wuldre* (victory reward in the glory of heaven [line 344]).

---

100 Cross, 'The Ethic of War in Old English,' 275; Chamberlain, '*Judith*,' 157.
101 Cf. Shepherd, 'Scriptural Poetry,' 42; Donald Scragg, 'The Nature of Old English Verse,' 66.

In the poet's antithetical treatment of Holofernes,[102] particularly memorable is the Assyrian leader's drunkenness at the feast and his helplessness as he lies in bed in his *burgeteld* (bower tent [lines 57, 248, and 276]), secluded by an exotic *fleohnet* (fly net [line 47]). This phase of the narration appears to be coloured by reminiscences of the Gothic Jǫrmunrekkr, as described in *Deor* and in the later Icelandic *Hamðismál*, or the Hunnish Atli, as described in *Atlakviða*, and therefore probably had counterparts in stories of these kings performed in tenth-century England or the Danelaw.[103] The Old English renderings of Orosius's *Historiae adversum paganos*, the *Dialogues of Gregory the Great*, and Boethius's *De Consolatione Philosophiae* may have contributed denigrations of Gothic kings as ardent heathens,[104] parallel to the condemnation of Holofernes as a *wærloga* (pledge-breaker [line 71]) or *hæðenan hund* (heathen dog [line 110]).[105]

These features may help to account for another legendary element in the text, the strangely cryptic and discordant phrase *ides ælfscinu* (elfbright lady [line 14]). Elves are understood as the agency of ailments (in the *Charms* and *Leechdoms*) and part of the kindred of Cain (*Beowulf*, line 112). The word *ælfig* is used to gloss *fanaticus*, in the sense of *minister templi futura præcinens*, literally 'temple-servant chanting future events.'[106] The compound *ælfscinu/-scieno*, as it occurs in *Judith* and *Genesis*, is explained in the *Dictionary of Old English* (see under *ælfscŷne*) as 'radiant or fair as an elf, beautiful'; the compilers note that the word has also been understood as 'delusive as an elf' or 'divinely inspired.' Within *Judith* it might suggest the captivation of Holofernes by the beauty of the heroine.[107] The story as told in the Vulgate already has a folktale tinge,[108] and possibly the English poet was allowing details to 'bleed in' from a folktale type that involved the undoing of a king by a bewitching maiden. Examples of this type are the legend of King Haraldr hárfagri's seduction by Snjófríðr, who is associated with dwarves, in *Ágrip, Heimskringla*, and

---

102 Griffith, *Judith*, 53; Fulk and Cain, *A History of Old English Literature*, 117; Orchard, *Pride and Prodigies*, 8–9; Paul Szarmach's essay in this volume.

103 Cf. John McKinnell, 'Eddic Poetry in Anglo-Scandinavian Northern England,' 327–44; Roberta Frank, 'Germanic Legend in Old English Literature,' 94.

104 M.R. Godden, 'The Anglo-Saxons and the Goths,' 63 and 67.

105 Cf. Orchard, *Pride and Prodigies*, 8.

106 Cf. *Dictionary of Old English*, s.v. *ælfig*.

107 Swanton, 'Die altenglische Judith,' 289; cf. Heather Stuart, 'The Anglo-Saxon Elf,' 313–20; Patricia A. Belanoff, '*Judith*,' 251; Chamberlain, '*Judith*,' 146.

108 Cf. Óskarsdóttir, 'The Book of Judith,' 84.

Flateyjarbók; and King Helgi's seduction by an unnamed elfin woman in *Hrólfs saga kraka*. Of a similar type, again involving dwarves, is the story in *Ynglinga saga* that describes how a Finnish woman called Skjálf avenges herself on the Swedish king Agni, who has abducted her and killed her father. Skjálf tricks Agni by asking him to arrange a funeral feast in honour of her father. He complies, gets drunk, and falls asleep in a tent (*landtjald*) under a tree. Skjálf and her men then hang him and make their escape.

The anticipatory contrition seen in Judith's prayer before she beheads Holofernes comes as a conspicuous corrective element, offsetting these more legendary motifs:

> Forgif me, swegles ealdor,
> sigor ond soðne geleafan,   þæt ic mid þys sweorde mote
> geheawan þysne morðres bryttan;   geunne me minra gesynta,
> þearlmod þeoden gumena.   Nahte ic þinre næfre
> miltse þon maran þearfe. (lines 88b–92a)

[Ruler of heaven, give me victory and true faith, that I with this sword may slay this dealer-out of murder; grant me my salvation, resolute lord of men. Never have I had greater need of your mercy.]

Our overall impression of this text, however, is that the homicide and subsequent fighting are viewed pragmatically for the most part, as instances of just warfare. The treatment of just wealth is just as fully pragmatic. Judith finds God's gifts in this world decidedly useful, in line with Ælfric's apparent 'belief that characters of extreme wealth and social privilege could serve as models across boundaries of both class and social station.'[109] On her arrival at Holofernes' tent, her wearing of conspicuous accessories – *beagum gehlæste, / hringum gehrodene* (laden with treasures, adorned with rings [lines 36–7]), also *golde gefrætewod* (adorned with gold [line 171b]) – is instrumental in Holofernes' undoing. Part of her prize at the end of the battle is his rich war equipment,[110] including his *side byrnan / gerenode readum golde* (broad mailshirts ornamented with red gold [lines 337–8]), but also treasure of a more general kind: *eal þæt se rinca baldor / swiðmod sinces ahte oððe sundoryrfes, / beaga ond beorhtra maðma* (all that the fierce leader of men possessed of jewels or private

---

109 Klein, 'Beauty,' 79.
110 Godden, 'Biblical Literature,' 221–2.

heirlooms, rings and glistening treasures [lines 338–40]). When Judith re-tains these riches, rather than practising unworldliness by giving them up, she may have a tacit recognition of the importance of booty to English leaders for territorial defence.[111] So, contrary to the Sermon on the Mount, the heroine will gain both earthly and heavenly rewards for her faith: 'mede on heofonum, / sigorlean in swegles wuldre, þæs þe heo ahte soðne geleafan / to ðam ælmihtigan; huru æt þam ende ne tweode / þæs leanes þe heo lange gyrnde' (reward in heaven, victory tribute in the glory of the firmament, because she had true faith in the Almighty; truly at the end she did not doubt of the reward that she long desired [lines 343–6]). Once again, here was an 'example' that could be reconciled with skaldic trad-itionalism in a way that the unworldliness of a St Martin could not be.

In Ælfric's homiletic version of the story we see similar potential for co-options towards purposes of skaldic encomium. Ælfric impresses upon his audience that Judith is doubly God's servant: she is exemplary not merely in her chastity but also in her continued trust in God at a time when the leadership of her people is contemplating submission to heathen domination. For many contemporary Anglo-Saxons, alarmed by a preva-lent loss of faith in Divine Providence,[112] these qualities would have marked Judith as a resolute leader for troubled times; so too for those who, like Ælfric himself, were dismayed at the ability of the heathen ar-mies to hold the English to scorn.[113] Hence perhaps his perfunctory miti-gation of the lies and prevarications that she resorts to in order to achieve her victory. 'Iudith behet ærest þam welhreowan ealdormen, þæt heo wolde hine gebringan binnan to hire folce. Ac hit næs na ealles leas, þæt þæt heo him behet, þa þa heo bær his heafod binnan þam weallum ·ond þam folce æteowde hu hire fylste God.'[114] (Judith first promised the savage ealdorman that she would bring him within to her people. But that was not entirely a lie, what she promised him, when she bore his head inside the walls and showed the people how God assisted her.) Ælfric shows without mitigation the heroine beheading the sleeping man with his own sword, calculatedly and in cold blood, and departing without declaring the

---

111 Chamberlain, 'Judith,' 156.
112 Godden, 'The Anglo-Saxons and the Goths,' 63.
113 Lawson, 'Archbishop Wulfstan,' 571.
114 Bruno Assmann, ed., Homily 9, in Angelsächsische Homilien und Heiligenleben, 3, 102–16; repr. 1964, 115, lines 420–2.

deed, something remarkable in a homilist who often toned down violence in his hagiographic sources.[115]

Iudith geseah þa, þa þa he on slæpe wæs, þæt hire wæs gerymed to hire ræde wel forð, and het hire þinene healdan þa duru and gelæhte his agen swurd and sloh to his hneccan and mid twam slegum forsloh him þone swuran and bewand þæt bodig mid ðam beddclaðum.[116]

[Judith saw then, when he was asleep, that an excellent opportunity for her plan had come about, and bade her servant hold the door, and took up his own sword and struck at his neck, and with two strokes cut off his neck, and wrapped the body up with the bedclothes.]

A key part in the rhetorical justification for the homicide is the praise for Judith as God's agent in the deed.[117] Of her personal triumph over Holofernes, Judith speaks in her own commendation: 'Godes engel soðlice me gescylde wið hine, þæt ic unwemme eft becom to eow, and god sylf ne geþafode, þæt ic gescynd wurde, ac butan besmitennysse he asende me ongean, on his sige blissigende and on eowre alysednysse.'[118] (Truly God's angel shielded me against him, so that I came back to you unharmed, and God himself did not permit that I was injured, but without taint he sent me back, rejoicing in his victory and in our release.) Of her people's triumph over the Assyrians, the text tells us: 'Israhela folc þa mid ænlicum sige wendon him hamweard'[119] (The Israelites then with that signal victory went home). It is true that in the Vulgate the Assyrians do not fight but merely retreat, but Ælfric, like the *Judith* poet, makes as much as he can of this limited military engagement.[120]

Judith's possession of just wealth is a legacy from her rich husband: 'He læfde þære wudewan unlytel on feo ond on oðrum æhtum, æfter his gebyrdum, mycele welan on manegum begeatum'[121] (He left the widow a large amount in money and in other possessions, in keeping with his [high]

---

115 Magennis, 'Warrior Saints,' 46–7; Earl, 'Violence and Non-violence,' 130.
116 Assmann, Homily 9, 111, lines 301–6.
117 Ibid., 112, lines 334–7.
118 Ibid., 112, lines 326–30.
119 Ibid., 113, lines 378–9.
120 Mary Clayton, 'Ælfric's *Judith*: Manipulative or Manipulated?' 218.
121 Assmann, Homily 9, 108, lines 200–2.

birth, great wealth in many items of property). She puts it to good use by dressing alluringly for her audience with Holofernes, *mid golde and mid purpuran and mid ænlicum gyrlum*[122] (with gold and purple and peerless adornments). Wealth acquired from heathens was evidently a more awkward topic, and in his epilogue Ælfric actually modifies the Vulgate account by having her decline the presentation of Holofernes' forfeited possessions: 'Heo nolde agan, swa swa us sægð seo racu, þæs wælhreowan hærereaf, þe þæt folc hire forgeaf ... nolde þurh his hæþenscype habban ænige synne'[123] (She did not wish, so the narrative tells us, to have the cruel man's war spoils, which the people gave her ... she did not wish to have any sin through his heathen beliefs).[124] Here he may have been deliberately altering the doctrinally dangerous detail present in the poetic version, as we know he did with other texts.

To sum up, a poem such as Sigvatr's *Nesjavísur* marks an abrupt shift from the type of encomium represented by Einarr skálaglamm's *Vellekla* or even by Hallfreðr's explicitly Christian *erfidrápa* for Óláfr Tryggvason. I have argued that Sigvatr could have evolved his new rhetoric in emulation of specifically Anglo-Saxon modes of Christian teaching. In Anglo-Saxon England and early Christian Scandinavia, although local heroes could be aggrandized to the status of types of Christ, as Edmund and Óláfr certainly were, their advocates must at least from time to time have felt embarrassed and inhibited by some conspicuously un-Christlike attributes of their subjects. In such cases, the Old Testament must have proved valuable in furnishing exemplary material of a less strictly hagiographic kind than that available in the New Testament. The older branch of scripture recounted plenty of literal battles, many of them against the heathens, and the fighting was often shown as led and resourced by patriarchs and other chieftain-like figures who could be restyled as wealthy magnates of a recognizably Anglo-Saxon and Scandinavian type. Also, Old Testament narratives lent themselves to the introduction of legendary material from English and Scandinavian vernacular sources, which may have broadened the narratives' appeal. By the time Christian doctrine found its way into skaldic hands it would necessarily have been shorn of much of its ethical, legal, and political refinement, but in this cruder expression it may have reflected not merely skaldic traditionalism but also

---

122 Ibid., lines 229–30; Griffith, *Judith*, 50.
123 Assmann, Homily 9, 115, lines 424–8.
124 Cf. Clayton, 'Ælfric's *Judith*,' 221.

some shades of contemporary Anglo-Danish and Norwegian thinking: witness the continued cultivation of skaldic poetry that was encouraged by Knútr during his reign in England.[125]

125 Roberta Frank, 'King Cnut in the Verse of His Skalds,' 106–24; Judith Jesch, 'Knútr in Poetry and History,' 243–56; also Matthew Townend, 'Whatever Happened to York Viking Poetry?' 48–90.

Happiness and the Psalms

STEPHEN J. HARRIS

Throughout Anglo-Saxon England, on each day of the year, at all hours of
the day, thousands of men and women sang the psalms. Harried school-
children fumbled with their styli as they scrawled psalm verses into the
hard wax of their tablets.[1] People in the midst of profound emotion recited
psalms, and during the daily liturgy and offices throughout Christendom
the psalms echoed off the walls of chapels and churches, cloisters and
cathedrals. If any poetry could be said to have saturated the Anglo-Saxon
literate classes, it was the poetry of King David and his psalmists. It is no
surprise, then, that the imagery of the psalms pervades Old English poetry.
Words and phrases that were an integral part of daily prayer sound in
the literary productions of those who prayed. Joseph Dyer reminds us,
'Years of daily encounters with the prayers of the psalmist fostered a rich

---

1 Six such tablets were found in Springmount Bog in County Antrim, Ireland. See George
Hardin Brown, 'The Psalms as the Foundation of Anglo-Saxon Learning,' 4. The Psalter
was one of the primary books in an Anglo-Saxon education. See Bede, *Historia ecclesiastica gentis Anglorum*, vol. 3, v; and Pierre Riché, *Education and Culture in the Barbarian
West*, 318. Cassiodorus says that students begin with the psalms: 'Psalterii quoque pro-
prium est quod per eum legis diuinae sanctitas introitur. Non enim tirones incohant a
Genesi, non ab apostolo, non inter ipsa initia auctorita euangelica sancta pulsatur; sed,
licet psalterium quartus codex sit auctoritatis diuinae, primum tamen tirones incohantes
scripturas sanctas, inde legendi faciunt decenter initium.' (A further peculiarity of the psalter is that it is the entry into the divine law. Novices do not begin with Genesis or St Paul;
initially we do not knock at the door of the sacred authority of the gospel. Though the
psalter is the fourth book authorized by God, it is fittingly the first with which novices
begin when embarking on the holy Scriptures.) 'Praefatio,' cap. xvi, in *Cassiodorus:
Explanation of the Psalms*, trans. Patrick G. Walsh, vol. 1, 41; *Magni Aurelii Cassiodori
expositio Psalmorum*, ed. Marcus Adriaen, 22.

contextuality of associations.'[2] These associations included not only words but also images, later partially reconstituted in vernacular poetry. When we look for the source of an image, we may do well to look in the Old Testament, perhaps among the psalms. Patrick Wormald wrote that an 'Old Testament model is always a likely inspiration for an image cultivated or a policy pursued.'[3] When we observe the same appositional and accumulative style in both Old English poetry and the psalms, we might wonder whether the songs of the scriptorium were implicitly measured against the songs of the psalter. In short, as Dyer writes, 'it would be difficult to overestimate the power of the psalms in the lives of those who prayed and sang the Office.'[4] A relation between Old English literature and the psalms is felicitous since images or phrases that are found both in the psalms and in the poetry can link us to a long intellectual tradition of Christian commentary. We can make sense of the poetry in part by making sense of the psalms. Whatever else an *eadig wer* might be in vernacular verse, he was primarily the figure of the first psalm: the blessed or happy man (*beatus uir*). Thus, when we read in *Andreas* that Matthew was *eadig ond onmod* (blessed and resolute [line 54a]), the first psalm hovers around that claim. Judith, too, is called *eadig*. Strangely, she is called *eadig* at the moment that she is threatened with rape. The poem *Judith* is not very clear on the subject of her happiness. However, commentary on the first psalm may help us to understand what may have been intended by the term at that moment in the poem.

Psalms in Anglo-Saxon England

How widely known were the psalms in Anglo-Saxon England? The psalms were extant there in dozens of manuscripts, in a number of versions, and in various books. The books in which psalms are found are chiefly psalters and breviaries, although psalms occasionally appear elsewhere, as well. A psalter is an independently bound liturgical book that contains all 150 psalms along with liturgical material such as calendars,

---

2 Joseph Dyer, 'The Singing of Psalms in the Early-Medieval Office,' 535.
3 Patrick Wormald, *The Making of English Law*, 122.
4 Dyer, 'The Singing of Psalms,' 538. Jean Châtillon says that the psalter sufficed for the education of most medieval monks; see his 'La Bible dans les écoles du xiie siècle,' 168. The close stylistic relation of Old English and Anglo-Latin poetry to scripture is famously made by David Howlett, *British Books in Biblical Style*.

canticles, and litanies.[5] Of the thirty-seven remaining Anglo-Saxon psalters and psalter fragments, about seventeen are wholly or partially glossed in Old English.[6] These include the famous eighth-century Vespasian Psalter from Canterbury and the tenth-century Junius Psalter from Winchester. On the third folio of the Vespasian Psalter, Cotton Vespasian A i, an anonymous scribe has written approvingly, 'Psalmus tranquilitas animarum est' (A psalm is stillness for the soul).[7] Most psalters are magnificent volumes meant for public display or private devotion. Perhaps the best-known Old English psalter includes a translation of the first fifty psalms into Old English prose by King Alfred. Alfred knew the psalms as a boy and collected them into a book that he is said to have carried with him.[8] His prose translation of the psalms are extant in the *Paris Psalter* (Paris BN lat. 8824, not to be confused with the other Paris Psalter, BN lat. 8846). A breviary is an independently bound liturgical book that contains all of the material necessary to perform monastic offices. Although none survives from Anglo-Saxon England, at least five books that are much like breviaries are mentioned in Anglo-Saxon records.[9] These likely would have included the *Trinia oratio* (prayers comprised of psalms and collects), the seven penitential psalms, and various psalms and psalm verses required in daily prayer and petition. Psalms could also be found in liturgical books such as pontificals, ordines, benedictionals, sacramentaries, and monastic *regulae*.

There was no standard book of psalms in Anglo-Saxon England. The psalms themselves were composed in Hebrew and were thought by early

---

5 Phillip Pulsiano, 'Psalters,' 45.

6 Phillip Pulsiano, 'Psalter Glosses' in *The Blackwell Encyclopaedia of Anglo-Saxon England*, ed. Michael Lapidge, John Blair et al., 380–1; Pulsiano, 'Psalters,' 61–85. See also Minnie Cate Morrell, *A Manual of Old English Biblical Materials*, 45. But see Mechthild Gretsch, 'The Junius Psalter Gloss,' 85–121, who claims that there are ten completely glossed psalters and two partially glossed psalters (85). Pulsiano, 'Psalters,' 70, records seventeen sigla for glossed psalters. Gretsch appears to discount twelfth-century psalters with Old English glosses, psalters brought to England in the tenth and eleventh centuries, and psalter fragments.

7 *Anglo-Saxon Manuscripts in Microfiche Facsimile*. I, f. 3. Tranquility is a reflex of the Greek notion of ataraxia, which was important to Epicurean and Stoic notions of happiness, discussed in terms of the psalms below.

8 The claim is made by William of Malmesbury (Allen J. Frantzen, *King Alfred*, 90). On Alfred's authorship of the first fifty Old English prose psalms, see Patrick P. O'Neill, *King Alfred's Old English Prose Translation of the First Fifty Psalms*, 73–96.

9 Alicia Corrêa, 'Daily Office Books: Collectars and Breviaries,' in *The Liturgical Books of Anglo-Saxon England*, ed. Richard W. Pfaff, 52.

medieval commentators to have been collected from numerous sources by the Old Testament prophet and scribe Ezra.[10] In ensuing centuries, several versions of the psalms circulated in late antique and early medieval Europe. After the Hebrew, the next major Western version known to us is the Septuagint Greek, translated into Alexandrian koine sometime during the second century. Of the psalms, there was no Old Latin version, per se, but many vulgar Latin translations from the Greek and Hebrew circulated – St Jerome, a fourth-century doctor of the Catholic church, joked that there were as many translations as manuscripts. These Old Latin texts are rare in Anglo-Saxon England, but the Venerable Bede and Bishop Boniface knew some of them.[11] Bede tells us that in the late seventh century, an Old Latin Bible came to his monastery at Wearmouth-Jarrow from Vivarium, Cassiodorus's monastery. Cassiodorus, author of a hugely influential commentary on the psalms, used both these Old Latin psalms and Jerome's Latin translation from the Hebrew. The Old Latin psalms were collected into an old Roman Psalter, so called by Jerome, which is close to the psalter used by Jerome's contemporary and doctor of the church, Saint Augustine of Hippo. By 392, Jerome had thrice translated the psalter into Latin at the behest of Pope Damasus, once when in Rome and twice again while he was living in Bethlehem. The first is known, as was its predecessor, as the Roman Psalter, and is probably Jerome's cursory revision of the

---

10 Hilary of Poitiers, *Tractatus super Psalmos*, in *Sancti Hilarii episcopi Pictaviensis Tractatus super Psalmos*, ed. Anton Zingerle, 9: 'Esdras enim, ut antiquæ traditiones ferunt, incompositos eos et pro auctorum ac temporum diuersitate dispersos in uolumen unum collegit et rettulit.' Jerome says the same thing in his second preface to the psalter; see *Biblia sacra iuxta uulgatam uersionem*, ed. R. Weber et al., 768.

11 Richard Marsden, *The Text of the Old Testament in Anglo-Saxon England*, 53 and 70. Old Latin psalm variants are recorded in the margins of an eighth- or ninth-century Visigothic psalter, the Codex Cavensis. See Samuel Berger, *Histoire de la Vulgate*, 15. Such mixed texts were popular in Ireland, as well; see Marsden, *The Text of the Old Testament*, 49. It is not unreasonable to assume such marginalia travelled in Anglo-Saxon England. Anglo-Saxons had little or no knowledge of Hebrew, with the important exception of that had from Jerome's writings on Hebrew words and letters. Folio 7 of Cotton Vespasian A.i lists 'Hebrew' letters and their meanings; the letters are Greek, and the Hebrew names do not correspond to the phonological value of the Greek letters. The source of the incorrect meanings seems to be a misreading of Jerome; for example, Beit is said to mean 'filius' (son). In Jerome's *Liber interpretationis hebraicorum nominum*, ed. P. de Lagarde, G. Morin, and M. Adriaen (119 and 130, respectively), Beth is said to mean 'domus' (house) and 'filia uel mensura' (daughter or measure). For a better appreciation of Hebrew in Anglo-Saxon England, we await a monograph by Damian Fleming of Indiana University-Purdue University Fort Wayne, who kindly advanced me his chapter on Hebrew letters.

Old Latin from the Greek Septuagint.[12] It is reprinted today in the Clementine Vulgate Bible. Jerome later modified the psalms further with the help of a multilingual Bible called the *Hexapla* in the library of Origen, the great Christian Platonist, in the holy land. This second version, introduced by Charlemagne into the Gaulish liturgy, became known as the Gallican Psalter, after its popularity in the early medieval Gaulish church. A third version follows the Hebrew directly and is known as the *Psalterium iuxta Hebraicum*; it is sometimes printed in the Clementine Vulgate alongside the Roman Psalter. No Western liturgy employs this third 'Hebrew' version.

Jerome's Vulgate was not readily accepted, and this antipathy continued into the ninth century. When Jerome's translation first arrived in Tripoli and her bishop read Jonah 4:6, a riot broke out – Jerome had corrected the Old Latin *cucurbita* (gourd) to the more accurate *hedera* (ivy). He was accused of sacrilege, and both Rufinus and Augustine chastised him publicly for his translation.[13] Christians were especially severe with Jerome when it came to the psalms, their most cherished songs. Jerome's *Commentarioli in Psalmos* was meant to redress his wounded dignity. However well Jerome may have translated them anew, the Old Latin psalms had already found their way into liturgical formulae and were thus frozen. In this antiquated guise they influenced Old English poems such as *Genesis* and *Exodus*.[14] Early Anglo-Saxon churches employed the Roman Psalter, while Gaul (and Ireland) most often employed the eponymous Gallican Psalter. It was not until tenth-century monastic reforms that the Gallican Psalter came to dominate English practice, and English psalters like the Bosworth Psalter were emended to reflect Gallican readings. The great exception is Bede, who compiled an abbreviated psalter from verses unique to Jerome's *Iuxta Hebraicum*. Sometimes known as the *psalterium idioticum*, it was entitled *Collectio psalterii Bedae seu parvuum psalterium* by Alcuin, Charlemagne's celebrated court scholar, in

---

12 The complicated history of the Old Latin psalms is discussed by Mechthild Gretsch, *The Intellectual Foundations of the English Benedictine Reform*, 21–5, esp. 24n46. Jerome was dissociated from this first revision by Donatien deBruyne, 'Le Problème du Psautier Romain,' 101–26; see Morrell, *A Manual of Old English Biblical Materials*, 211–12.

13 Stefan Rebenich, *Jerome*, 57. See also Germanus Morin, ed., 'Praefatio,' in *S. Hieronymi presbyteri commentarioli in Psalmos*, 167.

14 Marsden, *The Text of the Old Testament in Anglo-Saxon England*, 52–3; and Paul Remley, *Old English Biblical Verse*, 3–4.

a letter of 802.[15] Like Alcuin, Charlemagne's biographer Einhard was uneasy with Bede's version, which came to be known by the ninth century as the psalter of St Jerome.[16] Alcuin's own psalmic florilegium, made a generation later, follows not Jerome's Hebrew but the old Roman Psalter.[17] Perhaps Bede execrated Irish usage to such a degree that, in distinction to Irish practice, Bede championed the *Iuxta Hebraicum* psalter both in his own abbreviated psalter and in the Codex Amiatinus, the great pandect produced during his time at Wearmouth-Jarrow. He is likely also to have appreciated the fidelity of Jerome's translations to the Hebrew, and Bede's abbreviated psalter may simply have been a scholar's tool for remembering which verses differed among the versions. If Alcuin and Bede disagreed on the better version of the psalms, we are unlikely to find consensus among Anglo-Saxons generally.

Nevertheless, there is surprising consistency in Old English translations of the psalms.[18] The psalms were translated into Old English in two ways. First, the Latin psalms were glossed.[19] There are fourteen psalters with Old English interlinear glosses: Vespasian, Junius, Cambridge, Royal or Regius, Eadwine, Stowe or Spelman, Vitellius, Tiberius, Lambeth, Arundel, Salisbury, Bosworth, Blickling or Morgan, and Paris (BN lat. 8824). In addition, there are glosses to the fragmentary Sondershäuser Psalter and Cambridge Pembroke 312, along with a binding strip known as the Haarlem fragment. These glosses are not confined to the psalter. In the Junius Psalter, the Benedictine office of prime is given in full, and the prayers include psalm verses glossed in Old English. A second way in which the psalms were translated into Old English is represented in Paris BN lat. 8824, the

---

15 Edited by Fraipont, *Opera rhythmica Bedae uenerabilis*, 406: 'Insuper Alcuinus hoc opus Bedae anno 802 laudare uidetur his uerbis: "Psalterium paruum quod dicitur beati Bedae presbyteri, quod ille collegit per uersus dulces in laud Dei ex orationibus per singulos psalmos iuxta hebraicam ueritatem."' See also Alcuin, *Epistola* 156, 'Ad Aronem,' *PL* 100.407B; MGH Epist. IV, ed. Dümmler, 417.

16 Benedicta Ward, *Bede and the Psalter*, 13. The Codex Regius, a ninth- or tenth-century two-volume Bible (BN lat. 3563 and 3564), modelled on the revision by Theodulf of Orleans, contains a 'Hebrew' Psalter. See Berger, *Histoire de la Vulgate*, 97.

17 Marsden, *The Text of the Old Testament in Anglo-Saxon England*, 225. Alcuin was concerned that monks know and understand by heart what is sung by the mouth and tongue; see his *Enchiridion*, PL 100.345B.

18 Old English glosses are collated for the first fifty psalms by Phillip Pulsiano, *Old English Glossed Psalters*.

19 See Gretsch, *The Intellectual Foundations*, 26–7.

Paris Psalter, inscribed by Wulfwinus Cada in the eleventh century.[20] In this manuscript, two columns contain, in the first, the Roman Psalter corrected with Gallican and Hebrew variants and, in the second, an Old English prose translation of the first fifty psalms attributed to Alfred; these are followed by a verse translation of the remaining hundred. The complete psalter is followed by canticles, that is songs from other Old Testament books, as well as other liturgical material. Almost every psalm is prefaced by an Old English introduction that describes the meaning and use of the psalm. These introductions are distinct from the titles and introductory verses to the Vulgate psalms, which are called inscriptions to the psalms.[21] The third psalm, for example, begins in the Vulgate with an inscription noting that David sang the psalm when he fled from his son Absalom. The Old English prefaces that inscription with its own: 'David lamented this evil to God, as does each man who sings this psalm; his own difficulty, either of body or mind, he laments to God; just as Christ did when he sang the psalm: to the Jews he sang it, and to Judas Iscariot who betrayed him.'[22]

This Old English inscription and the traditional Latin inscriptions illustrate how a psalm was set into a wider theological and liturgical tradition. Each psalm, in fact, carried with it interpretations established by the church fathers.[23] Cassiodorus, one of the most prolific commentators on the psalms, wrote concerning the third psalm that when Absalom fled from David, he was ensnared around the neck by the branches of an oak tree. 'This was a prefiguration of the Lord's betrayer.'[24] Through the image of an ensnaring tree, Cassiodorus associates the third psalm with Judas,

---

20 Dating by N.R. Ker, *Catalogue of Manuscripts Containing Anglo-Saxon*; see Morrell, *A Manual of Old English Biblical Materials*, 134. A similar psalm is the so-called Kentish hymn, a paraphrase of Psalm 50, *The Anglo-Saxon Poetic Records*, vol. 6, 87. See Sarah Keefer, *Psalm-Poem and Psalter-Glosses*.

21 One of the only available commentaries dedicated to these inscriptions is *Gregory of Nyssa's Treatise on the Inscriptions of the Psalms*, trans. Ronald E. Heine.

22 O'Neill, *King Alfred's Old English Prose Translation*, 101: 'David ... seofode þa yrmðe to Drihtne; swa deþ ælc þæra manna, þe þisne sealm singð, his sylfes earfoðu, ægðer ge modes ge lichaman, he sofað to Drihtne; swa dyde Crist þonne he þysne sealm sang: be Iudeum he hine sang and by Iudan Scarioth þe hine lærde.' The phrase *be Iudeum he hine sang* may be clarified by O'Neill's note to the verse that cites a commentary, 'Aliter, uox Christi ad patrem de Iudaeis' (169).

23 Joseph Dyer, 'The Psalms in Monastic Prayer,' 66: 'As the Psalms began to take on an important role in the prayer life of the Christian church, there arose a considerable literature of Psalm commentaries that provied not only orthodox interpretations of every line of the psalms but also models of text interpretation.'

24 *Cassiodorus*, trans. P.G. Walsh, vol. 1, 68.

which is likely why the Old English inscription to this psalm mentions Judas, who hanged himself after betraying Christ. Other than Cassiodorus, major sources for psalm interpretations are Augustine, Jerome, and Hilary of Poitiers. Their works on the psalms were extant in Anglo-Saxon England. The Old English inscriptions to the psalms follow not these but an Irish compilation long attributed to Jerome, *Breviarium in Psalmos*.[25] Other sources for the Old English include an anonymous Gaulish commentary known as the *Glosa [sic] Psalmorum*; a seventh- or eighth-century anonymous commentary called the *Expositio Psalmorum*; and an incomplete, anonymous Latin Psalter commentary from Northumbria in the eighth century, now Vatican MS Palatinus latinus 68 (Gneuss, *Handlist of Anglo-Saxon Manuscripts*, 909).[26] In addition, there are dozens of medieval commentaries on particular psalms or groups of psalms, such as Alcuin's commentary on the seven penitential psalms and his commentary on the gradual psalms.[27] These offer literal, allegorical, and spiritual interpretations of various terms and phrases.

As a brief example of how such interpretations might illuminate Old English poetry for us, Psalm 50:17 (which Benedict, in his monastic rule, directs every monk to say upon arising) asks the Lord to 'open my lips, and my mouth shall speak out your praise.'[28] Alcuin comments that these are the lips of the prophet, which were closed by the condition of sin and are opened by forgiveness. Only when the lips are opened by forgiveness can the inner heart speak praises of the Lord.[29] The Junius Psalter glosses this verse, 'Dryhten **weleras** mine **ontyn** ðu & **muð** min bodað lof ðin' (emphasis mine). In the Old English poem *The Whale*, part of the Exeter Book's *Physiologus*, the poet remarks:

> þonne hine on holme hungor bysgað
> ond þone aglæcan ætes lysteþ,
> ðonne se mereweard **muð ontyneð**,
> wide **weleras**;

---

25 O'Neill, *King Alfred's Old English Prose Translation*, 35. It is number 629 in *Clavis Patrum Latinorum*, ed. Eligius Dekkers; ed. Vallarsi in *PL* 26.821–1270.

26 O'Neill, *King Alfred's Old English Prose Translation*, 34–44.

27 See Richard Sharpe, *A Handlist of the Latin Writers of Great Britain and Ireland*, 42. Alcuin's commentaries are printed in *PL* 100.

28 Jerusalem Bible translation; Psalm 51:15 in the Protestant reckoning. Here and hereafter I use the Vulgate numbers. The Benedictine *regula* was adopted for Anglo-Saxon use; the results are the *Regularis concordia*, ed. and trans. Thomas Symons.

29 *PL* 100.586B. Alcuin takes this directly from Cassiodorus.

[When hunger occupies him on the sea, and seduces the monster with food, then the sea warden **opens** his **mouth**, his wide **lips**.]

Then a sweet fragrance is emitted from deep inside the whale, and unwary prey are drawn in and trapped by this figure of the Devil.[30] This image is doubly strange: whales don't have lips. However, it begins to make more sense to us if we set the whale's open mouth in its psalmic context. The poet's appositive does not ask us merely to imagine a whale's lips but to recall the language of the daily monastic psalms. We can then observe a contrast between a physically alluring, appetitive fragrance of food and a spiritually alluring sweetness of prayer.[31] By invoking the first prayer of the monastic day, this portion of *The Whale* reminds hungry monks that upon waking, their minds should be on prayer, not on food.[32] Consistent with this image, the poem suggests allegorically that a change of heart brings God's immanent mercy, which gives salvation from the tempting mouth of hell.[33] In this example, then, the psalms offer us a wider field in which to observe the poem's images at play.

Eadig

References to the psalms are scattered throughout Anglo-Saxon poetry. They are unsurprisingly most frequent in poems like *Genesis* or *Christ* that deal directly with scripture, or poems like *Guthlac* or *Elene* that deal with explicitly Christian topics. Today's readers are less likely to recognize these allusions than were Anglo-Saxon monks whose common duty it was to memorize the entire psalter in Latin. The importance of these allusions can be illustrated by examining an intriguing instance of the first psalm's

---

30 Jerome associates the whale with the devil, as does this poet. See Jerome, *Commentaria in Ionam, PL* 25.1131B.

31 This metaphor is used by Cassiodorus of the psalms: 'Their marvellous sweetness does not grow bitter with worldly corruptions, but retains its worth and is continually enhanced with the grace of the purest sweetness' (Walsh, *Cassiodorus*, vol. 1, 25).

32 Thus Ephesians 5:14 reminds readers that sleepers should rise to be in Christ, and after waking (Eph. 5:19), 'speak to one another with psalms and hymns and spiritual songs.'

33 The whale is a site for conversion, as the Jonah story indicates. The significance of the Jonah story in Anglo-Saxon England is discussed by Paul Szarmach in 'Three Versions of the Jonah Story,' 183–92. This is the *significatio* given the same image in 'The Whale' of Arundel 292, a thirteenth-century English Physiologus. See Szarmach, 'The Whale,' 350–1. The whale 'doð men hungren and have ðrist, / And mani oðer sinful list; / Tolleð men to him wið his onde [breath], / Woso him folgeð, he findeð sonde [shame].'

first line in the Anglo-Saxon poem, *Judith*. In the Vulgate, the psalm begins, '[B]eatus uir qui non abiit in consilio impiorum et in uia peccatorum non stetit et in cathedra pestilentiae non sedit' (Blessed is the man that walketh not in the counsel of the ungodly, nor standeth in the way of sinners, nor sitteth in the seat of the scornful [1611 King James Version]). The first psalm is said to contain within it all other psalms, some say the entirety of scripture. Jerome writes in his homilies on the psalms that the psalter is like a mansion, and the 'main entrance to the mansion of the Psalter is the first psalm.'[34] Gregory of Nyssa writes in his *Treatise on the Inscriptions of the Psalms* that the psalter is 'arranged sequentially according to the logic of virtue.' The psalms, he continues, 'have been formed like a sculptor's tools for the true overseer who, like a craftsman, is carving our souls to the divine likeness.'[35] The first psalm directs the reader to that likeness.

Gregory writes, 'The goal of the virtuous life is blessedness.' The blessed man is the *beatus uir*. The Hebrew term behind *beatus* is *ashrei*, meaning 'happy or blessed,' but it implies 'fortune or luck.' *Happy* derives from the Old Norse *happ*, and it also means 'good luck or good fortune.'[36] *Ashrei* was translated into the Greek of the Septuagint as *makarios*, the same term used in the Beatitudes of Matthew, chapter 5, and Luke, chapter 6.[37] The Old English equivalent of this Greek term is *eadig*, an adjective cognate with Old High German *otag* and Gothic *audag*, presumably derived from the proto-Germanic *auđanaz.[38] All glossed Old English psalters gloss *beatus vir* as *eadig wer*.[39] In that consistency, we can presume a connection between Old English *eadig* and Latin *beatus* in the minds of literate Anglo-Saxons. King Alfred's *Paris Psalter* translates Psalm 1:1 as 'Eadig byð se wer þe ne gæð on geþeaht unrihtwisra.' The phrase *eadig bið se* is as ubiquitous in the psalter as it is in the Old English psalms (for example, Psalms 64:4, 83:5, 93:11, 111:1, 126:6, and 145:4). The phrase appears in

---

34 *The Homilies of St. Jerome*, trans. Sister Marie L. Ewald, vol. 1, 3.
35 *Gregory of Nyssa's Treatise*, II.cciii, 193, and II.cxxxvii, 165, respectively.
36 This is also the meaning of *beatus* in secular Roman school texts. Varro reports that *beatus* is a word having to do with fortune and luck. See Roland G. Kent, *Varro*, vol. 1, 88–9.
37 W.E. Vine, *Vine's Expository Dictionary of Old and New Testament Words*, s.v. 'Blessed.'
38 Sigund Feist, *Vergleichendes Wörterbuch der Gotischen Sprache*, s.v. 'audags.' See also Helmut Gneuss, *Lehnbildungen und Lehnbedeutungen im Altenglischen*, §21, 61–2.
39 Pulsiano, *Old English Glossed Psalters*, 1. Dialect variants are represented by the Eadwine Psalter, Cambridge, Trinity College R. 17.1 (which uses the term *Æði*), and the Arundel Psalter, London BL Arundel 60 (which uses the term *eadi*).

poems of the Exeter Book like *The Seafarer* ('eadig bið se þe eaþmod leo-faþ' [Blessed is he who lives humbly/obediently], line 107) and *Maxims I* ('eadig bið se þe in his eþle geþihð' [Blessed is he who thrives in his home-land], line 37). Old English *eadig bið se* maxims, it seems, ultimately take their form from the psalms.

Old English poems allude not only to a psalm, and do so across lan-guages, but also to the interpretative apparatus of a psalm. At the outset of the fragment *Judith*, neighbour to *Beowulf* in Cotton Vitellius A.xv, the poet characterizes Judith as an *eadigan mægð* (blessed maid [line 35a]).[40] It is a strange epithet at this particular point in the poem. The poem begins *in media res* in the fortress of Holofernes, with the depraved commander of the Assyrian forces threatening Judith's Hebrews. Holofernes is feast-ing with his thanes, as Belshazzar was in Daniel, chapter 5. He and his men become loud, *hlydde* (line 23a), so that they can be heard from far off. One is reminded here of Hrothgar's celebrations in *Beowulf*, during which Grendel hears from far off *hludne in healle* (loudness in the hall [line 89a]).[41] Loudness in both poems brings the downfall of the partygoers. This loudness recollects, and in *Judith* is distinguished from, the loud praise of God in Psalm 32 (33): 'Cantate ei canticum nouum bene psallite ei in uociferatione' (glossed in Old English in the Stowe Psalter, 'Syngað him canticc niwne well syngað him on stemne *hlud*re').[42] The same loud-ness characterizes the doomed soldiers as they wait outside the dead Holofernes' tent (line 270b). Now noisy, drunk, and lustful, Holofernes, looking to physical rather than to spiritual pleasure, threatens to rape Judith. The poem reads:

> Het ða niða geblonden
> þa **eadigan** mægðe   ofstum fetigan
> to his bedreste   **beagum** gehlæste,
> **hringum** gehrodene. (lines 34b–7a)

---

40 On the manuscript and major critical approaches to the poem, see Andy Orchard, *Pride and Prodigies: Studies in the Monsters of the Beowulf Manuscript*, 5–16.

41 A number of translators render *hlude* as 'laughter,' but there is no connotation of laughter to the term. Cocks crow with *hluda* voices, and the month of March is called *Hlyda* because of wind and storm. See Joseph Bosworth and T. Northcote Toller, *An Anglo-Saxon Dictionary*, s.v. 'hlud.'

42 Emphasis mine. Andrew C. Kimmens, *The Stowe Psalter*, 56. 'Sing unto Him a new song; play skilfully with a loud noise' (King James Version).

[The one corrupted by evil commanded then that the **blessed/happy** maid be fetched hastily to his bed, laden with **rings**, adorned with **bracelets** (emphasis mine).]

The passage is thick with biblical allusion, not only to Psalm 1:1 but, in lines 36b and 37a, possibly to the story of Tamar and Judah in Genesis, chapter 38. (In Old English, Judah is often spelled *Iudas*, just like Judas of the New Testament and of the Old English commentary on Psalm 3.)[43] The story of Tamar and the first psalm coincide in their portraits of blessed or happy persons. Tamar pretended to be a harlot so that she might conceive a child with Judah. Seeing her, not knowing who she was, and lustful for a harlot, Judah gave her his bracelets and rings as a token. The Old English Heptateuch translates the relevant scriptural passage as *ðinne hring & ðinne beah*.[44] In the Old English poem, Judith is adorned allusively with the same rings and bracelets as is Tamar. They signify Judith's blessedness and her role in the salvation of her people. Later in the scriptural story, Tamar reveals these rings and bracelets in public to shame Judah and to save her own life, using the same words Judah had once used to wound his own father, Jacob, as he presented Jacob with the bloody cloak of Joseph. Similarly, when Judith approaches Bethulia, the poet adds the extraneous detail that she and her handmaid are *beahhrodene* (ring adorned [line 138b]) as they approach the city gate to be identified. She is greeted by crowds who approach *ða Þeodenes mægð þusendmælum* (the Lord's maid in the thousands [line 165]). Why this poet, perhaps alone of all Old English poets, would number the crowd, is uncertain – perhaps in recollection of the crowds that gathered around Jesus or St Alban. However, the number may be read as more allusive than descriptive: *folc ... þusendmælum* (lines 163–5) recollects Psalm 3:7, *milia populi* (Old English, *þusenda folces*). And the psalm, like the poem, expresses the thought that the speaker will not be afraid of the Lord's enemies.

---

43 See for example, Matthew 26:47 in R.M. Liuzza, *The Old English Version of the Gospels*, vol. 1, 56.

44 Emphasis mine. Gen. 38:18. *The Old English Version of the Heptateuch*, ed. S.J. Crawford, 176. Fred Robinson argues that the rings are a means to allure men. See his 'Five Textual Notes on the Old English Judith,' 47–8.

An allusion to the story of Tamar (and possibly to Psalm 3) associates Judith with the righteous, the blessed, the *happy* women of history,[45] but it still does not reveal anything about the nature of early medieval happiness. After all, it is unlikely that at a tense moment, threatened with rape, Judith is experiencing an affective mental state synonymous with gladness, Old English *sælig*. Old English *eadig* is not synonymous with a pleasurable feeling, and this may be difficult for a twenty-first-century reader to appreciate. We tend to equate happiness with pleasure. This may be an effect of a semantic collapse among terms that once distinguished various sorts of pleasure – joy, contentment, glee, happiness, and so forth – but there may also be philosophical considerations. Nineteenth-century philosophers Jeremy Bentham and John Stuart Mill, like ancient Greek and Roman Epicureans, saw in happiness a close relation to pleasure. Bentham went further than the Epicureans and developed a calculus of pleasure by which he hoped to reach true happiness. He famously asserted that if one had more pleasure from playing push-pin (a pub game like skittles) than from reading Shakespeare, one should play push-pin. Mill, unconvinced by this hedonistic calculus, distinguished quantities of pleasure from qualities of pleasure, as well as higher pleasures from lower ones.[46] With contributions from Nietzsche and Hegel, the philosophy of happiness turned to physiology for evidence, and that turn eventually relegated happiness to the realm of psychology. This more recent physiological legacy more often than not alienates *Judith* from our empathetic appreciation of early medieval happiness. Chief among the difficulties that modern students of the poem seem to face in understanding medieval Christian happiness is modernity's secularization or abandonment of a human telos, an end to which all human life ought to tend. Alisdair MacIntyre famously argued that with 'the elimination of any notion of essential human nature and with it the abandonment of any notion of a telos leaves behind a moral scheme' alienated from its teleological context. Since nothing impels secular man to achieve salvation, the argument runs, he is without an idea of a human

---

45 Judith is called blessed by Hraban Maur in his *Expositio in librum Iudith*, PL 19.540D. The title of his eleventh chapter includes the phrase 'Judith, whose beauty and wisdom were admired by all.' On the influence of Maur, see Orchard, *Pride and Prodigies*, 6n42.
46 John Skorupski, 'John Stuart Mill,' 566–9. I follow Alasdair MacIntyre, *After Virtue*, 62–6. I would like to thank Professors Liam Harte of Westfield State College and Garreth Matthews of the University of Massachusetts for their guidance in the philosophy of happiness – all errors are my own.

nature that requires improvement.[47] This has been celebrated as the autonomy of the self, but one of its consequences is the equation of happiness with achieving pleasant emotion.[48] MacIntyre then deduces what he calls the 'emotivism' of contemporary life, a subject that bears significantly on our understanding of Judith's *eadignes*.

By supposing Judith's *eadignes* to be similar to a secular and affective, internal disposition towards happiness, we allow the possibility that Judith's motivation is ultimately self-serving rather than self-sacrificing. Of course, this makes no sense of the moment in the poem where her happiness seems predicated on a potential rape. Were one to try to formulate her happiness as self-serving, one might suggest that Judith desires to do what is right, and it is Holofernes' unintentional confirmation of that desire, by providing Judith with an antagonist for her virtue, which makes her happy. However, this formulation profoundly misrepresents the poem's Christian *eadignes*, not least because it is entirely possible that a Christian can feel miserable and yet be *eadig*. In the Old English poem *Andreas*, the apostle Matthew is pinioned by spears jutting through his hands before his eyes are gouged out, yet he is **eadig** *ond onmod* (happy and resolute [line 54a]). Guthlac, the English saint whose verse life appears in the Exeter Book, is racked with sickness and disease but, nevertheless, *eadig on elne* (happy/blessed in courage [line 1026a]) as he coughs and sputters. These examples illustrate that Christian, Anglo-Saxon *eadignes* is not a physical affect. Nor is it akin to Michel Foucault's idea of pleasure that derives ultimately from an exercise of power, which he suggests is the unfettered dominion of one body over another (be it a human body or an institution). Foucault's pursuit of power is analogous (but not equivalent) to a Benthamite pursuit of pleasure: both imagine pleasure as a telos of

---

47 MacIntyre, *After Virtue*, 54–5. Without an external telos, the inward turn of theology is fastened onto the self. In his *De vera religione* (xxxix, 72), Augustine famously says, 'Noli foras ire, in teipsum redi; in interiore homine habitat ueritas' (Do not go outward, return within yourself; in the inward man dwells truth [trans. Charles Taylor, *Sources of the Self*]). But he intends for each man to seek God from there. It was Descartes who argued that the moral order was not found externally but built internally. The self thus became the maker and justification of moral identity. See Charles Taylor, *Sources of the Self*, 129–44.

48 This argument is made by Kenneth Minogue, 'Ideal Communities and the Problem of Moral Identity,' 61. He is critiquing normativism, which 'misunderstands individualism by identifying it with the content of individual desires and satisfactions.' Normativism is 'the belief that moral and political philosophy should *demonstrate* the basic practical rules for distributing goods so as to constitute a just society' (41).

human activity; both suggest that a selfish pursuit of pleasure can be justified as a selfish pursuit of a common good.[49] In short, Judith's happiness has little to do with emotions, feelings, or self-interest.

What kind of happiness could Judith know at this moment of grave danger? Clearly, she is selflessly pursuing a course that she believes to be right, but is not her opinion of right and wrong culturally defined? Does her blind obedience to her religion not delude her into mistaking Christian opinion for universal moral truth? For those who reject or downplay the revelation of moral law in scripture, morality or immorality are arbitrated ultimately by reason (in which case happiness is either rational or irrational) or by shared feeling (in which case happiness is either a shared or inappropriate emotion). The eighteenth-century Scottish philosopher David Hume argued for arbitration by feeling. Sentiment, says Hume, is the gauge of morality (and sympathy with other people's pain and joy directs our reason). If we are happy at other people's pain, then our happiness is inappropriate. In this view, Judith's happiness would arise from her sensing the happiness of others – and the only one showing joy at this point in the poem seems to be Holofernes, leaving us with an inappropriate conclusion about the source of Judith's happiness.[50] Twentieth-century moral philosophers went further: Bertrand Russell argued that there are no 'moral facts,' that is, dispassionate criteria whereby something may be judged good or evil.[51] Morality, and the happiness had from its exercise, is in this view a matter of personal opinion. Accordingly, individuals are imagined to establish their own criteria for the pursuit of pleasure, and these criteria are valued differently by different individuals and are thus called *values*. Postmodern moral philosophers, inheritors of Hume and Russell's more materialistic views, are thus tasked with conceiving moral grounds for common action without privileging what philosopher Todd May calls 'incommensurable values.'[52] From this perspective, Judith's happiness

---

49 It is important to recognize that Foucault does not seek a common good. His program is, according to Allan Megill, more extreme than Marx's. Megill writes that for Foucault 'there is no ultimate social and political truth, no possibility of a final end of repression ... All one can do is struggle against the condition [of the extant social order], engaging in a continual guerrilla warfare, in a political theater of cruelty directed against the existing order' (Allan Megill, *Prophets of Extremity*, 188).

50 That is, Judith would be sympathetic to Holofernes' joy: she is happy because he is happy. Obviously, the potential victim of a rape does not feel happiness for the rapist. So, sympathetic or empathetic happiness is ludicrous in this instance.

51 Richard Norman, 'History of Moral Philosophy,' 590.

52 Todd May, *The Moral Theory of Poststructuralism*, 3.

would be of her own making and of equal moral worth to the happiness Holofernes takes in his wine and rapine. Any postmodern, non-traditional 'normative theories' that assent to a definition of happiness elastic enough for local variation would be entirely alien to the author of *Judith*. Consequently, they will not help us make sense of this poem.

Judith's Happiness

In both Christian and non-Christian early medieval contexts, *eadig* connotes wealth and happiness, joy and good luck. Its material sense is illustrated in *Beowulf*, line 1224, *eadig æþeling*, and line 2468, *eadig man*. Given the incommensurability of emotivist or materialist views of happiness with *Judith*, assessing the term's Christian connotations is essential to understanding how Judith can be thought happy when she is threatened with rape. Greek philosophers like Aristotle and Plato spoke of eudaimonia, which refers to long-term happiness, the sort of happiness one means when speaking of enjoying a happy life. Aristotle also uses the term *makarios* (used in the Septuagint Psalm 1:1) and uses *eudaimonia* and *makarios* interchangeably in his *Nichomachean Ethics* I, x. In a study of late antique and early medieval happiness Jiyuan Yu and Jorge Gracia write, 'It is a deeply rooted assumption of the Greeks that everyone has a final end in life and this end is happiness.'[53] John Calvin will write much the same thing almost two thousand years later.[54] Notably, Greek happiness is not an egoistic gratification of appetite but a pursuit of 'the gratification of the rational part of the soul.'[55] Reason was thought divine, and the pursuit of happiness was conceived as a pursuit of divinity. Later, among Christians, divinity was no longer thought to be pure reason but a being. Reason was subordinated to this being. Thus, to 'achieve happiness is not a result of cultivating reason, but rather it involves reestablishing a relationship with the divine persons.'[56] Reason might help an individual to

---

53 Editors' introduction to Jiyuan Yu and Jorge J.E. Gracia, eds., *Rationality and Happiness*, 3.

54 John Calvin, *Commentaries on the Epistle of Paul*, chap. 4.7 (96): 'And doubtless as the highest happiness of man is to be united to his God, so ought to be his ultimate end, to which he ought to refer all his thoughts and actions.' It is important to note that this ecstatic happiness comes to be associated with an internal affection as the moral law is internalized during the Reformation. See Jaroslav Pelikan, *Christian Doctrine and Modern Culture*, chapter 3.

55 Yu and Gracia, *Rationality and Happiness*, 4.

56 Ibid., 9.

achieve a relationship with the divine, but for Christian theologians the divine was beyond that which could be thought, to paraphrase Anselm of Canterbury. This early medieval sense of Christian happiness is most effectively described by Augustine.

Augustine considered happiness in both its experiential and formal aspects. In the first, Augustine inquired into the experience of happiness. He sought to know how the Platonic form of happiness manifests itself in human life. He distinguishes between pleasure (*gaudium*) and happiness (*beata uita* [a happy life]) and argues that hearing the term *beatus* recalls in each of us a memory of pleasure. In the *Confessions* he notes that while everyone wants happiness, each has his or her own memory of pleasure and therefore finds a different way to achieve happiness. Here, he seems to anticipate postmodern claims of a value-centred happiness: one can be happy insofar as one is free to pursue a self-gratifying pleasure. But Augustine makes an important distinction. Augustine proposes that perhaps what everyone wants is not really happiness but a revival of an experience of pleasure, 'to live according to one's own pleasure (*delectatio*).'[57] He distinguishes pleasure and pleasurable memories from happiness, in that happiness consists not only in having what one wants but also in ensuring that what one wants is good. In this last condition on happiness – that it aim at the good – Augustine takes happiness beyond an individual's orbit by positing an external 'good,' as can be found in Plato and Plotinus. The good is an objective standard beyond the exigencies of human appetite or of one's personal perspective. Thus, Augustine's second aspect of happiness is the rational pursuit of what is good for one;[58] he does not mean that one ought to rationalize personal pleasure. Augustine's second, formal aspect of happiness is fulfilled by rationally pursuing what has been set out through faith. Scripture and tradition tell a Christian that the greatest object of desire is God; thus the greatest happiness is had in His pursuit. Furthermore, true happiness, Augustine says, cannot be achieved on earth by our own means but only through Christ.[59] Christian happiness,

---

57 From his *Confessions*, 13.5.8, in Gareth B. Matthews, 'Two Concepts of Happiness in Augustine,' 169. I owe my understanding of this topic and my thanks for his guidance to Professor Matthews.

58 Matthews calls this Augustine's Formal Concept of Happiness, as opposed to his Experiential Concept of Happiness, described earlier. Augustine thus combines *beatitudo* with *felicitas*. See R. Spaemann, 'Glück, Glückseligkeit,' 691. Isidore of Seville follows suit in his *De differentis verborum*, PL 83.72.

59 John Bussanich, 'Happiness, Eudaimonism,' 413–14. See also Augustine, *Confessions*, trans. Pine-Coffin, IX, 4, 185–9. Happiness in Augustine has to do with the right use of the will; see his 'On Free Will,' in Augustine, ed. J.H.S. Burleigh, 130–1.

according to Augustine, requires one to set out on the road to salvation according to the mandates of revelation.

Augustinian and Greek views of happiness were combined uneasily in Anglo-Saxon England with the ninth-century translation of the *Consolation of Philosophy* of Boethius. Boethius was a Christian but wrote his *Consolatio* without reference either to God or to Christian doctrine. King Alfred translated all or most of the *Consolatio* into Old English and transformed it into a Christian text.[60] Throughout Alfred's dialogue, refashioned as between Mod (Mind) and Wisdom, happiness derived from earthly sources is pronounced false or illusory. As Allen Frantzen notes, 'Wisdom commands Mod to "study wisdom" because wisdom is the secret of happiness and the source of power.'[61] Wisdom's central lesson is that 'true power and happiness cannot be found in the rewards of the world, but only in the strength of the soul.'[62] Alfred introduces an image of a wheel to explain how happiness and a knowledge of God combine. Frantzen explains:

> The axle of the wheel represents God, the unchanging, unmoving center, outward from which, and along the wheel's spokes, are men. 'The nave moves nearest the axle; therefore it moves more surely and more securely than the rim; so the axle may be the highest good, which we call God, and the best men travel nearest to God, as the nave rotates nearest to the axle.' The farther men range from the axle, the greater their physical suffering and spiritual confusion ... The greater one's distance from the center, the greater one's difficulty in seeing God and understanding the workings of the universe.[63]

Alfred links proximity to God with wisdom, and wisdom with happiness. Happiness is had by seeking to know God's will. This is true happiness, as opposed to a false or illusory happiness had from material gain, wine, or lust. Let us call this latter sort *joy*.

Augustine's distinction between a *beata uita* and *gaudium* is borne out in *Judith*. His distinction is a function of the same distinction in the psalms and in psalm commentary. *Gaudium* is a sensual pleasure, a feeling of joy. In Christian contexts, the term is used to speak of spiritual joy, but also an

---

60 See Frantzen, *King Alfred*, 45.
61 Ibid., 53.
62 Ibid., 56. See also Matti Rissanen, 'In Search of *Happiness*,' 237–48.
63 Frantzen, *King Alfred*, 59.

imperfect joy.[64] It is the joy that accompanies the harp and drum in Genesis 31:27. It is the good fortune and abundance of the land in Deuteronomy 28:47. And it is the joy that Jesus saw before submitting himself to suffering on the cross, according to Paul's letter to the Hebrews 12:2. It is first and foremost a sensation prompted by physical or spiritual things. In Anglo-Saxon glosses, *gaudium* is often glossed *gefea* or *blisse*.[65] Anglo-Saxon hymns also tend to gloss *gaudium* as *gefea*.[66] In *Judith*, the term *gefea* describes the joy of the lean wolf as it rejoices in the forest before the Hebrews battle the troops of Holofernes (line 205b). Here the poet offers us an image of appetite at its most fundamental. There is nothing spiritual about this joy. The wolf anticipates slaughter, and that anticipation prompts its joy. The human correlative in *Judith* of joy had from anticipation is expressed with the term *bliðe*. When Judith returns home to Bethulia after being held by Holofernes, the poet tells us that the Jewish people were *bliðe* (line 159a); they anticipate victory, as Judith promises. Also *bliðe* is Holofernes; he anticipates raping Judith and becomes *on mode / bliðe* (joyful in his mind [lines 57b–8a]). However, these are short-term forms of joy that will be realized on earth. The wolf will eat his fill, the Hebrews will win their battle, and Holofernes hopes he will rape Judith. None of these expresses the long-term sense of *eadige* or *beatus*.

Also borne out in *Judith* is Alfred's link between wisdom and happiness. From an Augustinian perspective, Judith is *eadig* insofar as she pursues God in faith – and, as Augustine makes clear in his letters to his sister, in chastity. Her anticipation of happiness will be fulfilled only in heaven, not on earth. Her pursuit of God demands that she isolate herself from whatever is evil. Psalm 1 describes the just man and the wicked man, setting the image of one against the image of the other.[67] Gregory of Nyssa writes that the first psalm 'pronounces separation from evil to be blessed,

64 See s.v. 'gaudium' the *Oxford Latin Dictionary*; Alexander Souter, *A Glossary of Later Latin to 600 A.D.*; and R.E. Latham, *Revised Medieval Latin Word List from British and Irish Sources*. It is this sense of joy that C.S. Lewis pursues in *Surprised by Joy*.

65 The Lindisfarne Gospels (Skeat, *The Four Gospels*, 25–245), Matt. 5:12 and 18:13, etc. The Rushworth Gospels (Skeat, *The Four Gospels*, 25–245), Matt. 2:10, 13:14, 18:13, etc.

66 For example, Hymn 38, line 7; Hymn 73, line 10; Hymn 74, line 5; Hymn 75, lines 5 and 7, and so forth. Edition by Stevenson, The Latin Hymns, 1–147. See also Aldhelm, *De laude uirginitatis*, line 1346 (Arthur S. Napier, *Old English Glosses*, 36).

67 This is the substance of Jerome's homily on the first psalm, 'Homily 1,' in *The Homilies of St. Jerome*, trans. Ewald, esp. 10–11.

since this is the beginning of turning to what is better.'[68] Cassiodorus concurs after following Jerome's exposition of the tripartite disposition of sin that this verse suggests. Bede writes in a homily on the Gospel of Mark, 'The first hope of salvation for anyone is to desert those with vicious habits.'[69] And the Lord's Prayer famously asks for deliverance from evil. Likewise, the poet of *Judith* sets Judith's qualities firmly against those of Holofernes. As Lori Ann Garne points out, 'In a significant departure from the [Vulgate] *Liber Iudith*, the Old English poet further highlights Holofernes' inherent wickedness by removing Judith from the feast altogether.'[70] Thematically, however, the poet follows his or her immediate source very closely. The Old Testament book of Judith describes Nabuchodonosor's charge to Holofernes. Nabuchodonosor instructs Holofernes to go out against all the Western kings and to destroy all those who oppose him. The oppositions are clear in both scripture and in the Old English poem: good against evil, Judith against Holofernes, Hebrews against Assyrians, and God's power against secular power.

Where Chaucer or Shakespeare might have explored the complexities of an evil character like Holofernes, the Anglo-Saxon poet has no such interest. Holofernes is called *niða geblonden* (one corrupted by evil [line 34b]); *nergende lað* (loath to the Saviour [line 45b]); *se deofulcunda, / galferhð guðfreca* (the devil-kin one, licentious and destruction-greedy [line 61b]); *bealofull* (full of cruelty [line 63a]); *unsyfra / womfull* (unclean and impure [lines 76b–7a]). Holofernes, so obviously antithetical to Judith, wants only to defile Judith, to stain her with *womme* (sin [line 59a]). There is a similar phrase describing the cross in *Dream of the Rood*: *forwunded mid wommum* (thoroughly wounded with sin [line 14a]). Both Judith and the Rood, unlike those who merit the scourge of God, suffer undeservedly. Augustine makes a distinction between deserved and undeserved suffering in his tract on the happy life. Undeserved is 'the evil spirit which invades the soul from the outside,' while a soul 'defiled through vices and sins' deserves its own penance.[71] Holofernes is an evil spirit, a character like Iago who seeks to do others undeserved harm. In testament to Judith's undefiled soul, the Lord (promises the poet) restrains Holofernes in this

---

68 Heine, *Gregory of Nyssa's Treatise*, 85.
69 Bede, 'Homily II.6 on the Gospels,' in *Bede the Venerable*, trans. Lawrence T. Martin and David Hurst, vol. 2, 53.
70 Lori Ann Garne, 'The Art of Translation in the Old English *Judith*,' 175.
71 Augustine, *The Happy Life (De beata uita)*, trans. Ludwig Schopp, in *The Fathers of the Church*, vol. 5, 29–84 and 65–6.

act. However, the warlord's concupiscent urge is merely steered wide of its mark, not eliminated. Holofernes' wickedness is an irremediable quality of his person, of his devil kinship, as well as a quality of the acts he commits. The poem thus raises the question of the nature of sin – whether it is fated or chosen. Judith is clearly on the side of the elect, but what of Holofernes, the devil kin? Can he be redeemed, or is he destined to fulfil the mandate of his role? Lynn Grundy points out in her study of grace in Ælfric, 'Neither Augustine nor Ælfric is quite happy to say that the non-elect are predestined to evil, at least in the sense of being made capable of sin but incapable of redemption.'[72] But there is a compromise position. The constant, voluntary sin of a man is thought to make him hard-hearted, a condition that 'comes from within him, and is not imposed by God.'[73] This internal vice places blame squarely on Holofernes' shoulders, even though he seems to be acting according to God's plan.[74]

Judith is *eadig* primarily because she is wise. She knows to seek God. Happiness and wisdom are twinned in many Anglo-Saxon sources. The first psalm declares that blessed is she who does not take *consilo impiorum* (the counsel of the ungodly). *Impietas* also means 'cruelty or wickedness' and is glossed *arleas* in Old English psalters. Psalm 72:6 reads: 'Operti sunt iniquitate et impietate sua' (They are clad with their iniquity and their wickedness). Cain is called *arleas of earde* in the Old English poem *Genesis* (line 1018). Holofernes' equally damnable wickedness derives in part from his inability to take good counsel. It seems a strange detail to choose, but understandable in light of the psalm. The poet writes that once Holfernes

---

72 Lynne Grundy, *Books and Grace*, 130. See also Ælfric, 'Feria III de dominica oratione,' in *Ælfric's Catholic Homilies, The First Series*, ed. Peter Clemoes, 326: 'Witodlice se man þe deofle geefenlæcð. se bið deofles bearn. ná þurh gecynde. oððe þurh gesceapennysse. ac þurh ða geefenlæcunge. & yfelum geearnungum' (Truly, the man who imitates the devil, he is the devil's child, not through kinship or through creation, but through imitating and earning evil). In stessing imitation, Ælfric suggests the opposite of the *imitatio Christi*, as seen in Ambrose of Milan, *Explanatio super psalmos xii*, *PL* 14.941B: 'qui ergo beatus est, imitator erit Domini Iesu.'

73 Grundy, *Books and Grace*, 131. Ælfric's text is Romans 9:18, but the question is equally pertinent to the heart of Pharoah in Exodus 10:1, which is made stubborn or hard. The Latin is *induravi*, from *indurare* (to make hard); the Hebrew is from the verb *hobed* (to make heavy or unresponsive). One issue in this verse is pertinent to *Judith*: does Pharoah act as he does because he is unresponsive to God, because God has hardened his heart, or because he acts of his own accord?

74 This middle position is also King Alfred's. As Frantzen explains, Alfred 'did not believe that man was fated to a preordained role in the world, but rather that he had the power to make his own world, to do evil or to do good' (*King Alfred*, 65).

is thoroughly drunk, 'he nyste ræda nanne' (he did not know any counsel [line 69b]). Moments later in the poem, and in direct contrast to Holofernes, Judith is inspired by God precisely because she 'him to helpe seceð / **mid ræde** ond mid rihte geleafan' (seeks help from him / **with counsel** and correct faith [lines 97–8, emphasis mine]). *Rihte* is a word often used to imply lawfulness, and here implies orthodoxy, or correctness of belief. Judith has just spoken her prayer to God (lines 83–94). She has called on the Trinity in its parts – 'frymða God ond frofre Gæst, / Bearn Alwaldan' (God of created things and Holy Ghost, Son of the Almighty [lines 83–4]) – and as three in one, *Đrynesse* (line 86a). She has asked God for *soðne geleafan* (true belief [line 89a]). Thus, she appears not only as the vehicle of God's vengeance but also as the recipient of his true faith. In the end, the Hebrew victory is ascribed to *Judithe gleawe lare* (Judith [through her] wise/prudent doctrine/advice [line 333]).

Her wisdom is not a home-made thing but a gift of God. It is Judith's understanding of this gift, her ability to look beyond herself and to see her telos in the infinite divine, that enables her to succeed and to enjoy *eadignes*. Thus, Judith rightly gives thanks to God at the end of the poem (lines 341–2). But those who do not see beyond themselves, like Holofernes and his men, suffer the torments of hell. In a deservedly famous scene, Holofernes' soldiers wait uncomfortably outside his tent. They think he is lying with Judith, but he is fast dead. To wake Holofernes the soldiers begin to cough, to cry loudly, and to grind their teeth (lines 270–2). Literally, it seems a strange thing to do; after all, how loudly can one gnash teeth? But the psalms report that the wicked shall see the justice of God and gnash their teeth (111:10 [112:10]). The same psalm verse says that the wicked shall be grieved. The poet of *Judith* likewise says that the soldiers are not only gnashing teeth but also *torn þoligende* (suffering grief [line 272a]). And the Psalm verse concludes that the wicked man shall *tabescet* (melt/waste away). This short scene in *Judith* also concludes of the soldiers that 'Þa wæs hyra tires æt ende, / eades ond ellendæde' (Then was their glory at an end, / success and brave deeds [lines 272–3]). By reading this scene against Psalm 110, we come to see that the terrestrial lord of the soldiers, unlike the Lord of the psalms, does not answer the grieving of his supplicants. In fact, by this point in the poem Holofernes' spirit is deep under the ground, nethered and wound in torment, bound in punishments, imprisoned firmly in hell's burning brine (lines 112b–17a). Psalm 110, which provides some context to this scene in *Judith*, begins, 'Beatus uir qui timet Dominum in mandatis eius uolet nimis' (Happy/Blessed is the man who fears the Lord, that delights greatly in his commandments). It is

Judith's *rihte* faith, her delight in God's commandments, that makes her *beatus* (or, rather, *beata*). Her happiness arises solely from her service to God. The abstract level of her happiness is continually reinforced by the poet's reference to her mind and spirit, ubiquitous in the poem. In this more abstract notion of happiness she is contrasted to Holofernes, who is described chiefly through physical characteristics and who pursues physical pleasure. Judith is a type of the *beatus uir* of the psalms, and her happiness makes little sense to us today unless we define it in the context of the Old Testament and in the light of the psalms.

The Old English *Kentish Psalm* and Polysystems Theory

M.J. TOSWELL

Psalm translation has in every generation been a significant feature of what Itamar Even-Zohar would call the polysystem of English texts.[1] (Even-Zohar's theory of the polysystem and its interaction is more well known in his native Israel and in countries with overlapping cultural systems at work – notably in Europe and Asia. At its simplest, Even-Zohar's theory of the interaction of polysystems argues for approaching cultural systems both diachronically and synchronically, considering the dynamic interaction of texts in a complex of systems, so that sometimes a certain kind of text – biblical translation, for example – will be at the centre of the polysystem and at other times at the periphery, as a result of structural and sociocultural shifts in the polysystem.) Perhaps more intriguingly, until very recently in the long history of English literature and English approaches to biblical texts, psalter translation has almost always been a primary part of that polysystem, something not relegated to a second tier of the polysystem as a secondary text or set aside altogether as potentially heretical, dangerous, or likely to be misappropriated. Psalm translation has also from its inception in the vernacular involved both prose versions and poetic attempts to recreate the lyric poetry of the original.[2] Miles Coverdale, one of the earlier Bible translators in England, rendered the

---

1 See Itamar Even-Zohar, *Papers in Historical Poetics*. The collection reprints a series of papers read, and some of them published, between 1970 and 1977.
2 See Michael P. Kuczynski, *Prophetic Song*, and Rivkah Zim, *English Metrical Psalms*. A more general but quite useful study is William L. Holladay, *The Psalms through Three Thousand Years*. Two useful collections are Nancy van Deusen, ed., *The Place of the Psalms in the Intellectual Culture of the Middle Ages*, and Brendan Cassidy and Rosemary Muir Wright, eds., *Studies in the Illustration of the Psalter*.

psalms into verse. Queen Elizabeth I, on the other hand, translated the Latin psalms into her own devotional prose version of the psalter in English as an exercise in piety. One of her most famous courtiers, Sir Philip Sidney, translated some of the psalms into verse, the rest being completed by his sister, the Countess of Pembroke, after his untimely death. Their choice was to use the whole range of possible metrical and stylistic choices of lyric poetry for their renditions and also to work from pre-existing prose translations of the psalms. In his *Apology for Poetry (Defence of Poesy)*, Sidney explicitly speaks to the nexus of poetry and prophecy to be found in the psalms and links them directly to David:

> [T]he holy David's Psalms are a divine poem ... even the name of Psalms will speak for me, which, being interpreted, is nothing but Songs; then, that it is fully written in meter, as all learned Hebricians agree, although the rules be not yet fully found; lastly and principally, his handling his prophecy, which is merely poetical ... wherein almost he showeth himself a passionate lover of that unspeakable and everlasting beauty to be seen by the eyes of the mind, only cleared by Faith?[3]

For Sidney the psalms are songs, poems first and foremost, accomplished by David in metre to present the prophecy and the praise of God. Later, in the same text, he refers explicitly to Psalm 51 when he uses Nathan's chastising of David's adultery and murder, which makes David 'as in a glass see his own filthiness, as that heavenly Psalm of mercy well testifieth' (126), to demonstrate the utility of poetry, the way it leads to virtue. The poet, for Sidney, can lead the mind to delight and thence to virtue.

Sidney's argument is now a cornerstone of introductory theory courses, and it occasions much discussion as to the true utility of poetry. Less discussed, however, is the direct link he himself draws to the production of poetry by 'kings, emperors, senators, great captains' (144), starting with David and the explicit demand he makes that poetry should be 'lyrical kind of songs and sonnets' for 'singing the praises of the immortal beauty, the immortal goodness of that God who giveth us hands to write and wits to conceive' (152). For Sidney, the right and proper use of poetry is praise of God, and he concludes his work with a ringing endorsement of the ability of English to rise to the occasion and provide the flexibility of language and versification that is necessary for this high purpose. Before his death,

---

3 *Sir Philip Sidney*, ed. Robert Kimbrough, 106–7.

he had drafted translations of the first forty-three psalms; his sister, Mary Sidney Herbert, Countess of Pembroke, revised his work and translated the rest of the psalms. She used psalm translations and commentaries in her work, being particularly inspired by the mid-sixteenth-century metrical French renditions of Clément Marot and Théodore de Bèze (Beza). Following is the opening of her version of the *Miserere* psalm:

> O Lord, whose grace no limits comprehend;
>   Sweet Lord, whose mercies stand from measure free;
> To me that grace, to me that mercy send,
>   And wipe O Lord, my sins from sinful me,
>   O cleanse, O wash my foul iniquity:
> Cleanse still my spots, still wash away my stainings,
> Till stains and spots in me leave no remainings.[4]

This first stanza of the translation renders the first five verses of the psalm, summarizing and recasting the imagery very elegantly. The Countess uses anaphora, repeating O and also *cleanse*, and polyptoton with *sins* and *sinful* and also *stainings* and *stains*, and she produces exact iambic pentameter lines with *abaacc* rhymes until the feminine rhyme of *stainings/remainings* (an elegant final touch) – in all, a perfect rhyme royal stanza. Her version of the psalm is generally called a metaphrase, a term which might usefully be used to describe the psalm translation that is the focus here. The rendition is succinct and elegant, finding the core of the psalm's meaning and reconfiguring it for her age.[5] The work of the Kentish psalmist is less impressive in those terms, although it bears comparison with the Sidney psalms in two ways: it demonstrates no concern or anxiety about translation as a mode of activity, and it appears to serve the same dual purpose for the individual listener or reader of teaching and meditating on the psalm.

In both cases, the translators focused on the most well known of the penitential psalms, which is a group of seven psalms that is a subgroup of

---

4 Mary Sidney and Sir Philip Sidney, *The Sidney Psalms*. Another edition is J.C.A. Rathmell, *The Psalms of Sir Philip Sidney and the Countess of Pembroke*. For a discussion of the use of Psalm 51 in ritual executions, including its recitation by Lady Jane Grey in English on the scaffold, and an analysis of the obsession with death and with the completion of her brother's work which was so central to the accomplishments of the Countess of Pembroke, see Gavin Alexander, *Writing After Sidney*, 76–127, esp. 99–100.
5 For a more detailed analysis, see G.F. Waller, *Mary Sidney, Countess of Pembroke*, esp. 231–11.

the individualistic psalms of lamentation.[6] This particular psalm ends the
first third of the psalter (the first quinquagene), which in Irish usage and
very commonly in Anglo-Saxon psalters was split first into the 'three fif-
ties' and only secondarily or later divided according to the Benedictine
usage. Often seen as an autobiographical document in modern and early
modern commentaries, Psalm 51 is analysed for its psychological portrait
of betrayal and adultery in the first person, remorse, penitence, and potential consolation. In the psalm, David pleads for mercy for his misdeeds,
shifting back and forth between statements of his own uncleanness and
error and hopeful statements about God's cleansing of his sin, and concluding with an analysis of animal sacrifice, the sacrifice of righteousness with
which God will be pleased. The psalm is one of the most personal and typical lamentations in a very personal book of the Bible. Moreover, the
Miserere psalm is wholly Davidic, and wholly based on Old Testament history and focused on David. This is one psalm that does not readily prefigure
Christ and have a Christological interpretation, since the psalm is a kind of
justification of David, an extolling of the breadth and depth of his penitence
and also, to some extent, his accomplishments.

Psalm 51 seems to have been one of those psalms that was plucked out
of its context in the psalter early on for separate consideration – the *Kentish
Psalm 50* being a particularly striking example of that special treatment.
The *Miserere* is the first psalm directly referred to by Dante, for example,
who has the sinners in canto 5 of the *Purgatorio* crossing in front of
the narrator and his guide while chanting the *Miserere* antiphonally. The
psalm had tremendous power as a lament, as the chief of the penitential
psalms and one of four major lament psalms. It has David explicitly connecting his personal penance for his crimes of adultery and homicide with
his ability to serve as a moral guide for others, a communicator of moral
precepts, even a prophet. Michael Kuczynski argues that David's acts of

---

6 For studies of the psalms, see, for example, S.E. Gillingham, *The Poems and Psalms of
the Hebrew Bible.* For studies of Psalm 51 (usually numbered as 50 in Anglo-Saxon
psalter manuscripts), see Edward R. Dalglish, *Psalm Fifty-One in the Light of Ancient
Near Eastern Patternism.* Dalglish divides the psalm into the introduction (verses 3–4),
the confession (verses 5–8), the prayer (verses 9–14), the vow (verses 15–19), and a liturgical appendix (verses 20–1). This division reflects the commentary tradition. For a similar analysis of Psalm 51 as an autobiographical document, and the argument that the
abyss of misery invokes mercy and the abyss of scene invokes grace, see Girolamo
Savonarola, *Esposizione e meditazione del Salmo Miserere.*

contrition are never simply personal but always have social implications.[7] This psalm is perhaps the clearest statement concerning the psalms as public and private texts, as acts of devotion and of moral instruction. Augustine proposes that this is the psalm in which the public and private roles meet, in which the psalmist takes on the collective sin of the faithful (and thereby forges the Christological link that is otherwise difficult to determine).[8]

The Psalms were, in Anglo-Saxon England as in the Renaissance, the book of the Bible that was most frequently translated and commentated. The Psalter was also the book of the Bible most commonly to be found in parish churches, monasteries, and perhaps even in the hands of the secular nobility.[9] Its very ubiquity may well lead scholars to underestimate its profound and permanent significance for the medieval mind and heart. Bede, for example, produced what may be the first abbreviated psalter, a mnemonic device for remembering the beginning and principal themes of each psalm, and the psalms imbued his thinking and writing. Many of his principal examples of rhetoric and style, when he was demonstrating the persuasive and elegant techniques of Latin, came from the psalms.[10] Over

---

7 See Kuczynski, 'David "the Maker"' in *Prophetic Song*, 3–50, which focuses on Psalm 50 to introduce Middle English approaches to the psalms and to David. The importance of David in Anglo-Saxon England is well known but perhaps insufficiently studied. Art historians discuss the David miniatures in psalter manuscripts at great length, and literary scholars speculate as to the connection King Alfred must have seen between himself and his ancestor David (according to some Anglo-Saxon genealogies) as he translated the first fifty psalms.

8 Augustine makes this point throughout his exposition of this psalm, linking Christ to the miserable *I* of the psalmist (*Sancti Aurelii Augustini enarrationes in Psalmos*, ed. E. Dekkers and J. Fraipont).

9 This argument, often quoted, was famously first made by Kenneth Sisam in the edition he prepared with Celia Sisam, *The Salisbury Psalter*, 'Appendix II: The Gloss D and its relations,' 75. Scholars today phrase the point somewhat more cautiously but nonetheless mean the same thing. Thus, William Noel begins his study *The Harley Psalter* by noting the bequest of Ælfric, archbishop of Canterbury, to Wulfstan, archbishop of York, of a book of Psalms, and then stating, 'The book of Psalms was an appropriate part of Ælfric's bequest: more than any other book of the Middle Ages, the Psalter was at the centre of both public and private worship. It was recited in its entirely at least once a week in the performance of the liturgy, and it was extensively used for personal devotions' (1).

10 See, for example, Michael Lapidge, *Bede the Poet*, and Benedicta Ward, *Bede and the Psalter*, and her *Venerable Bede*. Ward provides a translation of Bede's abbreviated psalter as an appendix to *Bede and the Psalter*; for another, see Gerald M. Browne, trans. *The Abbreviated Psalter of the Venerable Bede*, which is based on his own critical edition of the Latin, *Collectio Psalterii Bedae Venerabili adscripta*.

two hundred years later, when King Alfred of Wessex established a circle of learning and translation at his court at the end of the ninth century, the translation and provision of brief prose commentaries for the first fifty psalms appears to have been his own chosen work. When Cnut wanted to impress foreign rulers with his magnificence and munificence on his European tour, he gifted them with de luxe copies of the psalms (among other manuscripts).[11] And when Christina of Markyate, fifty or so years after the end of the Anglo-Saxon period, wanted to embrace the eremitical life, the devil chose to intimidate her by sending toads to squat on her psalter.[12] The devil was singularly unsuccessful in his efforts. Perhaps knowingly, perhaps not, Christina copied the example of the Anglo-Saxon warrior saint Guthlac and used the power of the psalter to banish his manifestations.[13]

The psalms, however, demonstrate another feature of Anglo-Saxon literacy and one that is rarely acknowledged: a fearless willingness to translate into the vernacular. Only Ælfric objected, both philosophically and practically, to the idea of translation of both Latin thoughts and sacred expressions into the vernacular. His objections have been carefully studied and analysed, and to some extent his unease at the idea of translation has infected modern scholars with a pathology of dis-ease about rendering the Bible into the early medieval vernacular; they see biblical translation as already fraught with uncertainty.[14] Polysystems theory may be a useful

---

11 See, for example, Veronica Ortenberg, *The English Church and the Continent in the Tenth and Eleventh Centuries*, 62, 239, and 260.

12 See C.H. Talbot, ed. and trans., *The Life of Christina of Markyate*, 98.

13 See Bertram Colgrave, ed. *Felix's Life of Saint Guthlac*, 100–1.

14 A long history attends this point, most recently and perhaps best argued by Robert Stanton's *Culture of Translation in Anglo-Saxon England* (Cambridge: D.S. Brewer, 2002). Stanton argues initially for translation as an explanatory paradigm for thinking about Anglo-Saxon England, engaging in a close reading of the statements about translation by Cicero and Jerome and by Anglo-Saxon thinkers such as Bede, Aldhelm, and Alcuin. The argument turns, however, to a detailed discussion of decoding and rethinking the statements made by Alfred and Ælfric (both of whom at different times apologized for and justified their work in different ways), and the ways in which their statements are or are not reflected in their translations. Thus, Stanton follows the traditional approach of scholars such as Rita Copeland, beginning with the *fidus interpres* and considering how translators addressed their translations throughout the late classical and medieval periods. His focus then turns to the anxiety of authority and biblical translation (including a chapter on glossing that discusses the psalter glosses in particular). My argument here is that this kind of approach tends to be circular, and polysystems theory allows us to reframe the traditional questions about approaches to translated texts in Anglo-Saxon England.

way to consider the importance of translation, and especially psalm translation, in Anglo-Saxon England, by focusing on the *Kentish Psalm*.

Kentish Psalm is an introduction, translation, and to some extent a meditation on the *Miserere* psalm produced in the Kentish dialect, probably at the end of the tenth century at Canterbury.[15] It survives in one manuscript, British Library Cotton Vespasian D.vi, and does not appear to be a particularly learned product.[16] Using the typical Old English equivalents of particular lexemes in the psalms, as established over two centuries of a glossing tradition, it lays out, generally in one line, the Latin psalm verse and, in the ensuing two to six (at the most eight) lines, provides a translation into Old English metrical verse of that text – and then further expansion and repetition.[17] Furthermore, and particularly useful for a polysystem approach, there are three sets of comparanda for this vernacular version of the psalms: the glossed psalters, of which there are two generally accepted traditions and one very learned outlier, totalling some seventeen manuscripts;[18] the aforementioned prose psalms of King Alfred, which include the first nine verses of the *Miserere* psalm before a break in the manuscript in which they were copied – the so-called *Paris*

---

15 The only available edition is Elliott Van Kirk Dobbie, *The Anglo-Saxon Minor Poems*. The text is also presented but not re-edited, save for punctuation, in Sarah Larratt Keefer, *Psalm-Poem and Psalter-Glosses*. She is now preparing a new edition and discussion of the *Kentish Psalm* as part of a collection of liturgical verse in Anglo-Saxon England, a project begun with Patricia Hollahan.

16 The original context of the material is the second diachronic feature that polysystem theory considers. (The first diachronic feature is the historiography of the text, which will emerge later; this paper focuses rather on the synchronic features of the text – the analysis of the *Kentish Psalm* itself.) However, space does not permit full discussion of the manuscript, so I will simply note here (based on my own study of the codex in December 2005) that this manuscript would repay further study. It is a quarto-sized codex of only 125 folios, measuring only 180 mm × 132 mm, and closely resembling a prayerbook. Painted gold around all its edges, the manuscript has been cut down at top and bottom (and the gilding post-dates the cuts, indicating that the manuscript retained some considerable status). The scribe used blackish-brown ink, with orange colouring on selected letters throughout the manuscript; the page layout most closely resembles that of the Book of Cerne.

17 The only detailed study of the psalm and its treatment of the Latin source is Patricia Hollahan, 'The Anglo-Saxon Use of the Psalms,' 96–134.

18 The most recent list and discussion of the glossed psalters is Phillip Pulsiano, 'Psalters,' 61–85. See also M.J. Toswell, 'Psalter Manuscripts,' A25–33. The first volume of Pulsiano's projected four-volume edition of the glossed psalters is *Old English Glossed Psalters: Psalms 1–50*.

Psalter;[19] and the complete metrical translation of the Roman Psalter, which is often called the *Paris Psalter* because one hundred psalms of it survive in that manuscript. However, for the purpose of this analysis the metrical psalter more importantly includes the fragments that survive as part of a vernacular explanation of the Office, now improperly known as *The Benedictine Office*, the fuller version of which is extant in Bodleian Library MS Junius 121.[20] These other versions of the psalm not only demonstrate the apparent ease with which the Anglo-Saxons chose to translate this sacred scripture but also offer an opportunity to investigate closely the translation strategies and techniques of the anonymous Kentish poet who produced this text.

For example, the opening verse of the translation itself reads:

Miserere mei deus secundum magnam misericordiam tuam
'Miltsa ðu me, meahta walden[d],   nu ðu wast manna geðohtas,
help ðu, hælend min,   handgeweorces
þines anes,   ælmehtig god,
efter þinre ðære miclan   mildhiortnesse.' (lines 30a–4)

[*Have mercy on me, O God, according to thy great mercy.*
You, Lord of strengths, have mercy on me; now you know the purposes of men; my Saviour, Almighty God, help your own creation, according to your great mercy.]

The metrical psalter version, which also begins with the Latin psalm verse and then provides the translation in *The Benedictine Office*, has:

---

19 See Patrick P. O'Neill, ed., *King Alfred's Old English Prose Translation of the First Fifty Psalms*. Janet Bately established Alfred's authorship of the psalms in 'Lexical Evidence for the Authorship of the Prose Psalms in the Paris Psalter,' 69–95, following up the work of J.I.'a. Bromwich, 'Who Was the Translator?' 289–304.

20 George Philip Krapp, ed. *The Paris Psalter and the Meters of Boethius*, ASPR 5; Elliott Van Kirk Dobbie edits the fragments of the metrical psalter in *The Anglo-Saxon Minor Poems*, but the standard edition is J.P. Ure, ed., *The Benedictine Office*. Ure is also largely responsible for the poor title of these explications of the offices. For quotations from the *Kentish Psalm*, Dobbie's is the standard edition and the one I have used here, though with some reference to my own transcription from the manuscript. I have used the Latin from the manuscript as well; translations from the Latin Psalter are from the Rheims-Douay Version edited by Challoner and now available as *The Holy Bible* (Fitzwilliam, NH: Loreto Publications, 2007). Translations from the Old English are my own.

Miserere mei deus; secundum magnam misericordiam tuam.
Mildsa me mihtig drihten,   swa ðu manegum dydest,
æfter ðinre þære mycelan   mildheortnysse.

[*Have mercy on me, O God, according to thy great mercy.*
Mighty Lord, have mercy on me, just as you did for many others, according
to your great mercy.]

The parallel in translation of the second membrum is intriguing, especially
since in both cases an adjective and the noun it modifies break over the
caesura. The first half-line is also very similar, though the *Kentish Psalm*
repeats and elaborates the petition for an extra two lines. The similarities
should not of themselves be taken to reflect influence, since a limited range
of options existed for translation if consistency was an issue, and both
texts closely reflect the kind of language usage found in the glossed psalters. Thus, the Vespasian Psalter for this psalm has:

mildsa min god efter ðere miclan mildheortnisse ðinre (Miserere mei deus
secundum magnam misericordiam tuam)

[God have mercy on me according to your great mercy, *Have mercy on me,
O God, according to thy great mercy*][21]

Alfred is both more adventurous and more likely to use other resources
for his inspiration, but few options offer themselves here. The Latin
Psalter, a Roman Psalter, appears in the manuscript in a facing column:

Miltsa me, Drihten, æfter þinre mycelan mildheortnesse,

[Show mercy to me, Lord, on account of your great mercy,]

Of these, the *Kentish Psalm* is by far the longest and most discursive translation, but the additions are almost wholly repetition and variation. *Miltsa
ðu me* is varied by *help ðu*, and *meahta walden[d]* by *hælend min* and also
by *ælmehtig god*. The idea seems to be repetition, perhaps for meditation

---

21 See Sherman M. Kuhn, ed. *The Vespasian Psalter*, 47. I have also checked the readings
against the *Dictionary of Old English Corpus* (2004) found at http://www.doe
.utoronto.ca. Since Kuhn did not regularize his numbering to the Vulgate standard, as
did other psalter editors before and after him, for the Vespasian Psalter, I also use my
own private database of this material, which has the psalters aligned.

or for learning. The two additions, *nu ðu wast manna geðohtas* and *hand-geweorces þines anes*, do not seem to provide new information. Now that God knows the thoughts of men, he will be able to help through the use of his own handiwork. The last line of the verse suggests that the Kentish psalmist, like Alfred and the *Paris Psalter* translator, either knew the verse and its rendition very well or had recourse to one or more glossed psalters to help with the translation. The former seems slightly more likely since all the translators simply render the original word for word.

For verse 3, the *Kentish Psalm* has:

Amplius laua me ab iniustitia mea et a delicta mea munda mæ.
Aðweah me of sennum,   saule fram wammum,
gasta sceppend,   geltas geclansa,
þa ðe ic on aldre   æfre gefremede
ðurh lichaman   leðre geðohtas.

[*Wash me yet more from my iniquity, and cleanse me from my sin.*
Creator of spirits, wash me of my sins, my soul from stains; cleanse (me) of the offences which I constantly perpetrated in life by way of the wicked thoughts of the body.]

Alfred's prose psalter has:

And aðweah me clænran from minum unrihtwisnessum þonne ic ær ðysse scylde wæs, and of þysse scamleasan scylde geclænsa me,

[And wash me cleaner from my iniquities than I was before this crime, and cleanse me of this shameless crime]

The psalm poet again uses the epithet *gasta sceppend*, and both transla-tors use *aðweah* to render **laua**. However, here the *Kentish Psalm* prefers *saule from wammum* rather than *clæne* (although the term appears in *geclansa* as part of the variation in the next line). This departs also from the psalter glosses. More intriguingly, from both a poetic and a theo-logical point of view, the poet makes specific references to the soul (*gasta sceppend*) or shaper of spirits (souls), and to the performance that the sinner had previously made of wicked thoughts (*leðre geðohtas*) through-out the *lichama* (the home of the flesh, the body). The sins of the flesh, the body, require cleansing; the soul needs to be washed clean from the *wammum* (the wrongs) that were committed. The faint hint of the trope of the soul and body here recalls *Soul and Body*, I and II, and various homiletic references. For our purposes here, then, the translation demonstrates knowledge of a primary system in Old English (poetry) and a secondary system (homiletics and penitential texts).

The last verse that overlaps with Alfred's prose psalter (verse 10 in the Vulgate) is particularly intriguing since, unexpectedly for this verse, both Alfred and the *Kentish Psalm* poet range far from the source text, producing generalized meditations on its meaning.

> *Auditui meo dabis gaudium.*
> Ontyn nu, elmehtig,   earna hleoðor,
> þæt min gehernes   hehtful weorðe
> on gefean bliðse   forðweard to ðe;
> ðanne bioð on wenne,   waldend, simle
> þa gebrocenan ban,   bilwit dominus,
> ða þe on hænðum ær   hwile wæron.

> [*To my hearing thou shalt give joy and gladness.*
> Almighty, now open up song for my ears, so that my hearing will become joyful, in happiness of joy towards you; Ruler, gracious Lord, the broken bones will always be in a state of delight, those which earlier for a time were in a state of humiliation.]

> Syle minre gehyrnesse gefean and blisse, þæt ic gehyre þæt ic wylle, and eac oðre gehyron be me þæt þæt ic wilnige, swa swa hy ær gehyrdon þæt þæt ic nolde, þæt þonne mæge unrote mod blissian.[22]

> [Give to my hearing joy and bliss, so that I hear that which I desire, and also let the others hear about me that which I wish, just as they earlier heard that which I did not wish, so that the unhappy mind might be made happy.]

Alfred waxes philosophical and perhaps somewhat personal. The forlorn hope of kings that others should hear of them only what they choose

---

22 O'Neill in his annotation indicates that 'none of the commentaries have this lengthy and convoluted addition. What David desires to hear is news of God's willingness to forgive him; what he formerly did not want to hear was God's condemnation (through Nathan) of his sin' (*King Alfred's Old English Prose Translation*, 271). O'Neill then cites a parallel from the *Cura pastoralis*, though it parallels the thought of the verse rather than its vocabulary and expression.

to release seems to shine through in Alfred's rather anxious hope that this would make the sorrowful to rejoice. The psalm poet, however, waxes somewhat repetitive and poetic, repetition well beyond that provided for in the source text with *gefean, bliðse, wenne* (*wynn*), and the adjective *hehtful*. This verse also provides one of four occurrences of *dominus* as a loanword in the vernacular as part of an epithet. The *Kentish Psalm* appears to be alone in this usage, with *weoroda dominus* (in the introduction, line 16), *bilwit dominus* and *bilewit dominus* (lines 77 and 99), and *mæhtig dominus* (line 139). The usual translation for *dominus* in the psalter glosses is *drihten*; the poet freely uses *drihten* throughout the text, so the only possible conclusion is that for the psalm poet *dominus* was so familiar a word that it could be taken as part of the vernacular – although only as part of an epithet. From the point of view of polysystem theory, the psalm poet here occludes the lines between source and target text, even more strongly indicating that this text is part of the primary polysystem. Metrically speaking, these are perfectly acceptable Old English verses, with five out of six of the *b* verses being type A, and the sixth, *forðweard to ðe,* type E. The *a* verses have three light verses, but the fourth and fifth lines are type B, and the third line, with its emphasis on happiness, a type C: *on gefean bliðse.* The poet, then, could produce quite reasonable verse; unusually, in this verse the additions run throughout, and the translation of the source text is interspersed right to the last line.

The *Kentish Psalm* can also be compared to the only other poetic vernacular version of the psalms – the *Paris Psalter* – for a handful of verses that survive in the fragmentary psalms used in *The Benedictine Office.* Thus, verse 50.10 reads, first in the *Kentish Psalm* and second in the metrical psalter:

> *Auerte faciem tuam a peccatis meis et omnes.*
> Ahwerf nu fram synnum,   saula neriend,
> and fram misdedum   minra gylta
> þine ansione,   ælmeahtig god,
> and ðurh miltsunga   meahta þinra
> ðu unriht min   eall adilga.

> [*Turn away thy face from my sins: and ...*
> Saviour of souls, almighty God, turn away now your face from sins, and from misdeeds, from my crimes; and through the powers of your mercy wholly blot out my wickedness.]

Auerte faciem tuam a peccatis meis; et omnes iniquitates meas dele.
Awend þine ansyne   a fram minum
frǣcnum fyrenum;   and nu forð heonon
eall min unriht adwæsc   æghwær symle.

[*Turn away thy face from my sins; and blot out all my iniquities.* Turn your face always away from my terrible crimes; and now henceforth wholly quench my wickedness always everywhere.]

The similarities between the two texts are quite striking; both use the conventional language of Old English biblical vocabulary (as also exemplified in the psalter glosses) to render the Latin original; both also depart as they choose, so that the *Paris Psalter* poet has *awend* where the *Kentish Psalm* poet has *ahwerf*; they differ also with *fyrenum/misdedum* and with *adwæsc/adilga*. For the latter, the use of *adilga*, the *Kentish Psalm* agrees with Alfred's common usage. Otherwise, interestingly, given the frequency with which the *Paris Psalter* is decried as repetitive and long-winded, it is the *Kentish Psalm* that adds the epithets *saula neriend* and *ælmeahtig god* and expands elsewhere. The *Kentish Psalm* also avoids the awkward metre of *eall min unriht adwæsc*, which is probably an extended type B with the stress either on *un-* or on *riht*. While throughout the metrical psalter the stress can fall on either syllable of this most common word for alliterative purposes, usually the context makes clear the right metrical interpretation. Here the *Kentish Psalm*'s much simpler *ðu unriht min* is preferable, with the emphasis having to be on the first syllable of *unriht* for the vowel alliteration of the line.

The next verse, 50.11, demonstrates the same repetition on the part of the *Kentish Psalm* poet, an effort to rework and restate nearly every membrum of the verse:

Cor mundum crea in me deus et spiritum rectum.
Æc ðu, dryhten Crist,   clene hiortan
in me, mehtig god,   modswiðne geðanc
to ðolienne   ðinne willan
and to healdenne   halige domas,
and ðu rihtne gast,   rodera waldend,
in ferðe minum   feste geniowa.

[*Create a clean heart in me, O God; and renew a right spirit within my bowels.* But you, Lord Christ, mighty God, (make) in me a pure heart, a resolute will to endure your will and to maintain the holy judgments; and you, Lord of the heavens, firmly renew a correct spirit in my soul.]

Cor mundum crea in me, deus; et spiritum rectum innoua in uisceribus meis.
Syle me halig god   heortan clæne;
and rihtne gast,   god, geniwa
on minre gehigde   huru min drihten.

Create a clean heart in me, O God; and renew a right spirit within my bowels.
Holy God, give me a pure heart and a correct soul; God, my Lord, truly renew (me) in my mind.]

Interestingly, where even the fragments of psalms in the *Paris Psalter* text retain the entire Latin verse (and in the *Paris Psalter* manuscript the Latin faces the vernacular in a double psalter column format), the *Kentish Psalm* abbreviates the source text steadily more and more, focusing ever more intently on the new version in the vernacular. Also, unlike the *Paris Psalter*, this translator throughout makes the direct and clear linkage with Christ (here with the epithet *dryhten Crist*), demonstrating (perhaps following Augustine, though the translation does not demonstrate any direct parallels to the *Enarrationes*) that David prefigures Christ and that the misery of the narrative 'I' leads to forgiveness and to happiness forever. In this verse the poet even achieves linking alliteration between the second and third lines, carrying the ð of *geðanc* forward to *to ðolienne ðinne willan*, and then producing syntactic rhyme of the *a* verse with the next *a* verse, *and to healdenne*. Also, the *Kentish Psalm* produces another series of epithets: *dryhten Crist, mehtig god, rihtne gast,* and *rodera waldend*. The *Paris Psalter* text provides only *halig god* and *rihtne gast* – the latter an exact translation of the Latin epithet in the source – and, perhaps, if the definition of epithet is very loose indeed, *min drihten*.

Finally, the *Kentish Psalm* has been extensively compared to the glossed psalter tradition by Sarah Larratt Keefer, who elucidates the many similarities between the two kinds of texts. One example may, however, usefully point out how far the Canterbury translation deviates from the glossed psalter texts as represented by the three most prominent psalter glosses:

Vespasian Psalter 50.15:

Ic leru ða urehtwisan wegas ðine & ða arleasan to ðe bioð gecerde. *Doceam iniquos uias tuas, et impii ad te conuertentur.*

[I will teach the unjust thy ways: and the wicked shall be converted to thee. *I will teach your ways to the unjust and the impious will be converted to you.*]

Regius Psalter 50.15:

Ic lære unryhtwise wegas þine arlease to ðe beoð gecyrred. *Docebo iniquos uias tuas et impii ad te conuertentur.*

[I will teach the unjust thy ways: and the wicked shall be converted to thee. *I will teach your ways to the unjust; the impious will be converted to you.*]

Lambeth Psalter 50.15:

Ic lære þa unrihtwisan wegas ðine & arlease to þe sien gecyrrede. *Docebo iniquos uias tuas et impii ad te conuertentur.*[23]

[I will teach the unjust thy ways: and the wicked shall be converted to thee. *I will teach your ways to the unjust; and the impious will be converted to you.*]

Kentish Psalm:

Doceam iniquos uias tuas et impii ad te
Simle ic ðine weogas   wanhogan lærde
ðæt hio arlease   eft gecerdan
to hiora selfra   saula hiorde,
god selfa, to ðe   gastes mundberd
ðurh sibbe lufan   seocan scoldan.

[*I will teach the unjust thy ways and the impious to you.* Always I taught your ways to the ones weak in mind so that they, the impious ones, again would turn to the Guardian of their own souls, God himself; from you, they had to seek the protection of the spirit through the happiness of love.]

---

23 Kuhn, ed. *The Vespasian Psalter*, 48; Fritz Roeder, ed. *Altenglische Regius Psalter*, 94; U. Lindelöf, ed. *Text und Glossar.* A complete edition of the glossed psalters is also becoming available: see Philip Pulsiano, ed. *Old English Glossed Psalters: Psalms 1–50*, 723–39.

The first three lines of the psalm poem correspond very closely with the psalter gloss tradition, with all the texts rendering *doceam* with a form of *læran*; *uias tuas* with *wegas ðine*; *impii* with *arlease*; *ad te* with *to ðe*; and *conuertentur* with a form of *gecyrran*, although for the latter the *Kentish Psalm* stands alone in choosing to alter it to the active voice in the past tense rather than use the present passive of the source. However, where all the glosses agree on some form of *unrihtwis(an/e)* for *iniquos*, the poem chooses *wanhoganr* 'the ones weak in mind, the foolish ones,' which seems a greatly watered-down rendition of 'the evil ones.' More interestingly, once the translation is complete, the psalm poem adds fully three lines emphasizing the role of God himself and the soul, even using the epithet *gastes mundberd*. The *Kentish Psalm* poet is rather like the producer of the metrical psalter (though with more fidelity to the original) in clearly feeling perfectly free to elaborate and expand the text. Here, though, the added three lines also riff on the letter *s*, with linked alliteration playing through the lines, and real emphasis on the half-line *god selfa to ðe* – a type E verse that is particularly noteworthy since the rest of the psalm verse has light verses in the first half-lines, and type A verses in the second half-lines. The emphasis of the focus on God himself and the search for his love and mercy is clear.

Here, then, is a translation that is sure and clear and in acceptable Old English metre; it is neither inspired nor elegant, but the long history of psalm translation has many examples of similar levels of accomplishment. It uses many epithets, especially for God but also for other terms in the source, and freely elaborates. In the last line of the translation itself, unusually, David speaks of himself as someone who *glidan mote* (will be able to glide or will be able to slip) into forgiveness. The psalm poet had an unusual turn of vocabulary. Perhaps the poet lacks the elegance and metrical versatility of the Countess of Pembroke, but the poem forms part of the same extended polysystem.

Also unusually, the *Kentish Psalm* provides a paratext, a text introductory to and perhaps explanatory of the translation. Translation studies as a field tends to focus on paratexts because they provide some way into thinking about the purpose and approach of the translator. Old English texts are sadly lacking in paratexts. Here, however, the Kentish psalmist has thirty lines of introduction of the subject; following are the first eight:

Dauid wæs haten   diormod hæleð
Israela brega   æðelæ and rice
cyninga cynost   Criste liofost.
Wæs he under hiofenum   hearpera mærost

ðara we an folcum   gefrigen hæbben.
Sangere he wæs soðfæstest,   swiðe geðancol
to ðingienne   þiodum sinum
wið þane mildostan   manna sceppend.

[He was called David, a warrior bold in spirit, chief of the Israelites, noble
and powerful, most intelligent of kings, most beloved to Christ. He was the
most famous of harpers under the heavens, of those we have heard of in the
nations. He was the most righteous singer, very mindful in interceding for his
people with the most merciful creator of men.]

Nothing in the content of these lines provides information that is not
available in the Bible or more specifically in the psalms themselves. David
is introduced with a series of epithets, themselves a feature of Old English
verse that chimes well with biblical epithets. The sequence is perhaps less
illuminating than such sequences can be; the progression appears to move
from warrior qualities to kingly abilities to singing, which might perhaps
imply that singing God's praises is the highest of these callings. The metrical structure is perhaps most revealing: the eight *a* verses here include
four type A verses and four light verses, and every single *b* verse is type A.
Only two lines have double alliteration, and perhaps only one line, *cyninga cynost Criste liofost*, could be described as having some complexity,
with its internal rhyme of superlative endings and its link between David
as the most keen of kings and David as the most beloved of Christ in consequence. This is singularly uninteresting metre – in fact, less interesting
than the metre in some of the verses that are more complex because they
have to render a source text. In general, however, the poet in the paratext,
although not constrained by issues of translation and fidelity, produces
singularly uncreative verse. Further evidence for this is that only seven of
the thirty lines of this introductory section have double alliteration; fully
twenty-three lines have single alliteration. We have here a clear and un-
complicated, perhaps somewhat florid, opening enumeration of David's
good qualities. The coda or concluding text is similarly florid, as if re-
instating David in the reader's or listener's mind. Of course, the translation
proper, or metaphrase, which is the central section of the *Kentish Psalm*,
does its best to minimize the iniquities and maximize the joys and abilities
of David in his praise of God.

The rest of the introductory paratext describes David in extremely laud-
atory terms, working through his accomplishments in uniting the land and
leading it against its enemies, and then admitting sorrowfully that this
paragon also made errors. The prophet Nathan, who appears in nearly all

the surviving rubrics of this psalm, is not mentioned in the introductory verse paragraph; only David is. Nathan's role in bringing David to task is thus effaced. The focus is entirely on praising David's accomplishments, evaluating his estimable character, admitting his terrible error in having Uriah killed in battle so that he could take the widow, Bathsheba, as his wife, and turning very directly to introducing the psalm as the words David used to speak to God about his transgressions. At the end of the psalm, similarly, the twelve-line coda – the second piece of the paratext of this translation – describes David as having *þingode* (pled his case). The term almost has legal ramifications and nearly suggests that David has bargained with his God. Very briefly the coda refers to a Christological reading of the psalm (which as we have already noted is difficult) and turns to the moral lesson that the audience should draw from this penitential psalm. Elsewhere, epithets make the link to Christ but in a way that suggests only a general understanding of the typological linkage between the psalmist David and Christ. The florid enumeration of David's good qualities, even the adulation of his *georne* (eager) penance and recitation of crimes, keeps the focus on David, not on penance or on the lamentation of the evils that he did.

What, then, does the *Kentish Psalm* tell us about attitudes towards translation, and especially biblical translation, in late Anglo-Saxon England? Polysystems theory and its approach to translation may provide some answers. Polysystems theory is the brainchild of Itamar Even-Zohar, who considers first the content and approach of the primary system in a given nation or literature, describes its role and function, and then addresses the secondary or subsystems in that literature. A primary system is the most prevalent and widely operating system, while secondary systems provide different intersecting relationships with each other and with the primary system (graphically, this analysis would produce one large circle in a Venn diagram with overlapping smaller circles, some of which also intersect with each other). With respect to translated texts, Even-Zohar proposes first that translation maintains a primary position in a culture in three social circumstances: (1) the literature is 'young' or is in the process of being established, (2) the literature is 'peripheral' or 'weak,' or both, and (3) the literature is experiencing a crisis or turning point. Since the manuscript in which the psalm appears dates from the third quarter of the tenth century, and the poem does not seem greatly to predate the manuscript, this is clearly not a period of crisis. Nor does it seem appropriate to describe the vernacular literature of Anglo-Saxon England as either 'peripheral'or 'weak.' With regard to the specific subsystem of psalters, glossed versions of the Latin text had been circulating, apparently quite broadly, for the better part of two centuries. In the closing decades of the ninth century, King Alfred had signalled his approval first of a generalized translation program (thereby making translation a *primary* activity of the poly-system) and second – more specifically – of psalter translation as a sub-system (when he worked on his own translation). The third conclusion seems likely, that Anglo-Saxon literature qualified as 'young' or still in the process of being established. As a result, translations were probably not, to use Even-Zohar's terminology, secondary texts; translations were primary documents, more likely to be at the centre of literary – and in this case religious – concern than at the periphery.

Polysystems theory itself derives from Russian formalism as a way to ad-dress not just texts but whole literatures in interaction with other litera-tures. It brings a sociological element to the study of literature since it allows for canonized and non-canonized systems to be part of the same polysystem, the former as a primary system and the latter as secondary sys-tems. A defective polysystem lacks the secondary system; Even-Zohar cites Hebrew literature as only including canonized works, highly learned and elitist texts. Translated literature holds a shifting place in the polysystem: a large nation that is also old would have it in a secondary position, but a small nation, old or young, would have it as primary. The issue is the role that the system or genre plays within the literary polysystem. Primary ac-tivity involves innovation; secondary activity maintains the established code. Although his first priority is elucidating the role of Hebrew literature, especially with respect to Russia, Even-Zohar strangely does not directly address the ways in which religious choice affects polysystems. He notes that the normal position of translated literature is a secondary one in a polysystem and that the conditions referred to above are usually transitory. However, a system is never wholly homogeneous, and entropy is always at work in an existing system. In addition, polysystems theory cannot permit a rigid nomenclature, because the same arguments hold. Thus, although re-ligion is a system that is universal in the polysystems of Anglo-Saxon England, polysystems theory argues that human activity is always cultural first, no matter what the individual points of departure might be. Moreover, Even-Zohar argues that 'all literary systems strive to become polysystemic.' Individual Anglo-Saxon texts should be studied initially for how they fit into the polysystem and what they accomplish in their subsystems.

At a precise level, Even-Zohar distinguishes two kinds of literary con-tacts: those between systems that are relatively established and therefore relatively independent, and those between non-established or fluid sys-tems that are partly or wholly dependent on other systems. The system of vernacular texts in Anglo-Saxon England is both non-established with respect to the Latin Christian system and fluid with respect to the Germanic traditional narrative system. In this situation, Even-Zohar notes that a source language text can function for a target language text almost as though it were part of it. Thus, it may well be that the Latin text of *Kentish Psalm* was in the system of Anglo-Saxon thinking an Anglo-Saxon text, available to be treated as if it were part of the local system. Even-Zohar sees this as a kind of symbiosis used by a weak or defective polysystem as it moves towards filling in the gaps in its systems, and always as a result of sociocultural conditions. The Latin text functions here as a kind of superstratum, a source on which to model the target language text. However, although Even-Zohar does not consider it except by implication, it is clear that, in Anglo-Saxon England, texts such as the Latin psalms had this role as a superstratum, but so also did the system that involved Old English poetry.

Kentish Psalm therefore reflects at least two sets of systems, one of them admittedly a superstratum with all the prestige of that system, but the other equally powerful, if less fully articulated. Thus, where Even-Zohar points out that normally the target language text will simplify, regularize, or schematize a source language text, the existence of a separate system for Old English poetry means that *Kentish Psalm* may have elements of simplification of the source text, but it also has elements that make interpretation of the text much more complex and uncertain. While the text looks like what Even-Zohar would call the result of a bilingual polysystem – an attempt to fill an empty space in the system by using a text from another system in a symbiotic relationship – (each verse of the Latin Psalter appears before its translation), it moves beyond that simple kind of contact relationship by way of its use of other systems (for example, the translation is spaced out in the manuscript to indicate that it has priority, that it is the prestige text even though it might appear to be the dependent or secondary text). Even-Zohar argues that a symbiotic state can be replaced with a non-symbiotic dependent state, but here we have a dependent text that rejects its dependency by linking with another system, by appropriating the source text into its own pre-existing system, its own tradition.

One of the great benefits of polysystem theory is that it puts the focus squarely on the target text, concluding that infidelity is inescapable, presumed by the process itself. Thus, Edwin Gentzler, in his cogent analysis of the theory, notes the obvious:

> [T]ranslators do not work in ideal and abstract systems nor desire to be innocent, but have vested literary and cultural interests of their own, and *want* their

work to be accepted within another culture. Thus they manipulate the source text to inform as well as conform with the existing cultural constraints.[24]

Polysystems theory concludes that translators will indeed have an agenda, though its parameters may not wholly be available, and rather than investigate what is in the mind of the translator, polysystems analysis focuses on the sociological context, the text, and the role played in the literary system and polysystem. Polysystems theory is therefore fundamentally descriptive rather than prescriptive.

A detailed polysystemic analysis of the *Kentish Psalm*, using this descriptive approach rather than addressing what the translation should do or whether the translation should have been made, starts with two sets of diachronic features: the historiography of study of the text (which would not take long) and a consideration of the original context of the material in a very small high-status manuscript of learned Latin texts, and two short vernacular poems. Then, polysystems theory engages in a synchronic study of what the text actually includes and how it works. This text unusually has both an introduction and a conclusion, as well as a translation that extends into a meditation; these features separate it from the rest of the subsystem of psalter translation. However, uniting it to that subsystem in Anglo-Saxon England are very many features: the use of the Roman Psalter as the source text; the appearance of both the Latin and the vernacular texts in the manuscript, with the vernacular prioritized; the use of the common vocabulary of psalter glossing and psalter study in Old English; and the use, however unsophisticated, of Old English verse. The focus of polysystems theory on the target texts, on what the translators produced, and on what they did accomplish and in the context of which systems, allows us to point towards a clearer articulation of translated texts in the vernacular – and particularly the *Kentish Psalm*.

Polysystems theory is one approach, and by no means the best-known, in the burgeoning field of translation studies. Although Anglo-Saxonists, as well as scholars of the Renaissance, have certainly studied translations, there has been little interest in studying the ways in which the discipline of translation studies might provide useful paradigms. Specific analyses of individuals and of texts from Anglo-Saxon England have certainly been accomplished, including Ray St-Jacques on the Old English translation of Bede's *Ecclesiastical History*,[25] Jane Roberts on the prose vernacular

24 Edwin Gentzler, *Contemporary Translation Theories*, 134.
25 '*Hwilum word be worde, hwilum andgit of andgiete*,' 85–104.

version of Felix's *Vita sancti Guthlaci*,[26] Andy Orchard on *Cædmon's Hymn*,[27] Nicole Guenther Discenza on the *Metres of Boethius*,[28] and, especially, Richard Marsden's magisterial consideration of Ælfric and the book of Genesis.[29] The psalter glosses have been the focus of much comparative analysis, the best of it in recent years by Evert Wiesenekker and Mechthild Gretsch.[30] However, there has been little attempt to think about how translation functioned in the system of texts in Anglo-Saxon England. Rather, the focus has remained very tightly on what an individual writer intended by specific choices and approaches, all intended to suggest that a given Old English writer had changed the source for a good reason, misread the source, or simply could not be bothered with giving a good rendition of the source. The focus for translation analysis remains the source and fidelity to it. Constructing translation in this way, however, renders it a kind of reflection of language training that will, like training wheels on a bicycle, be left behind and disappear wholly once the individual has assimilated and engaged fully with the new language – in this case, the sacred language of the Anglo-Saxon Bible (something that to the modern eye and perhaps figures such as Jerome and Cassiodorus holds divine power in and of itself). The problem with this approach is that it fails fully to account for the actual practice as it survives in the manuscripts. It requires a kind of sotto voce commentary as to what the Anglo-Saxons really intended by their failure to provide us with more information about their approach to translation – especially biblical translation – and also a generalization about translation and interpretation in the whole time and space of Anglo-Saxon England.

---

26 'The Old English Prose Translation of Felix's *Vita sancti Guthlaci*,' 363–79.
27 Andy Orchard, 'Poetic Inspiration and Prosaic Translation,' 402–22.
28 Nicole Guenther Discenza, *The King's English*.
29 Richard Marsden, 'Ælfric as Translator,' 319–58. For an approach to the same writer but focusing on a different text, see also Jonathan Wilcox, 'A Reluctant Translator in Late Anglo-Saxon England,' 1–18. Wilcox also discusses translation and even hints at the existence of the field of translation studies in his edition *Ælfric's Prefaces*. More general studies do exist, but they tend to focus on the pragmatic issue of what an Anglo-Saxon translator was actually doing with the source text; hence Janet M. Bately's magisterial 'The Literary Prose of Alfred's Reign: Translation or Transformation?' Also, there are many translations from Old English as well as assessments of those translations. See, for example, Eric Stanley, 'Translation from Old English: "The Garbaging War-Hawk"'; and, more recently, for an analysis which does discuss some translation theory, Roy M. Liuzza, 'Lost in Translation,' 281–95.
30 Mechthild Gretsch, *The Intellectual Foundations of the English Benedictine Reform*, and Evert Wiesenekker, *Word be Worde, Andgit of Andgite*.

More than a whiff of prescriptivism, then, surrounds this approach to Anglo-Saxon translation. More than a hint of opprobrium attaches itself to a translator who does provide a paratext, indicating anxiety about the translation, yet proceeds to engage in the task anyway. Moreover, those who fail to express their anxiety and move forward with a translation are questioned or second-guessed: did they realize how badly they were behaving according to the very unclear directives of the church? Did they think about the complex reception issues? Did they really imagine themselves as having the authority to recreate the Word of God? These questions and others of their ilk tend to lie behind (sometimes quite explicitly, but generally not) all modern assessment of Old English translation texts. The tracks of the argument run deep and long. Polysystems theory, or its later development 'Descriptive Translation Studies' (as labelled by Gideon Toury), provides a way out of this prescriptivist approach, preferring to examine the texts and their context without venturing upon the uncertain ground of divination as to intent and audience.[31] Nor would such a shift be a return to uncritical description. Rather, in the way that prescriptive grammars and dictionaries in the eighteenth and early nineteenth centuries gave way to descriptive approaches of current usage and elucidation of what had and was then happening to a given word, the prescriptivism inherent in the paucity of attention that psalms and psalm translation from Anglo-Saxon England receives might give way to a descriptive analysis of how widespread and obviously significant this activity was for the individual Christian, and particularly for the individual monastic.[32]

---

31 See Gideon Toury, *Descriptive Translation Studies and Beyond*. Translation studies is a field in constant flux; a good introduction to it is Lawrence Venuti, *The Translator's Invisibility*; the central arguments are almost all found in *The Translation Studies Reader*, ed. Lawrence Venuti. Useful on the basics is *The Routledge Encyclopedia of Translation Studies*, ed. Mona Baker. Biblical translation and poetic translation are well discussed in Willis Barnstone, *The Poetics of Translation*.

32 Other theories of translation studies could potentially also be useful. For example (*pace* Stanton), in *Translation & Taboo*, Douglas Robinson proposes that translation studies must move away from the binary oppositions of describing a given text as source- or target-oriented, as literary or non-literary, as sacred or profane, and towards a descriptive approach that nonetheless acknowledges that translation is all about power. Stanton describes Robinson solely as considering biblical translation to be a taboo of the most awesome kind, something contested in every Christian age. However, Robinson makes a wider-ranging argument and essentially proposes that refiguring translation studies to a descriptive rather than prescriptive approach – something that linguistics accomplished some time ago as a general process – is the most appropriate way forward. In this respect he agrees with the basic premise of polysystem theory.

The last word should perhaps belong to an early reviewer of the Sidney psalms, who commented:

> They shew us Ilanders our joy, our King,
> They tell us *why*, and teach us *how* to sing;
> ... The songs are these, which heavens high holy Muse
> Whisper'd to *David*, *David* to the Jewes:
> And *Davids* Successors, in holy zeale,
> In formes of joy and art doe re-reveale
> To us so sweetly and sincerely too.[33]

John Donne had no qualms about psalter translation; rather, he saw its deeper pedagogical purpose both in connecting with a long tradition of praise of God and King that originated with David and in explaining why these 'formes of Joy' need constant repetition in order to reveal the psalms and permit meditation and contemplation of God through engagement with these songs. The *Kentish Psalm* forms an integral part of that tradition.

---

33 John Donne, 'Upon the Translation of the Psalmes by Sir Philip Sydney,' 33–5, lines 21–2, 31–5 (italics original).

Bibliography

Abrams, Lesley. 'The Anglo-Saxons and the Christianization of Scandinavia.'
Anglo-Saxon England 24 (1995): 213–50.

Adriaen, Marcus, ed. *Magni Aurelii Cassiodori exposition Psalmorum*. CCSL
97–98. Turnhout: Brepols, 1958.

Agaësse, Paul, and Aimé Solignac, eds. *La Genèse au sens littéral en douze livres*.
Bibliothèque Augustinienne 48–9. Paris: Institut d'études augustiniennes,
2000–1.

Alexander, Gavin. *Writing After Sidney: The Literary Response to Sir Philip
Sidney, 1586–1640*. Oxford: Oxford University Press, 2006.

Allen, Michael I., ed. *Frechulfi Lexoviensis episcopi opera omnia*. CCSL 169–
169A. 2 vols. Turnhout, Belgium: Brepols, 2002.

– 'Universal History, 300–1000: Origins and Western Developments.' In
Historiography in the Middle Ages, edited by Deborah M. Deliyannis. Leiden,
Netherlands: Brill, 2003.

Allen, Michael J.B., and Daniel G. Calder, trans. *Sources and Analogues of Old
English Poetry: The Major Latin Texts in Translation*. Cambridge: D.S. Brewer,
1976.

Ames, Ruth M., 'The Old Testament Christ and the Old English *Exodus*.' *Studies
in Medieval Culture* 10 (1977): 33–50.

Anderson, Earl. 'Style and Theme in the Old English *Daniel*.' *English Studies* 68
(1987): 1–23.

Andersson, Theodore M. 'Sources and Analogues.' In *A Beowulf Handbook*,
edited by Robert E. Bjork and John D. Niles, 125–48. Lincoln: University of
Nebraska Press, 1997.

– 'The Viking Policy of Ethelred the Unready.' *Scandinavian Studies* 59.3 (1987):
284–95, reprinted in *Anglo-Scandinavian England: Norse-English Relations in
the Period before the Conquest*, Old English Colloquium Series 4, edited by

John D. Niles and Mark Amodio, 1–11. Lanham, MD: University Press of America, 1989.

Anlezark, Daniel. 'Connecting the Patriarchs: Noah and Abraham in the Old English *Exodus*.' *JEGP* 104 (2005): 171–88.

Assmann, Bruno. 'Abt Ælfric's angelsächsische Homilie über das Buch Judith.' *Anglia* 10 (1888): 76–104.

– ed. *Angelsächsische Homilien und Heiligenleben, Bibliothek der angelsächsischen Prosa*. Kassel, Germany: Wigand, 1889; reprinted, with a supplementary introduction by Peter Clemoes, Darmstadt, Germany: Wissenschaftliche Buchgesellschaft, 1964.

Astell, Ann W. 'Holofernes' Head: *Tacen* and Teaching in the Old English *Judith*.' *ASE* 18 (1989): 117–33.

Aðalbjarnarson, Bjarni, ed. *Heimskringla*, Íslenzk fornrit v. 52. Reykjavik: Hið íslenzka fornritafélag, 1941–51.

Auerbach, Erich. 'Figura.' In *Scenes from the Drama of European Literature: Six Essays*, translated by Ralph Mannheim. 1959. Reprint, Minneapolis: University of Minnesota Press, 1984.

– *Mimesis: The Representation of Reality in Western Literature*. Translated by Willard R. Trask. Princeton: Princeton University Press, 1968.

Baker, Mona, ed. *Routledge Encyclopedia of Translation Studies*. With the assistance of Kirsten Malmkjær. London: Routledge, 1998.

Baker, Peter S. *Introduction to Old English*. 2nd ed. Oxford and Malden: Blackwell Publishing, 2007.

Bammesberger, Alfred. 'Die syntaktische Analyse von *Exodus* 1–7a.' In *Festgabe für Hans Pinsker zum 70: Geburtstag*, edited by R. Acobian, 6–15. Vienna: VWGÖ, 1979.

– 'Hidden Glosses in Manuscripts of Old English Poetry.' *ASE* 13 (1984): 43–9.

Banting, H.M.J., ed. *Two Anglo-Saxon Pontificals*. Henry Bradshaw Society 104. London: Boydell Press, 1989.

Barclay, John M.G. 'Paul and Philo on Circumcision: Romans 2.25–9 in Social and Cultural Context.' *New Testament Studies* 44.4 (1998): 536–56.

Barlow, Claude W., ed. *Martini Episcopi Bracarensis Opera Omnia*. New Haven, CT: Yale University Press, 1950.

Barnhouse, Rebecca. 'Shaping the Hexateuch Text for an Anglo-Saxon Audience.' In *The Old English Hexateuch: Aspects and Approaches*, edited by Rebecca Barnhouse and Benjamin C. Withers, 91–108. Kalamazoo, MI: Medieval Institute Publications, 2000.

Barnstone, Willis. *The Poetics of Translation: History, Theory, Practice*. New Haven, CT: Yale University Press, 1993.

Bately, Janet. 'Lexical Evidence for the Authorship of the Prose Psalms in the Paris Psalter.' *ASE* 10 (1982): 69–95.

– *The Literary Prose of Alfred's Reign: Translation or Transformation?* London: University of London King's College, 1980.

– 'World History in the *ASE*: Its Sources and Its Separateness from the Old English Orosius.' *ASE* 8 (1979): 177–94.

Battles, Paul. '*Genesis A* and the Anglo-Saxon "Migration Myth."' *ASE* 29 (2000): 43–66.

Bauer, J., ed. *Sancti Aurelii Augustini de catechizandis rudibus.* CCSL 46, 121–78. Turnhout, Belgium: Brepols, 1969.

Bayless, Martha, and Michael Lapidge, ed. and trans. *Collectanea Pseudo-Bedae.* Scriptores Latini Hiberniae 14. Dublin: Dublin Institute for Advanced Studies, 1998.

Bede. *De schematibus et tropis.* Ed. C.B. Kendall. CCSL 123A. Turnhout, Belgium: Brepols, 1975.

Bedingfield, M. Bradford. 'Reinventing the Gospel: Ælfric and the Liturgy.' *Medium Ævum* 68 (1999): 13–31.

Belanoff, Patricia A. '*Judith*: Sacred and Secular Heroine.' In *Heroic Poetry in the Anglo-Saxon Period: Studies in Honor of Jess B. Bessinger, Jr.*, edited by Helen Damico and John Leyerle, 247–64. Kalamazoo, MI: Medieval Institute Publications, 1993.

Berger, Samuel. *Histoire de la Vulgate.* New York: Burt Franklin, 1893.

Bethel, Patricia. 'Regnal and Divine Epithets in the Metrical Psalms and *Metres of Boethius*.' *Parergon* 9 (1991): 1–41.

Bethurum, Dorothy, ed. *The Homilies of Wulfstan.* Oxford: Clarendon Press, 1957.

Biddick, Kathleen. *The Typological Imaginary: Circumcision, Technology, History.* Philadelphia: University of Pennsylvania Press, 2003.

Bieler, Ludwig, ed. *Anicii Manlii Severeni Boethii philosophiae consolatio.* CCSL 94. Turnhout, Belgium: Brepols 1957.

Biggs, Frederick M. '*Englum gelice*: *Elene* Line 1320 and *Genesis A* Line 185.' *NM* 85 (1985): 447–52.

– 'The Passion of Andreas: *Andreas* 1398–1491.' *SP* 85 (1988): 413–27.

– *Sources of Anglo-Saxon Literary Culture: The Apocrypha.* Instrumenta Anglistica Mediaevalia I. Kalamazoo, MI: Medieval Institute Publications, 2007.

Biggs, Frederick M., Thomas D. Hill, and Paul E. Szarmach, eds. *Sources of Anglo-Saxon Literary Culture: A Trial Version.* Binghamton, NY: Center for Medieval and Early Renaissance Studies, 1990.

Bischoff, Bernhard, and Michael Lapidge, eds. and trans. *Biblical Commentaries from the Canterbury School of Theodore and Hadrian*. CSASE 10. Cambridge: Cambridge University Press, 1994.

Bjork, Robert E. 'Oppressed Hebrews and the Song of Azarias in the Old English *Daniel.' SP* 77 (1980): 213–26.

– 'Speech as Gift in *Beowulf.' Speculum* 69 (1994): 993–1022.

Blackburn, Francis A., ed. *Exodus and Daniel; Two Old English Poems Preserved in MS Junius 11 in the Bodleian Library of the University of Oxford, England*. Boston: D.C. Heath, 1907. Reprint, New York: AMS, 1972.

Blaise, Albert. *Manuel du latin chrétien*. Strasbourg: Le Latin Chrétien, 1955.

Blatt, Franz, ed. *Die lateinischen Bearbeitungen der Acta Andreae et Matthiae apud anthropophagos*. Giessen, Germany: Töpelmann, 1930.

Bloch, R. Howard. *Etymologies and Genealogies: A Literary Anthropology of the French Middle Ages*. Chicago: University of Chicago Press, 1983.

Bolintineanu, Alexandra. 'The Land of Mermedonia in the Old English *Andreas.' Neophilologus* 93 (2009): 149–64.

Bolton, Whitney F. *Alcuin and* Beowulf: *An Eighth Century View*. New Brunswick, NJ: Rutgers University Press, 1978.

Borgehammar, Stephan. *How the Holy Cross Was Found: From Event to Medieval Legend*. Stockholm: Almqvist & Wiksell, 1991.

Bosworth, Joseph, and T. Northcote Toller. *An Anglo-Saxon Dictionary*. Oxford: Oxford University Press, 1898.

Bouterwek, Karl W., ed. *Screadunga: Anglosaxonica maximam partem inedita*. Elberfeld, Germany: Samuel Lucas, 1858.

Boyarin, Jonathan, and Daniel Boyarin, eds. *Jews and Other Differences: The New Jewish Cultural Studies*. Minneapolis: University of Minnesota Press, 1997.

Boyd, Nina. 'Doctrine and Criticism: A Reevaluation of *"Genesis A.'" NM* 83 (1982): 230–8.

Bradley, H. 'The "Cædmonian" Genesis.' *Essays and Studies by Members of the English Association* 6 (1920): 7–29.

Bradley, S.A.J., ed. and trans. *Anglo-Saxon Poetry*. London: Dent, 1982.

– trans. *Old English Poetry: An Anthology of Old English Poems in Prose Translation*. London: Everyman, 1982.

Brearley, Denis, ed. *Commentum Sedulii Scotti in maiorem Donatum grammaticum*. Toronto: Pontifical Institute of Mediaeval Studies, 1975.

Bredehoft, Thomas A. 'Ælfric and Late Old English Verse.' *Anglo-Saxon England* 33 (2004): 77–107.

– *Early English Metre*. Toronto: University of Toronto Press, 2005.

Breeze, Andrew. 'The Book of Habakkuk and the Old English Exodus.' *ES* 75 (1994): 210–13.

Brehe, Steven. 'Rhythmical Alliteration: Ælfric's Prose and the Origins of Layamon's Metre.' In *The Text and Tradition of Layamon's Brut*, edited by F. Le Saux, 65–87. Cambridge and Rochester, NY: D.S. Brewer, 1994.

Bright, J.W. 'On the Anglo-Saxon Poem *Exodus.*' *MLN* 27 (1912): 13–19.

– 'The Relation of the Cædmonian *Exodus* to the Liturgy.' *MLN* 27 (1912): 97–103.

Brockman, Bennett. '"Heroic" and "Christian" in *Genesis A*: The Evidence of the Cain and Abel Episode.' *Modern Language Quarterly* 35 (1974): 115–28.

Bromwich, J.I'a. 'Who Was the Translator of the Prose Portion of the *Paris Psalter*?' In *The Early Cultures of Northwest Europe: H.M. Chadwick Memorial Studies,* ed. Sir Cyril Fox and Bruce Dickins, 289–304. Cambridge: Cambridge University Press, 1950.

Brooks, Kenneth R. *Andreas and the Fates of the Apostles.* Oxford: Clarendon Press, 1961.

Brotanek, R., ed. *Texte und Untersuchungen zur altenglischen Literatur und Kirchengeschichte.* Halle, Germany: M. Niemeyer, 1913.

Brown, George H. 'The Psalms as the Foundation of Anglo-Saxon Learning.' In *The Place of the Psalms in the Intellectual Culture of the Middle Ages*, edited by Nancy van Dusen, 1–24. New York: State University of New York Press, 1999.

Browne, Gerald M., trans. *The Abbreviated Psalter of the Venerable Bede.* Grand Rapids, MI: W.B. Eerdmans, 2002.

– ed. *Collectio Psalterii Bedae uenerabili adscripta.* Munich: K.G. Saur, 2001.

Bryk, Felix. *Circumcision in Man and Woman.* New York: American Ethnological Press, 1934.

Bugge, John. 'Virginity and Prophecy in the Old English *Daniel.*' *ES* 87 (2006): 127–47.

Burleigh, John H.S., ed. *Augustine: Earlier Writings.* Philadelphia: Westminster, 1953.

Burlin, Robert B. *The Old English Advent.* New Haven, CT: Yale University Press, 1968.

Burrus, Virginia. *The Sex Lives of Saints: An Erotics of Ancient Hagiography.* Philadelphia: University of Pennsylvania Press, 2004.

Bussanich, John. 'Happiness, Eudaimonism.' In *Augustine through the Ages*, edited by Allan D. Fitzgerald, 413–14. Grand Rapids, MI: Eerdmans, 1999.

Busse, Wilhelm. *Altenglische Literatur und ihre Geschichte: Zur Kritik des gegenwärtigen Deutungssystems.* Düsseldorf: Droste Verlag, 1987.

Bynum, Caroline W. 'The Body of Christ in the Later Middle Ages: A Reply to Leo Steinberg.' In *Fragmentation and Redemption: Essays on Gender and the*

Human Body in Medieval Religion, edited by Caroline W. Bynum, 79–343. New York: Zone Books, 1991.

Cabaniss, Allen. '*Beowulf* and the Liturgy.' *JEGP* 54 (1955): 195–201. Reprinted in *An Anthology of Beowulf Criticism*, ed. Lewis E. Nicholson, 223–32. Notre Dame, IN: University of Notre Dame Press, 1963.

Cable, Thomas. *The English Alliterative Tradition*. Philadelphia: University of Pennsylvania Press, 1991.

Caie, Graham. 'The Old English *Daniel*: A Warning Against Pride.' *ES* 59 (1978): 1–9.

Calder, Daniel G. 'Figurative Language and Its Contexts in *Andreas*: A Study in Medieval Expressionism.' In *Modes of Interpretation in Old English Literature: Essays in Honour of Stanley B. Greenfield*, edited by Phyllis R. Brown, Georgia R. Crampton, and Fred C. Robinson, 115–36. Toronto: University of Toronto Press, 1986.

Calvin, John. *Commentaries on the Epistle of Paul the Apostle to the Hebrews*. Ed. and trans. Rev. John Owen. Edinburgh: Calvin Translation Society, 1853.

Cameron, Angus, Ashley C. Amos, and Antonette diP. Healey, eds. *Dictionary of Old English, A–F, on CD-ROM*. Toronto: Pontifical Institute of Mediaeval Studies, 2003.

Campbell, Alistair, ed. *Aedilvulfus: De abbatibus*. Oxford: Clarendon Press, 1967.
– ed. *Breuiloquium uitæ beati Wilfredi*. Zurich: Thesaurus mundi, 1950.
– ed. *Encomium Emmae reginae*. With an introduction by Simon Keynes. Cambridge: Cambridge University Press, 1998.
– ed. *Narratio metrica de sancto Swithuno*. Zurich: Thesaurus mundi, 1950.

Carey, John. *The Irish National-Origin Legend: Synthetic Pseudohistory*. Cambridge: Quiggin Pamphlets on the Sources of Mediaeval Gaelic History, 1994.

Carleton Paget, J.N.B. 'Barnabas 9:4: A Peculiar Verse on Circumcision.' *Vigiliae Christianae* 45 (1991): 242–54.

Cassidy, Brendan, and Rosemary M. Wright, eds. *Studies in the Illustration of the Psalter*. Stamford, CT: Shaun Tyas, 2001.

Chamberlain, David. '*Judith*: A Fragmentary and Political Poem.' In *Anglo-Saxon Poetry: Essays in Appreciation for John C. McGalliard*, edited by Lewis E. Nicholson and Dolores W. Frese, 135–59. Notre Dame, IN: University of Notre Dame Press, 1975.

Chambers, Raymond W. *Beowulf: An Introduction to the Study of the Poem*. 3rd ed., with supplement by C.L. Wrenn. Cambridge: Cambridge University Press, 1963.

Charles, Robert H. *The Apocrypha and Pseudepigrapha of the Old Testament in English*. 2 vols. Oxford: Clarendon Press, 1913.

Châtillon, Jean. 'La Bible dans les écoles du xiie siècle.' In *Le Moyen Âge et la Bible*, edited by Pierre Riché and Guy Lobrichon, 163–97. Paris: Beauchesne, 1984.

Clark, M.J. 'The Commentaries on Peter Comestor's *Historia scholastica* of Stephen Langton, Pseudo-Langton, and Hugh of St. Cher.' *Sacris Erudiri* 44 (2005): 301–446.

Clayton, Mary. 'Ælfric's *De auguriis* and Cambridge, Corpus Christi College 178.' In *Latin Learning and English Lore*, edited by Katherine O'Brien O'Keeffe and Andy Orchard, II.376–94. Toronto: University of Toronto Press, 2005.

– 'Ælfric's *Judith*: Manipulative or Manipulated?' *ASE* 23 (1994): 215–28.

Clemoes, Peter. 'Ælfric.' In *Continuations and Beginnings: Studies in Old English Literature*, edited by Eric G. Stanley, 176–209. London: Nelson, 1966.

– ed. *Ælfric's Catholic Homilies: The First Series, Text*. EETS s.s. 17. Oxford: Oxford University Press, 1997.

– 'The Chronology of Ælfric's Works.' In *The Anglo-Saxons: Studies in Aspects of Their History and Culture Presented to Bruce Dickins*, 212–47. London: Bowes and Bowes, 1959. Reprinted in *Old English Prose: Basic Readings*, edited by Paul E. Szarmach, with the assistance of D.A. Oosterhouse, 29–72. New York and London: Garland, 2001.

– 'The Composition of the Old English Text.' In *The Old English Illustrated Hexateuch: British Museum Cotton Claudius B.iv*. EEMF 18, edited by C.R. Dodwell and Peter Clemoes, 42–53. Copenhagen: Rosenkilde and Bagger, 1974.

– 'Language in Context: *Her* in the 890 Anglo-Saxon Chronicle.' *Leeds Studies in English* 16 (1985): 27–36.

Cohen, Shaye J.D. *The Beginnings of Jewishness: Boundaries, Varieties, Uncertainties*. Berkeley: University of California Press, 1999.

Colgrave, Bertram, ed. *Felix's Life of Saint Guthlac*. Cambridge: Cambridge University Press, 1956.

– ed. *The Paris Psalter*. EEMF 8. Copenhagen: Rosenkilde & Bagger, 1958.

Colgrave, Bertram, and R.A.B. Mynors, ed. and trans. *Bede's Ecclesiastical History of the English Nation*. Oxford: Clarendon Press, 1969.

Colish, Marcia. *The Mirror of Language: A Study in the Medieval Theory of Knowledge*. New Haven, CT, and London: Yale University Press, 1968.

– '*Psalterium Scholasticorum*: Peter Lombard and the Emergence of Scholastic Psalms Exegesis.' *Speculum* 67 (1992): 531–48.

Collins, John F. *A Primer of Ecclesiastical Latin*. Washington, DC: Catholic University of America Press, 1985.

Collins, John J. *Daniel: A Commentary on the Book of Daniel.* Minneapolis, MN: Fortress Press, 1993.

Conti, Aidan. 'An Anonymous Homily for Palm Sunday, *The Dream of the Rood*, and the Progress of Ælfric's Reform.' *Notes and Queries* 48 (2001): 377–80.

Cook, Albert S, ed. *The Old English Elene, Phoenix, and Physiologus.* New Haven, CT: Yale University Press, 1919.

Corrêa, Alicia. 'Daily Office Books: Collectars and Breviaries.' In *The Liturgical Books of Anglo-Saxon England.* Old English Newsletter Subsidia 2, edited by Richard W. Pfaff, 45–60. Kalamazoo: Medieval Institute, Western Michigan University, 1995.

Coupland, Simon. *Carolingian Coinage and the Vikings: Studies on Power and Trade in the 9th Century.* Aldershot, UK: Ashgate Variorum, 2007.

Cowley, A.E., trans. *Gesenius' Hebrew Grammar as Edited and Enlarged by the Late E. Krautzsch.* 2nd ed. Oxford: Clarendon Press, 1910.

Craven, Toni. *Artistry and Faith in the Book of Judith.* Society of Biblical Literature Dissertation Series 70. Chico, CA: Scholars Press, 1988.

Crawford, Samuel J., ed. *The Old English Version of the Heptateuch: Ælfric's Treatise on the Old and New Testament, and His Preface to Genesis.* EETS o.s. 160. London: Oxford University Press, 1922. Reprinted, with transcriptions by N.R. Ker. London and New York: Oxford University Press, 1969.

Creed, Robert P. 'The Art of the Singer: Three Old English Tellings of the Offering of Isaac.' In *Old English Poetry: Fifteen Essays*, edited by Robert P. Creed, 69–82. Providence, RI: Brown University Press, 1967.

Cross, James E. 'Doctrine and Poetry.' *JEGP* 59 (1960): 561–4.

– 'The Ethic of War in Old English.' In *England before the Conquest: Studies in Primary Sources Presented to Dorothy Whitelock*, edited by Peter Clemoes and Kathleen Hughes, 269–82. Cambridge: Cambridge University Press, 1971.

– 'The Old English Period.' In *Sphere History of Literature in the English Language*, vol. 1, *The Middle Age*, edited by W.F. Bolton. London: Sphere Books, 1970.

– 'Oswald and Byrhtnoth: A Christian Saint and a Hero Who Is Christian.' *ES* 46 (1965): 93–109.

Cross, James E., and Thomas D. Hill, eds. *The Old English Prose Solomon and Saturn and Adrian and Ritheus.* McMaster Old English Studies and Texts 1. Toronto: University of Toronto Press, 1983.

Cross, James E., and Susie I. Tucker, 'Allegorical Tradition and the Old English *Exodus.*' *Neophilologus* 44 (1960): 122–7.

Cunningham, M.P., ed. *Aurelii Prudentii Clementis carmina.* CCSL 126. Turnhout, Belgium: Brepols, 1966.

Dalglish, Edward R. *Psalm Fifty-One in the Light of Ancient Near Eastern Patternism.* Leiden, Netherlands: Brill, 1962.

Damico, Helen, and Alexandra Hennessy Olsen, eds. *New Readings on Women in Old English Literature.* Bloomington and Indianapolis: Indiana University Press, 1990.

Daniélou, Jean. *The Bible and the Liturgy.* Notre Dame, IN: University of Notre Dame Press, 1956.

– *From Shadows to Reality: Studies in the Biblical Typology of the Fathers.* Translated by W. Hibberd. Westminster, MD: Newman, 1960.

– *Typology and English Medieval Literature.* Edited by Hugh T. Keenan. New York: AMS Press, 1992.

Davis, Craig R. 'Cultural Historicity in *The Battle of Maldon.*' *PQ* 78 (1999): 151–69.

Davis, Glenn M. 'Changing Senses in *Genesis B.*' *PQ* 80 (2001): 113–31.

Day, Virginia. 'The Influence of the Catechetical *Narratio* on Old English and Some Other Medieval Literature.' *ASE* 3 (1974): 51–61.

DeBruyne, Donatien. 'Le Problème du Psautier Romain.' *Revue Bénédictine* 42 (1930): 101–26.

DeGregorio, Scott. '*Þegenlic* or *flæsclic*: The Old English Prose Legends of St Andrew.' *JEGP* 103 (2003): 449–64.

Dehusses, Jean, ed. *Le Sacramentaire grégorien, ses principales formes d'après les plus anciens manuscrits.* Vol. 1, *Le Sacramentaire, le supplément d'Aniane.* Fribourg, Germany: Spicilegium Friburgense 16, 1971.

Dekkers, E. *Clavis Patrum Latinorum.* 3rd ed. Steenbrugge, Belgium: Brepols, 1995.

Dekkers, E., and J. Fraipont, eds. *Sancti Aurelii Augustini Enarrationes in Psalmos.* CCSL 38–40. Turnhout, Belgium: Brepols, 1956.

De Lagarde, P., G. Morin, M. Adriaen, eds. *Hieronymus: Hebraicae quaestiones in libro Geneseos. Liber interpretationis Hebraicorum nominum.* CCSL 72. Turnhout, Belgium: Brepols, 1959.

De Lubac, Henri. *Exégèse médiévale: Les quatre sens de l'Écriture.* 2 vols. in 4 parts. Paris: Aubier, 1959–64.

Del Zotto, Carla. 'Vom rex iustus zum Märtyrer: Das Heldenparadigma der christlichen Könige zwischen Hagiographie und Geschichte in den mittelalterlichen Quellen über die Bekehrung Skandinaviens.' In *Scandinavian and Christian Europe in the Middle Ages: Papers of the Twelfth International Saga Conference, Bonn/Germany, 28th July –2nd August 2003*, edited by Rudolf Simek and Judith Meurer, 115–28. Bonn: Hausdruckerei der Universität Bonn, 2003.

DeMarco, M., ed. *Ars Tatuini.* CCSL 133. Turnhout, Belgium: Brepols, 1968.

De Senneville-Grave, Ghislaine, ed. *Sulpice Sévère, Chroniques.* Sources chrétiennes 441. Paris: Éditions du Cerf, 1999.

DeWald, T. *The Illustrations of the Utrecht Psalter.* Princeton, NJ: Princeton
  University Press, 1932. Online facsimile at http://psalter.library.uu.nl/.
Discenza, Nicole G. *The King's English: Strategies of Translation in the Old
  English Boethius.* Albany: State University of New York Press, 2005.
Doane, Alger N., ed. *Genesis A: A New Edition.* Madison: University of Wisconsin
  Press, 1978.
– ed. *The Saxon Genesis.* Madison: University of Wisconsin Press, 1991.
Dobbie, E.v.K., ed. *The Anglo-Saxon Minor Poems.* ASPR VI. New York:
  Columbia University Press, 1942.
Dockray-Miller, Mary. 'Female Community in the Old English *Judith*.' *Studia
  Neophilologica* 70 (1998): 165–72.
Donne, John. 'Upon the Translation of the Psalmes by Sir Philip Sydney, and the
  Countesse of Pembroke His Sister.' In *The Divine Poems*, edited by H.
  Gardner, 2nd ed. Oxford: Clarendon Press, 1978.
Douglas, B.J. 'The Anglo-Saxon Version of the Book of Psalms Commonly
  Known as the Paris Psalter.' *PMLA* 9 (1894): 43–164.
Drijvers, Jan W. *Helena Augusta: The Mother of Constantine the Great and the
  Legend of Her Finding of the True Cross.* Leiden, Netherlands: E.J. Brill, 1992.
Dubs, K.E. '*Genesis B*: A Study in Grace.' *American Benedictine Review* 33
  (1982): 47–64.
Dümmler, Ernst., ed. *Alcuini Carmina.* MGH, Poeta I. Berlin: Weidmann, 1881.
– ed. *Alcuini epistolae.* MGH, *Epistolae* IV, *Epistolae karolini aeui* II. Berlin:
  Weidmann, 1895.
Dyer, Joseph. 'The Psalms in Monastic Prayer.' In *The Place of the Psalms in the
  Intellectual Culture in the Middle Ages*, edited by Nancy van Deusen, 59–89.
  Albany: State University of New York Press: 1999.
– 'The Singing of Psalms in the Early-Medieval Office.' *Speculum* 64 (1989):
  535–78.
Earl, James W. 'Christian Traditions in the Old English Exodus.' *NM* 71 (1970):
  541–70. Reprinted in *The Poems of MS Junius 11: Basic Readings*, edited by
  Roy M. Liuzza. London: Routledge, 2002.
– 'The Typological Structure of *Andreas*.' In *Old English Literature in Context*,
  edited by John D. Niles, 66–89. Cambridge: Boydell and Brewer, 1980.
– 'Violence and Non-violence in Anglo-Saxon England: Ælfric's "Passion of
  St. Edmund."' *PQ* 78 (1999): 125–49.
Ehwald, Rudolph, ed. *Aldhelmi Opera.* MGH, Auctores Antiquissimi 15. Berlin:
  Weidmann, 1919. Reprinted 1961.
Elliot, Alison G. 'A Brief Introduction to Medieval Latin Grammar.' In *Medieval
  Latin*, 2nd ed., revised by Joseph Pucci and K.P. Harrington. Chicago:
  University of Chicago Press, 1997.

Emerson, Oliver F. 'The Legend of Joseph's Bones in Old and Middle English.' *MLN* 14 (1899): 331–4.

Emmerson, Richard. 'From *Epistola* to *Sermo*: The Old English Version of Adso's *Libellus De Antichristo.*' *JEGP* 82 (1983): 1–10.

Erffa, Hans-Martin von. *Ikonologie der Genesis : Die christlichen Bildthemen aus dem Alten Testament und ihre Quellen.* 2 vols. Munich: Deutscher Kunstverlag, 1989.

Estes, Heide. 'Feasting with Holofernes: Digesting Judith in Anglo-Saxon England.' *Exemplaria* 15.2 (2003): 325–50.

– 'Lives in Translation: Jews in the Anglo-Saxon Literary Imagination.' PhD diss., New York University, 1998.

Even-Zohar, Itamar. *Papers in Historical Poetics.* Tel Aviv: Porter Israeli Institute for Poetics and Semiotics, Tel Aviv University, 1978.

Ewald, Marie L., trans. *The Homilies of St. Jerome.* Washington, DC: Catholic University of America, 1964.

Farrell, Robert T., ed. *Daniel and Azarias.* London: Methuen; New York: Harper & Row, 1974.

– 'The Unity of the Old English *Daniel.*' *RES* 18 (1967): 117–33.

Fee, Christopher. 'Productive Destruction: Torture, Text, and the Body in the Old English *Andreas.*' *Essays in Medieval Studies* 11 (1994): 51–62.

Feist, Sigund. *Vergleichendes Wörterbuch der Gotischen Sprache.* Leiden, Netherlands: E.J. Brill, 1939.

Ferguson, Paul F. 'Noah, Abraham, and the Crossing of the Red Sea.' *Neophilologus* 65 (1981): 282–7.

Fidjestøl, Bjarne. *Det norrøne fyrstediktet.* Øvre Ervik, Norway: Alvheim & Eide, 1982.

– '"Har du høyrt eit dyrare kvæde?" Litt om økonomien bak den eldste fyrstediktinga.' In *Festskrift til Ludvig Holm-Olsen på hans 70-årsdag den 9. juni 1984*, edited by Bjarne Fidjestøl et al., 61–73. Øvre Ervik, Norway: Alvheim & Eide, 1984. Translated by P. Foote as '"Have You Heard a Poem Worth More?" A Note on the Economic Background of Early Skaldic Praise-Poetry,' in *Bjarne Fidjestøl: Selected Papers*, edited by O. Haugen and E. Mundal. Odense, Denmark: Odense University Press, 1997.

– 'Kongetruskap og gullets makt: Om nokre Bibel-allusjoner hjå Sigvat skald.' *Maal og Minne* (1975): 4–11.

Finch, Roger G., ed. and trans. *The Saga of the Volsungs.* London: Nelson, 1965.

Finnegan, Robert E. 'The Old English *Daniel*: The King and His City.' *NM* 85 (1984): 194–211.

Fischer, Bonifatius, et al., eds. *Biblia sacra iuxta uulgatam uersionem.* Stuttgart: Deutsche Bibelgesellschaft, 1994.

Fleming, Damian. '"The Most Exalted Language": Anglo-Saxon Perceptions of Hebrew.' PhD diss., University of Toronto, 2006.

Foote, Peter. '"Have You Heard a Poem Worth More?" A Note on the Economic Background of Early Skaldic Praise-Poetry.' In *Bjarne Fidjestøl: Selected Papers*, edited by O. Haugen and E. Mundal, 117–32. Odense, Denmark: Odense University Press, 1997.

Foucault, Michel. *Discipline and Punish: The Birth of the Prison*. Translated by Alan Sheridan. New York: Vintage Books, 1979.

Fox, Michael. 'Ælfric on the Creation and Fall of the Angels.' *ASE* 31 (2002): 175–200.

– 'Alcuin as Exile and Educator: *uir undecumque doctissimus*.' In *Latin Learning and English Lore: Studies in Anglo-Saxon Literature for Michael Lapidge*, edited by Katherine O'Brien O'Keeffe and Andy Orchard, I.215–36. Toronto: University of Toronto Press, 2005.

– 'Alcuin's *Expositio in epistolam ad Hebraeos*.' *JMLat* 18 (2008): 326–45.

– 'Alcuin the Exegete: The Evidence of the *Quaestiones in Genesim*.' In *The Study of the Bible in the Carolingian Era*, edited by Celia Chazelle and Burton Van Name Edwards, 39–60. Turnhout, Belgium: Brepols, 2003.

Fraipont, J., ed. *Opera rhythmica Bedae uenerabilis. Liber hymnorum, rhythmi, uariae preces*. CCSL 122. Turnhout: Brepols, 1955.

Fraipont, J., and D. de Bruyne, eds. *Sancti Aurelii Augustini Quaestionum in Heptateuchum*. CCSL 33. Turnhout, Belgium: Brepols, 1958.

Frank, Roberta. 'The Blood-Eagle Again.' *Saga-Book* 22 (1988): 287–9.

– 'Germanic Legend in Old English Literature.' In *The Cambridge Companion to Old English Literature*, edited by Malcolm Godden and Michael Lapidge, 88–106. Cambridge: Cambridge University Press, 1991.

– 'The Ideal of Men Dying with Their Lord in *The Battle of Maldon*: Anachronism or *Nouvelle Vague*.' In *People and Places in Northern Europe, 500–1600: Essays in Honour of Peter Hayes Sawyer*, edited by Ian Wood and Niels Lund, 95–106. Woodbridge, UK: Boydell Press, 1991.

– 'King Cnut in the Verse of His Skalds.' In *The Reign of Cnut, King of England, Denmark and Norway*, edited by Alexander R. Rumble, 106–24. Leicester: Leicester University Press, 1994.

– 'Sex in the *Dictionary of Old English*.' In *Unlocking the Wordhord: Anglo-Saxon Studies in Memory of Edward B. Irving, Jr*, edited by Mark C. Amodio and Katherine O'Brien O'Keeffe, 302–12. Toronto: University of Toronto Press, 2003.

– 'Some Uses of Paronomasia in Old English Scriptural Verse.' *Speculum* 47.2 (1972): 207–26. Reprinted in *The Poems of MS Junius 11: Basic Readings*, edited by R.M. Liuzza, 69–98. New York: Routledge, 2002.

Frantzen, Allen J. *King Alfred*. Boston: Twayne, 1986.

Franzen, Christine. *The Tremulous Hand of Worcester: A Study of Old English in the Thirteenth Century*. Oxford and New York: Clarendon and Oxford University Press, 1991.

Frede, Hermann J. *Kirchenschriftsteller: Verzeichnis und Sigel*. 4th ed., Vetus Latina 1/1. Freiburg, Germany: Herder, 1996.

Frick, Karl. *Chronica minora: Accendunt Hippolyti Romani praeter canonem paschlem fragmenta chronologica*. Vol. 1. Bibliotheca scriptorum Graecorum et Romanorum Teubneriana. Leipzig: Teubner, 1892.

Fulk, Robert D. *A History of Old English Meter*. Philadelphia: University of Philadelphia Press, 1992.

Fulk, Robert D., Robert E. Bjork, and John D. Niles. *Klaeber's Beowulf and the Fight at Finnsburg*. 4th ed. Toronto: University of Toronto Press, 2008.

Fulk, Robert D., and Christopher M. Cain. *A History of Old English Literature*. Oxford: Blackwell, 2003.

Garde, Judith N. *Old English Poetry in Medieval Christian Perspective: A Doctrinal Approach*. Cambridge: D.S. Brewer, 1991.

Garde, Judith N., and Bernard J. Muir. 'Patristic Influence and the Poetic Intention in Old English Religious Verse.' *Literature and Theology* 2 (1988): 49–68.

Gardner, John. 'Cynewulf's *Elene*: Sources and Structure.' *Neophilologus* 54 (1970): 65–76.

Garner, Lori A. 'The Art of Translation in the Old English *Judith*.' *Studia Neophilologica* 73 (2001): 171–88.

– 'The Old English *Andreas* and the Mermedonian Cityscape.' *Essays in Medieval Studies* 24 (2007): 53–63.

Gatch, Milton McC. *Eschatology and Christian Nurture: Themes in Anglo-Saxon and Medieval Religious Life*. Variorum Collected Studies Series CS681. Aldershot, UK: Variorum, 2000.

– 'Noah's Raven in *Genesis A* and the Illustrated Old English Hexateuch.' *Gesta* 14 (1975): 3–15. Reprinted in Gatch, *Eschatology and Christian Nurture: Themes in Anglo-Saxon and Medieval Religious Life*, essay XI (repaginated 1–32). Aldershot, UK: 2000.

– 'The Office in Late Anglo-Saxon Monasticism.' In *Learning and Literature in Anglo-Saxon England: Studies Presented to Peter Clemoes*, edited by Michael Lapidge and Helmut Gneuss, 141–62. Cambridge: Cambridge University Press, 1983.

– *Preaching and Theology in Anglo-Saxon England: Ælfric and Wulfstan*. Toronto and Buffalo: University of Toronto Press, 1977.

Gebauer, G.J., and B. Löfstedt, eds. *Ars grammatica Bonifatii*. CCSL 133B, 1–99. Turnhout, Belgium: Brepols, 1980.

Gentzler, Edwin. *Contemporary Translation Theories*. London: Routledge, 1993.

George, Jodi-Anne. '*Hwalas ðec herigað*: Creation, Closure and the *Hapax Legomena* of the OE *Daniel*.' In *Lexis and Texts in Early English: Studies Presented to Jane Roberts*, edited by Christian J. Kay and Louise M. Sylvester, 105–16. Amsterdam: Rodopi, 2001.

Gibson, Margaret, T.A. Heslop, and Richard W. Pfaff, eds. *The Eadwine Psalter*. London, 1992.

Gibson-Wood, Carol. 'The Utrecht Psalter and the Art of Memory.' *Revue d'art canadienne/Canadian Art Review* 14 (1987): 9–15.

Gillingham, Susan E. *The Poems and Psalms of the Hebrew Bible*. Oxford: Oxford University Press, 1994.

Glick, Leonard B. *Marked in Your Flesh: Circumcision from Ancient Judea to Modern America*. Oxford and New York: Oxford University Press, 2005.

Glorie, Fr., ed. *Aenigmata*. CCSL 133–133A. Turnhout, Belgium: Brepols, 1968.

Gneuss, Helmut. '*Anglicae linguae interpretatio*: Language Contact, Lexical Borrowing and Glossing in Anglo-Saxon England.' In *Language and History in Early England*, 109–48. Aldershot, UK: Variorum, 1996.

– *Handlist of Anglo-Saxon Manuscripts: A List of Manuscripts and Manuscript Fragments Written or Owned in England up to 1100*. Tempe: Arizona Center for Medieval and Renaissance Studies, 2001.

– *Lehnbildungen und Lehnbedeutungen im Altenglischen*. Berlin: Erich Schmidt, 1955.

– 'The Study of Language in Anglo-Saxon England.' *Bulletin of the John Rylands Library* 72 (1990): 1–32.

Godden, Malcolm R., ed. *Ælfric's Catholic Homilies: Introduction, Commentary and Glossary*. EETS s.s. 18. Oxford: Oxford University Press, 2000.

– ed. *Ælfric's Catholic Homilies: The Second Series, Text*. EETS s.s. 5. Oxford: Oxford University Press, 1979.

– 'The Anglo-Saxons and the Goths: Rewriting the Sack of Rome.' *ASE* 31 (2002): 47–68.

– 'Biblical Literature: The Old Testament.' In *The Cambridge Companion to Old English Literature*, edited by Malcolm Godden and Michael Lapidge, 206–26. Cambridge: Cambridge University Press, 1991.

Gollancz, Sir Israel. *The Caedmon Manuscript of Anglo-Saxon Biblical Poetry, Junius XI in the Bodleian Library*. Oxford: Oxford University Press, 1927.

Godlove, Shannon N. 'Bodies as Borders: Cannibalism and Conversion in the Old English *Andreas*.' *SP* 106 (2009): 137–60.

Gordon, R.K. *Anglo-Saxon Poetry: Selected and Translated*. London: Everyman, 1926.

Gorman, Michael. 'Adomnán's *De locis sanctis*: The Diagrams and the Sources.' *Revue Bénédictine* 116 (2006): 5–41.

– 'The Canon of Bede's Works and the World of Ps. Bede.' *Revue Bénédictine* 111 (2001): 399–445.
– 'The Encyclopedic Commentary on Genesis Prepared for Charlemagne by Wigbod.' *Recherches Augustiniennes* 17 (1982): 173–201.
– 'An Unedited Fragment of an Irish Epitome of St. Augustine's *De Genesi ad litteram.*' *Revue des études Augustiniennes* 28 (1982): 76–85.
Gradon, P.O.E., ed. *Cynewulf's Elene*. London: Methuen, 1958.
Graham, Timothy. 'A Runic Entry in an Anglo-Saxon Manuscript from Abingdon and the Scandinavian Career of Abbot Rodolf (1051–2).' *Nottingham Mediaeval Studies* 40 (1996): 16–24.
Grau, Ángel Fábrega, ed. *Pasionario Hispánico*. Monumenta Hispaniae Sacra, Serié Litúrgica VI. Madrid, 1955.
Greene, David, and Fergus Kelly, eds. and trans. *The Irish Adam and Eve Story from Saltair na Rann*. 2 vols., with commentary by Brian Murdoch. Dublin: Dublin Institute for Advanced Studies, 1976.
Greenfield, Stanley B., and Daniel G. Calder. *A New Critical History of Old English Literature*. New York and London: New York University Press, 1986.
Gretsch, Mechthild. *The Intellectual Foundations of the English Benedictine Reform*. Cambridge: Cambridge University Press, 1999.
– 'The Junius Psalter Gloss: Its Historical and Cultural Context.' *ASE* 29 (2000): 85–121.
Griffith, Mark S. 'Ælfric's Preface to Genesis: Genre, Rhetoric, and the Origin of the *ars dictaminis*.' *ASE* 29 (2000): 215–34.
– ed. *Judith*. Exeter: University of Exeter Press, 1997.
– 'Poetic Language and the Paris Psalter: The Decay of the Old English Tradition.' *ASE* 20 (1991): 167–86.
Grundy, Lynne. *Books and Grace: Ælfric's Theology*. London: King's College, 1991.
Gwara, Scott, ed. *Aldhelmi Malmesbiriensis Prosa de Virginitate cum glosa latina atque anglosaxonica*. CCSL 124A. Turnhout, Belgium: Brepols, 2001.
– 'Glosses to Aldhelm's *Prosa de virginitate* and Glossaries from the Anglo Saxon Golden Age, ca. 670–800.' *Studi Medievali* 38 (1997): 561–645.
Häcker, Martina. 'The Original Length of the OE *Judith*: More Doubts on the "Missing Text."' *Leeds Studies in English* 27 (1996): 1–18.
Hagan, Hermann, ed. 'Ars Asperi grammatici.' In *Grammatici Latini*, vol. 8, edited by Heinrich Keil, 39–61. Leipzig: Teubner, 1857–80.
Haines, Dorothy. 'Unlocking *Exodus* ll. 516–32.' *JEGP* 98 (1999): 481–98.
Hall, J.R. 'The Old English Epic of Redemption: The Theological Unity of MS Junius 11.' *Traditio* 32 (1976): 185–208. Reprinted in *The Poems of MS Junius 11: Basic Readings*, edited by Roy M. Liuzza, 20–52. London: Routledge, 2002.

- '"The Old English Epic of Redemption": Twenty-Five Year Retrospective.' In *The Poems of MS Junius 11: Basic Readings*, edited by Roy M. Liuzza, 53–68. London: Routledge, 2002.
- 'Pauline Influence on *Exodus*, 523–48.' *ELN* 15 (1977): 84–8.

Hall, Thomas N. 'Biblical and Patristic Learning.' In *A Companion to Anglo-Saxon Literature*, edited by Philip Pulsiano and Elaine Treharne, 327–44. Oxford and Malden: Blackwell, 2001.

Halldórsson, Halldór. 'Determining the Lending Language.' In *The Nordic Languages and Modern Linguistics: Proceedings of the International Conference of Nordic and General Linguistics, University of Iceland, Reykjavík, July 6–11, 1969*, edited by Hreinn Benediktsson, 365–78. Reykjavík: Vísindafélag Íslendinga, 1970.

- 'Some Old Saxon Loanwords in Old Icelandic Poetry and Their Cultural Background.' In *Festschrift für Konstantin Reichardt*, edited by Christian Gellinek, 106–26. Berne: Francke, 1969.
- 'Synd – An Old Saxon Loanword.' *Scientia Islandica: Anniversary Volume*, 60–4. Reykjavík: Societas Scientarum Islandica, 1968.

Harbus, Antonina. 'A Mind for Hagiography: The Psychology of Resolution in *Andreas*.' In *Germanic Texts and Latin Models: Medieval Reconstructions*, edited by Karen E. Olsen, Antonina Harbus, and Tette Hofstra, 127–40. Groningen, Netherlands: Forster, 1999.

Hare, Michael. 'Cnut and Lotharingia: Two Notes.' *ASE* 29 (2000): 261–78.

Harris, Joseph. 'Love and Death in the Männerbund: An Essay with Special Reference to the *Bjarkamál* and *The Battle of Maldon*.' In *Heroic Poetry in the Anglo-Saxon Period: Studies in Honor of Jess B. Bessinger, Jr.*, edited by Helen Damico and John Leyerle, 77–114. Kalamazoo, MI: Medieval Institute Publications, 1993.

Harris, Nathaniel. *The Life and Works of Gustav Klimmt*. Bath: Paragon Books, 1993.

Harris, Stephen J. *Race and Ethnicity in Anglo-Saxon Literature*. Studies in Medieval History and Culture 24. London and New York: Routledge, 2003.

Hauer, Stanley R. 'The Patriarchal Digression in the Old English *Exodus*, Lines 362–446.' *SP* 78.5 (1981): 77–90.

Head, Thomas, ed. *Medieval Hagiography: An Anthology*. New York: Garland, 2000.

Heaney, Seamus. *Beowulf: A New Verse Translation*. New York: Farrar, Straus, and Giroux, 2000.

Heine, Ronald E., trans. *Gregory of Nyssa's Treatise on the Inscriptions of the Psalms*. Oxford: Clarendon, 1995.

Hellberg, Staffan. 'Kring tillkomsten av *Glælognskviða*.' *Arkiv för nordisk filologi* 99 (1984): 14–48.

– 'Tysk eller Engelsk mission? Om de tidliga kristna lånorden.' *Maal og minne* 1986, 42–9.

Helm, R. *Eusebius Werke.* Vol. 7, 3rd ed. Die griechischen christlichen Schriftsteller der ersten drei Jahrhunderte 47. Berlin: Akademie-Verlag, 1984.

– 'Tysk eller Engelsk mission? Om de tidliga kristna lånorden.' *Maal og minne* (1986): 42–9.

Herbison, Ivan. 'Generic Adaptation in *Andreas.*' In *Essays on Anglo-Saxon and Related Themes in Memory of Lynne Grundy*, edited by Jane Roberts and Janet Nelson, 181–211. London: King's College London, 2000.

Hermann, John P. *Allegories of War: Language and Violence in Old English Poetry.* Ann Arbor: University of Michigan Press, 1989.

– 'The Green Rod of Moses in the Old English *Exodus.*' *ELN* 12 (1975): 241–3.

Hieatt, Constance B. 'The Harrowing of Mermedonia: Typological Patterns in the Old English *Andreas.*' *NM* 77 (1976): 49–62.

Higley, Sarah L. 'The Mouthful of the Giants: Words and Space in Indo-European Revelation Discourse.' In *De Gustibus: Essays for Alain Renoir*, edited by John M. Foley, 266–303. New York: Garland, 1992.

Hill, Edmund, ed. *Saint Augustine: On Genesis.* Translated by Matthew O'Connell, with introductions by Michael Fiedrowicz. Hyde Park, NY: New City Press, 2002.

Hill, John M. *The Cultural World in Beowulf.* Toronto: University of Toronto Press, 1995.

– 'Social Milieu.' In *A Beowulf Handbook*, edited by Robert E. Bjork and John D. Niles, 255–70. Lincoln: University of Nebraska Press, 1997.

Hill, Joyce. 'Ælfric and Smaragdus.' *ASE* 21 (1992): 203–37.

– 'Confronting *Germania Latina*: Changing Responses to Old English Biblical Verse.' In *Latin Culture and Medieval Germanic Europe*, Germania Latina 1, edited by Richard North and Tette Hofstra. Groningen, Netherlands: John Benjamins, 1992.

– 'Lexical Choices for Holy Week: Studies in Old English Ecclesiastical Vocabulary.' In *Lexis and Texts in Early English: Studies Presented to Jane Roberts*, edited by Christian J. Kay and Louise M. Sylvester, 117–27. Amsterdam: Rodopi, 2001.

Hill, Thomas D. 'Bread and Stone, Again: *Elene* 611–18.' *NM* 81 (1980): 252–7.

– 'The Fall of the Angels and Man in the Old English *Genesis B.*' In *Anglo-Saxon Poetry: Essays in Appreciation for John C. McGalliard*, edited by Lewis E. Nicholson and Dolores W. Frese, 279–90. Notre Dame, IN: Notre Dame University Press, 1975.

– 'Figural Narrative in *Andreas.*' *NM* 70 (1969): 261–73.

– 'Literary History and Old English Poetry: The Case of *Christ I, II,* and *III.*' In *Sources of Anglo-Saxon Culture*, Studies in Medieval Culture 20, edited by Paul E. Szarmach, 1–22. Kalamazoo, MI: Medieval Institute Publications, 1986.

– 'The Myth of the Ark-Born Son of Noe and the West-Saxon Royal Genealogical Tables.' *Harvard Theological Review* 80 (1987): 379–83.

– 'The Sphragis as Apotropaic Sign: *Andreas* 1334–44.' *Anglia* 101 (1983): 147–51.

– 'The "Variegated Obit" as an Historiographic Motif in Old English Poetry and Anglo-Latin Historical Literature.' *Traditio* 44 (1988): 102–24.

– 'The *virga* of Moses and the Old English *Exodus*.' In *Old English Literature in Context: Ten Essays*, edited by John D. Niles, 57–65. Cambridge: D.S. Brewer, 1980.

Hoffman, Hartmut. 'Der älteste Textzeuge der Chronik des Sulpicius Severus.' *Deutsches Archiv für Erforschung des Mittelalters* 59 (2003): 447–58.

Hoffmann, Erich. *Die heilige Könige bei den Angelsachsen und den skandinavischen Völkern: Königsheiliger und Königshaus*. Neumünster, Germany: Wachholtz, 1975.

Hofmann, Dietrich. *Nordisch-englische Lehnbeziehungen der Wikingerzeit*. Copenhagen: Munksgaard, 1955.

Hofmann, Johann B. *Lateinische Syntax und Stilistik*. Revised by Anton Szantyr. Munich: C.H. Beck, 1965.

Holder, Alfred, ed. *Inventio sanctae crucis: Actorum Cyriaci pars I, latine et graece*. Leipzig: Teubner, 1889.

Holladay, William L. *The Psalms through Three Thousand Years: Prayerbook of a Cloud of Witnesses*. Minneapolis, MN: Fortress Press, 1996.

Hollahan, Patricia. 'The Anglo-Saxon Use of the Psalms: Liturgical Background and Poetic Use.' PhD diss., University of Illinois at Urbana-Champaign, 1977.

Holthausen, F. *Cynewulfs Elene (Kreuzauffindung) mit Einleitung, Glossar, Anmerkungen und der lateinischen Quelle*. Heidelberg: Carl Winter, 1936.

Holtz, Louis, ed. *In Donati artem maiorem*. CCCM 40. Turnhout, Belgium: Brepols, 1977.

Honderich, Ted, ed. *The Oxford Companion to Philosophy*. 2nd ed. Oxford: Oxford University Press, 2005.

Hostetler, Margaret. '*Nimað eow bysne be þyssere Iudith*: Deictic Shifting and Didactic Discourse in Ælfric's *Judith*.' *Studia Neophilologica* 76 (2004): 152–64.

Hourihane, Colum. '*De Camino Ignis*: The Iconography of the Three Children in the Fiery Furnace in Ninth-Century Ireland.' In *From Ireland Coming: Irish Art from the Early Christian to the Late Gothic Period*. Princeton, NJ: Princeton University Press, 2001.

Howe, Nicholas. *Migration and Mythmaking in Anglo-Saxon England*. New Haven, CT: Yale University Press, 1989.

- 'Rome: Capital of Anglo-Saxon England.' *Journal of Medieval and Early Modern Studies* 34 (2004): 147–72.

Howlett, David. *British Books in Biblical Style*. Dublin: Four Courts, 1997.

- 'Tres linguae sacrae and Threefold Play in Insular Latin.' *Peritia* 16 (2002): 94–115.

Huemer, J., ed. *Euangeliorum libri quattuor*. CSEL 24. Vienna: F. Tempsky, 1891.

- ed. *Sedulii opera omnia*. CSEL 10. Vienna: C. Gerold, 1885.

Hunt, Theodore W. *Caedmon's Exodus and Daniel*. Boston: Ginn, 1883.

Huppé, Bernard F. *Doctrine and Poetry: Augustine's Influence on Old English Poetry*. Albany: State University of New York Press, 1959.

Hurst, D., ed. *Bedae homiliae euangelii*. CCSL 122. Turnhout, Belgium: Brepols, 1955.

Hurt, James. *Ælfric*. New York: Twayne, 1972.

Irvine, Martin. 'Anglo-Saxon Literary Theory Exemplified in Old English Poems: Interpreting the Cross in *The Dream of the Rood* and *Elene*.' *Style* 20 (1986): 157–81. Reprinted in *Old English Shorter Poems*, edited by Katherine O'Brien O'Keeffe. New York and London: Garland, 1994.

- 'Medieval Textuality and the Archaeology of Textual Culture.' In *Speaking Two Languages: Traditional Disciplines and Contemporary Theory in Medieval Studies*, edited by Allen J. Frantzen, 181–210. Albany: State University of New York Press, 1991.

Irvine, Susan. 'The Sources of Anglo-Saxon Chronicle MS E.' *Fontes Anglo-Saxonici*. http://fontes.english.ox.ac.uk, accessed December 2006.

Irving, Edward B., Jr, ed. *The Old English Exodus*. New Haven, CT: Yale University Press, 1953.

Isaacs, J. 'The Authorized Version and After.' In *The Bible in Its Ancient and English Versions*, edited by H. Wheeler Robinson, 196–234. Oxford: Clarendon Press, 1940.

Jaager, Werner, ed. *Bedas metrische Vita sancti Cuthberti*. Leipzig: Mayer and Müller, 1935.

Jager, Eric. 'Speech and the Chest in Old English Poetry: Orality or Pectorality?' *Speculum* 65 (1990): 845–59.

- *The Tempter's Voice: Language and the Fall in Medieval Literature*. Ithaca and London: Cornell University Press, 1993.

James, M.R., ed. *The Canterbury Psalter*. London: Lund, 1935.

Jesch, Judith. 'Knútr in Poetry and History.' In *International Scandinavian and Medieval Studies in Memory of Gerd Wolfgang Weber*, edited by Michael Dallapiazza, Olaf Hansen, Preben Meulengracht Sørensen, and Yvonne S. Bonnetain, 243–56. Trieste: Parnaso, 2000.

Jewitt, R. 'The Agitators and the Galatian Congregation.' *New Testament Studies* 17 (1971): 198–212.

Johnson, David N. 'The Fall of Lucifer in *Genesis A* and Two Anglo-Latin Royal Charters.' *JEGP* 97 (1998): 500–21.

Jones, Alexander, ed. *The Jerusalem Bible*. Garden City, NJ: Doubleday, 1966.

Jones, Charles W., ed. *Bedae opera didascalica*. 3 vols, CCSL 123A–C. Turnhout, Belgium: Brepols, 1975–80.

– ed. *Bedae uenerabilis opera, pars II, opera exegetica: Libri quatuor in principium Genesis*. CCSL 118A. Turnhout, Belgium: Brepols, 1967.

– ed. *De temporum ratione*. CCSL 123B. Turnhout, Belgium: Brepols, 1977.

Jones, Christopher A. *Ælfric's Letter to the Monks of Eynsham*. CSASE 24. Cambridge: Cambridge University Press, 1998.

Jónsson, Finnur. *Den oldnorske og oldislandske Literaturs Historie*. 2nd ed., 3 vols. Copenhagen: Gad, 1920–4.

– ed. *Morkinskinna*. Samfund til Udgivelse af Gammel Nordisk Litteratur, 53. Copenhagen: Jørgensen, 1928–32.

– ed. *Skjaldedigtning: Den norsk-islandske skjaldedigtning*. Copenhagen: Gyldendal, 1912–15. Reprint. Copenhagen: Rosenkilde og Bagger, 1967, 1973.

Jost, David A. 'Biblical Sources of Old English *Daniel*, 1–78.' *ELN* 15 (1978): 257–63.

Jost, Karl, ed. *Die 'Institutes of Polity, Civil and Ecclesiastical': Ein Werk Erzbischof Wulfstan von York*. Swiss Studies in English 47. Berne: Francke Verlag, 1959.

Jungmann, Joseph A. *The Mass of the Roman Rite: Its Origins and Development*. Translated by Francis A. Brunner. New York: Benziger Brothers, 1955.

Kantorowicz, E.H. 'The King's Advent.' *The Art Bulletin* 26.4 (1944): 206–31.

Karkov, Catherine E. *Text and Picture in Anglo-Saxon England: Narrative Strategies in the Junius 11 Manuscript*. CSASE 31. Cambridge: Cambridge University Press, 2001.

Kaulen, Franz. *Sprachliches Handbuch zur biblischen Vulgata*. 1904. Reprint, Hildesheim, Germany: G. Olms, 1973.

Kazhdan, Alexander. 'Byzantine Hagiography and Sex in the Fifth to the Twelfth Centuries.' *Dumbarton Oaks Papers* 44 (1990): 131–43.

Kedar-Kopfstein, Benjamin. 'The Vulgate as a Translation: Some Semantic and Syntactical Aspects of Jerome's Version of the Hebrew Bible.' PhD diss., Hebrew University, 1968.

Keefer, Sarah Larratt. 'Assessing the Liturgical Canticles from the Old English *Hexateuch*.' In *The Old English Hexateuch*, edited by Rebecca Barnhouse and Benjamin C. Withers,109–43. Kalamazoo, MI: Medieval Institute Publications, 2000.

– 'Hebrew and the Hebraicum in Late Anglo-Saxon England.' *ASE* 19 (1990): 67–80.

– *Psalm-Poem and Psalter-Glosses: The Latin and Old English Psalter-Text Background to 'Kentish Psalm 50.'* New York: Peter Lang, 1991.

Keefer, Sarah Larratt, and Katherine O'Brien O'Keefe, eds. *New Approaches to Editing Old English Verse.* Cambridge: Boydell and Brewer, 1998.

Keil, Heinrich, ed. *Grammatici Latini.* 8 vols. Leipzig, 1857–80.

Kendall, Calvin B. 'The Responsibility of *Auctoritas*: Method and Meaning in Bede's Commentary on Genesis.' In *Innovation and Tradition in the Writings of the Venerable Bede*, edited by Scott DeGregorio, 101–20. Morgantown: West Virginia University Press, 2006.

Kennedy, Charles W. *The Caedmon Poems.* London: G. Routledge, 1916.

Kent, Charles W., ed. *Elene: An Old English Poem.* Boston: Ginn, 1897.

Kent, Roland G. *Varro: On the Latin Language.* 2 vols. Cambridge, MA: Harvard, 1972.

Ker, N.R. *Catalogue of Manuscripts Containing Anglo-Saxon.* Oxford: Clarendon Press, 1957. Reprinted 1992.

Keynes, Simon, and Michael Lapidge, trans. *Alfred the Great: Asser's Life of Alfred and Other Contemporary Sources.* Harmondsworth, UK: Penguin, 1983.

Kim, Susan. 'Bloody Signs: Circumcision and Pregnancy in the Old English *Judith*.' *Exemplaria* 11 (1999): 285–307.

Kimbrough, Robert, ed. *Sir Philip Sidney: Selected Prose and Poetry.* 2nd ed. Wisconsin, MI: University of Wisconsin Press, 1983.

Kimmens, Andrew C. *The Stowe Psalter.* Toronto Old English Series 3. Toronto: University of Toronto Press, 1979.

Kiser, Lisa J. '*Andreas* and the *Lifes Weg*.' *NM* 85 (1984): 65–75.

Klaeber, Friedrich, ed. *Beowulf.* 3rd ed. Boston: D.C. Heath, 1950.

– 'Die *Ältere Genesis* und der *Beowulf*.' *Englische Studien* 42 (1910): 321–38.

Klein, Stacy S. 'Ælfric's Sources and His Gendered Audiences.' *Essays in Medieval Studies* 13 (1996): 111–19.

– 'Beauty and the Banquet: Queenship and Social Reform in Ælfric's *Esther*.' *JEGP* 103 (2004): 77–105.

Kleist, Aaron. 'Ælfric's Corpus: A Conspectus.' *Florilegium* 18.2 (2001): 113–64.

– *Striving with Grace: Views of Free Will in Anglo-Saxon England.* Toronto: University of Toronto Press, 2008.

Koch, John, and John Carey, eds. and trans. *The Celtic Heroic Age: Literary Sources for Ancient Celtic Europe & Early Ireland and Wales.* 3rd ed. Oakville, CT: Celtic Studies Publications, 2000.

Kornexl, Lucia, ed. *Die Regularis concordia und ihre altenglische Interlinearversion.* Munich: W. Fink, 1993.

– 'The *Regularis Concordia* and Its Old English Gloss.' *ASE* 24 (1995): 95–130.

Krapp, George P., and Elliot Van Kirk Dobbie, eds. *The Anglo-Saxon Poetic Records: A Collective Edition.* 6 vols. New York: Columbia University Press, 1931–53.

Kristeva, Julia. *Powers of Horror: An Essay on Abjection.* Trans. Leon S. Roudiez. New York: Columbia University Press, 1982.

Krüger, Karl Heinrich. *Die Universalchroniken.* Typologie des sources du moyen âge occidental 16. Turnhout, Belgium: Brepols, 1976.

Krush, B., and W. Levison, eds. *Historia Francorum.* MGH, Scriptores rerum Merovingicarum 1/1, 2nd ed., vol. 1, 1–9. Hanover: Hahn, 1937–51.

Kuczynski, Michael P. *Prophetic Song: The Psalms as Moral Discourse in Late Medieval England.* Philadelphia: University of Pennsylvania Press, 1995.

Kuhn, Sherman M., ed. *The Vespasian Psalter.* Ann Arbor: University of Michigan Press, 1965.

– 'Was Ælfric a Poet?' *PQ* 52 (1973): 643–62. Reprinted in *Studies in the Language and Poetics of Anglo-Saxon England*, edited by R.E. Lewis, 186–205. Ann Arbor, MI: Karoma, 1984.

Lapidge, Michael. 'The Anglo-Latin Background.' In *A New Critical History of Old English Literature*, edited by Stanley B. Greenfield and Daniel G. Calder, 5–37. New York: New York University Press, 1986.

– *The Anglo-Saxon Library.* Oxford: Oxford University Press, 2006.

– *Bede the Poet.* Jarrow Lecture. Newcastle, UK: St Paul's Church, 1993.

– 'Byrhtferth and Oswald.' In *St. Oswald of Worcester: Life and Influence*, edited by Nicholas Brooks and Catherine Cubitt, 64–83. London: Leicester University Press, 1996.

– 'Israel the Grammarian in Anglo-Saxon England.' In *From Athens to Chartres: Neoplatonism and Medieval Thought; Studies in Honour of Edouard Jeauneau*, edited by H. J. Westra, 97–114. Leiden and New York: Brill, 1992.

– 'The School of Theodore and Hadrian.' *ASE* 15 (1986): 45–72.

– 'Versifying the Bible in the Middle Ages.' In *The Text in the Community: Essays on Medieval Works, Manuscripts, Authors, and Readers*, edited by Jill Mann and Maura Nolan, 11–40. Notre Dame, IN: Notre Dame University Press, 2006.

Lapidge, Michael, John Blair, Simon Keynes, and Donald Scragg, eds. *The Blackwell Encyclopaedia of Anglo-Saxon England.* Oxford: Blackwell, 1999.

Lapidge, Michael, and Helmut Gneuss, eds. *Learning and Literature in Anglo-Saxon England: Studies Presented to Peter Clemoes.* Cambridge: Cambridge University Press, 1983.

Lapidge, Michael, and Michael Herren, trans. *Aldhelm: The Prose Works.* Ipswich and Cambridge: D.S. Brewer, 1979.

Lapidge, Michael, and James L. Rosier, trans. *Aldhelm: The Poetic Works.* Appendix by Neil Wright. Cambridge: D.S. Brewer, 1985.

Larratt Keefer, Sarah. *Psalm-Poem and Psalter-Glosses: The Latin and Old English Psalter-Text Background to 'Kentish Psalm 50.'* New York: P. Lang, 1991.

Latham, R.E. *Revised Medieval Latin Word-List from British and Irish Sources, with Supplement.* Oxford: Oxford University Press, 2004.

Law, Vivien. *Grammar and Grammarians in the Early Middle Ages*. London: Longman, 1997.

- *The Insular Latin Grammarians*. Studies in Celtic History 3. Woodbridge, UK: Boydell, 1982.

- *Wisdom, Authority and Grammar in the Seventh Century: Decoding Virgilius Maro Grammaticus*. Cambridge: Cambridge University Press, 1995.

Lawson, M.K. 'Archbishop Wulfstan and the Homiletic Element in the Laws of Æthelred II and Cnut.' *English Historical Review* 424 (1992): 565–86.

- *Cnut: The Danes in England in the Early Eleventh Century*. London: Longman, 1993.

Lee, Stuart, ed. *Ælfric's Homilies on Judith, Esther, and the Macabees*. 1999. Available online at users.ox.ac.uk/~stuart/kings.

Lewis, C.S. *Surprised by Joy*. London: Harcourt Press, 1955.

Liebermann, Felix, ed., *Die Gesetze der Angelsachsen*, 3 vols. Halle, 1903; reprinted Aalen, Germany: Scientia, 1960.

- 'King Alfred and the Mosaic Law.' *Transactions of the Jewish Historical Society* 6 (1908–10): 21–31.

Lieu, Judith M. 'Circumcision, Women and Salvation.' *New Testament Studies* 40.3 (1994): 358–70.

Lindelöf, U., ed. *Der Lambeth-Psalter*. Vol. 1, *Text und Glossar*. Helsingfors: Acta Societatis Scientiarum Fennicæ, 1909.

Liuzza, R.M. 'Lost in Translation: Some Versions of *Beowulf* in the Nineteenth Century.' *ES* 83 (2002): 281–95.

- ed. *The Old English Version of the Gospels*. 2 vols. EETS o.s. 304, 314. Oxford: Oxford University Press, 1994 and 2000.

- ed. *The Poems of MS Junius 11: Basic Readings*. London: Routledge, 2002.

Lochrie, Karma. 'Gender, Sexual Violence, and the Politics of War in the OE *Judith*.' In *Class and Gender in Early English Literature: Intersections*, edited by Britton J. Harwood and Gillian R. Overing, 1–20. Bloomington: Indiana University Press, 1994.

Lockett, Leslie. 'An Integrated Re-examination of the Dating of Oxford, Bodleian Library, Junius 11.' *ASE* 31 (2002): 141–73.

Löfstedt, B., ed. *Ars Laureshamensis: Expositio in Donatum maiorem*. CCCM 40A. Turnhout, Belgium: Brepols, 1977.

- ed. *Virgilius Maro Grammaticus: Opera omnia*. Munich: K.G. Saur, 2003.

Löfstedt, B., L. Holtz, and A. Kibre, eds. *Liber in partibus Donati*. CCCM 68. Turnhout, Belgium: Brepols, 1986.

Lubac, Henri de. *Exégèse médiévale: Les quatre sens de l'Écriture*. 2 vols. in 4 parts. Paris: Aubier, 1959–64.

- *Medieval Exegesis*. Translated by E.M. Macierowski and Mark Sebanc. 3 vols. Grand Rapids, MI: W.B. Eerdmans, 1998–2000.

Lucas, Peter J. '*Daniel* 276.' *Notes and Queries* 221 (1976): 390–1.

– 'A Daniel Come to Judgement? Belshazzar's Feast in Old and Middle English.' In *Loyal Letters: Studies on Medieval Alliterative Poetry and Prose*, edited by L.A.J.R. Houwen and A.A. MacDonald, 71–91. Groningen, Netherlands: Egbert Forsten, 1994.

– ed. *Exodus.* 2nd rev. ed. Exeter: University of Exeter Press, 1994.

– 'Loyalty and Obedience in the Old English *Genesis* and the Interpolation of *Genesis B* into *Genesis A.*' *Neophilologus* 76 (1992): 121–35.

– 'On the Incomplete Ending of *Daniel* and the Addition of *Christ and Satan* to MS Junius 11.' *Anglia* 97 (1979): 46–59.

– 'The Place of *Judith* in the *Beowulf*-Manuscript.' *RES* 41 (1990): 463–78.

Lucken, Linus Urban. *Antichrist and the Prophets of Antichrist in the Chester Cycle.* Washington, DC: Catholic University of America Press, 1940.

Luria, M. 'The Old English *Exodus* as a Christian Poem: Notes towards a Reading.' *Neophilologus* 65 (1981): 600–6.

– 'Why Moses' Rod Is Green.' *ELN* 17 (1980): 161–3.

Lyonnet, S., and L. Sabourin. *Sin, Redemption, and Sacrifice: A Biblical and Patristic Study.* Rome: Biblical Institute Press, 1970.

Macalister, R.A.S, ed. and trans. *Lebor Gabála Érenn: The Book of the Taking of Ireland.* 5 vols. Irish Text Society 34, 35, 39, 41, 44. London, 1938–56.

MacIntyre, Alasdair. *After Virtue: A Study in Moral Theory.* 2nd ed. Notre Dame, IN: University of Notre Dame Press, 1984.

MacLean, George. 'Ælfric's Version of *Alcuini interrogationes Sigeuulfi in Genesin.*' *Anglia* 6 (1883): 425–73 (introduction and commentary), and *Anglia* 7 (1884): 1–59 (text).

Madan, F., H.H.E. Craster, and N. Denholm-Young. *A Summary Catalogue of Western Manuscripts in the Bodleian Library at Oxford.* Oxford: Clarendon, 1937.

Magennis, Hugh. 'Contrasting Narrative Emphases in the Old English Poem *Judith* and Ælfric's Paraphrase of the Book of Judith.' *NM* 96 (1995): 61–6.

– *Images of Community in Old English Poetry.* CSASE 18. Cambridge: Cambridge University Press, 1996.

– 'Warrior Saints, Warfare and the Hagiography of Ælfric of Eynsham.' *Traditio* 56 (2001): 27–51.

Magennis, Hugh, and Mary Swan, eds. *A Companion to Ælfric.* Leiden and Boston: Brill, 2009.

Major, Tristan. 'Rebuilding the Tower of Babel: Ælfric and Bible Translation.' *Florilegium* 23.2 (2006): 47–60.

Marsden, Richard. 'Ælfric as Translator: The Old English Prose *Genesis.*' *Anglia* 109 (1991): 319–58.

- 'Cain's Face and Other Problems: The Legacy of the Earliest Bible Translations.' *Reformation* 1 (1996): 2–51.
- *The Cambridge Old English Reader*. Cambridge: Cambridge University Press, 2004.
- '"In the Twinkling of an Eye": The English of Scripture before Tyndale.' *Leeds Studies in English* 31 (2000): 145–72.
- 'Old Latin Intervention in the Old English *Heptateuch*.' *ASE* 23 (1994): 229–64.
- *The Text of the Old Testament in Anglo-Saxon England*. CSASE 15. Cambridge: Cambridge University Press, 1995.
- 'Translation by Committee? The Anonymous Text of the Old English *Hexateuch*.' In *The Old English Hexateuch: Aspects and Approaches*, edited by Rebecca Barnhouse and Benjamin C. Withers, 41–90. Kalamazoo: Western Michigan University Press, 2000.
- Martin, José Carlos, ed. *Isidori Hispalensis chronica*. CCSL 112. Turnhout, Belgium: Brepols, 2003.
- Martin, Joseph, ed. *De doctrina christiana*. CCSL 32. Turnhout, Belgium: Brepols, 1962.
- Martin, Lawrence T., and David Hurst, trans. *Bede the Venerable: Homilies on the Gospels*. 2 vols. Kalamazoo, MI: Cistercian, 1991.
- Matthews, Gareth B. 'Two Concepts of Happiness in Augustine.' In *Rationality and Happiness: From the Ancients to the Early Medievals*, edited by Jiyuan Yu and Jorge J.E. Gracia, 161–74. Rochester, NY: University of Rochester Press, 2003.
- Mauss, M. *The Gift: Forms and Functions of Exchange in Archaic Societies*. Translated by I. Cunnison. New York: W.W. Norton, 1967.
- May, Herbert Gordon. 'The God of My Father: A Study of Patriarchal Religion.' *Journal of Bible and Religion* 9.3 (1941): 155–8 and 199–200.
- May, Todd. *The Moral Theory of Poststructuralism*. Philadelphia: Pennsylvania State University Press, 1995.
- McIntosh, Angus. 'Wulfstan's Prose.' *Proceedings of the British Academy* 35 (1949): 109–42.
- McKenna, Stephen. *St Augustine: The Trinity*. Washington, DC: Catholic University of America Press, 1963.
- McKill, L.N. 'The Artistry of the Noah Episode in *Genesis A*.' *English Studies in Canada* 13 (1987): 121–35.
- 'The Offering of Isaac and the Artistry of Old English *Genesis A*.' In *The Practical Vision: Essays in English Literature in Honour of Flora Roy*, edited by Jane Campbell and James Doyle, 1–11. Waterloo, ON: Wilfrid Laurier University Press, 1978.

McKinlay, Arthur P., ed. *Arator: De actibus apostolorum.* CSEL 72. Vienna: Hoelder, Pichler, Tempsky, 1951.

McKinnell, John. 'Eddic Poetry in Anglo-Scandinavian Northern England.' In *Vikings and the Danelaw: Select Papers from the Proceedings of the Thirteenth Viking Congress, Nottingham and York, 21–30 August 1997*, edited by J. Graham-Campbell, Richard Hall, Judith Jesch, and David Parsons, 327–44. Oxford: Oxbow, 2001.

McKitterick, Rosamond. *Perceptions of the Past in the Early Middle Ages.* Notre Dame, IN: University of Notre Dame Press, 2006.

Megill, Allan. *Prophets of Extremity: Neitzsche, Heidegger, Foucault, Derrida.* Berkeley: University of California, 1987.

Mellinkoff, Ruth. *The Mark of Cain.* Berkeley and Los Angeles: University of California Press, 1981.

– *Outcasts: Signs of Otherness in Northern European Art of the Later Middle Ages.* Berkeley: University of California Press, 1993.

Menner, Robert J., ed. *The Poetical Dialogues of Solomon and Saturn.* New York: Modern Language Association, 1941.

Meritt, Herbert Dean. *Fact and Lore about Old English Words.* Stanford, CA: Stanford University Press, 1954.

Migne, J.-P., ed. *Patrologia Latina.* 217 vols. Paris, 1844–64.

Minkoff, Harvey. 'An Example of Lating [*sic*] Influence on Ælfric's Translation Style.' *Neophilologus* 61 (1977): 127–42.

– 'Some Stylistic Consequences of Ælfric's Theory of Translation.' *SP* 73 (1976): 29–41.

Minogue, Kenneth. 'Ideal Communities and the Problem of Moral Identity.' *Nomos* 35 (1993): 41–66.

Mitchell, Bruce. *Old English Syntax.* 2 vols. Oxford: Clarendon Press, 1985.

Mitchell, Bruce, and Fred C. Robinson, eds. *A Guide to Old English.* 7th ed. Oxford and Malden: Blackwell, 2007.

Mitchell, F.H. *Älfrics Sigewulfi Interrogationes in Genesin: kritische Bearbeitung des Textes von MacLean mit Übersetzung und sprachlichen Bemerkungen.* Zurich: Schabelitz, 1888.

Mombritius, Bonino, ed. *Sanctuarium, seu Vitae sanctorum.* 2 vols. Hildesheim, Germany: G. Olms, 1978.

Mommsen, Theodor, ed. *Chronica minora, saec. iv, v, vi, vii.* 3 vols. MGH, Auctores antiquissimi 9, 11, 13. Berlin: Weidmann, 1892–8.

– ed. *Rufinus: Historia ecclesiastica.* In *Eusebius Werke*, vol. 2, Die griechischen christlichen Schriftsteller der ersten drei Jahrhunderte 9/1–3. Leipzig: J.C. Hinrichs, 1903–8.

Moore, Carey A. *Judith*. The Anchor Bible 40. Garden City, NY: Doubleday, 1985.

Morey, James H. *Book and Verse: A Guide to Middle English Biblical Literature*. Urbana: University of Illinois Press, 2000.

Morin, Germanus, ed. *S. Hieronymi presbyteri commentarioli in Psalmos*. CCSL 72, 163–245. Turnhout, Belgium: Brepols, 1959.

Morrell, Minnie Cate. *A Manual of Old English Biblical Materials*. Knoxville: University of Tennessee Press, 1965.

Morris, John. 'The Chronicle of Eusebius: Irish Fragments.' *Bulletin of the University of London Institute of Classical Studies* 19 (1972): 80–93.

Morris, Richard, ed. *Old English Homilies and Homiletic Treatises*. EETS o.s. 29, 34. London: N. Trubner, 1868.

– ed. *The Blickling Homilies of the Tenth Century*. EETS o.s. 58, 63 and 73. London: N. Trübner, 1880.

Mosshammer, Alden A. *The Chronicle of Eusebius and Greek Chronographic Tradition*. Lewisburg, PA: Bucknell University Press, 1979.

Muir, Bernard J., ed. *The Exeter Anthology of Old English Poetry*. 2 vols. 2nd ed. Exeter: University of Exeter Press, 2000.

– ed. *MS Junius 11*. CD-ROM. Oxford: Bodleian Library, 2004.

Murdoch, B. 'An Early Irish Adam and Eve: *Saltair na Rann* and the Tradition of the Fall.' *Medieval Studies* 35 (1973): 146–77.

– 'From the Flood to the Tower of Babel: Some Notes on *Saltair na Rann* XIII–XXIV.' *Ériu* 40 (1989): 69–92.

Mutzenbecher, A., ed. *Sancti Aurelii Augustini retractationum libri II*. CCSL 57. Turnhout, Belgium: Brepols, 1984.

Mynors, R.A.B., R.M. Thomson, and Michael Winterbottom, eds. *William of Malmesbury, Gesta regum Anglorum*. 2 vols. Oxford: Clarendon Press, 1998–9

Napier, Arthur S., ed. *Old English Glosses: Chiefly Unpublished*. Oxford: Clarendon Press, 1900.

– ed. *Wulfstan: Sammlung der ihm zugeschriebenen Homilien nebst Untersuchungen über ihre Echtheit*. Berlin: Weidmann, 1883. Reprint, Berlin: Weidmann, 1967.

Nelson, Janet L. *The Frankish World, 750–900*. London: Hambledon, 1996.

Nelson, Marie. 'Judith: A Story of a Secular Saint.' *Germanic Notes* 21 (1990): 12–13.

– *Judith, Juliana, and Elene: Three Fighting Saints*. American University Studies, Series IV: English Language and Literature, vol. 135. New York: Peter Lang, 1991.

Neuman de Vegvar, Carol. *The Northumbrian Renaissance: A Study in the Transmission of Style*. Selinsgrove, PA: Susquehanna University Press; London: Associated University Presses, 1987.

Niles, John D., and Mark Amodio, eds. *Anglo-Scandinavian England: Norse-English Relations in the Period before the Conquest*. Old English Colloquium Series 4. Lanham, MD: University of Press of America, 1988.

Noel, William. *The Harley Psalter*. Cambridge: Cambridge University Press, 1991.

Norman, Richard. 'History of Moral Philosophy.' In *Oxford Companion to Philosophy*, 586–91.

O'Brien O'Keeffe, Katherine, ed. *The Anglo-Saxon Chronicle: A Collaborative Edition 5, MS C*. Cambridge: Cambridge University Press, 2001.

– 'Body and Law in Late Anglo-Saxon England.' *ASE* 27 (1998): 214–25.

– 'The Book of Genesis in Anglo-Saxon England.' PhD diss., University of Pennsylvania, 1975.

– ed. *Old English Shorter Poems*. New York and London: Garland, 1994.

– 'Three English Writers on Genesis: Some Observations on Ælfric's Theological Legacy.' *Ball State University Forum* 19.3 (1978): 69–78.

– *Visible Song: Transitional Literacy in Old English Verse*. CSASE 4. Cambridge: Cambridge University Press, 1990.

Ó Cróinín, Dáibhí, ed. and trans. *The Irish Sex aetates mundi*. Dublin: Dublin Institute for Advanced Studies, 1983.

Ogilvy, J.D.A. *Books Known to the English, 597–1066*. Cambridge, MA: Mediaeval Academy of America, 1967.

O'Loughlin, Thomas. 'Christ as the Focus of Genesis Exegesis in Isidore of Seville.' In *Studies in Patrisitic Christology*, edited by Thomas Finan and Vincent Twomey, 144–62. Dublin: Four Courts Press, 1998.

O'Neill, Patrick P. 'The Old English Introductions to the Prose Psalms of the Paris Psalter: Sources, Structure, and Composition.' *SP* 78 (1981): 20–38.

– ed. *King Alfred's Old English Prose Translation of the First Fifty Psalms*. Cambridge, MA: Medieval Academy of America, 2001.

– 'Latin Learning at Winchester in the Early Eleventh Century: The Evidence of the Lambeth Psalter.' *ASE* 20 (1991): 143–66.

Opland, Jeff. *Anglo-Saxon Oral Poetry: A Study of the Traditions*. New Haven, CT: Yale University Press, 1980.

Orchard, Andy. 'Artful Alliteration in Anglo-Saxon Song and Story.' *Anglia* 113 (1995): 429–63.

– 'Conspicuous Heroism: Abraham, Prudentius, and the Old English Verse *Genesis*.' In *Heroes and Heroines in Medieval English Literature: A Festschrift Presented to André Crépin on the Occasion of His Sixty-Fifth Birthday*, edited by Leo Carruthers, 45–58. Woodbridge, Suffolk: Brewer, 1994. Reprinted in *The Poems of MS Junius 11*, edited by R.M. Liuzza, 119–36.

– *A Critical Companion to Beowulf*. Cambridge: D.S. Brewer, 2003.

– 'Intoxication, Fornication, and Multiplication: The Burgeoning Text of *Genesis A*.' In *Text, Image, Interpretation: Studies in Anglo-Saxon Literature and Its Insular Context in Honour of Éamonn Ó Carragáin*, ed. Alastair Minnis and Jane Roberts, 333–54. Turnhout, Belgium: Brepols, 2007.

– 'Poetic Inspiration and Prosaic Translation: The Making of Caedmon's Hymn.' In *Studies in English Language and Literature. 'Doubt Wisely': Papers in Honour of E.G. Stanley*, edited by M.J. Toswell and E.M. Tyler, 402–22. London: Routledge, 1996.

– *Pride and Prodigies: Studies in the Monsters of the Beowulf Manuscript*. Cambridge: D.S. Brewer, 1995. Reprinted Toronto: University of Toronto Press, 2003.

Orchard, Nicholas, ed. *The Leofric Missal II: Text*. Henry Bradshaw Society 114. London: Boydell, 2002.

Ortenberg, Veronica. *The English Church and the Continent in the Tenth and Eleventh Centuries: Cultural, Spiritual, and Artistic Exchanges*. Oxford: Clarendon Press, 1992.

Osborn, Marijane. 'The Great Feud: Scriptural History and Strife in *Beowulf*.' *Papers of the Modern Language Association* 93 (1978): 973–81.

Óskarsdóttir, Svanhildur. 'The Book of Judith: A Medieval Icelandic Translation.' *Gripla* 11 (2000): 79–124.

Overing, Gillian R. 'Nebuchadnezzar's Conversion in the Old English *Daniel*: A Psychological Portrait.' *Papers on Language and Literature* 20 (1984): 3–14.

Page, Raymond I. 'Anglo-Saxon Texts in Early Modern Transcripts.' *Transactions of the Royal Bibliographical Society* 6 (1973): 69–85.

Parkes, Malcolm B. '*Rædan, areccan, smeagan*: How the Anglo-Saxons Read.' *ASE* 26 (1997): 1–22.

Peiper, Rudolfus, ed. *Poematum libri VI*. MGH, Auct. antiq. 6.2, 203–74. Berlin: Weidmann, 1883.

Pelikan, Jaroslav. *Christian Doctrine and Modern Culture*. Chicago: University of Chicago Press, 1989.

Peltola, Niilo. 'Observations on Intensification in Old English Poetry.' *NM* 72 (1971): 649–90.

Pfaff, Richard W. 'Liturgical Books.' In *The Blackwell Encyclopaedia of Anglo-Saxon England*, edited by Michael Lapidge, John Blair, Simon Keynes, and Donald Scragg. Oxford: Blackwell, 1999.

– ed. *The Liturgical Books of Anglo-Saxon England*. Old English Newsletter Subsidia 23. Kalamazoo, MI: Medieval Institute Publications, 1995.

Pine-Coffin, R.S., trans. *St Augustine: Confessions*. Harmondsworth, UK: Penguin Classics, 1961.

Plater, W.E., and H.J. White. *A Grammar of the Vulgate*. Oxford: Clarendon Press, 1926.

Polara, G., ed. *Virgilio Marone grammatico: Epitomi ed epistole*. Naples: Pipola, 1979.

Poole, Russell. 'The *Nesjavísur* of Sigvatr Þórðarson.' *Mediaeval Scandinavia* 15 (2005): 171–98.

– 'Sigvatr, *Nesjavísur*.' In *Skaldic Poetry of the Scandinavian Middle Ages I: Poetry from the Kings' Sagas*, vol. 1, *From Mythical Times to c. 1035*, ed. Diana Whaley. Turnhout, Belgium: Brepols, forthcoming.

Pope, John C., ed. *The Homilies of Ælfric: A Supplementary Collection*. EETS o.s. 259–260. London: Oxford University Press, 1967–8.

Portnoy, Phyllis. *The Remnant: Essays on a Theme in Old English Verse*. London: Runetree Press, 2005.

– '"Remnant" and "Ritual": The Place of *Daniel* and *Christ and Satan* in the Junius Epic.' *ES* 75 (1994): 408–21.

– 'Ring Composition and the Digressions of *Exodus*: The "Legacy" of the "Remnant."' *ES* 82, no. 4 (2001): 289–307.

Powell, Alison. 'Verbal Parallels in *Andreas* and Its Relationship to *Beowulf* and *Cynewulf*.' PhD diss., University of Cambridge, 2002.

Pringle, Ian. '"Judith": The Homily and the Poem.' *Traditio* 21 (1975): 8–97.

Pulsiano, Philip. *Old English Glossed Psalters: Psalms 1–50*. Toronto: University of Toronto Press, 2001.

– 'Psalters.' In *The Liturgical Books of Anglo-Saxon England*, Old English Newsletter Subsidia 23, edited by Richard W. Pfaff, 61–84. Kalamazoo: Medieval Institute, Western Michigan University, 1995.

Rädle, Fidel. *Studien zu Smaragd von Saint-Mihiel*. Medium Aevum-Philologische Studien 29. Munich: W. Fink, 1974.

Rathmell, J.C.A. *The Psalms of Sir Philip Sidney and the Countess of Pembroke*. New York: New York University Press, 1963.

Raw, Barbara C. 'The Construction of Oxford, Bodleian Library, Junius 11.' *ASE* 13 (1984): 187–207.

– 'The Probable Derivation of Most of the Illustrations in Junius 11 from an Illustrated Old Saxon *Genesis*.' *ASE* 5 (1976): 187–207.

– *Trinity and Incarnation in Anglo-Saxon Art and Thought*. CSASE 21. Cambridge: Cambridge University Press, 1997.

Raynes, Enid M. 'MS. Boulogne-sur-Mer 63 and Ælfric.' *Medium Ævum* 26 (1957): 65–73.

Rebenich, Stefan. *Jerome*. London: Routledge, 2002.

Regan, Catharine A. 'Evangelicism as the Informing Principle of Cynewulf's *Elene.*' *Traditio* 29 (1973): 27–52.

Reinsma, Luke M. *Ælfric: An Annotated Bibliography*. New York and London: Garland, 1987.

Remley, Paul G. 'Aldhelm as Old English Poet: *Exodus*, Asser, and the *Dicta Ælfredi.*' In *Latin Learning and English Lore: Studies in Anglo-Saxon Literature for Michael Lapidge*, edited by Katherine O'Brien O'Keeffe and Andy Orchard, I.90–108. Toronto: University of Toronto Press, 2005.

– '*Daniel*, the *Three Youths* Fragment and the Transmission of Old English Verse.' *ASE* 31 (2002): 81–140.

– 'The Latin Textual Basis of *Genesis A*.' *ASE* 17 (1988): 163–89.

– *Old English Biblical Verse: Studies in Genesis, Exodus and Daniel*. CSASE 16. Cambridge: Cambridge University Press, 1996.

Renoir, Alain. '*Judith* and the Limits of Poetry.' *ES* 43 (1962): 145–55.

Reynolds, Roger E. *The Ordinals of Christ from Their Origins to the Twelfth Century*. Beiträge zur Geschichte und Quellenkunde des Mittelalters 7. Berlin: De Gruyter, 1978.

Riché, Pierre. *Education and Culture in the Barbarian West*. Translated by John J. Contreni. Columbia: University of South Carolina, 1976.

Richter, Gregor, and Albert Schönfelder, eds. *Sacramentarium Fuldense saeculi X*. Quellen und Abhandlungen zur Geschichte der Abtei und der Diözese Fulda 9. Fulda, Germany: Der Fuldaer Actiondruckerei,1912. Reprint, Henry Bradshaw Society 101. London: Boydell, 1972–7.

Richter, Michael, and Jean-Michel Picard, eds. *Ogma: Essays in Celtic Studies in Honour of Próinséas Ní Chatháin*. Dublin: Four Courts Press, 2002.

Riedinger, Anita R. '*Andreas* and the Formula in Transition.' In *Hermeneutics and Medieval Culture*, edited by Patrick J. Gallacher and Helen Damico, 183–91. Albany: State University of New York Press, 1989.

Rissanen, Matti. 'In Search of *Happiness*: *Felicitas* and *Beatitudo* in Early English Boethius Translations.' *Studia Anglica Posnaniensia* 31 (1997): 237–48.

Rist, Martin. 'The God of Abraham, Isaac and Jacob: A Liturgical and Magical Formula.' *Journal of Biblical Literature* 57 (1938): 289–303.

Robbins, Frank E. *The Hexaemeral Literature: A Study of the Greek and Latin Commentaries on Genesis*. Chicago: University of Chicago Press, 1912.

Roberts, Jane. 'The Old English Prose Translation of Felix's *Vita sancti Guthlaci*.' In *Studies in Earlier Old English Prose*, edited by Paul Szarmach, 363–79. Albany: State University of New York Press, 1986.

Roberts, Jane, Christian Kay, and Lynne Grundy, eds. *A Thesaurus of Old English*. London: King's College, 1995.

Robertson, D.W., Jr, trans. *On Christian Doctrine*. Indianapolis, IN: Bobbs Merrill, 1958.

Robinson, Douglas. *Translation and Taboo*. DeKalb: Northern Illinois University Press, 1996.

Robinson, Fred C. 'Five Textual Notes on the Old English Judith.' *American Notes & Queries* 15 (2002): 47–51.

– 'God, Death, and Loyalty in *The Battle of Maldon*.' In *J.R.R. Tolkien, Scholar and Storyteller: Essays in Memoriam*, edited by Mary Salu and Robert T. Farrell, 104–21. Ithaca, NY: Cornell University Press, 1979. Reprinted in Fred C. Robinson, *The Tomb of Beowulf and Other Essays on Old English*, 104–21. Cambridge, MA: Blackwell, 1993.

– 'Lexicography and Literary Criticism: A Caveat.' In *Philological Essays: Studies in Old and Middle English Language and Literature in Honour of Herbert Dean Meritt*, edited by James L. Rosier, 99–110. The Hague: Mouton, 1970. Reprinted in Fred C. Robinson, *The Tomb of Beowulf and Other Essays on Old English*, 140–52. Cambridge, MA: Blackwell, 1993.

– 'Notes on the Old English *Exodus*.' *Anglia* 80 (1962), 363–78.

– 'The Significance of Names in Old English Literature.' *Anglia* 76 (1968): 14–58.

– 'Some Aspects of the *Maldon* Poet's Artistry.' *JEGP* 75 (1976): 25–40.

– *The Tomb of Beowulf and Other Essays on Old English*. Oxford: Blackwell, 1993.

Roeder, Fritz, ed. *Altenglische Regius Psalter*. Halle, Germany: Max Niemeyer, 1904.

Rollinson, Philip B. 'The Influence of Christian Doctrine on Old English Poetry.' *ASE* 2 (1973): 271–84.

Rooth, Anna Birgitta. *The Raven and the Carcass: An Investigation of a Motif in the Deluge Myth in Europe, Asia, and North America*. Folklore Fellows Communications 77, no. 186. Helsinki: Suomalainen Tiedeakatemia, 1962.

Rosser, Susan. 'The Sources of Cynewulf's *Elene* (Cameron A.2.6).' *Fontes Anglo-Saxonici: World Wide Web Register*. Oxford: Fontes Anglo-Saxonici Project, English Faculty, Oxford University, 1990. http://fontes.english.ox.ac.uk/, accessed March 2004.

Savonarola, Girolamo. *Esposizione e meditazione del Salmo Miserere*. Florence: Libreria Editrice Fiorentina, 1968.

Schäfer, Gerd. *'König der Könige' – 'Lied der Lieder': Studien zum paronomatischen Intesitätsgenitiv*. Heidelberg: Carl Winter, 1974.

Scheil, Andrew P. 'Anti-Judaism in Ælfric's *Lives of the Saints*.' *ASE* 28 (1999): 65–86.

– 'Babylon and Anglo-Saxon England.' *Studies in the Literary Imagination* 36.1 (2003): 37–58.

- *The Footsteps of Israel: Understanding Jews in Anglo-Saxon England*. Ann Arbor: University of Michigan Press, 2004.
- 'The Historiographic Dimensions of *Beowulf*.' *JEGP* 107.3 (2008): 281–302.

Schoene, Alfred, ed. *Eusebi chronicorum libri duo*. Berlin: Weidmann, 1875.

Schopp, Ludwig, trans. *The Happy Life (De beata uita)*. In *The Fathers of the Church*, vol. 5, 29–84. New York: CIMA Publishers, 1948.

Schücking, Levin L. *Untersuchungen zur Bedeutungslehre der angelsächsischen Dichtersprache*. Heidelburg: Carl Winter, 1915.

Scragg, Donald G., ed. *The Battle of Maldon*. Manchester: Manchester University Press, 1981.
- 'The Nature of Old English Verse.' In *The Cambridge Companion to Old English Literature*, edited by Malcolm Godden and Michael Lapidge, 55–70. Cambridge: Cambridge University Press, 1991.
- ed. *The Vercelli Homilies and Related Texts*. EETS o.s. 300. Oxford: Oxford University Press, 1992.

Seow, Choon Leong. *Ecclesiastes: A New Translation with Introduction and Commentary*. New York: Doubleday, 1997.

Sharma, Manish. 'Nebuchadnezzar and the Defiance of Measure in the Old English *Daniel*.' *ES* 86 (2005): 103–26.

Sharpe, Richard. *A Handlist of the Latin Writers of Great Britain and Ireland before 1540*. Turnhout, Belgium: Brepols, 2001.

Shell, Marc. 'The Holy Foreskin: Or Money, Relics, and Judeo-Christianity.' In *Jews and Other Differences: The New Jewish Cultural Studies*, edited by Jonathan Boyarin and Daniel Boyarin, 345–59. Minneapolis: University of Minnesota Press, 1997.

Shepherd, Geoffrey. 'Scriptural Poetry.' In *Continuations and Beginnings: Studies in Old English Literature*, edited by Eric Gerald Stanley, 1–36. London: Nelson, 1966.

Shippey, Thomas A. *Old English Verse*. London: Hutchinson University Library, 1972.

Sidney, Mary, and Sir Philip Sidney. *The Sidney Psalms*. Edited by R.E. Pritchard. Manchester: Carcanet, 1992.

Sidney, Sir Philip. *Sir Philip Sidney: Selected Prose and Poetry*. Edited by Robert Kimbrough. New York: Holt, Rinehart and Winston, 1969.

Sievers, Eduard. *Der Heliand und die angelsächsische Genesis*. Halle, Germany: M. Niemeyer, 1875.

Sigurðsson, Jón et al., eds. *Edda Snorra Sturlusonar*. 3 vols. Copenhagen: Legatum Arnamagnæanum, 1848, 1852, 1880–87. Reprint, Osnabrück: Zeller, 1966.

Sisam, Kenneth, and Celia Sisam. *The Salisbury Psalter*. EETS o.s. 242. London: Oxford University Press, 1959.

Skeat, Walter W., ed. *Ælfric's Lives of Saints*. EETS o.s. 76, 82, 94, and 114.
  London: Oxford University Press, 1881–1900; reprint in two vols., 1966.
– *The Four Gospels in Anglo-Saxon, Northumbrian and Old Mercian Versions*.
  4 vols. Cambridge: Cambridge University Press, 1871–87.
Skemp, A.R. 'The Transformation of Scriptural Story, Motive and Conception in
  Anglo-Saxon Poetry.' *Modern Philology* 4 (1907): 423–70.
Skorupski, John. 'John Stuart Mill.' In *The Oxford Companion to Philosophy*,
  edited by Ted Honderich, 566–9. Oxford: Oxford University Press, 1995.
Smetana, C.L. 'Ælfric and the Early Medieval Homiliary.' *Traditio* 15 (1959):
  163–204.
– 'Ælfric and the Homiliary of Haymo of Halberstadt.' *Traditio* 17 (1961):
  457–69.
Solo, H.J. 'The Twice-Told Tale: A Reconsideration of Syntax and Style of the
  Old English *Daniel*, 245–429.' *Papers on Language and Literature* 9 (1973):
  347–64.
Souter, Alexander. *A Glossary of Later Latin to 600 A.D.* Oxford: Clarendon
  Press, 1949.
Spaemann, R. 'Glück, Glückseligkeit.' In *Historisches Wörterbuch der Philoso-
  phie*, edited by Joachim Ritter, 679–707. Stuttgart: Schwabe, 1971.
Speirs, Nancy J. *Hermeneutic Sensibility and the Old English 'Exodus.'* PhD
  diss., University of Toronto, 1992.
Spinks, Bryan D. *The Sanctus in the Eucharistic Prayer*. Cambridge: Cambridge
  University Press, 1991.
Stanley, Eric G., 'Ælfric on the Canonicity of the Book of Judith: *hit stent þus on
  ðære bibliothecan*.' *Notes and Queries* 230 (1985): 439.
– ed. *Continuations and Beginnings: Studies in Old English Literature*. London:
  Nelson, 1966.
– 'Translation from Old English: "The Garbaging War-Hawk" or the Literal
  Materials from Which the Reader Can Re-create the Poem.' In *Acts of
  Interpretation*, edited by Mary J. Carruthers and Elizabeth D. Kirk, 67–101.
  Norman, OK: Pilgrim Books, 1982.
Stanton, Robert. *The Culture of Translation in Anglo-Saxon England*. Cambridge:
  D.S. Brewer, 2002.
Staubach, Nikolaus. '*Christiana tempora*. Augustin und das Ende der alten
  Geschichte in der Weltchronik Frechulfs von Lisieux.' *Frühmittelalterliche
  Studien* 29 (1995): 167–206.
Steinberg, Leo. *The Sexuality of Christ in Renaissance Art and in Modern
  Oblivion*. 2nd ed. Chicago: University of Chicago Press, 1996.
Steinmeyer, Elias, and Eduard Sievers. *Die althochdeutschen Glossen*. 5 vols.
  Berlin: Weidmann, 1879–1922.

Stevenson, Jane, ed. *The 'Laterculus Malalianus' and the School of Archbishop Theodore*. CSASE 14. Cambridge: Cambridge University Press, 1995.

Stevenson, Joseph, ed. *The Latin Hymns of the Anglo-Saxon Church*. Durham: George Andrews, 1851.

Stevenson, William H., ed. *Asser's Life of King Alfred*. New impression with supplement by Dorothy Whitelock. Oxford: Clarendon Press, 1959.

St-Jacques, Ray. '*Hwilum word be worde, hwilum andgit of andgiete*: Bede's *Ecclesiastical History* and Its Old English Translator.' *Florilegium* 5 (1983): 85–104.

Stocker, Margarita, ed. *Judith, Sexual Warrior: Women and Power in Western Culture*. New Haven, CT, and London: Yale University Press, 1998.

Stokes, Whitley, ed. *The Saltair na Rann*. Anecdota Oxoniensia, Mediaeval and Modern Series, 1, part 3. Oxford: Clarendon Press, 1883.

Stoneman, William P. 'Another Old English Note Signed "Coleman."' *Medium Ævum* 56 (1987): 78–82.

– 'A Critical Edition of Ælfric's Translation of Alcuin's *Interrogationes Sigwulfi presbiteri* and of the Related Texts *De creatore et creatura* and *De sex aetatibus huius saeculi*.' PhD diss., University of Toronto, 1982.

Strecker, Karl, ed. *Miracula Nynie episcopi*. MGH, Poetae Latini Aevi Carolini 4.3. Berlin: Weidmann, 1923.

Stuart, Heather. 'The Anglo-Saxon Elf.' *Studia Neophilologica* 48 (1976): 313–20.

Swan, Mary, and Elaine Treharne, eds. *Rewriting Old English in the Twelfth Century*. Cambridge: Cambridge University Press, 2000.

Swanton, Michael. 'Die altenglische Judith: Weiblicher Held oder fräuliche Heldin.' In *Heldensage und Heldendichtung im Germanischen*, Ergänzungsbände zum Reallexikon der germanischen Altertumskunde 2, edited by Heinrich Beck, 289–304. Berlin: De Gruyter, 1988.

Swanton, Michael J. *English Literature before Chaucer*. London: Longman, 1986.

Sweet, Henry, ed. *King Alfred's West-Saxon Version of Gregory's Pastoral Care*. EETS o.s. 45, 50. London: N. Trübner, 1871–72.

– *Sweet's Anglo-Saxon Reader*. Rev. ed. edited by Dorothy Whitelock. Oxford: Clarendon Press, 1967.

Symons, Thomas, ed. and trans. *Regularis concordia*. London: Thomas Nelson, 1953.

Szarmach, Paul E. 'Abbot Ælfric's Rhythmical Prose and the Computer Age.' In *New Approaches to Editing Old English Verse*, edited by Sarah L. Keefer and Katherine O'Brien O'Keeffe, 95–108. Cambridge: Boydell and Brewer, 1998.

– ed. *Old English Prose: Basic Readings*. New York and London: Garland, 2000.

– 'Three Versions of the Jonah Story: An Investigation of Narrative Technique in Old English Homilies.' *ASE* 1 (1972): 183–92.

- 'The Whale.' In *Old and Middle English: An Anthology*, edited by Elaine Treharne, 350–1. Oxford: Blackwell, 2000.

Szittya, Penn. 'The Living Stone and the Patriarchs: Typological Imagery in *Andreas*, Lines 706–810.' *JEGP* 72 (1973): 167–75.

Talbot, Charles H., ed. and trans. *The Life of Christina of Markyate*. Oxford: Clarendon Press, 1959.

Taylor, Charles. *Sources of the Self: The Making of the Modern Identity*. Cambridge, MA: Harvard University Press, 1989.

Taylor, Paul Beekman. 'The Old English Poetic Vocabulary of Beauty.' In *New Readings on Women in Old English Literature*, edited by Helen Damico and Alexandra Hennessy Olsen, 211–21. Bloomington and Indianapolis: Indiana University Press, 1990.

Temple, E. *Anglo-Saxon Manuscripts 900–1066*. London: Harvey Miller, 1976.

Teske, Roland J., trans. *Saint Augustine on Genesis*. Washington, DC: Catholic University of America Press, 1991.

Tessman, A., ed. *Aelfrics altenglische Bearbeitung der Interrogationes Sigewulfi presbyteri in Genesin des Alcuin*. Berlin: Bernstein, 1891.

Thornbury, Emily. '*eald enta geweorc* and the Relics of Empire: Revisiting the Dragon's Lair in *Beowulf*.' *Quaestio* 1 (2000): 82–92.

Thorpe, Benjamin, ed. *The Homilies of the Anglo-Saxon Church. The First Part, Containing the Sermones Catholici*. 2 vols. London: Ælfric Society, 1844–6.

Thundy, Zacharias P. *Covenant in Anglo-Saxon Thought*. Madras: Macmillan, 1972.

Timmer, B.J. (Benno Johan), ed. *Judith*. London: Methuen, 1952.

Tolkien, J.R.R. *The Old English Exodus: Text, Translation and Commentary*. Edited by Joan Turville-Petre. Oxford: Clarendon Press, 1981.

Toller, T. Northcote. *An Anglo-Saxon Dictionary: Supplement*. Oxford: Oxford University Press, 1921.

Tonsfeldt, H. Ward. 'Ring Structure in *Beowulf*.' *Neophilologus* 6 (1977): 443–52.

Toswell, M. Jane. 'Psalter Manuscripts.' *Old English Newsletter* 28.1 (1995): A25–33.

- 'The Relationship of the Metrical Psalter to the Old English Glossed Psalters.' *English Studies* 78 (1997): 297–315.

Toury, Gideon. *Descriptive Translation Studies and Beyond*. Amsterdam: J. Benjamins Publishing, 1995.

Townend, Matthew. 'Like Father, Like Son? *Glælognskviða* and the Anglo-Danish Cult of Saints.' In *Scandinavian and Christian Europe in the Middle Ages: Papers of the Twelfth International Saga Conference, Bonn/Germany, 28th July–2nd August 2003*, edited by Rudolf Simek and Judith Meurer, 471–82. Bonn: Hausdruckerei der Universität Bonn, 2003.

- 'Whatever Happened to York Viking Poetry?' *Saga-Book* 27 (2003): 48–90.

Treschow, M. 'The Prologue to Alfred's Law Code.' *Florilegium* 13 (1994): 79–110.

Ure, James M., ed. *The Benedictine Office: An Old English Text*. Edinburgh: University Press, 1957.

Vaciago, Paolo, ed. *Glossae Biblicae*. CCCM 189A–B. Turnhout, Belgium: Brepols, 2004.

Vance, Eugene, ed. *Mervelous Signals: Poetics and Sign Theory in the Middle Ages*. Lincoln and London: University of Nebraska Press, 1986.

Van der Horst, K., W. Noel, and Wilhelmina C.M. Wustefeld, eds. The *Utrecht Psalter in Medieval Art*. Utrecht and Tuurdijk, Netherlands: HES, 1996.

Van Deusen, Nancy, ed. *The Place of the Psalms in the Intellectual Culture of the Middle Ages*. Albany: State University of New York Press, 1999.

Venuti, Lawrence, ed. *The Translation Studies Reader*. London: Routledge, 2000.

– *The Translator's Invisibility: A History of Translation*. London: Routledge, 1995.

Verhelst, D., ed. *Adso Deruensis, De ortu et tempore Antichrist*. CCCM 45. Turnhout, Belgium: Brepols, 1976.

Vickrey, John F. '*Exodus* and the Robe of Joseph.' *SP* 84 (1989): 1–17.

– '*Exodus* and the Treasure of Pharoah.' *ASE* 1 (1972): 159–65.

– '*Selfsceaft* in *Genesis B*.' *Anglia* 83 (1965): 154–71.

Vine, W.E. *Vine's Expository Dictionary of Old and New Testament Words*. Old Tappan, NJ: Fleming H. Revell, 1981.

Voigt, Edward Edgar. *The Latin Versions of Judith*. Leipzig: W. Drugulin, 1925.

Waller, G.F. *Mary Sidney, Countess of Pembroke: A Critical Study of Her Writings and Literary Milieu*. Salzburg: Institut für Anglistik und Amerikanistik, Universität Salzburg, 1979.

Walsh, Marie. 'The Baptismal Flood in the Old English *Andreas*: Liturgical and Typological Depths.' *Traditio* 33 (1977): 132–58.

Walsh, Patrick G., trans. *Cassiodorus: Explanation of the Psalms*. 3 vols. New York: Paulist Press, 1990–1.

Walton, Ann. 'The Three Hebrew Children in the Fiery Furnace: A Study in Christian Iconography.' In *The Medieval Mediterranean: Cross-Cultural Contacts*, ed. M.J. Chiat and K.L. Reyerson, 57–66. St Cloud, MN: North Star Press, 1998.

Wanley, Humfrey. *Librorum Veterum Septentrionalium Catologus*. In *Linguarum Veterum Septentrionalium Thesaurus*, vol. 2, edited by George Hickes. Oxford, 1705. Reprint, Menston, UK: Scholar Press, 1970.

Ward, Benedicta. *Bede and the Psalter*. Jarrow Lecture. Newcastle, UK: St Paul's Church, 1991.

– *The Venerable Bede*. Cistercian Studies 169. Kalamazoo: Western Michigan University Press, 1998.

Warner, Rubie D.-N., ed. *Early English Homilies from the Twelfth-Century MS Vespasian D.xiv*. EETS o.s. 152. London: Oxford University Press, 1917. Reprint, New York: Kraus Reprint, 1971.

Warren, Frederick E. *The Leofric Missal*. Oxford: Clarendon Press, 1883.

Wasserstein, David J. 'The First Jew in England: "The Game of the Evangel" and a Hiberno-Latin Contribution to Anglo-Saxon History.' In *Ogma: Essays in Celtic Studies in Honour of Próinséas Ní Chatháin*, edited by Michael Richter and Jean-Michel Picard, 283–8. Dublin: Four Courts Press, 2002.

Watkins, Calvert. *How to Kill a Dragon: Aspects of Indo-European Poetics*. Oxford: Oxford University Press, 1995.

Waugh, Robin. 'Word, Breath, and Vomit: Oral Competition in Old English and Old Norse Literature.' *Oral Tradition* 10 (1995): 359–86.

Weber, Dorothea, ed. *Augustinus: De Genesi contra Manichaeos*. CSEL 91. Vienna: Verlag der Österreichischen Akademie der Wissenschaften, 1998.

Weber, Robert, et al., eds. *Biblia sacra iuxta uulgatam uersionem*. 4th ed. Stuttgart: Deutsche Bibelgesellschaft, 1994.

Weinfield, Moshe. *Deuteronomy and the Deuteronomic School*. Oxford: Clarendon Press, 1972.

Whatley, Gordon, ed. and trans. 'Constantine the Great, the Empress Helena, and the Relics of the Holy Cross.' In *Medieval Hagiography: An Anthology*, Garland Reference Library of the Humanities vol. 1942, edited by Thomas Head, 77–95. New York: Garland, 2000.

– 'Cynewulf and Troy: A Note on *Elene* 642–61.' *Notes and Queries* 20 (1973): 203–5.

– 'The Figure of Constantine the Great in Cynewulf's *Elene*.' *Traditio* 37 (1981): 161–202.

Whitelock, Dorothy, ed. *Sermo Lupi ad Anglos*. London: Methuen, 1963.

Widengren, Geo. 'Yahweh's Gathering of the Dispersed.' In *In the Shelter of Elyon: Essays on Ancient Palestinian Life and Literature in Honor of G.W. Ahlström*, edited by W. Boyd Barrick and John R. Spencer, 227–45. Sheffield, UK: JSOT Press, 1984.

Wiesenekker, Evert. '*Word be Worde, Andgit of Andgite*': Translation Performance in the Old English Interlinear Glosses of the Vespasian, Regius and Lambeth Psalters. Huizen, Netherlands: Bout, 1991.

Wiethaus, Ulrike. *Agnes Blannbekin, Viennese Beguine: Life and Revelations*. Woodbridge, UK: D.S. Brewer, 2002.

Wilcox, Jonathan, ed. *Ælfric's Prefaces*. Durham Medieval Texts 9. Durham: Durham Medieval Texts, 1994.

– 'The First Laugh: Laughter in Genesis and the Old English Tradition.' In *The Old English Hexateuch: Aspects and Approaches*, ed. Rebecca Barnhouse and

Benjamin C. Withers, 239–70. Kalamazoo, MI: Medieval Institute Publications, 2000.

- 'Napier's "Wulfstan" Homilies XL and XLII: Two Anonymous Works from Winchester?' *JEGP* 90 (1991): 1–19.
- 'A Reluctant Translator in Late Anglo-Saxon England: Ælfric and Maccabees.' *Proceedings of the Medieval Association of the Midwest* 2 (1993): 1–18.
- 'Transmission of Literature and Learning: Anglo-Saxon Scribal Culture.' In *A Companion to Anglo-Saxon Literature*, edited by Phillip Pulsiano and Elaine Treharne, 50–70. Oxford and Malden: Blackwell, 2001.

Wilcox, Miranda. 'Vernacular Biblical Epics and the Production of Anglo-Saxon Cultural Exegesis.' PhD diss., Notre Dame University, 2005.

Williams, Ronald J. *Hebrew Syntax: An Outline*. Toronto: University of Toronto Press, 1967.

Wills, Jeffrey. *Repetition in Latin Poetry: Figures of Allusion*. Oxford: Clarendon Press, 1996.

Woolf, Rosemary. 'The Fall of Man in *Genesis B* and the *Mystère d'Adam*.' In *Studies in Old English Literature in Honor of Arthur G. Brodeur*, edited by S.B. Greenfield, 187–99. 1963. Reprint, New York: Russell and Russell, 1973.

- 'The Ideal of Men Dying with Their Lord in the *Germania* and in *The Battle of Maldon*.' *ASE* 5 (1976): 63–81.
- 'Saints' Lives.' In *Continuations and Beginnings: Studies in Old English Literature*, edited by E.G. Stanley, 37–66. London: Thomas Nelson, 1966.

Wormald, F. *English Drawings of the Tenth and Eleventh Centuries*. London: Faber and Faber, 1952.

Wormald, Patrick. 'Bede, the Bretwaldas and the Origins of the Gens Anglorum.' In *Ideal and Reality in Frankish and Anglo-Saxon Society: Studies Presented to J.M. Hadrill*, ed. P. Wormald, 99–129. Oxford: Blackwell, 1983.

- '*Lex Scripta* and *Verbum Regis*: Legislation and Germanic Kingship.' In *Early Medieval Kingship*, ed. Peter H. Sawyer and Ian N. Wood, 105–38. University of Leeds, 1977.
- *The Making of English Law: King Alfred to the Twelfth Century*. Oxford: Blackwell, 1999.
- 'The Venerable Bede and the "Church of the English."' In *The English Religious Tradition and the Genius of Anglicanism*, ed. G. Rowell, 13–32. Nashville, TN: Abingdon Press, 1992.

Wright, Charles D. 'The Blood of Abel and the Branches of Sin: *Genesis A, Maxims I* and Aldhelm's *Carmen de uirginitate*.' *ASE* 25 (1996): 7–19.

Wright, Cyril Ernest. *The Cultivation of Saga in ASE*. Edinburgh: Oliver and Boyd, 1939.

Yu, Jiyuan, and Jorge J.E. Gracia, eds. *Rationality and Happiness: From the Ancients to the Early Medievals*. Rochester, NY: University of Rochester Press, 2003.

Zacher, Samantha. 'The Chosen Peoples: Religious Identities.' In the *Oxford Handbook of Medieval English Literature*, ed. Elaine Treharne and Greg Walker. Oxford University Press, forthcoming.

– 'Cynewulf at the Interface of Literacy and Orality: The Evidence of the Puns in *Elene*.' *Oral Tradition* 17 (2002): 346–87.

– 'Sin, Syntax, and Synonyms: Rhetorical Style and Structure in Vercelli Homily X.' *JEGP* 103 (2004): 53–76.

Zangemeister, Karl, and W. Braune. 'Bruchstücke der altsächsischen Bibeldichtung aus der Bibliotheca Palatina.' *Neue Heidelberger Jahrbuch* 4 (1894): 205–94.

Zim, Rivkah. *English Metrical Psalms: Poetry as Praise and Prayer, 1535–1601*. Cambridge: Cambridge University Press, 1987.

Zingerle, Anton, ed. *Sancti Hilarii episcopi Pictaviensis Tractatus super psalmos*. CSEL 22. Vienna: F. Tempsky, 1891.

Zupitza, Julius, ed. *Ælfrics Grammatik und Glossar. Erste Abteilung: Text und Varianten*. Berlin: Weidmannsche Verlagsbuchhandlung, 1880.

– ed. *Cynewulfs Elene mit ein Glossar*. Berlin: Weidmannsche Verlagsbuchhandlung, 1883.

Zycha, Joseph, ed. *Sancti Aurelii Augustini De Genesi ad litteram imperfectus liber, De Genesi ad litteram, Locutiones in Heptateuchum*. CSEL 28. Vienna: F. Tempsky, 1894.

Index

Compiled by Michael D. Elliot

Toronto Anglo-Saxon Series

General Editor
ANDY ORCHARD

Editorial Board
ROBERTA FRANK
THOMAS N. HALL
ANTONETTE DIPAOLO HEALEY
MICHAEL LAPIDGE